FIFTH EDITION

CHILDREN'S BOOKS
in CHILDREN'S HANDS

A Brief Introduction to Their Literature

FIFTH EDITION

CHILDREN'S BOOKS *in* CHILDREN'S HANDS

A Brief Introduction to Their Literature

Charles Temple
Hobart and William Smith Colleges

Miriam Martinez
University of Texas at San Antonio

Junko Yokota
National Louis University

PEARSON

Boston • Columbus • Indianapolis • New York • San Francisco • Upper Saddle River
Amsterdam • Cape Town • Dubai • London • Madrid • Milan • Munich • Paris • Montréal • Toronto
Delhi • Mexico City • São Paulo • Sydney • Hong Kong • Seoul • Singapore • Taipei • Tokyo

Editor-in-Chief: Jeffery Johnston
Acquisitions Editor: Kathryn Boice
Development Editor: Jennifer Gessner
Editorial Assistant: Carolyn Schweitzer
Executive Marketing Manager: Krista Clark
Production Editor: Janet Domingo
Manufacturing Buyer: Linda Sager
Project Coordination and Electronic Page Makeup: Cenveo® Publisher Services
Interior Design: Carol Somberg
Cover Designer: Diane Lorenzo
Cover and Interior Illustrator: Franée Lessac

Credits and acknowledgments borrowed from other sources and reproduced, with permission, in this textbook appear on the appropriate page within text (or on pages 357–358).

Library of Congress Cataloging-in-Publication Data
Temple, Charles A.
  Children's Books in Children's Hands: a Brief Introduction to Their Literature/Charles Temple, Hobart and William Smith Colleges; Miriam Martinez, University of Texas at San Antonio; Junko Yokota, National-Louis University. -- Fifth Edition.
     pages cm
  Includes bibliographical references and index.
  ISBN 978-0-13-309851-8
  1. Children's literature--History and criticism. I. Martinez, Miriam G. II. Yokota, Junko. III. Title.
  PN1009.A1C5118 2014
  809'.89282--dc23
                    2014004961

10 9 8 7 6 5 4 3 2 1
V011

ISBN-10: 0-13-309851-6
ISBN-13: 978-0-13-309851-8

To Aurora Martinez: Thanks for all the books.
—C.T.

To Elena, Emma, Annabelle, and Elia and all the stories we will share
—M.M.

To Bill, for enriching my understanding of literature
—J.Y.

ABOUT
the AUTHORS

The authors of this text were drawn together by a love of children's books and a fascination with the people who make them and by the hope that another generation of students, teachers, librarians, and parents could be inspired to take up the challenge of getting those works into the hands of children.

Charles Temple is a banjo-picking storyteller and Education Professor at Hobart & William Smith Colleges in Upstate New York. He has co-authored many books in the field of reading and language arts, including *All Children Read, Understanding Reading Problems*, and *The Beginnings of Writing*. He has also published several books for children. Temple has worked over the years with teachers in Europe, Asia, Africa, and Latin America on initiatives to promote literacy and critical thinking. He currently works with writers, illustrators, and editors in East and West Africa who are producing books for children, and with teachers in the Caucasus region to develop literacy assessment tools and teaching strategies.

Favorite books as a child included: *The Broad Highway* by Jeffery Farnol; Uncle Wiggly Stories and Dr. Doolittle; and also Tom Swift, and the *All-About Books*.

Miriam Martinez is a teacher educator at the University of Texas at San Antonio who loves nothing more than getting lost in good books, including children's books, of course! She is recipient of the International Reading Association's Arbuthnot Award which honors outstanding university teachers of children's literature. Dr. Martinez coedited *Book Talk and Beyond: Children and Teachers Respond to Literature* (1995) and *What a Character! Character Study as a Gateway to Literary Understanding* (2005), both published by the International Reading Association. She served for seven years as the coeditor of "Bookalogues," a children's book review column in the journal *Language Arts*. She is co-editor of the *Journal of Children's Literature*. The focus of her research and writing is on ways of bringing children and books together to foster students' literary and literacy development.

Favorite books as a child included: *Horton Hatches the Egg* by Dr. Seuss; *The Four-Story Mistake* by Elizabeth Enright; *Then There Were Five* by Elizabeth Enright; *Dangerous Island* by Helen Mather-Smith Mindlin; and *The Bobbsey Twins in Mexico* by Laura Lee Hope.

Junko Yokota is the Director of the Center for Teaching through Children's Books and a Professor Emeritus of National Louis University in Chicago, Illinois. She was a classroom teacher and a school librarian during the first ten years of her career. She has published widely in a variety of reading/language arts and children's literature journals, chapters in professional books, and edited *Kaleidoscope: A Multicultural Booklist for Grades K–8* published by the National Council of Teachers of English. She has served on the Newbery Award Committee, chaired the Caldecott and the Batchelder Award Committees, and judged on the Audies Awards. Junko is past president of the United States Board on Books for Young People (the US national section of IBBY), and is a recipient of the Virginia Hamilton Award for Contribution to Multicultural Literature and the Reading the World Award. She has served two terms on the Hans Christian Andersen Jury to select the author and illustrator winners of the highest international award for children's literature.

Having grown up in Japan, her favorite childhood books were in her first language.

BRIEF CONTENTS

CONTENTS

5 International Literature

PART TWO
Exploring the Genres of Children's Literature   139

PREFACE

Imagine if every child and every young person were a reader. We don't mean people with the skills of decoding, fluency, comprehension, and the rest—we mean people who loved to read, and who *did* read, every chance they got. We're talking about children and young people you could find curled up on the sofa reading a book, or backpacking books on camping trips, or running back into the house to retrieve a Kindle before the family left on a vacation, or reading to a little brother or sister on a rainy afternoon in a city apartment.

We know some things that would be true about them. They would have rich imaginations. They would have big vocabularies, and those vocabularies would make them naturally curious about the large and small wonders of this world (because you notice and think about things when you have names for them). They would have a richer experience of other people, and understand themselves better. We know that as adults they would get along better with others, be healthier, be more productive, and generally be interesting people to talk to. We know these things because there are already such people in the world.

There just aren't enough of them.

Our job as writers of this book is to acquaint you with many, many books, and the riches they contain. We will give you roadmaps to their qualities and acquaint you with many of their writers, illustrators, editors, and critics so that you can begin to know your way around the world of children's literature. But above all we will introduce you to many, many books—the folktales, poems, picture books, multicultural books, novels about the range of human experiences, works of fantasy and science fiction, information books, and biographies. Think of this introduction as a handshake, as it were—after you are introduced, you can go off and get to know each other better. And then you can introduce children to the books, too.

New to This Edition

The UPS drivers in Geneva, New York, San Antonio, Texas, and Evanston, Illinois, can find our houses with their eyes closed. They have been stopping by almost daily for decades delivering new books. "New to this edition" most importantly are the new books we are reviewing and presenting—dozens of new titles and many new authors in each chapter.

There were two main ideas that motivated this fifth edition of *Children's Books in Children's Hands*. One was to make a shorter version of the book, to leave the students and the instructor time to read more children's books in your children's literature courses. The second was to update the book generally, to keep abreast of the thousands of new books published each year for children, and to keep it relevant to important changes in school classrooms.

- This fifth edition is over a hundred pages shorter than the previous one. While teaching ideas have been included in nearly every chapter, the former chapters on teaching with children's literature have left this edition and are being expanded into a book of their own.

- Just as in previous editions, there are hundreds of annotations of newer titles for children in *Children's Books in Children's Hands,* Fifth Edition, with a strong emphasis on books from many cultural groups. There are entire chapters on multicultural books and international books, and both are expanded from the last edition.
- Traditional genres of children's books are being challenged and reworked in exciting ways, and our presentation is updated to reflect changes in the genres.
- The chapter on nonfiction has been completely rewritten and expanded. Nonfiction books are a key change that is being promoted by the new Common Core Standards, and our revised chapter with its expanded list of annotated books will help teachers meet those standards.
- The Common Core Standards are addressed throughout the book in other ways. Since the standards ask children to be aware of different genres of literature, to understand how characters and settings are developed, to understand the dynamics of book illustration, to appreciate the craft of poetry, and to read nonfiction with confidence and understanding, these things are clearly presented in the chapters throughout the book and referenced to the standards.
- Throughout the book teachers are given suggestions for finding books that foreground the cultures of English language learners, and also for drawing English language learners into discussions of children's books.

How This Book Is Organized

PART 1 "Understanding Literature and the Child Reader," orients the reader to the study of children's literature, and gives you the critic's perspective. **Chapter 1,** "Children's Books in Children's Hands," introduces children's literature as a distinct category, and discusses the genres of children's books as well as their qualities. **Chapter 2,** "Literary Elements in Works for Children," introduces a set of literary concepts with which to approach children's books, describing how plots are organized, how characters are drawn, and how themes are developed. **Chapter 3,** "Picture Books," focuses on how art and text combine to form unique works. **Chapter 4,** "Literature Representing Diverse Perspectives," reflects this book's strong emphasis on multicultural literature. It investigates the ways various cultural groups are depicted in children's literature, highlights the progress that has been made in publishing children's books that represent various cultural groups more extensively and fairly, surveys the multicultural books that are available, and sets out guidelines for selecting high-quality multicultural books for children. **Chapter 5,** "International Literature," introduces books that come to us from other parts of the world. It investigates international children's literature, surveys the international books that are available, and sets out guidelines for selecting high-quality international books for children.

PART 2 "Exploring the Genres of Children's Literature," surveys the books that have been written for children, type by type or genre by genre. Each of the chapters in this part outlines the historical development of a particular genre, examines the literary qualities that distinguish the genre and the reading demands those qualities place on the child, reviews outstanding examples of works from the genre, and sets out criteria for selecting good works in the genre. Each chapter closes with an extensive annotated list of recommended books in the genre. **Chapter 6,** "Poetry for Children," surveys the genre from nursery rhymes to contemporary multicultural poetry for children. **Chapter 7**, "Traditional Literature," looks at folk literature from many times and cultures. **Chapter 8**, "Modern Fantasy and Science Fiction," considers the artistry that enables readers to enter hypothetical worlds. **Chapter 9**, "Contemporary Realistic Fiction," looks at ways authors create believable books that are set in the "here and now" and that address the wide-ranging problems and delights of today's children. Books set in times that may be many generations removed from our own are discussed in **Chapter 10**, "Historical Fiction," which explains the origins of the current emphasis on meticulous accuracy in this genre. Many highly imaginative works are explored in **Chapter 11**, Nonfiction," which surveys a growing area of children's literature, in which talented writers present the real world and its people to young readers in skillfully focused works that can be as riveting as fiction.

Pedagogical Enrichment and Features of This Book

The richly illustrated fifth edition is packed with practical applications and unique pedagogical features:

TOP SHELF 4.2

GROWING UP IN A WORLD OF POLITICAL OR SOCIAL UNREST

Before We Were Free by Julia Alvarez

Girl of Kosovo by Alice Mead

Grab Hands and Run by Frances Temple

The Other Side of Truth by Beverley Naidoo

Red Scarf Girl by Ji Li Jiang

Zlata's Diary: A Child's Life in Sarajevo by Zlata Filipovec

"Top Shelf" book lists in every chapter list our best picks of titles that exemplify a particular concept discussed in the chapter (e.g., Humorous Picture Books or Multicultural Audiobook).

 TEACHING IDEA 2.2

PLOTTING THE STORY JOURNEY

COMMON CORE STANDARD: *Key Ideas and Details, STANDARD 3*

Students can make a kind of graph to plot a story journey. Drawing a line from left to right across a chart, they can make the line go up for events when morale is high and down for events when morale is low. Above the line, they can write in what happened. Below the line, they can write in how a character felt or what she or he learned.

"Teaching Ideas" provide valuable, practical lessons and activities for sharing literature with children in the classroom.

"Technology in Practice" teaching tips in each chapter reflect our collective experience with the intersection of electronics and print, and provide activities for the classroom utilizing new media technology (e.g., how to create a student book referral database).

 TECHNOLOGY in PRACTICE 10.2

Many teachers are finding multiple uses for software programs that allow teachers and students to easily create graphic organizers that can be applied in any number of subject areas. Ready-made templates can be used, or designs can be customized.

Using such a program, create a Venn diagram of overlapping circles to compare a period of history with today. On one circle, write the things that were unique to the historical time period (e.g., traveling by wagon). In the other circle, write descriptors for the way things are today (e.g., traveling by car). In the center section created by the overlapping circles, write down things that both times have in common (e.g., going to school). Topics such as transportation, clothing, occupations, and men's and women's roles can be addressed. Comparisons between cultures can be made. Creating their own Venn diagrams engages students in the subject matter in more complex ways.

Ask *the* Author. . . Sharon Creech

Most of my stories begin with the image of a person and a place, and I write to discover the story. Very early on, the main character will mention other people, and I know that these people will have their own stories to tell. It is these stories that evolve into other strands of the plot.

Weaving them together is not as difficult as it might sound, because each day I merely pick up the previous strands and go wherever it feels right to go. If I feel the need to spend some time with the main character's grandparents, for example, I will do that, and then return to the central story. That central story will be affected by what I've learned from the grandparents, and so the different strands begin to intertwine.

Often I use the image of clearing a trail to describe the writing process. Like Zinny Taylor, who clears a long trail in *Chasing Redbird*, I am only clearing a little bit of the story trail at a time. Sometimes there are side paths that look interesting, and I'll follow those and then return to the main trail.

It is wonderful when you begin to see the patterns emerge—when you can see enough of the story to sense how one part relates to another. If I tried to predict the pattern—or the course of the story trail—in advance, I don't think I'd be so willing to allow it to change and evolve, and it is this changing and evolving that becomes most interesting to me. At the end, I can see how all the parts of the trail are connected, and then I revise, clearing patches that aren't yet smooth enough.

Sometimes students worry when they're writing their own stories that they have to know the whole story before they begin. I find it more exciting to know very little at the beginning, and to run down that trail wondering what I will find along the way.

Sharon Creech is the author of *Walk Two Moons*, which received the Newbery Medal; *The Wanderer*; *Absolutely Normal Chaos*; *Bloomability*; *Pleasing the Ghost*; and *Chasing Redbird*. After spending eighteen years teaching and writing in Europe, Sharon Creech returned with her family to the United States to live.

Each chapter includes an "Ask the Author" (or Illustrator, Editor, or Educator) box, in which a prominent children's author, illustrator, editor, or educator responds to a question related to the chapter content.

● ISSUE *to* CONSIDER

How Much Artistic License Should Be Given to Illustrators as They Create Images of a Culture?

Some illustrators argue that demands for absolute accuracy of every detail rob the illustrator of the right to use imagination and individual style in portraying an image. They contend that unless the illustrations are photographs, the style of illustration will influence the degree of attention to detail.

Others argue that accurate details in illustrations create the overall sense of cultural authenticity. They point out that misconceptions may develop from incorrect images. In some cases, highly regarded illustrators whose work is exceptional from an artistic viewpoint have been criticized for creating images that "mix" cultures. Critics say that this mixing of cultures robs each culture of its distinction. Yet the illustrators express their desire to create unified images of cultures that sometimes share a common voice. One example is *Brother*

Eagle, Sister Sky: A Message from Chief Seattle (1991) by Susan Jeffers. Controversy arose over the text because the words were based on a script for a 1971 television commercial decrying pollution. Controversy arose over the illustrations because of mixed images of Native American cultures that contained inaccuracies of both history and culture. Jeffers defended her position by stating that the important point is that the book reflects a Native American philosophy (Noll, 1995).

How do you view this issue of authenticity versus artistic license in children's book illustrations? How will the type of illustrations affect child readers who do not intimately know the culture portrayed? How will the illustrations affect child readers whose own cultures are portrayed?

What do you think?

"Issue to Consider" boxes in each chapter present a highly debated issue in children's literature.

EXPERIENCES FOR FURTHER LEARNING

1. Compile your own anthology of poems for children. Organize it around a theme or an issue—for example, poems for choral reading, poems from many cultures, or poems to celebrate holidays. So that you can become acquainted with contemporary poetry, use ten different sources, choose no more than two poems per source, and make sure they were published within the last fifteen years. (Thanks to Linnea Henderson for this suggestion.)

2. A good poem may sound natural, but on examination it is likely to turn out to have been very carefully crafted. Take a poem such as A. A. Milne's "Happiness" (from *When We Were Very Young*). Try substituting other words for any of Milne's. Does the poem sound as good?

"Experiences for Further Learning" are end-of-chapter activities that help readers deepen their own understanding of the chapter content.

RECOMMENDED BOOKS

* indicates a picture book; I indicates interest level (P = preschool; YA = young adult).

Comprehensive Anthologies

Berry, James, ed. *Classic Poems to Read Aloud*. Larousse Kingfisher, 2003. An excellent collection of poems from many cultures. (I: 10–YA)

Cullinan, Bernice, ed. *Another Jar of Tiny Stars: Poems from NCTE Award-Winning Poets*. Wordsong/Boyds Mills Press, 2009. An update to *A Jar of Tiny Stars*, published in 1996, this volume includes poems by all NCTE Poetry Award winners through 2009. (I: 6–13)

Kennedy, Caroline. *A Family of Poems: My Favorite Poetry for Children*. Illustrated by Jon J. Muth. Hyperion, 2005. This collection of over 100 classic and new poems is arranged into seven sections—About Me, That's So

Giovanni, Langston Hughes, and a dozen others who are better known to adults than to children, but who all celebrate the black experience. (I: 9–12)

Brooks, Gwendolyn. *Bronzeville Boys and Girls*. Illustrated by Faith Ringgold. Amistad, 2006. Poems for children first published in 1958 by the first African American woman to win a Pulitzer Prize. (I: 8–11)

*Bruchac, Joseph. *The Earth under Sky Bear's Feet: Native American Poems of the Land*. Illustrated by Thomas Locker. Puffin, 1998. Most of these poems are reflections on the Sky Bear constellation, also known as the Big Dipper. Some of Locker's rich oil paintings are magnificent. (I: 7–11)

Florian, Douglas. *Comets, Stars, the Moon, and Mars*. Harcourt, 2007. Florian's rich descriptions of heavenly bodies will enhance the study of space in any classroom.

Each chapter concludes with extensive lists of "Recommended Books" that offer publication data, a brief annotation, and interest level by age for every book listed. These lists have been extensively updated for the fifth edition with scores of new entries.

Children's Books in Children's Hands is available as a Pearson eText

The affordable, convenient, interactive version of this text includes tools to help navigate and understand important, current content. The Pearson eText is available with a black and white, loose-leaf printed version of the text.

Features of the Pearson eText include:

- Tools to take and share notes, highlight and bookmark chapter concepts, and search by keyword
- Accessible from your computer, iPad and Android tablets with the Pearson eText app
- More affordable than a traditional textbook
- Extended access upgrade is available

Enjoy the advantages of an eText, plus the benefits of print, all for less than the price of a traditional book!

Supplements to Aid Teachers and Students

Students and instructors will find these supplements invaluable:

Instructor's Manual and Test Bank provides a variety of instructional tools, including chapter overviews, "pre-reading" directions, questions for class discussion, classroom activities, extending the reading assignments, plus multiple choice and essay questions. (Available for download from the Instructor Resource Center at www.pearsonhighered.com/irc.)

Acknowledgments

Frances Temple (now deceased) and Nancy Roser helped shape our thinking early in the project; we are grateful to both. We also wish to thank Nancy for suggesting the title of the book, which so aptly captures our mission as the authors. Professor Bird Stasz has created instructors' manuals for this and many previous editions of the book, and has been a stalwart supporter of this work. We are grateful.

Joy Moss, teacher educator at the University of Rochester (New York) and an elementary school literature teacher, brought to bear her considerable experiences in sharing literature with children as she read and commented on the first edition of the book in its formative stages.

We have long admired the colorful and vibrant art of Franée Lessac, whose illustrations have graced all editions of the book. We are always delighted with the results of her work.

Thanks also go to the talented children's books authors, illustrators, editors, and educators who so generously shared their thoughts and experiences for "Ask the Author" features. In addition, several writer and illustrator friends gave us a look inside their craft: thanks to the Rochester Writers Group, especially Cynthia DeFelice, Ellen Stoll Walsh, M. J. Auch, Vivian Vande Velde, and Robin Pulver; also to Barbara Seuling and Bill Hooks. Several children's book editors did much the same thing; we wish to thank Matilda Welter, Refna Wilkin, Kent Brown, and Richard Jackson.

For their expert knowledge of children's books, our thanks go to the Friends of the Center for Teaching through Children's Books. For invaluable insights, thanks to Bill Teale, Gail Bush, and Toby Rajput.

We gratefully acknowledge the thoughtful and expert suggestions of the reviewers for this new edition: Marion Hussong, Richard Stockton College of New Jersey; Sharon F. O'Neal, Texas State University; Lisa L. Sandoval, Joliet Junior College; and Elizabeth A. Yanoff, The College of Saint Rose.

We also gratefully acknowledge those who reviewed previous editions: Alma Flor Ada, University of San Francisco; Paulette Babner, Cape Cod Community College; Erin Banks, Eastern Michigan University; John Beach, University of Nebraska at Omaha; Jessica Bevans, The Ohio State University; Celestine Cheeks, Towson University; Linda DeGroff, University of Georgia; Pat Farthing, Appalachian State University; Peter Fisher, National Louis University; Esther Fusco, Hofstra University; Connie Golden, Marietta College; Ambika Gopalakrishnan, California State University, Long Beach; M. Jean Greenlaw, University of North Texas; Dan Hade, Penn State University; Darwin L. Henderson, University of Cincinnati; Janet Hill, Kent State University; Judith Hillman, St. Michael's College; Miriam J. Johnson;

Bridgewater State College; Nancy J. Johnson, Western Washington University; Linda Leonard Lamme, University of Florida; Barbara A. Lehman, The Ohio State University; Susan Lehr, Skidmore College; Diane L. Lowe, Framingham State College; Amy A. McClure, Ohio Wesleyan University; Dianne L. Monson, University of Minnesota; Maria Offer, Northern Michigan University; Richard Osterburg, California State University, Fresno; Patricia J. Pollifrone, Gannon University; T. Gail Pritchard, University of Alabama; Roxanne Reedyk, Lakeland College; Mary Kate Sableski, University of Dayton; Olivia Saracho, University of Maryland; Sam Sebesta, University of Washington; Lesley Shapiro, National Louis University; Charlotte Skinner, Arkansas State University; Elizabeth A. Smith, Otterbein College; Jeff Smith, Roosevelt High School, Kent, Ohio; Karen J. Sweeney, Wayne State College, and Ian W. Wojcik-Andrews, Eastern Michigan University.

The professionals at Pearson deserve much credit for helping us pull this off: We thank our good friend Kathy Smith for taking such good care of our prose; Janet Domingo for managing the many pieces that go into an illustrated text; and especially our editors, Virginia Lanigan, Aurora Martinez Ramos, and Kathryn Boice for providing good cheer and good sense along the way.

Charles Temple
Miriam Martinez
Junko Yokota

PART ONE

Understanding Literature and the Child Reader

Children's Books in Children's Hands

A four-year-old child in her mother's lap hears Margaret Wise Brown's *Little Fur Family* and is filled with a secure feeling of being a special child, very much loved. In the coming months, the child picks up the book every now and then, and that same feeling of warmth and security comes over her each time she does.

In a first-grade classroom on the South Pacific island of Fiji, the teacher has created a hand-lettered enlarged version of Bill Martin, Jr.'s *Brown Bear, Brown Bear, What Do You See?* She reads it to her assembled class, pointing with a ruler to each word. Even before she has finished the first reading, children are anticipating what she is going to say next. The second time through, the children, supported by the patterned text and the illustrations, are reading along with her. There are no bears on Fiji, though, and soon the children are writing their own book based on Martin's pattern but featuring a mongoose, a mynah bird, an iguana, and other local animals. Martin's book has helped these children of Fiji learn to read and write.

> Trip-trap, trip-trap, trip-trap, trip-trap.
> "Who's that walking on my bridge?" roared the Troll.
> "It is I, Little Billy Goat Gruff."

In a South Texas classroom, Jackie murmurs, "Oh, good," when Ms. Sloan sends her group to the library center, a favorite in the classroom. Some of her fellow students browse through the collection looking for particular books. Jackie says, "Let's do 'Three Billy Goats Gruff.'" Four other children agree and cut short their search. Now the five children—three goats, one troll, and a narrator—are acting out this folktale that is so well known to them from their teacher's reading it aloud. And of course one performance will not do. Everyone wants a chance to be the troll!

A teacher reads aloud from Gloria Anzaldua's *Prietita and the Ghost Woman/ Prietita y La Llorona*, a modern tale that features the "Weeping Woman," a ghostly character familiar among Hispanic children in Mexico and the American Southwest. "We tell about *la Llorona* down in the valley at my *abuela's* house," says Ana Margarita. "But she's not nice like this lady. She's the one who catches little kids if they go out at night, especially near the water." Then she politely provides the pronunciation of *Llorona*, "You pronounce the double L like a 'Y,'" she says—and goes on to explain some of the other Spanish words such as *curandera* and *remedio* that are given in the book. She has a look on her face that says, "Isn't it great to discuss a book about things from *my* side of town?!"

In a fourth-grade classroom in Atlanta, a teacher has just finished reading Carmen Deedy's *Fourteen Cows for America* (2009) with two-page spreads of lifelike illustrations of a Maasai community in East Africa.

"Look closely in the eye of the person in the picture," she says.

"Oh!" says a student. "It's a tiny reflection of a building. It's burning, and you can see the smoke!"

"So the young man can still see the attack on the twin towers. It's still in his eyes, even when he's so far away from it in Africa," says another student.

"Was that a true story?" asks another.

"Yes, it was. Let's turn the page." The next pages give an account of a young man from the Maasai tribe who was studying medicine in the United States when he happened to witness the attack on the World Trade Center in New York. When he returned to his village a year later, his people were so moved by his descriptions that they donated some of their most valuable possessions—fourteen cows—to America.

"But where are the cows?" a student asks. Later the class looks up the event on the Internet and finds newspaper accounts of the

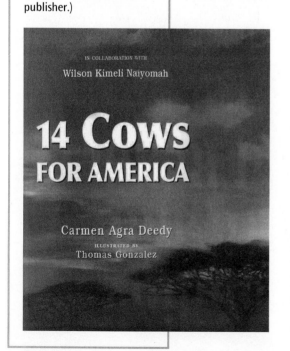

ILLUSTRATION 1.1
Generous Maasai herdsmen from Kenya donated cows to America as a gesture of solace after September 11, 2001, in this true story. (Cover image from "14 Cows for America" by Carmen Agra Deedy & Wilson Kimeli Naiyomah, illustrated by Thomas Gonzalez. Illustration copyright © 2009 by Thomas Gonzalez. Printed with permission from the publisher.)

IN COLLABORATION WITH
Wilson Kimeli Naiyomah

14 COWS FOR AMERICA

Carmen Agra Deedy
ILLUSTRATED BY
Thomas Gonzalez

TEACHING IDEA 1.1

ASK THE CHILDREN!

Have a conversation with a group of children about children's books. Ask these questions in a conversational way:

COMMON CORE STANDARD:
Craft and Structure,
STANDARD 5

1. How do you know a book is a children's book?
2. What are three of your favorite children's books?
3. What makes them good—that is, if you met someone who was going to write a book for children, what advice would you give her or him to make it a *good* book?
4. How do you feel after you've read a really good book? What are you thinking about?

Note carefully what the children say. Is there a difference in what children of different ages admire in books? How do their criteria for good children's books compare with those set out in this chapter?

Maasai village's generous act, entries about the Maasai people, and an entry about Wilson Kimeli Naiyomah, the young man in the story.

John Cunningham's sixth-grade class has finished Louis Sachar's *Holes* (2000), about a juvenile detention camp. Now he is reading them parts of Adam Rapp's *The Buffalo Tree* (1997), a book about "juvies," young people who are incarcerated in a juvenile detention home. One student sighs, shakes her head, and remarks, "This is more like what it must really be like to be locked up in one of those places. I mean, I loved *Holes*, but that book seems kind of like a dream in comparison—not a good dream, but like nothing is quite real. But this, this—you can almost smell the anger, almost taste the blood in your mouth."

Good books—like good paintings, plays, movies, sculptures, and other creative works—merit appreciation in their own right. But good books serve children in some specific ways. Good children's books can evoke strong feelings and come to stand for childhood emotions, much in the way a security blanket does. Good books can give children reference points for understanding their own experiences, lessons that may last a lifetime. Good books may make children proud of and knowledgeable about their own culture and open windows onto other cultures. Good books may help children understand how others live, and how they face the same issues in their lives. Good books, and the sharing of them, cultivate children's capacity for empathy and compassion. Good books educate the imagination, as children stretch to visualize what it would be like to walk in the shoes of a character in a book.

ILLUSTRATION 1.2 Adam Rapp's *The Buffalo Tree* is a book about "juvies," young people who are incarcerated in a juvenile detention home. (Used by permission of HarperCollins Publishers.)

> All great things that have happened in the world, happened first of all in someone's imagination, and the aspect of the world of tomorrow depends largely on the extent of the power of imagination of those who are just now learning to read. That is why children must have books, and why there must be people . . . who really care what kind of books are put into the children's hands. (Astrid Lindgren, author of *Pippi Longstocking*, from her acceptance speech for the Hans Christian Andersen Award in 1958)

Good books may give children much of the motivation and even the concepts they need to learn to read and the models that show them how to write. Good books offer children delight, mystery, charm, an experience of awe, and companionship. Good books invite children to play with language. Good picture books cultivate children's visual literacy and their aesthetic sense. Good books nurture children's appreciation of the author's craft.

What Are Good Books for Children?

For the student of children's literature, there is a lot to learn about. Let's identify some key questions here, and relate them to the upcoming chapters, where you will find answers.

What Are Good Books for Each Child?

Answering that question will require that we develop some criteria for quality in children's books. And since the answer depends partly on the age and interests of the child, we should consider ways in which readers respond to literature and how they differ in their responses at different ages. These issues will be the focus of this chapter.

Knowing what good books are for different children requires some intelligent way of talking about goodness and mediocrity in books—that is, we will need a

ISSUE *to* CONSIDER 1.1

*Even **Comic Books**?!*

Although children who are now in school think of Superman, Spiderman, Batman, and Catwoman as characters in action-packed movies, in previous generations young people knew the real score: These were characters from comic books, those pulpy-paged illustrated thrillers from the days before television, that cost only 10 cents—and then 15, and then 25, and then . . . they all but disappeared. Comic books were either a staple of life or a threat to civilization, depending on whom you asked. In the 1950s, during the McCarthy Era when people suspected that the moral fiber of our country was under attack from many quarters, a set of Congressional hearings were held in which comic books were accused of promoting amorality, lawlessness, and perversion. In 1954, the major comic book publishers agreed to police themselves and adopted the Comics Code Authority, which insists, among other things, that:

1. Crimes shall never be presented in such a way as to create sympathy for the criminal, to promote distrust of the forces of law and justice, or to inspire others with a desire to imitate criminals.
2. No comics shall explicitly present the unique details and methods of a crime.
3. Policemen, judges, government officials, and respected institutions shall never be presented in such a way as to create disrespect for established authority.
4. If crime is depicted it shall be as a sordid and unpleasant activity. (Comics Code Authority)

Source: Comix: A History of Comic Books in America, by Les Daniels, copyright 1971 by Les Daniels and Mad Peck Studios.

Many comic book publishers went out of business, and the rest quickly lost ground to the growing attraction of television—which, of course, some would argue has become an even greater threat to children's intellects and morals.

Now comic books are back in a new form, called *graphic novels.* They are being produced with some sophistication—printed on glossy paper and costing more money. Many graphic novels are reprints of comic books, with several episodes strung together as one volume. Others are newly created as graphic novels. Notable among these are *manga,* graphic novels from Japan.

The American Library Association is taking graphic novels seriously, and they put out an annual list of the best graphic novels (see the home page at <http://www.ala.org>). Graphic novels are reviewed in *School Library Journal* and *Kirkus.*

Some advocates of graphic novels are enthusiastic about their exciting multimedia formats. Others note their appeal to reluctant readers—especially children from 11 or 12 and up. (You can, after all, "read" them by only occasionally looking at the words.) Educators we talked to in an unscientific survey weren't sure. When we asked to review the graphic novels in one middle school library recently, the librarian confided that it was not yet possible: The principal had taken them all into his office, and was still trying to decide if they should go on the shelves.

What do you think: Should they?

serviceable set of terms to help us talk about literary features of children's books. Those will be the focus of Chapter 2.

Some of the most appealing books for children are illustrated books. Picture books are a unique art form, combining aspects of novels and movies. Appreciating the dynamics of picture books deserves its own focus, and that will be the topic of Chapter 3.

A huge contribution of children's literature is to help children understand themselves and appreciate people from other cultures. Multicultural books mostly written within North America will be the focus of Chapter 4. Because many good books are available to children from writers in other parts of the world, we will focus on international literature in Chapter 5.

Having considered those background issues, we will then look more closely at the books themselves: the kinds of books available (arranged by genre), the evolution of books over the years, and exemplary writers and illustrators of children's books. In the pages that follow, we will examine Poetry for Children (Chapter 6), Traditional Literature (Chapter 7), Modern Fantasy and Science Fiction (Chapter 8), Contemporary Realistic Fiction (Chapter 9), Historical Fiction (Chapter 10), and Informational Books and Biography (Chapter 11).

What Is Children's Literature?

It is surprisingly hard to define a children's book. In his own apology for not offering a straight answer to the question, "What *is* a children's book?" Peter Hunt (1995) writes,

> [T]he answer is that we all *know* what it is, but it is not very easy to *tell* what it is (or what it is not). . . . [I]t is everything from a Sixteenth Century chapbook to a twentieth century computer-based, interactive device. It is everything from the folk tale to the problem novel, from the picture book to the classroom poem, from the tract to the penny dreadful, from the classic to the comic. (p. ix)

Children's literature is the collection of books that are read to and by children. That collection is enormous: There are hundreds of thousands of English-language children's titles in print. Currently about 25,000 new titles are published every year in the English language alone (*Library and Book Trade Almanac*, 2010). And it is old: The tradition of publishing literature for English-speaking children dates back two and a half centuries, predating the founding of the American republic.

Children's literature spans the range from alphabet books and nursery rhyme collections for the very young through novels and informational books for adolescents (or young adults, as they are called in the book trade)—in other words, from birth to about age fifteen.

Today, most children's books are written expressly for children. But there are books written originally for adults that have become popular with children—from an earlier period, John Bunyan's *Pilgrim's Progress* and Daniel Defoe's *Robinson Crusoe* and, more recently, *Platero and I (Platero y yo)* by Juan Ramon Jimenez. Other works, such as Charles Perrault's "Sleeping Beauty in the Woods" and the anonymous *Arabian Nights*—were written for adults but have been adapted for children. And the oral tradition—myths, ballads, epics, and folktales—makes up a large body of material that was told to adults and children alike, including the well-known stories "Jack and the Beanstalk," "Rapunzel," "Brer Rabbit and the Briar Patch," "Cucarachita Martina and Ratoncito Perez," and "Anansi the Spider."

Today, children's books are published by the juvenile books branches of large publishing houses such as Random House and Houghton Mifflin, as well as by publishers that serve the children's market exclusively, such as Candlewick Press and Peachtree Press. Many publishers offer books published under imprints, which might, like Atheneum, be the name of an originally independent publisher that has been taken over by a larger house or, like Richard Jackson Books, Margaret K. McElderry Books, and Walter Lorraine Books, reflect arrangements by which publishers allow their most successful editors to publish books under their own names.

We should note that many titles of children's books are produced by publishing companies that have particular religious orientations. Such books may sell copies that number in the millions; however, because they are not usually purchased for use in public schools, or reviewed in professional journals on children's literature such as *The Horn Book* or *School Library Journal,* they are not treated in this text.

Qualities of Children's Literature

As teachers of college courses on children's literature, we sometimes catch ourselves smiling to see an adult student smuggling *Frog and Toad Are Friends* to class between a copy of *War and Peace* and a thick tome on organic chemistry. That image sometimes makes us stop to ask: What is the study of children's literature doing in a college curriculum? Just how significant is the quality of children's books? There are several ways to answer these questions.

First, although children's books might seem simple, their simplicity is achieved through hard work by talented writers. Many people try to produce books for children, but the percentage of manuscripts that are actually published is unbelievably small. In a recent year, one major publishing house received five thousand unsolicited manuscripts and published two of them.

TEACHING IDEA 1.2

INTERTEXTUALITY!

> **COMMON CORE STANDARD:**
> *Integration of Knowledge and Ideas, STANDARD 9*

"Intertextuality" is a term for the similarities between stories—the features like the problem situation (such as children being left at home alone), the plot structure (the hero as least-likely-to-succeed going on a quest and proving himself or herself a hero), the pattern of actions (such as one thing leading to another), the kinds of characters (such as a trickster spider), or even important details (such as a piece of clothing that identifies the true hero).

Read one of these collections of stories to children; then lead the class in completing a Venn diagram (two interlocking circles) about them.

For kindergarten through grade 3:

- *Hattie and the Fox,* by Mem Fox
- *The Little Red Hen,* retold and illustrated by Paul Galdone

It's not just the chicken heroes! It's also the pattern of the chicken-hero going to one character after another, and having them give the same lazy response that makes these stories similar.

For older students:

- *The Children's Homer,* by Padraic Colum
- *The Homecoming,* by Cynthia Voigt
- *Bud, Not Buddy,* by Christopher Paul Curtis
- *Parvana's Journey,* by Deborah Ellis

Here the pattern to observe is *the journey.* What sends each character or set of characters on their way? What discouragements and distractions do they face along the way? What faith sustains them? How do they grow and change as they travel? What turns out to be more important: the arrival or the journey?

Award-winning author Katherine Paterson (1988) compares writing a children's book to composing music. She suggests that a good children's book is like a score for a chamber quartet, rather than a work for a full symphony. The work for the chamber quartet is less elaborate, but if its melodies are pleasing and its harmonies apt, it will have no less quality than a full orchestral work. In the same way, a good children's book will have fewer layers of complexity than a good book for adults, but if it is created with great care, it can also have excellence.

Second, because much of our contemporary children's literature grew out of the folktales from oral traditions, children's books contain many timeless stories that know no age boundaries. In *The Anatomy of Criticism*, Northrop Frye (1957) wrote that all literature is one fabric, woven of many strands of plot, image, and theme that have been told over and over in stories around the world, throughout all time. The most essential stories—those that tell of virtue rewarded, of straying into danger and struggling to get back out, of learning to distinguish the things of lasting value, of finding one's true qualities and putting them to the service of others—are the materials out of which all literature is made. They are found in their purest form in myths and folktales from around the world, and in books for children.

Third, children's books are worthy of serious study because the education of children warrants society's best energies. Good books will help children by making them literate, giving them knowledge of the world and empathy for those with whom they share it, offering them stories and images to furnish their minds and nurture their imaginations, and kindling their appreciation for language used well. Given such worthy goals, such literature deserves attention and respect.

What makes a book a children's book? A children's book usually has these qualities:

- **A child protagonist and an issue that concerns children.** A children's book usually has a central character that is the age of the intended audience. Children identify more easily with one of their own. Even when the central character is not a child—as in "Cinderella," for example—children need to feel that the central issues of a story concern them in some way.
- **A straightforward story line, with a linear and limited time sequence in a confined setting.** Books for younger children usually focus on one or two main characters, cover short time sequences (they are usually—but not always—told straight through from problem to solution, without flashbacks), and most often are set in one place. When writing for older children, authors gradually take more license with time sequences and may interweave more than one plot strand, as Louis Sachar does in *Holes*.
- **Language that is concrete and vivid and not overly complex.** The words in children's books—especially in picture books—primarily name actors and actions. Books without pictures need to have more verbal description to help children visualize characters and settings. They use dialogue to move the story along. And they give glimpses of the characters' motives. In all these cases, readers see more of what characters do than of what they say, and certainly more of both than of what they think.

Qualities of Outstanding Children's Literature

What makes a good children's book? Qualities that make outstanding children's books apply to excellent literature for any age. If a book satisfies the following criteria, it is a good children's book:

- **Good books expand awareness.** Good books give children names for things in the world and for their own experiences. Good books take children inside other people's perspectives and let children "walk two moons" in their shoes. They broaden children's understanding of the world and their capacity for empathy.

- **Good books provide an enjoyable read that doesn't overtly teach or moralize.** Many children's books turn out to be about something—to have themes, in fact—and it is often possible to derive a lesson from them. But if a book seems too deliberately contrived in order to teach a lesson, children (and critics) will not tolerate it.
- **Good books tell the truth.** Outstanding children's books usually deal with significant truths about the human experience. Moreover, the characters in them are true to life, and the insights the books imply are accurate, perhaps even wise.
- **Good books embody quality.** The words are precisely chosen and often poetic in their sound and imagery; the plot is convincing, the characters believable, and the description telling.
- **Good books have integrity.** The genre, plot, language, characters, style, theme, and illustrations, if any, all come together to make a satisfying whole.
- **Good books show originality.** Excellent children's books introduce readers to unique characters or situations or show them the world from a unique viewpoint; they stretch the minds of readers, giving them new ways to think about the world and new possibilities to consider.

Children's Books and Childhood

The criteria for excellence just outlined have not always held true. That is because the life stage of childhood has evolved throughout history as adults changed their definition of *childhood* and their views of young people. Literature for children has changed, too, following the fortunes of childhood as a life stage. As Victor Watson writes, "Children's books reflect and are bound up in cultural changes; they are particularly susceptible to developing assumptions about the nature of childhood, adolescence, and education" (2001, p. vi).

Children in the Middle Ages

It has been said that until roughly five hundred years ago, childhood as we know it did not exist in the West (Aries, 1962). That is because up until the Renaissance, children's activities—the games they played and the stories they heard—were not separated from those of adults.

Children drank alcoholic beverages, smoked tobacco, and used coarse language. After the age of seven, most children were made to work in the kitchen, in the fields, or in shops. When the village storyteller could be persuaded to tell a tale, children and adults alike gathered around to hear it. In medieval England, games such as Red Rover could involve people of all ages in a village.

It is not surprising, then, that books were not written expressly for children in those times. The few children who could read had no choice but to turn to adult fare. The ballad "Robin Hood," for example, was known as far back as 1360 A.D., and three printed versions of the legend existed before 1534. Child readers, then as now, enjoyed and accepted the romantic concept of robbing the rich to help the poor. Other romantic stories circulating at the time were those about King Arthur and the Knights of the Round Table and about Bevis, a thirteenth-century hero who hacked his way out of dungeons and slew dragons.

In 1476, William Caxton established the first printing press in England, and in 1477, he published one of the earliest books expressly for children. Called *A Booke of Curteseye,* it was filled with do's and don'ts for an audience of aristocratic boys preparing for social engagements and military careers.

Ask *the* Critic . . . Betsy Hearne

Some critics, such as Northrop Frye and E. D. Hirsch, Jr., maintain that there are some stories that all Western children could benefit from being exposed to. Do you agree? Do you believe there are some core stories or works that all children should know, or do you see the issue another way?

The idea of canonizing stories that all Western children should know is understandably controversial. On the one hand, this would solve problems in defining curriculum, testing educational achievement, and establishing cultural frames of reference in a multicultural environment. Yet realizing such an idea raises as many questions as it answers. Literature is not a science with objective, quantifiable standards of measurement. Who will decide which stories belong in the canon? How do we incorporate individual differences (both adults' and children's) into the subjective task of assessing a story's importance? Is it possible to reconcile myriad conflicting values in a small selection or, conversely, reflect representative values in a large selection? In terms of use, a core of "approved" stories is bound to take precedence over other texts. What are the implications for publishing new texts? And how long do we wait before inducting a story? Some books and stories that are now considered classics met with a negative reaction when they were first published. This includes traditional fairy tales, picture books such as **Where the Wild Things Are**, and many examples of fiction across two centuries.

On the practical front, what are the effects of mandating stories to creative teachers, who may find such a prescription stifling? Sometimes it is more effective to study one story in depth, establishing a process and a set of principles that can then be applied broadly, than to cover a predetermined core, which can easily become an exercise in superficial exposure. Certainly, the identification of a canon of stories, those that have appealed to both critics and children over a long period of time, would require a balanced emphasis on the often warring factors of high quality and general appeal.

Proponents of a clearly defined—and, by implication, required—body of stories common to all children either believe that these questions are answerable or believe that the disadvantages of compromise are worth the advantages of commonality. My own experience of reviewing, teaching, and storytelling over several decades has persuaded me that adult consensus on these issues is rare, if not impossible, and that children and stories are a quirky, unpredictable match depending on personality, peer group, family environment, and many other factors. Of course every child needs some stories. But selecting the same stories for "all Western children" involves the kind of generalized social and aesthetic assumptions that have plagued efforts to establish a literary canon in higher education. I would suggest that a buffet of stories, from which children and adults can choose together, is preferable to a set menu.

Betsy Hearne is a professor in the Graduate School of Library and Information Science at the University of Illinois at Urbana-Champaign, where she teaches children's literature and storytelling. She is the author of numerous articles and books, including *Choosing Books for Children: A Commonsense Guide*; the folktale anthology *Beauties and Beasts*; several novels for children (most recently *Listening for Leroy* and *Wishes, Kisses, and Pigs*); and a picture book, *Seven Brave Women*, which won the 1998 Jane Addams Children's Book Award. The former children's book editor of *Booklist* and of *The Bulletin of the Center for Children's Books*, she has reviewed books for thirty years and contributes regularly to the *New York Times Book Review*.

Children in Puritan Times

By the seventeenth century, more works were being written for children, but most did not make for enjoyable reading. The Puritans, the stern religious exiles who established the English colonies in America, infused early American children's works with their certainty that the devil could enter young bodies. They even wrote poems exalting death at an early age—better to die innocent than grow up and be corrupted. Given the didactic and fiery messages of Puritan authors, it is not surprising that most of their works are no longer read. Here is an example of Puritan prose written in 1702 by one Thomas Parkhurst:

> My dear Children, consider what comfort it will be unto you when you have come to dye, that when other children have been playing, you have been praying. The time will come, for ought you know very shortly, . . . when thou shalt be sick upon thy bed, and thou shalt be struggling for life, thy poor little body will be trembling, so that the very bed will shake under thee, thine eyestrings will break, and then thy heartstrings will break; . . . then, O then, the remembrance of thy holy life will give thee reassurance of the love of God.

Despite this bleak view, nonetheless, there were some bright moments. Books were generally instructional and religious in nature, but many writers did sugarcoat their instruction with rhymes, riddles, and good stories. Also, children continued to find adult fare to their liking. John Bunyan's Christian allegory, *Pilgrim's Progress*, was read for centuries. What made it palatable to children was its portrayal of a sense of family. Children are presumed to have skipped over the lengthy religious commentary to savor the happy family life. Indeed, the story of Christian can still hold the imagination of children who read the adapted, abridged, and illustrated versions.

Children of the fifteenth to eighteenth centuries also turned to hornbooks and chapbooks for their reading fare. In both England and America, peddlers traveled from town to town selling items such as pots, pans, needles, medicine, and hornbooks—which looked like paddles, averaged two and a half by five inches, were usually made of wood, and often were attached to a leather thong so that children could hang them around the neck or wrist. The lesson sheet or story was pasted onto the flat surface, and then covered with horn, a film of protective material similar to animal horn. Hornbooks were filled with lessons in religion, manners, the alphabet, and reading.

The same traveling salesmen who peddled hornbooks inspired the invention of chapbooks ("chap" is derived from the word "cheap"). Chapbooks were made of folded sheets of paper and were inexpensive to produce and light to carry. They contained popular stories of the day, such as "Jack, the Giant Killer," "The History of Sir Richard Whittington," and "Saint George and the Dragon," and also large numbers of cautionary tales, illustrating the do's and don'ts of childhood. Contemporary author Gail E. Haley has written and illustrated *Dream Peddler*, about a fictitious chapbook peddler who was proud of his profession because he gave children fairy tales and adventures to cultivate their dreams.

Children in the Enlightenment

In 1693, John Locke published *Some Thoughts Concerning Education*, which influenced child-rearing practices on both sides of the Atlantic. The book's exhortation that "some easy pleasant book" be given to children was good for the circulation of children's books. Nonetheless, the books still promoted strict moralistic teachings, if in narrative form.

At the dawn of the eighteenth century, more playful and pleasurable literature began to emerge. The verses of Isaac Watts were popular, and although to a contemporary ear they sound overly moralistic and didactic, for their time they were less so than those of his predecessors. In 1743, Mary Cooper published *The Child's New Plaything, Being a Spelling Book Intended to Make the Learning to Read a Diversion.* An American edition of the book came out in 1750 with even more "diversions," reflecting a change in how stories for children were perceived. *The New England Primer*, which combined alphabet and catechism, was the most widely read book of the period, another indication of the instructive mindset of the eighteenth century.

During this period, children also continued to read books written for adults. Many of Daniel Defoe's works were popular with children. In fact, *The Life and Surprising Adventures of Robinson Crusoe of York, Marine,* with its fearless optimism and high adventure, proved popular with children for the better part of two centuries. Jonathan Swift's *Gulliver's Travels*, published in 1726, is another book that was written for adults but adopted by children. Although the book is filled with heavy satire that reflects Swift's quarrels with the imperfections of humankind in general and Englishmen in particular, its language and plot are irresistible.

Two and half centuries ago, an innovative entrepreneur named John Newbery (1713–1767) prepared the way for the blossoming of children's literature in the nineteenth and twentieth centuries. Newbery moved to London in 1744 and launched the first commercially successful company dedicated almost exclusively to publishing beautiful and pleasurable children's books. In his thirty-year career, Newbery published twenty titles for children in attractive, playful formats, including the accordion book, made of one long strip folded accordion-style to form "pages." He was the first to introduce illustrations by first-rate artists, and he published books in more permanent, attractive bindings than the popular, less expensive chapbooks.

In 1922, Frederick Melcher, the founder of *Publisher's Weekly*, made a donation to the American Library Association to establish an annual award for the most distinguished contribution to literature for children. Fittingly, the award was named after John Newbery. (A list of the award winners and the honor books over the past eight decades appears on our accompanying website.)

Newbery is believed also to have written some of the books he published, including *A Little Pretty Pocket-Book* and *The History of Little Goody Two-Shoes.* Read for the better part of a century in England and the United States, *Little Goody Two-Shoes* was the first best seller written for children (and one of the longest lasting). The book might not be familiar to you, but the phrase "goody two shoes" is still used to mean a person with overly refined behavior.

The "Golden Age of Children's Literature"

As the example of *Little Goody Two-Shoes* illustrates, children's books up until the 1800s were often strongly didactic—if not downright preachy. But in the 1800s, books for children became more entertaining. In the 1800s, delightful works written expressly for children emerged that still rank among the most popular books of all time. During the long reign of Queen Victoria from 1837 to her death in 1901, England enjoyed a period of stability. Parents began to sentimentalize childhood, creating what has been called "the cult of childhood." Some of the very best writers created books for children. Books written in the nineteenth century that still circulate briskly include Clement Moore's *The Night Before Christmas* (published in 1823), Hans Christian Andersen's *The Ugly Duckling* and *The Little Mermaid* (translated into English in 1846), Lewis Carroll's *Alice's Adventures in Wonderland* (published in 1865), Louisa May Alcott's *Little Women* (published in 1868), Mark Twain's *The Adventures of Tom Sawyer* (published in1876), Randolph Caldecott's *The House That Jack Built* (1878), Carlo Collodi's *The Adventures of Pinocchio* (1881), Robert Louis Stevenson's *Treasure Island* (1883), Joel Chandler Harris' *Uncle Remus: His Songs and Sayings* (1883), and Rudyard Kipling's *The Jungle Book* (1894).

TEACHING IDEA 1.3

EXPLORING LITERATURE FROM THE GOLDEN AGE

COMMON CORE STANDARD: *Craft and Structure, STANDARD 4*

Authors writing children's literature a century ago often used more elaborate language than contemporary children's book authors do. Such writing had its own virtue. Here is an experiment. For students in third grade and above, read a section from Kenneth Grahame's original *The Wind in the Willows*—the chapter "Dulce Domus" will do fine. Tell the children a little bit about the characters: Ratty is a "Hail fellow, well met" type who has invited his new friend Mole for an outing in the countryside, and now they are making their way home. Mole, of course, is naturally timid, and might have preferred to stay home in the first place. Ask the students to listen carefully and try to picture the scene in their minds. After you have finished reading, have them tell you what they envisioned. It may help to have them draw the scene first. Afterwards, ask if Grahame's writing "worked" for them.

This "Golden Age" of children's literature continued up until the 1920s. The early 1900s saw the publication of L. Frank Baum's *The Wizard of Oz* (1900), Beatrix Potter's *The Tale of Peter Rabbit* (1902), James Barrie's *Peter Pan in Kensington Garden* (1906), Kenneth Grahame's *The Wind in the Willows* (1908), Frances Hodgson Burnett's *The Secret Garden* (1910), Hugh Lofting's *The Story of Doctor Dolittle* (1920), Margery Williams' *The Velveteen Rabbit* (1922), and A. A. Milne's *Winnie the Pooh* (1926).

Although the "Golden Age" as a sort of distant period of excellence in children's literature may have ended with Milne, many other much-beloved books, especially picture books, emerged in the decades that followed. Hardie Gramatky's *Little Toot* came out in 1931. Dr. Seuss (Theodor Geisel) published *And to Think That I Saw It on Mulberry Street* and J. R. R. Tolkien published *The Hobbit* in 1937. Virginia Lee Burton's *Mike Mulligan and His Steam Shovel* dates from 1939, the same year Ludwig Bemelmans' *Madeline* appeared. Robert McCloskey's *Make Way for Ducklings* and H. A. Rey's *Curious George* both came out in 1941. Eleanor Estes won the Newbery Award with *The Hundred Dresses* in 1944. C. S. Lewis' *The Lion, the Witch, and the Wardrobe* was published in 1950, and E. B. White's *Charlotte's Web* followed two years later. All of these books are so popular with contemporary children that it may be hard to believe they delighted their great-grandparents, too.

Contemporary Children's Books

There is one obvious distinction between most of the books published for children through the 1950s and those that followed. Up until the early 1960s, in the United States, children's literature featured white children almost exclusively. Then in 1965, with the civil rights movement awakening mainstream Americans to the realization that their conception of "us" was largely limited to white, English-speaking children, Nancy Larrick wrote a path-breaking article for the *Saturday Review* in which she pointed out the paucity of nonwhite characters in books for children. Shortly afterward, the Council on Interracial Books for Children was established, with the goal of persuading writers and artists of color to produce works for children. In 1982, the American Library Association added to its Newbery and Caldecott Awards the Coretta Scott King Award, to celebrate books that honorably and accurately depict African American children (see Chapter 4).

These efforts opened the door to a wealth of talent. Not only has the representation of minority children in English-language children's literature increased substantially in the last thirty years, but the writers and artists of color who have broken into print are among the best we have. Children's books are written by, and feature, African Americans, Latinos, Asian Americans, and Native Americans, as well as children from families of limited means and those who otherwise depart from the older stereotype of white, middle-class, two-parent homes. Far more international literature is available for the American child reader—especially books from Latin America and Asia—and these books are written with greater sensitivity than in the past. Mostly gone are the stereotypical depictions of people from other continents; the norm is to have people from other cultures either write their own books or be portrayed as they would present themselves. Indeed, a whole subfield of multicultural children's literature has emerged to help librarians, teachers, and parents take advantage of the multicultural works that are available. (Chapter 4 of this book is devoted to that subject.)

Even as the "Golden Age of Children's Literature" was in full flower, there were, as Prime Minister Benjamin Disraeli acknowledged, "Two Nations" in nineteenth century England. The children of the aristocrats and the growing middle class were delving with delight into these wonderful new children's books, while the children of the poor from the age of five were working 16-hour days in the mines and factories. Today in North America, children's books are not enjoyed by all children, either—at least not in their homes. Although children's literature in America has exploded with color and diversity, many American children rarely see a children's book or hear one read aloud at home (Hart & Risley, 1995; Heath, 1983).

The Genres of Children's Literature

Genre in literature corresponds to the rules of play in a game: If you know the genre you are reading, you know what kinds of actions and realities to expect, and which ones are not allowed. But herein lies a problem: Rules (in games or in literature) are sometimes broken. The breaking of genre rules—or the blurring of genre lines—in literature results in what has been called blended genres, mixed genres, or hybrid books. While this is not a new phenomenon in literature, it seems to be occurring with increasing frequency.

One example of genre blending is the time travel book, in which a character is transported through time to another era or to a fantasy world. In Jane Yolen's *The Devil's Arithmetic* (2004), the story begins as a contemporary family gathers for a Passover Seder. Soon Hannah, the story's protagonist, is transported to a Polish village in 1940, where she is captured by the Nazis and taken to a death camp. In Susan Cooper's *King of Shadows,* the protagonist travels to contemporary England with an American drama troupe, only to find himself transported 400 years back in time to Shakespeare's London. Young readers also enjoy this type of blended genre, as evidenced by the popularity of series such as Jon Scieszka's *Time Warp Trio* series.

Magical realism is yet another example of genre blending. In magical realism the author creates a believable, realistic setting and then infuses elements into that setting that stretch the boundaries of believability. For example, in Polly Horvath's *The Pepins and Their Problems*, readers encounter a cow that produces lemonade. Cornelia Funke's *The Thief Lord* is largely a realistic story about two orphaned boys who run away to modern-day Venice and join a community of street children. Only at the end of story do magical elements come into play in this suspenseful adventure.

What is of particular note in contemporary children's literature is the way in which lines are being blurred across an increasingly wider range of genres. More and more contemporary authors are blurring the lines between poetry and other genres. In *Out of the Dust*, author Karen Hesse (1999) blends poetry and historical fiction, using free verse poetry to tell the story of the hardships faced by young Billie Jo in the midst of the Dust Bowl during the Great Depression. In *Dark Sons*, author Nikki Grimes (2005) further blurs genre boundaries as she uses free verse poetry to tell the story of two boys—modern day Sam and the Biblical Ishmael. In *Song of the Water Boatman and Other Pond Poems*,

ILLUSTRATION 1.3 Polly Horvath's *The Pepins and Their Problems* is written in a mix of genres. (Book cover of "The Pepins and Their Problems" by Polly Horvath, illustrated by Marylin Hafner. Square Fish [an imprint of Macmillan. All rights reserved.], 2008. (ISBN:0312377517).)

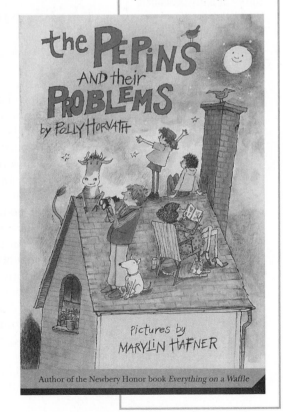

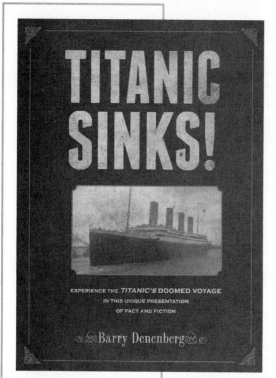

ILLUSTRATION 1.4 In *Titanic Sinks!* Barry Denenberg blurs the line between fact and fiction by creating a newspaper called the *Modern Times* that is used to convey information about the Titanic. ("Titanic Sinks!" by Barry Denenberg. Used by permission of Penguin Group (USA) Inc. All rights reserved.)

Joyce Sidman (2005) combines poetry and nonfiction. Sidman uses a variety of poetic forms to celebrate the plants and creatures commonly found in ponds. Each poem is accompanied by a paragraph that provides scientific information about the featured creature or plant.

In Jason Chin's picture book, *Coral Reefs*, a young girl at the library begins reading a book about coral reefs and suddenly finds herself immersed in the ocean and surrounded by plants and animals of the sea. So a fantasy framework becomes the vehicle for conveying information about the ocean. The line between fantasy and nonfiction are also blended in the popular *Magic School Bus* series by Joanna Cole.

While there has been some criticism of the blurring of genre boundaries in books such as these, we believe that children can readily distinguish between fact and fiction. Children know that school buses cannot really shrink down and carry the passengers into the human body! However, the blurring of boundaries can sometimes be cause for concern. In *Titanic Sinks!* Barry Denenberg (2011) blurs the line between fact and fiction by creating a newspaper called the *Modern Times,* which becomes the vehicle for conveying information about the Titanic. The author also infuses "journal entries" written by the editor of this fictitious newspaper throughout the book, which is made to appear to be a work of nonfiction by the inclusion of actual photographs from the era. And while the cover of the book notes that the book is a blend of "fact and fiction," young readers may not have the sophistication to untangle this blending.

Children's Books and English Language Learners

Two thirds of English language learners in American schools are born in the United States. But among those who were born elsewhere, as well as many who have grown up in relatively isolated communities in the United States, there are quite a few who may find books written for North American children to be puzzling or off-putting.

The genres of American children's books may be unfamiliar. In the countries outside North and South America, Europe, Australia and New Zealand, and Japan, realistic fiction is rarely found, so children from other parts of the world may be confused by books that *seem* true to life in every respect but actually are not true. Science fiction and fantasy genres may be unfamiliar, too. You may need to take the time to explain those genres to English language learners. Folktales, on the other hand, are common virtually everywhere.

The qualities of good children's books we described earlier in this chapter may not apply to stories that children from other parts of the world have heard or read. For example, books that are popular with children from Argentina, Mexico, and other Spanish-speaking countries may be startlingly unpredictable instead of linear, because their authors equate an unfettered imagination with creativity.

The moral orientation of American children's books may seem odd. Authors of mainstream children's literature in America downplay moral teaching, leaving room for readers to derive their own truths, but children raised in traditional societies more often expect stories to have clear moral messages.

The initiative taking and individualism of characters in American children's books may run counter to the cultural norms in many traditional societies, where children are taught to be stringently obedient to adults. Children from such cultures may find it hard to identify with characters like Marty in Phyllis Reynolds Naylor's *Shiloh* (2010), Opal in Kate DiCamillo's *Because of Winn-Dixie* (2010), and Jennifer Holm's Turtle in *Turtle in Paradise* (2010), each of whom is depicted with a strongly individualistic personality; in addition, each of these characters formulates and carries out plans that are daringly independent of adults.

Censorship: Which Books Will Make It into Children's Hands?

All teachers make decisions about which books to put into children's hands. Of course, teachers choose books that they think will interest children and that will appeal to the children's level of understanding. Of course, they choose books that they think have some sort of merit. But at the same time teachers make some books available, they deny children access to others. When teachers deny children access to books because they think those books are too risqué or controversial or when other adults put pressure on teachers to deny access to certain books, then we are dealing with the issue of censorship.

Simply put, censorship means to deny someone access to books or ideas (Naylor, 1991). The First Amendment of the Constitution of the United States states: "Congress shall make no law respecting an establishment of religion, or prohibiting the free exercise thereof; or abridging the freedom of speech, or of the press. . . ." This language suggests that individual freedom is at issue whenever teachers or other school officials deny children access to written materials. But many parents claim the right to expect teachers not to expose children to material on topics that the parents would rather handle more delicately at home or keep away from their children altogether. Teachers, for their part, may choose to introduce children to a book they know will stretch their minds and not to share books they consider trashy. Whose rights should prevail? And how should the issue of rights be squared with the requirements of responsible education?

Some topics seem to raise more pressures for censorship than others, and the controversial topics are not always the ones we might expect. In society at large, the areas in which the media feel the most pressure for censorship are sex and violence, especially in our entertainment. These topics seem to cause less controversy in schools, though (Traw, 1996), perhaps because there is something closer to a consensus among parents and teachers that books with more than trace amounts of sex and violence should not be circulated at school. It is true that there is the occasional book such as Judy Blume's *Forever* that describes sexual acts (and, sure enough, this book has suffered campaigns to get it off the shelves). But for the most part, in children's literature, sex is off limits, and few people want to argue about it. Other bodily functions seem to escape censorship, however. Taro Gomi's *Everyone Poops* and Shinta Cho's *The Gas We Pass* are sometimes found in school,

ILLUSTRATION 1.5   Books like the popular *Captain Underpants* series that deal with bodily functions are, surprisingly, seldom censored in schools. (Scholastic, Inc.)

and Dav Pilkey's *Captain Underpants* series, with titles such as *Captain Underpants and the Perilous Plot of Professor Poopypants*, is freely distributed during "Drop Everything and Read" time, even (especially!) in third grade.

The surprisingly difficult issue is religion. Religion seems to come up in two ways. We are familiar with the direct way, as exemplified by the state school board of Kansas's decision (later overturned) to require biology teachers to teach Creationism—the biblically based doctrine that God really did create man and woman in his own image—and not evolution—the theory that human beings descended from pre-human primates. The Louisiana Science Education Act allows but does not require teachers in that state to teach Creationism (and also to challenge the science behind claims that human activity has influenced climate change). Usually, religious censorship comes up in less direct ways, as groups of parents and other citizens campaign against books that they believe spread antireligious ideas. Especially vulnerable to censorship are books about magic and witches.

The *Harry Potter* books and even Tomie dePaola's *Strega Nona* books have evoked campaigns for removal from school libraries by people who believe the descriptions of magic that permeate them are not harmless fun but suggestive of Satanism. Sometimes the criticisms miss the target entirely. For instance, the storyteller Joseph Bruchac described visiting a school district in South Dakota where a citizens' group had demanded that the school remove all books from the library having to do with Transcendentalism. (The parents apparently confused the nineteenth-century literary movement led by Ralph Waldo Emerson with a popular method of meditation.) But whether the groups bringing complaints about books have done their homework or not, schools and teachers need to be prepared to defend their choice of books.

Arguments over religion and alleged Satanism may deflect attention from another kind of passive censorship that is also serious: What are we leaving out? James Loewen filled a book with teachings that were either distorted in or missing altogether from the typical American school curriculum. He entitled his book *Lies My Teacher Told Me: Everything Your American History Textbook Got Wrong* (Loewen, 1996). If our children are going to sharpen their minds and forge better ways of living in the future, they will need access to materials that challenge the status quo. But teachers who have been beleaguered by parents upset about Strega Nona or Harry Potter might not be very daring when it comes to looking at the true story of Christopher Columbus, the struggle to improve working conditions in America, or even the constructive role religion has played in U.S. life. Because censorship removes from consideration materials that might stretch children's minds, the American Library Association (ALA) has issued statements opposing it. Here is why:

> Why is censorship harmful?
> Censorship is harmful because it results in the opposite of true education and learning. In the process of acquiring knowledge and searching for truth, students can learn to discriminate—to make decisions rationally and logically in light of the evidence. By suppressing all materials containing ideas or themes with which they do not agree, censors produce a sterile conformity and a lack of intellectual and emotional growth in students. (ALA web page, November 2, 2000)

What seems clear is that in some districts, at least, there is less of a consensus about what schools should teach and less trust on the part of the parents than there was before the drumbeat of critiques of U.S. schools that began in the 1980s. How should teachers conduct themselves in the face of the occasional demands for censorship of children's reading fare in the schools?

We recommend the following steps:

1. Stay aware of what is in your classroom library and the groups of books you assign, and know why they are there. You should be confident that the books

you are making available have literary merit, are enjoyable, raise interesting and important themes, and broaden children's awareness of people and places and events. You should be confident that they are not mean spirited, racist, or prurient.

2. Make sure that your school has responsible guidelines for choosing books. One source of such guidelines is the National Council of Teachers of English (NCTE). NCTE has a special section on their Web site devoted to the topic of censorship, including suggested guidelines for choosing materials for students to read <www.ncte.org/censorship>.

3. Be prepared to speak up for the contribution that good books make to children's education. Also be prepared to explain the benefit to individual children and to society as a whole when students learn to distinguish what is worthwhile from what is not worthwhile and to entertain ideas and points of view that are different from their own.

4. Realize that others may disagree with your choice of a certain book, for reasons they believe are right. Be prepared to recognize their concern for their child and to respect that concern.

5. Be aware that, should the choice of books in your classroom or school be criticized in ways that you believe are unfair or misguided, and should calm conversation not resolve the problem, there are resources that can help. One is the American Library Association (ALA), which has an Office for Intellectual Freedom <www.ala.org>; the Office for Intellectual Freedom is also found on the ALA Web site. Another source of help is the National Council of Teachers of English <www.ncte.org>.

Resources for Children's Books

Studying children's literature in college differs in many ways from studying other literature, especially in that the focus is turned as much or more toward contemporary books for children as it is toward great works of the past. That is because—with the explosion in the number of books published for children, improvements in the technology of color reproduction, and a growing diversity in the range of people children need to know and care about—many of the very best books for contemporary children have appeared in the past twenty years. And they continue to be published every year. Therefore, to be well read in children's books, you must read backwards and forwards: Read the best of the books already published, and read the best of those just coming out. For the best books already published, you can count on the Recommended Books section at the end of each chapter (especially those in Chapters 5–11). The most important books in the development of each genre are discussed in each chapter in the section on historical development. If you want a historical perspective on children's literature, you should read those books as well. But what of the new books? How can you find your way to those that are best?

Several journals review children's books and promote the best ones. These journals, which include *The Horn Book Magazine*, *School Library Journal*, *Booklist*, and *Bookbird* as well as the book review sections of several professional magazines such as *The Reading Teacher* and *Language Arts*, have slightly different emphases and target audiences. Journals published by other teachers' organizations such as the National Council for the Social Studies <www.ncss.org> and the National Science Teachers Association <www.nsta.org> also list children's books that are keyed to topics from those subject areas.

Shaw, Nancy. (1997). *Sheep in a Jeep*. Illustrated by Margot Apple.

Willems, Mo. (2007). *I Am Invited to a Party*.

Wood, Audrey. (1999). *Silly Sally*.

Primary (books for reading aloud)

Avi. (2008). *The End of the Beginning: Being the Adventure of a Small Snail (and an Even Smaller Ant)*.

Cronin, Doreen. (2000). *Click, Clack, Moo: Cows That Type*. Illustrated by Betsy Lewin.

Henkes, Kevin. (1996). *Lilly's Purple Plastic Purse*.

Steig, William. (1990). *Doctor De Soto*.

Upper Elementary

Browne, Anthony. (2001). *Voices in the Park*.

Creech, Sharon. (2002). *Love that Dog*.

Sachar, Louis. (1998). *Holes*.

Wiles, Deborah. (2001). *Love, Ruby Lavender*.

Middle School

Avi. (1991). *Nothing But the Truth*.

Bartoletti, Susan Campbell. (2005). *Hitler Youth*.

Curtis, Christopher Paul. (1999). *Bud, Not Buddy*.

Walker, Sally M. (2005). *Secrets of a Civil War Submarine*.

TECHNOLOGY IN PRACTICE 1.1

LEARNING ABOUT BOOKS ONLINE

The online bookstore, <www.amazon.com>, is a valuable source of information about books. Click on "Books" from the menu of tabs arrayed horizontally across the top of the home page. When the window labeled "Books" opens on the left side of the page, immediately click "Advanced Search" underneath before entering other information. That will take you to another page where you can search for books by title, author, or subject. You can limit your search there to books on a certain topic for specific age groups, such as 4–8 or 9–12.

When you click on the title of a book, you will be taken to a page devoted to that book. If you click on the author's name at the top of the page, you will be taken to other titles by that author or illustrator. By scrolling down to the bottom of the page, you can usually find a publisher's description of the book and a review of the book, often by *School Library Journal, Publishers Weekly,* and others.

EXPERIENCES FOR FURTHER LEARNING

1. Reread the vignettes on page 4. Can you think of books that served you in each of those ways when you were a child? Are there other ways in which books appealed to you? Compare your answers with those of your classmates.
2. Pick a children's book. Evaluate it according to the criteria of a good children's book set out on pages 9–10. How does it fare? Are there other criteria of excellence that you would propose?
3. This chapter stated that children's books have changed throughout history, roughly as views of childhood changed. What trends do you see at work in society that may change children's literature in the next twenty years? What qualities or values would you expect to remain the same in children's literature?

4. Interview three teachers of the elementary grades. Ask them how many different ways they use children's books with their students. Compare their answers with the vignettes found on page 4.
5. Find a school librarian or a children's librarian who has worked in the field for thirty years or more. Ask her or him to talk about the ways in which books for children have changed, children's interests have changed, and parents' concerns about their children's reading materials have changed—and how these issues have remained the same. Prepare a two-column list of ways in which children's books have remained the same and ways in which they have changed. Share your list with your peers.

REFERENCES

Ainsworth, Mary D. S. "Attachment: Retrospect and Prospect." *The Place of Attachment in Human Behavior.* Ed. C. M. Parkes and J. Stevenson-Hinde. Basic Books, 1982.

Alcott, Louisa May. *Little Women.* Questar, 1868/1991.

Ancona, George. *Pablo Remembers: The Fiesta of the Day of the Dead.* Lothrop, Lee & Shepard, 1993.

Andersen, Hans Christian. *The Little Mermaid.* Random House, 1892/1993.

———. *The Ugly Duckling.* Dover, 1914/1992.

Anzaldua, Gloria. *Prietita and the Ghost Woman.* Illustrated by Maya Christina Gonzalez. Children's Book Press, 2001.

Applebee, Arthur. *The Child's Concept of Story.* University of Chicago Press, 1975.

Aries, Phillippe. *Centuries of Childhood: A Social History of Family Life.* Knopf, 1962.

Asbjornsen, Peter, and J. E. Moe. *The Three Billy Goats Gruff.* Illustrated by Glen Rounds. Holiday House, 1993.

Avi. *Nothing but the Truth.* Orchard Books, 1991.

Babbit, Natalie. *Tuck Everlasting.* Farrar, 1975.

Blume, Judy. *Forever.* Pocket Books, 1996.

Bogart, Dave (Ed.). *Library and Book Trade Almanac.* Information Sources, 2010.

Brown, Margaret Wise. *Goodnight, Moon*. HarperCollins, 1991.

———. *Little Fur Family*. Illustrated by Garth Williams. HarperCollins, 1991.

Bunyan, John. *Pilgrim's Progress*. Dent, 1678/1911.

Bus, Adriana G., and Marinus H. van IJzendoorn. "Mothers Reading to Their 3-Year-Olds: The Role of Mother-Child Attachment Security in Becoming Literate." *Reading Research Quarterly 30* (October/November/December 1995): 998–1015.

Carroll, Lewis. *Alice's Adventures in Wonderland*. Castle Books, 1865/1978.

Caxton, William. *A Booke of Curteseye*, 1477.

Chin, Jason. *Coral Reefs*. Flash Point, 2011.

Cho, Shinto. *The Gas We Pass*. Kane/Miller Book Publishers, 1994.

Collodi, Carlo. *The Adventures of Pinocchio*. Knopf, 1883/1988.

Cooper, Mary. *The Child's New Plaything, Being a Spelling Book Intended to Make the Learning to Read a Diversion*, 1743.

Cooper, Susan. *King of Shadows*. Margaret K. McElderry Books, 2001.

Creech, Sharon. *Walk Two Moons*. HarperCollins, 1994.

Daniels, Les. *Comix: A History of Comic Books in America*. Dutton, 1971.

Deedy, Carmen Agra, in association with Wilson Kimeli Naiyomah. *14 Cows for America*. Illustrated by Thomaz Gonzalez. Peachtree Publishers, 2009.

Defoe, Daniel. *Robinson Crusoe*. Running Press, 1719/1991.

Denenberg, Barry. *Titanic Sinks!* Viking Juvenile, 2011.

dePaola, Tomie. *Strega Nona*. Simon & Schuster, 1979.

DiCamillo, Kate. *Because of Winn Dixie*. Candlewick, 2010.

Dr. Seuss. *The Cat in the Hat*. Random House, 1957.

Eastman, P. D. *Are You My Mother?* Random House, 1988.

Egan, Kieran. "Individual Development in Literacy." *Stories and Readers*. Ed. Charles Temple and Patrick Collins. Christopher-Gordon, 1992.

Erikson, Erik. *Identity: Youth and Crisis*. Norton, 1968.

Frye, Northrop. *The Anatomy of Criticism*. Princeton University Press, 1957.

Funke, Cornelia. *The Thief Lord*. Scholastic, 2002.

Gomi, Taro. *Everyone Poops*. Kane/Miller Book Publishers, 1993.

Green, Norma. *The Hole in the Dike*. Scholastic, 1993.

Grimes, Nikki. *Dark Sons*. Jump at the Sun, 2005.

Haley, Gail E. *Dream Peddler*. Dutton, 1993.

Harris, Benjamin. *New England Primer*. 1686.

Hart, Betty, and Todd Risley. *Meaningful Differences in the Everyday Experience of Young American Children*. Brookes, 1995.

Heath, Shirley Brice. "What No Bedtime Story Means: Narrative Skills at Home and School." *Language in Society 11*(1) (April 1982): 49–76.

Hesse, Karen. *Out of the Dust*. Scholastic, 1999.

Hickman, Janet. "What Comes Naturally: Growth and Change in Children's Free Response to Literature." *Stories and Readers*. Ed. Charles Temple and Patrick Collins. Christopher-Gordon, 1992.

Hillman, Elizabeth. *Min Yo and the Moon Dragon*. Illustrated by John Wallner. Harcourt Brace, 1992.

Holm, Jennifer. *Turtle in Paradise*. Random House, 2010.

Horvath, Polly. *The Pepins and Their Problems*. Farrar, Straus and Giroux, 2002.

http://www.ala.org/alaorg/oif/intellectualfreedomandcensorship.html "Intellectual Freedom and Censorship Q and A."

Hunt, Peter. *Children's Literature: An Illustrated History*. Oxford University Press, 1995.

Jimenez, Juan Ramon. *Platero and I*. Translated by Antonio de Nicolas. Universe.com, 2000.

Kermode, Frank. *The Sense of an Ending*. Oxford University Press, 2000.

Larrick, Nancy. "The All-White World of Children's Books." *Saturday Review* (1965, September 11): 63–65.

Lehr, Susan. "The Child's Developing Sense of Theme as a Response to Literature." *Reading Research Quarterly 23*(3) (1988): 337–357.

Lionni, Leo. *Frederick*. Pantheon, 1967.

Locke, John. *Some Thoughts Concerning Education*, 1693.

Loewen, James. *Lies My Teacher Told Me: Everything Your American History Textbook Got Wrong*. Touchstone, 1996.

Luke, Alan. "Getting Over Method: Literacy Teaching as Work in New Times." *Language Arts 75*(4) (April 1998): 305–313.

Martin, Bill, Jr. *Brown Bear, Brown Bear, What Do You See?* Illustrated by Eric Carle. Henry Holt, 1983.

Meddaugh, Susan. *Hog-Eye*. Houghton Mifflin, 1995.

Mol, Suzanne E., Adriana G. Bus, and Maria T. de Jong. "Interactive Book Reading in Early Education: A Tool to Stimulate Print Knowledge as Well as Oral Language." *Review of Educational Research*. 79(2) (June 2009), 979–1008.

Myers, Walter Dean. *Harlem, A Poem*. Scholastic, 1997.

———. *Monster*. Amistad, 2001.

Naylor, Alice. "Censorship." *Children and Books* (8th ed.). Ed. Zena Sutherland and May Hill Arbuthnot. HarperCollins, 1991.

Naylor, Phyllis Reynolds. *Shiloh*. Atheneum, 1990.

Newbery, John. *The History of Little Goody Two-Shoes*. Singing Tree Press. 1766/1970.

———. *A Little Pretty Pocket-Book*. Harcourt, Brace & World, 1744/1967.

Paterson, Katherine. *The Gates of Excellence*. Dutton, 1988.

Paulsen, Gary. *Hatchet*. Macmillan Publishing Company, 1986.

Perrault, Charles. "Sleeping Beauty in the Woods" (La belle au bois dormant). Mercure gallant, February 1696.

Piaget, Jean. *The Language and Thought of the Child*. World, 1955.

Pilkey, Dav. *Captain Underpants and the Perilous Plot of Professor Poopypants: The Fourth Epic Novel*. Scholastic, 2000.

Rapp, Adam. *The Buffalo Tree*. Front Street, 2007.

Sachar, Louis. *Holes*. Farrar, Straus, & Giroux, 1998.

San Souci, Robert D. *The Samurai's Daughter: A Japanese Legend*. Dial, 1992.

———. *The Talking Eggs: A Folktale from the American South*. Illustrated by Jerry Pinkney. Dutton, 1989.

Shaw, Nancy. *Sheep in a Jeep*. Illustrated by Margot Apple. Houghton Mifflin, 1997.

Sidman, Joyce. *Song of the Water Boatman and Other Pond Poems*. Houghton Mifflin, 2005.

Spinelli, Jerry. *Maniac Magee*. Little, Brown & Company, 1991.

Steig, William. *The Real Thief*. Farrar, Straus, & Giroux, 1985.

———. *Sylvester and the Magic Pebble*. Simon and Schuster, 1969.

Steptoe, John. *Mufaro's Beautiful Daughters: An African Tale*. Lothrop, Lee, and Shepard, 1997.

Stern, Daniel. *The First Relationship*. Harvard University Press, 1977.

Swift, Jonathan. *Gulliver's Travels*. William Morrow, 1726/1983.

Temple, Charles. "What If 'Beauty' Had Been Ugly? Reading against the Grain of Gender Bias in Children's Books." *Language Arts* 70(2) (February 1993): 89–93.

Temple, Charles, Donna Ogle, Alan Crawford, and Penny Freppon. *All Children Read* (4th ed.). Allyn and Bacon, 2014.

Traw, Rick. "Beware! Here There Be Beasties: Responding to Fundamentalist Censors." *The New Advocate*, 9(1) (Winter 1996): 35–56.

Twain, Mark. *The Adventures of Huckleberry Finn*. Webster, 1885.

———. *The Adventures of Tom Sawyer*. American Publishing, 1876.

Watson, Victor. *The Cambridge Guide to Children's Books in English*. Cambridge University Press, 2001.

Wells, Rosemary. *Hazel's Amazing Mother*. Dial, 1985.

Yolen, Jane. *The Emperor and the Kite*. Illustrated by Ed Young. Putnam, 1988.

———. *The Devil's Arithmetic*. Puffin, 2004.

Zambo, Debby. Love, Language, and Emergent Literacy. *YC Young Children* 62(3) (May, 2007) 32–37.

Literary Elements in Works for Children

Kneeling in the sand, Paulie shredded dry seaweed and fluffed it into heap between the three black cooking stones, half forgetting that she had no food to cook. She broke palm fronds over the seaweed, then propped two pieces of driftwood with their tips just above the palm. Raking the sand together with her fingers, she built up a ring around the outside of the stones, careful to make room for the air to blow in and give life to the fire, a little and not too much.

Paulie leaned back, still kneeling, circling her upper arms in her hands to warm them. Night had come. The tree frogs stopped singing all at once.

"You got matches, Uncle?"

Paulie's uncle was washing in seawater from a bucket, pouring it down his back to get off the sweat and the sawdust, rinsing his arms.

"All the matches gone, Paulie."

"Go see if you can borrow a coal," her grandmother said. Sitting on the steps of her house, a cloth around her thin shoulders, Grann Adeline leaned toward the fire as if it were already lit. She frowned, slapped at a mosquito on her ankle. "Go on, girl. Ask sweetly and somebody bound to give you an ember."

Paulie wandered down the sand path. The small houses clustered under the trees were mostly dark. She could hear voices talking softly, a baby crying. A thin dog came out and sniffed at the backs of her knees. Paulie looked for the glow of a cook fire, smelled the breeze for one. She could feel the sea air, and hear the waves coming in, but it seemed like nobody was cooking.

Source: From *Tonight, by Sea,* by Frances Temple. Scholastic Inc./Orchard Books. Copyright © 1995 by Frances Temple. Reprinted by permission.

The Artistry of Literary Elements

Literature is a miracle. With words on a page, a writer can take readers to a place that never was, let them know people who never lived, and help them share adventures that never happened—and, in spite of the artifice, create something truer than life itself.

It can enhance our appreciation of a work to have a vocabulary and a set of concepts to help us admire its wonders, or note the shortcomings of a less-than-satisfactory work. In this chapter, we describe the literary qualities that critics and teachers most often refer to when they talk about texts, both narrative texts and informational ones. Knowing these characteristics will give us a vocabulary for exploring the elements of texts that move readers, and also for evaluating works for young readers.

The main elements of a literary work we will discuss are genre; setting; characterization; plot; theme; stance of the implied reader; point of view; the author's style, voice, tone, and mood; and intertextuality. Let's first take a closer look at each of these literary elements. Later we will consider some special literary features of informational books and poetry.

Genre: The "Rules of the Game"

Genres in literature are categories of writing recognized for their patterns of organization, their style, and their effects on readers. Genres matter. Imagine you are passing by a TV on a Saturday afternoon and see a game in progress. Your brain quickly registers what kind of game it is—football, baseball, soccer, tennis—whether it is played by women or men, and so on. Likewise, when you hear a story being told or come across one in a book, you soon decide whether it is truth or fiction, is based in fantasy or reality, is meant to be funny or scary, has human or animal characters, follows a dramatic plot or has a repeated series of actions, and so on. In your experiences with both sports and literature, you rely upon a set of categories to recognize what you are observing, what the rules are, and what you can expect to happen as well as not happen.

The genres most often treated in children's literature are folktales and other traditional literature, poetry, contemporary realistic fiction, fantasy, historical fiction, biography, and informational books. Genres let readers know what to expect as they read a work, and how to make sense of what happens.

In a work of fiction, the story usually begins with characters in a setting who soon face a problem. The reader implicitly appreciates the problem and begins to wonder about its solution. Like rules in different sports, the range of possible solutions of a literary work is controlled by the genre. If the work is realistic fiction, we expect a solution that would be possible in real life. If the work is a fairy tale, we know that the solution may be magical. If the work is fantasy, we are prepared for the story to take us into a kind of reality removed from our own, and then tell us, indirectly, something about our human nature or the world we live in.

Some works blur the distinction between realistic fiction and fantasy. *Magical realism* is the term used to describe works that mix the real and the magical. While true fantasies like J.K. Rowling's *Harry Potter* series and Philip Pullman's *His Dark Materials* take readers to a fantasy world, works of magical realism stay anchored in the real world but introduce just a touch of magical elements. For example, David Almond's *Skellig* is the story of ten-year-old Michael, whose sister has been born with a defective heart and is not expected to live. While the family fixes up a decrepit house, they are sleepwalking in the dread of impending tragedy. But Michael finds a tramp—a man looking like a dead thing—in a pile of junk in the falling-down garbage, and living, it turns out, on dead animals that the owls bring him. His name is Skellig, and he is an angel. Really.

Works may even keep the reader guessing as to what sort of genre they are reading. *The Magician's Nephew*, the first volume in C. S. Lewis's *Narnia* series, keeps readers wondering what is so peculiar about Uncle Andrew—until the two children slip on a magical ring and are transported to another world. In those early moments before the magical ring works its power, readers' curiosity is aroused as much by the questions of what *kinds of things* can happen (that is, "What genre is this, anyway?") as by the question of what *will* happen.

Note that picture books may be written in any of the genres: folktales, realistic fiction, poetry, informational books. Picture books are a kind of format rather than a genre, so they are not included in our list of genres. Figure 2.1 describes the main genres of literature for children.

Settings: How Do Authors Create Times and Places?

The setting is the time and place in which the events of a story occur. Because whatever is visualized must be seen in time and space, the setting of the story is part of the reader's invitation into an imaginary experience. If an author is successful in evoking a setting, the reader may subconsciously supply many details herself.

The development of settings varies from genre to genre. In a folktale, the setting may get scant mention, yet it can still have symbolic significance. In realistic fiction, the setting may be described more elaborately to add verisimilitude, or lifelikeness, to the story and make it easier for readers to believe in the events. In a survival story, the setting works against the main character or characters—almost as if it were a character

Genre	Definition	Subtype
Folktales	Works by anonymous authors that were passed on orally from generation to generation	**fairy tales:** tales in which magic is prominent **legends:** larger-than-life tales of famous people **fables:** stories with a moral **epics:** long, rhymed works that relate a hero's exploits **myths:** ancient stories about the gods **pourquoi stories:** stories lighter than myths that explain, often delightfully, about the reasons for things
Realistic Fiction	Fictional stories that *might have happened.* In realistic fiction, events are plausible, and settings are usually drawn from actual geography.	**adventure stories:** works that tell of a character's struggles against nature or other people **humorous stories:** works that are funny **relationship stories** (or other problem stories): works that focus on relations between people or a character's struggles with her own self-doubts **historical fiction:** works with realistic characters and plots set in a historical time and place
Fantasy	Works with otherworldly or supernatural elements	**high fantasy:** works that create a parallel universe alongside the real world **low fantasy:** works in which a magical element intrudes into life in the real world, and makes possible a series of events which otherwise stay very true to life **science fiction:** works that create a fictionalized setting or set of events based on some projection of scientific knowledge
Poetry	Works in verse	**narrative poems:** works that tell a story in verse **lyric or expressive poems:** verses that convey observations or express feelings **humorous poems:** jokes, funny riddles, or humorous stories in verse **novels in verse:** book-length poems that tell a story

FIGURE 2.1   Genres of Children's Literature

itself. In historical fiction or in stories from other cultures, the setting may share center stage with the characters and events, since readers may be as curious about what life is or was like in that setting as they are about what happens in the story. The same can be said of science fiction or fantasy—genres in which the author is free to make up whole new worlds. Let's look, then, at how settings vary with some of these genres.

Settings in Folktales and Fairy Tales

Settings in folktales are presented with few details. They represent everywhere and nowhere, but they often have particular associations. In European tales, *home* is where normal life is lived, securely. The *forest* is where one may be tested by sinister forces. The *country* is where simple but honest folk live, whereas the *town* is the place of sophisticated but possibly treacherous people. A *cottage* is a place one usually wants to rise above (but may have to learn to settle for), and a *palace* is the residence of those who were born privileged or who have had triumphant success.

Because the genre of folk stories tends to use these same settings with the same connotations again and again, the mere mention of them usually cues the reader to make these associations.

Settings in Realistic Fiction

Settings in realistic fiction are usually described in great detail. Just as the genre of a work sets and limits our expectations for what can happen in it, the way a setting is

TEACHING IDEA 2.1

EXPLORING FOLKTALE SETTINGS

COMMON CORE STANDARD: *Key Ideas and Details, STANDARD 3*

Have the students think of the settings in folktales they know, such as "Puss 'n Boots," "The Old Lady Who Lived in a Vinegar Bottle," or "Hans Clodhopper." Who lives in each setting? What takes place there? Make a chart like the one in Figure 2.2 in which students record findings about different settings. What generalizations can they draw?

	Who lives at home in a cottage? What happens at home?	Who lives in the forest? What happens in the forest?	Who lives in a castle? What happens there?
"Puss 'n Boots"			
"Sleeping Beauty"			
"Little Red Riding Hood"			
"The Gunny Wolf"			

FIGURE 2.2   Settings in Folktales and Fairy Tales

Ask *the* Editor . . . Richard W. Jackson

What was the best manuscript you ever received, and what qualities do you look for in an author?

The best manuscript I've received? Ever? You might have asked me to choose between my children! There are several bests. Paula Fox's *Maurice's Room*—she'd written only three chapters at the time I first saw it but I remember reading them aloud to my wife and saying, "This woman will win the Newbery medal someday." And she did. Such vividness in the people, such kindness in the humor. And such a voice. Also a favorite—the text for *The Relatives Came* by Cynthia Rylant, for somewhat the same reasons. I believe we didn't change a word, though "best" for me doesn't mean word perfect. More important than immediate perfection is the breath of life in a piece. Frances Temple's *Taste of Salt* was another revelation—a "breathing" book about modern Haiti, about brave young people whose lives were, at the time, largely unimaginable by Americans (of any age). The book is written in two first-person teenage voices, and there is urgency in every word. For "I" stories, urgency is crucial.

Even "light" books, such as Avi's *S.O.R. Losers* or Judy Blume's *Are You There God? It's Me, Margaret,* depend on urgency for their success. In funny stories as well as serious, you need to sense the narrator's urge to bend your ear. *Toning the Sweep* by Angela Johnson is another unique example of urgent voice. It began as a collection of quick scenes, poetic impressions, snippets of conversation about a girl witnessing her grandmother's struggle with cancer; it grew into a novel over several years. Thrilling years.

I look for long-term associations with writers or illustrators and rarely take on anyone published by many houses—for snobbish reasons, I suppose. I look for loyalty and for brains. For devotion to hard work and a certain delicacy of touch. I listen for voice. Just this minute the phone rang and—speaking of voice—a cheery one said, "I've figured out how to do it, the whole book. It was our conversation yesterday that helped." The caller was Theresa Nelson, a superb novelist whose first book, *The 25-cent Miracle,* is another best. She's written four beauties since. My response to such calls has remained unchanging since 1962: gratitude and joy.

Richard W. Jackson is editor of Richard Jackson Books, an imprint of Orchard Books, which publishes some thirty new titles a year. His articles have appeared in *The Horn Book Magazine, School Library Journal,* and *The New Advocate.*

---

described in realistic fiction sets up and limits our expectations for what can happen in that work. Aspects of a setting can include:

- the immediate social group (that is, the people immediately surrounding the character),
- the wider social setting (that is, the characters' nationality, race, and social class),
- the geography (including what kinds of activities typically happen there, as well as what has happened there in the past and how people feel about it), and
- the historical period (the current decade or earlier ones).

Rita Garcia-Williams' **One Crazy Summer** illustrates all of these aspects of settings. The immediate social setting is the family of Delphine, age ten, who has been thrust into the role of mothering her younger sisters, Vonetta and Fern. They live with their kind but somewhat aloof father and their conservative, disapproving grandmother in a crowded Brooklyn apartment. The grandmother and father had moved to Brooklyn from the South some years before. As for the wider social setting, they are African American, and they are keenly aware of their ethnicity whenever they are in the company of white people. The geographical setting shifts to Oakland, California, where the father has sent the children to visit their estranged mother, Cecile. Cecile seems to lack any capacity for kindness, even motherly instincts. The historical moment is the summer of 1968. A progressive young artist, Cecile is a radical women's liberationist, and the Black Panther movement is being born right in Cecile's neighborhood, even in her living room.

Settings as Important Features in Themselves

In some genres—especially realistic fiction, fiction based in history, multicultural fiction, and fantasy—settings can figure so strongly as to share attention with the characters in the story. Eugene Yelchin takes great care to paint a picture of life in the Soviet Union under Stalin's regime in *Breaking Stalin's Nose*:

> It's dinnertime, so the kitchen is crowded. Forty-eight hardworking, honest, Soviet citizens share the kitchen and single small toilet in our communal apartment we call *komunalka* for short. We live here as one large, happy family: We are all equal; we have no secrets. We know who gets up at what time, who eats what for dinner, and who said what in their rooms. The walls are thin; some don't go up to the ceiling. We even have a room cleverly divided with shelves of books about Stalin that two families can share. (Yelchin, 2011, p. 5)

Sometimes, the setting may become a metaphor for the meaning of the work. In Edward Bloor's *Tangerine*, the artificial gated community, Windsor Downs, was thrown together callously and dangerously over sinkholes and other natural threats in central Florida, a fact the residents try unsuccessfully to ignore. The setting finds a parallel in the life of protagonist Paul Fisher's family, with its veneer of normalcy built over terrible secrets.

In multicultural literature, details of the setting may seem commonplace to some readers but appear striking to others. For example, Alma Flor Ada's *My Name Is Maria Isabel* (1995) begins:

> Maria Isabel looked at the cup of coffee with milk and the buttered toast in front of her. But she couldn't bring herself to eat.
> Her mother said, "Maribel, cariño, hurry up."
> Her father added, "You don't want to be late on your first day, do you?" (p. 1)

Children from Latino lineage will find that scene reassuringly familiar. But other readers might be surprised that a young girl would drink coffee for breakfast, moved at the mother's affectionate shortening of the girl's name, and impressed that the mother speaks to her daughter in two languages. In effect, the setting is functioning almost as a character in the story.

In a historical novel, the details of the setting may also go a long way toward satisfying young readers' curiosity about a place that is far removed in time. The earthiness of English village life early in the fourteenth century is brought home in the first paragraph of Karen Cushman's *The Midwife's Apprentice* (1995):

> When animal droppings and garbage and spoiled straw are piled up in a great heap, the rotting and moiling give forth heat. Usually no one gets close enough to notice because of the stench. But the girl noticed and, on that frosty night, burrowed deep into the warm, rotting muck, heedless of the smell. (p. 1)

Here again, although the characters also do much to impress themselves on readers, the setting of this historical novel continually surprises and informs them.

TOP SHELF 2.1

BOOKS WITH MEMORABLE SETTINGS

Bloor, Edward (1997). *Tangerine*. Harcourt.

Ellis, Deborah (2000). *The Breadwinner*. Yearling.

Farmer, Nancy (2007). *Land of the Silver Apples*. Atheneum/Richard Jackson.

Fox, Paula (1993). *Monkey Island*. Yearling.

Gaiman, Neil (2008). *The Graveyard Book*. Harper-Collins.

Soto, Gary (2000). *Baseball in April and Other Stories*. Harcourt.

ILLUSTRATION 2.1 In *One Crazy Summer*, three sisters seek to reunite with their mother during the tumultuous 1960s in Oakland, California. (Used by permission of HarperCollins Publishers.)

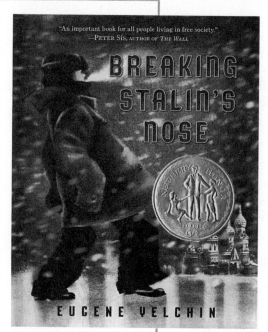

Characterization: How Do People Emerge from the Page?

Characterization is the art of creating people out of words on the page. When a writer has done a good job of characterization, readers feel as if they have gotten to know another person. How does a writer achieve that effect? Writers typically introduce characters to us in the same ways people become known to us in real life: by showing us what they do, by sharing their relationships with others, by revealing their inner thoughts and their general outlook, and by letting us hear them talk. Writers also give characters roles to play—protagonist, antagonist, helper, etc.—and this colors the way we feel about them. And, of course, writers come right out and describe characters. Let's look at each of these dimensions of characterization.

Characters: What They Do

Skillful writers show us, and don't tell us. In *The Breadwinner*, instead of telling us that Parvana's older sister is mean and insensitive, Deborah Ellis shows the sister badgering Parvana with cruel insults, even when Parvana cuts her hair, puts on boy's clothes, and risks her life to get provisions for her family in Taliban-controlled Kabul, Afghanistan. It is left to the reader to interpret these actions and decide what kind of character we are dealing with—just as it is with the people we meet in real life.

Characters: How They Relate to Others

Characters are also brought to life when readers see who "their people" are—and how they relate to those people. Marty in *Shiloh* (Naylor, 1991) is a member of a hard-working and frugal family in rural Appalachia. Bud, in *Bud, Not Buddy* (Curtis, 1999), is a member of the African American culture that conducts its affairs largely out of sight of the dominant white culture. But, as it turns out, his real people are a troupe of jazz musicians.

Often, book characters are portrayed as being out of harmony with their own group. Seventh grader Doug Swieteck in Gary Schmidt's *OK for Now* (2011) is not only more honest and peaceable than his delinquent older brother and his abusive and barely employable father, but he struggles not to be tarred by the low opinion people have of his family in their newly adopted town of Marysville, New York.

Characters: What They Think and Feel

Characters are revealed to us through their inner thoughts. Pause for a moment and note how rare that is. In real life, you can only know your own thoughts, not anyone else's, no matter how close you are to another person. But literature gives you the unique opportunity to go inside another person's head. And when you experience another's thoughts displayed in well-chosen words, you are likely to gain language for your own inner experiences, too. You become more self-reflective.

Doug Swieteck, just mentioned, has been learning to take a perspective on art and life by studying prints of birds by John James Audubon. As a disabled reader with an abusive father and a thug for a brother, Doug has enormous challenges in his life, just like the heron in a drawing that is about to intersect with the path of a hunter's shot. Doug says:

> May be the Snowy Heron is going to come off pretty badly when the planes come together. Maybe. But he's still proud and beautiful. His head is high, and he's got this sharp beak that's facing out to the world. He's OK for now. (Schmidt, 2011).

Characters: What They Say and How They Say It

Literature lets us hear what characters say and how they say it, and we can infer how they think and feel from those utterances. Listen to the words we hear from Caitlin, a child with Asperger Syndrome, in Kathryn Erskine's *Mockingbird* (2011), who is being visited by her classroom teacher after her brother Devon has died:

> She doesn't move. This means she is waiting for me to say something. I hate that. It makes my underarms prickle and get wet. I almost start sucking my sleeve like I do at recess but then I remember. *You're welcome*, I say.
>
> She moves away.
>
> I got it right! I go to the refrigerator and put a smiley face sticker on my chart under YOUR MANNERS. Seven more and I get to watch a video. (Erskine, 2010, pp. 7–8).

With no description at all supplied by the author, we know that even simple social interactions are to Caitlin like advanced calculus is to many of us. We know that Caitlin has been trained in procedures for simple conversations, and we also know that she wants to do the right thing.

Characters: The Roles They Play in the Plot

If a character in a story is cast in the role of the protagonist, or the hero, readers are inclined to be sympathetic toward him or her. If the character is cast as the antagonist (the villain or the hero's rival), readers are disposed to "fill in the blanks" of that character's personality with *bad* qualities. (This happens in real life, too: Just listen to what emotional sports fans say about players on the opposing team!)

In Gary Schmidt's *The Wednesday Wars* (2007), Holling Hoodhood's teacher Mrs. Baker is described at first as his enemy. He says, "She hates my guts" (and she really seems to!), but later she becomes his larger-than-life advocate.

Characters: As the Author Describes Them

Authors sometimes give readers descriptions of their characters. J.K. Rowling introduces Dudley Dursley, the spoiled and overstuffed son of Harry Potter's guardians, this way:

> Dudley looked a lot like Uncle Vernon. He had a large pink face, not much neck, small, water blue eyes, and thick blond hair that lay smoothly on his thick, fat head. Aunt Petunia often said that Dudley looked like a baby angel—Harry often said that Dudley looked like a pig in a wig. (*Harry Potter and the Sorcerer's Stone*, p. 21)

In case the reader needs more clues to Dudley's personality, he is immediately shown counting his Christmas presents—and finding that he's come up two short from last year. Then his fawning mother slips more presents into the pile—so we see his relationship to this overindulgent woman, as well.

ILLUSTRATION 2.3 The young protagonist of *Mockingbird* has Asperger Syndrome, and since the death of her brother, she feels there is no one to help her deal with the world around her. ("Mockingbird" by Kathryn Erskine. Used by permission of Penguin Group (USA) Inc. All rights reserved.)

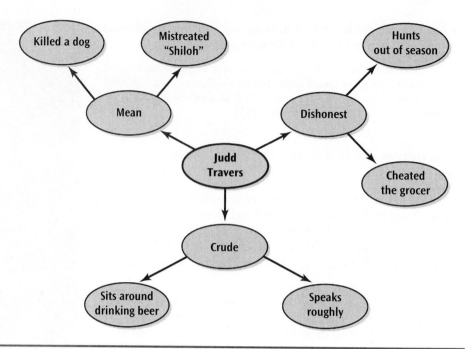

FIGURE 2.3 Character Map for Judd Travers from Phyllis Reynolds Naylor's *Shiloh*.

Round Characters and Flat Characters

Round characters in a story are actors whom we really get to know, along with their pasts, their relationships, their motives, their inner thoughts, and the changes they go through during the story. *Flat characters* are the opposite: They are introduced in a story and then they act predictably, as if they are needed as foils for the more prominent characters to play off. We learn little about them, except for their effects on other characters. For example, in Mildred Taylor's ***Roll of Thunder, Hear My Cry*** (2001), the Wallace boys are mean and violent racists who prey on black people, and who hide behind the privileges of being white. The Wallaces are flat characters. The author, Mildred Taylor, doesn't show us why the Wallaces are racist. They are described only enough to show what the other characters in the story are up against.

Contrasted with flat characters are round characters, whose motives are explained, who are seen from many points of view, and who usually develop and change as the story progresses. In ***Roll of Thunder, Hear My Cry***, Cassie Logan is the protagonist of the story. We are let in on her thoughts. We see what she does, why she does it, and what she thinks about her actions. Cassie's awareness of herself and others expands as she goes through the story, so that she is wiser by the end. She is a round character.

Round Characters Undergo Changes

The protagonists in many books undergo changes as their stories progress. For example, in Kate DiCamillo's ***Because of Winn-Dixie*** (2010), Opal learns to move past her feelings of abandonment and become a provider of comfort to others. In Cynthia Lord's ***Rules*** (2006), Catherine learns that the way to cope with her brother's autism is to expand her own capacity to relate to people who are different, to become their ally.

Often, a story demonstrates how events helped a main character to change. This is one of the main ways that stories teach, even when they do not appear to be didactic. The German term

ILLUSTRATION 2.4 In *Rules*, a young girl learns that the way to cope with her brother's autism is to expand her own capacity to relate to people who are different. (Scholastic, Inc.)

bildungsroman is used by literary scholars as the name for a work that chronicles a young character's growth from immaturity and naiveté to maturity and wisdom, and the lessons learned along the way. The term literally means "educational novel."

In some books, flat characters can suddenly become round. The series of quirky strangers in *Because of Winn-Dixie* all undergo transformations from flat characters to people with histories and personalities—and indeed, much of the power of the book is in the message that everyone "has a life." In Rebecca Stead's *When You Reach Me* (2009), the anonymous street bully who slugs Miranda's best friend Sal eventually gets a name, a history, and a set of motives, and he even becomes a pivotal character in the work.

Plots: How Do Stories Happen?

A plot is a meaningful ordering of events with their consequences, a "who did what, and why." A plot is the conveyor belt that pulls readers through the text, helping them get to know characters and scenes along the way, before arriving at a cumulative insight.

In this section, we look at plots in several ways. We look first at the conflicts that give rise to plots; then we examine the structure of plots. Common plot types will be the next topic, followed by a consideration of some of the twists and turns of plots that authors have at their disposal—techniques such as episodes within plots and surface stories with underlying plots.

Plots and Conflicts

Plots unfold when a character is drawn toward a significant goal but faces some kind of conflict in reaching it. Conflicts in fiction usually take one of four different forms: between the character and some rival person, between the character and himself or herself, between the character and the environment, or between the character and society.

Conflict between Characters. In J.K. Rowling's *Harry Potter and the Sorcerer's Stone* (1998), the ultimate conflict is between Harry Potter and Voldemort, the wicked sorcerer who killed Harry's parents and who is intent on doing further evil in the world. Along the way, there are other conflicts: between Harry and his stepfamily, the Dursleys, and between Harry and his friends and the residents of Slytherin Hall, a rival dormitory within Hogwarts School.

Roald Dahl's books often introduce conflicts between characters: between Danny and his father and Victor Hazlett, the wealthy landowner, in *Danny the Champion of the World* (1978) or between Matilda and her ghastly parents in *Matilda* (1988). As we note below, Dahl's willingness to portray really awful characters that children love to hate makes some parents and teachers uneasy—and by comparison makes us realize how many contemporary children's books portray antagonists with at least some redeeming characteristics.

Conflict within a Character. In Pam Muñoz Ryan's *Esperanza Rising* (2002), the heroine struggles with overcoming her social class prejudice and her sense of entitlement and accepting her lot as a field hand. She resolves the conflict when she realizes she can move on with her life but keep the core strengths and traditions her loved ones have always shared.

Conflict between a Character and Nature. Books with survival themes pit their protagonists against nature. Gary Paulsen's books do this brilliantly, as in *Hatchet*, (1987) in which a boy learns to survive in the woods after an airplane crash, and

The Voyage of the Frog (1990), in which a boy survives an ocean crossing on a sailboat. In Jean Craighead George's *Julie of the Wolves* (1972), the heroine survives in the Arctic tundra by adopting the ways of the wolves. In Theodore Taylor's *The Cay* (2002), eleven-year-old Phillip survives on a desert island in the Caribbean with the help of Timothy, an older islander. And in Margi Preus's *Heart of a Samurai* (2010), in the mid-1800s Manjiro survives being shipwrecked on an island, only to be rescued and carried to America, where the challenge is to understand and thrive in a new land.

Conflict between a Character and Society. Characters in books are often at odds with society. Sometimes society embraces some evil or prejudice against which the character must struggle. Such is the case in Afghanistan under the rule of the Taliban in *The Breadwinner.* In other books, the struggle with society comes about not because society is particularly evil, but just because it is what it is. In Vera Williams' *A Chair for My Mother* (1982), a young girl mobilizes her neighbors to raise enough nickels and dimes to buy a chair, so her mother can sit down comfortably at the end of a long day working as a waitress. While poverty is never mentioned, the plot would make no sense without the family's abject shortage of funds. What rises from the pages is a spirit of community, of the strength of people looking out for each other against a background of need.

Plot Structures

Plots have universal features, which literary scholars tend to describe this way. A plot begins with an *exposition* or *introduction*, which provides the information necessary to understand the story. Then comes the *complication*, in which some conflict is introduced and the character or characters begin their attempts to resolve it. The *rising action* follows from the complication, as the characters work their way through the situation in which they find themselves and pursue their goal. Most of the way through the book comes the *climax*, the point of maximum tension, when the character tries to resolve the conflict and things seem to be most at stake. After the climax comes a rapid series of events that can be called the *falling action*, which culminate in the *dénouement* (French for "untying," because finally the tensions introduced in the story are relaxed). The dénouement can also be called the *resolution*. Either way, here is where the problem is solved and the conflict resolved (see Figure 2.4).

In Alma Flor Ada's *The Gold Coin* (1991), the *exposition* is the part where Juan approaches a hut he plans to rob and spies an old woman inside holding a gold coin and saying, "I must be the richest person in the world." The *complication* comes when Juan breaks into the hut after the woman leaves and finds no gold coin. Now, in order to

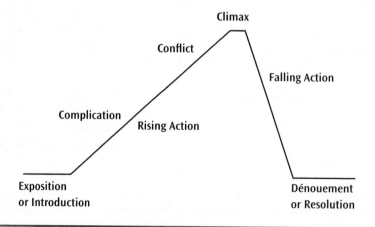

FIGURE 2.4 Typical Plot Structure

meet his goal of stealing her riches (or so he thinks), he must follow the old woman. Tensions mount (the *rising action*) throughout the story as Juan follows the old woman, Doña Josefa, to one farm after another—where he is told of a generous and helpful act she has just performed and is given work to do to pass the time before the farmers can take him to his next destination. The *climax* is the surprising events that befall Juan when he catches up with Doña Josefa alone on the road. And the *falling action* follows when Juan realizes that he has been transformed. The *dénouement* or *resolution* is tactfully left for the reader to imagine. How will Juan lead his life, now that he has learned the value of being trusted by others, of being generous?

Recurring Plots

Some plot forms are used again and again in stories. To lump them together by their common forms is to take nothing away from them; on the contrary, it may point out their larger psychic meaning and their contribution to our understanding of the human drama.

The Initiation Story. Children's literature is full of *initiation stories*, in which a young character is given some challenge to get through; having successfully met the challenge, she or he is recognized as being more mature or more worthy—and the reader learns lessons about growing up. "Jack and the Beanstalk" and "Hansel and Gretel" are initiation stories.

Becoming initiated sometimes implies trade-offs: The protagonist must trade innocence for experience. Hansel and Gretel lost their childhood and experienced horror before they could be reunited with their father, in what must have been an uneasy relationship. Growing up requires pain and struggle, embracing some things and giving up others—scary steps for a child. Initiation stories point the way, not by revealing the particular path a child will take, because that is necessarily unique to each person, but by offering the hope and assurance that there is sunlight above the clouds.

The Journey. Another metaphor for arduous progress and change is the journey. People all over the world have been motivated by deep urges to uproot themselves and travel long distances. As hunter-gatherers, humans ranged widely over the landscape, following animals or seeking greener habitats. Since ancient times, different cultures have had the custom of making pilgrimages to religious places—to Canterbury, Mecca, Santiago de Compostela—a practice that survives today. Voyages of discovery, for trade, to make war or bring comfort to the suffering—all seem to follow some deep-seated human urge to go, to see, and to be changed along the way.

Frances Temple's *The Ramsay Scallop* (1994b) goes to the roots of the tradition, as it recounts a young betrothed couple's pilgrimage from England to Spain in the year 1299. Rodman Philbrick's *The Mostly True Adventures of Homer P. Figg* (2009) chronicles the namesake character's journey from his cruel uncle's farm in Pine Swamp, Maine, south to Gettysburg to find his brother, who was illegally conscripted into the Union Army in 1863. Christopher Paul Curtis won a Newbery Award in 1999 for

TEACHING IDEA 2.2

PLOTTING THE STORY JOURNEY

COMMON CORE STANDARD: *Key Ideas and Details, STANDARD 3*

Students can make a kind of graph to plot a story journey. Drawing a line from left to right across a chart, they can make the line go up for events when morale is high and down for events when morale is low. Above the line, they can write in what happened. Below the line, they can write in how a character felt or what she or he learned.

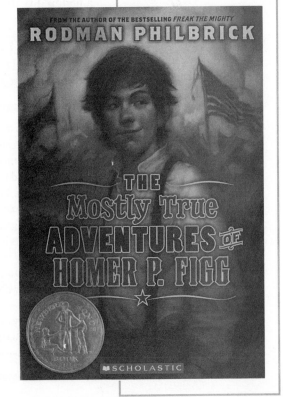

ILLUSTRATION 2.5 *The Mostly True Adventures of Homer P. Figg* chronicles a boy's journey to find his brother who was illegally conscripted into the Union Army in 1863. (Scholastic, Inc.)

Bud, Not Buddy, the story of an orphaned African American boy's odyssey across Michigan in the 1930s to find some remnants of his family. In *Parvana's Journey* (2003), the sequel to *The Breadwinner* (2001) by Deborah Ellis, the children's travel across war-torn Afghanistan is fraught with land mines below, bombs raining from above, and uneasy relations among the children themselves. In all of these stories, with every challenge they meet along the way, the characters grow in their awareness of other people, the circumstances that surround them, and themselves.

Episodes: Stories within Stories

Many books, especially those for older children, give us patterns of episodes within larger plots. Francisco Jiménez's *The Circuit* (1999) is a series of small stories all framed by the reality of a childhood in an undocumented migrant worker family in California. In fact, two episodes from this book have been made into stand-alone picture books.

Jennifer Holm's *Turtle in Paradise* is a series of episodes—about a business of taking care of inconsolable babies, curing bungy rash, relating to an eccentric and dyspeptic old bed-ridden relative, riding out a hurricane on a mangrove island, and finding pirate's treasure—all tied together by the fact that eleven-year-old Turtle is plunked down with relatives who weren't expecting her in Depression-era Key West.

Layered Stories: Surface Plots and Underlying Stories

Some stories have characters proceed through a series of events and then discover clues that lead to another series of events that happened at a different time. Detective fiction in adult literature regularly works on two levels. On one level, the detective is given a set of clues. By following the good clues and rejecting the misleading ones, the detective constructs another story, the story of the crime, and solves the mystery.

In children's literature, one of the best examples of a story with two layers of plot is Louis Sachar's *Holes* (2000), in which Stanley Yelnats, the young prisoner at Camp Green Lake, digs a series of holes that literally unearths an older story from a hundred years before.

TECHNOLOGY in PRACTICE 2.1

PLOT GENERATORS

Getting started is the hardest part. Many writers are fully advised about plot structures—they know that they need protagonists and antagonists, problems and attempts, resolutions and consequences—but they still have trouble getting a story started. Several years ago, writing teachers Anne Bernays and Pamela Painter in Writing *What If? Exercises for Fiction Writers* (1991) came up with the idea of a story generator, where writers are invited to mix and match striking characters with imaginative actions, until they find a combination that gets them going. Now there are several online story generators that randomly produce characters and situations to inspire story writers. Once students have the basics of plotting, using a story generator can be a fun way to inspire story writing, and help students learn to appreciate the creativity that is possible even within the constraints of a story structure. Some recommended sites are:

(For younger writers)
Story Maker—<http://learnenglishkids.britishcouncil.org>
Seussville Story Maker—<http://www.seussville.com>
(For older writers)
Writers' Plot Generator—<http://funstuff.pantomimepony.co.uk>

Themes: How Do Stories Convey Meaning?

Beyond the question "What happened to whom and why?" readers sometimes ask, "What is this work really about?" "What does it mean?" or even "Why did the author write this work?" Answers to those questions are usually statements of theme. Here is Rebecca Lukens's definition: "Theme in literature is the idea that holds the story together, such as a comment about society, human nature, or the human condition. It is the main idea or central meaning of a piece of writing" (Lukens, 2003, p. 129).

Explicit and Implicit Themes

Themes may be stated explicitly or suggested implicitly by the text. Explicit themes were once far more common than they are now. In the 1700s Madame Le Prince de Beaumont closed *La Belle et La Bête*, an early and popular version of *Beauty and the Beast*, with a lavish statement of what she took to be the moral of the story, namely that Beauty was of such a sterling and obedient character that she deserved the happily-ever-after life she went on to enjoy with her handsome and well-off partner.

"Cendrillon," a version of "Cinderella" by Charles Perrault that is a close source of the versions known in the United States, ends with not one stated moral but two: first, it's better to be virtuous than beautiful; and second, that even if you are virtuous and beautiful it helps to have a fairy godmother.

Most modern readers don't like to have the morals of stories dictated to them, and explicit themes have largely fallen out of favor.

An *implicit theme* is an idea that is strongly suggested but not explicitly stated. In Harriet Ziefert's *A New Coat for Anna* (1988), a reader can infer a theme that doing something for the good of a child pulls war-weary citizens out of their doldrums and creates a community. But there is also the theme that the mother must trade away sad memories of the past and go forward to build a new life, for the benefit of her daughter, her neighbors, and herself. These themes are suggested as much by Anita Lobel's brilliant illustrations as they are by the text.

Especially in contemporary literature, stating what themes are is not always an easy or foolproof matter. Good writers rarely start with explicit themes in mind. Author Frances Temple (1994a) explained her approach to themes this way: "At first, I'm just getting out the story. Once it's written down, I can go through and see what the story is adding up to—and then as I rewrite I can make sure that what stays in the book pulls more or less in the same direction."

Many authors express surprise, however, at the themes others find in their works. For instance, author Charles Temple was surprised to read in a review of his *Shanty Boat* (illustrated by Melanie Hall) that the work was about the importance of respecting differences. Temple had thought it was just a rhyme about a quirky old guy who lived on a boat; he had created it as an exaggerated portrait of his own brother.

Themes are sometimes represented or symbolized by an image in a story. In Natalie Babbitt's *Tuck Everlasting* (1975), the image of the wheel is used again and

TOP SHELF 2.2

again—presumably to symbolize the life cycle and the sad consequences of stepping off it. In Cynthia Lord's **Rules,** the rules themselves come to stand for the girl protagonist's attempts to impose boundaries on her autistic brother; finally she realizes that it is she who has been too hemmed in by an overly ordered view of what behavior is acceptable, who is a friend, and in what form joy may come.

Reading against the Grain

The explicit and implicit themes described above were the sort many authors might have agreed were present in their work. But if we define a theme, as the critic Rebecca Lukens does, as a source of "insight into people and how they think and feel" (Lukens, 1990), then there are other layers of themes that we must take into account. Some of these may be insights that the authors did not intend.

Almost every work of literature takes some stance toward the social order—toward the relative roles and attributes of males and females, old and young, rich and poor, and so on. Of course, those stances are not always explicit. A work of literature may overtly argue for the status quo, may implicitly take the status quo for granted, or may argue for a different social order. Reading against the grain is a way to examine the unexamined, question the unquestioned, and hold up to scrutiny the unspoken assertions the text is making about the way lives are lived in society. Reading against the grain means asking, "Is this book a true portrait of how people behave? Is it a portrait of how they ought to behave?"

"Suppose This Happened to Someone Else?" A useful way to examine the unexamined is to ask, "What would have been different if these events had happened to another character?" For example, in Phyllis Reynolds Naylor's **Shiloh,** what if Marty's little sister, Dara Lynn, had found the dog instead of Marty? Would her parents have taken her devotion to the dog as seriously? Would she have had the freedom to keep it secretly and arrange to give it food? What does this tell the reader about the range of activity boys and girls are permitted? What if Marty's upper middle class friend David Howard had found Shiloh, instead of Marty, whose family shares a cramped cottage on the edge of the woods? Would David have gone to so much trouble not to confront Judd Travers with his mistreatment of animals—or would he simply have called the authorities? Would he and his family have been so careful not to make an enemy of Judd? What does this tell us about the range of options open to people from different social classes?

Readers can ask how any story would play out if one or more key characters were changed, in terms of the following:

- Switching males and females,
- Old people and young people,
- People of different social classes,
- People of different races,
- Americans and residents of developing countries, and
- People who are differently abled.

"What Did They Do? What Did They Get?" Another way to read against the grain is to list the actions taken by different classes of characters in the story (male and female, black and white, young and old) and then to match those actions with the rewards the characters receive. Looking at the story "Beauty and the Beast" in this way, we see that males were rewarded for going after what they wanted—although they had to learn the hard way to be respectful of all sorts of people. Women, though, were rewarded for **not** going after what they wanted—for focusing on serving others and being pure. Is that always the way women should behave?

A text is a piece of virtual experience that can be held up and examined from many angles. As the questions above make clear, readers can find interesting meanings to talk about in almost any text, regardless of whether an author intended to stress those meanings.

The Stance of the Implied Reader

The stance of the implied reader is one more device written into a work besides the plot, the setting, the characters, and the theme (Booth, 1961; Iser, 1974). The implied reader is the ideal interpreter of a work, as imagined by the author. The implied reader is not usually mentioned in the text, but his or her activity is essential if the text is to "work." If events or characters in a text are exciting, funny, sad, suspenseful, heroic, blameworthy, or even understandable, those events or characters must be perceived in those ways *by some reader*. Those qualities do not exist except as responses of a reader to a work. Therefore, in constructing a piece of literature, the writer must consciously or unconsciously keep an ideal reader in mind and arrange the details of the work in such a way as to evoke the desired responses from that reader.

As they begin to read a work, actual readers implicitly take the perspective of the implied reader and begin to have emotional and intellectual reactions to the work in ways the author has scripted for them. Or else they don't: If a book is too silly, too "hard," or too far outside their usual way of seeing things, the actual readers might not be willing or able to take the stance of the implied reader, and the book will not work for them.

There are at least three ways in which an actual reader can take the stance of the implied reader. The first is by identifying with characters. The second is by taking a moral perspective on the story. The third is by filling in gaps to make the story "work."

Identifying with Characters

Identification with one or more characters in a text is an important function of the implied reader. When actual readers step into the shoes of a character, they suffer what that character suffers, face the dilemmas that character faces, and feel the consequences of the choices they (the character and, vicariously, the readers) have made. For example, the reader of Jack Gantos's *Joey Pigza Swallowed the Key* identifies with Joey because of his first-person narrative (see pages 40–41), but then may react in horror as Joey, his impulse control severely limited by his Attention Deficit Disorder, goes from disaster to disaster, including injuring a classmate while running with open scissors. The reader who stays with Joey will gain understanding and sympathy for a boy who struggles with challenges most of us don't.

Taking the Intended Moral Stance

Another way in which the text influences readers is by inviting them to take a moral stance on the story—a stance the author has staked out as part of the construction of the work. As we noted above, for a story to work, the author has to be able to count on readers to believe that some goals are worthwhile, that some events are exciting, that some things people say are funny or sad or shocking. If readers adopt these views—if only for the duration of the reading—the book will come together for them. If they don't, it won't. So far, so good.

But no readers hold precisely the orientations asked of them by all books. They occasionally have to stretch to accept a certain point of view for the time during which they participate in a certain book. This stretching has consequences. We have all had the experience of being told a joke that was so sexist, racist, or otherwise mean-spirited that we had to decide whether to keep listening, scold the teller, or walk away. It's the times we didn't quite muster the energy to do either of the latter two that are most bothersome. If, for the sake of the humor, we temporarily agree to take the stance the joke requires of us, we may give a polite laugh, but feel compromised. That is because we have just agreed to live the life of a bigot, if only for two minutes.

Many of Roald Dahl's perennially popular books, such as *Danny the Champion of the World, Matilda, George's Marvelous Medicine,* and *Charlie and the Chocolate Factory,* present truly awful characters with no redeeming features as antagonists to the main character. Sometimes they are other children, sometimes teachers, sometimes relatives, sometimes parents. Each of these characters harms the main character in some way, and each of them receives a bad outcome of one sort or another. In the meantime, we readers are invited to hate these characters and to delight in the terrible if quirky things that befall them. For many readers, though—especially those who try to respond to people who annoy us not with hatred but with understanding—Dahl's books raise moral challenges. The challenge is not in what Dahl says explicitly, but in the emotional stance he sets out for readers to take. Some readers are unwilling to adopt this stance.

Filling in the Gaps

The implied reader functions in one last way. A writer friend of ours says, "You have to trust your readers to figure some things out for themselves. They'll feel more like they're with you if you let them have the fun of figuring things out. Telling them too much spoils the fun." Writers leave gaps in their work to be filled in by the reader's realizations. In Maurice Sendak's *Where the Wild Things Are,* for example, a visual clue is given early in the book as to where the Wild Things came from. (Can you find it?)

In Harry Allard and James Marshall's *Miss Nelson Is Missing!,* readers are never told where Miss Viola Swamp, the no-nonsense substitute teacher, came from—or, for that matter, where she went. But at the end of the story the reader sees Miss Nelson reading in bed, next to a closet with an ugly black dress hanging in it—just like the one Viola Swamp wore. And there's a box on the shelf marked in upside-down letters that spell "WIG."

Point of View

Point of view is the perspective from which the events in a story are perceived and narrated. The choices of point of view are *first person* (in which one of the characters in the work narrates the story, using the first-person pronoun "I"), *second person* (addressed to "you"), and *third person* (in which a narrator outside the story relates events that happened to those in it, using the third-person pronouns "she," "he" and "they"). When the author's knowledge of events shifts freely between different characters' points of view and the author describes events no one character could have known, he or she is writing from the point of view known as *third-person omniscient* ("all-knowing").

Stories in the First Person

Stories in the first person, such as Clare Vanderpool's *Moon Over Manifest* (2010) and Gary Schmidt's *OK for Now* (2011) tell the tale through a character's voice.

Narration in the first person lends immediacy to the action and lets readers know what the character is feeling. But it also limits readers to that character's perspective.

Stories in the Second Person

The least commonly used voice is the second person, "you." Judy Allen and Tudor Humphreys use the second person both delightfully and informingly in *Are You a Spider?* (2003).

> "Are you a spider? If you are, your mother looks like this [picture of a spider] and spins webs."

The book goes on to share information about spiders, while titillating its young audience with the suggestions that they might have eight hairy legs, eat flies, and so on.

Stories in the Third Person

Most of the time, authors describe the action as happening to someone else. This point of view is called narration in the *third person*. Deborah Ellis narrated *I Am a Taxi* in the third person. She did not narrate the story using the voice of Diego (the taxi) in the first person, but she did stick strictly to his point of view. The author never tells us anything that Diego himself did not know.

Third-person omniscient narration occurs when authors tell stories from the point of view of a narrator who knows more than any one character could. Louis Sachar narrated *Holes* in the third-person omniscient voice, as he was able to tell different stories from different time periods that only later came together in an explanatory whole.

Writing in the third person gives the author a broad range of choices of what to show the reader. Nonetheless, skilled writers usually narrate events as if from one character's point of view at a time. When an author changes the perspective of the narration from one character to another, the results can radically change the meaning. Philip Pullman's *I Was a Rat!* (2002) reminds us that even a bit player in a story—like a coachman Cinderella's fairy godmother left in human form—may have an entirely different take on events. Jon Scieszka's *The True Story of the Three Little Pigs (By A. Wolf)* (1989) and Rachel Mortimer's *Three Billy Goats Fluff* (2011) tell familiar tales from the antagonist's point of view, with humorous results.

Style

Style is not *what* is said, but *how* it is said. When a book makes you hear a distinct voice in your head or when you find a passage so good you want to read it out loud to a friend, chances are you're responding to style. Style is not the same thing as talent. A talented author may write in different styles and may have a gift for matching a style with the content of each book she or he writes.

Some of the elements of style are words, images, metaphors, sounds, and voice. Let's look at each.

Words

The poet William Carlos Williams wrote, "Each object in nature and each idea has an exact name." Good writers behave as if that were true, and they strive to name experiences exactly. Mark Twain wrote, "The difference between the right word, and almost the right word, is the difference between the lightning bug and the lightning."

But what makes a word "right"? Good word choices are concrete and vivid—they show, rather than sum up and judge. Or if they sum up and judge, they do so exactly. Good words create fresh images. Good writing crackles with insight.

Writing can be sparse or rich, as writers use few words or many to create impressions. Rich writing was more common in the nineteenth century and early in the twentieth. Note this passage from Kenneth Grahame's immortal *The Wind in the Willows*:

> Never in his life had he seen a river before—this sleek, sinuous, full-bodied animal, chasing and chuckling, gripping things with a gurgle and leaving them with a laugh, to fling itself on fresh playmates that shook themselves free, and were caught and held again. All was a-shake and a-shiver—glints and gleams and sparkles, rustle and swirl, chatter and bubble. (pp. 3–4)

Grahame's language consists of long sentences awash with colorful adjectives, images, and metaphors.

Spare writing can also be powerful. Frances Temple told *Grab Hands and Run* in the voice of twelve-year-old Felipe, and so the words she chose are simple and direct. Here is a scene from a parsonage in Guatemala, where refugees from the civil war in El Salvador find momentary protection:

> Another little girl comes in, a child with big dark eyes, younger than Romy. Father Ramon opens his arms to her and speaks gently, but at the sight of him she begins to scream and fastens herself around the leg of a table. Her screams are terrible, and no one can stop them.
>
> Father Ramon looks so upset that I follow him into the courtyard.
>
> "Why does she scream, Padre?" I ask him. "Can I help?"
>
> "Ask the soldiers why she screams, son," says Father Ramon. I have never heard anyone sound so sad. (p. 62)

Word choice doesn't depend on a fancy vocabulary—just on exact descriptions.

Images

Imagery is the art of making readers experience details as if through their own five senses. Alexander Carmichael had a good phrase for it: "bringing the different characters before the mind as clearly as the sculptor brings the figure before the eye" (quoted in Briggs, 1977, p. 10). The writer mentions, however offhandedly, how things smelled, felt, tasted, sounded, and looked. But the effect is of living the moments described, rather than hearing a summary of them. Here is a moment from *Tuck Everlasting*:

> Shifting his position, he turned his attention to a little pile of pebbles next to him. As Winnie watched, scarcely breathing, he moved the pile carefully to one side, pebble by pebble. Beneath the pile, the ground was shiny wet. The boy lifted a final stone and Winnie saw a low spurt of water, arching up and returning, like a fountain, into the ground. He bent and put his lips to the spurt, drinking noiselessly, and then he sat up again and drew his shirt sleeve across his mouth. As he did this, he turned his face in her direction—and their eyes met. (p. 26)

Read that passage again, and see how many senses it appeals to.

Metaphors

To use a metaphor is to describe one thing in terms of something else. Technically, there is a distinction between a *simile*, which is an overt comparison that says, "X is like Y"; a true *metaphor*, which talks about X as if it were Y; and *personification*, which ascribes human features, actions, or motives to something that isn't human.

Here is *Tuck Everlasting* again:

> The road that led to Treegap had been trod out long before by a herd of cows who were, to say the least, relaxed. It wandered along in curves and easy angles, swayed off and up in a pleasant tangent to the top of a small hill, ambled down again between fringes of bee-hung clover, and then cut sidewise across a meadow. (p. 5)

This isn't quite personification: The road is described as if it were not a person, but a cow—wandering, swaying, and ambling. To describe the road this way is to enliven the writing with unobtrusive magic.

Voice, Tone, and Mood

The author's *voice* in a literary work corresponds to the way an author would sound if she were speaking aloud. Daniel Pinkwater's voice in *Fat Camp Commandoes* (2001) is funny and sarcastic. Adam Rapp's voice in *The Buffalo Tree* (1997), set in a juvenile detention facility, is "wired," pushed to the limit.

The author's *tone* refers to the author's apparent attitude toward the contents of the work, and also toward the audience. Joanna Galdone's tone in the African American ghost story *The Tailypo* (1984) is somber (although her voice is folksy). Lemony Snickett's tone in the *Series of Unfortunate Events* is also somber—but we would also call it ironic, too, because he has a tacit agreement with the readers that these works are spoofs on older melodramas (a *melodrama* is an overly suspenseful adventure with exaggerated good and evil)—he is writing with his tongue in his cheek. Margaret Wise Brown's tone in *Little Fur Family* is protective and maternal.

The *mood* refers to the emotional state the work is likely to evoke in the reader. *Little Fur Family* evokes a mood that is cozy and safe, which makes it a favorite bedtime read. The mood of Cornelia Funke's *The Thief Lord* is enchanting and romantic (in the sense of being emotionally engaging), as it takes us through the canals and streets, backstage in a grand abandoned theater, and behind the ornate doors of aristocratic townhouses.

Intertextuality

Intertextuality is a literary term for the tendency of writers and illustrators to relate aspects of one work to aspects of another. Sometimes the references are *allusions*: the text or the picture refers explicitly to other works. There is an allusion in Gary Schmidt's *The Wednesday Wars* when seventh grader Holling Hoodhood is asked to diagram a much harder sentence than his classmates. His reads, "For it so falls out That what we have we prize not to the worth whiles we enjoy it, but being lack'd and lost, why, then we rack the value, then we find the virtue that possession would not show us whiles it was ours," which comes from Act IV, Scene 1 of *Much Ado About Nothing*, although the author doesn't say so. It figures in the book, though, because the overly demanding teacher, Mrs. Baker, turns out to be a fan of Shakespeare. There are many visual allusions in Anthony Browne's *Voices in the Park*, as images of King Kong, the *Mona Lisa*, and le Jardin des Tuileries pass through the book's illustrations.

Other kinds of intertextuality can be more subtle. David Almond was influenced not only by the style of Gabriel Garcia Marquez's magical realism when he created *Skellig*, but also, as Don Lehman (2011) suggests, by a short story by Marquez. There is nothing wrong with this; on the contrary, intertextuality is a way writers reward readers by helping them to develop a fabric of literary understanding, and also pay homage to other writers and artists.

Visual Literacy

Picture books have another set of features of their own. In Chapter 3 we will explore the visual language of picture books—or, to put it more properly, the verbal-and-visual language of picture books. The pictures have visual dynamics that communicate to readers: the colors that are used, the kinds of lines that are drawn, the placement of characters and objects on the page, the flow from page to page, the title page, the back cover, and the end papers—all are used by skillful illustrators and bookmakers to create a pleasing whole. Add to that the interaction of text and illustration; for example, often things are shown in the illustrations that complement or even contradict what is said in print—and there is a kind of language of expression used in picture books that needs to be explored in its own right.

For ENGLISH LANGUAGE LEARNERS

- American and European stories typically feature deserving characters who strive against adversity through a logical and predictable series of events, actions, and consequences, and are eventually rewarded. In stories from other cultures, though, characters may strive against adversity and not be rewarded at all. Characters may break even, at best, or perish; or the stories may be simply a string of imaginative and unpredictable events rather than problems and solutions. English language learners who are newcomers to Western stories may find them hard to follow. Invite English language learners to tell stories from their own cultures—or to invite family members or neighbors to come to class and do so. Engage the class in discussing similarities and differences between stories read in America and stories from elsewhere.

- American children's books include many works of realistic fiction—stories set in contemporary times with true-to-life characters. But realistic fiction for children is rare outside the more developed countries, and newcomers to the United States from many countries may be puzzled by stories about characters who seem like real people, but aren't. Works of realistic fiction often reveal characters' inner thoughts and motives, but traditional tales rarely do—and traditional tales are what most children in the world know when it comes to fiction. Teachers will need to take extra care with English language learners who have difficulty talking about characters' inner lives.

- American children's books often celebrate individuality and competition: The youngest child is the hero, or the unlikely character turns out to be the winner. In many parts of the world, though, individuality and competition are discouraged and the stories focus on the successes of the group, or on an individual's contribution to the group's success. Similarly, American children's books give children strong roles as agents and problem solvers, but in many cultures children are expected to follow adult direction, and it is considered inappropriate for children to take initiative. Teachers should take opportunities to have English language learners talk about stories that are popular in their own cultures, and discuss how they differ from stories read in America.

EXPERIENCES FOR FURTHER LEARNING

1. Make three columns on a piece of paper. In the left-hand column, list three male and three female characters in *Shiloh.* In the middle column, write two or three major actions these people took in the book. In the right-hand column, list the rewards or punishments they received at the end. Discuss these results. Can you formulate a statement that explains the pattern of who is rewarded and who is not in the story?

2. Choose a short but poignant scene from *Tuck Everlasting*. (Chapter 12 will work nicely.) Think through the scene from a different character's point of view—visualize the scene, for example, from Tuck's point of view rather than Winnie's. Which of Tuck's concerns come to the surface that do not emerge in the scene as written? How does Winnie appear?

RESOURCES AND REFERENCES

Ada, Alma Flor. *The Gold Coin*. Atheneum, 1991.

_____. *My Name Is Maria Isabel*. Atheneum, 1995.

Allard, Harry. *Miss Nelson Is Missing!* Illustrated by James Marshall. Houghton Mifflin, 1977.

Allen, Judy, and Tudor Humphreys. *Are You a Spider?* Kingfisher, 2003.

Almond, David. *Skellig*. Delacorte, 2009.

Babbitt, Natalie. *Tuck Everlasting*. Farrar, Strauss, and Giroux. 1975.

Barthes, Roland. *S/Z*. Trans. Richard Miller. Hill & Wang, 1974.

Bernays, Anne, and Pamela Painter. *What If? Exercises for Fiction Writers*. William Morrow, 1991.

Booth, Wayne. *The Rhetoric of Fiction*. University of Chicago Press, 1961.

Briggs, Katherine. *British Folktales*. Pantheon, 1977.

Curtis, Christopher Paul. *Bud, Not Buddy*. Delacourt, 1999.

Cushman, Karen. *The Midwife's Apprentice*. Clarion, 1995.

Dahl, Roald. *Danny the Champion of the World*. Bantam, 1978.

_____. *Charlie and the Chocolate Factory*. Knopf, 1985.

_____. *George's Marvelous Medicine*. Knopf, 1982.

_____. *Matilda*. Viking, 1988.

DiCamillo, Kate. *Because of Winn-Dixie*. Candlewick, 2009.

Egoff, Sheila, G. T. Stubbs, and L. F. Ashley. *Only Connect: Readings on Children's Literature* (2nd ed.). Oxford University Press, 1980.

Ellis, Deborah. *The Breadwinner*. Groundwood Books, 2001.

_____. *I Am a Taxi*. Groundwood Books, 2006.

_____. *Parvana's Journey*. Groundwood Books, 2003.

Erskine, Kathryn. *The Mockingbird*. Puffin, 2011.

Frye, Northrop. *The Educated Imagination*. Indiana University Press, 1964.

Galdone, Joanna. *The Tailypo*. Sandpiper, 1984.

Gantos, Jack. *Joey Pigza Swallowed the Key*. Square Fish, 2011.

Garcia-Williams, Rita. *One Crazy Summer*. Amistad, 2010.

George, Jean Craighead. *Julie of the Wolves*. HarperCollins, 1974.

Grahame, Kenneth. *The Wind in the Willows*. Scribner's, 1908/1953.

Grimm, Jacob, and Wilhelm Grimm. *The Complete Grimms' Fairy Tales*. Pantheon, 1972.

Hearne, Betsy, and Marilyn Kaye. *Celebrating Children's Literature*. Lothrop, Lee, & Shepard, 1981.

Holm, Jennifer. *Turtle in Paradise*. Random House, 2010.

Hunt, Peter. *Children's Literature: The Development of Criticism*. Routledge, 1990.

Iser, Wolfgang. *The Implied Reader: Patterns of Communication in Prose Fiction from Bunyan to Beckett*. Johns Hopkins University Press, 1974.

Jimenez, Francisco. *The Circuit*. Houghton Mifflin, 1999.

Lord, Cynthia. *Rules*. Scholastic, 2006.

Lowry, Lois. *The Giver*. Houghton Mifflin, 1993.

Lukens, Rebecca. *A Critical Handbook to Children's Literature* (6th ed.) HarperCollins, 2012.

MacLachlan, Patricia. *What You Know First*. Illustrated by Barry Moser. HarperCollins, 1995.

McGraw, Eloise. *The Moorchild*, Aladdin, 1998.

May, Jill. *Children's Literature and Critical Theory*. Oxford University Press, 1995.

Mortimer, Rachel. *Three Billy Goats Fluff*. Illustrated by Liz Pichon. Tiger Tales, 2011.

Naylor, Phyllis Reynolds. *Shiloh*. Atheneum, 1991.

Nodelman, Perry, ed. *Touchstones: Reflections on the Best in Children's Literature*. Children's Literature Association, 1985.

Paulsen, Gary. *Hatchet*. Simon and Schuster, 1987.

_____. *Voyage of the Frog*. Yearling, 1990.

Philbrick, Rodman. *The Mostly True Adventures Of Homer P. Figg*. Blue Sky, 2009.

Pinkwater, Daniel. *Fat Camp Commandoes*. Scholastic, 2002.

Preus, Margi. *Heart of a Samurai*. Amulet, 2010.

Pullman, Phillip. *I Was a Rat!* Yearling, 2002.

Rapp, Adam. *The Buffalo Tree*, Front Street, 1997.

Rodanas, Kristina. *The Dragonfly's Tale*. Clarion, 1992.

Rowling, J.K. *Harry Potter and the Sorcerer's Stone*. Scholastic, 1998.

Ryan, Pam Muñoz. *Esperanza Rising*. Scholastic, 2002.

Sachar, Louis. *Holes*. Dell Yearling, 2000.

Sale, Roger. *Fairy Tales and After: Snow White to E. B. White*. Harvard University Press, 1978.

Schmidt, Gary. *The Wednesday Wars*. Clarion, 2007.

_____. *OK for Now*. Clarion, 2011.

Scholes, Robert. *Structuralism in Literature*. Yale University Press, 1974.

Scieszka, Jon. *The True Story of the Three Little Pigs, by A. Wolf*. Illustrated by Lane Smith. Dutton, 1995.

Sendak, Maurice. *Where the Wild Things Are*. Harper & Row, 1963. Souriau, Etienne. *Les Deux Cent Milles Situations Dramatiques*. Flammarion, 1955.

Spinelli, Jerry. *Maniac Magee*. Little, Brown, 1990.

Stead, Rebecca. *When You Reach Me*. Wendy Lamb, 2009.

Taylor, Mildred. *Roll of Thunder, Hear My Cry*. Dial, 2001.

Taylor, Theodore. *The Cay*. Yearling, 2002.

Temple, Charles. *Shanty Boat*. Illustrated by Melanie Hall. Houghton Mifflin, 1993a.

_____. "'What If Beauty Had Been Ugly?' Reading against the Grain of Gender Bias in Children's Books." *Language Arts 70* (February 1993b): 89–93.

Temple, Charles, and Patrick Collins, eds. *Stories and Readers.* Christopher-Gordon, 1992.

Temple, Frances. Personal communication. 1994a.

_____. *Grab Hands and Run!* HarperCollins, 1995.

_____. *The Ramsay Scallop.* Orchard, 1994b.

Turnbull, Colin. *The Human Cycle.* HarperCollins, 1982.

Vanderpool, Clare. *Moon Over Manifest.* Delacorte, 2010.

Yelchin, Eugene. *Breaking Stalin's Nose.* Henry Holt, 2011.

Williams, Vera. *A Chair for My Mother.* Greenwillow, 1982.

Ziefert, Harriet. *A New Coat for Anna.* Dragonfly, 1988.

Picture Books

66 *The gratifying thing about good art is the longer one looks at it the more one sees, the more one sees, the deeper one feels, and the deeper one feels the more profoundly one thinks. Looking at art is everything!* 99

—from *Picture Books for Children*, 4th ed. by Patricia J. Cianciolo

What Are Picture Books?

Today's picture books are filled with good art—art that invites repeated lingering, elicits a depth of feeling, and promotes profound thinking. A picture book can take many forms. It can be a wordless book, which tells a story solely through illustrations. It can be an illustrated book, in which the words carry most of the message, but illustrations either depict what is stated in the text or decorate the page. It can be a picture storybook, in which a story is told through a combination of illustrations and text, each amplifying the other to create a unified whole. Much of the discussion in this chapter focuses on the picture storybook.

Picture books are also characterized by a unique use of language. *Wordless books* are marked by the absence of written language; however, language is implied through the illustrations, so it exists within the book, but not in a visible text. *Concept books* have language that is unique in its ability to convey the meaning of concepts such as the alphabet, numbers, shapes, or colors. *Beginning Readers* are books that use controlled language to enable children to practice reading independently. The best *picture storybooks* have language that is rich in its ability to tell the story well. They may include vocabulary that is beyond the child's independent reading level, but is valuable in helping nurture a depth of understanding achievable only by precise language use.

Picture books are types of books, and there are picture books as a book type within each of the genres discussed in later chapters: picture books that are historical fiction, picture books that are fantasies, and so on. This chapter focuses on building a depth of understanding about picture books as a form rather than concentrating on the content, which will be addressed within the genre chapters.

The Evolution of Picture Books

Since the publication of the first picture book in 1658, many factors have influenced the evolution of these books for children. Picture books have changed as their creators have explored the interplay of text and illustrations and refined their concepts of picture books. Developments in printing technology have influenced the technical as well as the artistic aspects of creating picture books.

The Development of the Concept of the Picture Book

What is generally considered the first picture book is **Orbis Sensualium Pictus (The Visible World in Pictures**), published in 1658 by Johannes Amos Comenius (1592–1670), a visionary educator from what is now the Republic of Slovakia. Comenius believed that in addition to the "dead" languages, history, and catechisms that were popular subjects for instruction at the time, children should be taught about practical matters in the language they used daily. He added illustrations to informational text to increase children's understanding and pleasure. Following the lead of Comenius, most picture books of the seventeenth and eighteenth centuries were created to educate children and guide their moral behavior.

Children's book publishing advanced dramatically under the leadership of John Newbery (1713–1767). In 1744, Newbery established a company in London dedicated almost exclusively to publishing beautiful children's books. He created books for children in attractive, playful formats, including the accordion book, which was a long strip folded accordion-like to form "pages." He was the first to introduce illustrations by accomplished artists, and his books had permanent, attractive bindings.

Picture books flourished in England during the nineteenth century. Much of the credit for changes in picture books is given to Edmund Evans (1826–1905), an artist, publisher, and printer. Evans advanced the development of picture books by recognizing the importance of the relationship between illustration and book design. In addition, using photographic techniques, he created copies that closely resembled the original illustrations to improve the color printing process. Evans persuaded artists such as Randolph Caldecott (1846–1886), Walter Crane (1845–1915), and Kate Greenaway (1846–1901) to create books for children (Kiefer, 1995).

The picture book form made the greatest leap toward its modern manifestation in the hands of English illustrator Randolph Caldecott, of whom Maurice Sendak (1990) wrote:

> He devised an ingenious juxtaposition of picture and word, a counterpoint that never happened before. Words are left out—but the picture says it. Pictures are left out—but the word says it. In short, it is the invention of the picture book. (p. 21)

Caldecott built on Crane's ideas about book design, perfecting the unification of text and illustration and allowing illustrations to interpret and extend the text beyond what the words implied. Also, Caldecott created illustrations that were not contained within borders, so characters virtually bounced off the pages.

Later, another English illustrator, Beatrix Potter (1866–1943), recognized the need to consider the audience when creating children's books. She insisted that her books be appropriately sized for little hands. Potter's stories of woodland animals are endearing not only because of the well-written text, but also because of the meticulously drawn illustrations.

By the 1930s, the concept of the modern picture book had basically taken shape. The illustrations extended the text, the text and illustrations were interdependent, and the importance of the book's entire design was recognized (Schwartz, 1982).

Changes in Printing and Technology

Improvements in printing technology over the years account for great changes in the appearance of picture books. Paper, the use of color, printing quality, and art styles have contributed to the evolution of the picture book.

Illustrations in early picture books were created using a relief method such as wood-block printing. Artists carved illustrations on wood blocks by cutting away the background. The resulting images, which stood above the rest of the block, were inked and impressed on paper by printing machines. Every book was colored by hand; ironically, some of those hands belonged to children who worked under sweatshop conditions.

In the late nineteenth century, metal plates and metal engravings were used. William Blake used etchings on metal plates to illustrate his *Songs of Innocence.* Walter Crane's illustrations in *Absurd ABC* were hand-colored, and the typography in that book was considered to be as excellent as the pictures. John Tenniel's illustrations of Lewis Carroll's *Alice's Adventures in Wonderland* were printed by letterpress from metal engravings.

Lithography, a process invented in the late eighteenth century, allowed artists to work on flat stones that had a very hard, smoothly polished surface. Images were drawn on the stone with wax crayons or touche, a crayonlike liquid material. The ink adhered to the waxed portions of the stone; images were then printed on dampened paper using enormous pressure. One example of fine lithography is found in Hans Fischer's 1958 illustrations for Charles Perrault's *Puss in Boots.*

The use of photography and letterpress printing revolutionized the printing of picture books in the early twentieth century. At first, colors had to be separated by hand,

TECHNOLOGY in PRACTICE 3.1

DIGITIZED PICTURE BOOKS

Find a Web site that has picture books online; for example, Tumble Books <www.tumblebooks.com> or One More Story <www.onemorestory.com>. These sites provide a trial book for free, or your public library Web site may give you access through your library card. Once you are familiar with the numerous ways in which readers can interact with digitized books, weigh the pros and cons of each type of interaction. Consider which outcomes are educational and which ones focus on entertainment or motivation. Decide how you will introduce such books to your students, what parameters you will set, and how you will promote the most positive features of digitized picture books. Introduce the digitized book to students along with the traditional book version and engage students in discussions of what each type of "reading experience" has to offer. For more information see Yokota, J. & Teale, W. H. (in press, 2014). Picture Books and the Digital World: Educators Making Informed Choices. *The Reading Teacher.*

and the process was both tedious and expensive. It was not until illustrators could turn color separation over to machines that the number of full-color illustrations in picture books increased. Photography and later the laser scanner made the greatest impacts on the quality of art reproduction.

In the twentieth and early twenty-first centuries, printing technology improved tremendously: Art is now reproduced so that it closely resembles its original form. Picture books have become objects of great beauty. The use of computer technology to create picture books has led to a new era of book illustration. Since the advent of the laser scanner, the printing process imposes few limitations on the artist. It is amazing what illustrators have been able to use: Imaginative picture books have been made with collages of cardboard, cereal, and plastic, as David Diaz did in illustrating Eve Bunting's *Smoky Night,* the 1995 Caldecott-winning book, or even wood veneers, which is what Paul O. Zelinsky used to illustrate Anne Isaacs's *Swamp Angel,* a 1995 Caldecott Honor Book.

Computer technology itself offers illustrators a new medium. Artists have different reactions to the use of computers to create art. Some suggest that technology separates the artist too much from the reader and that children will always prefer illustrations in which "the hand of the artist" is recognizable. On the other hand, some highly regarded and established illustrators have made such a complete transition to computer-generated art that they have given up paintbrushes entirely. Others have merged their work by creating illustrations by hand and then scanning and manipulating them on-screen. More recently, a new generation of illustrators who create their art solely digitally has emerged. As technology changes rapidly and new possibilities are constantly made available, it's likely that the interactivity possible in the digital world of ebooks and apps will influence what's created for children to read and enjoy.

Authors and Illustrators Who Have Defined the Field

The work of many early authors and illustrators has contributed to the shaping and defining of the field of picture books. Some early works continue to be enjoyed by children today—evidence of the timeless appeal of these creations.

Beatrix Potter's 1902 publication of *The Tale of Peter Rabbit* is celebrated as her debut as a creator of children's books, although her first book was published earlier. This story originally appeared in a series of letters in 1893 to Noel, the son of her former governess, and was intended to cheer him up when he was ill with scarlet fever. Potter included black-and-white drawings to accompany the story. Years later, after several publication rejections, she used her own funds to have the book published. Frederick Warne & Co. agreed to publish this "little book for little hands" on the condition that Potter provide color illustrations. More than twenty other books followed. The tales of such animal characters as Pigling Bland, Squirrel Nutkin, Jemima Puddleduck, Benjamin Bunny, Hunca Munca, and Jeremy Fisher are known by children all around the world.

Before the 1930s, the picture books that were available to children in the United States were typically imported from England and other European countries. However, between 1930 and 1960, many authors and illustrators came from Europe and joined those working in the United States to establish a solid foundation of American picture books. Ludwig Bemelmans, Roger Duvoisin, Feodor Rojankovsky, and Tomi Ungerer were among those who emigrated from Europe. American picture book creators of that time were Robert McCloskey, Wanda Gág, Robert Lawson, Virginia Lee Burton, Marie Hall Ets, and Margaret Wise Brown. Many of the books created during that era continue to be popular with children.

Wanda Gág's 1929 book *Millions of Cats* still delights readers with the repeated phrases "Hundreds of cats, Thousands of cats, Millions and billions and trillions of cats." The lonely man who sets out to find a cat to keep him and his wife company simply cannot choose from among the millions of cats, each with unique qualities. The lines of the hills and roads in the black-and-white illustrations show the long distance the man travels in search of a cat and echo the long line of cats that follow him home.

Many adults today remember reading Virginia Lee Burton's 1939 story of *Mike Mulligan and His Steam Shovel* as they grew up. When new electric and diesel shovels take jobs away from steam shovels, Mike takes his steam shovel, Mary Anne, to Popperville and proves that she can dig "as much in one day as a hundred men could dig in a week." The house in Burton's 1942 *The Little House* was said to be so well built that the "great-great-grandchildren's great-great-grandchildren" would live there. Although both of these works are much more than a half-century old, they meet contemporary criteria for good picture books.

Of the many books written by Margaret Wise Brown, the one most cherished by millions of readers over the years is *Goodnight Moon.* In this bedtime story, published in 1947, a little rabbit is in bed, saying goodnight to each item in the bedroom and outside the window. Gradually, the lights dim until it is dark in the room, and the rabbit falls asleep.

Robert McCloskey's 1942 Caldecott-winning *Make Way for Ducklings* made the Boston Public Garden famous all over the world to children who read and reread the endearing story of a duck family in search of a place to live. Among McCloskey's other books from the 1940s and 1950s that continue to enjoy wide popularity are *Blueberries for Sal* and *Time of Wonder,* both depicting life in rural Maine.

Marcia Brown's first book was published in 1946, and only one year later she produced her first Caldecott Honor Book, *Stone Soup: An Old Tale.* Her interest in folktales and fairy tales continued in the many books that followed. In fact, all three of Brown's Caldecott Medal books are folktales or fairy tales: *Cinderella*, created with watercolors in 1955, *Once a Mouse* with woodcut-style illustrations in 1962, and *Shadow*, which mixes collage, paint and print in 1983.

Ezra Jack Keats is known for his distinctive collages, but it is his depictions of the daily life of inner-city children that was ground breaking for the 1960s. In the 1963 Caldecott winner, *The Snowy Day,* Keats used a variety of papers—gift wrap, wallpaper, and other printed papers—to add color and texture to his illustrations. In this story, Peter wakes up, sees a snowy scene outside his window, and spends the day playing in the snow. Peter's experiences are often universal—getting a new baby sister in *Peter's Chair* and playing in the neighborhood in *Apt. 3*—but the details of the setting clearly place these stories in city neighborhoods.

John Steptoe knew from the time he was in high school that he wanted to write and illustrate books for African American children; he realized there was a great need for books these children could relate to. Immediately after high school, Steptoe published his first book, *Stevie.* Although the theme—a boy's jealousy at having to share his mother's attention with a younger boy—is universal and can be appreciated by all children regardless of race, the book uses language to which African American children can relate directly.

Tomie dePaola has written over one hundred books and illustrated over two hundred books for children. His artwork is characteristically done in watercolor in a folk art style. dePaola's loving family relationships are the root of many of his books, including *Nana Upstairs & Nana Downstairs* and *Tom,* which depict an intergenerational affection and bond and loss brought about by death. His Italian and Irish heritages are the source of his interest in those cultures, which several of his books reflect. Perhaps the best known is *Strega Nona*, a Caldecott Honor Book in which an Italian "Grandma Witch" with a magical touch leaves her helper, Big Anthony, home alone with a magic pot that can cook pasta by itself. dePaola's years in a Benedictine monastery influenced the eventual creation of books with religious stories or themes such as *Patrick, Patron Saint of Ireland*. In the early 1970s, *The Cloud Book, Charlie Needs a Cloak,* and *The Popcorn Book* made Tomie dePaola an early leader in writing narrative informational books—books with the intent of offering information to children, but that are set to a story.

Leo Lionni's career as a children's book author and illustrator began when he told a story to his grandchildren to pass the time while they were traveling together by train. Later published as a book, the story was about two children depicted as colors—blue and yellow—who hug and become green. *Little Blue and Little Yellow* was illustrated with torn-paper collage, which portrayed human emotions abstractly. Lionni continued to write and illustrate many books whose characters embodied concepts important in human relationships. In *Swimmy*, a school of fish gathers into a formation resembling a large fish to fend off predators who have eaten Swimmy's family. The combination of sponge printing and watercolor in this book effectively depicts the underwater world. *Frederick* is particularly well known for both its collage artwork and the story: As a family of mice gathers supplies to prepare for the coming winter, Frederick "stores up" stories and poetry as his contribution.

Categories of Picture Books

Picture books have a range of purposes, from introducing rhymes and serving as manipulative toys to helping children learn concepts. In this section, we organize picture books into five groups: early childhood books, wordless books, picture books with minimal text, beginning readers' books, and picture storybooks.

Early Childhood Books

Many children enjoy books from the moment they are nestled in an adult's lap and have a book shared with them or are able to hold a book on their own. Some books are particularly appropriate for young children, because of both their form and their content.

Toy Books. Preschoolers can become acquainted with books very early, thanks to cloth, vinyl, and board books. These books are typically eight to ten pages long and often have a sturdy or washable construction and simple pictures. If there are any words, they may simply label objects on the page. For slightly older children, pop-ups, pull-tabs, flaps to lift, half-pages, and other gadgets invite playful manipulation. Classic toy books include Dorothy Kunhardt's *Pat the Bunny,* a tactile and participatory book that is still in print more than seventy years after its first edition, and *The Nutshell Library,* a boxed set of miniature books by Maurice Sendak that generations of children have enjoyed for over fifty years.

For very young children, there are board books that often come in series of three to four titles centered on topics of immediate interest to them, such as animals, things babies do, or family members. Tana Hoban created two books for newborns: *Black on White* and *White on Black*. Both books show shadows of objects on solid backgrounds, creating high contrast between black and white. For preschoolers, there are replicas of hardcover picture books, such as the board book version of Eric Carle's *The Very Busy Spider* or Peggy Rathmann's *Good Night, Gorilla*. Some books have pages that are thicker and glossier than usual book pages. Cut-out shapes layer and unlayer on sixteen boldly colored pages to create various animal faces in *Color Zoo* by Lois Ehlert, a Caldecott Honor Book.

Some pop-up books are fairly straightforward, with single-fold pop-ups; other paper-engineered pop-ups are more elaborate, often with moving parts. One particularly popular series is by Eric Hill. In *Where's Spot?*, children lift flaps to help mother dog Sally open the door, look inside a wardrobe, and peek under the bed to search for her pup Spot. Laura Vaccaro Seeger has created a well-designed concept book entitled *Black? White! Day? Night! A Book of Opposites.* With cutouts and lift-the-flap features, the concept of opposites is explored in clever but clearly defined ways. Particularly fine examples of complex paper-engineered books are created by Robert Sabuda. For the most part, they are intended for an older audience than toddlers—in fact, the elaborate and complex designs appeal to all ages. *Dinosaurs* includes smaller pop-up books within the main pop-up book, adding layers of intrigue. Some books combine pop-ups with pull-tabs, flaps, and other parts to be manipulated. One example is Paul Zelinsky's *The Wheels on the Bus.* In addition to wheels that turn, the book has a bus door that swings open, passengers who board, wipers that swish, babies who cry open-mouthed, and mothers who shake their fingers.

Eric Carle's picture books have toy components that are integral to the story line. In *The Very Hungry Caterpillar,* actual holes in a series of illustrations of food indicate where the caterpillar dined. *The Very Quiet Cricket* searches for a friend until he finally meets another cricket; at that point, readers hear the sound of a cricket (produced by a computer chip embedded in the book).

Some books are toys themselves. *Maisy's House and Garden Pop-Up Playset,* by Lucy Cousins, looks like a book but opens up to serve as a two-story house, complete with furniture and garden for Maisy the mouse. The toy book stimulates children to create their own stories as they play with it.

Some books with toy components are for a little older audience, but they still include the toy component in a manner that best utilizes the device to contribute to the book's overall experience. In Emily Gravett's *Meerkat Mail,* a meerkat in the Kalahari Desert ventures away from home and sends postcards to her family; both sides of each postcard can be seen through the effective use of "lift-the-flap" style. Using the device of postcards as the format, information about each place in the world visited is presented, and meerkat's text contributes to the story. Visual humor and anticipation is implied through the image of the jackal that lurks in the background, with its potential prey, the meerkat, completely oblivious to it.

ILLUSTRATION 3.1 In an interactive mode of introducing the concept of changes, die-cut holes throughout the book depict the life cycle change from egg to chick to chicken, and more such changes. (Book cover of "First the Egg" by Laura Vaccaro Seegar. A Neal Porter Book, published by Roaring Brook Press [a division of Holtzbrinck Publishing Holdings Limited Partnership. All rights reserved.], 2007. (ISBN: 1596432721).)

Concept Books. Concept books convey knowledge, answering the question "What's that?" They cover a wide range of topics—the alphabet, numbers, colors, shapes, and opposites, to name a few. To appreciate the contribution of these picture books, you need only think about how difficult it is sometimes to describe and convey the meaning of concepts in words alone. Because of their significance and abundance, alphabet and counting books are discussed separately in this section. The important thing to remember when evaluating concept books is how clearly the information is presented and how appropriate it is to the reader's conceptual development.

Two concept books that explore the primary colors and how colors mix within a story arc are Ann Jonas's *Color Dance* and Ellen Stoll Walsh's *Mouse Paint.* In *Color Dance,* three girls dance with red, yellow, and blue sheets of sheer fabric. As they dance and their sheets cross, new colors are made. In *Mouse Paint,* three mice splash around in red, yellow, and blue paint. When they dance around in each other's puddles, new colors are made.

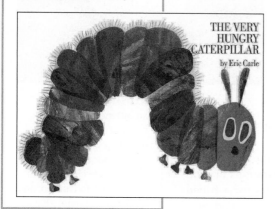

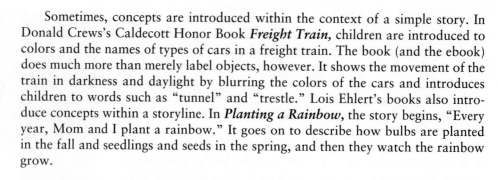

Sometimes, concepts are introduced within the context of a simple story. In Donald Crews's Caldecott Honor Book *Freight Train,* children are introduced to colors and the names of types of cars in a freight train. The book (and the ebook) does much more than merely label objects, however. It shows the movement of the train in darkness and daylight by blurring the colors of the cars and introduces children to words such as "tunnel" and "trestle." Lois Ehlert's books also introduce concepts within a storyline. In *Planting a Rainbow,* the story begins, "Every year, Mom and I plant a rainbow." It goes on to describe how bulbs are planted in the fall and seedlings and seeds in the spring, and then they watch the rainbow grow.

Alphabet Books. Alphabet books are one of the oldest and most popular varieties of concept books. Preschoolers are often first exposed to the alphabet through picture books, and such books are available in large numbers. A traditional alphabet book shows a one-to-one correspondence between a letter and an object whose name begins with that letter. Typically, there is one letter and one object per page or half page, clearly showing letter-picture match. One example is *Eric Carle's ABC.* More complex alphabet books show more objects per page to illustrate the featured letter; the "B" may be represented by a bicycle as a central picture, but birds, bells, and beans may be found in the border; *Anno's Alphabet* is subtitled "An Adventure in Imagination." These pictures are often too sophisticated for simple letter-sound associations and are intended for children to extend their alphabet knowledge. Finally, some alphabet books challenge readers to discover as many objects as they can find hidden within a very busy illustration that includes numerous objects with names that begin with the featured letter. In *Animalia* by Graeme Base, "Beautiful Blue Butterflies Basking by a Babbling Brook," has hidden objects that begin with "B"—baboon, bassoon, bee, beetle, book, bear, bonnet.

Many books play with the sounds of language while introducing the alphabet. A popular one is Bill Martin, Jr., and John Archambault's *Chicka Chicka Boom Boom.* Children especially enjoy the rhythmic, rhyming text that tells the story of alphabet letters vying to see which can climb to the top of the coconut tree first. A similar rhyming book featuring the letters of the alphabet is Jane Bayer's *A, My Name Is Alice,* whose alphabet rhymes are illustrated by Steven Kellogg. The rhymes are traditional accompaniments to playground games such as jump rope or ball bouncing games: "A, my name is Alice and my husband's name is Alex. We come from Alaska and we sell ants. Alice is an Ape. Alex is an Anteater." A different way of playing with the sounds of language is through alliteration, such as in Maurice Sendak's *Alligators All Around,* from the Nutshell Library.

A large variety of themed alphabet books are also available. One book with a food theme is *Eating the Alphabet: Fruits and Vegetables from A to Z,* by Lois Ehlert, which shows a variety of fruits and vegetables in alphabetical order. The alphabet is used to organize all kinds of information at many conceptual levels; there is a rich array of alphabet books for all ages.

Counting Books. Counting books introduce children to a mathematical concept. The most basic counting books clearly show a number along with easily identifiable objects to count, without much background clutter to confuse children. Eric Carle's *1, 2, 3 to the Zoo* is about animals aboard a train on their way to the zoo. Each double-page spread shows a number on the upper left and a boxcar with the correct number of a particular animal on board. The eleventh page is a foldout in which children can see all the animals in their zoo home and the empty train.

Denise Fleming's *Count!* encourages children to count from one to ten vibrantly colored, action-oriented creatures. Then the book continues counting by tens to fifty. Lois Ehlert's *Fish Eyes: A Book You Can Count On* encourages children to count the fish on a page, then add one more by counting the narrator fish. The illustrations have cut-out eyes for children to count. Books like Eric Carle's *The Very Hungry Caterpillar* offer children an opportunity to count numbers within a story line. Children can count the fruit the caterpillar eats, while listening to the story being read.

Wordless Books

The pictures tell everything in wordless books, and it is an artistic feat to make the stories intriguing, understandable, and satisfying. The text is created in the mind of the reader. Wordless books give children the opportunity to be flexible in their interpretation of a story: They can discuss possibilities for the text, look for clues in the illustrations, and practice storytelling. Wordless books have been popular for years; Pat Hutchins's *Changes, Changes* remains, after over forty years, one of the best wordless picture books. The characters and setting are established with images made from wood blocks. The story line of two wooden figures resourcefully creating objects to fit varying dilemmas is action packed, and the theme is easily grasped, yet thought provoking.

David Wiesner's *Tuesday* won the Caldecott Medal in 1992. The only text is the notation about time of day on Tuesday. The hilarious exploits of a community of frogs who fly hither and yon on lily pads linger in the reader's visual memory as the many shades of green immerse the reader in the frog world.

Wordless storybooks such as these offer children many opportunities to imagine what the text could be. Note, however, that not all wordless books contain stories. Some wordless books are simply a themed set of pictures.

Picture Books with Minimal Text

Books with minimal text are related to the category of wordless books. The story is told predominantly through the illustrations, as in wordless books, but a few words are strategically included. In some cases, those few words are critical to the story; in other cases, they amplify the story, but are not critical to its success. In Peggy Rathmann's *Good Night, Gorilla,* the zookeeper walks from cage to cage wishing the animals good night, oblivious to the fact that the gorilla has taken his keys and is letting each animal out. The animals follow the zookeeper home and into the bedroom, where his wife discovers the animals. She then leads them back to the zoo. The only text is the repeated refrain, "Good night _____." This story would work even without the text, because the humor is obvious in the illustrations alone. In David Shannon's *No, David!,* Mother is always having to tell her rambunctious son, "No, David, no!" "No! No! No!" "I said no, David!" The other lines in the book are all cautionary commands—that is, all except the last line of the story.

Molly Bang's story of Sophie's anger at being required to share her toy with her sister is expressed precisely in the minimal text that accompanies the expressive illustrations in *When Sophie Gets Angry—Really, Really Angry.* Her explosive anger is vividly portrayed in the illustrations, and the accompanying text endorses the emotion. Rachel Vail's *Sometimes I'm Bombaloo,* illustrated by Yumi Heo, offers an interesting emotional comparison to this book but with more text.

ILLUSTRATION 3.3 In Jeremy Tankard's *Grumpy Bird*, a bird is followed around by various animal friends who imitate his antics, and before long, his mood changes as he has fun with an impromptu game of "follow the leader." (Scholastic, Inc.)

Emotions are clearly expressed through the art even with minimal text, and the plot is also clear in books such as Jeremy Tankard's *Grumpy Bird*, which shows a very grumpy bird's change of mood as his friends play along with him in follow-the-leader, even flying off at the end with him. In Jon Klassen's *I Want My Hat Back*, emotion is elicited in the reader without necessarily using text or illustration to explicitly depict emotion.

Beginning Readers' Books

Children need books they can read independently as they practice their emerging reading abilities. Some books are more likely to be a success with beginning readers because of their predictable format. Other books are more likely to be accessible to beginning readers because of their controlled vocabulary.

Predictable Books

Predictable books have highly structured or repetitive texts that are easy for fledgling readers to read independently. For children, being able to predict what will happen serves as a motivation to read and provides great satisfaction. Predictable books often use rhythms and rhymes or simple story structures to make it easy for the young reader to perceive the pattern of the text and use it to guess upcoming words. Such factors encourage emerging readers to take risks—and the reward is being in on what is happening.

A pioneer writer in this format is children's author and educator Bill Martin, Jr. Over four decades ago, Martin set out to write a series of books that would be easy for beginners to read. Of these Instant Readers, perhaps the best known is *Brown Bear, Brown Bear, What Do You See?* On one page, the text says, "Brown Bear, Brown Bear, what do you see?" The next page reads, "I see a yellow duck looking at me," and on that page readers find a yellow duck created by illustrator Eric Carle. The language pattern and illustrations work together so nicely that countless beginning readers have been able to recite/read the book after a brief introduction.

Uri Shulevitz's *One Monday Morning* uses a cumulative pattern and supportive illustrations to enumerate the important people who come to visit the young narrator in his urban apartment. *The Napping House,* by Audrey and Don Wood, repeats the phrase "In a napping house, where everyone is sleeping" and builds a story by adding a new sleepy character on each page—along with an array of interesting words about sleeping, such as "dozing," "napping," and "snoring."

Easy Readers. Easy readers are often among the first books that children read independently. Although they are not strictly picture storybooks as described later in this chapter, they have a formula that includes a generous amount of illustration throughout the book. They typically have some kind of controlled vocabulary; that is, the number of words, the types of words, and the sentence structure and length are determined by a formula that estimates the relative reading level of a book. The controlled vocabulary can result in poor writing, and some easy reader books are reminiscent of basal readers of the past. However, many easy readers combine literary merit with an opportunity for beginning readers to read on their own successfully.

One of the most innovative and famous writers of easy reader books was Dr. Seuss (a pseudonym for Theodor Seuss Geisel). In the 1930s, Dr. Seuss wrote such children's books as *The Five Hundred Hats of Bartholomew Cubbins* and *And to Think That I Saw It on Mulberry Street.* In 1957, convinced that beginning readers were being given uninteresting stories stifled by controlled vocabulary in basal readers of the time, Dr. Seuss changed the outlook on easy reader books when he published *The Cat in the Hat.* With a limited number of words, he tells the story of a cat whose outlandish behavior stuns two well-behaved children who have been left alone in their house for a short while. His impact in the field of beginning readers was so significant that the American Library Association named the (Theodor Seuss) Geisel award in his honor.

Since then, many easy readers have been written. *Henry and Mudge: The First Book of Their Adventures,* by Cynthia Rylant, is the first of a series of easy readers by this award-winning author. The text uses limited vocabulary, yet has the qualities of poetry. The friendly crayon line drawings by Sucie Stevenson enliven the text and encourage fledgling readers by giving visual clues to what the words must be.

Arnold Lobel wrote brilliantly within the constraints of limited numbers of words and simple sentence structures. In 1971, his *Frog and Toad Are Friends* was named a Caldecott Honor Book for its illustrations; *Frog and Toad Together* was a 1973 Newbery Honor Book for its text.

James Marshall's wit and creativity are evident in his many humorous easy-reading books. His text and illustrations are seemingly simple, yet the character and plot development is rich and complete. In *Three by the Sea* (written under the pseudonym Edward Marshall), readers meet Lolly, Spider, and Sam, who are having a picnic at the beach. Children are propelled to continue reading as they anticipate what will happen when a rat buys a cat to be his friend or when a monster comes out of the sea and finds three children on a beach. Young readers are equally motivated to read about Fox attempting to make money at various jobs so that he can buy a new bike in *Fox on the Job.*

Mo Willems created the Elephant and Piggie books in which the two humorously interact through engaging and entertaining dialogue, even on such seemingly mundane subjects as the weather. Piggie considers the weather and is undecided about playing outside as Gerald continuously wonders, *Are You Ready to Play Outside?*

Some easy readers are more advanced, to meet the needs of children's developing reading ability. Although these "transitional chapter books" (Roser, Martinez, McDonnald & Fuhrken, 2004) are longer and include more complex words, the qualities that make easy readers readable are still present. More complex easy readers include the *Mr. Putter and Tabby* series by Cynthia Rylant, and *Ling & Ting* by Grace Lin.

Some books "play" with the use of text and illustration in a way that directly gets at the close examination of words. In *One Boy,* Laura Seeger uses a clever format of covering most of the previous page's text, but leaving open a "mask" as a hole, allowing readers to see that part of each second set of lines is taken from words in the first line. For example, the book begins, "One boy, all alone" with the "one" showing through the box. The closing, "All done" allows adults to convey to beginning readers the notion of words that look alike but don't sound alike.

Books like these fill a vital need. Many preschoolers have grown accustomed to having their parents and teachers read fascinating and eloquent books to them, and when children reach school age, we hope parents and teachers will continue to read to them, for it will take much time and hard practice before they will be able to read such books for themselves. Easy readers, though, can be interesting and pithy books in highly readable language. It can be difficult to maintain quality in a format in which simplicity is paramount, but the continued efforts of such authors as Grace

TOP SHELF 3.1

PICTURE BOOKS WITH ADULT APPEAL

The Gardener by Sarah Stewart, Illustrated by David Small

Mysterious Thelonius by Chris Raschka

The Wall by Peter Sís

TEACHING IDEA 3.1

COMPARING ILLUSTRATIONS IN DIFFERENT VERSIONS OF THE SAME STORY

COMMON CORE STANDARD:
Craft and Structure,
STANDARD 6

Common Core Standard 6 calls for readers to "assess how point of view or purpose shapes the content and style of a text." Given that text includes visual as well as verbal text, consider how an illustrator's point of view or purpose shapes which details are included and what style of illustration is employed. Have children examine three or more illustrated versions of a common story, such as *Hansel and Gretel*; for example, look at editions by Paul Zelinsky, James Marshall, Anthony Browne, and Rachel Isadora. Have children note differences that inform viewers of the illustrator's perspective and interpretation of the story. Are there details that clearly set the story in a particular culture or time period? How do differences in artistic media or artistic style influence the viewers' interpretation of the story? Do differences in the illustration style make each of the books more appropriate for some audiences than others?

Lin, Laura Seeger, and Mo Willems are rewarded when young readers can enjoy interesting content in well-crafted language.

Picture Storybooks

There are more picture storybooks than any other type of picture book. As defined earlier, a picture storybook is one in which the text and the illustrations work together to amplify each other; in other words, part of the story is told through the illustrations and part is told through the text. Text and illustrations do not merely reflect each other; rather, combined, they tell a story that goes beyond what each one tells alone. The text of picture storybooks is best when it is rich in language use.

Visual Literacy

Since the days of cave paintings, communicating through visual images has been important, and it is an ability that everyone must continuously expand. The need to develop an understanding of visuals has been less emphasized in schools than text comprehension. Yet children are constantly being asked to rely on their visual comprehension skills, whether it is overtly or implied. Just as there are components of written communication that readers must know how to interpret, there are also parallel components of visual communication that must be interpreted.

In this section, we present an overview of some of the major artistic elements of design; later, we explore them in more detail and apply them to comprehending the illustrations in picture books in the section "How Picture Storybooks Work." Elements that apply to visual literacy in informational books are examined in Chapter 11.

ILLUSTRATION 3.4 Leo and Diane Dillon used stylized watercolor paintings patterned after batik art to illustrate this winner of the Caldecott Medal. ("Why Mosquitoes Buzz in People's Ears: A West African Tale" by Verna Aardema, Illustrated by Leo and Diane Dillon. Used by permission of Penguin Group (USA) Inc. All rights reserved.)

Elements of Design

Artists rely on various elements of design to communicate with their audience. When artwork is done well, the reader can enjoy the aesthetics of the illustrations and appreciate the emotions conveyed through the manipulation of artistic elements. The elements of design are line, shape, color, light, and texture, and together, they combine to create *composition*.

ILLUSTRATION 3.5 Dav Pilkey used line effectively in *The Paperboy* to convey the impression of depth and movement. (Scholastic, Inc.)

Let's examine one book in some depth and look at the use of these elements. In *The Paperboy,* Dav Pilkey presents the story of a paperboy's morning. As the story begins, the paperboy is asleep in his bed; readers see him rising, eating breakfast, folding papers, delivering on his route, returning home, and getting back into bed for some "time for dreaming." Throughout all of this, he is accompanied by his dog.

Line. Lines can be thin and light or heavy and bold; they can be straight, jagged, or curved. Line is used effectively in *The Paperboy* to create the rolling shapes of the hills in the background, which give a sense of long distances. Line also conveys the sense of fast movement when the paperboy and his dog are returning home: The dog's tail is horizontal, and the paperboy's empty bag is flying behind him.

Shape. Shape is created when spaces are contained by a combination of lines. The triangular roof, the side-by-side arrangement of the rectangular doors in the hallway, the two square windows in the kitchen, and the big rectangular work table in the garage all combine with the center gutter of the book to give the house in *The Paperboy* a symmetrical feel—one that creates a sense of solid security in the paperboy's home. In the opening double-page spread, the predictable shapes of the houses give a sense of a solid community life. The rolling shapes of the land separate the houses and give a sense of distance between them, even though they are painted close together on the page. The sense of distance and spaciousness leads the reader to think that this is more a rural area than an urban one.

ILLUSTRATION 3.6 In this illustration, Pilkey has a nightlight create the small amount of light in the hallway, signifying the darkness of the early morning hour. (Scholastic, Inc.)

Color. Color can range over the full spectrum, or it can be limited to a defined range—for example, black and white and the various shades of gray in between that characterize what "value" means. Color conveys emotions and establishes mood. One instance of dramatic use of color in *The Paperboy* is the single beam of the yellow headlight from the paperboy's bicycle, seen against the dark colors of the neighborhood before dawn.

Light. Light impacts the values of color in its gradations. Pilkey uses light to show the time of day in *The Paperboy.* When the lamp beside the boy's bed is turned on, his room lights up, but it is dark outside. Only a nightlight gives light in the hallway when the paperboy is getting up in the morning. By the time he returns from his route, though, light is peeking from underneath his parents' door, and the light in his sister's room can be seen beyond the doorway.

ILLUSTRATION 3.7 Through lines and shading, Pilkey gives texture to the wood boards of the ceiling and floor. (Scholastic, Inc.)

Texture. Texture is the illusion of a tactile surface created in an illustration. In ***The Paperboy,*** texture in the wood boards of the ceiling and floor is created through the use of lines and shading. The shading of the trees also contributes texture.

Composition. Composition is when line, shape, color, light, and texture are combined to create an overall effect. Unity is influenced by how the artistic elements are used to show balance, proportion, emphasis and contrast.

Appreciating the Artistic Craft of the Picture Book

The illustrations in picture books for children have become increasingly sophisticated over the years as the picture book has developed as a format. In addition, changes in printing technology have made it possible to reproduce a much greater range of artwork. This section focuses on two aspects of art in picture books: artistic media and artistic style.

Artistic Media

The artists who create picture books rely on a number of media to express their visions of the stories. Some illustrators use a "signature" medium almost exclusively; others select different media depending on how they want to express their views of the particular story. The examples in this section vary from informational books to various genres of fiction and are not necessarily from picture storybooks.

ILLUSTRATION 3.8 Burningham's paintings throughout the book convey the story of what a cat does at night in a magical fantasy played out in a world created by mixed media. ("It's a Secret!" Copyright © 2009 John Burningham. Reproduced by permission of the publisher, Candlewick Press, on behalf of Walker Books, London.)

Painting: Watercolor, Gouache, Oil, and Other Paints. More children's books are illustrated with watercolor than with any other medium. Watercolor paintings can be solidly intense or thin and fluid, depending on the amount of water used. Gouache is a type of watercolor paint that contains an added white powder to create a more opaque finished product. Artists who desire an opaque look may also use acrylic paints or oil paints.

Frané Lessac uses gouache to create vividly colorful images of the Caribbean Islands in many books, such as ***The Chalk Doll*** by Charlotte Pomerantz, in which a mother reminisces about her childhood in Jamaica. In ***Caribbean Alphabet,*** she uses the alphabet to list unique qualities of the islands—for example, breadfruit, hibiscus, reggae, and steel bands. In Susan Guevara's illustrations in acrylic paint on scratchboard for Gary Soto's ***Chato's Kitchen,*** readers see the lines that mark the movement of the paintbrush. These marks, and the heavy use of color, add to the vibrancy and energy of the book.

Thomas Locker characteristically uses oil paintings that give viewers a sense of wide landscapes. Paul Zelinsky's ***Rumpelstiltskin*** is also rendered in oil paint, an appropriate medium to complement the medieval setting. Floyd Cooper employs a variation on oil painting in which he applies a very thin layer of paint to a surface and, when it dries, creates shape and areas of light by using an eraser; he then adds color at the end. Some illustrators paint on surfaces other than

paper. In *The Pot of Wisdom: Ananse Stories,* Adwoa Badoe recounts stories of the trickster spider, and Baba Wagué Diakité paints on ceramic tiles. Paul Zelinsky's illustrations in the Caldecott Honor Book *Swamp Angel* by Anne Isaacs were painted on wood veneers.

Drawing: Pencil, Pen and Ink, Crayon, Chalk, etc. Stephen Gammell uses pencils to convey a range of emotions, from the happy, nostalgic feel of Karen Ackerman's *Song and Dance Man* to the sinister, gory tone of Alvin Schwartz's *Scary Stories* series. Pencils can be used to create strong lines, shaded areas, smudged shadows, and fine details. Readers sense the warmth of relationships in various books depicting family events, illustrated by Gammell with colored pencils. For instance, in *Song and Dance Man,* pastel hues against the white background give a soft glow to the attic in which the grandfather and his grandchildren share a moment from the past, as the grandfather dances and reminisces about the time when he was a song and dance man. Few areas are solidly shaded; rather, visible lines help guide the reader's eyes to areas of focus and give dimension to objects. Gammell's work in Schwartz's *Scary Stories to Tell in the Dark* seems a far cry from *Song and Dance Man,* even though both are pencil illustrations. In the *Scary Stories* book, the black-and-white images have unfinished lines, supporting the sense of the haunted as being unpredictably present and only partially visible. Even without color, we can clearly visualize the blood dripping. The jagged lines create feelings of horror. In these two examples, Gammell shows the range of artistic expression possible with one medium.

ILLUSTRATION 3.9 In illustrating *Scary Stories to Tell in the Dark*, Stephen Gammell used black-and-white pencil drawings to create a mood of impending peril. (Illustrations copyright © 1981 by Stephen Gammell. Used by permission of HarperCollins Publishers.)

Paper Crafts: Collage, Papermaking, Cut Paper. Various forms of paper crafts are used by illustrators of children's books. The most commonly used form is collage, in which, traditionally, various types of paper are cut or torn and pieced together onto a background to create a picture, as in the art of Ezra Jack Keats, Eric Carle, and Leo Lionni. The papers may be of varying weights and colors—anything from gift wrap to wallpaper to handmade paper. To create the art for *Saint Valentine,* Robert Sabuda cut marbleized and handmade paper into tiny squares and created a mosaic for each illustration, using over a thousand paper bits for each full-page illustration. To create the art for *Wings,* Christopher Myers used magazine pictures, paper of varying types, and even paper that presumably comes from an envelope on which the U.S. Post Office had printed the coding for mail.

Australian author/illustrator Jeannie Baker's books such as *Where the Forest Meets the Sea* are focused on the theme of taking care of the environment for future generations. Appropriately, she creates her illustrations with relief collages of amazing details, using natural materials like stone, plaster from old walls, grass, leaves, cracked paint, earth, knitted wool, natural vegetation, and hair. She has learned how to preserve and add permanent color to natural plants in order to combine the naturalness in texture while offering a wider range of color with which to illustrate.

Illustrator Denise Fleming creates vibrant illustrations by making a sheet of handmade paper for each illustration. She makes a pulp out of cotton rag fiber and water, adds color, and spreads the pulp out on a framed wire screen to create a background. Using plastic squeeze bottles filled with colored pulp, she pours shapes on the background or fills in her hand-cut stencils, sometimes adding other objects to create interesting textures. Fleming's book *In the Small, Small Pond,* a Caldecott Honor Book, shows the creatures of a small pond in their daily environment. Fleming mirrors their movements with alliterative and rhyming phrases—for example, "lash, lunge, herons plunge" and "sweep, swoop, swallows scoop."

ILLUSTRATION 3.10 Brian Pinkney's illustrations and Andrea Davis Pinkney's text combine to tell the powerful story of four friends who staged a peaceful protest against segregation by ordering at a Woolworth's lunch counter during the days of segregation. ("Sit-In: How Four Friends Stood Up by Sitting Down" by Andrea Davis Pinkney, illustrated by Brian Pinkney. Little, Brown and Company, a division of Hachette Book Group, Inc.)

David Wisniewski used cut paper to create the illustrations for his 1997 Caldecott Medal winner, *The Golem,* as well as for his other books. He uses an X-Acto knife to cut intricate designs and layers pieces to achieve a three-dimensional effect. Robert Sabuda created the art for *The Paper Dragon,* by Marguerite W. Davol, in the style of Chinese paper-cut art, by making precise and detailed cuts in tissue paper he painted. Each illustration is three pages long; the double spreads have a page that folds out, thereby creating a scroll-like effect.

Three-Dimensional Art. As book production technology advanced, the possibilities of artistic media became much less limited. Just about anything of any size can now be photographed, copied, or digitally manipulated for reproduction in a picture book. Thus, in recent times, there has been an increase in the use of three-dimensional art.

Many illustrators do not limit themselves to paper when creating collages, but employ a wide range of materials, including three-dimensional objects. For his 1995 Caldecott-winning book *Smoky Night,* written by Eve Bunting, David Diaz used matches, plastic bags, hangers, cereal, bubble wrap, and shoe soles, in addition to a variety of papers, to create collage backgrounds to frame his acrylic paintings and the text in this book depicting the 1992 Los Angeles riots. Lois Ehlert's *Snowballs* shows a family of snowpeople—complete with dog and cat—created with birdseed, a knit hat, seashells, a compass, a cinnamon stick, a pinecone, luggage claim checks, plastic forks, and toy fish, among other things.

In Joan Steiner's *Look-Alikes,* the double spreads look, at first glance, like scenes such as a train station, a playground, or a street. Closer inspection reveals that the picture is made entirely by using real objects to create a world of miniature scale; cinnamon sticks serve as logs, and a razor blade is converted into a vacuum cleaner.

Scratchboard. Brian Pinkney is known for using scratchboard as his signature medium. Scratchboard pictures are created by using sharp instruments to scratch away the top surface of a board, leaving precise lines on the surface. Pinkney believes that his passion for drawing, etching, and sculpting come together in scratchboard: He carves the pictures and then uses a photographic technique to paint color onto a print of the original scratchboard piece to produce the finished product. He used this technique to illustrate *Alvin Ailey,* by Andrea Davis Pinkney, but with a vivid use of colors to give a more painted effect. Beth Krommes uses scratchboard effectively in *Swirl by Swirl: Spirals in Nature.* In it, she captures the swirl patterns in black and white scratchboard and adds colored highlights to show the colors of the natural world.

Printmaking

Printmaking was the original method by which books for children were illustrated. Originals have been made on stone, metal, wood, sponge, potato, and a range of materials. Ink is added to the raised surface, pressed against a sheet of paper, and a reverse image appears on the paper.

Woodcut illustrations were particularly common in books of the past, but are still used today. Marcia Brown's *Once a Mouse,* rendered in woodcut, was awarded the 1962 Caldecott Medal. Ed Emberley used woodcuts to illustrate Barbara Emberley's *Drummer Hoff,* which won a Caldecott Medal in 1968. Gail E. Haley's *A Story, a Story,* the 1971 Caldecott winner, has illustrations carved on wood blocks.

Margaret Chodos-Irvine used a variety of print-making techniques, including linoleum blocks, to create her Caldecott Honor-winning book, *Ella Sarah Gets Dressed.* Ella Sarah is a little girl who asserts her independence by choosing the clothes she wants to wear. She announces, "I want to wear my pink polka-dot pants, my dress with orange-and-green flowers, my purple-and-blue striped socks, my yellow shoes, and my red hat." Chodos-Irvine, whose own daughter Ella Sarah served as the inspiration for the book, employs several different print-making methods to visually tell this story.

Photography. Several children's book illustrators use photography to create visual images or to convey information. George Ancona uses photographs to depict cultures outside the United States and to offer an immediacy of the setting. Nic Bishop photographs living things to offer real images for his informational picture books. Photography has also been used to capture images of original three-dimensional art; in such cases, photography serves as the vehicle for exhibiting the original art. One example is the cut-paper art that David Wisnewski created for his books and then had photographed by a professional photographer. The photographer gets name credit for his role in bringing the original images to the book form, but it is Wisnewski who is considered the illustrator.

Computer-Generated Art. Many newcomers to the field of book illustrating are generating art on the computer, along with veteran illustrators who are trying this new medium. Nina Crews created ***The Neighborhood Mother Goose*** by taking original photographs and digitally manipulating the proportions and placement of the people and settings on her computer to create a collage. Janet Stevens relies on a computer to embellish her paintings in ***Cook-a-Doodle-Doo!,*** a humorous twist on the "Little Red Hen" story. Along the sidebars that border the main story, cooking tips are included. Her detailed explanation of how she creates her books can be found at her Web site. Some artists, like South African illustrator Niki Daly, use the computer only in the planning stages of their work. He uses a stylus and pad to draft his preliminary sketches and finds the ability to easily manipulate the proportions and positions (he says, without all that "rubbing and erasing") to be helpful in planning his final artwork, which he completes in watercolor. William Low, illustrator of such books as ***Machines Go To Work,*** was trained as a traditional painter but now uses the Photoshop program to paint with a stylus and a touch screen. He finds that being able to undo steps allows him to paint freely, always knowing he can go back to an earlier version, and be more experimental.

Mixed Media. Illustrators often combine different media in creating their work. Many illustrators combine pen and ink with watercolor washes. Patricia Polacco uses pencil to create initial sketches and then finishes them with watercolors, but the original pencil markings are often visible as part of the final product. Eric Carle paints on his tissue papers and then pencils in details on his collages. In his 2000 Caldecott-winning book, ***Joseph Had a Little Overcoat,*** Simms Taback used watercolor, gouache, pencil, ink, and collages—of photographs of people, handmade paper, and pictures of textured items like braided rugs and sweaters.

British author/illustrator Lauren Child creates books in collage media. She draws the characters and collages them onto backgrounds that are created with paper, fabric, photographs, and other drawn materials. The seeming simplicity of the way she depicts her characters has an informality and childlike appeal and complements her humorous storytelling style.

Increasingly, we see digital media as part of "mixed media" used by artists such as Jeremy Tankard, who employs a combination of photography, paints, and digital media to create his finished images in ***Grumpy Bird***. Similarly, ***Knuffle Bunny*** has photographs that have been digitally incorporated (and enhanced/cleaned up!) that Mo Willems uses as background, but he paints the characters and the focal point of the story, creating an interesting contrast of setting with character.

Artistic Style

The artistic style used by the illustrator conveys much of the aesthetic impact on the reader/viewer's understanding as well as his or her emotional engagement and response. When we refer to *style*, we mean the impression created by the combined effect of visual elements discussed previously: line, shape, color, light, and texture. Style is important in conveying the mood of the story and in contextualizing the setting, as well as in defining characters. In well-crafted picture books, the style amplifies the text and works in harmony with it. The styles that are most frequently found in picture books for children are realism, impressionism, expressionism, cartoon, folk art, naïve art, surrealism, abstract art, romanticism, and postmodernism. It is important to remember that just as texts can cross genres and include elements of multiple genres, illustrations can have elements of more than one style. Some artists have created a personal style that is so distinct that their work is instantly recognizable: The illustrations of Tomie dePaola, Lois Ehlert, and Gerald McDermott remain consistent throughout the body of their work. Others, like David Shannon or Ed Young, tend to vary their styles to match each book.

Realism. Perhaps the most commonly used style in illustrated books for children, realism presents the world as realistically as possible. Artists do research to make their work accurately representative of their subject, especially when depicting historical settings or culturally specific ones. Allen Say's images of Japan and of Asians in America have a near-photographic quality to them. In his Caldecott-winning book *Grandfather's Journey*, Say tells the story of how his grandfather left Japan and made the United States his home. When the grandfather visited Japan years later, World War II prohibited him from returning to the United States. When his grandson follows in his path he realizes, "The funny thing is, the moment I am in one country, I am homesick for the other." The story is realistic in theme, setting, and portrayal of each country's natural beauty depicted in watercolor views of ocean, mountains, and greenery.

Impressionism. The style of Impressionism began with a group of painters who wanted to work in less restrictive ways than realism permitted, desiring to capture the moment in which they painted. Often working with looser interpretations and with less defined lines than realism, these artists did not labor over details as long as the overall effect—the impression—worked. An example of impressionism can be found in the work of Jerry Pinkney. In his interpretation of *The Ugly Duckling,* more emphasis is placed on the interplay of light and color—particularly on the endpapers where the images depict the ducks swimming and how they appear above/below waterlines—rather than near-exact representations of details such as all of the duck feathers. Impressionism works particularly well in representing this story, as the viewer interprets the spontaneity of living creatures in motion.

Expressionism. In expressionistic art, emotions, often deeply felt, are shown in the ways in which the artist portrays different aspects of the illustration to communicate feelings or mood. Things may be slightly out of proportion or given emphasis through devices that include placement or more detail of certain elements. The artist draws the attention of the viewer through such devices. In his work in *Encounter*, David Shannon focuses the viewer's attention on specific elements that guide the reader on an emotional path through the book. In telling the story of the aftermath of the atomic bomb in Hiroshima, Toshi Maruki's *Hiroshima no Pika* employs expressionistic style to powerfully convey deep emotion.

Cartoon. Many children find cartoon art appealing for its liveliness and playfulness, often expressing humor and fast-paced action along with rapidly changing moods. Line is used to effectively portray emotion, and proportions are sometimes exaggerated to emphasize story elements. Kevin Henkes masterfully pairs cartoon art with his text to tell a complete story. Readers will quickly realize how Henkes manipulates line to show readers the emotions of characters

ILLUSTRATION 3.11
Using watercolor and pen, Kevin Henkes creates memorable mice characters such as lively Lilly, who loves school—and her teacher. (Used by permission of HarperCollins Publishers.)

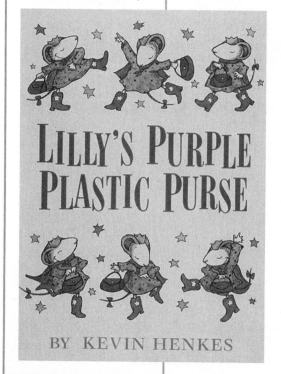

TABLE 3.1 *Examples of Artistic Styles*

ARTISTIC STYLE	TITLE	ILLUSTRATOR
Realism	*Mufaro's Beautiful Daughters*	John Steptoe
	Grandfather's Journey	Allen Say
Impressionism	*Mirette on the High Wire*	Emily Arnold McCully
	Mr. Rabbit and the Lovely Present	Maurice Sendak
Expressionism	*Hiroshima no Pika*	Toshi Maruki
	Chato's Kitchen (by Gary Soto)	Susan Guevara
Cartoon	*Click Clack Moo (by Doreen Cronin)*	Betsy Lewin
	Sylvester and the Magic Pebble	William Steig
Folk Art	*The Pot of Wisdom*	Baba Wagué Diakité
	Just in Case	Yuyi Morales
Naïve Art	*A Chair for My Mother*	Vera Williams
	Two of Everything	Lily Toy Hong
Surrealism	*Changes*	Anthony Browne
	Frida	Ana Juan
Abstract Art	*Mysterious Thelonius*	Chris Raschka
	The Green Frogs: A Korean Folktale	Yumi Heo
Romanticism	*The Tale of the Firebird*	Gennady Spirin
	Cinderella	Kinuko Craft
Postmodernism	*And the Dish Ran Away With the Spoon*	Janet Stevens and Susan Stevens Crummel
	Black and White	David Macaulay

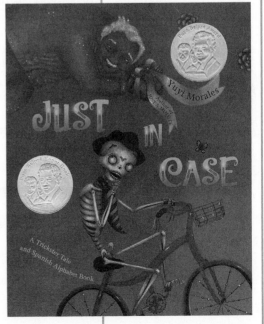

ILLUSTRATION 3.12 Yuyi Morales employs her trademark rendition of Mexican folk art in *Just in Case, a Spanish Alphabet Book* with trickster character Señor Calvera thinking up a gift for Grandma Beetle, one from each letter of the alphabet. (Book cover of "Just in Case: A Trickster Tale and Spanish Alphabet Book" by Yuyi Morales. A Neal Porter Book, published by Roaring Brook Press [a division of Holtzbrinck Publishing Holdings Limited Partnership. All rights reserved.], 2008. (ISBN: 1596433299).)

in the story. In *Lilly's Purple Plastic Purse,* Lilly's emotions change from disappointment to fury to sadness, sometimes by mere changes in eyebrows and head position. He also uses proportion to show how Lilly feels about the earlier attitude she displayed toward her teacher when she discovers a note from him in her purse.

Folk Art. Illustrators rely on folk art to partner with a story that is steeped in heritage—one that projects generations of traditions and cultural roots being passed down. Often, the culture portrayed is isolated from others in time or place so that the motifs, colors, and symbols remain specific and pure, and not influenced by others. Sometimes, there is a primitive quality to folk art. Barbara Cooney's illustrations in *The Ox-Cart Man* by Donald Hall do just that. They clearly set a time and place through both overall impression and details so that viewers understand the setting completely. Details that show what he packs on his wagon (barrel of apples, bag of goose feathers, and cabbages, for example), or big impressions of the life that was led on the farm (carving a new yoke, making flax into linen, and tapping the sugar maple trees) all contribute to assisting readers in understanding the setting. In another example, in the trickster tale and counting book *Just a Minute* by Yuyi Morales, Grandma Beetle convinces Señor Calavera to wait until preparations are completed for the birthday party. The book's illustrations are filled with motifs and colors that represent the Mexican culture.

ILLUSTRATION 3.13 The illustrations in Anthony Browne's *Voices in the Park* are an example of surrealism as he offers four different perspectives of lives that converge at one moment in the park. (Copyright © 2013 by DK Publishing and Anthony Browne. All Rights Reserved.)

Naïve Art. Flat, two-dimensional art that has a child-like quality to it is referred to as naïve art. Sometimes, it is self-taught artists who use naïve art; at other times, illustrators employ naïve art style to match the mood of a book's text. Figures are usually depicted from the front, back, or side, but always without a three-dimensional quality. Illustrator Frané Lessac's work can be seen on the cover of our textbook and throughout the book, and is an example of naïve art.

Surrealism. Unreal, unexpected, and sometimes even bizarre elements are part of surrealistic art. The illustrator may manipulate these "never could happen" aspects of the imagination in order to express internal feelings or thoughts; it may represent symbolism for the viewer to ponder, or it may be used to move the action of the story along. Anthony Browne's books are examples of surrealism. Gorillas float in the air, trunks of trees in wooded forests disappear, and humans turn into pigs. Likewise, Chris Van Allsburg's work represents surrealism as ships and trains fly through the air and weather changes unexplainably.

Abstract Art. Images are recognizable, but altered from realism in works of abstract art. Illustrators portray images in ways that create ambience and evoke mood. Chris Raschka's work often employs abstract art. He uses shapes and colors that evoke images and represent feelings. Vladimir Radunsky uses shapes in vaguely representational ways, but they are not accurate representations of objects or human bodies as we know them.

Romanticism. Often used with realism or impressionism, romanticism ignores the blemishes in the world and flourishes the best of what might be. Rich palettes of color are used to enhance the feeling of luxurious extravagance. Traditional tales with "happily ever after" endings are often the candidates for romanticized style. K. Y. Craft sets her *Cinderella* book in seventeenth–eighteenth century France and employs a romanticized style. Colors almost glitter and glow on the pages, and details like lace, flowers, and billowing fabric softly accentuate all edges so they are flowing and rounded.

Postmodernism. In recent times, illustrators have moved from traditional notions of artwork in picture books to break new ground. McCallum (1996) describes postmodernism as having the following features: "narrative fragmentation and discontinuity, disorder and chaos, code mixing and absurdity." These illustrators have mixed styles, borrowed from others' works, and they push the viewer to make sense of illustrations that are out of traditional bounds. *The Three Pigs* by Wiesner is an example of such a book. This book breaks the rules for how picture books typically develop by having the characters "fly" out of their story on a paper airplane, only to enter other stories of traditional literature that have related characters. Readers are required to bring their knowledge of these stories into play in order to make the transition along with the characters.

How Picture Storybooks Work

When we read a story that moves us deeply, we often speak of how the setting, characters, plot, and other elements of the book contributed to its effect. But if a picture moves us, most of us do not have a set of terms readily available to describe what caused the picture's effect. Picture books afford readers the opportunity to deepen their understanding of visual communication—their visual literacy. Knowing some terms can help teachers and parents talk as knowledgeably about pictures as they do about texts and better appreciate the principles that govern how picture book illustrations communicate meaning. The following elements of visual communication will concern us here:

- Book design/*peritextual* elements—book size and shape, book covers and jackets, endpapers, borders, text layout and typeface; elements of paging: single/double page spreads, page turns, final page
- Picture/text relationships—that is, which aspects of the communication are carried by the text and which are conveyed by the pictures, and how the pictures and text interact
- Visualization of literary elements—characterization, setting, plot, perspective, mood

Clearly, much goes into the creation of picture books. Many people besides the author and illustrator are involved in creating the final product. Editors, art directors, designers, and printers all have professional roles. Decisions about the book size, paper type, endpapers, font, and book jacket all contribute to the visual impact of the finished book.

Book Design

Children's books are printed in multiples of sixteen pages, and picture books are typically thirty-two pages long. One page is taken up by the title page, a second by the copyright information, and often another by the dedication—leaving the illustrator of most picture books a little less than thirty pages to work with. Within these few pages, the illustrator creates a visual world.

Book Size and Shape. The size and shape of a book has impact both in conveying content information and in eliciting the reader/viewer's emotional and aesthetic response. Tall books like Mordicai Gerstein's *The Man Who Walked Between the Towers* match the image of skyscrapers; at one point, Gerstein has readers turn the book and inserts a gatefold to create four pages together to increase the impact even more. Suzy Lee's *Wave* uses both the book's dimensions of being short and extra wide along with spreading each illustration being shown as double-spread units to convey a sense of the horizon and its vastness. In *Freight Train*, Donald Crews effectively used the wide double-spread to show a train in movement, colors bleeding from one train to another in fast motion to give illusion of new colors. Creating illustrations in large books like *Make Way for Ducklings* allowed author/illustrator Robert McCloskey to show readers Mr. and Mrs. Mallard flying over Boston, and also present all eight of the ducklings following their mother, while the height of the book allows us to see Michael halting oncoming traffic. Beatrix Potter created *The Tale of Peter Rabbit* as "small books for small hands" to emphasize the size appropriateness for her audience.

Book Covers and Jackets. Readers are first introduced to a book by its cover and jacket, and they serve as an invitation into the book. Covers on picture books offer a sample of what's inside—somewhat of a "window" to what lies within the covers. This may be particularly important for children who engage with pictures

 TECHNOLOGY in PRACTICE 3.2

DIGITAL STORYTELLING THROUGH eBOOKS AND APPS

With the advent of tablet computers, apps became immensely popular and offered possibilities that ebook platforms at the time did not support. Over time and with technological advances, this gap has decreased and the line between what apps and ebooks can offer has blurred. Find access to a tablet with picture book apps on it (try a library or bookstore for a demo) and find an app for which you can also get the print book to have in hand while studying the two experiences. Compare the app experience with the print book experience from a child's point of view as well as from an adult educator's perspective. In what ways do they differ, and are some features better in one format than another?

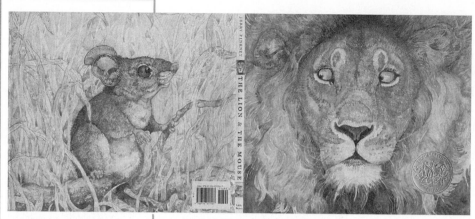

ILLUSTRATION 3.14 The front and back covers of Jerry Pinkney's ***The Lion and the Mouse*** feature portraits of the two animals, that when opened flat, show them looking at each other. The dramatic change to true proportionate size accentuates the idea that the mouse is not as "small" in spirit nor the lion so "large" when comparing the action each takes. ("The Lion & the Mouse" by Jerry Pinkney. Little, Brown and Company, a division of Hachette Book Group, Inc.)

even before they consider the text, and for those who form a physical engagement with the book through its cover (Powers, 2003). As an atypical but very appropriate example, in *The Lion and the Mouse,* the cover does not include the title and author/illustrator information. The wordless cover matches the interior of the book, where nearly wordlessly, the illustrations convey and carry the story. Book jackets often provide a lot of information beyond the book cover: They may include additional information about the author and illustrator; they typically include a write-up to "hook" a reader into the book; and they may include information on other books the author or illustrator has created and even some excerpts of reviews. Sometimes there are even clues and foreshadowing to lead into the story.

Endpapers. In function, the endpapers connect the pages of the book to the cover. Many also serve as prologues/epilogues to the content of the pages. Kevin Henkes created the opening endpapers for *Old Bear* using dark brown on medium brown outlines of leaves, suggesting the autumn season that leads into a bear's hibernation cycle. The closing endpaper for the book shows purple outlines of flowers, implying the arrival of spring. Both endpapers are subtly single toned and effective without attracting inordinate attention, adding to the overall "satisfying wholeness" of the reader's experience with the book.

Borders. Borders around pictures offer a means for the illustrator to control how intimately readers feel involved with the pictures. Some illustrators put decorative borders around four sides. These may put the action at some distance, sentimentalize it, or make it clear that the time period or place depicted is remote. Some authors like Jan Brett employ borders as an illustration device for foreshadowing what follows.

Trina Schart Hyman uses borders in an interesting way in Margaret Hodges's *St. George and the Dragon.* Each border suggests a stained glass window, and she reinforces this impression by sometimes drawing smaller images in the border panels in a way that embellishes the images in the center panel, but this also makes it seem as if the images were painted on the glass, rather than viewed through a window. On other pages, though, the images in the center intrude into the borders, and then we get the impression that we are looking not at static images in a stained glass window but through clear leaded glass at real figures just on the other side.

In *Where the Wild Things Are,* author and illustrator Maurice Sendak uses borders in a striking way. The sizes of the borders wax and wane with the crescendo and decrescendo of Max's wild adventures. In the opening pages, plain white borders contain relatively small pictures of Max. As his fantasy grows, though, so do the pictures—first filling a page, then spilling onto the opposite page, until the "wild rumpus" in the middle of the book pushes margins and words off the double-page spreads. As order returns, so do the borders—until, on the last page, the pictures are gone, leaving nothing but text.

In other books, the lack of borders conveys informality and communicates a sense of the picture going beyond the pages of the book. Jerry Pinkney's illustrations for Hans Christian Andersen's *The Ugly Duckling* bleed off the edges of the paper, and readers suppose that they were cut off from the world beyond the pages, restricted by the page size. This format seems especially fitting for a glimpse of the natural world.

Text Layout and Typeface. The visual aspect of text can convey messages to the reader. Typically, text is presented in a straightforward, horizontal manner with most line breaks determined by the side margins. Sometimes, illustrators use the text layout in ways that integrate the text into the illustrations. Some of those instances include speech bubbles within the illustration (as in the *Magic School Bus* books by Joanna Cole and illustrated by Bruce Degen) or letters or journal entries printed as the illustration as well as the text on a given page. At other times, the artistic placement, font, and color of the text is visually integrated into the illustration in such a way that the text is an important part of the visual presentation. Peter Sís creates hand-lettered fonts that do just that, as does Chris Raschka. In *The Maestro Plays*, Vladimir Randusky places Bill Martin's words in ways that emulate the movements of various circus actors. Similarly, in Lloyd Moss's *Zin! Zin! Zin! A Violin*, Marjorie Priceman incorporates text into illustrations in fluid ways. The typeface design, color, and size also communicate as part of the artistic style and mood of the text.

ILLUSTRATION 3.15 Trina Schart Hyman's borders in *St. George and the Dragon* remind viewers of stained glass images on church windows. ("St. George and the Dragon" by Margaret Hodges, illustrated by Trina Schart Hyman. Text copyright ©1984 by Margaret Hodges; Illustrations copyright © 1984 by Trina Schart Hyman. By permission of Little, Brown and Company. All rights reserved.)

Single Pages and Double-Page Spreads. As a rule in terms of pacing the story, putting a picture on each page propels readers through the story at an even pace, whereas putting more than one picture on a page is a way to depict a series of actions or the rapid occurrence of actions. Spreading a single picture across two facing pages (a double-page spread) can signal a pause—a moment to ponder the events. In *The Amazing Bone*, written and illustrated by William Steig, a succession of one-page illustrations shows Pearl's quick progress through the bustle of town life. A double-page spread showing Pearl sitting on the ground in the woods under trees raining wild cherry blossoms conveys a sense of her being overwhelmed by the beauty (and the seeming innocence) of nature.

Page Turns. Page turns allow an illustrator to create and relieve suspense. William Moebius (1986) called this phenomenon "the drama of the turning page." Many illustrators make use of this technique to add dramatic interest. One such example can be found in the pacing of Nancy Winslow Parker's illustrations of John Langstaff's text *Oh, A-Hunting We Will Go*. With each verse, children are implicitly challenged to guess where each animal will be put before they turn the

ISSUE *to* CONSIDER

Should Teachers Take the Time to Teach Students How to Interpret and "Read" the Illustrations in Picture Books?

Illustrators take great care to do their part in telling the story within a book. Designers work with book elements to influence the overall effect on the viewer's understanding and experience with the book. All in all, there is a lot for students to consider as the visual literacy of understanding the book.

Whoever helps students learn to become visually literate must also study how picture books work through the visual elements of art: design, medium, and style. This requires some basic understandings of the visual communication medium. Focusing on the text alone leaves out much that is presented to the reader only through the visual aspects of the illustration or book design. But does too much emphasis on the visual side take away from a focus on comprehending the text?

What do you think? Teachers are already challenged with teaching their students to read and understand the text. Is it their responsibility to also teach their students how to "read" the visual messages found in the illustrations? If so, how will teachers gain the background knowledge necessary to do so? If not, who will help students take steps toward visual literacy?

page and read the completed rhyme (e.g., fox-box). Sometimes, an illustrator will include clues that lead readers to the next page. In the Australian book *I Went Walking* by Sue Williams, within the background of the each page, Julie Vivas gives readers a glimpse of a portion of the animal that will be on the following page.

The Last Page. The last page of a picture book is often used for something of an afterword. Many illustrators reserve this last page for an epilogue, a comment on what has gone before. Maurice Sendak used the last page of *Where the Wild Things Are* to tell the reader that Max's supper was still hot after he returned from his antics with the Wild Things. Dav Pilkey used the last page of *The Paperboy* to show readers that after finishing his route, the paperboy went back to bed and entered a dream world. At times, authors and illustrators create an explicit epilogue. Kevin Henkes creates such a statement in *Chrysanthemum,* so readers know "what happened" beyond the denouement concluding Chrysanthemum's name dilemma.

Picture/Text Relationships

Illustrations and text have relationships that convey the story together. Often, key elements of the story are expressed only through text, and at other times, only through illustration, but often, through the interplay of both. Children will be more actively engaged if part of the meaning of the story is left for them to infer from the illustrations.

In *Where the Wild Things Are,* the hand drawing of a Wild Thing "by Max" on the wall is a clue to the observant reader that the wild things Max encounters have been created out of his imagination. Throughout the book, much of the story is revealed only through illustration. In the same vein, in Harry Allard's *Miss Nelson Is Missing!,* artist James Marshall drew a box marked "wig" in upside-down letters next to an ugly black dress in the open closet next to Miss Nelson's bed. Observant readers will pick up this clue to solve the mystery of the identity of Miss Viola Swamp, Miss Nelson's harsh alter ego.

That night, Officer Buckle watched himself on the 10 o'clock news.

The 1996 Caldecott Medal winner, *Officer Buckle and Gloria* by Peggy Rathmann, tells of a police officer who makes tiresome speeches about home and school safety. Interest in his presentations suddenly increases a hundredfold when he begins to take a police dog, Gloria, with him. Because Gloria stands just behind him, Officer Buckle doesn't see that the dog is pantomiming and generally cutting up while he gives his otherwise boring speech. The text doesn't mention Gloria's antics, either. We readers are in on a secret that Officer Buckle doesn't know, because we are informed by the pictures as well as the text. The most telling picture of all is the one in which Officer Buckle discovers, by way of television, what Gloria has been up to. In addition to depicting Officer Buckle's reaction and Gloria's response, the picture includes the large mirror that hangs on the wall behind the couch, which allows the reader to see what is showing on the television screen.

ILLUSTRATION 3.18
Mouse narrates a story about his friend, rabbit, who means well but gets into trouble. Illustrations convey much of the humor and tell part of the story in a way that shows the importance of the relationship between text and illustration in working together to convey the whole story. (Book cover of "My Friend, Rabbit" by Eric Rohmann. Roaring Brook Press [a division of Holtzbrinck Publishing Holdings Limited Partnership. All rights reserved.], 2002. (ISBN: 0439579309).)

In *The Journey of Oliver K. Woodman,* Uncle Ray is unable to accept his niece Tamika's invitation to visit, so he creates a wooden man to send. Oliver K. Woodman is accompanied by a note asking that travelers help him get from the west coast to the east, and for them to send his creator, Ray, a postcard letting him know of his progress to his destination. What readers see is interplay between text and illustration, with some of the text (the letters and postcards) being shown as the illustration itself. In several situations, details and emotions are shown only through the illustrations. In fact, Tamika is portrayed as a biracial child only through the illustrations.

Visual Representations of Literary Elements

Typically, we think of text when referring to literary elements, but visual representations of literary elements play a large part in picture books. Here, we look at a few examples of how to understand how character, setting, and perspective play out in illustrations.

Characterization. Characterization refers to the way in which an illustrator helps readers identify a particular character and continue to recognize that character throughout the changes of scene or status in the whole book. This is not easy. Leonardo da Vinci painted only one *Mona Lisa*, but would we always recognize the *Mona Lisa* if da Vinci had depicted her fifteen or twenty times, in different perspectives and in different circumstances? This is the challenge faced by the illustrator of virtually every picture book. To meet that challenge, some artists, such as Ted Lewin, hire models to pose for their drawings in different settings. Others, such as Jerry Pinkney, rely on family members to serve as models. He has them don various costumes and pose so that he can photograph them and use the photographs as references as he draws. When artists work purely from the imagination, though, they must decide on identifying features by which readers will immediately know their characters. When reading Arnold Lobel's books, for instance, we can keep Frog and Toad straight in our minds because Frog is always green and Toad is always brown.

Features of a character may become so recognizable that even a part of a character may serve to identify the whole. In James Marshall's *Fox and His Friends,* for example, readers can recognize little sister Louise just from the tip of her tail hanging down into the frame from her perch atop a telephone pole. Similarly, in Mem Fox's *Hattie and the Fox,* just the presence of a nose in the bushes signals that a fox is stalking the barnyard animals.

Mo Willems masterfully creates characterization, largely evident through illustration. In *Knuffle Bunny,* readers can clearly understand preschooler Trixie's emotional journey despite the fact that her verbal expressions are all

TOP SHELF 3.3

CREATIVE INTERPLAY OF TEXT WITH ILLUSTRATIONS

Come Away from the Water, Shirley by John Burningham

My Friend Rabbit by Eric Rohmann

Rosie's Walk by Pat Hutchins

Voices in the Park by Anthony Browne

TEACHING IDEA 3.2

INTERPRETING THE STORY AS TOLD THROUGH ILLUSTRATION

COMMON CORE STANDARD:
Integration of Knowledge and Ideas, STANDARD 7

Common Core Standard 7 recognizes that in picture storybooks, pictures and text work together to tell the story. Select some books from Top Shelf 3.3 in which some critical story events emerge through the illustrations while others emerge through the text. Have children examine the illustrations without reading the text and ask them to tell the story as they see it. Some teachers call this prereading strategy of predicting the text by previewing the illustrations a "picture walk." Then read the text and discuss how the story is similar to or different from the story they interpreted through illustration alone. Go back through the book and see what roles the text and illustrations had in contributing to understanding the whole story.

babbling. Likewise, in ***Don't Let the Pigeon Drive the Bus,*** the pigeon's emotional range from pleading to conniving to angry outbursts are all depicted through the illustrations.

Setting. Characters are often identified by the objects that surround them. In William Steig's ***The Amazing Bone,*** Pearl seems most at home in the spring forest, gently showered by cherry blossoms. In spite of his dapper appearance, the loathsome wolf that accosts her lives in a ramshackle cottage with the screen door hanging from one hinge and trash scattered about the overgrown front yard. His slovenly surroundings indicate an uncaring heart. In ***Where the Wild Things Are,*** Max's room becomes overgrown with trees and bushes, a signal that wildness is taking hold of him.

White space is a negative space use of background, or the absence of a specific background in order to achieve focus on the illustration within the white space. Emily Gravett is especially masterful in employing white space effectively, as evidenced in ***Monkey and Me.*** The little girl plays with her stuffed monkey as they describe having been to see various animals that they pretend to be. The spacing of illustrations on the double spread and the amount of white space invites readers to enter the story and participate.

Perspective. Illustrators use a variety of perspectives to give readers different vantage points from which to view the situation. In Chris Van Allsburg's ***Two Bad Ants,*** two ants decide to stay behind in a kitchen when their fellow ants return to the colony with crystals requested by the queen. The two ants find themselves being scooped out of the bed of crystals into a boiling lake of brown bitter water. Thus begins their dangerous adventure, which moves from coffee cup to toaster to garbage disposal to electrical outlet. Readers watch the ants' adventure from various perspectives—looking down to see the ants on the ground and up to see them on the kitchen counter. When the ants are in the coffee cup being rushed toward the mouth of the coffee drinker, the perspective is from directly behind the ants, and readers see the mouth just as the ants see it. Then the view is from inside the toaster, and the ants are seen sitting on top of the bread crust. The close-up view of the water faucet makes it easy to see why the ants might mistake it for a waterfall.

In Mordicai Gerstein's Caldecott-winning ***The Man Who Walked Between the Towers,*** the reader is shown the story from shifting perspectives that heighten each illustration's impact on how the reader understands the experience. From the cover art, Gerstein invites readers to stand and balance with Philippe on the wire, looking down on the city below. Readers also see the towers from the ground up, so they understand the height; they are shown the towers from the side so they understand the distance between the two. But in the most dramatic spread that is four pages wide, readers join Philippe a quarter mile high and experience the awe he must have felt.

Criteria for Evaluating Picture Books

Picture books are evaluated for their illustrations as well as for their text (except in the case of wordless books). But it is more than the sum of the two; it is the way that they are integrated to create a "satisfying whole" that is at the heart of evaluating picture books. The main points can be summarized as follows:

- Is the story well written according to the literary standards outlined in Chapter 2?
- Text (literary elements): Is the language of the text skillfully crafted?
- Illustrations (artistic elements): Do the illustrations communicate not just literally but symbolically through the use of colors, framing, shading, and other visual elements?
- Integration of text and illustrations: Do the pictures interplay with the text and do the text and the pictures seem to clarify, enhance, and extend each other?

Major Creators of Picture Books

CREATOR	PRIMARILY CREATES …	MAJOR WORKS INCLUDE
Eric Carle	Carle's signature style is painted tissue collage with toy elements such as die cut pages, short pages, pop-ups, and electronic sound chips, often focused on aspects of nature.	• *The Grouchy Ladybug* • *The Very Hungry Caterpillar* • *The Very Quiet Cricket*
Leo and Diane Dillon	The Dillons collaborate as a "third artist" in a way that combines both of their styles such that one may begin a line and the other complete it without discernible interruption.	• *Ashanti to Zulu* • *The People Could Fly* • *Why Mosquitoes Buzz in People's Ears*
Lois Ehlert	Ehlert's collages of real artifacts (buttons, birdseed, leaves, etc.), dazzling colors, and graphic illustrations convey information embedded within stories.	• *Eating the Alphabet* • *Red Leaf, Yellow Leaf* • *Color Zoo*
Emily Gravett	Pencils and watercolor are the tools Gravett uses to create the artwork, and white space usually serves as the background.	• *Monkey and Me* • *The Odd Egg* • *Wolves*
Kevin Henkes	Henkes's cartoon style pen and ink with watercolor paintings portray mice in real-life, childlike situations, depicted with fine-tuned emotional resonance.	• *Chrysanthemum* • *Kitten's First Full Moon* • *Lilly's Purple Plastic Purse*
Jerry Pinkney	Pinkney's watercolor paintings of nature and its inhabitants depict human and animal stories. He often focuses on African American stories.	• *The Lion and the Mouse* • *Mirandy and Brother Wind* • *The Talking Eggs*
Maurice Sendak	Sendak creates illustrations and text that interplay to tell stories of individualistic, clever, and imaginative characters.	• *Chicken Soup with Rice* • *In the Night Kitchen* • *Where the Wild Things Are*
Peter Sís.	Intricate pen and ink and mixed media provide extraordinarily fine details that often include visual mysteries that intrigue viewers.	• *The Wall* • *Madlenka* • *Starry Messenger*
William Steig	Steig's signature cartoon style depicts anthropomorphized animals to tell humorous tales of moral behavior. His illustrations' doodling quality conveys spontaneity and movement.	• *Doctor DeSoto* • *Shrek!* • *Sylvester and the Magic Pebble*
Chris Van Allsburg	Van Allsburg predominantly uses charcoal pencil and pen and ink to create monochromatic narrative illustrations.	• *Jumanji* • *The Mysteries of Harris Burdick* • *The Polar Express*
David Wiesner	With minimal or no text but a strong visual narrative, Wiesner invites viewers to look closely, carefully, and critically to "read" the illustrations for the story within.	• *Flotsam* • *The Three Pigs* • *Tuesday*
Mo Willems	Willems's cartoon characters take center stage as they connect with readers in ways that evoke emotional responses.	• *Don't Let the Pigeon Drive the Bus* • *Elephant and Piggie books* • *Knuffle Bunny*
Ed Young	Known for matching style and medium to each story and varying from book to book, Young's work employs a diverse range of media from chalk, watercolor, and collage to mixed media.	• *The Emperor and the Kite* • *Lon Po Po* • *Seven Blind Mice*

Ask *the* Author/Ask the Illustrator
Jon Scieszka and Lane Smith

How do you come up with such imaginative and unique books?

I would love to describe how I get up before dawn every day, light my special candle of inspiration, and sit down to write for twelve hours. But I never do that. Then I could say I sit in a little shed and write on an old board I put across my lap, but Roald Dahl already said that. Maybe I used to work at an ad agency and someone challenged me to write a book for kids using only 100 different words. Nah. That was Dr. Seuss.

I don't know. Lane, how do we come up with such imaginative and unique books?

"I get up before dawn every day, light my special candle of inspiration, and sit down to paint and draw for twelve hours."

You do not.

"I go out to my little shed and draw on an old board I put across my lap?"

No.

"I used to work in an ad agency..."

Thanks for your help, Dr. Seuss.

I've never really given much thought to how we put our books together. I do the writing thing just like most other authors—writing, rewriting, reading the stuff to kids and teachers, then rewriting some more. And Lane does the sketching, painting, and repainting thing like most other illustrators.

But, now that I think of it, we do have two secret ingredients that set us apart from those other Brand X books.

One, Lane and I are friends and work together. After I get a story to where I like it, I give it to Lane. He thinks about it, fools around with different ways to illustrate it; then we talk and goof around with changes in both the writing and the illustration to fit the new ideas. A lot of authors and illustrators never get this chance to work together.

Two, we have a secret weapon—our designer Molly Leach (who also happens to be Lane's wife and my wife's best friend and part of the reason Lane

and I met and started working together and . . . that's a whole other story). As the designer, Molly is the one who takes the text and the illustrations and decides how to weave them together and present them on the page so everything works together.

So, in *The Stinky Cheese Man*, it was Molly who came up with the idea to have the type grow and shrink to fit the page. And when Jack was telling his story endlessly over and over and over, I thought it would be funny if the text just ran off the page. Molly showed us how it would look better if the type got smaller and smaller.

For a book like *Math Curse*, the story stayed pretty close to the early finished draft. Lane came up with the idea to show the narrator under the spell of the curse. And we left it up to Molly to figure out how to cram all of the words, problems, and paintings into a picture book that looked kind of like a math book but not so ugly or so much like a math book that it would scare all of our readers away.

Our books look unique because we get to work in a unique way. Three people collaborate on getting the text, the illustration, and the design working to tell one story.

So, in conclusion, Lane and I make our imaginative and unique books by getting up before dawn every day, sitting in a little shed, working for an ad agency, and thanking our lucky stars that we get to work together and with Ace Designer, Molly Leach.

Jon Scieszka is the author of *The True Story of the 3 Little Pigs!; The Frog Prince, Continued; The Stinky Cheese Man and Other Fairly Stupid Tales; The Book That Jack Wrote; Math Curse;* and the *Time Warp Trio* series. He's a lumberjack in his spare time. He once climbed Mount Everest in his bare feet. And he enjoys potato chips and making up lies. Lane Smith's bio is exactly the same as Jon's, except a couple of the book titles are different.

EXPERIENCES FOR FURTHER LEARNING

1. Study some illustrations and practice using the vocabulary that describes what you see. Try seeing if you can identify the artistic media and the style. Then see if you can talk with others about the influence of the media and the style on your overall impression of the book. Remember that what matters is not so much whether you can classify a book correctly, but whether you can articulate how the art influences your understanding of the story as the reader. This is particularly true when considering that artists sometimes use mixed media and some illustrators' work can be interpreted as being influenced by more than one artistic style.

2. Select a book from an earlier era, such as the ones discussed in the section of this chapter entitled "Authors and Illustrators Who Have Defined the Field." What qualities still appeal to readers today? What qualities appear dated? What qualities in recently published books are likely to remain popular in future years? What qualities are likely to be time sensitive?

RECOMMENDED BOOKS

I indicates interest level by age (P = preschool, YA = young adult)

The picture books in this chapter are not marked with an asterisk since all are picture books. The picture books that are listed within the genre chapters that follow are marked with an asterisk.

Toy Books

Ahlberg, Janet, and Allan Ahlberg. *The Jolly Postman or Other People's Letters*. Little, Brown, 1986. A postman delivers letters to and from various fairy tale characters. Miniature letters, cards, and postcards are included. (I: P–8)

Cousins, Lucy. *Maisy's House and Garden Pop Up Play Set*. A Carousel Book, 2008. This book turns into a pop-up play house and garden, complete with furniture. (I: P)

Ehlert, Lois. *Color Zoo*. HarperCollins, 1989. As they turn the pages, children see various shapes that unlayer to reveal different animal faces. Shape names and animal names are included. A related title is *Color Farm* (1990). (I: P)

Gravett, Emily. *Meerkat Mail*. Simon, 2007. Postcards are used as a toy component both to offer information and to advance the story of a meerkat who leaves home and travels the world. (I: K–7)

Hill, Eric. *Where's Spot?* Putnam, 1980. Sally looks for Spot, who has not eaten his dinner. Children lift flaps to help search for the missing puppy. Over twenty other books about Spot (with Spanish versions of some titles) are available. (I: P)

Hoban, Tana. *Black on White*. Greenwillow, 1993. This board book shows black shapes of familiar objects such as an elephant, a butterfly, and a leaf on a white background. Its companion books are *White on Black* (1993) and *Black and White* (2007). (I: P)

Park, Linda Sue. *Mung-Mung: A Fold-Out Book of Animal Sounds*. Clarion, 2006. This guessing-game format book features animal sounds from around the world. (I: P–7)

Sabuda, Robert and Matthew Reinhart. *Encyclopedia Prehistorica Dinosaurs*. Candlewick, 2005. An amazingly accomplished piece of engineering, with many smaller pop-up books within the main pop-up book, offering three-dimensional art to accompany the lively text on dinosaurs. (I: K–8)

Seeger, Laura Vaccaro. *One Boy*. Roaring Brook, 2008. Using cutout windows to mask and unveil word parts, Seeger offers opportunities for beginning readers to examine words and word parts. (I: K–7)

Sendak, Maurice. *The Nutshell Library*. Harper & Row, 1962. A set of four miniature books: *Alligators All Around, Chicken Soup with Rice: A Book of Months, One Was Johnny: A Counting Book*, and *Pierre: A Cautionary Tale*. The first is an alphabet book; the second is a series of poems about enjoying chicken soup all the months of the year; the third is a counting book; and the fourth is a cautionary tale. (I: P–7)

Zelinsky, Paul O. *The Wheels on the Bus*. Dutton, 1990. This pop-up rendition of a popular action song shows movements for each verse as readers push, pull, or lift tabs on the pages. (I: P–6)

Alphabet Books

Base, Graeme. *Animalia*. Abrams, 1987. For each letter of the alphabet, an alliterative phrase describes what various animals are doing. Illustrations are filled with items beginning with the featured letter. (I: all ages)

Carle, Eric. *Eric Carle's ABC*. Grosset & Dunlap, 2007. Simple letter-to-picture matching in a board book format. (I: P–K)

Ehlert, Lois. *Eating the Alphabet: Fruits and Vegetables from A to Z*. Harcourt, 1989. Fruits and vegetables are displayed in alphabetical order. (I: P–7)

Ernst, Lisa Campbell. *The Turn-Around, Upside-Down, Alphabet Book*. Simon & Schuster, 2004. Using graphic representations of each letter, a reimagining of what that image represents pictorially. (I: P–7)

Fleming, Denise. *Alphabet Under Construction*. Holt, 2002. A mouse playfully constructs an alphabet—"airbrushing the A, buttoning the B," etc. in this brilliantly colored alphabet book. (I: P–7)

Floca, Brian. *The Racecar Alphabet*. Atheneum, 2003. Through alliterative text and energetic watercolors, cars race through the alphabet from a 1901 Ford 999 to a 2001 Ferrari F1. (I: 6–10)

Lessac, Frané. *Caribbean Alphabet*. Tambourine, 1989. The alphabet is used to organize images of the Caribbean islands, from food and animals to popular culture. (I: P–8)

Lobel, Arnold. *On Market Street*. Illustrated by Anita Lobel. Greenwillow, 1981. Alphabet letters are depicted as people whose bodies are made up of objects beginning with that letter. (I: P–7)

McMullan, Kate. *I Stink!* Illustrated by Jim McMullan. HarperCollins, 2002. A garbage truck goes out on the night route, picking up trash from A to Z. (I: P–7)

Martin, Bill, Jr., and John Archambault. *Chicka Chicka Boom Boom*. Illustrated by Lois Ehlert. Simon & Schuster, 1989. The alphabet letters race up a coconut tree in this rhythmic, rhyming verse. (I: P–7)

Morales, Yuyi. *Just in Case: A Trickster Tale and Spanish Alphabet Book*. Roaring Brook, 2008. Señor Calvera, a trickster skeleton from the Day of the Dead, seeks a birthday gift representing each letter of the alphabet for Grandma Beetle. (I: P–8)

Rankin, Laura. *The Handmade Alphabet*. Dial, 1991. The American Sign Language hand sign for each letter of the alphabet is shown, along with an item whose name begins with the letter. (I: P–9)

Seeger, Laura Vaccaro. *The Hidden Alphabet*. Porter/Roaring Brook, 2003. This lift-the-flap book cleverly shows a portion of the picture first so readers can engage in guessing what the entire picture representing the letter of the alphabet is. (I: K–7)

Counting Books

Anno, Mitsumasa. *Anno's Counting Book*. Crowell, 1977. Illustrations of landscapes include objects that can be counted. (I: P)

Bang, Molly. *Ten, Nine, Eight*. Greenwillow, 1983. Objects are counted backwards in this bedtime story. (I: P)

Carle, Eric. *1, 2, 3 to the Zoo*. Putnam, 1968. Beginning with one elephant and ending with ten birds, each car in the train has one more zoo animal than the one before it. At the end, readers unfold a page to see all the animals at their destination and an empty train along the bottom of the page. (I: P)

Christelow, Eileen. *Five Little Monkeys Jumping on the Bed*. Clarion, 1989. Humorous illustrations accompany this familiar chant of what happens when, one by one, the monkeys fall off and hit their heads. (I: P–7)

Fleming, Denise. *Count!* Holt, 1992. This vibrantly colored counting book shows one through ten animals to be counted. There are also small creatures to be counted by tens. (I: P)

Sayre, April Pulley, and Jeff Sayre. *One Is a Snail, Ten Is a Crab: A Counting by Feet Book*. Illustrated by Randy Cecil. Candlewick, 2003. Various creatures bicycle, limbo, and play volleyball on the beach as readers count, add, and multiply their feet. (I: P–7)

Walsh, Ellen Stoll. *Mouse Count*. Harcourt, 1991. A hungry snake counts mice. After they trick the snake into looking for more mice to fill up his jar, the mice tumble out as they "uncount" themselves. (I: P–7)

Concept Books

Crews, Donald. *Freight Train*. Greenwillow, 1978. As a freight train passes by, readers are introduced to colors, names of train cars, and the concepts of darkness and light. (I: P–7)

Cumpiano, Ina. *Quinito, Day and Night/Quinito, día y noche*. Illustrated by José Ramírez. Children's Book Press, 2008. Bilingually told in Spanish and in English, Quinito's day is portrayed through opposites. (I: P–6)

Ehlert, Lois. *Planting a Rainbow*. Harcourt, 1988. As the colored strips—in rainbow order—are flipped, flowers in the featured color appear. (I: P–5)

———. *26 Letters and 99 Cents*. Greenwillow, 1987. Open the book one way, and find letters of the alphabet matched with objects whose names begin with each letter. Turn the book over and open it from the opposite end, and count money up to 99 cents. (I: P–8)

Hall, Michael. *My Heart is Like a Zoo*. Greenwillow, 2009. Similes compare the emotions of a heart to 20 animals, and illustrations depict those animals, created with varying sizes and colors of heart shapes. (I: K–8)

Jonas, Ann. *Color Dance*. Greenwillow, 1989. Dancers with colored scarves introduce the primary colors. When their scarves overlap, the secondary colors are visible. (I: P–5)

Seeger, Laura Vaccaro. *First the Egg*. Roaring Brook, 2007. This concept book explores the relationship between what comes first and what follows, making a full circle to end with, "First the chicken, then the egg." (I: P–7)

Walsh, Ellen Stoll. *Mouse Paint*. Harcourt, 1989. Three white mice splash around in primary colored paint. When they dance in each other's colors, they make new colors. But when the cat comes around, they must find a way to keep from being seen. (I: P–5)

Wordless and Nearly Wordless Books

Anno, Mitsumasa. *Anno's Journey*. Philomel, 1978. The small towns and cities of Europe are shown, with cultural and historic details hidden throughout each page. (I: 7 and up)

Baker, Jeannie. *Window*. Greenwillow, 1991. Collage illustrations show environmental changes as seen through a window of a house, as the boy who lives there grows from babyhood to adulthood. See also *Where the Forest Meets the Sea* (1988) and *Home* (2004). (I: 6–9)

Banyai, Istvan. *Zoom*. Viking, 1995. Like a camera's zoom lens, each page backs up to show more and more of the big picture so that readers are challenged to think about what they see as part of a larger scene. See also *Rezoom* (1995). (I: 7 and up)

dePaola, Tomie. *Pancakes for Breakfast*. Harcourt, 1978. This wordless book tells a story of how pancakes are made. (I: P–6)

Hutchins, Pat. *Changes, Changes*. Simon, 1971. A story unfolds as two wooden dolls continuously change the things they create out of wooden blocks. (I: P–7)

Jenkins, Steve. *Looking Down*. Houghton Mifflin, 1995. The book begins by looking down onto earth from space, and gradually focuses closer and closer until it ends on a ladybug. (I: P–8)

Lee, Suzy. *Wave*. Chronicle, 2008. A little girl plays with a wave as if it were a playmate on the beach in this simply yet evocatively illustrated story. (I: P–6)

McCully, Emily Arnold. *Picnic*. Harper & Row, 1984. When the family goes on a picnic, one mouse is bumped out of the car and left behind. The mice are also featured in *School* (1987). (I: P–8)

Pinkney, Jerry. *The Lion and the Mouse*. Dial, 2009. Across the landscape of Africa, the folktale of the lion and the mouse is told nearly wordlessly with only the onomatopoeic sounds made by the animals. (I: P–8)

Raschka, Chris. *A Ball for Daisy*. Schwartz & Wade/Random House, 2011. Narrative visuals expressively tell the story of a dog's fondness for a favorite toy, her sense of loss over the demise of that ball, and her joy with the replacement "ball for Daisy." (I: P–7)

Rohmann, Eric. *My Friend Rabbit*. Roaring Brook, 2002. When Mouse's friend Rabbit gets a toy airplane caught in a tree, they must work together with others to solve the dilemma. (I: P–7)

Wiesner, David. *Flotsam*. Clarion, 2006. A magnifying glass, binoculars, microscope, camera—all add up to encourage viewers to consider the various ways in which we view this particular story that is set on the seaside, but also look at how we view the world in which we live. (I: K–9)

————. *Tuesday*. Clarion, 1991. On a mysterious Tuesday night, frogs float through the air on their lily pads. The mystery of this strange occurrence is complicated when the book closes with shadows of flying pigs. (I: P–9)

Yum, Hyewon. *Last Night*. Foster/Farrar, 2008. Linocut illustrations expressively tell the story of a girl who is sent to bed when she does not like her dinner, and embarks on a dream adventure. (I: P–6)

Books with Minimal Text

Bang, Molly. *When Sophie Gets Angry—Really, Really Angry*. Scholastic, 1999. The power of a young child's emotional outpouring when required to share a toy is realistically presented. (I: P–7)

Dunrea, Olivier. *Gossie*. Houghton Mifflin, 2002. An endearing gosling discovers one red boot missing one day—only to find it on the foot of another gosling—Gertie. See also *Gossie and Gertie* (2002) and others. (I: P–7)

Gravett, Emily. *Monkey and Me*. Simon & Schuster, 2007. A little girl and her stuffed monkey tell about having been to see the penguins, elephants, kangaroos, and monkeys and then coming home to tea. (I: P–6)

Portis, Antoinette. *Not a Box*. HarperCollins, 2006. Through spare design and minimal text, this book portrays a rabbit playing with a simple cardboard box with a consistent message of using one's imagination when playing. See also *Not a Stick* (2007). (I: P–7)

Raschka, Chris. *Yo! Yes?* Orchard, 1993. Two boys use expressive body language and one- and two-word utterances to communicate. One is lonely; the other offers to be his friend. (I: P–7)

Rathmann, Peggy. *Good Night, Gorilla*. Putnam, 1994. In this nearly wordless story, as a zookeeper says good night to the animals in the zoo, the gorilla follows, unlocking their cages so that the animals can follow the zookeeper home. (I: P)

Rosenthal, Amy Krouse. *Duck! Rabbit!* Illustrated by Tom Lichtenheld. Chronicle, 2009. Arguing back and forth, two voices claim that the one figure they see is a duck—or a rabbit—and each side's viewpoint is reinforced by how one looks at the pictures. (I: P–6)

Shannon, David. *No, David!* Blue Sky/Scholastic, 1998. Mother must repeatedly tell her preschool son "No" in an attempt to stop his inappropriate behavior. See also *David Goes to School* (1999) and *David Gets in Trouble* (2002) (I: P–6)

Tafuri, Nancy. *Have You Seen My Duckling?* Greenwillow, 1984. A mother duck leads her ducklings around the lake as they search for a missing duckling. (I: P)

Tankard, Jeremy. *Grumpy Bird*. Scholastic, 2007. Wonderfully visually descriptive story about a grumpy bird that is greeted by various animals who play "follow the leader" until their bird leader snaps out of his grumpiness and they all fly off with him. (I: P–2)

Predictable Books

Fox, Mem. *Hattie and the Fox*. Illustrated by Patricia Mullins. Bradbury, 1987. As Hattie the hen tries to warn the barnyard animals of danger, more and more of a fox is revealed in the bushes. (I: P–7)

Langstaff, John. *Oh, A-Hunting We Will Go*. Illustrated by Nancy Winslow Parker. Simon, 1974. Rhyming couplets in this folk song tell of a group of children who go hunting and find various animals they place somewhere temporarily—for example, "We'll catch a goat, and put him in a boat, and then we'll let him go." (I: P–8)

Martin, Bill, Jr. *Brown Bear, Brown Bear, What Do You See?* Illustrated by Eric Carle. Holt, 1967/1983. Patterned, repetitive language is used to introduce colors and animal names. See also *Polar Bear, Polar Bear, What Do You Hear?* (1991) and *Panda Bear, Panda Bear, What Do You See?* (2003). (I: P–7)

Numeroff, Laura Joffe. *If You Give a Mouse a Cookie*. Illustrated by Felicia Bond. Harper, 1985. A circular story of cause and effect, beginning and ending with a mouse and a cookie. (I: P–8)

Shulevitz, Uri. *One Monday Morning*. Macmillan, 1967. Repetitive text depicts visitors on one Monday morning. (I: P–6)

Williams, Sue. *I Went Walking*. Illustrated by Julie Vivas. Harcourt, 1990. A child goes walking and encounters a series of animals, with their tails showing on the previous page to offer clues of what animal is next. (I: P–7)

Wood, Audrey. *The Napping House*. Illustrated by Don Wood. Harcourt, 1984. It is naptime, and the little boy, his granny, and various animals are piled on the bed. One wakeful flea causes everyone to spring up from naptime. (I: P–7)

Easy Readers

Baker, Keith. *Meet Mr. and Mrs. Green*. Harcourt, 2002. Three short stories with two fun-loving alligators with a delightful relationship. First in a series. (I: K–7)

Bang-Campbell, Monika. *Little Rat Sets Sail*. Illustrated by Molly Bang. Harcourt, 2002. Little Rat learns to overcome her fear of water as she learns to sail. See also *Little Rat Rides* (2006), *Little Rat Makes Music* (2007). (I: 6–9)

Kvasnosky, Laura McGee. "*Zelda and Ivy*" series. Candlewick, 1998–2011. Three short stories focus on the day-to-day events that show the bond as well as sibling rivalry between two fox sisters, Zelda and Ivy. (I: P–7)

Lin, Grace. *Ling & Ting: Not Exactly the Same!* Little Brown, 2009. Ling and Ting are twins whose stories are told in short vignettes. Some are culturally grounded, such as making Chinese dumplings and eating with chopsticks, while most are culturally generic experiences such as haircuts, library visits, etc. (I: P–6)

Lobel, Arnold. *Frog and Toad Are Friends*. HarperCollins, 1970/1979. Five short stories tell of the friendship between Frog and Toad. Sequels are *Frog and Toad Together* (1972) and *Frog and Toad All Year* (1976). (I: P–8)

Marshall, (James) Edward. *Fox and His Friends*. Illustrated by James Marshall. Dial, 1982. In this humorous story, Fox wishes his tag-along sister would not be with him when he plays with his friends. There are numerous other books about Fox. (I: 6–8)

_____. *Three by the Sea*. Illustrated by James Marshall. Dial, 1981. Lolly, Spider, and Sam go to the seashore and try to outdo each other in telling the most interesting story. See also *Four on the Shore* (1985). (I: 6–8)

Rylant, Cynthia. *Henry and Mudge: The First Book of Their Adventures*. Illustrated by Sucie Stevenson. Simon & Schuster/Aladdin, 1987–2008. A lonely boy named Henry finds companionship with a big dog named Mudge in this popular series. (I: 6–8)

_____. *Mr. Putter and Tabby* has over 15 titles in this popular series. (I: 6–8)

Seeger, Laura Vaccaro. *Dog and Bear: Two Friends, Three Stories*. Roaring Brook, 2007. A toy patchwork bear and a real dachshund humorously interact in stories that model how good friends interact. (I: P–2)

Seuss, Dr. *The Cat in the Hat*. Random House, 1957. One rainy day, when two children are home alone, an entertaining cat comes and creates chaos and wild fun. The sequel is *The Cat in the Hat Comes Back* (1958). (I: P–8)

Willems, Mo. *Are You Ready to Play Outside?* and other titles in the "Elephant and Piggie" books. Hyperion, 2007–2011. These stories of friendship appeal on every level—with readable, humorous, and emotionally satisfying episodes. (I: P–7)

Picture Storybooks

Aardema, Verna. *Why Mosquitoes Buzz in People's Ears: A West African Tale*. Illustrated by Leo and Diane Dillon. Dial, 1987. A mosquito tells a lie to an iguana and sets off a chain of events. (I: 6–9)

Ackerman, Karen. *Song and Dance Man*. Illustrated by Stephen Gammell. Knopf, 1992. Grandpa reminisces about the bygone days when he danced in vaudeville. (I: 6–8)

Allard, Harry. *Miss Nelson Is Missing!* Illustrated by James Marshall. Houghton Mifflin, 1977. The children behave badly, and their sweet teacher, Miss Nelson, disappears. She is replaced by Miss Viola Swamp, who is out to set the children straight. First in a series. (I: 6–9)

Baker, Jeannie. *Where the Forest Meets the Sea*. Greenwillow, 1988. Exquisitely detailed and textured collage illustrations show an Australian forest. (I: 6–9)

Barnett, Mac. *Extra Yarn*. Illustrated by Jon Klassen. HarperCollins, 2012. Annabelle transforms her drab world by knitting colorful creations made from her "extra yarn" that seems to be endlessly available for her to use for her magical creations. She begins by knitting a sweater and goes beyond the usual creations for humans to creating for animals and even buildings. (I: P – 8)

Best, Cari. *Three Cheers for Catherine the Great!* Illustrated by Giselle Potter. DK Ink, 1999. When Grandma Catherine announces No Presents for her birthday, Sara must creatively think of a way to celebrate her grandmother's birthday. (I: 6–9)

Brett, Jan. *The Mitten*. Putnam, 1989. Nicki's lost mitten provides snug shelter for various animals until a bear sneezes. See also *The Hat* (1997). (I: P–8)

Brown, Marcia. *Once a Mouse*. Scribner's, 1961. This fable from India, in which a mouse that keeps changing into other animals learns a lesson about vanity, is illustrated with woodcuts. (I: 6–9)

_____, translator and illustrator. *Shadow*. Macmillan, 1982. Brown's translation of a poem by French poet Blaise Cendrars is about a dancing image, Shadow, that rises from ashes, brought to life by African storytellers. (I: 7–9)

Brown, Margaret Wise. *Goodnight Moon*. Illustrated by Clement Hurd. Harper, 1947. A young rabbit says good night to various objects in the room and outside the window. (I: P)

Brown, Peter. *Mr. Tiger Goes Wild*. Little, Brown, 2013. Stylized illustrations depict a tiger who tires of the "proper" Victorian lifestyle and wants to go wild. (I: K–7)

Browne, Anthony. *Voices in the Park*. Knopf, 1998. A mother and her daughter take their dog to the park, and a father and his son take their dog to the park. This book depicts four points of view on this singular event. (I: 6–9)

Bunting, Eve. *Smoky Night*. Illustrated by David Diaz. Harcourt, 1994. The Los Angeles riots provided the impetus for the creation of this book. Families learn about acceptance and being good neighbors in order to survive difficult times. (I: 9–11)

Burningham, John. *Come Away from the Water, Shirley*. Crowell, 1977. There are two stories in this family's trip to the beach. One is Shirley's daydreaming about pirate ships and gangplanks; the other is about the actual events and the parental warnings about how to behave at the beach. See also *Time to Get Out of the Bath, Shirley* (1978). (I: P–8)

_____. *Mr. Gumpy's Outing*. Harper, 1976. Mr. Gumpy meets many animals that ask to go along on his boat outing. A related title is *Mr. Gumpy's Motor Car* (1976). (I: P–6)

Burton, Virginia Lee. *The Little House*. Houghton Mifflin, 1942/1978. A house that was built in the countryside finds that, as the years go by, it is becoming run-down and is being surrounded by a city. (I: P–7)

_____. *Mike Mulligan and His Steam Shovel*. Houghton Mifflin, 1939. Mike Mulligan and his steam shovel, Mary Anne, prove that they can dig more in one day than one hundred men can dig in a week. (I: P–7)

Carle, Eric. *The Very Hungry Caterpillar*. Philomel, 1984. A little caterpillar eats "holes" through the food on the pages, and the cycle of metamorphosis is explained when the caterpillar emerges from a cocoon as a butterfly. See also *The Very Busy Spider* (1985), *The Very Quiet Cricket* (1990), *The Very Lonely Firefly* (1995), and *The Very Clumsy Click Beetle* (1999). (I: P–7)

Cherry, Lynne. *The Great Kapok Tree: A Tale of the Amazon Rain Forest*. Harcourt, 1990. When a man takes a nap before cutting down the great kapok tree in the rain forest, the animals that depend on the tree for their survival appear in a dream and convince him not to chop it down. (I: 6–9)

Child, Lauren. *Who's Afraid of the Big, Bad Book?* Hyperion, 2003. A boy falls asleep and enters into the world of his fairy tale book; he wakes up resolved to fix all of his mischievous markings and cutouts that changed the lives of the characters. See also *Beware of the Storybook Wolves* (2001). (I: 7–10)

Chodos-Irvine, Margaret. *Ella Sarah Gets Dressed*. Harcourt. 2003. Chodos-Irvine employs a variety of printmaking techniques to show Ella Sarah's confidence in cheerfully selecting her own attire for the day. (I: P–7)

Cooney, Barbara. *Miss Rumphius*. Viking, 1982. Miss Rumphius travels the world, making it more beautiful as she plants lupines. (I: 6–9)

Cronin, Doreen. *Click, Clack, Moo: Cows That Type*. Illustrated by Betsy Lewin. Simon, 2000. Farmer Brown's cows have gotten a hold of a typewriter that they use to negotiate in getting their needs met. (I: 6–9)

dePaola, Tomie. *Nana Upstairs and Nana Downstairs*. Autobiographical stories of Tomie's relationship with his grandmothers. Putnam, 1973. See also *Tom* (1993). (I: 6–8)

_____. *Strega Nona*. Simon & Schuster, 1979. "Grandma Witch" hires a helper, Big Anthony, who thinks that he has found the secret of how to make the magic pot cook pasta. What he doesn't know is how to make it stop. Several sequels were published between 1996–2006. (I: P–7)

Duvoisin, Roger. *Petunia*. Knopf, 1950. Petunia is a silly goose who thinks that all she has to do to gain wisdom is carry a book. (I: P–7)

Ehlert, Lois. *Snowballs*. Harcourt, 1995. Children create a snow family, using a large variety of items they had saved: a luggage tag, a toy fish, popcorn, etc. (I: P–6)

Emberley, Barbara. *Drummer Hoff*. Illustrated by Ed Emberley. Simon & Schuster, 1967. The story of how a cannon is fired is told through rhyming couplets in cumulative text. (I: 5–8)

Ernst, Lisa Campbell. *Zinnia and Dot*. Viking Penguin, 1992. Zinnia and Dot are two hens that are full of pride. When a weasel steals their eggs, they must learn to cooperate to save the one egg that is left behind. (I: 6–9)

Falconer, Ian. *Olivia*. Atheneum, 2000. Through text and illustration, readers see Olivia as a little pig whose daily life is lived fully and expressively. (I: P–8)

Fleming, Denise. *Barnyard Banter*. Holt, 1994. Barnyard animals noisily occupy their places on the farm, but the goose is missing. See also *In the Tall, Tall Grass* (1991), *In the Small, Small Pond* (1993). (I: P–6)

Fox, Mem. *Wilfrid Gordon McDonald Partridge*. Illustrated by Julie Vivas. Kane/Miller, 1985. Wilfrid Gordon McDonald Partridge is worried because everyone is talking about Miss Nancy's lost memory. In his attempt to find out what "memory" is, he restores Miss Nancy's memory in an unusual way. (I: 6–9)

Frazee, Marla. *A Couple of Boys Have the Best Week Ever*. Harcourt, 2008. Cartoon illustrations and upbeat text portray two boys enjoying a week of bonding through their various explorations at "nature camp." (I: K–7)

Gág, Wanda. *Millions of Cats*. Coward, McCann, 1929. When a lonely old man cannot choose among hundreds of cats, thousands of cats, millions and billions and trillions of cats, the cats fight it out as each claims to be the prettiest. (I: P–7)

Gerstein, Mordicai. *The Man Who Walked Between the Towers*. Roaring Brook Press, 2003. This true story shows the courage of a young Frenchman who walked on a tightrope between the World Trade Center Towers in 1974. (I: 7–10)

Graham, Bob. *"Let's Get a Pup!" Said Kate*. Candlewick, 2001. Even though Kate and her parents find the perfect pup at The Rescue Center, they cannot forget the old, gray dog they passed up. (I: P–8)

Gravett, Emily. *Wolves*. Simon & Schuster, 2007. A rabbit goes to the library and discovers information about wolves that is distressing. (I: P–7)

_____. *The Odd Egg*. Simon & Schuster, 2009. When a duck is unable to lay an egg, he adopts a huge spotted egg and all get a surprise ending. (I: P–7)

Hall, Donald. *The Ox-Cart Man*. Illustrated by Barbara Cooney. Viking, 1979. In nineteenth-century New England, a family fills an ox cart with the extra things they have grown or made during the previous year. After everything in the cart is sold, the family purchases supplies and goes through another year of growing things and making things to sell. (I: 6–8)

Henkes, Kevin. *Kitten's First Full Moon*. Greenwillow, 2004. Kitten mistakes a full moon for a bowl of milk and sets off on a quest to reach it. (I: P–8)

_____. *Lilly's Purple Plastic Purse*. Greenwillow, 1996. Lilly disrupts class to show off her new purple plastic purse and is devastated when Mr. Slinger, the teacher whom she idolizes, confiscates the purse until the end of the day. Numerous other related books include *Wemberley Worried* (2000) and *Penny* (2012). (I: P–8)

_____. *Old Bear.* Greenwillow, 2008. A bear in hibernation dreams of the passing of seasons. (I: P–6)

Ho, Minfong. *Hush!* Illustrated by Holly Meade. Orchard, 1996. In this lullaby set in Thailand, a mother tries to quiet the animals so that her baby can sleep. (I: P–8)

Hodges, Margaret. *St. George and the Dragon.* Illustrated by Trina Schart Hyman. Little, Brown, 1984. This adaptation of Edmund Spenser's *Faerie Queene* tells how the Red Cross Knight slays the dragon and ends its terrorizing of the English countryside. (I: 8–12)

Isaacs, Anne. *Swamp Angel.* Illustrated by Paul O. Zelinsky. Dutton, 1994. A tall tale about a bear-wrestling heroine who helps settlers in Tennessee. (I: 6–9)

Johnson, Crockett. *Harold and the Purple Crayon.* Harper & Row, 1958. Harold goes on a walk, using his purple crayon to draw pictures that create an adventure. (I: P–7)

Jonas, Ann. *Round Trip.* Greenwillow, 1983. The journey begins at dawn in a quiet neighborhood and passes through the countryside on the way to the city. Then readers turn the book upside down and see what the illustrations depict when viewed from the opposite direction, completing a round trip back to the neighborhood. (I: P–9)

Kasza, Keiko. *A Mother for Choco.* Putnam, 1992. Choco goes in search of mother, only to find that nobody looks like him. Instead, he meets a mother who asks what a mother would do. (I: P–7)

_____. *Wolf's Chicken Stew.* Putnam, 1987. Wolf is very hungry for chicken stew and finds the perfect chicken. His attempts to fatten her up backfire. (I: P–7)

Keats, Ezra Jack. *Goggles!* Macmillan, 1969. Archie and Willie are met by bullies and must think quickly to return home safely. (I: P–7)

_____. *Peter's Chair.* Harper, 1967. Peter is jealous of his new baby sister and refuses to give her his chair until he discovers that he has outgrown it. (I: P–7)

_____. *The Snowy Day.* Viking, 1962. Peter plays outside following a big snowfall. (I: P–7)

Kellogg, Steven. *Island of the Skog.* Puffin, 1973/1993. Mice sail in search of a safe home, only to find that their "unhabited" island has giant footprints, launching an attack plan that ends in a surprise. (I: P–9)

Klassen, Jon. *I Want My Hat Back.* Candlewick, 2011. A bear is missing its hat and asks various animals if they have seen it, and the ending implies who was responsible for the missing hat. (I: P–7) See also: *This Is Not My Hat*, 2012.

Landowne, Youme. *Selavi, That Is Life: A Haitian Story of Hope.* Illustrated by Youme Landowne. Cinco Puntos, 2004. This story of homeless children in Haiti depicts children who work together and care for each other. (I: K–8)

Lionni, Leo. *Frederick.* Knopf, 1967. The field mice work hard to prepare for winter, and it appears that Frederick is shirking his responsibilities. However, when winter comes, he is able to entertain the other mice with his poems describing the warmth of the sun and the colors of the flowers. A sequel is *Frederick and His Friends* (1981). (I: P–7)

_____. *Swimmy.* Pantheon, 1963. A little fish comes up with a clever plan to protect the small fish in the school from being eaten by larger fish: They swim together in the formation of a giant fish. (I: P–7)

Lobel, Arnold. *The Rose in My Garden.* Illustrated by Anita Lobel. Greenwillow, 1984. Cumulative text tells the story of a bee asleep on a rose in the garden—until a cat chases a mouse through the garden. (I: P–8)

Macaulay, David. *Black and White.* Houghton Mifflin, 1990. This Caldecott winner presents four separate stories—or one intertwined story—about children, parents, trains, and cows. (I: 8–12)

Marshall, James. *George and Martha.* Houghton Mifflin, 1972. George and Martha are two hippos who share a fun-filled day. Other titles in the series. (I: P–8)

Martin, Bill, Jr., and John Archambault. *The Ghost-Eye Tree.* Illustrated by Ted Rand. Holt, 1985. When a brother and sister are sent to fetch a pail of milk one dark and spooky night, their imaginations run wild as they hurry past the Ghost-Eye Tree. (I: P–8)

McCloskey, Robert. *Blueberries for Sal.* Viking, 1948. A little girl goes blueberry picking with her mother and a little bear follows its mother, but the two children get their mothers mixed up! (I: P–7)

_____. *Make Way for Ducklings.* Viking, 1941. Mr. and Mrs. Mallard set off in search of a perfect place to raise their family. They find that Boston Public Garden provides just the right home. (I: P–8)

McCully, Emily Arnold. *Mirette on the High Wire.* Putnam, 1992. When a formerly great tightrope artist becomes fearful of walking the rope, it is a little girl, Mirette, who must help him overcome his fears. (I: 6–9)

McLerran, Alice. *Roxaboxen.* Illustrated by Barbara Cooney. Lothrop, 1991. Marian and her sisters enjoy imaginary play with their friends as they create a community out of rocks on a hill. (I: 6–9)

McPhail, David. *Fix-It.* Dutton, 1984. Emma Bear is distressed to find that the television won't turn on, until Mother Bear reads her a good book. (I: P–6)

Meddaugh, Susan. *Hog-Eye.* Houghton Mifflin, 1995. When the family demands an explanation for why a little pig missed school one day, she launches into a wild story of how she got on the wrong bus, took a shortcut through the forest, and met a wolf who tied her up and made her teach him how to make soup. The pig tells how she outwitted the wolf through the magic of "Hog-Eye." (I: 6–9)

_____. *Martha Speaks.* Houghton Mifflin, 1992. Martha the dog is able to speak after eating alphabet soup. Her family is thrilled to be able to communicate with her verbally and hear her thoughts on various subjects. Sequels are *Martha Calling* (1994), *Martha Blah Blah* (1996), *Martha Walks the Dog* (1998), and *Martha and Skits* (2000). (I: 6–9)

Morales, Yuyi. *Just a Minute!: A Trickster Tale and Counting Book.* Chronicle, 2003. When Señor Calavera comes for Grandma Beetle, she tricks him into waiting just one more minute . . . . (I: P–8)

Moss, Lloyd. *Zin! Zin! Zin! a Violin.* Illustrated by Marjorie Priceman. Simon & Schuster, 1995. A trombone begins playing solo and is joined by the trumpet, French horn, cello, violin, flute, clarinet, oboe, bassoon, and harp. (I: P–8)

Myers, Christopher. *Wings*. Scholastic, 2000. Ikarus Jackson is mocked for being different from others: He has wings. When the narrator learns to stand up for Ikarus, they both understand the power of embracing differences and celebrating individuality. (I: 6–10)

Pattison, Darcy. *The Journey of Oliver K. Woodman*. Illustrated by Joe Cepeda. Harcourt, 2003. Uncle Ray sends a wooden man to his niece via various travelers who are driving from coast to coast, sending postcards along the way. (I: 6–9)

Perkins, Lynne Rae. *Pictures from Our Vacation*. Greenwillow, 2007. Mother gives the children cameras and notebooks to document memories of their family trip, but it isn't until they connect with family members that the true experiences get captured in their memories. (I: K–8)

Pilkey, Dav. *The Paperboy*. Orchard, 1996. Readers get a sense of ritual as a boy gets out of bed and goes about his daily routine of delivering the newspaper. (I: P–8)

Polacco, Patricia. *The Keeping Quilt*. Simon & Schuster, 1998/2008. A quilt made of patchwork pieces from various family members' clothing helps Anna stay connected with her homeland of Russia, and becomes a centerpiece of important family traditions in the new land from picnic blanket to Sabbath tablecloth to wedding chuppah to christening blanket. (I: 6–9)

————. *Thunder Cake*. Philomel, 1993. Grandmother helps her granddaughter overcome her fear of thunder. (I: 6–9)

Pomerantz, Charlotte. *The Chalk Doll*. Illustrated by Frané Lessac. Lippincott, 1989. Rose asks her mother to talk about her childhood in Jamaica. (I: 6–8)

Potter, Beatrix. *The Tale of Peter Rabbit*. Warne, 1902/1986. This is the story of Peter, a naughty rabbit who disobeys his mother and ends up caught in Mr. McGregor's garden. (I: P–8)

Ransome, Arthur. *The Fool of the World and the Flying Ship*. Illustrated by Uri Shulevitz. Farrar, 1968. A Russian boy of poor background marries the czar's daughter. (I: 7–10)

Rathmann, Peggy. *Officer Buckle and Gloria*. Putnam, 1995. Officer Buckle makes school rounds, giving safety tips to children. His dog, Gloria, pantomimes the safety tips and is the one who actually keeps the children amused. (I: 6–9)

Rinker, Shelley Dunskey. *Goodnight, Goodnight, Construction Site*. Illustrated by Tom Lichtenheld. A good night book of construction site vehicles told through rhyming text. (I: P–7)

Rosen, Michael. *We're Going on a Bear Hunt*. Illustrated by Helen Oxenbury. Macmillan, 1989. A father takes his children on an imaginary bear hunt. They bravely go through various obstacles until they encounter the bear and make a mad dash home. Alternating full-color and black-and-white illustrations depict what part of the story actually happens and what part is imagination. (I: P–6)

Schaefer, Carole Lexa. *The Squiggle*. Illustrated by Pierr Morgan. Crown, 1996. On an outing with her class, a little girl finds a rope that she imagines to be part of a dragon, the Great Wall of China, and various other things. See also *Someone Says* (2003). (I: P–7)

Sendak, Maurice. *Where the Wild Things Are*. Harper & Row, 1963/1989. When he is punished and sent to bed without supper, Max sails off to an imaginary world where he is the king of the Wild Things. (I: P–8)

Seuss, Dr. *And to Think That I Saw It on Mulberry Street*. Vanguard, 1937. A little boy imagines what would happen if the horse and cart he sees on his street were transformed into a circus bandwagon. (I: P–8)

————. *Horton Hatches the Egg*. 1940/1968. Random House. Mayzie the bird leaves for a vacation and leaves Horton the elephant to sit on her nest and tend her egg. (I: P–8)

Shulevitz, Uri. *Snow*. Farrar, Straus, & Giroux, 1998. A little boy discovers a snowflake falling, but the adults do not pay attention. Soon, the boy is delightedly playing in snow with Mother Goose characters from a sign that come and join him. (I: P–7)

Soto, Gary. *Chato and the Party Animals*. Illustrated by Susan Guevara. Putnam, 2000. Chato, the coolest cat in el barrio, throws a surprise party for his friend, Novio Boy. See also *Chato's Kitchen* (1995). (I: 6–10)

Stead, Philip C. *A Sick Day for Amos McGee*. Illustrated by Erin E. Stead. Roaring Brook, 2010. Amos takes time for his animal friends at the zoo where he works, and when he is ill, they take a bus to visit him and offer their companionship. Softly colored woodblock print illustrations tell the gentle tale of friendship. (I: P–7)

Steig, William. *Sylvester and the Magic Pebble*. Simon & Schuster, 1969. When Sylvester, a donkey, makes a wish while holding an extraordinary rock and turns himself into a rock, he finds that he is unable to turn himself back into a donkey. (I: 6–9)

Steptoe, John. *Stevie*. Harper, 1969. A small boy resents having to share his mother with a little boy who is temporarily staying with them, until he realizes that the little boy is "kinda like a brother." (I: P–7)

Stevens, Janet. *And the Dish Ran Away With the Spoon*. Harcourt, 2001. When dish and spoon run away at the end of the traditional rhyme, they do not return, so dog, cat, and cow set off in search of them and encounter various other nursery rhyme characters along the way. (I: 6–9)

————. *Tops & Bottoms*. Harcourt, 1995. Clever and hard-working Hare outsmarts the land-rich but lazy Bear in order to "cash in" on the crops he grows. (I: 6–9)

Stevens, Janet and Susan Stevens Crummel. *Cook-a-Doodle-Doo!* Illustrated by Janet Stevens. Harcourt Brace, 1999. A hungry rooster seeks help in cooking up Great Granny's recipe for strawberry shortcake in this twist on the story of "The Little Red Hen." (I: 6–9)

Stevenson, James. *Could Be Worse!* Greenwillow, 1977. Grandpa tells his grandchildren a wild story. (I: 6–8)

Stewart, Sarah. *The Gardener*. Illustrated by David Small. Farrar, 1997. When Lydia is sent to live in an unfamiliar city and work for her uncle, she brightens her life and her surroundings with her garden. (I: 6–9)

Taback, Simms. *There Was an Old Lady Who Swallowed a Fly*. Viking, 1997. The familiar folk song of an old woman who swallows a fly, and increasingly larger living creatures to catch each other is depicted with clever cutouts in illustration. (I: P–8)

Teague, Mark. *Dear Mrs. LaRue: Letters from Obedience School*. Scholastic, 2002. A dog writes letters from obedience school to his owner, depicting a jail-like place instead of the spa-like reality. (I: 6–10)

Tunnell, Michael O. *Mailing May*. Illustrated by Ted Rand. Tambourine/Greenwillow, 1997. Based on a true story, this book tells of a little girl sent on a train by parcel post mail in 1914 so that she can visit her grandmother. (I: 6–9)

Vail, Rachel. *Sometimes I'm Bombaloo*. Illustrated by Yumi Heo. Scholastic, 2002. Dealing with strong emotions can be hard for a young child to learn, and sometimes it becomes "bombaloo" before things calm down again. (I: P–7)

Van Allsburg, Chris. *Jumanji*. Houghton Mifflin, 1981. Peter and Judy find an unusual board game that comes alive and turns the house into a jungle. (I: 7–10)

———. *Two Bad Ants*. Houghton Mifflin, 1988. Two ants in search of sugar crystals for their queen divert from the path to seek adventure in the house. Their experiences prove terrifying. (I: 7–10)

Waddell, Martin. *Farmer Duck*. Illustrated by Helen Oxenbury. Candlewick, 1992. A duck is overworked by a lazy farmer, and the barnyard animals rescue the duck and keep his family intact. (I: P–7)

Watt, Mélanie. *Scaredy Squirrel*. Kids Can, 2006. Engaging illustrations capture the emotions of a squirrel who overcomes the fear of going beyond the security of his own oak tree. (I: P–7)

Wells, Rosemary. *Bunny Cakes*. Dial, 1997. In an effort to decorate his earthworm cake for Grandma's birthday, Max repeatedly attempts to write "Red-Hot Marshmallow Squirters" on the grocery list. See also *Bunny Money* (1997) and *Bunny Party* (2001). (I: P–8)

Wiesner, David. *The Three Pigs*. Clarion, 2001. The traditional story of the three pigs takes a twist when the pigs fly out of the story and into other stories. (I: 6–9)

———. *Tuesday*. Clarion, 1991. One Tuesday, a surreal scene of frogs flying on lily pads startle those they encounter. (I: 6–9)

Willems, Mo. *Don't Let the Pigeon Drive the Bus!* Hyperion, 2003. A very persistent pigeon uses a full range of tactics to get to drive the bus. (I: P–8)

———. *Knuffle Bunny: A Cautionary Tale*. Trixie's beloved "knuffle bunny" gets left behind at a laundromat, causing emotional distress that her babbling cannot communicate to her father. See also *Knuffle Bunny, Too: A Case of Mistaken Identity* (2007). (I: P–7)

Williams, Vera B. *"More More More," Said the Baby: Three Love Stories*. Greenwillow, 1990. Three love stories show the loving relationships between each child and his or her parent. (I: P)

Wisniewski, David. *The Golem*. Clarion, 1996. A rabbi creates a clay giant, the golem, and brings it to life to help protect the Jews in Prague during the sixteenth century. (I: 9–12)

Yolen, Jane. *The Emperor and the Kite*. Illustrated by Ed Young. Putnam, 1967/1988. The diligence and loyalty of the emperor's smallest daughter allow him to rule the land again after being overthrown by evil plotters. The watercolor paintings are reminiscent of Chinese cut-paper art. (I: 6–9)

———. *Owl Moon*. Illustrated by John Schoenherr. Philomel, 1987. A young boy goes "owling" with his father. (I: 7–9)

Young, Ed. *Seven Blind Mice*. Philomel, 1992. One by one, the blind mice feel the "thing" and describe various body parts they each feel. (I: P–9)

———. *What About Me?* Putnam, 2002. In this Sufi tale, a young boy in search of wisdom is sent off to embark on a circular story by a Grand Master. (I: 7–10)

Zelinsky, Paul. *Rumpelstiltskin*. Dutton, 1986. Zelinsky's oil paintings richly depict this familiar tale of a young woman who must either discover the name of the little man or give him her first-born child in exchange for assistance in weaving straw into gold. (I: 7–9)

Zolotow, Charlotte. *Mr. Rabbit and the Lovely Present*. Illustrated by Maurice Sendak. HarperCollins, 1977. A little girl in search of a birthday present for her mother encounters a rabbit and asks for help. (I: 7–9)

CHILDREN'S BOOKS REFERENCES

Andersen, Hans Christian. *The Ugly Duckling*. Adapted and illustrated by Jerry Pinkney. Morrow, 1999.

Badoe, Adwoa. *The Pot of Wisdom: Ananse Stories*. Illustrated by Baba Wagué Diakité. Groundwood, 2008.

Brown, Marcia. *Stone Soup: An Old Tale*. Aladdin, 1947/1987.

Bunting, Eve. *Smoky Night*. Illustrated by David Diaz. Harcourt, 1994.

Carroll, Lewis. *Alice's Adventures in Wonderland*. Illustrated by John Tenniel. Macmillan, 1865.

Craft, K. Y. (Illustrator). *Cinderella*. New York: Sea Star, 2000.

Crews, Nina. *The Neighborhood Mother Goose*. Greenwillow, 2003.

Davol, Marguerite W. *The Paper Dragon*. Illustrated by Robert Sabuda. Atheneum, 1997.

de Paola, Tomie. *Charlie Needs a Cloak*. Prentice-Hall, 1973.

_____. *The Cloud Book*. Holiday House, 1975.

_____. *Patrick: Patron Saint of Ireland*. Holiday House, 1994.

_____. *The Popcorn Book*. Holiday House, 1988.

Heo, Yumi. *The Green Frogs: A Korean Folktale*. Houghton Mifflin, 1996.

Keats, Ezra Jack. *Apt. 3*. Viking, 1974/1999.

Kunhardt, Dorothy. *Pat the Bunny*. Golden Books, 1940/2001.

Lester, Julius. *John Henry*. Illustrated by Jerry Pinkney. Dial, 1994.

_____. *The Tales of Uncle Remus: The Adventures of Brer Rabbit*. Illustrated by Jerry Pinkney. Dutton, 1987.

Louie, Ai-Ling. *Yeh-Shen: A Cinderella Story from China*. Illustrated by Ed Young. Putnam, 1982.

Martin, Jr., Bill. *The Maestro Plays*. Illustrated by Vladimir Radunsky. Holt, 1994.

McCloskey, Robert. *Time of Wonder*. Viking, 1957.

Moebius, William. "Introduction to Picturebook Codes." *Word & Image* 2.2 (1986): 141–152.

Perrault, Charles. *Cinderella*. Illustrated by Marcia Brown. Scribner's, 1954.

_____. *Puss in Boots*. Illustrated by Fred Marcellino. Translated by Malcolm Arthur. Farrar, 1990.

_____. *Puss in Boots*. Illustrated by Hans Fischer. Translated by Anthea Bell. North-South Books, 1958/1996.

Pinkney, Andrea Davis. *Alvin Ailey*. Hyperion, 1993.

_____. *Sit-In: How Four Friends Stood Up by Sitting Down*. Illustrated by Brian Pinkney. Little Brown, 2010.

Sabuda, Robert. *Saint Valentine*. Aladdin, 1992.

San Souci, Robert D. *The Talking Eggs: A Folktale from the American South*. Illustrated by Jerry Pinkney. Dial, 1989.

Schwartz, Alvin. *Scary Stories to Tell in the Dark*. Illustrated by Stephen Gammell. HarperCollins, 1985.

Sendak, Maurice. *In the Night Kitchen*. Harper, 1970.

Spirin, Gennady. *The Tale of the Firebird*. Philomel, 2002.

Steiner, Joan. *Look-Alikes*. Little, Brown, 1998.

Toy Hong, Lily. *Two of Everything*. Whitman, 1993.

Winter, Jonah. *Frida*. Illustrated by Ana Juan. Levine/Scholastic, 2002.

RESOURCES AND REFERENCES

Bang, Molly. *Picture This: Perception and Composition.* Sea Star Books, 1991/2000.

Blake, William. *Songs of Innocence and Songs of Experience.* Dover, 1789/1992.

Cianciolo, Patricia J. *Picture Books for Children.* 4th ed. American Library Association, 1997.

Crane, Walter. *Absurd ABC.* George Routledge & Sons, c. 1865.

Cummins, Julie. *Children's Book Illustration and Design* (2 vols.). PBC International, 1998.

Evans, Dilys. *Show & Tell: Exploring the Fine Art of Children's Book Illustration.* Chronicle Books, 2008.

Kiefer, Barbara Z. *The Potential of Picturebooks: From Visual Literacy to Aesthetic Understanding.* Merrill/Prentice-Hall, 1995.

Marcus, Leonard S. *Show Me a Story! Why Picture Books Matter: Conversations with 21 of the World's Most Celebrated Illustrators.* Candlewick, 2012.

McCallum, Robyn. "Metafiction and Experimental Work." In *International Companion Encyclopedia of Children's Literature.* Ed. Peter Hunt. London and New York: Routledge, 1996, pp. 397–409.

McCloud, Scott. *Understanding Comics: The Invisible Art.* Morrow, 1994.

Nikolajeva, Maria, and Carole Scott. *How Picturebooks Work.* Routledge, 2001.

Nodleman, Perry. *Words about Pictures: The Narrative Art of Children's Picture Books.* Univ. of Georgia Press, 1988.

Powers, Alan. *Children's Book Covers: Great Book Jacket and Cover Design.* London: Mitchell Beazley, 2003.

Roser, N. L., Martinez, M., McDonnald, K., & Fuhrken, C. (2004). Beginning chapter books: Their features and their support of children's reading. In Fairbanks, C. M., Worthy, J., Malock, B., Hoffman, J. V., & Schallert, D. L. (Eds.) *53rd Yearbook of the National Reading Conference.* Oak Creek, WI: National Reading Conference.

Schwartz, Joseph H. *Ways of the Illustrator: Visual Communication in Children's Literature.* American Library Association, 1982.

Sendak, Maurice. *Caldecott and Co.* Farrar, Straus, & Giroux, 1990.

Shulevitz, Uri. *Writing with Pictures: How to Write and Illustrate Children's Books.* Watson-Guptill, 1985/1997.

Silvey, Anita. *Children's Books and Their Creators.* Houghton Mifflin, 1995.

Sipe, Lawrence and Sylvia Pantaleo, eds. *Postmodern Picturebooks: Play, Parody, and Self-Referentiality.* Routledge, 2008.

Styles, Morag, and Eve Bearne, eds. *Art, Narrative and Childhood.* Trentham Books, 2003.

Yokota, J. and W. H. Teale. Picture Books and the Digital World: Educators Making Informed Choices. *The Reading Teacher.* (in press, 2014).

Literature Representing Diverse Perspectives

> ❝ I'm a sophomore," Sheila said. "Three more years in this place."
>
> "And you just got here, Maizon," Charli said, bouncing down next to me. She had more energy than Li'l Jay.
>
> "Buckle your seat belt, girlfriend, 'cause you in for one heck of a ride."
>
> "Charli. You're slipping," Marie said, frowning.
>
> "Oh, chill out, Marie." Charli waved her hand and lay back on the bed. "We're among our own. ❞

—from *Maizon at Blue Hill* by Jacqueline Woodson

I n *Maizon at Blue Hill,* a girl enters a private academy and discovers that she is one of only five African American students there. Incidents throughout the book reveal how she feels in this situation, how she sees her place in this setting, and how she interacts with others. The passage above implies that people feel and act differently when they are able to say, "We're among our own." How does being among people whose perspectives are different from your own make you feel? Reading and discussing books such as *Maizon at Blue Hill* allows children to reflect on what it means to live in a diverse world and to consider how issues of diversity affect them.

Why should we have multicultural literature, really? That is a fair question. Some critics worry that the rise of multicultural education in the United States may fragment our loyalties and loosen our civic ties to each other. For example, a noted historian wrote a book entitled *The Disuniting of America* (Schlesinger, 1991) that offers this premise. But James Banks (2000), an energetic proponent of multicultural education, argues that multicultural education is fully American because the United States is a society that was founded on the premise of providing justice and the pursuit of happiness for its citizens; therefore, recognizing the culture and potential of different groups is necessary to their pursuit of happiness and justice.

Multicultural children's books can make a contribution here. Beverly Tatum, a psychologist who has studied racism, explains why. Most of us live in racially segregated neighborhoods (Tatum, 1999). Tatum suggests that our earliest experiences take place among people of the same race as ourselves. We count on secondhand sources—books, movies, and television—for our impressions about people from other races, ethnic groups, or religious backgrounds. If those sources give caricatured representations of other races or leave them out altogether, we are likely as children to form deep-seated notions that people of other races are silly, unimportant, or, at the very least, much different than we are. If we belong to a race that is caricatured or excluded, we might internalize the idea that we are unimportant in the eyes of the world.

The best defense against allowing racist views to take hold of our children is to surround them with rich, realistic information about children from many other races. If they have that information, then the concepts or preconceptions they form will more genuinely reflect people from other races as they are, with their differences, similarities, and individuality. This is the role that multicultural literature needs to fill.

Diverse Perspectives in the United States

Schools in the United States are experiencing a tremendous increase in the cultural and ethnic diversity of the children they serve. According to the 2010 census, almost 25% of the U.S. population is composed of people who claim a race other than White. More than 20% of families with children age 5 or older speak a language other than English in the home. That reality, along with our expanding relationships with countries around the world, increases the need for children to perceive themselves as members of a multicultural global community. Because good literature reaches the minds and hearts of its readers, reading and discussing multicultural literature will broaden children's perspectives and increase their understanding in a way that affects—for the better, we hope—how people live in this pluralistic society. Yet the books being published do not reflect the depth and breadth of our diversity. The Cooperative Children's Book Council in Wisconsin maintains annual statistics on the publication of multicultural books because of its commitment to raising awareness for the continuing need for representations of multicultural experiences.

Ask *the* Author: Alma Flor Ada

How do you feel about the argument that one has to be a member of a culture to write about it?

The more intimately connected an author is with the reality she explores, the greater the possibility to portray it authentically and to make a positive impression on the reader. Does this require that the author be a member of a specific culture? Not necessarily. If an author possesses ample knowledge about a culture and can develop the understanding of its intricacies, she will be able to write with a responsible degree of authenticity.

Otherwise, authors would be tremendously restricted about what they can write: Men could not write about women, nor women about men, and historical novels would not be possible.

Children who belong to minority cultures and see themselves and their people constantly stereotyped, ignored, or misrepresented deserve to hear authentic voices showing the complexity and richness of their experience. Children who may have limited or dubious understanding of other cultures deserve to get to know them from those who can best represent them.

In the multicultural society of the United States, many times the books we have are visions from specific cultures, but we still are short on books that portray the cultures interacting with each other: the friendships, rivalry, love, sharing, losses, experienced by characters of diverse backgrounds as they come together.

It is not only a matter of cultural background, but of the responsibility one takes in learning, observing, reflecting, experiencing, suffering, struggling to understand that makes the vision of an author sincere. But let's be aware that authors frequently write about another culture opportunistically, because there is an interest or a demand, because the culture seems colorful or appealing.

It is very difficult to become intimately familiar with another culture, even after living many years in its midst. Therefore, there is a great risk that, in spite of the best intentions, the author who writes from outside a culture may not do justice to its essence. Even while knowing many things factually about a culture, an author can miss the intrinsic expression of the cultural values that make all the difference.

What must not be forgotten is that children always deserve the truth at its best.

Perhaps better than reclaiming the right to write about the other, we would do well in writing about us in relationship to the other, or about us as someone else's other, until such glorious day in which there will be no other, but us, each in our radiant uniqueness, enriched by our past and our culture, but equally central, equally respected, equally valued and embraced in brotherly, in sisterly, love.

Alma Flor Ada is the author of many award-winning books for children and adolescents including childhood memories *Under the Royal Palms* and *Where the Flame Trees Bloom*; whimsical letter collections *Dear Peter Rabbit* and *Yours Truly, Goldilocks*; and beloved stories such as *The Gold Coin* and *My Name Is Maria Isabel*. Alma Flor, a retired professor at the University of San Francisco, attributes her productivity to the support of her four children and now rejoices in sharing her books with her eight grandchildren.

Multicultural education theorists define *pluralism* as diversity in "ethnic, racial, linguistic, religious, economic, and gender [characteristics], among others" (Nieto, 1996). Nieto argues "that all students of all backgrounds, languages, and experiences need to be acknowledged, valued, and used as important sources of their education" (p. 8). This inclusive definition of pluralism correlates with beliefs about the need for diverse perspectives in education. Banks (1999) asks that multicultural

TOP SHELF 4.1

MULTIRACIAL CHARACTERS

Aneesa Lee and the Weaver's Gift by Nikki Grimes. Illustrated by Ashley Bryan

black is brown is tan by Arnold Adoff. Illustrated by Emily Arnold McCully

Habibi by Naomi Shihab Nye

I Love Saturdays y domingos by Alma Flor Ada. Illustrated by Elivia Savadier

Molly Bannaky by Alice McGill. Illustrated by Chris Soentpiet

education include voices that have been marginalized in the past, but urges that it not ignore the achievements of Western civilization in doing so. The goal of multi-cultural education is freedom—helping students develop the knowledge, attitudes, and skills that will allow them to participate in a democratic and free society. Banks acknowledges that students should know their own culture before they can success-fully participate in other cultures.

The United States is a diverse society, and this diversity has many sources. The obvious ways in which both the general and school populations are diverse are gen-der, culture, ethnic and racial background, language, and physical and mental abili-ties. Less often acknowledged are differences in social class. All of these differences can affect the ways people see themselves and others. And all must be taken into account in forging a working democracy or maintaining a harmonious classroom.

The Role of Schools in Presenting Multiple Perspectives

Schools face many demands in shaping the curriculum. Some of these demands are made by people who want the curriculum to be presented from one perspective—their own. Multiple viewpoints serve students best. If only male, white, able-bodied characters are presented in a curriculum, then female students, children of ethnic diversity, students with disabilities, and children with learning exceptionalities are likely to feel that the school day is not planned with them in mind. They may even feel that their place in society in general is questionable. Although strides have been made in creating an anti-bias curriculum that promotes social justice, more work is needed. Schools can be instrumental in providing opportunities for students to read and discuss material from multiple viewpoints. Such discussions are important in de-veloping attitudes of open-mindedness about diversity. This chapter (and this book) recommends books that offer multiple perspectives.

Literature's Potential for Influencing the Reader's Perspective

What role does literature have in influencing children's understanding of diverse perspectives? Depending on their experiences, some children feel uncomfortable when presented with an opportunity to interact with someone who is different from them. How can children resolve their misunderstanding, lack of understanding, or fear? Developing a hypersensitivity that leads to avoidance is a serious mistake. "Many people have an inhibition about talking with someone in a wheelchair. They don't know quite what to say, so they don't say anything at all and ignore both the person and the chair" (Haldane, 1991, n. pag.). People may respond to any kind of diversity in this way. Although it is a vicarious experience, interacting with diverse people through literature can help. Literature that portrays diversity in natural ways can provide realistic images as well as inspire discussion.

Fiction and informational books are powerful vehicles for helping students understand other cultures because they offer cultural insights in natural ways. Such books should not be narrowly viewed as replacements for social studies textbooks; too often, students miss the richness of the writing if they read merely to locate cul-tural information. However, fiction and informational books can enhance children's understanding of cultures by involving them emotionally. The narrower focus of such books allows for deeper exploration of the thoughts, feelings, and experiences of people from diverse groups. Thus, through story, readers take an emotional stake in understanding how and why people live as they do. Julius Lester (2004) sees the power of story in helping us "to reach out to others and forge relationships." He describes how the intimacy of storytelling binds us to others: "We need to share our stories because in so doing, we hope to be understood, and being understood we are no longer so alone."

Milton Meltzer (1989) believes that the writer has a social responsibility and that "writing about social issues need not depress and dispirit readers; it should provide them with courage. If they learn to confront life as it is, it may give them the heart to strive to make it better" (p. 157). Meltzer is saying that literature is a powerful vehicle when it treats issues honestly. But, as Jean Little (1990) points out, literature that is designed to present object lessons, in which teachers point out the "good messages," appears self-righteous and rarely changes people's opinions. Well-written books that speak from the writer's vision pull readers into the characters' experiences and emotions and build compassion, thereby having a lasting effect on readers' understandings of the world in which they live.

Books depicting diverse perspectives are found in all genres of children's literature. In this chapter, we will examine the criteria for viewing multicultural and international issues in children's books. These criteria form a foundation for evaluating the literature you encounter in all the genre chapters that follow.

What Is Multicultural Literature?

Although there is general agreement that multicultural literature is about people who are not in the mainstream, there is no consensus as to what constitutes non-mainstream populations (Cai & Sims Bishop, 1994). Some contend that multicultural literature is written by or about people of color in the United States. Many include literature about religious minorities (such as the Amish and Jews) or about people who live in specific regions of the United States (such as Appalachia). Some include literature about diverse lifestyles (such as families headed by same-sex parents or people with disabilities). Some include books about people in countries outside the United States. There is value in having an inclusive definition when considering issues of diversity; however, too broad a definition dilutes the focus.

We define multicultural literature as works that reflect the multitude of cultural groups within the United States. To address the issues of multiculturalism that are most salient to our study of children's literature, we will focus on literature that reflects ethnic and regional groups whose cultures historically have been less represented than European cultures. A related body of literature is international literature—literature that was originally written and published in countries outside the United States. This type of literature will be discussed in the next chapter.

One reason we focus on books about ethnic groups within the United States is that these books reflect experiences

TECHNOLOGY in PRACTICE 4.1

WEB SITES RELATED TO MULTICULTURAL LITERATURE: WWW.OYATE.ORG

Oyate is an organization committed to portraying the lives and histories of Native people in honest ways. Members review and evaluate books, texts, and other teaching materials to check for authentic portrayals. They disseminate information through their resource center, examination library, and publications. This Web site serves as a way to reach a wider audience than would be reached through teacher workshops. Teachers can use this site to learn how to critique books about Native Americans. First, read a book from the "books to avoid" list without reading the critique and jot down your impressions. Then click on the book title and read the critique that is written from a Native perspective. Compare it with your own earlier opinion and consider what the similarities and differences in the opinions mean. Reread the book with the Oyate critique in mind. How does the interaction with the Oyate Web site influence your critique of books about Native Americans?

of the children in U.S. schools today, since most were either born or raised in this country. Often, books of this type are classified as African American, Asian American, Latino/a, or Native American. We use the term "multicultural" rather than "minority," with its implied reference to groups that have been historically "minor" in number compared to the "majority." Some groups that historically have been considered "minorities" are no longer numerically in the minority. Unfortunately, however, underrepresentation and misrepresentation of these groups continue. Virginia Hamilton's (1993) term "parallel cultures" has been preferred by many because it defines various cultures as parallel to the mainstream, rather than in a minority status. However, in reality, we have not yet reached Hamilton's ideal for parallel status of the various cultural groups. In addition, the ideal is not to simply exist on parallel planes; rather, it is interactions between cultures that lead to interdependence.

The Value of Multicultural Literature

Why should children's books deliberately include the perspectives of people from many backgrounds? This continues to be a legitimate question, despite political movement that seemed to take our society forward, beyond tolerance, and toward acceptance of diversity. Decades after the notion was challenged, some still believe that the old analogy to a "melting pot" is the target that literature should strive for; that we shouldn't accentuate ethnic and cultural differences because these differences emphasize the stresses that are tearing apart the fabric of society.

We believe that there are two compelling reasons for making sure children's literature includes the perspectives of people from many groups. First, students feel welcome in school to the extent to which they find themselves and their experiences represented in the books and materials they find there. Second, students need to understand and empathize with people who are different from them. If books do not portray differences, students cannot learn to transcend them.

Rudine Sims Bishop (1990) uses the metaphor of mirrors and windows to emphasize these two values of multicultural literature. *Mirrors* let readers see reflections of their own lives; windows let them see others' lives. Multicultural literature provides both types of experience. What value is there in seeing oneself represented in literature? Quite simply, it engenders a sense of pride. When readers encounter images of people they consider like themselves in a book, they take more interest in the book and feel a sense of involvement in the literary discussion that follows their reading. What value is there in seeing others represented in literature? Books that act as *windows* into experiences that are different from our own stretch the range of experiences we have had. Lee Galda (2000) makes an interesting analogy connecting windows with mirrors: In certain types of light, windows show reflections of self in varying degrees of clarity. Likewise, books that are windows to outside experiences should offer the possibility that readers will see some type of reflection of themselves.

Seeing ourselves and others portrayed authentically is only one of the values of multicultural literature. The greatest value of multicultural literature lies in the opportunities for extension that these books offer. In what ways can quality multicultural books elicit insights about our world and ourselves? What kinds of discussion are elicited by reading these books? Many multicultural books have the potential to serve as springboards for considering issues of social justice. Perhaps most important, many works of

ILLUSTRATION 4.1 In *We Are the Ship*, readers learn of the talent, determination, and dedication of the players in baseball's Negro Leagues despite the discrimination, circumstances and obstacles they faced. ("We Are the Ship," words and paintings by Kadir Nelson. Jacket illustration © 2008 by Kadir Nelson. Reprinted by permission of Disney. Hyperion Books, an imprint of Disney Book Group, LLC. All Rights reserved.)

multicultural literature can nudge readers to take action when social justice issues are explored in thought-provoking ways. If multicultural literature is to make a difference in our world, then the value of such books must go beyond the artifact of the book and extend to the way these books make a difference in the lives of the people who read them.

Identifying Multicultural Books

All multicultural books depict people of diverse cultures, but the degree to which such books focus on cultural or social issues varies significantly. It is not enough to count the diverse faces in a book; the important thing is how the members of various cultures are portrayed. There is a range of degrees of cultural specificity in books, from merely visual inclusion that shows diverse faces to books that are entirely based on specific cultural aspects. The full range of depicting diversity is needed, but books differ in the degree and the specificity of their emphasis and, accordingly, in the cultural understandings that they offer to the reader. In some books, people of different cultures are deliberately included so that the illustrations appear visually diverse, but the text does not specify that characters be of a particular culture. Diversity is incidentally depicted. In others, the culture is more than highlighted; it is central to the book. All details in the book focus on the culture. At the two ends of the continuum of specificity in depicting diversity are "culturally generic books" and "culturally specific books."

Culturally Generic Books

Culturally generic books are "generically American" in theme and plot (Sims Bishop, 1992). Sometimes, the inclusion of diversity appears to be merely incidental, and at other times, it purposefully and prominently features multicultural characters, but in all cases the theme remains generic to any culture. An example of a culturally generic book is *Emma's Rug* by Allen Say. In the story, Emma is an artistic child who finds inspiration by gazing at the shadows in a small white rug she has always had in her room. One day, her mother washes the rug, and Emma is sure that her inspiration can no longer be found in the very clean rug. Visually, Emma is portrayed as an Asian American child, but no details in the text identify Emma by a particular ethnicity. Emma's struggle is universal—one that children could experience regardless of their culture. Still, books that depict multicultural inclusiveness—even when the focus is not on any aspect of diversity—are important because they increase readers' exposure and awareness. In addition, books that show the universality of experiences allow students to find connections across cultures.

Culturally Specific Books

Culturally specific books illuminate the experience of members of a particular cultural group (Sims Bishop, 1992). The nuances of daily life are captured accurately, reflecting language use, attitudes, values, and beliefs of members of the group portrayed. Such details add texture to the writing, making the stories more real and more believable and therefore making it more likely that readers will see the stories as authentic. An example of a culturally specific book is Mildred Taylor's *Roll of Thunder, Hear My Cry*. Not only are the descriptions of situations and events historically accurate, but the character names, the forms of address, the dialogue, and the interactions are true to the culture of the people whose lives are reflected.

Although they differ in the depth of the cultural experiences they provide to readers, the full range of inclusiveness in multicultural books contributes to readers' understandings of their own and others' cultures. Sometimes, readers see themselves and others as sharing universal experiences, and therefore cultural group membership need not be explicitly discussed. But it is culturally specific books that offer the insights necessary to truly further readers' understanding of different cultures.

Evolution of Multicultural Literature

From the time children's books were first published in this country until well after World War II, most reflected mainstream characters, settings, values, and lifestyles. Children usually learned to read from books that presented primarily European American lifestyles and values. People who did not resemble the so-called American ideal—people of African, Asian, Latino/a, and Southern European origins, as well as Native Americans—were regularly singled out for discrimination. Likewise, early portrayals of nonmainstream characters tended to be highly stereotypical. Such characters were portrayed as cute, savage, primitive, uncouth, untrustworthy, or underdeveloped. Since the late 1960s, increasing efforts have been made to include honest depictions of people from all cultural groups in children's books—not simply to talk about them, but to narrate their perspectives and experiences through their eyes and in their voices.

Although several individuals (for example, Augusta Baker, Virginia Lacy, and Charlemae Rollins) campaigned for inclusion of people of diversity in children's books before 1965, the wake-up call that made the U.S. public aware of the situation is usually considered to be Nancy Larrick's 1965 article in the *Saturday Review*, "The All-White World of Children's Books." In her study, Larrick found that only 6.7% of children's books published between 1962 and 1964 included any African Americans in illustrations or text, and just 0.9% depicted African Americans in contemporary settings. Other cultural groups were represented even less. The decade that followed saw an increase in the number of books that included people of diversity. The Council on Interracial Books for Children was founded in 1966 to heighten public awareness of diversity issues related to children's books. The Coretta Scott King Award was established in 1969 to give annual recognition to an African American author and an African American illustrator who contributed the most distinguished work during the previous year.

Larrick's study was replicated a decade later in order to examine how things had changed (Chall, Radwin, French, & Hall, 1985). The percentages had more than doubled: 14.4% of all children's books published from 1973 to 1975 included African Americans in text or illustrations, and 4% showed African Americans in contemporary settings. This increase was attributed in part to the civil rights movement, along with long overdue recognition of the inequities highlighted by Larrick and others. However, Rollock (1984) found that these increases were only temporary and that in the five years after the Chall study, between 1979 and 1984, only 1.5% of newly published children's books included African Americans. The politically conservative 1980s fostered a decline in the publication of multicultural literature.

Limited data are available on representation in children's books of groups other than African Americans. But sources such as the Council on Interracial Books for Children (1975), Nieto (1983), Schon (1988), and Sims (1985) indicate that there has been even less representation of groups such as Asian Americans, Native Americans, and Latinos/as. Quiroa (2004) notes that the numbers of Latino-themed books published in the United States comprised .02% of children's literature published between 1990 and 2000, and these numbers have not kept pace with the increases in this population. The Cooperative Children's Book Center of the University of Wisconsin has maintained annual statistics about the publication of African American literature since 1985, and statistics about the publication of literature by and about Asian Pacific Americans, American Indians, and Latinos since 1994. This information can be accessed on the center's Web site at <http://www.soemadison.wisc.edu/ccbc/pcstats.htm>.

The beginning of the 1990s saw the largest surge to date in multicultural publishing in the children's book field. Sims Bishop's (1991) note of optimism reflected a general increase in the level of awareness and understanding of the importance of multicultural literature. But despite the increase in numbers of multicultural publications, a study by Reimer (1992) revealed a lack of multicultural representation in popular booklists such as the International Reading Association's annual "Children's Choices" (the 1989 list was used in her study), Jim Trelease's *The New Read-Aloud Handbook* (1989), and former U.S. Secretary of Education William Bennett's list of recommended reading for elementary students (Bennett, 1988).

Other problems were highlighted in the early 1990s. Because of the predominance of European American writers and illustrators, multicultural literature was presented primarily from an "outside" perspective. Related to this problem was the fact that some Native Americans believed that mainstream authors had "stolen" stories without considering the cultural rules regarding who had access to those stories. Another problem was the grouping of related but distinctly separate cultures under one label (for example, labeling Mexican Americans, Puerto Rican Americans, and Cuban Americans as "Hispanic"). In addition, there was a lack of teacher awareness of the importance of including multiple cultural perspectives in the classroom (Harris, 1997; Reimer, 1992; Sims Bishop, 1992). Unfortunately, inaccuracies, stereotypes, tokenism, bias, language flaws, and narrowness of representation continued to plague some books (Barrera, Thompson, & Dressman, 1997).

Although the total number of multicultural books published has declined during the last decade in number <http://www.education.wisc.edu/ccbc/books/pcstats.asp>, authors, illustrators, publishers, and educators are paying more attention to the issues of "authenticity" that were raised in the early 1990s and before. And authors and illustrators from diverse cultures are accepting the call to create culturally authentic work. (Ironically, many had tried unsuccessfully to have their work published in earlier years. In numerous cases, it was the annual contest sponsored by the Council on Interracial Books for Children that led to the publication of books written by people from diverse cultures.) Today, publishers are seeking ways both to encourage new multicultural authors and to ensure authenticity in the books they produce. For example, Lee and Low Publishers sponsors a New Voices award and the winners receive a cash award and a contract for publishing their book. Librarians and reviewers are recognizing authenticity as a critical criterion in evaluating multicultural books. And teachers are working to include authentic multicultural books as featured reading materials in their classrooms. However, librarians and teachers should also look critically at the books from years past that are still found on the shelves of many school libraries and in classrooms. Although such books have value in specialized collections that allow people to see historic trends in the publication of multicultural books, teachers should make sure that young readers are not exposed to these books without some discussion of the damaging racist or stereotypical images they contain. In an interview by K. T. Horning (2008), Rudine Sims Bishop talks about African American literature being purposeful. "Sewn throughout the fiction are threads of African American history, mentions of African American heroes,

ILLUSTRATION 4.2 Readers learn about aviator Bessie Coleman as her family, friends, and others share their memories of her from various perspectives. (Scholastic, Inc.)

and references to African American music, so that there's a whole idea of making sure that Black children have a sense of the culture in which they live. It's that notion again of being teachy but not preachy, of giving information and trying to empower them without preaching at them." (p. 256) Despite the rise in African American literature from that of decades past, Sims Bishop still cautions reviewers to be sensitive to the historical context of African American literature and to take the context into consideration. She expresses hope for more quantity, availability, and marketing because they continue to be "perennially . . . underrepresented in the field."

Issues Related to Multicultural Literature

To evaluate the influence of multicultural literature on children's understanding of the world around them and to establish criteria for good multicultural literature, we need to consider several issues: (1) whether a work presents cultural details authentically, (2) whether the author writes from an inside or an outside perspective, (3) whether a work promotes stereotypes, and (4) which cultural group is being described in the work. Consideration of these issues can guide teachers in selecting multicultural literature and facilitating discussions of such literature among their students.

Cultural Authenticity

When a book presents a theme that is true to a culture and is filled with specific details that are authentic, members of that culture who read it feel that their experiences have been genuinely reflected and illuminated for others to share. Culturally authentic books are written by authors who have developed a "culturally conscious" way to "provide exceptional aesthetic experiences: [to] entertain, educate, and inform; and . . . engender racial pride" (Harris, 1990, p. 551). However, when a book distorts or misrepresents information about a culture, such misinformation leads to misunderstandings about that culture by those from other cultures and makes members of the misrepresented culture feel betrayed.

Examples of culturally authentic books are Carmen Lomas Garza's *In My Family/En mi familia* and her earlier book *Family Pictures/Cuadros de familia.* Based on the author's life in South Texas, these books include various paintings that illustrate events in her childhood, accompanied by bilingual text. In *Family Pictures/ Cuadros de familia,* the page entitled "Birthday Party/Cumpleaños" begins with "That's me hitting the piñata at my sixth birthday party." Following the English text is the Spanish translation: "Ésa soy yo, pegándole a la piñata en la fiesta que me dieron cuando cumplí seis años." Readers can identify specific details, such as the framed picture of the Last Supper, the flamenco dancers on the calendar, and the assembling of the tamales, all of which are culturally authentic. Through illustrations and text, *In My Family/En mi familia* tells about the making of empañadas, birthday barbecue parties, and summer dance time. Mexican American readers can feel a sense of kinship with the creator of such books—a sense of shared experiences and understandings. Readers outside the culture can gain new insights from these authentic depictions of the culture.

When a book lacks authenticity, it is likely to convey misleading images of a culture. Sometimes, the text gives readers a stereotyped or dated image of a culture; other times, confused illustrations depict a culture in inappropriate ways. Readers outside the portrayed culture might not be able to discern what is authentic and

ISSUE *to* CONSIDER

How Much Artistic License Should Be Given to Illustrators as They Create Images of a Culture?

Some illustrators argue that demands for absolute accuracy of every detail rob the illustrator of the right to use imagination and individual style in portraying an image. They contend that unless the illustrations are photographs, the style of illustration will influence the degree of attention to detail.

Others argue that accurate details in illustrations create the overall sense of cultural authenticity. They point out that misconceptions may develop from incorrect images. In some cases, highly regarded illustrators whose work is exceptional from an artistic viewpoint have been criticized for creating images that "mix" cultures. Critics say that this mixing of cultures robs each culture of its distinction. Yet the illustrators express their desire to create unified images of cultures that sometimes share a common voice. One example is *Brother*

Eagle, Sister Sky: A Message from Chief Seattle (1991) by Susan Jeffers. Controversy arose over the text because the words were based on a script for a 1971 television commercial decrying pollution. Controversy arose over the illustrations because of mixed images of Native American cultures that contained inaccuracies of both history and culture. Jeffers defended her position by stating that the important point is that the book reflects a Native American philosophy (Noll, 1995).

How do you view this issue of authenticity versus artistic license in children's book illustrations? How will the type of illustrations affect child readers who do not intimately know the culture portrayed? How will the illustrations affect child readers whose own cultures are portrayed?

What do you think?

what is not. In such cases, misinformed and inauthentic images continue to perpetuate and negatively influence readers' beliefs and understandings about that culture.

Perspective: Insider or Outsider

The perspective of the writer has become a major issue in multicultural literature: Does the author have an "inside" or an "outside" perspective on the culture being portrayed? An author with an inside perspective writes as a member of the culture and therefore is more likely to portray the cultural group authentically. An author with an outside perspective writes from a point of view of a nonmember of the group being portrayed. But even among those inside a culture, the range of cultural experiences and opinions regarding the depictions of the culture may vary, revealing the multidimensionality of any culture (Noll, 1995).

Members of the dominant culture have had multiple opportunities to see their world interpreted through eyes like their own. But they may not have had the experience of being wrongly portrayed, and therefore they may not know the feeling of betrayal at having their culture misrepresented. An outsider might miss the rhythm, accent, and flavor that enliven the ethnic experience for the insider audience. An outsider's interpretation of an ethnic experience may be filled with details that are factually accurate, but the presentation may be bland and dry, lacking the cultural nuances that would make it come alive. A simple missed or misrepresented detail may be enough to negate authenticity for members of the culture being portrayed (Kaplan, 1995).

In his article "Can We Fly across Cultural Gaps on the Wings of Imagination? Ethnicity, Experience, and Cultural Authenticity," Cai (1995) compares a novel by Laurence Yep, an insider of the Chinese culture, to one by Vanya Oakes, an outsider. Through detailed comparisons, Cai clearly outlines the differences between the inside and outside perspectives. Can those born outside a culture produce authentic material about that culture? Some say no. Others, such as scholar Henry Louis Gates, Jr., W. E. B. Du Bois Professor of Literature at Harvard, believe that an inside perspective can be gained by cultural outsiders. Gates believes that "no human culture is inaccessible to someone who makes the effort to understand, to learn, to inhabit

Ask *the* Author: Julius Lester

You must know how grateful readers are to you for rescuing the Uncle Remus stories from the patronizing traditions through which they came down to us. How did you find the original stories and the voice to tell them in? What was most challenging about it?

Retelling the Uncle Remus stories was relatively easy. It is a project that came naturally to me because I grew up in the southern black storytelling tradition and I had previously done retellings of stories in *Black Folktales* (1969) and *The Knee High Man* (1972). So, I don't know that there was anything especially challenging involved. It was a fun project and relatively easy to do.

As for how I did it, it has been quite a few years since I did those books, but as I recall they were the first books I did using a computer. This was back in 1986 or so.

The how of doing any book is essentially the same. Sit in the chair and work, work, work.

Julius Lester Born in St. Louis, Missouri, the son of a Methodist minister, Lester later converted to Judaism. Lester spent much of his childhood in the South of the 1940s and 1950s, where he dealt firsthand with Southern attitudes about race and segregation. In 1960, Lester graduated from Fisk University with a degree in English. He became politically active in the civil rights movement. In the mid-1960s, he joined SNCC, the Student Non-Violent Coordinating Committee, where he served as head of their photo department. Lester originally was a musician who recorded two albums, performed with Pete Seeger, Phil Ochs, and Judy Collins, and worked as a radio announcer in New York City. His first book, *The 12-String Guitar as Played by Leadbelly: An Instructional Manual*, dealt with black folk music. Most of Lester's earlier works were written for adults. In 1969, he published two works that established his success as a children's author. These two works were *To Be a Slave*, a Newbery Honor Book, and *Black Folktales*. His subsequent works continued to show his interest in African American history, folklore, and politics. Since the early 1970s, Lester has served as a professor at the University of Massachusetts at Amherst.

another world" (cited in Sims Bishop, 1992, p. 42). Certainly, stereotypes do not exist in all books by mainstream writers and illustrators that depict diversity. Good depictions can be found in the works of Ezra Jack Keats and Demi. Some, through their own life experiences and extensive research, have been able to create culturally authentic portrayals of a group different from the one into which they were born. Many African Americans view Arnold Adoff's writing as having an inside perspective, yet he is not African American. Many of his books, such as **black is brown is tan,** speak from his biracial family's experiences. Similarly, Demi's picture books, such as **The Empty Pot**, are set in China. Although Demi was not born Chinese, her thoroughness of research is evident, and readers who are Chinese find that her work reflects the perspective of insiders. Author Laura Krauss Melmed (1999) documents the thoroughness of research that she and illustrator Jim LaMarche completed in creating a picture book set in Japan, *Little Oh*.

Clearly, the issue of insider versus outsider authorship is complex. However, books that present authentic voices and images—no matter who created them—offer a uniquely valuable contribution to literature about a culture. They allow readers within the culture to enjoy the sense of kinship and pride that come from having one's own experience accurately portrayed. They also broaden the perspective of readers from other cultures and offer them fresh insights about the cultural group depicted.

Stereotyping and Other Unacceptable Depictions of Cultural Groups

When a single set of attributes is assigned to an entire cultural group, diversity and individuality are overlooked, and stereotyping results. A stereotyped impression of a cultural group may be created by how characters are portrayed, how characters interact with one another, how a book's setting is described, how a theme is treated, or simply how information is conveyed. It is important to remember, though, that stereotypes often originate in some kernel of behavior that is true to a culture. How do we distinguish between details that make up cultural specificity and globalized stereotypes? Usually, negative (but sometimes positive) attributes that are assumed always to be true simply because of their association with a cultural group are stereotypes. It is sometimes very difficult to distinguish between cultural details and stereotypes. One way to make this distinction is by finding out whether members of the cultural group embrace that attribute as defining themselves.

ILLUSTRATION 4.3 Pablo goes about his town near Oaxaca, Mexico, gathering special food and preparing for the big festivities of The Day of The Dead. (Used by permission of HarperCollins Publishers.)

In the past, literature often depicted nonmainstream cultures in patronizing and condescending ways. Stereotypes abounded in images created by mainstream writers and illustrators. Books such as the 1899 book by Bannerman, *The Story of Little Black Sambo,* and Bishop's 1938 *The Five Chinese Brothers* presented negative and stereotyped images of blacks and Asians, respectively. Although *The Story of Little Black Sambo* is set in India, the illustrations in the original edition depict negative caricatures of African Americans. The story line of *The Five Chinese Brothers* requires that the brothers look alike; however, the book depicts all the Chinese people of the village as identical and with yellow skin. Some more recent books are also controversial because of their stereotyped images. Despite the explanations at the end of the book that document distinctions among ten of the tribes, Native Americans believe that Virginia Grossman and Sylvia Long's 1991 book, *Ten Little Rabbits,* is problematic. Too often, Native American characters are portrayed as animals or depicted as something to be "counted," perpetuating the myth that all Native American people are alike—in this case, "they just wear different blankets" (McCarty, 1995). Stereotyped images of Latinos were identified by the influential (but now defunct) Council on Interracial Books for Children in 1974 and includes "Mexican men wearing wide-brimmed hats snoozing under a giant cactus" and images of "sarapes, piñatas, burros, bare feet, and broken English."

Many books that present stereotypical images of a cultural group are still in print and may be on the shelf of your local bookstore, school library, or public library. Sometimes, adults purchase these books because they remember them from their childhood and want to share them with young children. However, having loved a book as a child is not in itself an adequate selection criterion, unless you are prepared to take advantage of this teachable moment to discuss stereotypes in older books that represent dominant cultural mores of those times. Ginny Moore Kruse, Director of the Cooperative Children's Book Center at the University of Wisconsin, Madison, cautions against the use of materials that contain "hurtful images" or perpetuate erroneous information about cultures (1991/1997).

In recent years, efforts have been made to remedy stereotyped images in old stories by publishing new versions of these stories. Sometimes, the original author/illustrator team creates the revised version, as in the case of a story set in Alaska titled *On Mother's Lap,* written by Ann Herbert Scott and illustrated by Glo Coalson. Margaret Mahy provided new text for *The Seven Chinese Brothers,* which was illustrated by Jean and Mou-sien Tseng. Julius Lester and Jerry Pinkney collaborated in the creation of *Sam and the Tigers,* a retelling of the Sambo story in the African American tradition. In *The Story of Little Babaji,* Fred Marcellino re-illustrated

Helen Bannerman's original text for the Sambo story, renaming the characters with Indian names and depicting the setting in India, as the text indicates. Khorana (1996) asserts that the stereotype now has moved from caricatures of African Americans to reflect British colonialism in illustrations that depict the boy (Little Babaji) as a royal maharajah instead of a village boy as the story indicates. Khorana reports that "cultural details are used for their exotic appeal and are inconsistent with the professional and socioeconomic status of the family in the story."

Identification of Cultural Groups

For some time, there has been ongoing discussion as to which groups should be included under the "multicultural literature" umbrella. African Americans, Asian Americans, Latinos/as, and Native Americans are always included. An extensive bibliography at the end of this chapter lists recommended books that represent these cultural groups. As our population shifts to include less represented groups, their stories are also needed. For example, Muslim Americans are seldom found in ethnic American literature. There are other groups outside the mainstream that have also been underrepresented and misrepresented in children's literature and therefore deserve attention as teachers and librarians evaluate and select multicultural literature. Reading and discussing books that are culturally and historically distinct helps readers gain insights that "mainstream" literature alone cannot provide.

Jewish Americans. Because of the years of oppression and misrepresentation they have experienced, attention needs to be given to books that authentically reflect the history, religion, and culture of Jewish people. Books such as Lois Lowry's *Number the Stars* share an important part of Jewish history with readers who may or may not be familiar with the Holocaust. The story is about both a strong friendship and people who help others who are facing unjust treatment. The specific circumstances focus on the Danish resistance to the Holocaust, but the themes are universal.

Some contemporary works are important in that they offer possibilities for understanding the lives of Jewish Americans today. Patricia Polacco tells of her own Jewish Russian family's heritage and traditions in most of her books, including *The Keeping Quilt.* Passing on the traditions of her heritage is the important theme of this book, which is filled with such cultural markers as a babushka and a wedding huppa.

Other religious groups, such as the Amish and Mennonites, are also misunderstood and need better representation. In Sarah Stewart's *The Journey,* a young Amish girl makes a trip to the city of Chicago. Although it is quite improbable that two Amish women would travel to a city merely for sightseeing, the comparisons and contrasts of the city to the girl's home show readers how differently we view a world outside our own experiences. Raymond Bial's informational books such as *Amish Home* and *Visit to Amish Country* also help readers to understand the Amish world through nonfiction descriptions.

Appalachian Americans. Another group that has historically been underrepresented in children's literature is the people of the Appalachian region of the United States, who have a distinct culture and way of life. Cynthia Rylant, George Ella Lyon, and Gloria Houston have written books that authentically reflect this group's experiences. In Gloria Houston's *My Great-Aunt Arizona,* for example, details of the schoolhouse are accurately depicted. Also, the fact that five generations of the family in the book attended the same school and had Aunt Arizona as their teacher is typical of real-life Appalachian families of the era. *The Relatives Came* by Cynthia Rylant reflects the universal experience of family members coming together for a reunion. However, that experience takes on a special meaning from the fact that Appalachian people are separated from their neighbors by mountains and therefore often live in relative isolation. Both text and illustrations support the sense of distance traveled along small mountain roads. But it is the activities of the family—"hugging and eating and breathing together"—that give readers vivid insight into the experience.

Two books that offer authentic historic fiction are *Spitting Image* and *Ghost Girl*. In Shutta Crum's *Spitting Image*, twelve-year-old Jessie's concern for the well-being of her family and that of her neighbors leads her to be a helpful informant for a government program intended to offer assistance to those in poverty. But her plan to help others backfires and national publicity portrays the people she loves in a negative light that brings them embarrassment and shame. Likewise, *Ghost Girl* by Delia Ray is set in the Blue Ridge Mountains, and the extreme poverty of the region results in a lack of resources for the community. When President and Mrs. Hoover build a school and April hopes for her first real chance to attend one, she must face opposing forces in her mother, who does not approve her enrolling in a school, and her grandmother, who wants April to get her education. Issues such as this one are always complicated by other matters, and in this case, it is the death (and the untold secret about the death) of a sibling that must be dealt with.

European Americans. European American cultures have been excluded from the multicultural umbrella because they generally have been well represented in the literature. Because such literature most frequently depicted a generic American experience, not much separate attention was given to European American cultures. Therefore, although literature about European American cultural groups does not need the corrective attention that misrepresented or underrepresented groups might call for, teachers and librarians should not overlook books that give insight into the experiences of specific European American cultures. More recent stories from Europe have culturally and historically specific details that distinguish them from culturally generic stories of mainstream life. *Girl of Kosovo* by Alice Mead is an example of a book that is about the ethnic cleansing war that took place in Kosovo in 1999, seen from the point of view of eleven-year-old Zana, who wonders why the world sends reporters to record the devastation and death, but not give help to her people. Books like this one depict a culturally distinct experience and should be considered as meeting the goals for multicultural literature.

Muslim Americans and the Middle East. The Muslims in America and in the Middle East have long been underrepresented. In Naomi Shihab Nye's *Habibi,* biracial Liyana explores what it means to move to Jerusalem as a teenager when she has been raised in St. Louis, and recounts how she struggles to understand cultural differences and the way they affect her identity. Books like Mary Hoffman's *The Color of Home* show readers that despite language barriers, the basic human need to communicate about things that are important to each of us—home, family, community—can be done through illustration and interpreters. In her *Breadwinner* trilogy, Deborah Ellis explores what it means to be a female child, living in modern-day Afghanistan under the Taliban regime. In *The Breadwinner,* eleven-year-old Parvana hides her gender identity in order to obtain a job to feed her family when her father is suddenly taken away. In *Parvana's Journey,* after her father's death, she sets out to find her missing family. *Mud City* switches to the story of Parvana's friend, Shauzia, and describes how she survives life in the streets as she longs to escape to France.

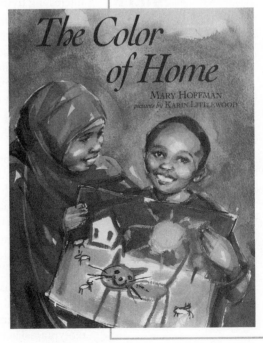

ILLUSTRATION 4.4   A new child from Somalia finds a way to communicate with his classmates through his drawing of his homeland. (*"The Color of Home"* by Mary Hoffman, illustrated by Karin Littlewood. Used with permission by Penguin Group (USA). All rights reserved.)

Criteria for Evaluating and Selecting Multicultural Literature

With the growth in the number of multicultural books, it is important to select those of high quality. Naturally, when judging the quality of multicultural books, a teacher should apply the criteria for evaluating the various genres of children's literature that are discussed throughout this text. In addition, there are specific questions to consider regarding multicultural books:

- Do the author and illustrator present authentic perspectives?
- Is the culture portrayed multidimensionally?
- Are cultural details naturally integrated?
- Are details accurate and is the interpretation current?
- Is language used authentically?
- Is the collection balanced?

Do the Author and Illustrator Present Authentic Perspectives?

The author should maintain an insider's mindset and point of view when writing about a cultural group in order to portray it authentically. Voices such as Patricia Polacco's and Pat Mora's convey an insider's perspective because these authors write of experiences based on their own heritage. Polacco's *The Keeping Quilt* and Mora's *A Birthday Basket for Tía* both tell of the authors' personal lives. However, as we discussed earlier in this chapter, the crucial issue is not heritage by fact of birth, but whether the author thinks as a member of the group or as an outsider looking in. Careful research and experience living within the culture contribute to Demi's insider voice in a book such as *Liang and the Magic Paintbrush.* Outsider perspective that offers authentic portrayals include contemporary photo essays such as those by Diane Hoyt-Goldsmith, in which she depicts the daily lives of children who have a particularly strong ethnic heritage. Her subjects vary from Vietnamese Americans to different Native American tribes, but in each case, she offers as true a portrayal as possible, highlighting things that would be interesting to those both within and outside the culture.

Illustrations should be accurate, true to the time period portrayed, and culturally authentic. They must not stereotype, homogenize, or ridicule any cultural group. Racial groups should be depicted with a variety of physical features that are not overemphasized. Illustrations play a major role in transmitting cultural images, especially in picture books. Often, a book's cover illustration sends an immediate message about the book's perspective.

Is the Culture Portrayed Multidimensionally?

Cultural groups should be presented multidimensionally to help readers realize the depth and breadth of experiences within cultures. For example, *El Chino,* a biography of Billy Wong by Allen Say, tells the story of a son of Chinese immigrants who became a bullfighter despite the expectations others had of him. To pursue his dream, he had to clash with those expectations. Others said, "Who's ever heard of a Chinese athlete?" and "Only the Spaniards can become true matadors." But he remembered what his father had said: "In America, you can be anything you want to be." Presenting a culture's multidimensionality means portraying the members of that culture in a range of ways. A book should especially be free of any tokenism, in which cultures might be represented only in order to give a head count for politically correct inclusion.

Cultural groups should not be presented through images that could lead to stereotyping. There is no particular experience that is so universal that it can be defined

TOP SHELF 4.2

GROWING UP IN A WORLD OF POLITICAL OR SOCIAL UNREST

Before We Were Free by Julia Alvarez

Girl of Kosovo by Alice Mead

Grab Hands and Run by Frances Temple

The Other Side of Truth by Beverley Naidoo

Red Scarf Girl by Ji Li Jiang

Zlata's Diary: A Child's Life in Sarajevo by Zlata Filipovec as "The _____ Experience." Rather, multiple dimensions of all cultures should be presented objectively, without bias. Roles of cultural members should also be varied, as in Mildred Pitts Walter's *Justin and the Best Biscuits in the World,* in which the African American grandfather serves as an important role model for his ten-year-old grandson. During a visit to his grandfather's ranch, Justin discovers that cowboys must become self-sufficient by learning to do the jobs that Justin had earlier deemed were "women's work."

Are Cultural Details Naturally Integrated?

The cultural details necessary to make a story come alive should not impede the flow of the story. These details should be presented in context so that cumbersome explanations are not necessary. If longer explanations are needed, footnotes or endnotes can serve to clarify. Laurence Yep's *Dragon's Gate* is filled with cultural details. The hardships endured, the power relationships and the actions they lead to, the dialogues among the Chinese workers, and the dialogues between the Chinese workers and their white bosses are all described with a completeness that gives readers insight into the lives of the men who left their families behind in the hope of getting rich in a foreign land. These details are necessary for readers to deepen their understanding and empathy.

Are Details Accurate and Is the Interpretation Current?

Details must be accurate and true to the situation in which they are presented. Factual errors, omissions, and changes may indicate sloppy research and presentation. Sometimes, these problems may actually reflect an attempt on the author's part to meet the expectations of a mainstream readership that has preconceived notions of cultures. Series books that focus on children in various countries are sometimes guilty of such intentional errors. One book featuring a child in the Netherlands included all the preconceived images that mainstream readers might expect to find: A blonde girl wakes up, puts on her wooden shoes, and passes a windmill and a field of tulips on her way to school!

There are also series books that are written according to a formula, such as books about other countries in which authors fill in the blanks of standardized formats. In many cases, these authors have no firsthand experience with the country they are discussing. Currency of interpretation can sometimes be evaluated by considering how recently the book was published and assessing the thoroughness of the revision. Books that claim to cite "current" statistics should be carefully analyzed to determine whether the statistic reported is still appropriate, years after the book is published. Sometimes, the interpretation of factual information is more influential than the facts themselves. The author's understanding of the culture determines his or her choice of words, which

TEACHING IDEA 4.1

CONNECT BOOKS WITH SIMILAR THEMES, ACROSS DIFFERING CULTURES

Present a set of books that have similar themes, but represent different cultures. Examples of themes are the search for freedom, immigration, coming of age, friendships/peer relationships, and intergenerational relationships. Have children realize the universality of many themes, but also how the details of the stories differ if they are culturally bound. For example, collect immigrant stories. Be sure to include stories of immigrants who came through Ellis Island generations ago, immigrants who came more recently under dangerous circumstances, and recent immigrants who are fortunate enough to freely travel back and forth to their homelands. Consider the variety of reasons and ways in which people have immigrated to the United States. Find similarities in their experiences as well as differences. Share books like *Grandfather's Journey* by Allen Say that speak to nearly every first-generation immigrant's feelings when it closes, "As soon as I am in one place, I'm homesick for the other."

TEACHING IDEA 4.2

IDENTIFY CULTURAL MARKERS

Cultural markers are found in culturally authentic books. They are the details that are true to a culture—artifacts, character behavior, language use, and physical descriptions. Select a picture book that includes many cultural markers and have children list all that they encounter in either the text or the illustrations. Remove the cultural markers and retell the story without the details that make the story rooted in a specific culture. Discuss how the details personalized the story to a specific culture. Try substituting equivalent details from another culture, and consistently make those changes throughout the story (names, places, language, foods, etc.). Some students may want to try their hand at re-illustrating the story to fit the revised version. See if they can include illustration details that are also culturally specific.

in turn influences the readers' perceptions. For example, reference to a Japanese father as "honorable father" is a literal translation of the word *otoosan*. The "o" at the beginning of the word for *father* denotes the honoring of the person addressed. However, constantly referring to each adult as "honorable" may lead readers to an exaggerated, stereotypical view that is not in keeping with the actual personal interactions described in the story.

Is Language Used Authentically?

The language and dialect spoken by characters should authentically portray the kinds of interactions that are typical of those characters, and terminology that refers to aspects of culture should be acceptable by contemporary standards. For example, Gary Soto writes from the perspective of a Mexican American who grew up in California. Readers who have a background similar to his sense a true voice of their experiences. In his book *Pacific Crossing,* Soto portrays two teenage Mexican American boys as foreign exchange students in Japan. Soto uses terminology and phrases that Mexican Americans might use to communicate with each other. He also follows the Japanese language's very strict rules of verbal exchange, which take into consideration the gender, the age, and the familiarity of the speakers. Spanish-speaking readers often note that when English language books insert the Spanish word, but then follow it up in English, that "double word use" is unnatural and inauthentic.

Is the Collection Balanced?

It is important to present children with a balanced collection of multicultural books. The term "collection" refers to the books that are available in a school, classroom, or public library as well as the books selected to serve as teaching units within a classroom. Budget constraints, space limitations, and the need to present readers with the best possible choices make careful decisions regarding book collections a necessity. Readers need to be able to find recommended books readily, not buried under an avalanche of mediocre books. It is generally accepted that purchasing multiple copies of excellent books is better than including mediocre books simply to increase the size of the collection. Because a great number of high-quality multicultural books are available today, there is no need to include books simply to fulfill a quota.

To compile a balanced multicultural collection, a teacher or librarian should assess needs and match available quality books with those identified needs. In assessing needs, consideration should be given to (1) readers' preferences, (2) existing multicultural books in the collection, (3) curricular needs, (4) the availability of quality multicultural books, and (5) provision of a strong selection across genres. In addition, the compiler should ensure that adequate numbers of books are available for recreational reading, for teacher read-alouds, and for placement in the classroom library.

Consider Readers' Preferences. Both teachers and librarians need to acquire an understanding of the general background knowledge and the preferences of the readers for whom the particular collection is being developed, including the range of materials they enjoy and the types of books they choose. Often, children will be interested in reading books about their own cultural group, but that is not always the case. Some readers will voluntarily read books about other cultural groups; others might need to be introduced to and encouraged to select such books.

Survey Multicultural Books Already in the Collection. Multicultural books that are already in the collection form the core of the collection and help to determine what is needed. Overselecting or underselecting certain types of books can be avoided by conducting a careful inventory of existing books in the collection. Is there an

TOP SHELF 4.3

IMMIGRANT STORIES

Grandfather's Journey by Allen Say

In the Year of the Boar and Jackie Robinson by Bette Bao Lord

Journey of the Sparrows by Fran Leeper Buss

overabundance of folktales from various cultures? Are there enough contemporary stories about people of diversity? Are there books that show multiple perspectives? Familiarity with the existing collection also enables a teacher or librarian to weed out and discard books that are not culturally appropriate.

Assess Curricular Needs. It is important to assess curricular needs to determine what is needed to supplement units of study. Literature-based curriculum calls for high-quality books to be used in all curricular areas. As teachers and librarians work together to obtain books that fit the needs of the curriculum, they should attempt to include books that extend beyond the basic information and enhance multicultural understanding.

Determine the Availability of High-Quality Multicultural Books. Determine the availability of quality multicultural books because no matter what the needs are, only high-quality books should be considered. Obtaining lower-quality books simply to fill a shelf is not recommended.

Provide a Strong Selection Across Genres. Another goal in establishing a balanced collection of multicultural books is to provide a variety of different genres. For example, when creating a collection of books about Mexico, the teacher or librarian should make a point to include folklore, history, informational books, picture books, historical fiction, biography, poetry, and modern realistic fiction. There should be books set in Mexico as well as books about Mexican Americans. The books must represent a broad range of experiences and voices if readers are to understand the diverse nature of Mexico and its people.

Awards for Multicultural Literature

Multicultural books qualify for all of the general awards that are given to children's literature, such as the Caldecott, Newbery, or Sibert Medals. Several multicultural books have been recipients of such awards. For example, Ed Young was presented the Caldecott Medal for *Lon Po Po: A Red-Riding Hood Story from China.* Linda Sue Park was presented the Newbery Medal for *A Single Shard.* The same year, An Na was presented the Sibert Medal for *A Step from Heaven.* Such recognitions have caused some to question the continuation of ethnicity-based awards (Aronson, 2001). However, the need for awards that are designated specifically for the purpose of examining and awarding books and their creators for the criteria of cultural depiction continues. Awards are sometimes given to previously unpublished authors and illustrators to encourage the writing and illustrating of books on multicultural subjects, and have played an important role in launching the careers of authors and illustrators. Awards provide public recognition for a book, author, or illustrator and serve as selection and evaluation tools.

ILLUSTRATION 4.5 Children can share in other countries' heritages by reading folktales from those cultures, such as *Lon Po Po*, the Chinese "Little Red Riding Hood." ("*Lon Po Po*" by Ed Young. Used by permission of Penguin Group (USA), Inc. All Rights Reserved.)

The Coretta Scott King Award

At an American Library Association conference in 1969, after lamenting the fact that a "minority" author or illustrator had never been awarded the Newbery or Caldecott Medal, school librarians Mabel McKissick and Glyndon Greer were encouraged by publisher John Carroll to launch a new award highlighting the accomplishments of African American authors and illustrators. The award was named in honor of Coretta Scott King to "commemorate the life and work of Martin Luther King, Jr." as well as to honor his wife for "courage and determination in continuing to work for peace and brotherhood" (Smith, 2004). The Coretta Scott King Award has been presented at the annual meeting of the American Library Association since 1972 and has been recognized as an official ALA award since 1982. Selection criteria for the award have evolved with the increase in the number of books from which to choose. In the beginning, any book that reflected some aspect of the black experience or embraced concepts of brotherhood was considered. In recent years, however, the criteria have become more stringent and now specify that "recipients are African American authors and illustrators whose distinguished books promote an understanding and appreciation of the culture and contribution of all people to the realization of the 'American dream.'"

Since 1993, the Genesis Award certificate of recognition has been given to African American authors and illustrators who show significant promise in their work. Basic criteria for this award are the same as for the Coretta Scott King Award, but winners can have no more than three published works.

The Pura Belpré Award

The Pura Belpré Award, established in 1996, is sponsored jointly by Reforma (a national association to promote library services to Spanish speakers) and the American Library Association's Association of Library Services to Children. It is awarded biannually to a Latino/a writer and illustrator whose work best depicts and celebrates Latino heritage. A complete list of past winners can be found in the Appendix.

Tomás Rivera Mexican American Children's Book Award

This award was established in 1995 at Texas State University—San Marcos, in honor of a distinguished alumnus who published widely on topics relevant to the lives of Mexican Americans. It is awarded annually to the author/illustrator of the book selected as the most distinguished book of the previous publication year that authentically reflects the lives of Mexican American children and young adults in the southwestern United States. A complete list of past winners can be found in the Appendix.

The Américas Book Award for Children's and Young Adult Literature

This award was established in 1993 and is sponsored by the National Consortium of Latin American Studies Programs, a United States Department of Education National Resource Center housed at the University of Wisconsin. Winners and commended titles are announced annually to recognize works that were published in either English or Spanish in the previous publication year and that portray Latin America, the Caribbean, or Latinos in the United States authentically and engagingly. The intent is to focus on cultural heritage and to acknowledge the link of the Americas. In addition to recognizing literary merit, exceptional design, and cultural context, the potential for classroom use is considered. A complete list of past winners can be found in the Appendix.

The Asian Pacific American Literary Award

The Asian Pacific American Award for Literature was presented for the first time in 2001 by the National Conference on Asian Pacific American Librarians. It is given every three years to Asian Pacific American writers in three categories, one of which is literature for children and young adults. Authors of fiction and nonfiction books are eligible, and both the author and the illustrator of picture books are jointly eligible.

The American Indian Youth Literature Award

This award was created to identify and honor the best books written and illustrated by and about American Indians. Books are to depict American Indians in the "fullness of their humanity, in either past or present contexts." Every two years, up to three books can be recognized for the award in the following categories: Best Picture Book, Best Middle School Book, and Best Young Adult Book. The first awards were named in 2006.

The Jane Addams Children's Book Award

Since 1953, the Jane Addams Children's Book Award has been presented annually by the Women's International League for Peace and Freedom (WILPF) and the Jane Addams Peace Association to the children's book published during the preceding year that most effectively promotes the cause of peace, social justice, and world community. A picture book category was added in 1993. The award honors Jane Addams, who in 1931 became the first woman to win the Nobel Peace Prize. The Jane Addams Peace Association was founded for the purpose of promoting understanding among the people of the world, with the goal of avoiding wars and living in peace. A complete list of past winners can be found in the Appendix.

Although the numbers have decreased in recent years, more multicultural books were published in the last decade than in any previous decade. Thus, teachers and parents have both the opportunity and the responsibility to select high-quality multicultural books. In her book *Against Borders,* Hazel Rochman (1993) suggests that teachers and parents look for books that fight against the idea of borders that separate people and seek out books that help readers tear down those borders by enabling them to understand people around the world.

Educators' Roles in Presenting Multiple and Diverse Perspectives

It is important for educators to read a wide variety of books. Personal reading of high-quality adult books depicting diverse perspectives enhances our understanding of the world. In addition, professional reading offers teachers theories on why reading a broad range of books is helpful and often provides suggestions for how to expand the canon. Reading children's books allows teachers to identify texts appropriate in content and level for the children with whom they will be shared. All in all, educators who are committed to sharing diverse perspectives have many opportunities for reading at the personal and professional levels. To read more about international books, see Chapter 5.

Understanding Diverse Perspectives through Adult Literature

Reading is important both to enhance current understandings and to add new perspectives on the world. Teachers frequently seek out books that provide such reading experiences for their students. But it is also important for teachers to read adult books so that they can better understand diverse perspectives, too. A children's book offers a certain level of insight into diversity. A young adult book allows more space and time to reflect on issues. But an adult book allows readers to think about these issues in even greater depth.

Research indicates that students frequently relate best to a teacher's messages when the students' cultural background is similar to that of the teacher (Au, 1993; Delpit, 1988). Teachers understand the world from their own cultural perspectives, and it is impossible to share the background of each of their students. One way in which teachers can try to build their understanding is by joining a discussion group that examines adult books depicting diverse viewpoints; such discussions take the understandings gained from reading to a deeper level. By building their own understanding, teachers can enhance their ability to facilitate discussions of literature with their students.

Understanding Diverse Perspectives through Professional Literature

Teachers can choose from a variety of professional materials dealing with literature that reflects diversity. Such professional materials discuss the importance of reading multicultural literature; recommend criteria for evaluation and selection; and present methods for discussing and eliciting responses to the literature. Often, there are annotated bibliographies to help teachers identify books that may interest students. Professional materials promote an understanding of the critical role teachers play in making multicultural literature accessible to children.

Helping Children Gain Diverse Perspectives

It is generally accepted that children's reading choices are often based on recommendations of peers and influential adults. Therefore, teachers, library media specialists, and other influential adults have a responsibility to be knowledgeable about books that offer a wide variety of perspectives.

Teachers can help to ensure that their students gain a variety of perspectives by keeping diversity in mind when they are selecting reading material for the whole class and when they are deciding what choices to offer to students in literature circles and for individual free choice reading. The importance of the school librarian or media specialist in acting as a consultant to both the teacher and individual students in choosing reading materials cannot be overlooked.

Here are some steps that lead to a richer sense of the role reading about diversity plays in children's developing an understanding of the world in which they live:

1. Begin by being inclusive when collecting books for the classroom library. This makes multicultural books accessible to all students.
2. Read multicultural books aloud to the class and/or choose them as book selections for literature circles. Then facilitate a discussion in which students have opportunities to consider their own ideas about diversity and to learn by engaging in talk with each other.
3. Connect various multicultural books to each other in order to deepen thematic understanding.
4. Make an action plan for putting into practice a commitment to making a difference in the world by becoming advocates and activists.

EXPERIENCES FOR FURTHER LEARNING

Storytelling is popular throughout the world, and many cultures have unique ways of telling stories. Select a story to tell, study the culture's storytelling style, and practice presenting the story to others. Resources that may be of help include Anne Pellowski's *Hidden Stories in Plants*, *Family Story-Telling Handbook,* and *The Story Vine*. Be sure to visit the resources at the Web site: <http://www.ala.org/ala/alsc/alscresources/forlibrarians/StorytellingResources.htm> and Web sites of storytelling publishers such as August House.

RECOMMENDED BOOKS

* indicates a picture book; I indicates interest level
(P = preschool, YA = young adult)

Multicultural literature and literature portraying various types of diversity can be found throughout this textbook. These lists represent a sampling of recommended books. In particular, Chapter 9, "Contemporary Realistic Fiction," includes titles that depict realistic portrayals of people of diversity. A list of recommended books can be found at the end of that chapter.

African and African American

*Aardema, Verna. *Who's in Rabbit's House? A Masai Tale.* Illustrated by Leo Dillon and Diane Dillon. Dial, 1977. Rabbit's friends try to get rid of a mysterious Long One that is occupying Rabbit's House—and the solution is a surprising one. The illustrations portray this story as a play, acted out by Masai wearing masks. (I: P–8)

*Adoff, Arnold, ed. *My Black Me: A Beginning Book of Black Poetry.* Dutton, 1974/1994. This anthology opens with Adoff's words "This book of Black is for you." Poets such as Langston Hughes, Lucille Clifton, Nikki Giovanni, and Imamu Amiri Baraka contributed to the anthology. (I: 9–YA)

Alexander, Elizabeth and Marilyn Nelson. *Miss Crandall's School for Young Ladies and Little Misses of Color.* Illustrated by Floyd Cooper. Wordsong/Boyds Mills, 2007. In highly prejudiced 1830s Connecticut, Miss Crandall accepts African American women into her school, believing in their right to an education. (I: 10–YA)

Brimner, Larry Dane. *We Are One: The Story of Bayard Rustin.* Calkins Creek, 2007. Bayard Rustin's commitment to nonviolent activism and his perseverance are portrayed in this informational book. (I: 9–13)

*Bryan, Ashley. *Ashley Bryan: Words to My Life's Song.* Atheneum, 2009. Bryan's autobiography is a celebration of his love of art, nature and community, told in scrapbook album style. (I: All ages)

Cameron, Ann. *Gloria's Way.* Illustrated by Lil Toft. Foster/Farrar, 2000. Six warm-hearted short stories are about Gloria and her parents and friends Julian, Huey, and Latisha from Cameron's earlier books. See also *The Stories Julian Tells* (1981), *The Stories Huey Tells* (1995), etc. (I: 6–8)

*Cooper, Floyd. *Coming Home: From the Life of Langston Hughes.* Philomel, 1994. This picture book biography of the African American poet describes his childhood and his search for "home." (I: 7–10)

*Crews, Donald. *Bigmama's.* Greenwillow, 1991. This is an autobiographical story about going to "Bigmama's" house and visiting with relatives in the summertime during Donald Crews's youth. Also by Crews is *Shortcut* (1992). (I: P–8)

Curtis, Christopher Paul. *The Watsons Go to Birmingham–1963.* Delacorte, 1995. The Watsons are an African American family from Flint, Michigan. Their 1963 summer visit to Grandmother in Alabama changes their lives dramatically. (I: 10–YA)

*Diakité, Penda. *I Lost My Tooth in Africa.* Illustrated by Baba Wagué Diakité. Scholastic, 2006. When Amina loses her tooth on vacation in Mali, she hides it under a calabash and the tooth fairy brings her a chicken. (I: P–7)

*Elliott, Zetta. *Bird.* Illustrated by Shadra Strickland. Lee & Low, 2008. Bird, nickname for a young African American boy, relies on his love of drawing as he deals with trying to make sense of his older brother's drug addiction and the death of his grandfather. (I: 8–11)

*Evans, Shane. *Underground.* Roaring Brook, 2011. A nighttime escape of slaves heading to freedom is depicted through poetic, brief text and symbolic illustrations. (I: 6–10)

Feelings, Tom. *The Middle Passage: White Ships Black Cargo.* Dial, 1995. This wordless book dramatically depicts the hardships of the journey across the Atlantic Ocean made by Africans bound for slavery in America. (I: 10–YA)

*———. *Soul Looks Back in Wonder.* Dial, 1993. Feelings created the stunning art, which is accompanied by the voices of noted poets, including Maya Angelou, Langston Hughes, and Lucille Clifton, who write of their African American heritage. (I: 9–YA)

*Flournoy, Valerie. *The Patchwork Quilt.* Illustrated by Jerry Pinkney. Dial, 1985. As Tanya helps her mother and grandmother create a quilt from the scraps of their family's clothes, she comes to realize the stories and memories the quilt holds. A sequel is *Tanya's Reunion* (1995). (I: 6–9)

*Giovanni, Nikki. *Spin a Soft Black Song*. Illustrated by George Martins. HarperCollins, 1971/1985. This is a collection of poems reflecting African American children's everyday thoughts in their own voices. (I: 6–10)

Govenar, Alan (collector and editor). *Osceola: Memories of a Sharecropper's Daughter*. Illustrated by Shane W. Evans. Jump at the Sun/Hyperion, 2000. In her straightforward and personal voice, Osceola Mays recalls a childhood in the early 1900s as a sharecropper's daughter. (I: 8–12)

*Greenfield, Eloise. *Honey, I Love and Other Love Poems*. Illustrated by Diane Dillon and Leo Dillon. Harper, 1978. These poems, narrated by a young African American girl, tell of love and friendship. (I: 7–9)

*Grimes, Nikki. *My Man Blue: Poems*. Illustrated by Jerome Lagarrigue. Dial, 1999. Damon, a boy without a father, and Blue, a man who lost his son to the streets, form a unique friendship and bond with each other. (I: 6–9)

*_____. *Talkin' About Bessie: The Story of Aviator Elizabeth Coleman*. Illustrated by E. B. Lewis. Orchard/Scholastic, 2002. Following her funeral, various people reflect on their memories of who Bessie Coleman was through monologues that reveal many sides of her. (I: 7 and up)

Hamilton, Virginia. *Her Stories: African American Folktales, Fairy Tales, and True Tales*. Illustrated by Leo and Diane Dillon. Scholastic, 1995. This collection of stories is about women in African American folktales, fairy tales, animal stories, supernatural tales, legends, and biographical accounts. (I: 9–YA)

_____. *M. C. Higgins, the Great*. Macmillan, 1974. M. C. has to reconcile his love for his mountain home with its pending destruction by a slag heap. (I: 10–12)

*Hill, Laban Carrick. *Dave the Potter: Artist, Poet, Slave*. Illustrated by Bryan Collier. Little, Brown and Co., 2010. At a time when it was illegal for slaves to read and write, Dave perseveres and fights the odds with his ability to write poetry and create beautiful pottery. (I: 7 and up)

*Hoffman, Mary. *The Color of Home*. Illustrated by Karin Littlewood. Fogelman/Penguin, 2002. Hassan, a recent immigrant from Somalia, has an interpreter to help him communicate about his illustrations to his new classmates. (I: P–8)

Hurmence, Belinda. *Slavery Time When I Was Chillun*. Putnam, 1997. This is a selection of twelve oral histories from former slaves, taken from the over 2,000 that were collected by the Library of Congress in 1936. (I: 10 and up)

*Johnson, Angela. *Do Like Kyla*. Illustrated by James E. Ransome. Orchard, 1990. All day long, a little girl follows her big sister Kyla around, "doing like Kyla," but at the end of the day, "Kyla does just like me." See also: *One of Three*. Illustrated by David Soman. Orchard, 1991. (I: P–7)

_____. *Heaven*. Simon & Schuster, 1998. Twelve-year-old Marley's understanding of her life turns upside down when she discovers that the people she believed were her parents are actually her aunt and uncle. (I: 12–YA)

Jurmain, Suzanne. *The Forbidden Schoolhouse: The True and Dramatic Story of Prudence Crandall and Her Students*. Houghton Mifflin, 2005. The story of a Miss Crandall and her belief in offering education to African American girls during the racist 1830s is dramatically portrayed in this book. (I: 12–YA)

*Lawrence, Jacob. *Harriet and the Promised Land*. Simon & Schuster, 1968. The life of Harriet Tubman is described in verse, and the story of her commitment to helping fellow slaves to freedom is told. (I: 9–11)

Lester, Julius. *The Blues Singers: Ten Who Rocked the World*. Illustrated by Lisa Cohen. Jump at the Sun/Hyperion, 2001. This book features ten blues singers who became "legends" and explores the blues as an art form. (I: All ages)

_____. *Long Journey Home: Stories from Black History*. Dial, 1972/1993. Six stories, based on the lives of real people, tell about the impact of escaping from slavery on the lives of individuals and families. (I: 11–YA)

*_____. *Sam and the Tigers*. Illustrated by Jerry Pinkney. Dial, 1996. Based on the story "Little Black Sambo," this new version is told in Lester's "Southern black storytelling voice," with Pinkney's illustrations setting the story in the mythical land of Sam-sam-sa-mara. (I: 6–9)

*Levine, Ellen. *Henry's Freedom Box: A True Story from the Underground Railroad*. Illustrated by Kadir Nelson. Scholastic, 2007. Henry decides to have himself put in a box and mailed along a dangerous path to freedom. (I: 7–9)

Mathis, Sharon Bell. *The Hundred Penny Box*. Illustrated by Leo and Diane Dillon. Puffin, 1975. Great-great-aunt Dew is a hundred years old and has a box with a penny in it for each of her birthdays. Michael loves to listen to the stories each penny holds and intercedes on her behalf when his mother wants to throw out the old "hundred penny box" and buy a new one. (I: 8–10)

Mattox, Cheryl Warren. *Shake It to the One That You Love the Best: Play Songs and Lullabies from Black Musical Traditions*. Illustrated by Varnette P. Honeywood and Brenda Joysmith. Sobrante, CA: Warren-Mattox, 1989. African American songs that accompany jump rope, hopscotch, and other games are featured in this collection. (I: P–9)

*McCully, Emily Arnold. *The Escape of Oney Judge: Martha Washington's Slave Finds Freedom*. FSG, 2007. Raised to be the personal slave of the nation's First Lady, Oney faces a difficult decision when Martha Washington's death leads to being her resold rather than receiving freedom. (I: 7–10)

*McKissack, Patricia. *Flossie and the Fox*. Illustrated by Rachel Isadora. Dial, 1986. A little girl meets a creature in the woods and insists on his proof of identity as a fox before she will give up her eggs. (I: 7–9)

*_____. *Someplace Special*. Illustrated by Jerry Pinkney. Atheneum, 2001. During the 1950s amidst Jim Crow segregation laws in the South, "Tricia Ann sets off on her first solo trip by bus to go someplace special—the 'Public Library: All Are Welcome.'" (I: 7–9)

*Mollel, Tololwa M. *My Rows and Piles of Coins*. Illustrated by E. B. Lewis. Clarion, 1999. Saruni saves his piles of coins, arranged in rows, in hopes of buying a bicycle to help his mother carry heavy goods to market in Tanzania. (I: 6–9)

*Myers, Walter Dean. *Harlem*. Illustrated by Christopher Myers. Scholastic, 1997. Poetic text and vibrant collage illustrations offer vivid images of everyday life, as well as the art, music, and literature that define Harlem. (I: 12 and up)

*_____. *Jazz*. Illustrated by Christopher Myers. Holiday House, 2006. Through musical poetry and accompanying illustration, the father-son team introduce jazz, its history, background and features. (I: 10–YA)

_____. *Malcolm X: By Any Means Necessary*. Scholastic, 1993. This is the story of the famous civil rights leader Malcolm X. (I: 9–11)

Naidoo, Beverley. *Journey to Jo'burg: A South African Story*. Harper, 1986. Naledi travels from her South African village to Johannesburg to deliver news of her baby sister's near-death from an illness to her mother, who works and lives in the home of some white people. (I: 9–11)

Nelson, Kadir. *Heart and Soul: The Story of America and African Americans*. HarperCollins, 2011. An elderly woman tells the story of African American history, through rich descriptions of the extraordinary strength of past generations it has taken to go beyond endurance to thriving in the world. (I: 9 and up)

_____. *We Are the Ship: The Story of Negro League Baseball*. Jump at the Sun/Hyperion, 2008. The talent, determination and dedication of the players in baseball's Negro Leagues allowed them to rise above the discrimination, circumstances, and obstacles they faced. (I: 9–YA)

Nelson, Marilyn. *Carver: A Life in Poems*. Front Street, 2001. 44 poems from different voices paint a picture of George Washington Carver, son of slaves who became a famous scientist, inventor, botanist, painter, musician, and educator. (I: 13–YA)

*Nelson, Vaunda Micheaux. *Almost to Freedom*. Illustrated by Colin Bootman. Carolrhoda, 2003. Sally is a beloved rag doll who is accidentally left behind when her owner escapes North to freedom, but becomes a companion for another child who stops at the Underground Railroad stop and needs to find comfort. (I: 6–9)

_____. *Bad News for Outlaws*. Illustrated by R. Gregory Christie. Carolrhoda, 2010. (I: 10–13)

*Nivola, Claire A. *Planting the Trees of Kenya: The Story of Wangari Maathai*. Farrar, Straus, & Giroux, 2008. The extraordinary work of a Nobel Peace Prize winner, a Kenyan woman who mobilized the people in her country to plant trees to save the land from environmental damage. (I: 7–10)

*Pinkney, Andrea Davis. *Dear Benjamin Banneker*. Illustrated by Brian Pinkney. Harcourt, 1994. Benjamin Banneker was an accomplished mathematician and astronomer and also the first black creator of an almanac. When he realized the injustice of the words in the Declaration of Independence proclaiming that "all men are created equal," he wrote to Secretary of State Thomas Jefferson. (I: 7–9)

_____. *Let It Shine: Stories of Black Women Freedom Fighters*. Illustrated by Stephen Alcorn. Harcourt, 2000. This collection of brief biographies describes how black women like Sojourner Truth, Harriet Tubman, Rosa Parks, and Shirley Chisholm have fought for freedom. (I: 10–13)

*_____. *Seven Candles for Kwanzaa*. Illustrated by Brian Pinkney. Dial, 1993. This book describes the seven-day festival of Kwanzaa, a holiday during which Americans of African descent celebrate their ancestral values. (I: 6–9)

*Rappaport, Doreen. *Martin's Big Words: The Life of Dr. Martin Luther King, Jr.* Illustrated by Bryan Collier. Hyperion, 2001. Text pulled from King's speeches, paired with illustrations, offers an image of a man who used "big words" to powerfully make his views known. (I: 6 and up)

*Ringgold, Faith. *Tar Beach*. Crown, 1991. A young girl remembers spending summer evenings on the "tar beach" on the roof of their apartment building, imagining that she could fly over Manhattan and claim all she saw for herself and her family. (I: 6–9)

*Sisulu, Elinor Batezat. *The Day Gogo Went to Vote: South Africa*. Illustrated by Sharon Wilson. Little, Brown, 1996. Thembi and her great-grandmother participate in the election on the historic day on which black South Africans were allowed to vote for the first time. (I: 7–10)

*Steptoe, Javaka, illustrator. *In Daddy's Arms I Am Tall: African Americans Celebrating Fathers*. Lee & Low, 1997. A collection of poetry focusing on the important role of fathers in the lives of their children. (I: P–10)

*Steptoe, John. *Baby Says*. Lothrop, Lee & Shepard, 1988. In this nearly wordless book, a baby and his big brother learn to play together. (I: P)

Taylor, Mildred. *The Friendship*. Illustrated by Max Ginsburg. Dial, 1987. In 1930s rural Mississippi, the four Logan children witness a confrontation when Mr. Tom Bee, an elderly black man, calls a white storekeeper by his first name. Other titles about the Logans include *Road to Memphis* (1990) and *The Well* (1995). (I: 8–11)

_____. *The Gold Cadillac*. Illustrated by Michael Hays. Dial, 1987. Father brings home a new gold Cadillac, and 'Lois and Wilmato are proud to be riding in it. But driving south from Ohio to Mississippi to visit relatives, the family faces prejudice and racism and must temporarily trade the Cadillac for a less conspicuous car. (I: 8–11)

_____. *Mississippi Bridge*. Illustrated by Max Ginsburg. Dial, 1990. In the 1930s, amidst racial tension, black passengers are ordered off a bus to accommodate white passengers. Crossing the flooded river on a weak bridge, the bus is swept off and the passengers die. (I: 10–12)

_____. *Roll of Thunder, Hear My Cry*. Illustrated by Jerry Pinkney. Dial, 1976. The Logan family faces many problems associated with being black in the rural South during the Depression. The sequel is *Let the Circle Be Unbroken* (1981). See also the prequel, *The Land* (2005) and *Song of the Trees* (1975). (I: 11–13)

Walter, Mildred Pitts. *Justin and the Best Biscuits in the World*. Illustrated by Catherine Stock. Lothrop, Lee & Shepard, 1986. Justin lives in a house full of women and considers cooking and cleaning to be "women's work." Spending time on his grandfather's ranch shows Justin a different view of work. (I: 9–11)

*Weatherford, Carole Boston. *Moses: When Harriet Tubman Led Her People to Freedom*. Illustrated by Kadir Nelson. Hyperion/Jump at the Sun, 2006. Harriet Tubman's spiritual strength is depicted as she follows God's call for her to be the "Moses" of her people and to lead them to freedom. (I: 7–10)

Williams-Garcia, Rita. *One Crazy Summer*. HarperCollins, 2010. Delphine and her younger sisters are sent to spend the summer of 1968 in California with their mother who left them years before, and find a world in the midst of the Civil Rights Movement. (I: 11–YA)

*Winter, Jonah. *Dizzy*. Illustrated by Sean Qualls. Scholastic/Arthur A. Levine, 2006. This picture book biography depicts the life of jazz musician Dizzy Gillespie, from his abusive childhood to his brilliant creation of bebop through musically portrayed text and illustration. (I: 8–11)

Woodson, Jacqueline. *Last Summer with Maizon*. Delacorte, 1992/2002. Margaret knows that after the summer ends, her best friend, Maizon, will be leaving their neighborhood in Brooklyn to attend a boarding school to which she has won a scholarship. See also *Maizon at Blue Hill* (1992/2002) and *Between Madison and Palmetto* (1995/2002). (I: 11–YA)

*_____. *The Other Side*. Illustrated by E. B. Lewis. Putnam, 2001. In the days of segregation, two girls are told not to cross the fence, so they find a way to befriend one another without going to the other side. (I: 7–9)

Asian and Asian American

*Coerr, Eleanor. *Sadako*. Illustrated by Ed Young. Putnam, 1993. Believing in the Japanese tradition that folding a thousand origami cranes will restore her health, a little girl named Sadako tries to survive the leukemia that resulted from the bombing of Hiroshima. See also the novel *Sadako and the Thousand Paper Cranes*. (I: 9–12)

Compestine, Ying Chang. *Revolution Is Not a Dinner Party*. Holt, 2007. Set in China during the days of the Cultural Revolution, Ling describes her daily life and the persecution her family and neighbors endure. (I: 12–YA)

*Demi. *The Empty Pot*. Holt, 1990. The Emperor distributes seeds to children across China, and the one who grows the best flower will inherit the kingdom. Ping finds that he must face the emperor honestly with his empty pot when springtime comes, as nothing has grown from the seed he was given. (I: 6–9)

*_____. *Liang and the Magic Paintbrush*. Holt, 1980. A small boy in China is given a paintbrush, and everything he paints magically comes to life. (I: 6–9)

*Hamanaka, Sheila. *The Journey*. Orchard, 1990. A historical look at Japanese Americans is provided through close-up details of an actual mural, accompanied by text explaining the significance of each section. (I: 10–YA)

*Heo, Yumi, reteller. *The Green Frogs: A Korean Folktale*. Houghton Mifflin, 1996. In this pourquoi tale, two frog sons always do the opposite of what their mother

requests, so disobedient children in Korea today are called "green frogs." (I: 6–10)

*Hong, Lily Toy. *Two of Everything*. Whitman, 1993. While digging in his field, Mr. Haktak finds a big pot, and everything he puts in it comes out doubled. He faces a dilemma when his wife falls into the pot! (I: 6–9)

Kadohata, Cynthia. *Weedflower*. Atheneum, 2006. Sumiko and her family are sent to live in a Japanese internment camp, where she develops an unexpected friendship with a Native American boy who is curious about the people he has been hired to fence in. (I: 10–13)

Lin, Grace. *The Year of the Dog*. Little Brown, 2005. Grace is an American girl of Taiwanese heritage, and throughout the "year of the dog" in the Chinese calendar, she navigates the differences of her two cultures. Sequel: *The Year of the Rat* (2008). (I: 8–10)

*Lo, Ginnie. *Auntie Yang's Great Soybean Picnic*. Illustrated by Beth Lo. Lee & Low, 2012. A Chinese immigrant family is delighted to discover soybeans growing in a field in Illinois, and this leads to annual picnics involving more and more neighbors over the years. Painted on ceramic, the illustrations delightfully match the tone for the story. (I: 6–10)

*Look, Lenore. *Uncle Peter's Amazing Chinese Wedding*. Illustrated by Yumi Heo. Simon & Schuster/Anne Schwartz, 2006. The marriage of Uncle Peter brings uncertain feelings to Jenny when the celebration takes place in traditional Chinese style. (I: K–8)

Lord, Betty Bao. *In the Year of the Boar and Jackie Robinson*. HarperCollins, 1984. In 1947, ten-year-old Chinese immigrant Shirley Temple Wong finds inspiration in Jackie Robinson, a grandson of a slave who has become an American hero, and she vows to view America as a land of opportunity. (I: 9–11)

*Mahy, Margaret. *The Seven Chinese Brothers*. Illustrated by Jean and Mou-sien Tseng. Scholastic, 1990. When one brother is ordered to be executed, the seven brothers take turns escaping death by virtue of their extraordinary abilities. (I: 6–9)

*Mochizuki, Ken. *Baseball Saved Us*. Illustrated by Dom Lee. Lee & Low, 1993. While forced to live in an internment camp for Japanese Americans during World War II, a young boy learns to play baseball. (I: 6–9)

*Morimoto, Junko. *My Hiroshima*. Viking, 1987. The author recalls her childhood in Hiroshima and what happened on the day the atomic bomb was dropped. (I: 9–12)

Park, Linda Sue. *A Single Shard*. Clarion, 2001. An orphan living under a bridge is struck by the incredible beauty of pottery and works to apprentice himself to a master celadon potter, enduring hardships and showing strength. (I: 10–12)

Perkins, Mitali. *Bamboo People*. Charlesbridge, 2010. Military rule governs in a story of two boys coming of age, forging an unlikely friendship among politically defined roles they were born into. (I: 10–12)

*Say, Allen. *El Chino*. Houghton Mifflin, 1990. This picture book biography of Bong Way "Bill" Wong tells how he became a famous Chinese American bullfighter in Spain. (I: 6–9)

*_____. *Emma's Rug*. Houghton Mifflin, 1996. Emma finds artistic inspiration in her small white rug, but when her mother washes it clean, Emma is sure that she can no longer draw or paint. (I: 6–9)

*_____. *Grandfather's Journey*. Houghton Mifflin, 1993. A Japanese man immigrates to the United States and learns to love his new home, but still misses his homeland. When visiting Japan, he finds that the war will keep him from returning to the United States. A related title is *Tree of Cranes* (1991). (I: 6–9)

*_____. *Tea with Milk*. Houghton Mifflin, 1999. A Japanese American woman returns with her parents to Japan in the 1950s and resolves conflicts between her American ways and the customs of women in Japan. (I: 9–12)

*Shea, Pegi Deitz. *The Whispering Cloth: A Refugee's Story*. Illustrated by Anita Riggio. Stitched by You Yang. Boyds Mills, 1995. Mai practices stitching borders in embroidered story cloths while in a Thai refugee camp with her grandmother. She finds a story within herself so that she, too, can stitch her own pa'ndau. (I: 7–10)

*Uchida, Yoshiko. *The Bracelet*. Illustrated by Joanna Yardley. Philomel, 1976/1993. Emi and her family are sent to an internment camp during World War II. Emi loses the bracelet that was a gift from her best friend, but she comes to realize that she does not need the physical reminder of her friendship in order to remember. (I: 6–9)

_____. *A Jar of Dreams*. Macmillan, 1981. Faced with the prejudice against Japanese in the 1930s in California, Rinko wants to be as American as possible. When Aunt Waka visits from Japan, Rinko begins to understand the strength of her family and the Japanese American community. Related titles are *The Best Bad Thing* (1983) and *The Happiest Ending* (1985). (I: 9–11)

*Wong, Janet. *Apple Pie, Fourth of July*. Illustrated by Margaret Chodos-Irvine. Harcourt, 2002. A young girl thinks that nobody will want to come to their Chinese restaurant on the Fourth of July but is pleasantly surprised. (I: 6–9)

*_____. *The Trip Back Home*. Illustrated by Bo Jia. Harcourt, 2000. A Korean American child visits her mother's homeland with her. (I: 6–9)

*Xiong, Blia. *Nine-in-One, Grr! Grr! A Folktale from the Hmong People of Laos*. Adapted by Cathy Spagnoli. Illustrated by Nancy Hom. Children's Book Press, 1989. Tiger is promised nine cubs a year by the god, Shao. Bird fears that tigers will overtake the land and tries to think of a way to prevent that from happening. (I: 6–10)

Yep, Laurence. *Angelfish*. Putnam, 2001. In this continued story of a biracial Chinese American girl, her ballet dancing brings about new understandings for herself and her neighbor who had been "reeducated" during the Cultural Revolution in China. See earlier books: *Ribbons* (1996) and *The Cook's Family* (1998). (I: 10–13)

_____. *Dragon's Gate*. HarperCollins, 1993. In 1867, Chinese men came to the United States and found work digging and dynamiting tunnels through the rocks of the Sierra Mountains so that the railroad could cross the nation. (I: 11–YA)

_____. *Dragonwings*. Harper, 1975/1987. Moon Shadow leaves his remote Chinese village in 1903 to join his father, Windrider, in California. Together, they survive the 1906 earthquake and the hardships of life in the "Golden Mountain" as they work to realize their dream of building a dragon-like flying machine. (I: 10–12)

*Young, Ed. *Cat and Rat: The Legend of the Chinese Zodiac*. Holt, 1995. This is the story of how the twelve animals became part of the Chinese zodiac. (I: 7–10)

*_____. *Lon Po Po: A Red-Riding Hood Story from China*. Philomel, 1989. When mother leaves the children at home, a wolf enters their house. The children must think quickly and come up with a plan to outsmart the wolf. (I: 7–10)

*_____. *Monkey King*. HarperCollins, 2001. This picture book version of the Chinese epic, *Journey to the West,* tells the beginning of the monkey king's pursuit of an enlightened state.

Latino/Latina

*Ada, Alma Flor. *The Gold Coin*. Atheneum, 1991. When a thief follows a healer woman in an attempt to steal her gold coin, he finds himself transformed by witnessing her acts of kindness. (I: 7–10)

_____. *My Name Is María Isabel/Me llamo María Isabel*. Atheneum, 1993. When María Isabel Salazar Lopez enters a new classroom, the teacher decides to call her "Mary Lopez" because there are already two girls named Maria in the class. (I: 7–10)

_____. *Under the Royal Palms: A Childhood in Cuba*. Atheneum, 1998. Author Ada offers a memoir of her childhood, with vivid descriptions of island life with her family. This is a companion book to *Where the Flame Trees Bloom* (1994). (I: 9–12)

Alvarez, Julia. *Before We Were Free*. Knopf, 2002. Twelve-year-old Anita lives in the Dominican Republic in the 1960s when freedom was controlled by the government (I: 12–YA)

_____. *How Tía Lola Came to Visit Stay*. Knopf, 2001. When his parents divorce, Tía Lola comes from the Dominican Republic to Vermont to help out with the boys, who try to keep their flamboyant aunt out of their friends' sight. (I: 9–12).

*Ancona, George. *Pablo Remembers: The Fiesta of the Day of the Dead*. Lothrop, Lee & Shepard, 1993. Pablo and his family prepare for the three-day fiesta of El Día de Los Muertos, a festival to honor the spirits of the dead. (I: 6–9)

*_____. *The Piñata Maker/El piñatero*. Harcourt, 1994. Don Ricardo is a craftsman in Ejutla de Crespo in southern Mexico. He makes piñatas for birthday parties and other fiestas. Bilingual text. (I: 6–9)

Andrews-Goebel, Nancy. *The Pot That Juan Built*. Illustrated by David Diaz. Lee & Low, 2002. Two parallel texts exist throughout the book; one is a cumulative story about the creating of a pot in the style of "The House that Jack Built" and the other a biography of the potter, Juan Quezada. (I: 6–9)

*Cowley, Joy. *Gracias, the Thanksgiving Turkey*. Illustrated by Joe Cepeda. Scholastic, 1996. Papa sends Miguel a turkey with instructions to fatten the bird for Thanksgiving dinner, but Miguel becomes attached to his new pet. (I: 6–9)

*Delacre, Lulu. *Arroz con leche: Popular Songs and Rhymes from Latin America*. Scholastic, 1989. The songs and rhymes in this bilingual collection are known throughout the Spanish-speaking countries. A related title is *Las Navidades: Popular Christmas Songs from Latin America* (1990). (I: P–8)

_____. *Golden Tales: Myths, Legends and Folktales from Latin America*. Scholastic, 1996. The twelve classic tales in this collection come from four cultures of Latin America—Taino, Zapotec, Muisca, and Inca—and from many different countries. (I: 9–12)

Engle, Margarita. *The Poet Slave of Cuba: A Biography of Juan Francisco Manzano*. Illustrated by Sean Qualls. Holt, 2006. Told through multiple-voiced poetry, the horrors and pain of slavery are powerfully reflected on. (I: 12–YA)

_____. *The Surrender Tree*. Holt, 2008. Poetic telling of the hardships of life in Cuba during the War for Independence in the latter 1800s. (I: 11–YA)

*Garza, Carmen Lomas. *Family Pictures/Cuadros de familia*. Spanish language text by Rosalma Zubizarreta. Children's Book Press, 1990. Bilingual text accompanies folk art illustrations depicting the author's experiences of growing up Mexican American in South Texas. Another book by Garza is *In My Family/En mi familia* (1996). (I: 6–10)

González, Lucía M. *Señor Cat's Romance and Other Favorite Stories from Latin America*. Illustrated by Lulu Delacre. Scholastic, 1997. Each of the six tales about outrageous Señor Cat, silly Juan Bobo, and others is followed by a note about the culture it comes from. (I: 6–9)

Jimenez, Francisco. *The Circuit: Stories from the Life of a Migrant Child*. Houghton Mifflin, 1999. An autobiographical account of a childhood journey from Mexico to California in a migrant farm family in the 1940s. See also *Breaking Through* (2001). (I: 11–13)

*Krull, Kathleen. *Harvesting Hope*. Illustrated by Yuyi Morales. Harcourt, 2003. This biography focuses on the role that Cesar Chavez played in the 1965 nonviolent protest against poor working conditions for migrant farm workers. (I: 7–10)

*Martinez, Alejandro Cruz. *The Woman Who Outshone the Sun/La mujer que brillaba aún más que el sol*. Illustrated by Fernando Olivera. Story by Rosalma Zubizarreta, Harriet Rohmer, and David Schecter from a poem by Alejandro Cruz Martinez. Children's Book Press, 1991. This retelling of a Zapotec Indian legend from Mexico is the story of Lucia Zenteno, a beautiful woman who possesses magical powers. When she is sent away from a mountain village, she takes its water away in punishment. (I: 7–10)

Mohr, Nicholasa. *Felita*. 1979. Bantam, 1990. Moving is always hard, but when Felita's family moves to an area where there aren't other Puerto Rican families speaking Spanish, the adjustment feels even more lonely. Also by Mohr is *Going Home* (1986). (I: 9–12)

*Mora, Pat. *A Birthday Basket for Tía*. Illustrated by Cecily Lan. Macmillan, 1992. Cecila wants to find the perfect present for her great-aunt's ninetieth birthday. (I: P–6)

*_____. *Tómas and the Library Lady*. Illustrated by Raúl Colón. Knopf, 1997. A librarian helps Tómas connect his life with books while living in Iowa as a migrant farm worker. (I: 6–9)

Ryan, Pam Muñoz. *Becoming Naomi Leon*. Scholastic, 2004. When Naomi Leon's mother reappears after a seven-year absence and threatens to change the peaceful life Naomi Leon has had with her younger brother and her Gram, a journey to Mexico in search of an estranged father helps her define who she is and where she belongs. (I: 10–13)

_____. *Esperanza Rising*. Scholastic, 2000. Esperanza lives a privileged and wealthy life in Mexico; then, circumstances force her to flee to California with her mother and work in a farm labor camp. (I: 12–YA)

Soto, Gary. *Baseball in April and Other Stories*. Harcourt, 1990. The eleven short stories in this collection tell of the author's experiences growing up Mexican American in Fresno, California. (I: 9–12)

*_____. *Chato's Kitchen*. Putnam, 1995. Illustrated by Susan Guevara. Cool cat Chato is thrilled to see who has moved into the barrio—a family of tasty-looking mice. When they accept a dinner invitation, Chato is filled with anticipation as he prepares the frijoles, guacamole, arroz, tortillas, and more, but things go differently than he expects when the mice's friend shows up. (I: 7–9)

_____. *Neighborhood Odes*. Illustrated by David Diaz. Harcourt, 1992. These twenty-one poems describe various everyday joys of growing up in a Mexican American neighborhood. (I: 9–YA)

*_____. *The Old Man and His Door*. Illustrated by Joe Cepeda. Putnam, 1996. The story is based on a Mexican song that goes "La puerta. El puerco. There's no difference to el viejo." Misunderstanding his wife's instructions on what to take to a party, an old man takes a door instead of a pig. But the door proves useful along the way, and the old man has many surprises for his wife. (I: P–8)

*_____. *Too Many Tamales*. Illustrated by Ed Martinez. Putnam, 1993. While helping to make tamales, Maria slips her mother's diamond ring on her hand to admire it. When she realizes that the ring is missing, she enlists the help of her cousins in eating the tamales until the ring is found. (I: 6–9)

*Tonatiuh, Duncan. *Diego Rivera: His World and Ours*. Abrams, 2011. This look at the young life of a famous Mexican painter connects to contemporary readers by considering what would be today's depictions in murals. (I: 6–9)

*Torres, Leyla. *Saturday Sancocho*. Mirasol/Farrar, 1995. María Líli's mother decides to make sancocho but needs a chicken; the two go to the marketplace to trade eggs for a series of items. (I: 6–9)

Native American

Alexie, Sherman. *The Absolutely True Diary of a Part-Time Indian*. Illustrated by Ellen Forney. Little Brown, 2007. This is a work of fiction, but with elements autobiographical to the author's growing up on a reservation and going to school outside, feeling bullied and trying to figure out where he belonged and what his identity was. (I: 12–YA)

*Begay, Shonto. *Navajo: Visions and Voices across the Mesa*. Scholastic, 1995. Twenty paintings and original poems are paired to present a personal voice of what it means to live as a Navajo in today's world. (I: 10 and up)

Bierhorst, John. *The Deetkatoo: Native American Stories about Little People*. Illustrated by Ron Hilbert Coy. Morrow, 1998. This book compiles twenty-two stories of little people from fourteen different native cultures and is well documented with notes, a guide to cultures, and a bibliography. (I: 10 and up)

Bruchac, James, and Joseph Bruchac. *The Girl Who Helped Thunder and Other Native American Folktales*. Illustrated by Stefano Vitale. Sterling, 2008. This is a collection of retold Native American folktales across many tribal groups. (I: 9–12)

*Bruchac, Joseph. *A Boy Called Slow*. Illustrated by Rocco Baviera. Philomel, 1994. A Lakota boy's childhood name "Slow" is changed to "Sitting Bull" as he matures because of his deeds. (I: 9–12)

_____. *Eagle Song*. Dial, 1997. Fourth-grade Danny Bigtree leaves the Mohawk Reservation and moves to Brooklyn and must learn to balance pride in his heritage with life in a new, urban environment. (I: 9–13)

_____. *In the Heart of a Chief*. Dial, 1998. This story of a contemporary eleven-year-old boy explores what it means to be a Penacook Indian who lives on a reservation, but encounters conflicts with schoolmates outside the reservation. (I: 10–13)

*_____, and Jonathan London. *Thirteen Moons on Turtle's Back: A Native American Year of Moons*. Illustrated by Thomas Locker. Philomel, 1992. Many Native American tribes relate the thirteen moons of the year to the pattern of thirteen large scales on the turtle's back. Poems—each based on a story from a different Native American nation, such as the Cherokee, Cree, or Sioux—make up the text for this book. (I: 8–10)

Caduto, Michael J., and Joseph Bruchac. *Keepers of Life: Discovering Plants through Native American Stories and Earth Activities for Children*. Illustrated by John Kahionhes Fadden and David Kahionhes Fadden. Fulcrum, 1997. This book's purpose is to teach children about Native American cultures and the link between humans and nature through an interdisciplinary approach. Twenty-three sets of lessons each feature a story followed by suggested activities to enhance learning. One in a series. (I: 6–12)

*Cohen, Caron Lee. *The Mud Pony*. Illustrated by Shonto Begay. Scholastic, 1988. A poor boy creates a mud pony and cares for it as if it were real. He dreams that the pony comes alive, and he awakens to find that it will guide him through many ordeals. (I: 6–9)

Dorris, Michael. *Morning Girl*. Hyperion, 1992. Morning Girl and her younger brother Star Boy describe their island life in alternating chapters. The story closes with the arrival of the first Europeans to her world. (I: 9–12)

*Ekoomiak, Normee. *Arctic Memories*. Holt, 1988. Appliqued, stitched, and painted illustrations show every-

day and special events in the lives of Inuits of the past. Through bilingual Inuktitut and English text, the author/illustrator describes his memories of childhood in an Inuit community in northern Quebec. (I: 7–10)

Erdrich, Louise. *The Birchbark House*. Hyperion, 1999. Seven-year-old Omakayas is an Ojibwa girl whose daily life on an island in Lake Superior is depicted during the U.S. westward movement. Sequels: *The Game of Silence* (2005), *The Porcupine Year* (2008). (I: 7–10)

*Goble, Paul. *Death of the Iron Horse*. Bradbury, 1987. Fearful of what will happen as the white men approach their territory, a group of Cheyenne braves derail a freight train in 1867, believing it to be an Iron Horse whose rails are binding Mother Earth. (I: 8–10)

*_____. *The Girl Who Loved Wild Horses*. Macmillan, 1978. A girl's love of horses leads her to be among them, where her family finds her. She finds that she feels a sense of belonging when she is with the horses. (I: 6–8)

*Littlechild, George. *This Land Is My Land*. Children's Book Press, 1993. Through striking illustrations and accompanying essays, Littlechild recounts historical events and their implications on his people. (I: 9–12)

*Ortiz, Simon. *The People Shall Continue*. Children's Book Press, 1988. This book briefly presents an overview of the history of the North American Indians from Creation to the present. (I: 9–12)

*Ross, Gayle. *How Rabbit Tricked Otter*. Illustrated by Murv Jacob. Parabola, 2003. Fifteen tales about Rabbit from the Cherokee storytelling tradition. (I: 6–9)

*Scott, Ann Herbert. *On Mother's Lap*. Illustrated by Glo Coalson. Clarion, 1972/1992. Michael enjoys rocking in Mother's lap—along with Dolly, Boat, reindeer blanket, and puppy—until Mother hears the baby crying. The illustrator created the original sketches while living in an Inuit village. (I: P–6)

*Steptoe, John. *The Story of Jumping Mouse: A Native American Legend*. Lothrop, Lee & Shepard, 1984. Jumping Mouse sets out to find the "far-off land." He finds that his generosity pays off as each of the animals he encounters bestows a gift to ensure his safe passage to his "far-off land." (I: 9–13)

*Tingle, Tim. *Crossing Bok Chitto: A Choctaw Tale of Friendship & Freedom*. Illustrated by Jeanne Rorex Bridges. Cinco Puntos, 2008. A Choctaw guides slaves to freedom in the1800s, when the Bok Chitto River in Mississippi represented the border between plantation slavery and freedom, where the Choctaws lived. (I: 7–11)

*_____. *Saltypie: A Choctaw Journey from Darkness into Light*. Illustrated by Karen Clarkson. Cinco Puntos, 2010. A contemporary story describing a boy's recollection of his grandmother whose childhood had included Indian Boarding School, racial discrimination, and eventual blindness that was later addressed through a transplant. (I: 7–11)

*Yolen, Jane. *Encounter*. Illustrated by David Shannon. Harcourt, 1992. This story is narrated by a young Taino boy, who tells of the arrival of Columbus and his ships in 1492. (I: 7–11)

Other Cultural Groups
Appalachian and Other Specific Regional and Religious Cultural Groups

Crum, Shutta. *Spitting Image*. Clarion, 2003. Twelve-year-old Jessie is mortified when her intended plan to help her neighbors in the poverty-ridden Appalachians backfires and brings them shame and embarrassment during the days of President Johnson's War on Poverty. (I: 10–13)

*Houston, Gloria. *My Great-Aunt Arizona*. Illustrated by Susan Condie Lamb. Harper, 1992. Arizona Houston Hughes was born in a log cabin in the Blue Ridge Mountains, and she grew up to become a teacher in the one-room school she had attended as a child. Arizona inspires generations of children to imagine the faraway places they will someday visit. (I: 6–9)

Ray, Delia. *Ghost Girl*. Clarion, 2003. When President and Mrs. Hoover build a school in the Blue Ridge Mountains, April realizes her first opportunity to attend school. She faces the opposition of her mother, but has the support of her grandmother. (I: 10–13)

*Rylant, Cynthia. *The Relatives Came*. Illustrated by Stephen Gammell. Bradbury, 1985. This book celebrates a family reunion in the Appalachian Mountains, where relatives must travel over winding mountain roads for a visit. (I: P–8)

Caribbean

*Landowne, Youme. *Sélavi, That is Life: . . . A Haitian Story of Hope*. Cinco Puntos Press, 2005. The street children in Haiti tolerate inhumane treatment and brutality, but the loving support of some people help them band together for hope and survival. (I: K–7)

*San Souci, Robert D. *The Faithful Friend*. Illustrated by Brian Pinkney. Simon & Schuster, 1995. In this traditional tale from the French West Indies island of Martinique, Clemente and Hippolyte are friends who find love, strange zombies, and danger. (I: 7–10)

European Americans

*Best, Cari. *Three Cheers for Catherine the Great!* Illustrated by Giselle Potter. Kroupa/DK Ink, 1999. Sara's beloved Russian grandmother asks for "no presents," but Sara finds a special present: She and her grandmother exchange language lessons. (I: 6–9)

*Polacco, Patricia. *The Keeping Quilt*. Simon & Schuster, 1988. A quilt made of scraps from clothes of family members left behind in Russia is passed down through the generations. The quilt serves a multitude of purposes: to welcome babies into the world, as a tent during play time, as a picnic cloth for a romantic date, and as a wedding chuppah. (I: 7–10)

*Sís, Peter. *The Wall: Growing Up Behind the Iron Curtain*. Farrar, 2007. Through images and text, Sís describes the experiences of his childhood in Prague during the communist era, and his search for artistic expression.

Jewish and Jewish Americans

Lowry, Lois. *Number the Stars*. Houghton Mifflin, 1989. When the Nazis come to find the Jews, ten-year-old Annemarie's family shelters a Jewish girl and participates as part of the Danish resistance in helping Jews escape to Sweden. (I: 10–13)

*Polacco, Patricia. *Mrs. Katz and Tush*. Bantam, 1992. A lonely Jewish widow gains companionship when an African American boy gives her a kitten. (I: 6–9)

The Middle East

*Alalou, Elizabeth, and Ali Alalou. *The Butter Man*. Illustrated by Julie Klear Essakalli. Charlesbridge, 2008. While Nora anxiously waits for her baba to finish making the couscous and vegetables dinner, her father tells the story of his childhood in Morocco and waiting hungrily for the butter man to come by. (I: P–8)

Barakat, Ibtisam. *Tasting the Sky: A Palestinian Childhood*. FSG, 2007. Set during the horror of war and occupation during the Arab-Israeli Six-Day War, this memoir recounts various episodes that define what the experience meant to her personally. (I: 12–YA)

Budhos, Marina. *Ask Me No Questions*. Simon & Schuster/Ginee Seo, 2006. Following 9/11, Muslim men were required to register with the U.S. government. When their father, an illegal immigrant from Bangladesh, is detained for attempting to leave the country, 14-year-old Nadira and her older sister must make a case for his release. (I: 12–YA)

Ellis, Deborah. *The Breadwinner*. Groundwood, 2001. Trapped inside the one-room family home after the Taliban takeover of Afghanistan, Parvana must bravely make a dangerous decision when her breadwinner father is taken away. See also: *Parvana's Journey* (2003) and *Mud City* (2004) (I: 10–12)

Nye, Naomi Shihab. *Habibi*. Simon & Schuster, 1998. Liyana and her family move from St. Louis to Jerusalem because her father wants his children to know the other half of their heritage. (I: 12–YA)

*_____. *Sitti's Secrets*. Illustrated by Nancy Carpenter. Four Winds, 1994. An American girl can't speak Arabic, the language of her grandmother—her sitti—but she remembers that they learned to communicate during the time they spent together in Palestine. (I: 6–9)

*Rumford, James. *Silent Music*. Roaring Brook, 2008. In a contemporary story set in Baghdad, Ali loves soccer, dancing, and especially calligraphy. The story reflects on Iraq's long history of valuing literacy as a powerful means of communication. (I: 7–10)

Multiple Cultures/Multiracial

*Ada, Alma Flor. *I Love Saturdays y domingos*. Illustrated by Elivia Savadier. Atheneum, 2002. A biracial girl visits her European American grandparents on Saturdays and her Mexican American abuelo and abuela on domingos (Sundays). (I: P–8)

*Adoff, Arnold. *black is brown is tan*. Illustrated by Emily Arnold McCully. Harper, 1973. Two children with a "chocolate momma," a "white" daddy, and "granny white and grandma black" share the joys of being a family. (I: 6–9)

*Dooley, Norah. *Everybody Cooks Rice*. Illustrated by Peter J. Thornton. Carolrhoda, 1991. It is dinner time and Carrie sets out to find her little brother. At each home, she finds that rice is part of the family's evening meal, but that it is prepared differently because of the various cultural backgrounds of the families. A related title is *Everybody Bakes Bread* (1996). (I: 6–9)

*Grimes, Nikki. *Aneesa Lee and the Weaver's Gift*. Illustrated by Ashley Bryan. HarperCollins, 1999. A multiethnic girl—black, white, Asian—is a talented weaver, and her beautiful tapestries form a metaphor for the range of experiences and emotions she expresses. (I: 6–9)

Hamilton, Virginia. *Plain City*. Scholastic, 1993. Buhlaire, a child of mixed racial heritage, is ostracized by her peers for her family's unusual habits. Her mother sings in clubs, and she thinks her father is Missing in Action—until one day, a homeless man appears. (I: 11–YA)

Kuklin, Susan. *Families*. Hyperion, 2006. Double-paged spreads with photographs introduce fifteen families of varying composition, including divorced parents, stepfamilies, gay parents, adopted children, immigrants, and special needs children. (I: K–9)

Kurtz, Jane. *The Storyteller's Beads*. Gulliver/Harcourt, 1998. Sahay realizes that she must flee to Sudan for her survival when her family is violently killed during a time of famine in Ethiopia. Rahel, who is blind and Jewish, is fleeing also, but with hopes of getting to Israel to escape prejudice as well as hunger. The story is set in the 1980s during the Israeli airlifts. (I: 12 and up)

*McGill, Alice. *Molly Bannaky*. Illustrated by Chris K. Soentpiet. Houghton Mifflin, 1999. Molly is banished from England for the punishable crime of a cow upsetting the milk pail. As an indentured servant in America, she buys and (illegally) marries a slave, and a Benjamin Banneker eventually is born as her grandson. (I: 8–10)

Nelson, Vaunda Micheaux. *Mayfield Crossing*. Illustrated by Leonard Jenkins. Putnam, 1993. When the school in Mayfield Crossing closes and its black students are sent to another school, they face racial and socioeconomic prejudices for the first time. See also *Beyond Mayfield* (1999). (I: 8–12)

*Nikola-Lisa, W. *Bein' with You This Way*. Illustrated by Michael Bryant. Lee & Low, 1994. Through upbeat rhythm, the text points out and celebrates people's physical similarities and differences. (I: P–8)

*Tingle, Tim. *Crossing Bok Chitto: A Choctaw Tale of Friendship & Freedom*. Illustrated by Jeanne Rorex Bridges. Cinco Puntos, 2006. When a Choctaw girl hears that a slave boy's mother is to be sold, she leads the family across the Bok Chitto River that forms the divide between freedom and slavery. (I: 8–11)

Woodson, Jacqueline. *Maizon at Blue Hill*. Delacorte, 1992/2002. Maizon enters a private boarding school and learns to deal with being one of only five African American students. She spends much time reflecting on what it feels like to be different from most. (I: 11–YA)

World Cultures Compared/Contrasted

*Anno, Mitsumasa. *All in a Day*. Philomel, 1986. The narrator, on a deserted island near the International Date Line, describes how children in eight countries celebrate New Year's Day. (I: 6–9)

*Lankford, Mary. *Mazes around the World*. Illustrated by Karen Dugan. HarperCollins, 2008. This series makes comparisons of practices around the world, and includes notes on geography, history, and cultural traditions for each topic in the series. See also: *Hopscotch Around the World* (1992) and *Dominoes Around the World* (1998) among others. (I: 6–10)

*Lewin, Ted. *Visiting Markets Around the World!* HarperCollins, 2006. A look at marketplaces around the world, showing the various things people bring to sell or trade. Companion book to *Market!* (I: 6–9)

*Morris, Ann. *Houses and Homes*. Photography by Ken Heyman. Lothrop, Lee & Shepard, 1992. Through photographs and simple text, readers are introduced to the varieties of homes in which people around the world live, ranging from Buckingham Palace to houses on stilts, houses on boats, and straw huts. Morris and Heyman have created several other books in the same format. (I: 5–9)

Nye, Naomi Shihab, ed. *This Same Sky: A Collection of Poems from Around the World*. Four Winds, 1992. The many forms of life under "this same sky"—human, animal, and nature—are reflected in poems written by 129 poets from 68 different countries. (I: 10–YA)

Smith, David J. *If the World Were a Village: A Book About the World's People*. Illustrated by Shelagh Armstrong. Kids Can Press, 2002. Translating the various statistics of our world's population into a village of 100 people, this book presents facts about language, economics, and how people live on this planet in numbers that are easier for children to understand. (I: 6–10)

Growing Up in a World of Political or Social Unrest

Alvarez, Julia. *Before We Were Free*. Knopf, 2002. In 1960 in the Dominican Republic, twelve-year-old Anita wonders what it would be like to be "free" of a terrifying dictator and the secret police. (I: 11–YA)

Buss, Fran Leeper. *Journey of the Sparrows*. Penguin/Lodestar, 1991. Three siblings escape the war in El Salvador and head for the hope of new life, nailed into a crate on the back of a truck. They end up in Chicago, where they live a new life as illegal immigrants. (I: 12–YA)

Filipovec, Zlata. *Zlata's Diary: A Child's Life in Sarajevo*. Viking, 1994. A ten-year-old Croatian girl begins her diary during prewar times and continues writing for three years until her family flees the former Yugoslavia and goes to Paris. (I: 11–YA)

Ho, Minfong. *The Clay Marble*. Farrar, 1991. Rebuilding homes and lives in a camp near the Thai border, families struggle to survive the destruction of war. A marble made from clay serves as a toy and a gesture of friendship between children in this camp. (I: 12–YA)

Jiang, Ji Li. *Red Scarf Girl: A Memoir of the Cultural Revolution*. HarperCollins, 1997. Ji Li wore her red scarf as the emblem of her devoted membership in the Young Pioneers, committed to the future of Communist China, when the course of her entire world changed with the beginning of the Chinese Cultural Revolution in 1966. (I: 10–YA)

Mead, Alice. *Girl of Kosovo*. Farrar, Straus, & Giroux, 2001. Eleven-year-old Zana struggles to survive and make sense of a world that seems to stand by as family members are killed and ethnic Albanians are nearly wiped out. (I: 11–YA)

Naidoo, Beverley. *The Other Side of Truth*. HarperCollins, 2001. Twelve-year-old Sade's father criticizes the government in their homeland of Nigeria and a bullet intended for him hits and kills her mother. The children are sent to London for safekeeping, but are placed in foster care. (I: 12 and up)

Temple, Frances. *Grab Hands and Run*. Orchard, 1993. Felipe and his family face threats to their lives at their home in El Salvador. He tells the story of their escape and the dangerous journey to Canada. (I: 12–YA)

———. *Tonight, by Sea*. Orchard, 1995. Poverty and government brutality make life in Haiti unbearable, so Paulie and other villagers help her uncle build a boat so that they can secretly attempt to escape to the United States. (I: 12–YA)

Social and Economic Diversity

*Dugan, Barbara. *Loop the Loop*. Illustrated by James Stevenson. Greenwillow, 1992. While playing outside, Anne encounters Mrs. Simpson, a woman who rides in a wheelchair, claims to be 969 years old, and performs fabulous tricks with a yo-yo. When Mrs. Simpson breaks her hip, Anne takes Mrs. Simpson's cat and a yo-yo to the hospital. (I: 6–9)

*Hausherr, Rosemarie. *Celebrating Families*. Scholastic, 1997. Color photos and accompanying text introduce children from single-parent families, adoptive families, extended families, and other types of families. (I: 6–9)

Holt, Kimberly Willis. *When Zachary Beaver Came to Town*. Holt, 1999. In west Texas in 1971, Toby deals with his mother's departure and befriends 600-pound Zachary Beaver. (I: 9–12)

Paterson, Katherine. *The Flip Flop Girl*. Viking, 1994. Father's death is hard enough to cope with, but moving to a new place, living with grandmother, and dealing with poverty make life even more difficult. (I: 9–12)

———. *The Great Gilly Hopkins*. Crowell, 1978. Gilly's attempts to be difficult and unlikable lead to her being moved from one foster home to another. Trotter, a foster mother, helps Gilly accept the love and security she craves. (I: 9–12)

*Pearson, Susan. *Happy Birthday, Grampie*. Illustrated by Ronald Himler. Dial, 1987. Age has taken away Grampie's vision, and he has forgotten English and reverted to his mother tongue, Swedish. Martha makes Grampie a card he can feel and hopes that it will communicate her birthday wishes. (I: 6–9)

Gender Issues and Portrayals of Same-Sex Parents

*Isadora, Rachel. *Max*. Macmillan, 1976. Max finds that taking dance lessons with his sister is a nice warm-up to his afternoon baseball games. (I: 5–8)

*Martin, Rafe. *Storytelling Princess*. Illustrated by Kimberly Bulcken Root. Putnam, 2001. A strong-willed princess refuses to accept her parents' choice in a negotiated arranged marriage, and circumstances allow her to make her own choice in a groom who values her intellect and personality. (I: 6–9)

*Paterson, Katherine. *The King's Equal*. Illustrated by Vladimir Vagin. HarperCollins, 1992. A prince in search of a princess to be his equal finds that he must prove to be her equal as well. (I: 7–10)

*Polacco, Patricia. *In Our Mothers' House*. Philomel, 2009. Two mothers lovingly raise a mixed-race family of adopted children in an idealized world. (I: K–7)

*Richardson, Justin, and Peter Parnell. *And Tango Makes Three*. Illustrated by Henry Cole. Simon & Schuster, 2005. Two male penguins in NYC Central Zoo are given an egg to hatch and raise when it becomes obvious that they want to raise a young one together. (I: K–8)

*Setterington, Ken. *Mom and Mum are Getting Married*. Illustrated by Alice Priestley. Rosie celebrates the marriage of her Mum and Mom in a joyful celebration. (I: P–2)

*Willhoite, Michael. *Daddy's Roommate*. Alyson Wonderland, 1990. Following a divorce, Daddy lives with another man. (I: P–8)

Woodson, Jacqueline. *From the Notebooks of Melanin Sun*. Scholastic/Blue Sky, 1995. Melanin Sun faces the everyday challenges of a thirteen-year-old growing up, but life is complicated when he hears rumors about his mother's love for a woman of a different race. (I: 12–YA)

Exceptional Learners

Billingsley, Franny. *Well Wished*. Atheneum, 1997. When Nuria wishes at a magical well that wheelchair-bound Catty could have a body like hers, the two girls surprisingly end up in each other's body. (I: 9–12)

*Booth, B. D. *Mandy*. Illustrated by Jim LaMerche. Lothrop, Lee & Shepard, 1991. Mandy's musings about why she fears the dark and her wonderings about the sounds of the world allow readers to get inside the thinking of a child with hearing loss. (I: 6–8)

*Brown, Tricia. *Someone Special Just Like You*. Photographs by Fran Ortiz. Holt, 1982. Photographs and simple text addressed to the reader show children with various disabilities engaged in activities in which all children participate. (I: P–6)

Byars, Betsy. *Summer of the Swans*. Illustrated by Ted CoConis. Viking, 1970. Sara learns to cope with her feelings of resentment toward her younger brother, who is developmentally delayed. (I: 10–13)

*Cohen, Miriam. *See You Tomorrow, Charles*. Illustrated by Lillian Hoban. Greenwillow, 1983. In this book (part of a series), Charles is a child with vision loss in a class of first-graders who learn with and from each other. (I: 5–7)

Fleischman, Paul. *Mind's Eye*. Holt, 1999. Courtney is paralyzed at sixteen, and her eighty-eight-year-old roommate teaches her to rely on her mind in order to survive. (I: YA)

*Fleming, Virginia. *Be Good to Eddie Lee*. Illustrated by Floyd Cooper. Philomel, 1993. Christy learns to appreciate the sensitive heart of Eddie Lee, a child with Down syndrome, when he noisily tags along on a visit to the woods in search of frog eggs. (I: 7–9)

*Fraustino, Lisa Rowe. *The Hickory Chair*. Illustrated by Benny Andrews. Levine/Scholastic, 2001. An African American boy who is blind shares a loving relationship with his grandmother, and a special way of communication that his grandmother calls "blind sight." (I: 7–9)

*Haldane, Suzanne. *Helping Hands: How Monkeys Assist People Who Are Disabled*. Dutton, 1991. A teen boy with quadriplegia performs daily routines with the aid of a monkey. (I: 6–12)

*Krull, Kathleen. *Wilma Unlimited*. Illustrated by David Diaz. Harcourt Brace, 1997. Wilma overcomes wearing braces on her legs to become a winning Olympic runner. (I: 6–10)

Martin, Ann. *A Corner of the Universe*. Scholastic, 2002. In the summer of 1960, twelve-year-old Hattie meets her twenty-one-year-old Uncle Adam, whose mental and emotional disabilities result in behaviors that are both endearing and frightening. (I: 10 and up)

McMahon, Patricia. *Dancing Wheels*. Illustrated with photographs by John Godt. Houghton Mifflin, 2000. The Dancing Wheels dance company includes both "standing" dancers and "sitting" dancers, who travel across the country, performing with energy and commitment. (I: 8–12)

*Miller, Mary Beth, and George Ancona. *Handtalk School*. Four Winds, 1991. A guide to a day in a boarding school for children with hearing loss shows, through color photographs, the use of American Sign Language to communicate. (I: All ages)

Miller, Sarah. *Miss Spitfire: Reaching Helen Keller*. Atheneum, 2007. This biography describes how Annie Sullivan, a half-blind orphan, taught a deaf, blind, and completely incorrigible child to communicate. (I: 9–12)

*Millman, Isaac. *Moses Goes to School*. Foster/Farrar, 2000. Moses and other deaf children in his school are shown communicating in ASL and learning to read and write in Standard English. American Sign Language accompanies the text and illustrations. See also *Moses Goes to a Concert* (1998) and *Moses Goes to the Circus* (2003). (I: P–8)

Philbrick, Rodman. *Freak the Mighty*. Blue Sky Press/Scholastic, 1993. A boy with physical size and might and a boy with intellectual brilliance are the book's main characters. Separately, each lacks what the other has, but together they become "Freak the Mighty." (I: 10–14)

Slote, Alfred. *Hang Tough, Paul Mather*. HarperCollins, 1973/1985. Twelve-year-old Paul's enthusiasm for baseball helps him through the difficulty of living with treatments for leukemia. (I: 9–11)

Trueman, Terry. *Stuck in Neutral*. HarperCollins, 2000. Narrator fourteen-year-old Shawn describes his exceptional ability to remember all he hears, but the world believes that he is retarded because cerebral palsy has left him with a total inability to control his muscles in any communicable way. (I: 12–YA)

*Willis, Jeanne, and Tony Ross. *Susan Laughs*. Andersen Press, 1999. (UK) Brief text describes all the things that Susan does, and the closing illustration depicts Susan in a wheelchair, "like me and you." (I: P–7)

RESOURCES

Austin, Patricia. (2010). Opening the Door to Tolerance. *Book Links, 19*(2), 42–45.

Cai, Mingshui. *Multicultural Literature for Children and Young Adults: Reflections on Critical Issues.* Greenwood, 2002.

Fox, Dana L., and Kathy G. Short. *Stories Matter: The Complexities of Cultural Authenticity in Children's Literature.* National Council of Teachers of English, 2003.

Henkin, Roxanne, and Junko Yokota. "Inclusive Reading: Literature Portraying Families with Gay and Lesbian Parents." *Democracy & Education, 13*(3) (1999): 60–61.

Jones, Guy W., and Sally Moomaw. *Lessons from Turtle Island: Native Curriculum in Early Childhood Classrooms.* Red Leaf Press, 2002.

Kruse, Ginny Moore, Kathleen T. Horning, and Megan Schliesman, with Tana Elias. *Multicultural Literature for Children and Young Adults: A Selected Listing of Books by and about People of Color, Volume 2.* Cooperative Children's Book Center, 1997.

Pellowski, Anne. *The Family Story-Telling Handbook: How to Use Stories, Anecdotes, Rhymes, Handkerchiefs, Paper, and Other Objects to Enrich Your Family Traditions.* Illustrated by Lynn Sweat. Macmillan, 1987.

_____. *Hidden Stories in Plants: Unusual and Easy-to-Tell Stories from around the World Together with Creative Things to Do While Telling Them.* Macmillan, 1990.

Rochman, Hazel. *Against Borders: Promoting Books for a Multicultural World.* American Library Association, 1993.

Rudman, Masha Kabakow. *Children's Literature: An Issues Approach* (3rd ed.). Longman, 1995.

Schon, Isabel. *The Best of the Latino Heritage 1996–2002: A Guide to the Best Juvenile Books about Latino People and Cultures.* Scarecrow Press, 2003.

_____. *Recommended Books in Spanish for Children and Young Adults: 2000–2004.* Scarecrow Press, 2004.

Seale, Doris, and Beverly Slapin. *A Broken Flute: The Native Experience in Books for Children.* Alta Mira Press, 2004.

Sims Bishop, Rudine. *Free Within Ourselves: The Development of African American Children's Literature.* Greenwood, 2007.

Slapin, Beverly, and Doris Seale. *Through Indian Eyes: The Native Experience in Books for Children.* American Indian Studies Center, University of California, 1998.

Smith, Henrietta M., ed. *The Coretta Scott King Awards: 1970–2004* (4th ed.). American Library Association, 2009.

Tikvah: Children's Book Creators Reflect on Human Rights. Introduction by Elie Wiesel. Jacket Art by Leo and Diane Dillon. SeaStar/North-South Books, 2001.

Yokota, Junko. "Issues in Selecting Multicultural Children's Literature." *Language Arts 70* (1993): 156–167.

_____, ed. *Kaleidoscope: A Multicultural Booklist for Grades K–8* (3rd ed.). National Council of Teachers of English, 2000.

_____, and Ann Bates. *Asian American Literature: Voices and Images of Authenticity.* In Darwin L. Henderson and Jill P. May (Eds.), *Exploring Culturally Diverse Literature for Children and Adolescents: Learning to Listen in New Ways.* Allyn & Bacon, 2005, pp. 323–335.

_____, and Mingshui Cai. (2002). "Social Justice in Children's Books." *Language Arts, 79*(5), 72–78.

_____, and Shari Frost. (2003). "Multiracial Characters in Children's Literature." *Book Links, 12*(3), 51–57.

_____, and Miriam Martinez. (2004). "Multicultural Audio Books: How Does the Reader Affect the Listeners' Sense of Culture?" *Book Links, 13*(3), 30–34.

REFERENCES

Aronson, Marc. "Slippery Slopes and Proliferating Prizes." *Horn Book,* 2001.

Au, Kathryn H. *Literacy Instruction in Multicultural Settings.* Harcourt, 1993.

Banks, James. *Cultural Diversity and Education: Foundations, Curriculum, and Teaching.* Allyn & Bacon, 2000.

_____. *An Introduction to Multicultural Education.* 5th ed. Pearson, 2013.

Bannerman, Helen. *The Story of Little Babaji.* Illustrated by Fred Marcellino. HarperCollins, 1996.

_____. *The Story of Little Black Sambo.* HarperCollins, 1899.

Barrera, Rosalinda B., Verlinda D. Thompson, and Mark Dressman, eds. *Kaleidoscope: A Multicultural Booklist for Grades K–8* (2nd ed.). National Council of Teachers of English, 1997.

Bennett, William. "Education Secretary Bennett's Suggested List for Elementary-School Pupils." *Chronicle of Higher Education* (1988, September 14): B3.

Bial, Raymond. *Amish Home.* Houghton Mifflin, 1993. and *Visit to Amish Country.* Phoenix Publishing, 1995.

Bishop, Claire Huchet. *The Five Chinese Brothers.* Illustrated by Kurt Wiese. Coward, 1938.

Brenner, Barbara, and Julia Takaya. *Chibi: A True Story from Japan.* Illustrated by June Otani. Clarion, 1999.

Browne, Anthony. *Piggybook.* Knopf, 1986.

Bruchac, Joseph. *Bowman's Store: A Journey to Myself.* Lee & Low, 1997/2001.

Cai, Mingshui. "Can We Fly across Cultural Gaps on the Wings of Imagination? Ethnicity, Experience, and Cultural Authenticity." *The New Advocate* 8.1 (1995): 1–16.

_____. "Multiple Definitions of Multicultural Literacy: Is the Debate Really Just 'Ivory Tower' Bickering?" *The New Advocate* 11 (1998): 311–324.

_____, and Rudine Sims Bishop. "Multicultural Literature for Children: Towards a Clarification of the Concept." *The Need for Story: Cultural Diversity in Classroom and Community.* Ed. Anne Haas Dyson and Celia Genishi. National Council of Teachers of English, 1994.

Chall, Jeanne S., Eugene Radwin, V. W. French, and C. R. Hall. "Blacks in the World of Children's Books." *The Black American in Books for Children* (2nd ed.). Ed. Donnarae MacCann and G. Woodard. Scarecrow, 1985, pp. 211–221.

Council on Interracial Books for Children. Special Issue on Chicano Materials. *Bulletin of the Council on Interracial Books for Children 5* (1975).

_____. Special Issue on Puerto Rican Materials. *Bulletin of the Council on Interracial Books for Children 4* (1974).

Delpit, Lisa D. "The Silenced Dialogue: Power and Pedagogy in Educating Other People's Children." *Harvard Educational Review 58* (1988): 280–298.

Galda, Lee. Personal communication, November 2000.

Gollub, Matthew. *Cool Melons Turn to Frogs! The Life and Poems of Issa.* Illustrated by Kazuko G. Stone. Lee & Low, 1998.

Grossman, Virginia, and Sylvia Long. *Ten Little Rabbits.* New York: Chronicle, 1991.

Hamilton, Virginia. "Everything of Value: Moral Realism in Literature for Children" (May Hill Arbuthnot Lecture). *Journal of Youth Services in Libraries 6* (Summer 1993): 363–377.

Harris, Violet J. "African American Children's Literature: The First One Hundred Years." *Journal of Negro Education 59* (1990): 540–555.

_____. *Using Multicultural Literature in the K–8 Classroom.* Christopher-Gordon Publishers, 1997.

Henkin, Roxanne. "Who's Invited to Share?": Using Literacy to Teach for Equity and Social Justice. Heinemann, 1998.

_____, ed. *Using Multiethnic Literature in the K–8 Classroom.* Christopher-Gordon Publishers, 1997.

Horning, K. T. (2008). An interview with Rudine Sims Bishop. *Hornbook, 84*(3), 247–259.

Jeffers, Susan. *Brother Eagle, Sister Sky: A Message from Chief Seattle.* Dial, 1991.

Kaplan, Esther. Personal communication, December 1995.

Khorana, Meena G. Editorial. *Bookbird* 34.4 (1996): 2–3.

Kruse, Ginny M., and Kathleen T. Horning, with Megan Schliesman. *Multicultural Literature for Children and Young Adults Vol. 2 1991–1996.* Cooperative Children's Book Center, 1997.

Larrick, Nancy. "The All-White World of Children's Books." *Saturday Review* (1965, September 11): 63–65.

Lester, Julius. *On Writing for Children & Other People.* Dial, 2004.

Little, Jean. *Little by Little: A Writer's Education.* Penguin, 1987.

_____. "A Writer's Social Responsibility." *The New Advocate* 3.2 (1990): 79–88.

McCarty, Teresa L. "What's Wrong with Ten Little Rabbits?" *The New Advocate* 8.2 (1995): 97–98.

McCloskey, Robert. *Make Way for Ducklings.* Viking, 1941.

Melmed, Laura Krauss. "Little Oh: A Story Unfolds." *Book Links* (1999): 4–44.

Meltzer, Milton. "The Social Responsibility of the Writer." *The New Advocate* 2.3 (1989): 155–157.

Na, An. *A Step From Heaven.* Front Street, 2000.

Nieto, Sonia. *Affirming Diversity.* 2nd ed. Longman, 1996.

_____. "Puerto Ricans in Children's Literature and History Texts: A Ten-Year Update." *Bulletin of the Council on Interracial Books for Children 14* (1983).

Noll, Elizabeth. "Accuracy and Authenticity in American Indian Children's Literature: The Social Responsibility of Authors and Illustrators." *The New Advocate* 8.1 (1995): 29–43.

Pallas, A. M., G. Natriello, and E. L. McDill. "The Changing Nature of the Disadvantaged Population: Current Dimensions and Future Trends." *Educational Researcher* 18.5 (1989): 16–22.

Quiroa, Ruth. "Painting a Picture of Mexican American-themed Children's Literature: Trends, Issues and a Historical Overview." National-Louis University, Wheaton, IL. May 10, 2004.

Reimer, K. M. "Multiethnic Literature: Holding Fast to Dreams." *Language Arts* 69 (1992): 14–21.

Rochman, Hazel. *Against Borders: Promoting Books for a Multicultural World.* American Library Association, 1993.

Rollock, Barbara. *The Black Experience in Children's Books* (2nd ed.). New York Public Library, 1984.

Rudman, Masha Kabakow. *Children's Literature: An Issues Approach* (3rd ed.). Longman, 1995.

Schlesinger, Arthur M. *The Disuniting of America.* The Larger Agenda Publishers, 1991.

Schon, Isabel. *A Hispanic Heritage: A Guide to Juvenile Books about Hispanic People and Culture* (3rd ed.). Scarecrow, 1988.

Sims, Rudine. "Children's Books about Blacks: A Mid-Eighties Status Report." *Children's Literature Review 8* (1985): 9–13.

_____. *Shadow and Substance: Afro-American Experience in Contemporary Children's Fiction* (2nd ed.). National Council of Teachers of English/American Library Association, 1982.

Sims Bishop, Rudine. "African American Literature for Children: Anchor, Compass, and Sail." *Perspectives 7* (1991): ix–xii.

_____. "Mirrors, Windows, and Sliding Glass Doors." *Perspectives 6* (1990): ix–xi.

_____. "Multicultural Literature for Children: Making Informed Choices." *Teaching Multicultural Literature in Grades K–8.* Ed. Violet Harris. Christopher-Gordon, 1992, pp. 37–54.

Smith, Henrietta M., ed. *The Coretta Scott King Awards: 1970–2004* (3rd ed.). American Library Association, 2004.

Soto, Gary. *Pacific Crossing.* Harcourt, 1992/Houghton Mifflin Harcourt, 2003.

Stewart, Sarah. *The Journey.* Illustrated by David Small. FSG, 2001.

Tatum, Beverly. *Why Are All the Black Kids Sitting Together in the Cafeteria?* St. Martins, 1999.

Trelease, Jim. *The New Read-Aloud Handbook.* 5th ed. Viking Penguin, 2001.

International Literature

ISSUE *to* CONSIDER

Why Take the Extra Effort to Find International Books?

International books are a sampling of the best books read by children around the world. Often, they offer a different perspective or a distinctive portrayal than what might be familiar. Sometimes, they exhibit diverse artistic sensibilities or different literary traditions. But always, they offer readers a connection to what children in other countries are reading.

Learning about international books takes a little more commitment and effort than learning about books published in your own country. There are organizations, booklists, and even conferences focused on international books, but some consider them to be "areas of specialties" rather than the norm. Teachers committed to bringing international books to the attention of readers must learn how to go about finding these books, obtaining them, and incorporating them into their teaching.

What do you think? International books are not always easily identified as such, and they are sometimes more difficult to obtain, although Internet booksellers are making it more accessible than in the past. Is it their publishers' responsibility to make these books accessible to students when there are already many good books readily available? If so, how will students obtain them and if not, who will make them accessible to students?

What Is International Literature?

J.K. Rowling, Margaret Mahy, Mitsumasa Anno, Polly Horvath, and Garth Nix are just a few of the well-known authors who reside in countries outside North America. Their works form a category of literature that can provide readers a different way of looking at the world, through the eyes of observers who live or have lived in different corners of it. Traditionally, the term "international literature" has meant books written and originally published outside the United States or Canada (Tomlinson, 1998). Originally published in English but from outside the United States, A.A. Milne's *Winnie the Pooh* and P.L. Travers's *Mary Poppins* are examples of international books. Some international books, such as Swiss author Johanna Spyri's *Heidi*, Swedish author Astrid Lindgren's *Pippi Longstocking*, and Swedish author Christina Bjork's *Linnea in Monet's Garden* were initially written in a language other than English and were translated for the U.S. audience. German author Cornelia Funke's books *The Thief Lord* and *Inkheart* have sold well in North America in English translation. Mem Fox's *Possum Magic* is an English-language book originally published in Australia. Importing books from abroad makes the works of the best authors and illustrators in the world available to children in the United States.

The primary purpose for all international books is the same: to tell a compelling story. Many times, international literature opens the eyes of readers in the United States to circumstances in countries of which they have very limited knowledge. In Beverley Naidoo's book, *The Other Side of Truth,* a man speaks out against his government in Nigeria, and the bullet intended for him strikes his wife and kills her. His daughters are sent to London, but the mysterious disappearance of their uncle results in the girls being placed in foster care. When their father arrives in England through illegal means, twelve-year-old Sade must fight to keep him from being deported. Circumstances such as these are not often the direct experience of readers in the United States. But through international literature, all readers can hear a first-hand telling and expand their understanding of the world around them.

Teacher/Librarian Partnership

Making International Books Accessible

Because some international books are difficult to obtain, your own school or public library may not have them on the shelves. Librarians are prepared to request interlibrary loans from outside their libraries, and serve a critical role in making hard-to-obtain books more accessible to readers. Depending on the policy of the interlibrary loan, books can be sent from another library in the system, even across city, state, and country borders! Teachers and librarians working together can support one another in making international books more readily available by promoting them to their students.

Evolution of International Literature

The world continues to read the "cornerstone" stories from various countries: *Pippi Longstocking* from Sweden, *Finn Family Moomintroll* from Finland, *The Wonderful World of Nils* from Sweden, *Pinocchio* from Italy, *A Bell for Ursli* from Switzerland, *Emil and the Detectives* from Germany, and many others. Stories that have roots in folklore but were later written down and published as books include the Anansi stories from various parts of Africa and Monkey King stories from China. Although these books have been translated into English, children in North America are less familiar with them as part of their literary heritage. However, countries that are more openly embracing of books that are in translation provide their readers with numerous editions that are readily available.

In many English-speaking countries, there is a wealth of literature for children and adolescents available, and the publishing industry has developed sufficiently to offer a rich legacy of quality books to young readers. This lack of need for new materials has precipitated the abundance of what is already at hand. This abundance—coupled with a seeming lack of urgency to learn about the world or to engage in international conversations—has led to an insular sensibility of focusing on literature that was exclusively written and created for our own audiences. Ultimately, it means that in the United States, there was very little literature available for our readers that originated from outside the country. In fact, prior to the publication of the *Harry Potter* books from the UK, less than 1% of books published in the United States had their roots outside the country (Tomlinson, 1998). Although there has been a small increase in those numbers, international books, especially translated ones, still rarely make it onto our bookshelves. Differences in sensibility of story structure, literary language, and thematic importance led to many books being rejected by publishers. Artistic sensibility and difference in interpretation of visual narrative also impacted what appealed to acquisition editors. And even at the level of details, there was rejection of word use and illustration that was viewed as "inappropriate." The United States is noted for its protective attitude toward the content of reading and viewing materials for children; this attitude is regarded as startling to individuals in other countries where showing the reality of life is viewed as natural. Details such as alcohol consumption (i.e., a can of beer in an urban street scene, the drinking of wine with a meal) or nudity (i.e., a bathing scene, breastfeeding an infant) were rejected and either removed or re-illustrated to adapt a book for U.S. audiences. Even vocabulary differences between British English and American English were changed (i.e., *lift–elevator, lorrie–truck*).

Various efforts have been made over the years for international literature to have its place in the United States. Committed editors have been making their way to the Bologna Book Fair, Frankfurt Book Fair, and other places where they seek books that are likely to appeal to readers in the United States or that the editors hope to introduce to new readers. Often, this has been done in the face of possible financial risk. In earlier eras, publishers were able to "balance the books" for the company when they knew that some books would make enough money to enable them to publish others that would fulfill the company's editorial vision and goals even though it was unlikely they would regain the revenue from the new books. A complicating factor is that few editors

ILLUSTRATION 5.1 *The Story of Nils* is alluded to on the cover of *A Bridge of Children's Books*, the autobiography of Jella Lepman. It represents an international story well known around the world. (By arrangement with the O'Brien Press Ltd., Dublin, and the International Youth Library.)

TEACHING IDEA 5.1

LINK TO INTERNATIONAL BOOKS

Scholars such as Carl Tomlinson, Carol Lynch-Brown, and Susan Stan have long advocated the pairing of books that may seem unfamiliar with those that are more familiar.

- Pair a U.S. book with an international book with similar themes: *Make Way for Ducklings* could be paired with *Chibi: A True Story from Japan*. A setting like Boston Public Garden or other American public gardens may well be familiar to many children, and they will find a parallel story of ducklings in search of a safe home at the Imperial Palace moat in Japan.
- Pair the same book published in different languages: Find foreign language translations of books the children might know in their original English editions. Show how children in other countries are reading books that they may also have read. Try the reverse: Find books that are international books published in the United States and emphasize the country of origin so that children can understand that readers in other countries have also enjoyed the same book.

TEACHING IDEA 5.2

POINT IT OUT!

Sometimes, readers are not aware that a book originates outside their own country. One way to highlight the origin of a book is to note the information on the back flap of a book that states where the author and illustrator live and work. Other information, such as the details on the Library of Congress Cataloging in Publication information on the copyright page, explicitly state the original country of publication. Teachers who note such details and explain it to students are able to quickly note that the book is one that children in other countries are also reading. Using a map at this point to simply point to the country may visually help readers see the relative location of a country outside their own.

were able to read multiple languages well enough to make independent assessments of books from non-English language countries. The search for people who had language expertise, an understanding of the children's literature field, and the ability to make recommendations regarding the viability of a book's acceptance in a new country was easier for some languages than for others. Initial assessments were often made based on "rough translations" in which editors had to determine whether thorough translations would lead to better text. In those early post-war years, the profession as a whole sought to appreciate and reward such efforts; the American Library Association established the Mildred Batchelder Award to applaud publishers who provided the best translated book for readers in the United States.

The 1990s saw the conglomeration of publishing companies in which smaller, independent children's book publishers became entities within larger corporations. This move meant that the responsibility of overseeing financial decisions was no longer solely within the children's divisions; rather, it was viewed through the lens of financial viability from a different perspective. Each book was examined for its likelihood of sales, and editorial vision had to be fiscally responsible at the "individual" book level rather than at the "group of books published within each season" level. Publishers sought books they knew would sell, and sales popularity became an increasingly dominant factor in acquisition decisions.

In the early years of the twenty-first century, we became progressively aware of our need and desire for access to the wealth of good literature available around the world, a more international perspective for our young people to see and read about, and a commitment to making extra efforts to maintain the purity of the artistic conceptualization of the original book. However, major changes in the publishing industry resulting in fewer publishers have meant that editors could no longer "balance the books" by having bestsellers offset the small sales of international books they believed in unless each book resulted in adequate sales. International books are among those that are well suited for the digital age; perhaps it will bring about new possibilities for such books.

Issues Related to International Literature

The primary areas of concern related to international literature are predominantly about *access*: that there are so few books that are translated into English, and that when they are, relatively few are published in the United States and only a rare few

TECHNOLOGY in PRACTICE 5.1

THE INTERNATIONAL CHILDREN'S DIGITAL LIBRARY

The International Children's Digital Library's Web site, launched in November 2002, offers digitized children's picture books from around the world. Their goal is to house approximately 10,000 books from 100 cultures. The University of Maryland's Human-Computer Interaction Lab and the Internet Archive, a nonprofit organization based in San Francisco, are responsible for the conception, design, data entry, and management. Children contributed ideas and feedback during the early stages of development by indicating the types of books they wanted, how they wanted to search for them, and how they wanted to read them. One nine-year-old commented that "the book is never checked out" and others remarked that there is access to books beyond what your local library has physically available.

The books available span quite a range: from classics with expired copyrights and now in the public domain to newer books still under copyright but donated to the project by various publishers. Books from various countries have been donated by international libraries and organizations. Despite some questions that are still being addressed regarding focus, design, use, and accessibility, the site is ready for those who have cable modem or DSL connections. Link: International Children's Digital Library <http://www.icdlbooks.org>

make it into children's hands. The question of access will likely take on new possibilities with the rise of ebooks, though, as translation and international sales are finding new avenues previously unavailable. But ultimately, "making it into children's hands" is still largely the responsibility of those who serve as gatekeepers, who make decisions about which books to review, purchase, and promote to readers. Just as in multicultural literature, the more different the experience, the more scaffolding and recommendation is required to successfully connect the material to new audiences.

A related issue regarding access has to do with *balance*. Regarding genre balance, most of the international books available in English are in the categories of folklore, historical fiction, and fantasy. Just as in multicultural literature, they lend an air of "long ago and far away," forgoing the idea that there are contemporary stories of realistic fiction that would allow us to take a peek into the lives of people in various parts of the world today. But even beyond genre balance, when considering what is available in terms of subject matter, there are certain topics that are more frequently made available from outside the United States. For example, many books about World War II have been imported, creating a wealth of perspectives, but skewing the numbers of books from outside the United States in terms of representing varying time periods and topics. And finally, the need for balance also implies the importance of understanding that no one book can fairly represent a country, and the more books of wide range that are made available, the better off the readers are in terms of trying to see the complexity of how books represent countries and their literature.

Another area of concern is in creating *relevance* of international books for a new audience. Books that are uniquely situated in one country and of primary importance to those who live there may still be thematically important in another; if details are considered "intriguing" rather than deeming them as "foreign," then they can be seen as enriching the story and grounding it in a particular setting. Lesley Beake's *Home Now* may be focused on the AIDS orphans in various African nations, but if you consider the

ILLUSTRATION 5.2 *Samir and Yonatan* by Daniella Carmi is a story of an Israeli boy and a Palestinian boy who end up side-by-side in a Jewish hospital in Israel. (Scholastic, Inc.)

theme of identifying "home" more broadly, this particular story deepens all readers' understanding of what it means to have to shift a child's understanding of "home" in ways that are universal, even though the details of the story will be rarely the same for many readers.

Some are concerned about international books and *comprehensibility* to a new audience—-that references to details that are "foreign" to young children may make a book incomprehensible. For example, in Jackie French's *Josephine Wants to Dance*, Josephine is a kangaroo who loves to dance, despite her younger brother Joey saying that "kangaroos don't wear tutus and they never wear silk ballet shoes." She remains determined, and ends up stepping in to fill the lead role when the prima ballerina twists her ankle. She had learned to dance from and with the brolgas, lyrebirds, and emus, and practiced and practiced. This reference to animals unknown to young children in countries outside of Australia may feel like too much new information at one time, but the introduction to new concepts through a quality picture book can be a welcome introduction to things newly encountered. Thematically, this book works well when compared to Mary Hoffman's *Amazing Grace*, illustrated by Caroline Binch. In this realistic story, a young girl wants to be Peter Pan in the school play, but is told by some that she can't get the role; her belief that she can is rewarded when she wins the part through her hard work and determination. Both of these books originate outside the United States; the realistic fiction picture book is from the United Kingdom and requires less new background knowledge for readers in the United States. Introducing these two books together allows readers to make thematic connections of perseverance, hard work, and believing in oneself.

Criteria for Evaluating International Literature

With the exception of authenticity, the evaluation and selection issues previously discussed in connection with multicultural literature are also important for international literature originating outside the United States. Although many countries publish material that is about cultures other than their own, the books that are exported to other countries tend to be about native experiences. When one's own country is the setting, cultural authenticity is expected, as both author and illustrator have an insider perspective. Three crucial issues specific to international literature focus on audience, illustrations, and the translation of non-English text.

■ How well does the book work for the new audience?

An international book is originally written from the perspective of an author within the country, with readers in that country as the intended audience. Only later is the book taken abroad to other countries. When a book travels away from its intended audience, sometimes readers in the new audience need support to help them understand it. Teachers should consider these questions: Is the book geared specifically toward readers in the book's country of origin, or does it make the transition to a broader audience outside of that country? Who will be able to empathize and identify with the story? Books written in the United States and intended for American children often include references to things that American readers take for granted. Similarly, books originally written for readers in another country often assume understandings that only the original intended audience would have. Sometimes, misinterpretations may occur when details are not understood; at other times, an inability to pick up details doesn't detract from the reader's understanding of the story as a whole.

As an example, let's examine Akiko Hayashi's illustrations of the series of books about Anna. The pictures are laden with cultural details—a mailbox attached to the inside of the front door, slippers in the entryway, artificial flowers on the street light, a place where children wash their hands at the park. Even the way Anna steps on the back of her shoes signifies that she is rushing as she tries to discover the identity of her new friend in *Anna's Secret Friend*. Japanese children would pick up these details because they are very natural to their understanding of home and community. American children might not take particular note of these details or might find them interesting, but not different enough to interfere with their understanding of the story.

Sometimes, certain details in the original edition of a book that would be innately understood by the original audience are explained when the book is prepared in an international edition. Uri Orlev's Batchelder Award book *The Lady with the Hat* has two characters stopping for a meal while on a trip in a remote area of Palestine. Foods such as hummus, tahini, shashlik, kebab, baklava, and Turkish coffee are described for readers who are unfamiliar with them—for example, "small cakes filled with pistachio nuts and honey that were called baklava."

■ Do the illustrations communicate as intended in its original context?

Artistic sensibilities and how art conveys emotion are often interpreted differently in various contexts. Sometimes, those contexts vary by cultures. Color may signify one thing in one country, and yet the same color may signify a completely opposite thing in another. Images may elicit particular emotions in one culture; they may elicit an entirely different feeling in another. Considering the impact of visual literacy across different cultures is an important aspect of evaluating how well a book crosses to a new audience.

■ How well does the translation work?

An issue of critical concern with international books is translation. When a book was originally published in a language other than English, the translator who makes it available to English-language readers plays an important role in the way the material is received by the new audience. The translator is as important as the author and illustrator in presenting the story. A skilled translator does not merely present the author's words in another language, but instead interprets the words, selecting ways to evoke images and emotions that reflect the author's original intent. The translator must consider several things:

■ Creating a flow in the translated language, despite differences in the sentence structures of the two languages
■ Balancing the amount of "foreign" information to maintain readability and reader attention while retaining the unique details that make the work authentic
■ Explaining foreign situations that are unknown to readers while maintaining the pace of the original text

Even when a book is from another English-language country, some differences in language use are noticeable to U.S. readers. Should these differences be changed? When comprehension may suffer significantly, the answer is yes. But maintaining as much of the original language as possible is part of maintaining the authenticity of the book. In Mem Fox's book, *Shoes from Grandpa*, originally published in Australia, the family

ILLUSTRATION 5.4 Mitsumasa Anno created *All in a Day* because he believes that world understanding begins with children imagining the lives of other children around the world. ("*All In A Day*" by Mitsumasa Anno. Used by permission of Penguin Group (USA), Inc. All rights reserved.)

ILLUSTRATION 5.5 Knowledge of history and popular culture will enable readers to find many interesting details in this double-page picture of New York City by Anno. ("Anno's USA" by Mitsumasa Anno. Used by permission of Penguin Group (USA), Inc. All rights reserved.)

TOP SHELF 5.1

DEPICTIONS OF WAR IN PICTURE BOOKS

Rose Blanche by Christophe Gallaz. Illustrated by Roberto Innocenti

Hiroshima No Pika written and illustrated by Toshi Maruki

The Donkey of Gallipoli: A True Story of Courage in World War I by Mark Greenwood. Illustrated by Frané Lessac

TOP SHELF 5.2

STORIES OF FRIENDSHIPS

Manolita Four Eyes by Elvira Lindo

Secret Letters, 0-10 by Susie Morgenstern

The Friends by Kazumi Yumoto

was enjoying a "barbie." A U.S. audience, unexposed to this name for a barbecue, might imagine the doll known as Barbie. The word was changed in this case. Yet in another of Mem Fox's books, *Possum Magic,* references to Australian foods such as "mornay, vegemite and pavlova" were maintained in the U.S. version. Although these words are unfamiliar to most American children, they do not interfere with an understanding of the story. With the words left in, the story remains true to the original context of the Australian culture. A benefit of this approach is that U.S. children are introduced to vocabulary that expands their knowledge of another country.

It does require extra effort to make international books accessible to U.S. audiences, but the benefits gained from including international books in children's repertoire make the extra effort worthwhile. One notable example of an international book is Mitsumasa Anno's *All in a Day.* A young child is on a deserted island, somewhere near the International Date Line. Each double-page spread shows this child in the center section, with text to one side. Across the top and the bottom of the spread are depictions of what New Year's Day might be like for children in eight different countries; each picture is by an illustrator from that country. Each time the reader turns a page, three hours have passed. In the preface to the book, Anno asks readers to consider the fact that while some children sleep, others play, and while some swim, others build snowmen. He points out that differences exist around the world in homes, clothes, languages, and other aspects of life, but he also notes that there are some things that remain the same around the world, such as facial expressions, the sounds of laughing or crying, and the moon and the sun in the sky. Anno and his team of illustrators offer a note of optimism. Their hope—and ours as well—is that by the time the children of today grow up, the world will have become a better place. This book exemplifies a sense of world community from a child's point of view. Although the book was originally published in Japanese, the composition of the illustration team and the theme make this book truly international.

Authors and Illustrators of International Literature

Mitsumasa Anno

Mitsumasa Anno, a Japanese author and illustrator, is a world-renowned contributor to the picture book field. He is best known for his wordless "journey" books, mathematical game books, and books with playful twists of visual perceptions. Anno's highly detailed and imaginative work appeals to all ages because his books offer multiple levels of humor and intrigue. His books combine technical sophistication with creative text, illustrations, and design. Many also include detailed historic, scientific, or mathematical information for adult readers who share them with children.

Anno delights in including mathematical and scientific details to make learning these ways of thinking enjoyable and interesting. In *Anno's Counting House,* the reader first sees all ten children living in the house on the left side of the double-page spread, and then watches them move into the house on the right one by one. Children can see who has moved and what belongings the child has taken, but they can also note that the total number of children shown in both houses is always ten.

Anno also manipulates visual perception in a way that makes the physically impossible seem probable. For example, *Upside-Downers: More Pictures to Stretch the Imagination* is a book that bends the "rules" for enjoying books. A pair of jokers and the four kings leave a deck of cards, but nobody can tell what's up and what's down. In the author's postscript, Anno suggests that a child can sit opposite a parent and they can read the book to each other at the same time—or a child can read alone, turn the book around, and then read it from the other direction, upside down.

Anno's Journey begins a series of books that are filled with images of the countries he visits. Historical events, literary figures, and cultural markers fill the pages of the wordless books simply titled *Anno's U.S.A., Anno's Italy,* and *Anno's Britain.* On the double-page spread depicting New York City in *Anno's U.S.A.,* readers will delight in discovering the surprises embedded in the art: the Macy's Thanksgiving Day Parade with floats representing characters from *Where the Wild Things Are,* Tarzan, and the New York Public Library lions; Marilyn Monroe standing on a street corner with the wind sweeping her skirt up; and Native Americans selling Manhattan island.

Anno was born and raised in a small town in western Japan. He taught art at an elementary school in Tokyo for ten years before becoming a full-time artist. In addition to his numerous picture books, Anno creates many other works of art such as paintings, calendars, and stationery. In 1985, he was awarded the Hans Christian Andersen Award for Illustration, given by the International Board on Books for Young People to honor an illustrator who has made a significant contribution to children's literature worldwide.

Ana Maria Machado

Born in 1941 in Rio de Janeiro, Ana Maria Machado is widely recognized as one of the most influential writers not only in her native Brazil and in South America, but also around the world. She began her career as a painter and later as a journalist, but by 1969, she had started to focus on writing for children. "I belong to that generation of writers who began to write during the military dictatorship, as children's literature, alongside poetry and song texts, were amongst the few literary forms with which, through the poetic and symbolic use of language, you could make the ideas of a joie de vivre, individual freedom and respect for human rights known" (10th International Literature Festival, Berlin <http://www.literaturfestival.com/bios1_3_6_456.html>). Clearly, her writing has political themes and social implications that prompt readers to think about their world; but Machado focuses on telling a story, and trusts her young readers to be able to think for themselves.

Perhaps her best known picture book abroad is *Nina Bonita,* in which a white rabbit falls in love with a dark-skinned girl, asking her to reveal her beauty secrets. The rabbit goes on to marry a black rabbit, and they produce children of various mixes of their colors.

In *From Another World,* Machado explores Brazil's history through the device of a contemporary setting with the ghost story revealing historic experiences. When Mariano's mother and friend purchase a historic homestead and convert it into an inn, the ghost of a nineteenth century slave girl appears and relays the story of her family's demise, appealing for help to Mariano and his friends. Similarly, *Me in the Middle* relies on elements of fantasy to connect the past, present, and future. Bel is nearly thirteen, and finds that she hears the voice of her grandmother, as well as that of her future great granddaughter, and both offer advice as they compete for Bel's attention while Bel learns to live in the present.

Ana Maria Machado's books for children and adults number over a hundred, and have been translated and published in seventeen countries. The Hans Christian Andersen Award was bestowed on her in 2000, in worldwide recognition of her contribution to children's literature.

Authors from Past Decades

Many authors and illustrators from decades past have made a mark on children's literature around the world in translation. Those who have defined the field in this way include Astrid Lindgren, Johanna Spyri, Erik Kästner, and many others. Some we may know better because their work was originally written in English and therefore was more accessible include A.A. Milne, P.L. Travers, and James Barrie.

In the chart below, we have listed authors and illustrators by their countries of original publication; many are well known and are sometimes featured within separate genre chapters (i.e., in the fantasy chapter: Philip Pullman, Cornelia Funke, Roald Dahl, Eva Ibbotson, Diana Wynne Jones, Brian Jacques, J.K. Rowling).

COUNTRIES FROM WHICH ENGLISH LANGUAGE BOOKS ARE AVAILABLE IN THE UNITED STATES:

Australia: Jeannie Baker, Graeme Base, Mem Fox, Jackie French, Bob Graham, Sonia Hartnett, Robert Ingpen, Shaun Tan, Patricia Wrightson, Markus Zusak

Canada: Brian Doyle, Deborah Ellis, Sarah Ellis, Polly Horvath, Jean Little, Tim Wynne-Jones, Paul Yee

Ireland: Eoin Colfer, P.J. Lynch, Siobhán Parkinson, Kate Thompson, Martin Waddell

New Zealand: Bernard Beckett, Joy Cowley, Margaret Mahy

South Africa: Niki Daly, Piet Grobler, Beverley Naidoo

United Kingdom: David Almond, Quentin Blake, Anthony Browne, John Burningham, Aidan Chambers, Lauren Child, Roald Dahl, Michael Foreman, Emily Gravett, Mini Grey, Shirley Hughes, Eva Ibbotson, Hilary McKay, David McKee, Michael Morpurgo, Terry Pratchett, Philip Pullman, Michael Rosen, J.K. Rowling, Jacqueline Wilson

COUNTRIES FROM WHICH THERE ARE BOOKS TRANSLATED INTO ENGLISH:

Argentina: Isol

Austria: Linda Wolfsgruber, Lisbeth Zwerger

Belgium: Carl Cneut, Kitty Crowther, Bart Moeyaert, Klaas Verplancke

Brazil: Ana Maria Machado, Lygia Bojunga Nunes

Canada (French): Marie-Louise Gay

Czech Republic: Kveta Pacovská

Denmark: Svend Otto S., Bjarne Reuter

Estonia: Piet Raud

Finland: Tove Jansson

France: Chen Jianghong (from China), Susie Morgenstern, Tomi Ungerer

Germany: Jutta Bauer, Rotraut Susanne Berner, Michael Ende, Wolf Erlbruch, Cornelia Funke, Peter Härtling, Erich Kästner, Mirjam Pressler, Binette Schroeder

Greece: Eugene Trivizas

Israel: Uri Orlev

Italy: Roberto Innocenti

Japan: Suekichi Akaba, Mitsumasa Anno, Taro Gomi, Akiko Hayashi, Kazuo Iwamura, Michio Mado, Komako Sakai, Shuntaro Tanikawa, Nahoko Uehashi, Kazumi Yumoto

Korea: Eun-hee Choung

Mongolia: Dashdondog Jamba

Netherlands: Guus Kuijer, Joke Van Leeuwen, Max Velthuijs

Norway: Stian Hole

Russia: Nicolai Popov, Gennadij Spirin

Slovenia: Lila Prap

Sweden: Lennart Hellsing, Astrid Lindgren, Barbro Lindgren, Eva Eriksson

Switzerland: Alois Carigiet, Etienne Delessert, Jürg Schubiger

Turkey: Feridun Oral

Ask *the* Author: Beverley Naidoo

You were born in South Africa during the apartheid, and raised in a world where "white privilege" was the norm. What compels you to write the stories you do about South Africa, racism, and politics?

As a child, I believe I was schooled, not educated. I grew up very blinkered to the world around me. I cried over *The Diary of Anne Frank* without realizing that there were atrocities all around me. When I came to the age of reason and began to be challenged to see the world around me for what it was, I felt angry that the adult society, including teachers, had not encouraged me to question. Then,

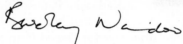

finding myself in exile in England, how could I tell my own children and the children of South Africa the stories of what was really going on? I have always loved story and thought of it as the way to opening up the world.

The issues I write about (the breaking up of families, war, and so forth) are very fundamental issues, not just to do with South Africa. My first novel was set in South Africa, but its meaning carries across time and place. It resonates with witness literature from other places; for example, Mildred Taylor's work, set in the United States but fundamentally about the same issues, spoke to me.

Books are like a window onto the world, and writers can invite us in. The important thing to me is to say that not only is this person's pain important but also to begin to connect us. Some of my books, such as *The Other Side* and *Web of Lies*, are largely set in London. But the fundamental themes of families and dislocation carry across time and place. The universal story of building walls by the "haves" who think they can ignore the "have nots" on the other side is what I care about. The building of these walls is not going to be the solution.

Witness literature is a genre of circumstance, of time and place. It is literature that connects umbilically with the society; in other words, it is not just literature about characters (stories about self) but about how characters connect to wider society (stories that examine an individual person's consciousness as it relates to

the larger society). My writing especially is about experiences that fracture society. Although individuals have the experiences, what they go through reflects issues and movements in that wider society. Much more African literature is written from a witness literature perspective than that which emanates from Western industrialized countries. Witness literature is about seeing things, observing and noting what is happening in this human condition so that you can't say, "I didn't know." It is a dramatic story and a personal story that is contextualized to relate to larger perspectives.

I always consider the questions, "Who is telling the story, and whose story is it?" It takes a tremendous amount of sensitivity, awareness, and research to know what you don't know.

I agree that white writers do not have that sense of firsthand detail and can't write it in that way that a person from the culture can, but a white writer can enter a story in a different way. We have to consider to what extent we can get into each other's lives; can we imagine each other's lives—whether it is a difference of class, culture, geography or some other factor. The key is authenticity.

Beverley Naidoo grew up in South Africa under the apartheid system. An active resister to apartheid, she lived in her home country until departing to study at the University of York in England. There she began writing in exile and in 1985 published her first children's book, the award-winning *Journey to Jo'burg*, which was dedicated to her nanny's two daughters who died from diphtheria because only white people were inoculated at the time. *Journey to Jo'burg* was banned in South Africa until 1991. Beverley Naidoo has taught primary and secondary school in London and worked as an Advisor for English and Cultural Diversity in Dorset. She has a Ph.D. in exploring issues of racism with young people through literature and works tirelessly to promote children's entitlement to grow up free from racism and injustice. Her novel *The Other Side of Truth* won the prestigious Carnegie Medal.

Awards for International Literature

The Hans Christian Andersen Award

The International Board on Books for Young People (IBBY) established the Hans Christian Andersen Award in 1956. The purpose of this international award is to honor an author who has made a significant contribution to children's literature; an award for illustrators has been offered since 1966. The entire body of work by an author or an illustrator is considered, and national IBBY chapters nominate an author and an illustrator from their country. This award is given every two years at the IBBY World Congress, which is held in various locations throughout the world. Past U.S. winners include author Meindert DeJong in 1962, illustrator Maurice Sendak in 1970, author Scott O'Dell in 1972, author Paula Fox in 1978, author Virginia Hamilton in 1992, and author Katherine Paterson in 1998. Some winners from other countries have had books published in the United States, including Astrid Lindgren from Sweden, Svend Otto S. from Denmark, Suekichi Akaba and Mitsumasa Anno from Japan, Lygia Bojunga Nunes from Brazil, Patricia Wrightson and Robert Ingpen from Australia, Lisbeth Zwerger from Austria, and Anthony Browne from England. A complete list of past winners can be found at the website for ibby.org.

The Astrid Lindgren Memorial Award

Astrid Lindgren, author of such famous books as *Pippi Longstocking* and *Ronia, the Robber's Daughter,* is Sweden's best-known author for children. This award was established to honor her memory and as a gift from the people of Sweden to the world of international children's literature as an encouragement for reading. It carries a significant monetary award of five million Swedish crowns and is the largest monetary award for children's literature in the world; it is the second largest literary prize in general. Because of its broad goals, not only are authors eligible, but also illustrators, storytellers, and individuals or organizations that promote reading. In fact, in its first several years, among the winners have been noted U.S. illustrator/author Maurice Sendak, U.S. author Katherine Paterson, Austrian author Christine Nöstlinger, UK author Philip Pullman, Japanese illustrator Ryoji Arai, the Venezuelan reading promotion organization Banco del libro, and Australian author Sonya Hartnett.

The Mildred Batchelder Award

The Mildred Batchelder Award was established in 1966 by the American Library Association's Association of Library Services to Children (ALSC) to promote international exchange of books for young people; it has been given to a U.S. publisher annually since 1968, unless no book is deemed worthy in a particular year. The award is named in honor of a former executive director of the ALSC. Books originally published in a foreign language in a foreign country and translated and published in the United States in the year preceding the award are considered. The citation is given to publishers to recognize their commitment to bringing books from abroad and making them available to young people in this country. With the exception of a few picture books, including the 1983 winner *Hiroshima No Pika* by Toshi Maruki and the 1987 winner *Rose Blanche* by Roberto Innocenti, most books are novels for older children.

The White Ravens Award

The International Youth Library in Munich, Germany, annually names books from around the world that have a universal theme and exceptional or innovative artistic and literary style and design. The books are noted in the following ways:

- *Special Mention:* Books to which the language specialists at the International Youth Library wish to draw special attention.
- *International Understanding:* Books that have content that is likely to contribute to understanding among cultures and people; such books are most likely to fit the mission under which Jella Lepman founded the library.
- *Easily Understandable:* Books for which the text is easy to understand but the content appeals to older readers, making such books particularly important for foreign language collections in libraries around the world.

These books are notable in that they are considered with one set of criteria, but across languages and cultures in their original version. The list is announced annually at the Bologna Children's Book Festival and is on exhibit at the library in Munich afterward. The complete list of past winners can be linked, with annotation, through the Web site of the International Children's Digital Library. The online catalogue includes nearly 4,000 annotations for books from over 80 countries in 60 languages, published since 1993 and can be accessed at <http://www.icdlbooks.org/servlet/WhiteRavens>.

Other International Book Awards

Many countries have book awards equivalent to the Caldecott and Newbery Medals. Great Britain has the Kate Greenaway Medal and the Carnegie Medal. Canada has the Amelia Frances Howard-Gibbon Medal and the Canadian Children's Book of the Year award. Australia has the Picture Book of the Year award and the Australian Children's Book of the Year for Young Readers award.

Outstanding International Books for Children

Each year, a committee of USBBY (United States Board on Books for Young People) selects approximately 25 outstanding books that they want to feature and recommend to children and young people and that are published in the United States, following an international original publication. Many of these books come from countries in which they were published in English originally—the United King-

ILLUSTRATION 5.8 Roberto Innocenti, world-renowned winner of the Hans Christian Andersen Award for Illustration, teams with Christophe Gallaz to tell a story not usually found in picture books in the English language, depicting war, Holocaust victims, and death. (Copyright © 2013 The Creative Editions is an imprint of The Creative Company, Mankato, MN.)

ILLUSTRATION 5.9 In *The Composition* by Antonio Skarmeta, illustrated by Alfonso Ruano, students read about military dictatorship and what it means to the lives of children in such countries. (Cover of "The Composition" reproduced with permission from Groundwood Books, Toronto.)

ILLUSTRATION 5.10 USBBY is the United States national section of the International Board on Books for Young People, IBBY. (United States Board on Books for Young People [USBBY].)

dom, Ireland, Canada, Australia, and so on. Others were originally published in various languages, but have been translated and are made available in English in the United States now. The award was begun with the intent of publicizing and recommending high quality books that originate from outside the United States. These titles are announced at the USBBY meeting at the American Library Association's Midwinter Conference each year, and published as an annotated set of reviews in *School Library Journal*'s February issue. The annual lists are also available in bookmark format at <www.usbby.org>.

EXPERIENCES FOR FURTHER LEARNING

1. Choose a theme from which you will select books across country origins. Try to pick a broad theme that can be interpreted in many ways, such as "effects of war," "immigration," or "international boundary crossing." Or you can pick a theme that is universal enough to comprise books that are not necessarily about being from a specific country, such as "intergenerational relationship," "bedtime stories," or "coming of age." Your selection of books should include several different countries, and show different ways of looking at your theme. When possible, include books across genre lines as well so that informational books and poetry are included along with works of fiction.

2. Read a variety of international books. Select one for which you can find a "partner book(s)" that you already know. Think of ways in which you can make connections between your known book and your new book, taking into consideration the differences and similarities that exist in the two books. Are any of the distinctions due to differences of country origin, or to other factors? Plan ways in which you might be able to support children who are reading the "partnered" books.

3. Read a variety of international books that have won international awards. You may want to begin with winners of the Batchelder Award and those on the Outstanding International Books for Children list, as those books are readily available in English in the United States. Consider ways in which you can incorporate the reading aloud of these books, or passages from longer works, to introduce them to students. Keep in mind that the more a book is different from their past reading materials, the more they will need an adult to scaffold the new book experience for them.

RECOMMENDED BOOKS

*indicates a picture book; I indicates interest level
(P = preschool, YA = young adult)
International literature can also be found at the end of other chapters. All titles included here are available in English. (Many international books have also been recommended within the various genre chapters.)

*Aldana, Patsy (ed.). *Under the Spell of the Moon: Art for Children from the World's Great Illustrators*. Groundwood, 2004. (Canada) This collection includes illustrators representing more than 25 countries, accompanied by poetry or brief text bilingually presented in the illustrator's own language and in English. Katherine Paterson's introduction describes the vision of Jella Lepman in founding IBBY (International Board on Books for Young People). (I: All ages)

*Anno, Mitsumasa. *Anno's Journey*. Philomel, 1977. (Japan) This wordless book depicts a rider crossing Europe, encountering various scenes from famous paintings, children's games and stories, and historical events. The detail-filled double spreads offer glimpses that add up to an overall sense of a traveler, looking into various parts of Europe. (I: All ages)

————. *Math Games, I–III*. Philomel, 1987, 1989, 1991. (Japan) Various mathematical concepts are explored playfully and imaginatively, and the focus is on intuitive understanding of mathematics rather than on accuracy of answers. (I: P–9)

Arni, Samhita, and Moyna Chitrakar. *Sita's Ramayana*. Tara Books, 2011. (India) This graphic novel represents the story of the Hindu Ramayana, told from the point of view of Queen Sita. (I: 12–YA)

*Baasansuren, Bolormaa. *My Little Round House*. Adapted by Helen Mixter. Groundwood, 2009. (Japan) Set in Mongolia, this book portrays the nomadic lifestyle of Jilu's first year from his point of view. (I: P–6)

*Bae, Hyun-Joo. *New Clothes for New Year's Day*. Kane/Miller, 2007. (Korea) A young girl in Korea enthusiastically prepares for Lunar New Year and dons her new "traditional" clothes. (I: P–7)

*Beake, Lesley. *Home Now*. Illustrated by Karin Littlewood. Charlesbridge, 2007. (UK) An AIDS-orphaned child in a South African township relates to an orphaned baby elephant and comes to realize that her aunt is providing "home now." An Author's Note helps provide additional support information on the AIDS crisis. (I: K–7)

Beckett, Bernard. *Genesis*. Houghton Mifflin Harcourt, 2009. (New Zealand). In a futuristic world in which only a small segment is saved following worldwide disasters, Anaximander is taking an oral examination to try for a spot in an exclusive training academy. Explores in depth many questions of science, philosophy, and artificial intelligence within moral decision making. (I: 12–YA)

*Berner, Rotraut Susanne. *In the Town All Year 'Round*. Translated by Neeltje Konings & Nick Elliott. Chronicle, 2008. (Germany) Wordless book of illustrations invites viewers to follow characters in vignettes within larger scenes, with various activities that change by seasons. (I: P–6)

*Bjork, Christina. *Linnea in Monet's Garden*. Illustrated by Lena Anderson. Farrar, Straus, & Giroux, 1987. (Sweden) Linnea visits impressionist painter Claude Monet's home and garden in Giverny, France, and readers learn about his art. (I: 9–12)

*Brenner, Barbara, and Julia Takaya. *Chibi: A True Story from Japan*. Illustrated by June Otani. Clarion, 1996. (Japan) In a story reminiscent of McCloskey's *Make Way for Ducklings,* a wild duck family seeks a safe home in the Imperial Palace moat in downtown Tokyo. (I: P–8)

*Browne, Anthony. *Willy the Wimp*. Walker, 2008. (UK) From the popular series about Willy, a chimp, this book explores the balance of bullies and bullied when Willy feels compelled to take a body-building class in an attempt at fighting against bullies. (I: P–8)

*Burningham, John. *It's a Secret*. Candlewick, 2009. (UK) Marie Elaine wonders, "Where do cats go at night?" Seeing Malcolm, her cat, all dressed up in fancy clothes, she asks where he is going. He replies that "It's a secret" but she gets herself invited to go along and join in the festivities. Mixed media illustrations of paints, pencils, and collage create a visual treat. (I: P–7)

*Campbell, Nicola I. *Shin-chi's Canoe*. Illustrated by Kim LaFave. Groundwood, 2008. (Canada) Shi-shi-etko prepares her six-year-old brother for the strength he will need to retain his spirit as they are put on a cattle truck to go to a mandatory residential school for Native children in Canada (as was also done in the United States). A purposeful story, it describes the injustice done to Native people, the separation of family members, and the loss of culture and language they were forced to endure. (I: 1–3)

Carroll, Lewis. *Alice in Wonderland*. Illustrated by Lisbeth Zwerger. Penguin, 2007. (Switzerland) The classic tale of fantasy in which Alice embarks on a magical adventure has been illustrated by world famous artist, Lisbeth Zwerger, in her signature style and palette. (I: 9–12)

*Chen, Jianghong. *The Magic Horse of Han Gan*. Enchanted Lion, 2006. (France) Chinese illustrator Chen illustrates the story of a classic painter whose realistic portrayals of tethered horses respond to a challenge to bring one to life. (I: 9–12)

*Choung, Eun-hee. *Minji's Salon*. Kane/Miller, 2008. (Korea) Parallel images show that when Minji sees her mother getting her hair done at a salon, she engages in make-believe play with her dog, using ice cream for color and crayons as rollers. (I: P–7)

*Daly, Niki. *Jamela's Dress*. Farrar, Straus, & Giroux, 2004. (South Africa) Jamela can't resist playing with her mother's new fabric, intended for a wedding. See also *Happy Birthday, Jamela* (2006). (I: P–8)

*De Déu Prats, Joan. *Sebastian's Roller Skates*. Illustrated by Francesc Rovira. Kane/Miller, 2005. (Spain) Sebastian is a shy boy who gains confidence when he finds a pair of abandoned roller skates and learns how to use them. (I: K–8)

Ellis, Deborah. *Three Wishes: Palestinian and Israeli Children Speak*. Frances Lincoln, 2007. (Canada) Ellis shares the viewpoints of Palestinian and Israeli youth, age 8 to 18, who describe three wishes for their lives amidst the tension and war they live in. (I: 11–YA)

*Foreman, Michael. *Mia's Story: A Sketchbook of Hopes and Dreams*. Candlewick, 2006. (UK) Set in the Andes, Mia and her family live near the city dump and each day, they gather usable items that they then take into the city to sell. (I: 8–10)

*Fox, Mem. *Possum Magic*. Illustrated by Julie Vivas. Harcourt, 1991. (Australia) Hush is an invisible possum whose request to Grandma Poss to make her visible again leads them on a quest, searching Australian cities for Australian foods for the solution. (I: P–8)

*French, Jackie. *Diary of a Wombat*. Illustrated by Bruce Whatley. Clarion, 2003. (Australia) Diary entries describe a wombat day: slept, slept, ate grass, scratched, ate grass, slept. When humans move in, the wombat discovers that they make good pets and are easily trainable to provide carrots or rolled oats upon demand. (I: P–7)

*_____. *Josephine Wants to Dance*. Illustrated by Bruce Whatley. HarperCollins, 2006. (Australia) Josephine the kangaroo loves to dance, and is able to take what she has learned from the brolgas, lyrebirds, and emus to fill the lead role when the prima ballerina twists her ankle. (I: P–7)

Funke, Cornelia. *The Thief Lord*. Translated from German by Oliver Latsch. Chicken House/Scholastic, 2002. (Germany) A thirteen-year-old "Thief Lord" serves as a leader for a group of runaway and homeless children in Venice. (I: 10 and up)

*Gallaz, Christophe, and Roberto Innocenti. *Rose Blanche*. Illustrated by Roberto Innocenti. Creative Education, 1985. (Italy) In a story set in World War II Germany, Rose's curiosity leads her to follow a truck and discover a concentration camp, where she is compelled to try to help by sharing her food. (I: 10 and up)

*Gay, Marie-Louise. *When Stella was Very, Very Small*. Groundwood, 2011. (Canada). Readers ponder the unique perspectives of seeing the world's possibilities through Stella as a young child in this book from the "Stella and Sam" stories. (I: P–7)

*Gomi, Taro. *Spring is Here*. Chronicle, 1999. (Japan). Simple text and graphic illustrations depict the passage of the seasons, shown on the body of a calf. (I: P–6)

Goscinny, René. *Nicholas*. Translated by Anthea Bell. Illustrated by Jean-Jacques Sempé. Phaidon, 2005. (France) For almost half a century, this book, set in an all boys' school, has been a favorite among French school children. This translation introduces American readers to a boy and his classmates at an all-boys' school. A 2006 Batchelder Honor Book. (I: 9–11)

*Graham, Bob. *Greetings from Sandy Beach*. Kane/Miller, 1992. (Australia) A family takes a vacation at the beach, and meets unlikely heroes—a motorbike group who turn out to be friendly and helpful. (I: 6–9)

*_____. *How to Heal a Broken Wing*. Candlewick, 2008. (Australia). Will finds a bird with a broken wing and takes it home to nurse it back to health. (I: P–7)

*Gravett, Emily. *Meerkat Mail*. Simon, 2007. (UK). A meerkat who lives with his family in the Kalahari Desert decides to venture out on his own. He sends home a series of postcards that show the various places he travels. Gravett incorporates information throughout the book, alongside the story of Sunny the meerkat. Observant viewers will notice that there is a jackal that is lurking dangerously throughout the book. Sunny returns home with deepened appreciation for his family.

*Greenwood, Mark. *The Donkey of Gallipoli: A True Story of Courage in World War I*. Illustrated by Frané Lessac. Candlewick, 2008. (Australia) The story of two boyhood friends who grow up in England, selling donkey rides across the beach, and ends with the two young men during wartime, with one leading a donkey carrying the other on his back in Turkey. Front endpapers and back endpapers reflect the opening and closing of the story setting. (I: 8–11).

*Grimm, Jakob and Wilhelm. *Little Red Riding Hood*. Retold and Illustrated by Bernadette Watts. NorthSouth, 2009. (Switzerland) This familiar folk tale is retold and drawn with oil pastel illustrations that have a charming appeal. (I: P–8)

*Heydlauff, Lisa. *Going to School in India*. Illustrated by Nitin Upadhye. Charlesbridge, 2005. (India) This informational book weaves together photographs, first-person narrative, and information about the culture studied. (I: 8–11)

*Hole, Stian. *Garmann's Summer*. Illustrated by the author. Translated by Don Barlett. Eerdmans, 2008. (Norway) Garmann considers his fear of starting school as the familiar routines of summer end. Collage illustrations effectively contrast the soothing and predictable patterns with slightly off-proportioned figures to contrast the familiar with the unexpected. See also *Garmann's Street*, 2010. (I: K–7).

*Ichikawa, Satomi. *My Father's Shop*. Kane/Miller, 2008. (France) Mustafa goes through the market, draped with a Moroccan rug from his father's shop. A rooster follows him, and tourists along the way share the different ways in which a rooster's crowing is depicted in their own countries. (I: K–7)

*Krishnaswami, Uma. *Out of the Way! Out of the Way!* Illustrated by Uma Krishnaswamy. Groundwood, 2012 (India) Folk art and lively text combine to tell the story of change over the years: a small path into a major road, a sapling into a sheltering tree.

*Kwon, Yoon-duck. *My Cat Copies Me*. Kane/Miller, 2008. (South Korea) A girl begins a game in which her cat plays with her, but then the roles reverse and the girl takes the cat's perspective as she copies her cat. (I: K–7)

*Lee, Suzy. *The Zoo*. Kane/Miller, 2007. (Korea) While visiting the zoo with her parents, a little girl runs off for a surreal adventure with the animals before collapsing into a dream world on a bench, where her worried parents find her. (I: K–8)

Lindgren, Astrid. *Pippi Longstocking*. Translated by Florence Lamborn. Illustrated by Louis S. Glanzman. Viking, 1950/1997. (Sweden) Pippi has extraordinary physical strength and engages in unpredictable antics that living alone permits her to do. (I: 8–12)

Lindo, Elvira. *Manolito Four-Eyes*. Translated by Joanne Moriarty. Illustrated by Emilio Urberuaga. Marshall Cavendish, 2008. (Spain) Humorous episodes tell of the everyday life of 10-year-old Manolito, who lives in Madrid with his family. (I: 8–10)

*Louis, Catherine. *Liu and the Bird: A Journey in Chinese Calligraphy*. Calligraphy by Feng Xiao Min. Translated by Sibylle Kazeroid. (France) The origin and evolution of Chinese writing is engagingly told through the story of a child who visits her grandfather. The picture transformation into calligraphic characters is symbolic and understandable. (I: 6–10)

Machado, Ana Maria. *From Another World*. Illustrated by Lucía Brandâo. Translated from Portuguese by Luisa Baeta. Groundwood, 2005. (Brazil) When Mariano and friends stay overnight in a building designated to be turned into an inn by Mariano's mother, they are confronted by the ghost of a nineteenth century slave girl who tells her tragic story and seeks their help. (I: 9–13)

_____. *Me in the Middle*. Illustrated by Caroline Merola. Translated from Portuguese by David Unger. Groundwood, 2003. (Brazil) In this fantasy story, an almost-13-year-old Bel comes to realize who she is in this present day while her grandmother relays wisdom and life from the last century and her great granddaughter offers words of the future. (I: 9–12)

_____. *Nina Bonita*. Illustrated by Rosana Faría. Kane Miller, 1996. (Brazil) A white rabbit falls in love with a dark-skinned girl and learns that the root of her physical beauty lies in her heritage. (I: K–7)

*Mahy, Margaret. *Bubble Trouble*. Illustrated by Polly Dunbar. Clarion, 2009. (UK) When Mabel blows a bubble that envelops her baby brother, mayhem ensues as the baby's bubble goes bouncing around and is chased by neighbors and family fearing for the baby's safety. (I: P–6)

*Maruki, Toshi. *Hiroshima No Pika*. Illustrated by Toshi Maruki. Lothrop/Morrow, 1982. (Japan) The effect of the atomic bombing of Hiroshima is described, including what happens to seven-year-old Mii and her parents. (I: 10 and up)

*Milway, Katie Smith. *One Hen: How One Small Loan Made a Big Difference*. Illustrated by Eugenie Fernandes. Kids Can, 2008. (Canada). Kojo is a small boy in Ghana, and he and his mother sell firewood for their livelihood. A small loan allows him to buy one hen, and selling the eggs allows him to buy more hens. The profits build and this example of microfinance shows the impact a small loan makes on a large future. In addition to the narrative that explains the concept of microfinance, the cumulative text format of building on one line of text is appropriate for paralleling this story's theme. (I: K–8)

Morgenstern, Susie. *A Book of Coupons*. Illustrated by Serge Bloch. Translated from French by Gill Rosner. Penguin Putnam, 2001. (France) An unconventional teacher gives each student a gift-wrapped book of coupons that excuse them from various behaviors like being late, forgetting homework, etc. (I: 9–12)

_____. *Secret Letters from 0 to 10*. Translated from French by Gill Rosner. Penguin Putnam, 2000. (France) Ten-year-old Ernest leads a mundane life when vivacious Victoria enters his life and helps him to see the joy of living. (I: 10–13)

Naidoo, Beverley. *Journey to Jo'burg*. HarperCollins, 1988. (South Africa) When their baby sister is gravely ill, and grandmother has no money for medicine or doctors, Naledi and Dineo walk more than 300 km to seek the help of their mother, who lives with the white family she works for. The sequel is *Chain of Fire* (1990). (I: 9–11)

_____. *The Other Side of Truth*. HarperCollins, 2001. (UK). When terrorists miss their intended target, their journalist father, Sade and Femi lose their mother instead. The children are sent to London, but when they arrive, the uncle who is to care for them has mysteriously disappeared. *Web of Lies* is the sequel. (I: 12–YA)

Naidoo, Beverley, and Maya Naidoo. *Baba's Gift*. Illustrated by Karin Littlewood. Viking, 2004. (South Africa) Lindi and Themba receive a handmade gift from their grandfather, but inadvertently lose it while playing with a new friend. (I: P–6).

Orlev, Uri. *The Lady with the Hat*. Translated by Hillel Halkin. Houghton Mifflin, 1995. (Israel) Seventeen-year-old Yulek is a concentration camp survivor who resolves to begin a new life in a Palestinian kibbutz, despite the British blockade. See also *The Man from the Other Side* (1991). (I: 12 and up)

*Pacovská, Kveta. *The Little Flower King*. Minedition, 2007. (Czech Republic) A king who fills his world with flowers realizes he needs something else for true happiness. He sets out in search of a princess, and finds his true love among his tulips. (I: P–8)

*Prap, Lila. *Why?* Kane-Miller, 2009. (Slovenia). A series of questions that children might have about animals are answered playfully, varying from real answers to silly ones. (I: P–7)

*Rao, Sandhya. *My Mother's Sari*. Illustrated by Nina Sabnani. NorthSouth, 2006. (India) Children use their mothers' saris as they play in various imaginary ways—train, stage backdrop, a place to hide, etc. (I: P–7)

*Ravishankar, Anushka. *Elephants Never Forget!* Illustrated by Christiane Pieper. Houghton Mifflin, 2008. (India) A lonely elephant feels at home with a herd of buffaloes he joins, but when encountering a herd of elephants, he must make a choice. (I: P–7)

*Rinck, Maranke. *I Feel a Foot!* Illustrated by Martijn van der Linden. Boyds Mills/Lemniscaat. (The Netherlands) Five animal friends meet up with a huge something in the dark, and each "feels" that it is a giant version of themselves. (I: P–7)

Rivera, Raquel. *Arctic Adventures: Tales from the Lives of Inuit Artists*. Illustrated by Jirina Marton. Groundwood, 2008. (Canada) Four modern artists from the Canadian Arctic portray themselves, their work, and stories from their culture. (I: 8–11)

*Rosen, Michael. *Michael Rosen's Sad Book*. Illustrated by Quentin Blake. Candlewick, 2005. (UK) Author Michael Rosen presents the emotions of love, anger, and grief as he reflects on the death of his teenage son. (I: 9–12)

*Sakai, Komako. *The Snow Day*. Levine/Scholastic, 2009. (Japan) A little rabbit wakes to find a wonderous world filled with snow, and kindergarten class canceled for the day. (I: P-6)

*Sellier, Marie. *Legend of the Chinese Dragon*. Translated by Sibylle Kazeroid. Illustrated by Catherine Louis. Calligraphy and chop marks by Wang Fei. NorthSouth, 2008. (France) The legend of the Chinese dragon describes how warring factions of the past united under one spirit. The illustrator uses stunning lino-block prints to accompany the bilingually presented text with Chinese calligraphy. (I: 8–10)

*Sellier, Marie, Catherine Louis, and Wang Fei. *What the Rat Told Me: A Legend of the Chinese Zodiac.* North-South, 2009. (France) This pourquoi tale adaptation from the Chinese Buddhist legend tells of twelve animals who responded to an invitation from the Great Emperor of Heaven to become the symbols of the Chinese zodiac. Beautiful black and red linoleum prints on cream paper ground the story in its Chinese roots. (I: 6–10)

Tan, Shaun. *Tales from Outer Suburbia.* Arthur A. Levine/Scholastic. (Australia) Fifteen illustrated short stories take place in a surreal suburban world where inexplicable events occur regularly. (I: 9–12)

Thompson, Kate. *The New Policeman.* Greenwillow/HarperCollins, 2008. (Ireland) Descendant in a family of musicians, 15-year-old Liddy sets off to fulfill his mother's birthday wish for "more time." Unknowingly, he set off on a quest that reveals family secrets and unrealized identities. Elements of Irish mythology and culture are important to the story. See also *The Last of the High Kings* (2009). (I: 13–YA)

*Tjong-Khing, Thé. *Where is the Cake?* Abrams, 2007. (Netherlands) This wordless book begins by asking the reader to find out what happened to the cake and where it is. But as viewers follow the visual maze, many other stories are revealed, and the puzzle becomes increasingly curious and entertaining. See also *Where is the Cake Now?* (2009). (I: P–8)

*Tullet, Húrve. *Press Here.* Chronicle, 2011. (France) Simple instructions to the reader to "press here" or "shake" result in changes as the pages are turned. The ebook edition exemplifies movement that is imagined in the book edition. (I: P–6)

Uehashi, Nahoko. *Moribito: Guardian of the Spirit.* Translated from Japanese by Cathy Hirano. Arthur A. Levine/Scholastic, 2008. (Japan) Balsa is a warrior who is compelled to save others in atonement for past lives lost. She saves a prince and serves as his bodyguard to protect him from the emperor, his father, who wants him dead. The first in the ten-volume *Guardian* fantasy series, it is popular also as radio, manga, and anime adaptations. See also *Moribito II: Guardian of the Darkness.* (I: 7–YA)

Varmer, Hjørdis. *Hans Christian Andersen: His Fairy Tale Life.* Translated from Danish by Tiina Nunnally. Illustrated by Lilian Brøgger. Groundwood, 2005. (Denmark) Hans Christian Andersen's own true-life fairy tale biography is told in this engaging book, complete with illustrations both reminiscent of Andersen's cut paper style, as well as some original ones by Andersen. (I: 10–13)

*Velthuijs, Max. *Frog in Love.* Holt, 2004. (Netherlands) Frog does not understand why his insides are "thump thumping" and he is turning hot and cold when Piglet diagnoses the symptoms as "being in love" with Duck. See also many other books about Frog. (I: P–6)

*Verplancke, Klaas. *Applesauce.* Groundwood, 2012. (Belgium) A father and son's relationship is joyfully explored and depicted as having many dimensions. Ultimately, the assuredness of fatherly love scaffolds the son's growth. (I: P–8)

*Waddell, Martin. *Can't You Sleep, Little Bear?* Illustrated by Barbara Firth. Candlewick, 1992. (Ireland) Little Bear's fear of the dark keeps him from falling asleep until Big Bear takes him outside to see the moon and stars. (I: P–6).

*Wild, Margaret. *Bobbie Dazzler.* Illustrated by Janine Dawson. Kane Miller, 2007. (Australia) Bobbie the kangaroo wants to be able to do a split. Despite her efforts, she cannot. Finally, when her persistence pays off, koala, wombat, and possum follow her example. (I: P–7)

Wilson, Jacqueline. *Candyfloss.* Illustrated by Nick Sharratt. Deborah Brodie/Roaring Brook, 2008. (UK). Flossie's mother, stepdad, and half-brother are moving to Australia for six months and Flossie stays in London with her father because of her allegiance to and adoration of her best friend. When her father's inability to care for them means that Flossie is snubbed by her former social circle, her new friend helps Flossie to realize what friendship can and should be. (I: 9–11)

RESOURCES AND REFERENCES

Anno, Mitsumasa. *All in a Day.* Philomel, 1986.

Fox, Mem. *Shoes from Grandpa.* Illustrated by Patricia Mullins. Orchard, 1990.

Freeman, Evelyn, and Barbara Lehman. *Global Perspectives in Children's Literature.* Allyn & Bacon, 2001.

Freeman, Evelyn, Barbara Lehman, and Pat Scharer. Panel Presentation at the IBBY (International Board on Books for Young People) Congress, Cape Town, South Africa, 2001.

Gebel, Doris, ed. *Crossing Boundaries with Children's Books.* Scarecrow, 2006.

Hoffman, Mary. *Amazing Grace.* Illustrated by Caroline Binch. Dial, 1991.

Pavonetti, Linda, ed. *Bridges to Understanding: Envisioning the World through Children's Books.* Scarecrow, 2011.

Pellowski, Anne. *The Story Vine: A Source Book of Unusual and Easy-to-Tell Stories from around the World.* Illustrated by Lynn Sweat. Macmillan, 1984.

Stan, Susan, ed. *The World Through Children's Books.* Scarecrow, 2002.

Tomlinson, Carl M., ed. *Children's Books from Other Countries.* Scarecrow, 1998.

Yokota, Junko. International literature: Inviting students into the global community. In S. Lehr (Ed.), *Shattering the looking glass: Challenges, risk and controversy in children's literature* (pp. 242–253). Christopher-Gordon, 2008.

_____. "Ten International Books for Children." *Journal of Children's Literature,* 25(1) (1999): 48–54.

Tsutsui, Yoriko. *Anna's Secret Friend.* Illustrated by Akiko Hayashi. Viking, 1987.

PART TWO

Exploring
the Genres
of Children's
Literature

Poetry for Children

What Is Poetry?

It is challenging to think of a definition of poetry that some poem or other won't evade. We might say that poems are made of rhymed language—but poems like this one are not:

"February Morning"

> Snowboots snuggled over fat wool socks
> Closed mouth muffled by a scratchy scarf
> Arms pulled back by a bulging bookbag
> Fingers slotted into gloves' thin sleeves
> Hat scrunched low
> Ready, set, go
> Straight out the door
> To the grumbling bus.

We might say that poems are words arranged in a visually striking fashion that is different from the arrangement of prose—but some poems aren't. Take "Football" by Walt Mason:

"Football"

> The game was ended, and the noise at last had died away, and now they gathered up the boys where they in pieces lay. And one was hammered in the ground by many a jolt and jar; some fragments never have been found, they flew away so far. They found a stack of tawny hair, some fourteen cubits high; it was the halfback, lying there, where he had crawled to die. They placed the pieces on a door, and from the crimson field, that hero then they gently bore, like soldier on his shield. The surgeon toiled the livelong night above the gory wreck; he got the ribs adjusted right, the wishbone, and the neck. He soldered on the ears and toes, and got the spine in place, and fixed a gutta-percha nose upon the mangled face. And then he washed his hands and said: "I'm glad that task is done!" The halfback raised his fractured head, and cried: "I call this fun!"

We might say poems wed image and sound in especially pleasing ways—but good prose often does this, too. For example, consider this excerpt from *Charlotte's Web*, by E. B. White:

> The barn was very large. It was very old. It smelled of hay and it smelled of manure. It smelled of perspiration of tired horses and the wonderful sweet breath of patient cows. It often had a sort of peaceful smell—as though nothing bad could happen ever again in the world. (p. 13)

Still, we know poetry when we see it. Poetry is a precise form of language, with intense feeling, imagery, and qualities of sound that bounce pleasingly off the tongue, tickle the ear, and leave the mind something to ponder. Poetry is a memorable structure for language: Things we want to remember and want our children to remember have always been put in poetic form and passed on. Poetry is the pinnacle of language use: From the communication tool we billions of humans use unthinkingly throughout the day, a few choice items are elegantly constructed, to be admired for their beauty, artistry, and power. Poetry is a celebration of awareness: Poets regularly name things people have felt but could not name, and thus they expand our consciousness and our discerning. Often with bouncing rhythms and sparkling words, poetry has a special appeal to children—yet it also inspired the great American poet Emily Dickinson to exclaim, "If I read a book and it makes my whole body so cold no fire can ever warm me, I know that it is poetry."

Poetry has a special place in children's education. Through the daily barrage of language to which people young and old are subjected—the purring lies of advertisements, the tone-deaf and bloodless facts of textbooks, the obtuse obscenities shouted down mean streets—it would be easy to lose our reverence for language, to leave mostly unexplored the half million (and counting) English words—each one an invitation to pay attention, to notice a nuance that might go undetected. We need poetry to help children celebrate what is clear, precise, beautiful, artful, and true in our language.

Categories of Poetry for Children

Children enjoy several acknowledged kinds of poetry: nursery rhymes, jump-rope rhymes, folk poems, lyric poems, narrative poems, and nonsense verse. Poems can also be classified by their forms: sonnets, limericks, haiku, concrete poems, and others. Some poems, of course, resist easy categorization.

Mother Goose Rhymes and Other Rhymes of the Nursery

Babies love to be bounced on grownups' knees, and the bouncers need rhythms and poems to sustain that rhythmic motion. Perhaps that is how nursery rhymes were born. Nursery rhymes are verses by anonymous poets that are highly rhythmic, tightly rhymed, and popular with small children. Although nursery rhymes have been recited to and by children since medieval times in English, they were associated with the name "Mother Goose" when the publisher John Newbery borrowed the name from quite a different publication (see Illustration 6.1).

Why Do We Call Them "Mother Goose" Rhymes?

The Frenchman Charles Perrault first used the name "Mother Goose" in the title of a collection of eight tales (not rhymes) that included "Cinderella," "The Sleeping Beauty in the Woods," and "Little Red Riding Hood." Perrault called his collection *Histoires ou Contes du Temps Passé, Avec des Moralités: Contes de Ma Mère l'Oye (Stories or Tales of Times Past, With Moral: Tales of My Mother Goose).* This collection was published in France in 1697, and was translated and published in England by Robert Samber as *Histories, or Stories of Times Past,* in 1729. Still, they were popularly called "Mother Goose Stories." Publisher John Newbery had found it profitable to publish books for the children of England's growing middle class, and when he brought out a collection of nursery rhymes for children, he appropriated Perrault's popular title and named it *Mother Goose's Melody, or Sonnets for the Cradle.* This was a collection of rhymes and jingles, which began the association of the name "Mother Goose" with highly rhythmic nursery rhymes.

Indeed, the associations in many nursery rhymes can be traced back several centuries.

Baa, baa, black sheep, have you any wool?
Yes, sir, yes, sir—three bags full.
One for my master and one for my dame,
And one for the little boy who lives down the lane.

This traditional rhyme dates from feudal times, when vassals paid shares of their produce to the powerful lords and ladies (masters and dames) who owned the lands of England.

Ring around the roses,
Pocket full of posies,
Ashes, ashes,
We all fall down.

This rhyme is said to refer to the Black Death, the bubonic plague, which killed a fourth of the population of England in the fourteenth century. The ring around the roses was a telltale rash of an infected person; the pocket full of posies was for protection against the "bad airs" that were believed to spread the sickness; and the ashes and falling down refer to the people who were stricken and died with dramatic suddenness (the disease ran its course in four days) and whose bodies were piled up and burned. Maybe so, but centuries of children have kept it alive out of fascination with its rhythms and their accompanying movements.

Nursery rhymes have pleasing sounds. This one sends the tongue tapping around all parts of the mouth—perhaps that is why small children love to recite it:

Polly put the kettle on,
Polly put the kettle on,
Polly put the kettle on,
We'll all have tea.
Sukey take it off again,
Sukey take it off again,
Sukey take it off again,
They've all gone away.

Many traditional rhymes also have accompanying motions. This one is a favorite when bouncing small children on one's knees:

This is the way the ladies ride,
Tri, tre, tre, tree!
Tri, tre, tre, tree!
This is the way the ladies ride,
Tri, tre, tre, tree!

And small children delight in having their toes wiggled to "This Little Piggie":

This little piggy went to market.
This little piggy stayed home.
This little piggy ate roast beef.
This little piggy ate none.
This little piggy cried "Wee! wee! wee!"
All the way home.

ILLUSTRATION 6.1   The illustrations of works for children by Joseph Bronheim (1810–1869) were popular for a hundred years. This little piggy is having roast beef. ("The Little Pig who had Roast Beef" illustrated by Joseph Martin Kronheim (1810–1896), from "My First Picture Book With Thirty-six Pages of Pictures Printed in Colours" by Kronheim, London & New York: George Routledge and Sons.)

Mother Goose Rhymes through the Years.   For well over a century, many of the greatest illustrators of children's books have published editions of these familiar rhymes. Randolph Caldecott's picture book **Hey Diddle Diddle** was published in 1882. In the same year, Kate Greenaway produced a beautiful version of **Mother Goose or the Old Nursery Rhymes.** Arthur Rackham's **Mother Goose: The Old Nursery Rhymes** was originally published around the end of the nineteenth century. Other classic versions were created by Tasha Tudor, Blanche Fisher Wright, and Feodor Rojankovsky. Chris Duffey recently assembled a version of 50 nursery rhymes rendered in cartoons.

Mother Goose equivalents and nursery rhymes are found in cultures around the world, and they developed separately from the ones known in the Western world.

Jump-Rope and Counting-Out Rhymes

Unlike nursery rhymes, which are usually introduced to children by their parents or sitters, children's folk rhymes are anonymous verses passed on from child to child. Thus, they constitute—as *The Lore and Language of School Children* (2001), the title of the well-known book by British experts Iona and Peter Opie, suggests—an actual folklore that is the province of children themselves.

Hand-clapping rhymes such as this one often accompany children's play:

> My boyfriend's name is Davy
> He's in the U.S. Navy
> With a pickle for his nose, cherries on his toes
> That's the way my story goes.

Counting-out rhymes are perennially popular, too:

> Bubble gum, bubble gum in a dish
> How many pieces do you wish?
> 1, 2, 3 . . .

Children also enjoy rhythmic alphabet games such as this one:

> A, my name is Annie,
> And my husband's name is Al.
> We come from Arkansas,
> And we sell apples.
> B, my name is Barbara,
> And my husband's name is Bill . . .

And here's a popular jump-rope rhyme:

> Cinderella
> Dressed in yellow
> Went upstairs
> And kissed a fellow
> Made a mistake and kissed a snake.
> Came back down with a belly ache.
> How many doctors does it take?
> One . . . Two . . . Three . . . Four . . .

Francelia Butler's *Skipping around the World* has 350 skipping rhymes collected over forty years from seventy countries, and many of them turn out to have reworked adult themes, including historic military campaigns, politics, death, love, and sex.

Several collections of children's folk rhymes are currently in print (see the Recommended Books list at the end of this chapter). That these rhymes have to be written down at all shows adults' recognition that children's oral traditions need some bolstering against the inroads of canned commercial media.

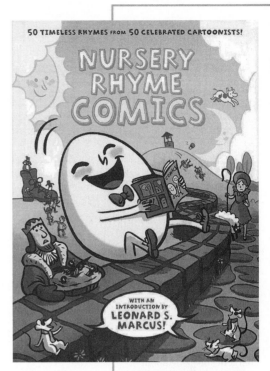

ILLUSTRATION 6.2 This collection of 50 nursery rhymes illustrated in comic format will keep young children chuckling. (Book cover of "Nursery Rhyme Comics: 50 Timeless Rhymes from 50 Celebrated Cartoonists" edited by Chris Duffey. First Second [an imprint of Roaring Brook Press, a division of Holtzbrinck Publishing Holdings Limited Partnership. All rights reserved.], 2011. (ISBN: 159643600X).)

Folk Songs Popular among Children

Another source of folk rhymes is folk songs that are popular with children. Some children's folk songs go back hundreds of years. "Oats, Peas, Beans, and Barley Grow" was sung in medieval times in England. Perhaps it's no coincidence that the plants in the song are mentioned in just the order of proper crop rotation practiced by farmers for centuries.

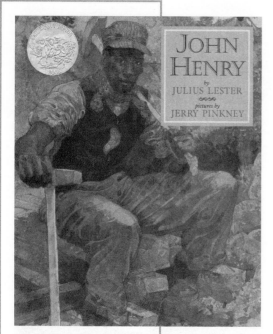

ILLUSTRATION 6.3 This energetic folk song about John Henry is beautifully illustrated by Jerry Pinkney. ("John Henry" by Julius Lester. Used by permission of Penguin Group (USA), Inc. All rights reserved.)

Other folk songs that are popular with children are from more recent times. The song about the legendary John Henry, a mythical turn-of-the-century African American railroad worker, has been made into picture books by different illustrators:

When John Henry was a little baby
Sittin' on his mama's knee,
He picked up a hammer and a little piece of steel
And said, "Hammerin's gonna be the death of me, Lord, Lord,
Hammerin's gonna be the death of me."

Lyric or Expressive Poems

The original lyrics were Greek poems that were accompanied on the lyre, a small harp. Today's lyric or expressive poems are works of emotion, observation, or insight. The category includes a huge number of poems—just about any poem that is not narrative, or nonsense, or does not follow a recognized form is likely to be a lyric poem if it conveys the poet's observation or thoughts on a topic.

Many of the entries in Robert Louis Stevenson's *A Child's Garden of Verses* are good examples of lyric poems.

"Rain"

The rain is raining all around
It rains on field and tree
It rains on the umbrellas here
And on the ships at sea.

Narrative Poems

Poems that tell stories are among the oldest of all poems, and at one time nearly all stories that were passed from generation to generation were told in verse form. **The Odyssey, The Iliad, Beowulf,** and the **Poema de Mio Cid** were all originally told in verse. In the Middle Ages, ballads—long narrative poems—told the stories of Robin Hood, Lord Randall, and other heroes.

TEACHING IDEA 6.1

USING FOLK MUSIC IN THE CLASSROOM

Folk songs connect students to both the emotions and the esthetic tone of historical periods. Learning and singing folk songs makes an excellent enhancement to reading books on historical periods or different parts of the world.

For a study of the Civil War, for example, novels like Irene Hunt's *Across Five Aprils*, Mary Pope Osborne's *After the Rain*, and Paul Fleischman's *Bull Run* can make history come alive for the reader through individual narratives. And students can sing folk songs as they read novels to make the stories feel even more alive. Fitting songs for the Civil War period include "Tenting Tonight on the Old Campground," which was sung by exhausted soldiers on both sides of the conflict. "Eating Goober Peas" was popular with Confederate troops, and "The Battle Hymn of the Republic" inspired the Northern troops. A good source of these songs and other folk songs is Peter Blood's *Rise Up Singing*.

Narrative poetry written expressly for children began in the nineteenth century. Clement Clarke Moore's "A Visit from St. Nicholas, or 'Twas the Night before Christmas," published in 1822, not only helped to establish the genre of narrative poetry for children but also contributed to the Santa Claus lore that is still widely circulated in North America. Robert Service's poems have long been popular for their exciting plots involving tough men in wilderness settings: the Yukon and the old West. The most famous of his poems, *The Cremation of Sam McGee*, was most recently brought out as a picture book with inspired illustrations by Ted Harrison. Here is a sample of the poem:

> There are strange things done
> in the midnight sun
> By the men who moil for gold;
> The arctic trails have their secret tales
>   That would make your blood run cold;
> The Northern Lights
>   have seen queer sights,
>   But the queerest they ever did see
> Was that night on the marge of Lake Lebarge
> I cremated Sam McGee.

One of the great American narrative poems is Ernest Lawrence Thayer's "Casey at the Bat," a favorite of generations of young people:

> The outlook wasn't brilliant for the Mudville nine that day;
> The score stood four to two with but one inning left to play . . .

Ludwig Bemelmans popularized rhyming narratives for modern children with his many books about Madeline, the feisty young resident of the convent school in Paris. And Roy Gerrard turned out imaginative contributions to the narrative poem genre: *Rosy and the Rustlers, Sir Frances Drake,* and others, until his death in 1997.

Novels in Verse

In recent years, several novels in verse have been written for upper elementary, middle-grade readers. Some of these books are by authors who have achieved acclaim with their more conventional novels for young people.

Karen Hesse had written a dozen successful novels for young people before she won the Newbery Medal in 1998 for *Out of the Dust*. Through the first-person voice of fourteen-year-old Billy Jo, the reader experiences firsthand the calamity of the Dust Bowl on the hard-bitten farmers who tried to survive it. Hesse followed with *Aleutian Sparrow* (2003), another novel in a difficult historical setting—this one about the Aleuts, the native people of the Aleutian Islands, who were forcibly removed from their homes during World War II by the U.S. government and put in settlement camps, where many died. Hesse's *The Cats in Krasinski Square* (2004), written in free verse, is a picture book telling a little-known story of the Holocaust from Poland.

Love That Dog (2001), by Newbery Award Winner Sharon Creech (author of *Walk Two Moons*) is a celebration of poetry itself that appeals to fourth- through sixth-grade readers. And *Locomotion* (2003), by Coretta Scott King Award winner Jacqueline Woodson, uses several forms of poetry—like Creech, with the sensitive agency of an insightful teacher who encourages her students to write it—for eleven-year-old Lonnie Collins Motion (AKA "Locomotion") to unburden himself of a story of tragedy and loss. Nikki Grimes (see page 164), NCTE Poetry Award winner, has used blank verse to create *Bronx Masquerade* and *What Is Goodbye?*, both exploring the lives and relationships of urban middle and high school students.

Ask *the* Poet . . . Naomi Shihab Nye

What advice do you have for teachers who want to help children appreciate poetry that isn't necessarily playful?

Poems have as many moods as people do. Often, when we're little, we learn nursery rhymes and funny, bouncy poems. We like repeating rhythms, even nonsense words—poems that make us laugh and stretch the boundaries of language. Some of us continue to like these poems no matter what age we are.

But there is much more to poetry. As we grow, hopefully we have a chance to read poems of many styles which echo all the varieties of human experience. Poems may help us understand universal human moods such as sadness, loneliness, alienation, anger, confusion better and more quickly than any other kind of writing, since poetry is such an intimate, immediate kind of writing. Surprisingly, poems about silence and emptiness can be some of the most moving poems! Many teenagers say they write best when they are depressed because a "negative emotion" often causes them to focus intensely. After writing, people often feel better, too, because that "serious emotion" found a shape for itself, a simple, comforting outlet, in words.

Naomi Shihab Nye

As readers, we bring our own experiences to every poem that we read. Quickly we understand that not all people will respond to every poem or understand every poem in the same way. Some poems may not "touch us" at all. A lot depends on what we have experienced ourselves, our individuality, our personal taste. Sometimes a single image will invite us into a poem. A metaphor or simile may awaken a fresh understanding of something we thought we knew. Reading poems makes us larger people—It extends our empathy, helping us understand how others feel and giving us insight into the many worlds within and around all of us, whether the subjects and moods are things we too have experienced or things we learn about mostly through reading.

Naomi Shihab Nye has written poems since she was six years old. Her most recent collections of poems are *Fuel* and *Red Suitcase*. She has also edited anthologies of poetry for young readers, including *This Same Sky, The Tree Is Older Than You Are,* and *What Have You Lost?* She also writes children's books, essays, and novels for teens. She lives in San Antonio with her husband and son.

Nonsense Verse

In the middle of the last century, the English poet Edward Lear was the first to publish nonsense verse. Lear's "The Jumblies" is also known as "They Went to Sea in a Sieve":

> They went to sea in a sieve, they did;
>   In a sieve they went to sea;
> In spite of all their friends would say,
> On a winter's morn, on a stormy day,
>   In a sieve they went to sea.

Nonsense poetry is alive and well among modern writers. Here is North Carolina poet Bucksnort Trout's tongue-in-cheek protest against too much television ("telly") watching:

> Nelly watched the telly
> 'Til her brains turned to jelly
> 'Til they flowed through her nose

And ran down her belly.
Mama said, "Hey, Nelly!"
Nelly said, "Huh? What?"
Then she sat there a-staring
Like some kind of a nut.

Nonsense verse and other humorous poetry have always been popular with children. The late Shel Silverstein was and still is immensely popular, and America's children's poet laureate, Jack Prelutsky, is a master of nonsense verse.

Form Poems: Limericks

Up until the beginning of the twentieth century, most poems in English had identifiable rhyme schemes and rhythmic patterns. Today, poetry is more varied in its structure and use of sounds. A few common forms of poetry persist, however. Limericks came into being in the early nineteenth century and found an early champion at midcentury in the nonsense poet Edward Lear. Lear so popularized the form that it is closely identified with him. Here is one of his limericks:

There was an Old Man who said, "Hush!
I perceive a young bird in this bush!"
When they said, "Is it small?"
He replied, "Not at all;
It is four times as big as the bush!"

Form Poems: Haiku

Another common form of poetry is the haiku, a three-line non-rhyming poem developed in Japan. Haiku poems traditionally contain seventeen syllables, five in the first line, seven in the middle, and five in the last (although English-language haiku don't always follow that requirement). Most haiku make an observation about nature in a particular moment and at a particular place:

Now at the black pond
twilight slowly abandons
the lone blue heron.

ISSUE *to* CONSIDER

Should We Distinguish between "Poems" and "Rhymes"?

When Emily Dickinson spoke of poetry as writing that made her so cold no fire could ever warm her, presumably she didn't mean the likes of "Jack Sprat could eat no fat/His wife could eat no lean." Some authorities would say that this is not real poetry but rather should be called "verse" or "rhyme" (Lukens, 1992). According to that way of thinking, "poetry" is written expression that strikes readers in many ways at once—with sound, image, and meaning—and that repays careful rereading to savor the artistry and ponder the associations. Works that fall short—although perhaps very enjoyable—should be called "verse" or "rhymes."

The "Emily Dickinson test" might work with most nursery rhymes, but how would the Belle of Amherst's body temperature have responded to the poems of Shel Silverstein or Jack Prelutsky or David McCord or Eve Merriam? And if it could be proved—as some claim to have done—that many nursery rhymes contain cleverly encoded social and political messages, would we still be content to call these works mere rhymes?

The poem-versus-rhyme distinction is useful if it keeps us from expecting too much from every bit of verse we read. But the distinction is bound to lead to some unhappiness, as someone sniffs that one of your favorite poems is not a poem at all, but only a rhyme.

What do you think? Should we make a distinction between poems and rhymes?

TEACHING IDEA 6.2

A POETRY SLAM

For the past 20 years or so, urban poets from all across the country have been engaging in a highly energetic competition based on performance poetry. Called Poetry Slams, the events give several poets limited amounts of time to hurl their poems into eager crowds, who then serve as juries and render scores for each performance. As the sponsoring group, Poetry Slam, Inc., defines it, "Simply put, a poetry slam is the competitive art of performance poetry. It puts dual emphasis on writing and performance, encouraging poets to focus on what they're saying and how they're saying it. A poetry slam is an event in which poets perform their work and are judged by members of the audience. . . ."

To host a Poetry Slam in a classroom, prepare students to present their poems—either individually or in teams—during a competition in which they are given fixed amounts of time, such as two minutes. (Points may be subtracted if they go over the time limit.)

The performances can be scored by a panel of judges, usually students—although a teacher or two may participate. Judges are given rubrics on which to score each poet. The criteria should deal with both presentation and content (assuming the student wrote the poem). If a panel of judges gives the scores, then the audience may be instructed to respond as follows:

a. Rubbing your hands on your legs means mild enthusiasm.
b. Snapping your fingers means more enthusiasm.
c. Slapping your hands on your thighs means still more enthusiasm.
d. Stomping your feet means the most enthusiasm.

More information on Poetry Slams is available from Poetry Slam, Inc., at <http://www.poetryslam.com>.

Concrete Poems

When letters and words are arranged on the page so that they physically resemble the subject, we have a concrete poem.

LION: # DID ANYBODY SEE A MOUSE?

MOUSE: no.

Dialogue Poems

Poems for two or more voices are enjoyable to read aloud. Dialogue poems are as old as Mother Goose rhymes:

"Old woman, old woman,
Shall we go a'shearing?"
"Speak a little louder sir,
I'm very hard of hearing."
"Old woman, old woman,
Shall I kiss you dearly?"
"Yes, sir, yes, sir,
I hear you very clearly."

Dialogue poems are sometimes used to highlight social issues. For example, here is a dialogue poem showing a conversation between two children.

My mother is nice
    My mother is a farmer
My mother drives me to school
    My mother carries my sister in a sling on her back when we chase birds from the rice field
My mother commutes to work on a train
    My mother walks ten kilometers to fetch water
My mother cooks dinner in a microwave
    My mother gathers sticks and makes a fire to boil our rice
My mother is trying to lose weight
    My mother sometimes sweats and trembles with malaria
My mother reads to me at night
    My mother sings to me in the dark
I love my mother
    I love my mother, too

Free Verse

Poetry that has no discernible form at all is free verse. Free verse has no rhyme or particular rhythm, but makes its impressions with an intensity of insight or feeling, a clarity of vision, and sounds and rhythms that ebb and flow with the pulse of the poet's feelings about the subject matter. Here is an example of free verse by Valerie Worth from *All the Small Poems:*

"Dog"

Under a maple tree
The dog lies down,
Lolls his limp
Tongue, yawns,
Rests his long chin carefully between
Front paws:
Looks up, alert;
Chops, with heavy
Jaws, at a slow fly,
Blinks, rolls
On his side,
Sighs, closes
His eyes: sleeps
All afternoon
In his loose skin.

With no meter or rhyme scheme to worry about, the poet can let the poem take its own shape. She sets out a series of images. She makes cadences in patterns and then suddenly breaks them, reflecting the erratic behavior of the poem's subject. She uses a series of sounds that echo each other (the dog lies down . . . Lolls his limp. . .), and then she shifts to other sounds.

Poetry Collections

Themed poetry collections make it easier to find poems related to topics in the curriculum. Integration of science and social studies curriculum with language arts instruction is now being undertaken in many schools in America,

TEACHING IDEA 6.3

WRITING DIALOGUE POEMS

Children can write dialogue poems between any two characters: a hunter and a deer, or a plate of food and a diner. They will write more powerful poems if they are given powerful subjects. After reading Robert Coles's *The Story of Ruby Bridges* (illustrated by George Ford), the students can write a dialogue between Ruby and one of the white parents who are heckling this young African American girl each day as she is escorted by federal marshals to a previously all-white New Orleans school. The dialogue poems can each be written by a single student, or by having each student write one speaker's lines.

TEACHING IDEA 6.4

USING POETRY ANTHOLOGIES

Choose one topic you will be teaching. It doesn't have to be a literary one, or even a touchy-feely social one. It might be a geometric pattern, or an insect. Find three poems that relate to that topic. Try to find at least one that is fairly literal, and one that is metaphorical. Have the students compare what they learn about the same concept from the two different poems.

If the topic is circles, for instance, you might use Barbara Juster Esbensen's "Think of a Circle" (from *Dance With Me* by B. J. Esbensen, illustrated by M. Lloyd, 1995) and "Circles" by Myra Cohn Livingston (from M. C. Livingston, *There Was a Place and Other Poems*, 1988).

thanks especially to the Common Core Standards. Fortunately, creative artists and children's publishers have already been producing attractive books for children and young people on a range of academic subjects. Many of them are books of poetry, organized around topics or themes.

Editors of some of the larger anthologies have thoughtfully included topical indexes. *The Random House Book of Poetry for Children* (selected by Jack Prelutsky and illustrated by Arnold Lobel) has 572 poems, along with an index that locates poems on such finely tuned topics as "Death, Dinosaurs, Dogs, Dreams, Fall, Family, Fantasy, Fathers, February, Fire, Fish. . . ."

You can also seek out thematically selected anthologies. Poetry anthologies are available on a host of topics. Marilyn Singer has written themed collections about fire and heat in *Central Heating: Poems About Fire and Warmth* (Singer, 2005), about the natural places on the earth in *Footprints on the Roof* (2002), and about playing outside in *A Stick Is an Excellent Thing: Poems Celebrating Outdoor Play* (2012). Jack Prelutsky, too, celebrates active movement in *Good Sports: Rhymes about Running, Jumping, Throwing and More* (2011).

Brian Karas has a collection of poems about the earth for young children (*On Earth*, 2008), and about the Atlantic Ocean for somewhat older children (*Atlantic*, 2004). Using the rhythms of jazz and blues, Walter Dean Myers' collection *Harlem* (1997) celebrates black traditions in that urban cultural cauldron, and *Blues Journey* (2007) sings the long history of African Americans. Months of the year are beautifully brought to life in poems by the late John Updike in *A Child's Calendar* (1999, illustrated by the late Trina Schart Hyman).

Collections of poems on science topics abound. Joyce Sidman has been prodigious in this vein, with *Swirl by Swirl: Spirals in Nature* (2011), *Dark Emperor and Other Poems of Night* (2010), and *Song of the Water Boatman and Other Pond Poems* (2005). The poetry of George Ella Lyon's *All the Water in the World* (2011) will engage children's fascination with the water cycle. Susan Stockdale's *Bring on the Birds* (2011) uses rhymes to introduce young readers to a variety of feathered creatures; and Mary Lynn Ray's *Stars* (2011) uses poetry to focus young readers' wonder on the night sky.

Biography is another organizing principal for poetry collections. Marilyn Nelson's *Carver: A Life in Poems* (2001) recounts the life of the ingenious African American plant scientist. Her *Sweethearts of Rhythm: The Story of the World's Greatest All-Girl Swing Band* (2009) uses rhythmic poetry to chronicle the amazing success of an inter-racial women's group in the 1940s. Carmen Bernier-Grand published a collection of poems on the Mexican populist painter of murals, Diego Rivera (*Diego: Bigger Than Life*, 2009), and another about Rivera's artistic companion, Frida Kahlo, *Frida: ¡Viva la Vida!* (2007). Leo Dillon features "Mister Bojangles," in *Rap a Tap Tap: Here's Bojangles—Think of That!* (2002), about the popular African American tap dance artist, Bill Robinson. Laban Carrick Hill's poems tell the fascinating story of a little-known potter, poet, and slave from South Carolina in *Dave the Potter: Artist, Poet, Slave* (2010).

The Evolution of Children's Poetry

Early Poetry for Children

A historical review of poems written in the English language for children does not begin well. Up until William Blake published *Songs of Innocence,* in 1789, children's poems from Great Britain were often cheerless, moralistic, didactic, and often downright mean-spirited. Here, for instance, is the beginning of an alphabet poem from around 1700:

> A was an Archer, and shot at a frog,
> B was a Blindman, and led by a dog,
> C was a Cutpurse, and lived in disgrace,
> D was a Drunkard, and had a red face.
> E was an Eater, a glutton was he,
> F was a Fighter, and fought with a flea,
> G was a Giant, and pulled down a house . . .

Early American poems for children were every bit as dour. Some poems exalted early death as the greatest aspiration of a young child, for by dying young, children reduced their chances of falling into sin. Other poems impressed on children the horrors of eternal damnation for their "original sin."

More Sympathetic Voices

The poems of the English poet William Blake (1757–1827) were something new. They addressed topics that appealed to children and approached childhood with sympathy.

> "The Lamb"
>
> Little Lamb who made thee?
> Dost thou know who made thee?
> Gave thee life and bid thee feed
> By the stream and o'er the mead;
> Gave thee clothing of delight,
> Softest clothing woolly bright;
> Gave thee such a tender voice,
> Making all the vales rejoice.
> Little Lamb who made thee?
> Dost thou know who made thee?

Blake's sympathy for children led him to become a voice for social justice. His poem, "The Chimney Sweeper," helped begin the long struggle in England to ban the worst forms of child labor:

> "The Chimney Sweeper"
>
> When my mother died I was very young,
> And my father sold me while yet my tongue
> Could scarcely cry "'weep!'weep!'weep!'weep!"
> So your chimneys I sweep, and in soot I sleep.
>
> . . .

The better poets from Blake's time on left off the moralizing and wrote for children's enjoyment. The long narrative poems of Robert Browning (1812–1889) are imaginative and entertaining. Here is the beginning of *The Pied Piper of Hamelin:*

Poetry. Perennial, 2000. First published over 40 years ago, poet Kenneth Koch's unconventional ideas for exercising different aspects of a poet's art are illustrated with the New York City children's poems they inspired.

McClure, Amy. *Sunrises and Songs: Reading and Writing Poetry in an Elementary Classroom*. Heinemann, 1990. By sharing evocative poetry with children, Amy McClure inspires children to get their own feelings and observations out in verse form.

Wolf, Alan. *It's Show Time! Poetry From Page to Stage*. Poetry Alive Publications, 1993. Poetry Alive! is a theater company that brings poetry to life through lively performances. Alan Wolf, one of the troupe's arrangers, shows teachers how to direct students in sharing poems through voice choirs and dramatizations.

> Hamelin Town's in Brunswick,
>   By famous Hanover city;
> The river Weser, deep and wide,
> Washes its wall by the southern side;
> A pleasanter spot you never spied;
>   But, when begins my ditty,
> Almost five hundred years ago,
> To see the townsfolk suffer so
>   From vermin, was a pity.
>   Rats!
> They fought the dogs and killed the cats,
>   And bit the babies in their cradles,
> And ate the cheeses out of vats,
>   And licked the soup from cooks' own ladles,
> Split open kegs of salted sprats,
> Made nests inside men's Sunday hats,
> And even spoiled the women's chats
>   By drowning their speaking
>   With shrieking and squeaking
> In fifty different sharps and flats . . .

From the mid-nineteenth century on, the poetry gets more and more delightful. We've already mentioned Edward Lear's nonsense verse, which plays with language and enlivens the imagination. In *Alice's Adventures in Wonderland* (1865), Lewis Carroll (1832–1898) confidently spoofed the moralistic doggerel that was so prominent in poetry for children just a short time before:

> Speak roughly to your little boy,
> And beat him when he sneezes:
> He only does it to annoy,
> Because he knows it teases.

Here is an excerpt from the poem that Carroll was spoofing.

> "Speak Gently"
>
> Speak gently to the little child!
> Its love be sure to gain;
> Teach it in accents soft and mild: —
> It may not long remain.
>
> Speak gently to the young, for they
> Will have enough to bear —
> Pass through this life as best they may,
> 'T is full of anxious care!
>   David Bates (1809–1870)

Christina Rossetti (1830–1894) could be thoughtful and accessible at the same time, as in "The Wind" (from *Complete Poems of Christina Rossetti*):

> Who has seen the wind?
>   Neither you nor I;
> But when the leaves hang trembling
>   The wind is passing through.
> Who has seen the wind?
>   Neither you nor I;
> But when the trees bow down their heads
>   The wind is passing by.

Robert Louis Stevenson (1850–1894) gave us the great adventure novels *Treasure Island* and *Kidnapped*. His *A Child's Garden of Verses*, written at the end of the nineteenth century, is still much admired; through the middle of the twentieth century, it was among the most widely read of poetry collections. Stevenson could be gentle, yet savvy to a child's point of view:

"Looking Forward"

When I am grown to man's estate
I shall be very proud and great,
And tell the other girls and boys
Not to meddle with my toys.

At the turn of the century and after, Rudyard Kipling, A. A. Milne, T. S. Eliot, and others appealed to children with exciting and delightful poems, with words and rhythms well suited to their themes.

Kipling's poems reflected the high adventure of a life lived in exotic places, as this fragment of "The Smuggler's Song" (from *Puck of Pook's Hill*) shows:

If you wake at midnight and hear horses' feet,
Don't go drawing back the blind, or looking in the street,
Them that asks no questions isn't told a lie.
Watch the wall, my darling, while the Gentlemen go by!
Five and twenty ponies,
Trotting through the dark—
Brandy for the parson,
'Baccy for the Clerk
Laces for a lady; letters for a spy;
And watch the wall, my darling, while the Gentlemen go by!

Contemporary Poetry for Children

During the twentieth century, poetry for children continued to evolve. One noticeable change was freedom from formality: Non-rhyming poems became more common, and the language of poetry more folksy. Beginning with the poetry of Langston Hughes in the 1920s, published children's poems began representing the experiences of children who were not white and were not middle class. Yet another change was a more honest and direct voice in the poetry. As we saw, in earlier centuries, the attitude of the poet could be aloof and punishing. Later, it became sentimental and reassuring. In the contemporary era, the voice of the poet has become more honest and confiding; both poet and child live in a troubled world, and even adults sometimes feel powerless. Modern poets may try to be hopeful, but they do not offer a naive reassurance they do not feel. For example, the voice of Langston Hughes's narrator in "Mother to Son" (from *The Dream Keeper and Other Poems*) reflects the shift. The narrator is teaching a message of optimism, but the optimism is based on perseverance in grim circumstances. This world is a far cry from the cozy, sheltered world of the imagination constructed by poets in the nineteenth century. Hughes uses a staircase in a slum dwelling as a metaphor for a hard life.

The honest and not superior voice is evident in the work of many modern poets who write for children, such as Nikki Giovanni, Nikki Grimes, Janet Wong, and Gary Soto.

Contemporary children's poets still write with insight and humor about the joys and scrapes of childhood. The humor is more biting than in previous generations, and sometimes more irreverent—see for example the poems of Shel Silverstein and Jack Prelutsky. And much of it is very funny, such as Nikki Grimes's poem "True Love Blues" (from *Hopscotch Love*):

"True Love Blues"

Love means putting others first—
That's what love's about.

Lord says you gotta put me first
'Cause that's what love's about.
But the way you hog that apple pie
Proves you still ain't figured that out.

Elements of Poetry

Ask yourself this question: What do you like about a favorite poem? If you can't quite put your finger on it, consider the main features that critics agree make up a good poem: sounds, images, and forms.

Sounds

Most poetry for children is crafted with a keen ear for sound. That's why it is usually best read aloud. Sounds are the musical aspect of poetry. Just as music is said to speak the language of the emotions, so the sounds of poetry—rhythm, rhyme, alliteration, and onomatopoeia—choreograph much of the listener's emotional experience.

Rhythm. Rhythm, the pattern of stressed and unstressed syllables, is the beat of a poem. Rhythm can be a direct route to the emotions. The rhythm of a slow heartbeat has a calming effect even on a newborn baby, whereas the sound of a fast heartbeat causes anxiety. The pulse of a graduation march sweeps us along with dignity and pride; the pounding of a military drum keeps soldiers advancing in step with one another. The rhythm of a marching band makes us want to run to get a better look.

Rhythm is prominent in many children's poems—and perhaps nowhere more so than in the work of NCTE award-winner David McCord. In his poem "The Pickety Fence" (from *One at a Time*), you can hear the rhythm of a stick dragging staccato across the pickets:

> The pickety fence
> The pickety fence
> Give it a lick it's
> The pickety fence
> Give it a lick it's
> A clickety fence
> Give it a lick it's
> A lickety fence
> Give it a lick
> Give it a lick
> Give it a lick
> With a rickety stick
> Pickety
> Pickety
> Pickety
> Pick

Children delight in clapping along to the rhythm of such poetry.

Rhythm makes music possible, and dancing. Rhythm is used to structure the stories we are told: the epics of *Gilgamesh*, the *Odyssey*, and the *Iliad* used rhythm as a code to help tellers retrieve and tell them for hours and days on end. Rhythm still fills the radio waves, and wiggles restless school children's knees up and down under their desks.

We have names for rhythms: *iambs, trochees, anapests,* and *dactyls* are terms for patterns of rhythm or *feet*, as they are technically called, that we have had since the Greeks mapped the rhythms of poetry 2500 years ago.

Iambs or **iambic feet** are made of one unstressed syllable followed by a stressed one.

> "A horse, a horse!" the captain cried . . .

Trochees are feet made up of a stressed syllable followed by an unstressed one:

> Cinderella dressed in yella
> Went upstairs and kissed a fella.

Anapests or **anapestic feet** are made up of two unstressed and one stressed syllable:

> In the cool of the day
> When the swallows come swirling . . .

Dactyls or **dactylic feet** have a stressed syllable followed by two unstressed syllables:

> Pulling a pig out of
> Piles of old pineapples . . .

Some common technical terms for the number of feet in a line are *dimeter* (two feet per line), *trimeter* (three feet), *tetrameter* (four feet), and *pentameter* (five feet). Thus, *dactylic tetrameter* would be a line made up of four feet, with each foot consisting of one stressed and two unstressed syllables, and so on.

Rhyme. Along with rhythm, rhyme lends a musical quality to poetry by building patterns of repetition. Rhymes delight us—but they do more. Rhymes function in a poem to link words, to play them against each other, and to build on their emotional content, as we see in this poem by Walter de la Mare (1923):

> "The Horseman"
>
> I heard a horseman
> Ride over the hill;
> The moon shone clear,
> The night was still;
> His helm was silver,
> And pale was he;
> And the horse he rode
> Was of ivory.

Rhymes are most pleasing when they surprise us. Note the rhymes on lines nine and ten and sixteen and seventeen of Bucksnort Trout's "Pickup Truck."

> "Pickup Truck"
>
> Climb in Uncle Ezra's pickup truck.
> Take your seat and trust your luck.
> Look out for the gearshift, easy with the door.
> Mind you don't step through the floor.
> Watch out where you sit. That furry hat?
> That's Dungeon Breath–Half dog, half rat.
> Careful of the coil spring poking thru the seat—
> You sit on that, you're gonna jump two feet.
> The roof is mighty low, or you'd jump higher.
> That's how those dents got there. That wire
> is hotter than a waffle iron. Do not touch!
> Hey, I never saw anybody *sweat* so much.
> You feeling all right? Here. Climb back out.
> You need some air. Breathe in. . . ., breathe out . . .
> There. Now you're looking better—
> But what are you sayin'?
> You're gonna walk, in all this rain?

Of course, the rhyming words should suit the meaning of the poem, and not be included merely for the sake of sound. The rhymes in Christina Rossetti's "Caterpillar" (from *Complete Poems of Christina Rossetti*) are skillfully done:

Brown and furry
Caterpillar in a hurry,
Take your walk
To the shady leaf, or stalk,
Or what not,
Which may be the chosen spot.
No toad spy you,
Hovering bird of prey pass by you;
Spin and die,
To live again a butterfly.

Contemporary poetry, including poetry for children, is less likely than older poetry to follow fixed rhymes schemes or rhythmic patterns.

Alliteration. Poems also may have repeated sounds that are more subtle than rhymes. These repeated sounds come in two common forms: *consonance,* the stringing together of similar consonant sounds, and *assonance,* the making of a series of similar vowel sounds. Together, consonance and assonance are known as *alliteration.*

Listen to this line from a poem by Rowena Bennett: "There once was a witch of Willowby Wood. . . ." A series of similar consonant sounds ties her words together; this is an example of consonance. No matter that "once" begins with *o*; the initial *w* sounds knit Bennett's words into a sonorous fabric. The poem we met at the opening of this chapter favored alliteration—consonance—over rhymes:

Snowboots snuggled over fat wool socks
Closed mouth muffled by a scratchy scarf
Arms pulled back by a bulging bookbag

A succession of percussive consonants can sound like feet walking on dry sticks, as in this anonymous Welsh poem translated by Gwyn Williams (in *The Rattle Bag,* edited by Heaney and Hughes):

Dinogad's speckled petticoat
was made of skins and speckled stoat:
whip whip whipalong
eight times we'll sing the song.

The succession of consonant clusters in Alfred, Lord Tennyson's "The Eagle" (1851) helps us to see and feel the bird's harsh, desolate perch; when the consonants give way to smoother sounds, they suggest the expansive beauty of the landscape below:

He clasps the crag with crooked hands;
Close to the sun in lonely lands,
Ringed with the azure world, he stands . . .

Assonance, the use of a series of similar vowel sounds, also ties the words in a line together. Note the repeated short vowel sounds in "clasps," "crag," and "hands" in Tennyson's poem. Assonance in William Blake's "The Lamb" ties words together:

Little Lamb who made thee?
Dost thou know who made thee?
Gave thee life and bid thee feed
By the stream and o'er the mead;

Onomatopoeia. When words in a poem imitate actual sounds of things (such as "moo," "oink," "bam"), the poet is using onomatopoeia, as you see in the first two lines of this poem:

"4 a.m."

Screech, roar, whoop, wham!
Whomp, whir, slam, bam!
Hey, why can't you folks be quiet?
Collecting trash is loud. You try it!

In sum, poets use sounds deliberately to approximate the emotional qualities of their subjects and to weave words together into tight compositions. Good poets blend sounds so skillfully that we feel the effects without being aware of the devices they have used.

Images

When a poem seems to "put us in the picture," chances are the poet has used imagery, an appeal to the senses, employing details that enable us to imagine how things look, sound, feel, smell, or taste.

"Dove"

The dove flew straight and quick
Rapid rhythmic rowing 'cross a red fall sky
Then "pop, pop, podop, pop"
Rang out and ricocheted around the hills.
At once the dove was not a dove
But feathers and flesh
Flailing and falling like a failed dream.

Comparisons

Imagery is one of poetry's great contributions to our awareness of the world. With imagery, poems name sensations and expand people's consciousness of their minute-to-minute experiences. Toddlers have the wonderful power to put words together in new ways: A naked child spread his arms and proclaimed, "I'm barefoot all over!" Making words do new work is one of the poet's greatest talents, too. Poets often use language in fresh ways by making comparisons: similes and metaphors and personifications.

The definitions of these terms never do justice to their power. A *simile* is defined as an explicit comparison, using the word "like" or "as." A *metaphor* omits those two words and describes one thing as if it were another. *Personification* is a sort of metaphor in which an inanimate thing is described as if it were human (or, at least, had sensations and a will). But look what writers do with these literary devices. Practically all mythology is built on personification. The ancient Norse myths, for example, personified the reckless forces of nature in the character of Thor. Most religious writing is built around metaphor and simile: Having no direct experience of any world but this one, religious writers use familiar terms to speak of things beyond.

The Scottish poet and song writer Robert Burns gave us two famous similes in "Red, Red Rose." Don't be troubled by the archaic spelling of *love*).

O my Luve's like a red, red rose,
That's newly sprung in June:
O my Luve's like the melodie,
That's sweetly play'd in tune.

Metaphors are the use of one object or idea (usually something concrete) to stand in for another idea (usually more abstract). For example, an old folk hymn says,

Bright morning stars are rising
Bright morning stars are rising
Bright morning stars are rising
Day is a-breaking in my soul.

TEACHING IDEA 6.5

CREATING A POEM COLLAGE

One way to interrupt children's expectations that a poem will have a literal meaning is by having them play with parts of poems out of order. Invite the students to make a poem collage. Pass out copies of a lyric or expressive poem. Ask the children to read it aloud, with each child taking a line. Then go around the room, having each child chant out a line or phrase he or she found especially striking. Finally, invite them to cut the poems apart and reassemble the lines or phrases as they see fit. If they want, they may repeat a line or phrase, for special emphasis.

"Bright morning stars" may mean good things that are happening or good insights that are occurring to the narrator. "Day . . . breaking in [the narrator's] soul" can mean a great sense of relief or a better state of affairs. In the case of these metaphors, the bright morning stars and the daybreak are not compared to events and feelings but rather stand for them.

Personification is speaking of inanimate objects as if they had human-like will and emotions. The sea chantey, "Rolling Home," contains this verse:

> And the waves that rise to join us seem to murmur as they rise
> We have tarried here to bear you to the land you dearly prize.

Here waves have human-like personalities, as they might to a person who spends his life at sea.

In summary, all of these ways of making likenesses—similes, metaphors, and personification—expand the power of language. In so doing, they expand our perceptions, too: They make us, the readers and hearers, experience the world in new ways.

Forms

The arrangement of words on the page affects their look, readers' progress through them with rushes and pauses, and the emphasis given to some of the words. Some poems imitate their themes with the array of words on the page. Note how the layout of this poem suggests the whimsical paths of falling leaves:

"Leaves"

We sipped life from sun light all summer long,
and waved the wind on its way
Then cold nights came and numbed our stems.
We put on cheerful garments, then. Gold and orange, we showed forth
our last best beauty,
and launched ourselves like lazy fall fireworks,
            showering
                    spiralling
                        spinning
                                wafting
                    drifting
                dancing
dazzling
                    and gently settling, fading, browning, melting, and
            merging
                    with our forebears
into the forest floor.
(Anonymous)

Insight

Above and beyond the effects of particular literary devices, poems often startle us with insight—a noticing of something that makes us say, "Yes—that's it! But I never found a way of saying it before." Some insights are simple but still surprising, like this one in Philip Whalen's poem "Early Spring" (in Paul Janeczko's *This Delicious Day*):

The dog writes on the window with his nose.

Some insights are more complicated, such as those in this poem by Naomi Shihab Nye (from *Words under the Words*):

"Famous"

The river is famous to the fish.
The loud voice is famous to silence,
which knew it would inherit the earth
before anybody said so.
The cat sleeping on the fence is famous to the birds
watching him from the birdhouse.
The tear is famous, briefly, to the cheek.
The idea you carry close to your bosom
is famous to your bosom.
The boot is famous to the earth,
more famous than the dress shoe,
which is famous only to floors.
The bent photograph is famous to the one who carries it
and not at all famous to the one who is pictured.
I want to be famous to shuffling men
who smile while crossing streets,
sticky children in grocery lines,
famous as the one who smiled back.
I want to be famous the way a pulley is famous,
or a buttonhole, not because it did anything spectacular,
but because it never forgot what it could do.

Imagery is one of poetry's great values, but insight is even greater. Good poems are often noteworthy for their concentrated clarity of understanding. The insight expressed in Naomi Shihab Nye's poem might well have been elaborated by another writer into a book-length manuscript.

Children's Preferences in Poetry

Very young children often love poetry. But their delight may not survive middle childhood, when the poetry moves beyond the merely playful toward more ambitious forms and uses.

 TECHNOLOGY in PRACTICE 6.1

FORM POEMS ON THE WEB

It can be interesting to sample ideas for teaching children to write poetry from different parts of the country and even different parts of the world. Two interesting Web sites on writing form poems are found at: http://www.poetspath.com (see Magnificent Rainbow Exhibits). http://www.standards.dfes.gov.uk/ (see Primary Resources for teaching writing/shape poems).

What sorts of poetry do elementary school children like? Most popular are narrative poems, poems with rhyme and rhythm, humor, and poems about familiar experiences. Children often dislike abstraction—too much imagery and figurative language (Kutiper & Wilson, 1993; Terry, 1974).

How can teachers expand the range of the poetry children can appreciate? One way is to share poetry informally with children every chance you get. Children will appreciate poems if you offer them for their content—for the insights and feelings they communicate—rather than as complex objects to be analyzed. A second way to promote poetry is to have children practice choral speaking and performance. Most poetry is best read aloud, and the variations possible with a voice choir can make poems sound magnificent. A third way is to encourage children to create their own. Writing poetry gives children a connection to what poets are trying to do.

CRITERIA FOR SELECTING POETRY FOR CHILDREN

1. **Honesty** Poems should avoid sentimentality or talking down to the child.
2. **A positive spirit** There are many poems that appeal mainly to children's mischievous side, but the better ones feature creative word play or illuminating observations or both.
3. **Sounds** Sounds should support the sense of the poem. Any rhymes should be precise, and also fresh (not predictable). Alliteration can be used carefully.
4. **Images** Language should bring clear images to the mind's eye.
5. **Insight** Good poems should surprise readers by pointing out things readers didn't realize or had overlooked.
6. **Relevance** While not essential, poems can be chosen that are relevant to what is happening in the world, among the students, or in the curriculum.

ISSUE to CONSIDER

How Can We Keep Children's Liking for Poetry Alive?

Jack Prelutsky, a very popular poet among North American children, explains the problem this way (1983, p. 18):

For very young children, poetry is as natural as breathing. . . . But then something happens to this early love affair with poetry. At some point during their school careers, many children seem to lose their interest and enthusiasm for poetry and their easygoing pleasure in its sounds and images.

What is to be done? What kinds of poems will keep children's interest alive? Here is Prelutsky's answer (1983, p. 18):

. . . poems that evoke laughter and delight, poems that cause a palpable ripple of surprise by the unexpected comparisons they make, poems that paint pictures with words that are as vivid as brushstrokes, poems that re-awaken pleasure in the sounds and meanings of language.

A contrasting opinion was expressed by Myra Cohn Livingston (1992, p. 9):

[Poetry] is now pouring from the publishers, but much of it is little more than prose arranged as poetry, overblown metaphors, tired clichés, and light verse that caters to many of the baser emotions, calculated to give children a quick laugh. It has, in many instances, no sign of helping children evolve, but on the contrary [allows them to] remain in the same old place.

Prelutsky and Livingston have written very different poetry. Prelutsky creates rhymed and rhythmic poems that are noted for their humor and surprising twists. Livingston's poems take more varied forms, including blank verse, and most of them explore serious themes. One has the feeling, reading their comments, that each might consider the other's poetry part of the problem.

What do you think? In order to keep children's interest in poetry alive, should we offer them mostly poems that are enjoyable? Or should we offer them mostly poems that take their inner complexities seriously? Should the poems be immediately rewarding? Or should they challenge children to ponder their meanings and associations? Or is there some middle ground?

Major Children's Poets and Their Works

Hundreds of poets have written for children, but we will look closely at only a handful who are especially noteworthy, both for their insight and literary skill and for their acceptance by children over the years.

POET	ABOUT THE POET	NOTABLE WORKS
Nikki Grimes	Winner of the NCTE Poetry Award, Nikki Grimes writes poems from an African American perspective with universal appeal. Born in Harlem, she lives in Corona, California.	*It's Raining Laughter*, with photographs by Myles Pinkney; *A Dime a Dozen*, illustrated by Angelo; *Hopscotch Love: A Family Treasury of Love Poems*, illustrated by Melodye Benson Rosales; *Meet Danitra Brown*, illustrated by Floyd Cooper (winner of the Coretta Scott King Award). Also has written novels in verse: *Bronx Masquerade* and *What Is Goodbye?*
Naomi Shihab Nye	Palestinian American poet from San Antonio whose sensitive poems appeal to upper elementary aged children through adults.	*Fuel, The Red Suitcase, Words under the Words, A Maze Me: Poems for Girls.* She has edited collections, including *This Same Sky*, poems from many countries; and *The Tree Is Older Than You Are*, Spanish-English bilingual poems; and poems written by young poets—*Salting the Ocean.*
Paul Janeczko	A former high school teacher, Janeczko writes poems in a range of forms from haiku to concrete poems to blank verse organized around themes. He also writes about writing poetry.	*A Poke in the I: Concrete Poems, Stone Bench in an Empty Park, Don't Forget to Fly: A Cycle of Modern Poems, This Delicious Day: 65 Poems, A Kick in the Head, A Foot in the Mouth*, and *The Music of What Happens: Poems That Tell Stories.* Also, *The Place My Words Are Looking For: What Poets Say about and through Their Work, Poetspeak: In Their Work, About Their Work*, and *Poetry from A to Z: A Guide for Young Writers.*
Janet Wong	A former lawyer from California with Chinese and Korean ancestry, Wong often writes poems from the point of view of non-white children, with a solid commitment to an open and egalitarian society. She also writes delightful and funny poems for children of all ages.	*The Dumpster Diver, A Suitcase of Seaweed, Good Luck Gold, Buzz, The Rainbow Hand—Poems About Mothers and Children*, and *Knock on Wood.*
Jack Prelutsky	Jack Prelutsky was a photographer, folk singer, and truck driver before becoming a popular creator of humorous poetry and poetry collections for children. In 2006 he was named the first Children's Poet Laureate by the Poetry Foundation. He lives in Seattle.	*My Dog May Be a Genius, It's Raining Pigs and Noodles, A Pizza the Size of the Sun, The Baby Uggs Are Hatching, Beneath a Blue Umbrella, The Dragons Are Singing Tonight*, and *Be Glad Your Nose Is on Your Face and Other Poems: Some of the Best of Jack Prelutsky.* He has also edited *For Laughing Out Loud* and *The Random House Book of Poetry for Children.* Prelutsky has written guides to help children write poetry, including *Pizza, Pigs, and Poetry: How to Write a Poem* and *Read a Rhyme, Write a Rhyme.*
Shel Silverstein	Silverstein was a cartoonist, songwriter, and children's poet. Known for humorous, irreverent, and mischievous poetry for children; he also penned the song "A Boy Named Sue" for Johnny Cash and was long a cartoonist for *Playboy* magazine.	*Where the Sidewalk Ends* and *A Light in the Attic.*
Lee Bennett Hopkins	Winner of the NCTE Poetry Award, Hopkins is most notable as a collector of poems for children. He has been an effective champion of children's poetry for many decades. A former classroom teacher, a curriculum specialist, a poetry anthologist, a poet, a consultant to publishers, a television show host, and a patron of two prestigious awards for poets and poems in his long career, he has published over 80 books for children, most of them poetry collections.	*Wonderful Words: Poems About Reading, Writing, Speaking, and Listening; Good Books, Good Times; My America; Spectacular Science; Marvelous Math; Weather; Sports! Sports! Sports!; Lives*, and *Hoofbeats, Claws, and Rippled Fins.*

Ask *the* Poet . . . Nikki Grimes

Some material is drawn from my own life ("Sister Love," Jazmin's Notebook, A Dime a Dozen—the only truly autobiographical work I've written to date). Most of my material, though, derives from a lifelong discipline of observing people around me, both young and old.

When I was in my early teens, my father encouraged me to develop a writer's eye and a writer's ear, to always be attentive, watchful, listening. It's second nature to me, now. I'm forever picking up snatches of dialogue, of dialect, forever noticing certain gestures, mannerisms, and so on. I file them all away in my memory for later use. When I sit down to write a new poem, a new story, these observances come forth, unbidden. The voices I've heard suddenly ring in my ear, the swagger I've seen passes before my eyes yet again. The encyclopedia of my memory provides everything I need.

Having my senses "on" at all times may sound like a lot of work, but it's automatic, at this point. I'm hardly aware that I'm doing it, anymore!

Great advice, Dad. Thanks!

Nikki Grimes does not consider herself a bona fide storyteller, but, as she told an audience at the Library of Congress, she is happy to own the title Poet. Born and raised in New York City, Nikki began composing verse at the age of six and has been writing ever since. She has received extraordinary acclaim for her poetry and novels for children and young adults. She won the 2006 NCTE Award for Excellence in Poetry for Children. Her works have been designated

as ALA Notable books and have won the Coretta Scott King Award. Her most recent honored works are *What Is Goodbye?* (an ALA Notable book), *Jazmin's Notebook*, *Dark Sons*, and *The Road to Paris* (Coretta Scott King Author Honor Books). Other honored works are the novels *Bronx Masquerade* (Dial), winner of the 2003 Coretta Scott King Author Award, and *Jazmin's Notebook* (Dial), a Coretta Scott King honor book and Bank Street College Book of the Year; the popular poetry collections *Danitra Brown Leaves Town* (HarperCollins) and *Meet Danitra Brown* (Lothrop), an ALA Notable and Coretta Scott King honor book, *Hopscotch Love* (Lothrop); *Under the Christmas Tree* (Harper); *Talkin' About Bessie*, the 2003 Coretta Scott King Illustrator Award winner and Author Award honor book, and Horn Book Fanfare book (Orchard); *Aneesa Lee & the Weaver's Gift*, an American Bookseller Pick of the List (Lothrop); *From a Child's Heart* (Just Us Books); *A Dime A Dozen, My Man Blue* (Dial); *Come Sunday* (Eerdman's), an ALA Notable book; *At Break of Day and When Daddy Prays* (Eerdman's). An accomplished and widely anthologized poet of both children's and adult verse, Grimes has conducted poetry readings and lectures at international schools in Russia, China, Sweden and Tanzania, while short-term mission projects have taken her to such trouble spots as Haiti. Ms. Grimes lives in Corona, California.

EXPERIENCES FOR FURTHER LEARNING

1. Compile your own anthology of poems for children. Organize it around a theme or an issue—for example, poems for choral reading, poems from many cultures, or poems to celebrate holidays. So that you can become acquainted with contemporary poetry, use ten different sources, choose no more than two poems per source, and make sure they were published within the last fifteen years. (Thanks to Linnea Henderson for this suggestion.)

2. A good poem may sound natural, but on examination it is likely to turn out to have been very carefully crafted. Take a poem such as A. A. Milne's "Happiness" (from *When We Were Very Young*). Try substituting other words for any of Milne's. Does the poem sound as good?

RECOMMENDED BOOKS

* indicates a picture book; I indicates interest level
(P = preschool; YA = young adult).

Comprehensive Anthologies

Berry, James, ed. *Classic Poems to Read Aloud*. Larousse Kingfisher, 2003. An excellent collection of poems from many cultures. (I: 10–YA)

Cullinan, Bernice, ed. *Another Jar of Tiny Stars: Poems from NCTE Award-Winning Poets*. Wordsong/Boyds Mills Press, 2009. An update to *A Jar of Tiny* Stars, published in 1996, this volume includes poems by all NCTE Poetry Award winners through 2009. (I: 6–13)

Kennedy, Caroline. *A Family of Poems: My Favorite Poetry for Children*. Illustrated by Jon J. Muth. Hyperion, 2005. This collection of over 100 classic and new poems is arranged into seven sections—About Me, That's So Silly!, Animals, The Seasons, The Seashore, Adventure, and Bedtime. (I: 5–12)

Kennedy, X. J., and Dorothy Kennedy, eds. *Knock at a Star* (2nd ed.). Little, Brown, 1999. This welcome second edition is a fine collection of poems organized by categories, with helpful commentary by the authors, themselves established poets. Nearly half of the poems have been changed from the first edition, which appeared in 1982, and the editors have included several more accessible poems. (I: 9–YA)

Prelutsky, Jack, ed. *The Random House Book of Poetry for Children*. Illustrated by Arnold Lobel. Random House, 1983. An extensive anthology collected by one of America's favorite children's poets. (I: 7–12)

Yolen, Jane, and Andrew Fusek Peters, eds. *Here's a Little Poem: A Very First Book of Poetry*. Illustrated by Polly Dunbar. Candlewick, 2007. More than 60 poems by noted poets arranged by topic: "Me, Myself, and I," Who Lives in My House?", "I Go Outside," and "Time for Bed." (I: 3–6).

Themed Collections

*Adoff, Arnold, ed. *My Black Me: A Beginning Book of Black Poetry*, rev. ed. Puffin, 1995. Adoff includes poems by Imamu Amiri Baraka, Lucille Clifton, Nikki Giovanni, Langston Hughes, and a dozen others who are better known to adults than to children, but who all celebrate the black experience. (I: 9–12)

Brooks, Gwendolyn. *Bronzeville Boys and Girls*. Illustrated by Faith Ringgold. Amistad, 2006. Poems for children first published in 1958 by the first African American woman to win a Pulitzer Prize. (I: 8–11)

*Bruchac, Joseph. *The Earth under Sky Bear's Feet: Native American Poems of the Land*. Illustrated by Thomas Locker. Puffin, 1998. Most of these poems are reflections on the Sky Bear constellation, also known as the Big Dipper. Some of Locker's rich oil paintings are magnificent. (I: 7–11)

Florian, Douglas. *Comets, Stars, the Moon, and Mars*. Harcourt, 2007. Florian's rich descriptions of heavenly bodies will enhance the study of space in any classroom. (I: 6–10)

*_____. *Mammalabilia*. Harcourt, 2000. These poems are also whimsical, funny, and wonderfully illustrated. (I: 8–11)

*_____. *Poetrees*. Beach Lane, 2010. Poems about trees, with cheerful word play. (I: 8–11)

George, Kristine O'Connell. *Hummingbird Nest: A Journal of Poems*. Illustrated by Barry Moser. Harcourt, 2004. This poetic journal chronicles the drama of hummingbirds building a nest, hatching their eggs, and watching the babies grow, learn to fly, and finally, leave their safe and secure nest. (I: 8–12)

*Greenfield, Eloise. *Honey, I Love and Other Poems*. Illustrated by Leo and Diane Dillon. Harper Trophy, 1986. Poems celebrating favorite things in a child's life in a perennially favorite collection by a highly esteemed African American poet. (I: 6–10)

_____. *In the Land of Words*. Illustrated by Jan Spivey Gilchrist. HarperCollins, 2004. This collection, which includes new poems as well as familiar favorites, celebrates the power of language and literacy. The poet explains the inspiration for each one.

*Grimes, Nikki. *Meet Danitra Brown*. Illustrated by Floyd Cooper. Mulberry, 1997. Danitra Brown is described in a series of poems in the voice of Danitra's best friend, with details that reveal much about what character means in a young person. (I: 7–9)

*Hoberman, Mary Ann. *Forget-Me-Nots: Poems to Learn by Heart*. Illustrated by Michael Emberley. Little, Brown, 2012. Celebrated children's port Mary Ann Hoberman has chosen 123 poems from contemporary and older generations that children can memorize and recite. (I: 6–10)

Hopkins, Lee Bennett, ed. *Hoofbeats, Claws, and Rippled Fins: Creature Poems*. Illustrated by Stephen Alcorn. HarperCollins, 2002. Thirteen poets were commissioned to match poems about animals to Alcorn's etchings. There are poems here about buffaloes, anteaters, camels, and frogs. (I: 8-11).

Hovey, Kate. *Voices of the Trojan War*. Illustrated by Leonid Gore. Simon and Schuster, 2004. Participants in the saga of ancient Troy each tell their story in a variety of forms—free verse, rhymed, metered, shaped, and other forms. (I: 10 and up)

Lewis, J. Patrick. *Monumental Verses*. National Geographic, 2005. Monuments from the modern and ancient worlds are celebrated in this collection including Stonehenge, the Great Pyramid of Cheops, the Golden Gate Bridge, the Eiffel Tower, and others. Photographs accompany each poem. Lewis won the 2011 NCTE Poetry Award. (I: 9–12)

Livingston, Myra Cohn. *Calendar*. Illustrated by Will Hildebrand. Holiday House, 2007. A poem about the seasons by an NCTE award-winning poet, expanded to picture book length. (I: 6–9)

*Mora, Pat. *Confetti: Poems for Children*. Illustrated by Enrique O. Sanchez. Lee and Low, 1996. A baker's dozen of short poems celebrate life in English, with Spanish words and a glossary. (I: 5–8)

*_____. *Yum! Mmmm! ¡Que Rico! Americas' Sproutings*. Illustrated by Rafael Lopez. Lee and Low, 2007. Celebrates 14 kinds of food that are native to the Americas. (I: 7–11)

Myers, Walter Dean. *Blues Journey*. Illustrated by Christopher Myers. Holiday House, 2003. This collection of 20 poems, penned in the traditional blues call-and-response style, celebrates and commemorates the range of African American history and experience. (I: 10 and up)

Noda, Takayo. *Dear World*. Dial, 2003. Illustrator Takayo Noda uses a young child's voice to address celebrations to the tulips, the birds, and the earth itself. This book will easily inspire writing exercises, as children craft their own "Dear _____ " poems. (I: 5–8)

Nye, Naomi Shihab, and Paul Janeczko, eds. *I Feel a Little Jumpy around You: A Book of Her Poems & His Poems Collected in Pairs*. Simon & Schuster, 1996. A fascinating collection of 96 paired poems, one from a young woman's perspective and the other from a young man's, on a range of topics, including relationships. (I: 12–YA)

*Rosenthal, Betsy R. *My House Is Singing*. Illustrated by Margaret Chodos-Irvine. Harcourt, 2004. This collection is a tribute to the ordinary places, spaces, and objects that define home—the laundry room, the smoke detector, the vacuum cleaner, a hideaway, the hallway chair. (I: 5–9)

*Sidman, Joyce. *Swirl by Swirl: Spirals in Nature*. Illustrated by Beth Krommes. Houghton Mifflin, 2011. Insightful poems about geometric expressions in nature, illustrated with scratchboard drawings. (I: 7–11)

*_____. *Dark Emperor and Other Poems of the Night*. Illustrated by Rick Allen. Houghton Mifflin, 2010. Twelve poems on the nocturnal habits of twelve different creatures supply accurate details that will inspire both further study and careful observation. Accompanied by a glossary. Winner of the Caldecott award. (I: 6–12)

*_____. *Song of the Water Boatman & Other Pond Poems*. Illustrated by Beckie Prange. Houghton Mifflin, 2005. This collection of poems chronicles plant and animal life in the pond throughout the seasons. Each double-page spread focuses on one plant or animal and includes a poem as well as a paragraph containing related scientific information. (I: 7–12)

*Singer, Marilyn. *A Stick Is an Excellent Thing: Poems Celebrating Outdoor Play*. Illustrated by LeUven Pham. Clarion, 2012. These eighteen poems might have been inspired by Michelle Obama—lively language celebrates the fun things children can do outdoors in all seasons. (I: 5–9)

*_____. *Central Heating: Poems About Fire and Warmth*. Illustrated by Meilo So. Knopf, 2005. Nineteen poems explore all sides of fire, from life-giving warmth to destructive terror. (I: 9–13)

*_____. *Footprints on the Roof: Poems About the Earth*. Illustrated by Meilo So. Knopf, 2002. Poems in free verse explore the variety of natural places on the planet. (I: 8–12)

*Wong, Janet S. *Buzz*. Illustrated by Margaret Chodos-Irvine. Harcourt, 2000. A celebration of household sounds, most sounding like "buzzzz." A popular poet's first offering for young children. (I: 4–7)

_____. *Good Luck Gold*. Create Space, 2012. These 42 poems by a widely recognized Asian American poet were first published more than 20 years ago. They are valued for their insights on growing up as a person of Asian origin in America. (I: 8–11)

*_____. *Twist*. Illustrated by Julie Paschkis. Margaret K. McElderry, 2007. Each poem in this collection presents a picture and a story focused on a yoga pose. Vibrant illustrations accompany each poem. (I: 6 and up)

A Poet's Collected Works

Farjeon, Eleanor. *Eleanor Farjeon's Poems for Children*. Lippincott, 1951. Farjeon won the first Hans Christian Andersen Award for her contribution to children's literature of the world. The poems are touching, funny, and insightful. (I: 7–11)

*Giovanni, Nikki. *Ego-Tripping and Other Poems for the Young*. Illustrated by George Ford. Lawrence Hill, 1993. Thirty-three poems in the lively and direct voice of a gifted urban poet. (I: 10–YA)

*_____. *Spin a Soft Black Song*. Illustrated by George Martins. Farrar, 1985. Fine poems for children by a noted African American poet. (I: 8–12)

Hughes, Langston. *The Dream Keeper and Other Poems*. Illustrated by Jerry Pinkney. Knopf, 1996. Poems suitable for young people by one of America's greatest poets, who was a leader of the Harlem Renaissance. (I: 8–YA)

*Prelutsky, Jack. *Be Glad Your Nose Is on Your Face and Other Poems: Some of the Best of Jack Prelutsky*.

Illustrated by Brandon Dorman. Greenwillow, 2008. Over a hundred of Prelutsky's favorite poems plus 15 new ones. (I: 5–11)

Roethke, Theodore. *The Collected Poems of Theodore Roethke*. Doubleday, 1946. Not all of these poems were written for children; nonetheless, they are full of rich imagery and sometimes startling insights. (I: 10–YA)

Sandburg, Carl. *Rainbows Are Made: Poems*. Selected by Lee Bennett Hopkins. Harcourt, 1982. A good source of poems for children by one of America's great poets. Includes poems not often anthologized. (I: 9–12)

*Stevenson, Robert Louis. *A Child's Garden of Verses*. Illustrated by Tasha Tudor. Simon & Schuster, 1999. Probably the most enduringly popular collection of poems for children in the English language, charmingly illustrated by Tasha Tudor. Though over a hundred years old, most of the poems are still enjoyable. (I: 4–adult)

Songs and Song Collections

*dePaola, Tomie. *The Friendly Beasts*. Puffin, 1998. This lovely old English carol of the Christmas story is a favorite of many children. With music for piano. (I: 5–6)

*Guthrie, Woody. *This Land Is Your Land*. Illustrated by Kathy Jakobsen. Little, Brown, 2008. A fascinating tribute to America's most prolific folk singer and the times that shaped him: the Depression Era and the Dust Bowl. (I: All ages)

*Langstaff, John. *Oh, A-Hunting We Will Go*. Illustrated by Nancy Winslow Parker. Aladdin, 1974/1991. An English folk song in picture book form. The couplets are spread across page turns, inviting the children to guess the endings. (I: 4–9)

Patterson, Annie, and Peter Blood. *Rise Up Singing*. Sing Out!, 2005. Hundreds of folk songs, some with music and all with guitar chords. Recordings of the songs are available. (I: All ages)

Seeger, Ruth Crawford. *American Folksongs for Children*. Music Sales America, 2002. A fine collection of folk songs with accompanying games. Music and guitar chords are included. (I: All ages)

*Stotts, Stuart. *We Shall Overcome: A Song That Changed the World*. Illustrated by Terrance Cummings. Clarion, 2010. Chronicles the old gospel and labor song that was reshaped at the Highlander Folk School into the battle hymn of the Civil Rights movement. (I: 7–12)

*Zelinsky, Paul. *Knick-Knack Paddy Whack*. Dutton, 2002. An award-winning illustrator enlivens this favorite children's song. (I: 3–9)

Narrative Poems

*Service, Robert W. *The Cremation of Sam McGee*. Illustrated by Ted Harrison. Kids Can Press, 2006. Originally published in 1907, this narrative poem turns out to be a tall tale with a surprise ending. The illustrations are abstract but colorful. (I: All ages)

Sidman, Joyce. *Meow Ruff: A Story in Concrete Poetry*. Illustrated by Michelle Berg. Houghton Mifflin, 2006. Through concrete poetry, Sidman tells the story of an unlikely friendship between a puppy and an abandoned kitten. (I: 6–9)

*Thayer, Ernest L. *Casey at the Bat: A Ballad of the Republic Sung in 1888*. Illustrated C. F. Payne. Simon and Schuster, 2003. A classic American baseball story set to verse. (I: 8–YA)

Poems About People

*Bernier-Grand, Carmen T. *Diego: Bigger Than Life*. Illustrated by David Diaz. Marshall Cavendish, 2009. A biography in free verse of the famous Mexican painter whose murals celebrated common people. (I: 8–11)

_____. *Frida: Viva la Vida! Long Live Life!* Marshall Cavendish, 2007. A biography in verse of Frida Kahlo, the Mexican artist and consort of Diego Rivera. (I: 8–11)

*Hill, Laban Carrick. *Dave the Potter: Artist, Poet, Slave*. Illustrated by Bryan Collier. Little, Brown, 2010. Dave lived in South Carolina in the 1800s and was a master potter and a sensitive poet. A biographical essay is included. (I: 6–10)

Nelson, Marilyn. *Carver: A Life in Poems*. Front Street, 2001. Forty-four poems elucidate the life of the remarkable African American genius of agriculture, George Washington Carver. (I: 9–12).

*_____. *Sweethearts of Rhythm: The Story of the Greatest All-Girl Swing Band in the World*. Illustrated by Jerry Pinkney. Dial, 2009. A story in verse about an interracial all-female jazz band that endured the hardships of the Jim Crow laws to tour the United States in the 1940s. (I: 8–12)

*Shange, Ntozake. *Ellington Was Not a Street*. Illustrated by Kadir Nelson. Simon and Schuster, 2004. The poet recalls the great African American and African movers and shakers that she remembers from her childhood and youth—people whose memories have been reduced to street names for the present generation of children. (I: 8–12)

Form Poems

Burg, Brad. *Outside the Lines: Poetry at Play*. Illustrated by Rebecca Gibbon. Putnam, 2002. These are poems about play, but they also play with the arrangement of the words on the page. (I: 7–11)

Grandits, John. *Technically, It's Not My Fault: Concrete Poems*. Clarion Books, 2004. Each of these 27 concrete poems—with very idiosyncratic content—is written from the viewpoint of an eleven-year-old. (I: 10–12)

*Janeczko, Paul, ed. *Stone Bench in an Empty Park*. Illustrated by Henri Silberman. Orchard, 2000. Janeczko has directed the insight-bearing light of the haiku form to urban scenes and matched poems from Nikki Grimes, Issa, and others to black-and-white photographs by Henri Silberman. (I: 12–YA)

Nelson, Marilyn. *A Wreath for Emmett Till*. Illustrated by Philippe Lardy. Houghton Mifflin, 2005. This deeply moving tribute to Emmett Till, whose murder galvanized the Civil Rights movement, is written in a highly structured and unusual poetic form called a heroic crown of sonnets. (I: 12 and up)

Prelutsky, Jack. *If Not for the Cat*. Illustrated by Ted Rand. HarperCollins, 2004. Each of the haiku in this collection poses a simple riddle about an animal. Individual haiku appear on double-page spreads accompanied by an illustration of the creature. (I: 5–12)

Humorous Poems

*Ciardi, John. *Doodle Soup*. Illustrated by Merle Nacht. Houghton Mifflin, 1985. Funny poems by a master of the genre. (I: 6–8)

Dahl, Roald. *Revolting Rhymes*. Bantam, 1983. If you like Roald Dahl, you'll like this hilarious collection of poems—some of which are in dubious taste. (I: 9–12)

Langsty, Bruce. *If Pigs Could Fly . . . And Other Deep Thoughts*. Illustrated by Stephen Carpenter. Maedow-brook, 2006. These really are funny poems, and they're fine for reading aloud. This collection, says the author, was nominated for inclusion by 1,000 children. (I: 5–9)

Scieszka, Jon. *Science Verse*. Illustrated by Lane Smith. Penguin Putnam, 2004. Parody is the name of the game in this collection of songs, rhymes, and poems based on Mother Goose, Ernest Lawrence Thayer, and Edgar Allan Poe—to name but a few of the original inspirations. (I: 5 and up)

Silverstein, Shel. *Where the Sidewalk Ends*. HarperCollins, 1974. Funny and irreverent poems by one of the most popular of children's poets. (I: 5–12)

*Viorst, Judith. *If I Were in Charge of the World and Other Worries*. Illustrated by Lynne Cherry. Atheneum, 1981. Viorst penetrates to the heart of the foibles of children and their parents. (I: 12–YA)

Street Rhymes and Nursery Rhymes

*Cole, Joanna, and Stephanie Calmenson. *Miss Mary Mack and Other Children's Street Rhymes*. Illustrated by Alan Tiegreen. Morrow/Beech Tree, 1990. Jump-rope rhymes and more from city streets. (I: 4–8)

_____. *The Inner City Mother Goose*. Simon & Schuster, 1969. Poems on urban themes patterned on older forms and with an ironic flavor. (I: 9–YA)

*Crews, Nina. *The Neighborhood Mother Goose*. Amistad, 2003. Computer-enhanced photographs create a fanciful urban backdrop—photographs from the artist's neighborhood in Brooklyn—for the rollicking rhymes. (I: P–7)

*Duffey, Chris. *Nursery Rhyme Comics: 50 Timeless Rhymes from 50 Celebrated Cartoonists*. First Second, 2011. Fifty traditional rhymes are brought to life in cartoon form by noted graphic artists. (I: 5–10)

*Manor, Sally. *Pocket Full of Posies: A Treasury of Nursery Rhymes*. Houghton Mifflin, 2010. Classic nursery rhymes illustrated with hand-sewn and crafted illustrations. (I: 5–7)

Milne, A. A. *Now We Are Six*. Illustrated by Ernest H. Shepard. E. P. Dutton, 1988. Short rhythmic poems from a child's point of view, from the author of *The House at Pooh Corner*. (I: 4–7)

_____. *When We Were Very Young*. Illustrated by Ernest H. Shepard. E. P. Dutton, 1988. Lively poems about lively children, these poems were originally published in 1924 and constitute some of the best-selling children's poem collections of all time. (I: 4–7)

Poems Arranged for Reading Aloud and for Memorizing

Ciardi, John. *You Read to Me, I'll Read to You*. Harper Trophy, 1987. Favorite poems for children by a much-loved poet. (I: 7–11)

*Fleischman, Paul. *Big Talk: Poems for Four Voices*. Illustrated by Beppe Giaccobe. Boston: Candlewick, 2000. Fleischman expands the size of the performance troupe with this set of poems for four (or more, or fewer) voices. (I: 9–12)

*_____. *I Am Phoenix: Poems for Two Voices*. Illustrated by Ken Nutt. Harper Trophy, 1989. Poems about birds, set for two voices. (I: 9–12)

*_____. *Joyful Noise: Poems for Two Voices*. Harper, 1988. This book of poems about insects won a Newbery Medal. (I: 9–12)

_____. *Side by Side: Poems to Read Together*. Simon & Schuster, 1988. Another fine collection by a noted children's poet and anthologist. (I: 7–10)

Giovanni, Nikki. *Hip Hop Speaks to Children: A Celebration of Poetry With a Beat*. Sourcebooks Jabberwocky, 2008. With an accompanying CD, this collection features poets of the African American experience from Langston Hughes to Queen Latifah. It's Giovanni's answer to *Poetry Speaks to Children*, to which she was a contributor. (I: All ages)

*Hoberman, Mary Ann. *Forget-Me-Nots: Poems to Learn by Heart*. Illustrated by Michael Emberley. Little, Brown, 2012. Here are 123 memorable poems from recent years and older generations, intended for children of all ages to memorize. Learning poems is a nearly forgotten way to furnish the memory with apt images and skillfully used language. (I: 6–12)

Paschen, Elise, and Dominique Raccah. *Poetry Speaks to Children: A Celebration of Poetry With a Beat*. Illustrated by Wendy Rasmussen, Judy Love, and Paula Wendgrand. Sourcebooks Media Fusion, 2005. With an accompanying CD, this collection features a cross-cultural range of poets living and dead, from James Berry with his Caribbean poem, to Nikki Giovanni, to J.R.R. Tolkien. (I: All ages)

Novels in Verse

Creech, Sharon. *Love That Dog*. Joanna Cotler, 2001. A boy finds his voice through poetry in this spare rhymed novel, expresses grief over his dog, and utter delight when the writer Walter Dean Myers visits his school. (I: 9–12)

Grimes, Nikki. *Bronx Masquerade*. The lives of 18 urban teenagers are portrayed through verse and essay. (I: 12–YA)

*_____. *Jazmin's Notebook*. Dial, 1998. Fourteen-year-old Jazmin, a resident of Harlem in the 1960s, puts down sketches of the people and events in her neighborhood in verse and musings. A Coretta Scott King Honor Book. (I: 1–14)

Hesse, Karen. *Aleutian Sparrow*. Margaret McElderry, 2003. During World War II, the inhabitants of the Aleutian Islands of Alaska were evacuated by the U.S. government "in order to save them." This novel in verse chronicles their dislocation. (I: 9–12)

_____. *Out of the Dust*. Scholastic, 1997. In this novel in verse set in the Dust Bowl of the 1930s, Billy Jo, a fourteen-year-old piano player, endures grief and guilt over the loss of her mother. Winner of the 1998 Newbery Medal. (I: 9–12)

Roy, Jennifer. *Yellow Star*. Marshall Cavendish, 2010. The story, told in blank verse, of one of the very few child survivors of the ghetto at Lodz, Poland, during the Holocaust. (I: 10–adult)

Smith, Hope Anita. *The Way a Door Closes*. Illustrated by Shane W. Evans. Henry Holt, 2003. This novel, a collection of 34 poems told from the perspective of a thirteen-year-old boy, chronicles the joys and struggle of an African American family. (I: 10 and up)

Williams, Vera. *Amber Was Brave, Essie Was Smart*. Greenwillow, 2001. The lives of two latchkey children are chronicled in this novel in verse. (I: 9–12)

Woodson, Jacqueline. *Locomotion*. Putnam, 2003. A fifth grader in a New York City school is helped by his teacher to write poetry in order to come to grips with his grief over his parents' death in a fire. (I: 9–13)

Books About Poets and Poetry

Janeczko, Paul. *A Kick in the Head: An Everyday Guide to Poetic Forms*. Illustrated by Chris Raschka. Candlewick, 2005. This guide to poetic forms, which features 29 forms, includes familiar forms such as the couplet and limerick, as well as less familiar forms such as the tercet and triolet. For each form, Janeczko includes an example of the form, an illustration (often humorous), and a footnote that offers a definition. (I: 10 and up)

_____. *The Place My Words Are Looking For: What Poets Say about and through Their Work*. Bradbury, 1990. Poems by Cynthia Rylant, Gary Soto, Gwendolyn Brooks, Myra Cohn Livingston, Naomi Shihab Nye, and others, with comments by the poets. (I: 12–YA).

_____. *Poetry from A to Z: A Guide for Young Writers*. Bradbury, 1994. Poems by Naomi Shihab Nye, Lilian Moore, Patricia Hubbell, and Myra Cohn Livingston are given, along with comments by the poets and suggestions for writing poems. (I: 11–YA)

*Kerley, Beverly. *Walt Whitman: Words for America*. Illustrated by Brian Selznick. Scholastic, 2004. The amazing life of Walt Whitman, the exuberant poet of the mid-nineteenth century, is sketched along with snatches of his poetry. (I: 10–13)

Poems by Children

*The Children of Terezin Concentration Camp. *I Never Saw Another Butterfly*,(2nd ed.). Schocken, 1993. 15,000 Jewish children passed through the Nazi concentration camp of Terezin, outside of Prague. With the help of a remarkable teacher, children learned to express themselves through art and poetry, and some of their works are reproduced here. For most of the children, these poems were all that survived. (I: 9–YA)

Lyne, Sanford. *Ten Second Rainshowers: Poems by Young People*. Illustrated by Virginia Halstead. Simon & Schuster, 1996. Lyne has worked for many years as a poet in the schools, and here he collects poems from 130 young poets aged 8 to 18. Full-color illustrations set off each section. (I: 6–11)

Nye, Naomi Shihab, ed. *Salting the Ocean: 100 Poems by Young Poets*. Illustrated by Ashley Bryan. Greenwillow, 2000. Nye presents poems collected from her extensive work as a poet in the schools. The poems are lively celebrations of insight into sound, and hearing them is an invitation to other young people to take leaps with language. (I: 6–10)

International, Multicultural, and Bilingual Poems

*Alarcón, Francisco X. *Poems to Dream Together: Poemas Para Soñar Juntos*. Illustrated by Paula Barragán. Lee & Low, 2005. This is a wide-ranging, thought-provoking collection of bilingual poems that explores the everyday world of family and community as well as broader social issues. (I: 8–12)

*_____. *Laughing Tomatoes: And Other Spring Poems/Jitomates Risuenos: Y Otros Poemas de Primavera*. Illustrated by Maya Cristina Gonzales. Children's Book Press, 2005. Alarcón has written bilingual collections of poems for each of the seasons, drawing on experiences in California and Mexico. These are poems of summer. (I: 5–8)

*_____. *Angels Ride Bikes: And Other Fall Poems/Los Angeles Andan en Bicicleta: Y Otros Poems del Otoño*. Illustrated by Maya Christina Gonzales. Lee and Low, 2005. Poems about fall in California, from Alarcón and Maya's series of bilingual poems on the seasons. (I: 6–10).

*_____. *Iguanas in the Snow: And Other Winter Poems/Iguanas en el Nieve: Y Otros Poems del Invierno*. Illustrated by Maya Christina Gonzales. Lee and Low, 2005. Winter poems from Alarcón and Maya's series of bilingual poems on the seasons. Childhood in Mexico is remembered from life in California.

Delacre, Lulu. *Arroz con leche: Popular Songs and Rhythms from Latin America*. Scholastic, 1989. Twelve poems from Puerto Rico, Mexico, and Argentina are first presented as verses in English and Spanish; then as musical scores, with simple guitar arrangements.

*Jaramillo, Nelly Palacio, ed. *Grandmother's Nursery Rhymes/Las Nanas de Abuelita: Lullabies, Tongue Twisters, and Riddles from South America*. Illustrated by Elivia Savadier. Holt, 1996. A bilingual book of poems from Latin America with lively illustrations. (I: 4–8)

Nye, Naomi Shihab, ed. *This Same Sky: A Collection of Poems from around the World*. Macmillan, 1992. English translations of more than one hundred poems from all of the continents except North America. (I: 8–YA)

_____, ed. *The Tree Is Older than You Are: Bilingual Poems from Mexico*. Simon & Schuster, 1995. A wonderfully illustrated collection of poems from Mexico, in Spanish with side-by-side translation. (I: 8–YA)

Soto, Gary. *A Fire in My Hands*. Harcourt, 2006. In this revised and expanded edition of his 1999 volume of poetry, Soto brings to life everyday experiences of Mexican American youth. (I: 12 and up)

Tadjo, Véronique, ed. *Talking Drums: A Selection of Poems from Africa South of the Sahara*. Bloomsbury, 2004. The poems in this multinational anthology range from praise songs to children's games to love poems to laments. They reflect the complexities of a complex land. (I: 8 and up)

REFERENCES

Blake, William. *Songs of Innocence and Songs of Experience.* Dover, 1789/1992.

Browning, Robert. *The Pied Piper of Hamelin.* Routledge, 1888.

Butler, Francelia. *Skipping around the World: The Ritual Nature of Folk Rhymes.* Ballantine, 1989.

Carroll, Lewis. *Alice's Adventures in Wonderland.* Illustrated by Sir John Tenniel. Dover, 1865/1993.

Ciardi, John. *The Monster Den; or, Look What Happened at My House—and to It.* Illustrated by Edward Gorey. Lippincott, 1966.

———. *The Reason for the Pelican.* Illustrated by Dominic Catalano. Wordsong/Boyds Mills, 1994.

Creech, Sharon. *Walk Two Moons.* Harper Collins, 1995.

de la Mare, Walter. *Peacock Pie.* Holt, 1923.

Dillon, Leo. *Rap a Tap Tap: Here's Bojangles—Think of That!* Illustrated by Diane Dillon. Blue Sky Press, 1995.

Esbensen, Barbara Juster. *Who Shrank My Grandmother's House?: Poems of Discovery.* Illustrated by Eric Beddows. HarperCollins, 1992.

Grimes, Nikki. *Hopscotch Love: A Family Treasury of Love Songs.* Illustrated by Melodye Benson Rosales. Scholastic, 2000.

———. *What Is Goodbye?* Illustrated by Raúl Colón. Disney-Hyperion, 2004.

Guthrie, Woody. (1944). This land is your land. Song lyrics recorded in 1944, and republished in Elizabeth Partridge, *This Land Was Made for You and Me: The Life & Songs of Woody Guthrie* (New York: Viking, 2002), p. 85.

———, and Kathy Jakobsen. *This land is your land, 10th Anniversary Edition.* Little, Brown, 2008.

Hall, Donald, ed. *The Oxford Book of Children's Verse in America.* Oxford Univ. Press, 1985.

Heaney, Seamus, and Ted Hughes. *The Rattle Bag.* Faber and Faber, 2005.

Hesse, Karen. *The Cats in Krasinski Square.* Wendy Watson, illustrator. Scholastic, 2004.

Janeczko, Paul. *This Delicious Day.* Orchard, 1987.

Karas, G. Brian. *On Earth.* Puffin, 2008.

Kipling, Rudyard. *Puck of Pook's Hill.* Doubleday, 1906.

Lyon, George Ella. *All the Water in the World.* Illustrated by Katherine Tillotson. Atheneum/Richard Jackson Books, 2011.

Mason, Walt. "Football." *The Random House Book of Poetry for Children.* Ed. Jack Prelutsky. Illustrated by Arnold Lobel. Random House, 1983.

McCord, David. *All Small: Poems by David McCord.* Illustrated by Madelaine Gill Linden. Little, Brown, 1986.

———. *One at a Time.* Illustrated by Henry Bugbee Kane. Little, Brown, 1986.

Moore, Clement Clarke. "A Visit from St. Nicholas, or 'Twas the Night before Christmas." *The Oxford Book of Children's Verse in America.* Ed. Donald Hall. Oxford Univ. Press, 1985.

Myers, Walter Dean. *Harlem.* Illustrated by Christopher Myers. Scholastic, 1997.

Nye, Naomi Shihab. *Words under the Words.* Eighth Mountain Press, 1994.

Opie, Peter, and Iona Opie. *The Lore and Language of Schoolchildren.* New York Review of Books, 2001.

Ray, Mary Lynn. *Stars.* Illustrated by Marla Frazee. Beach Lane Books, 2011.

Rosetti, Christina. *The Complete Poems of Christina Rossetti.* Digireads, 2011.

Sandburg, Carl. *The Complete Poems of Carl Sandburg.* Harcourt Brace Jovanovich, 1970.

Stevens, Wallace. *The Collected Poems of Wallace Stevens.* Vintage, 1990.

Stockdale, Susan. *Bring on the Birds.* Peachtree, 2011.

Swados, Elizabeth. *Hey, You! C'Mere! A Poetry Slam.* Levine, 2002.

Tennyson, Alfred. "The Eagle." 1851. *Poems of Tennyson: 1830–1870.* Ed. T. Herbert Warren. Oxford University Press, 1912.

Terry, Ann. *Children's Poetry Preferences: A National Survey of the Upper Elementary Grades.* National Council of Teachers of English, 1974.

Updike, John. *A Child's Calendar.* Illustrated by Trina Schart Hyman. Holiday House, 2002.

White, E. B. *Charlotte's Web.* Harper Trophy, 1952.

Worth, Valerie. *All the Small Poems.* Illustrated by Natalie Babbitt. Sunburst, 1987.

———. *Small Poems Again.* Illustrated by Natalie Babbitt. Farrar, Straus, & Giroux, 1985.

Traditional Literature

What Is Traditional Literature?

West African storytellers wear ornaments on their hats; an audience member chooses an ornament, and the teller shares the corresponding story. Native American storytellers from the Seneca tribe reach into a story bag, pull out an object, and tell the story it symbolizes. Storytellers in traditional Scottish island communities specialized: you went to this teller's house to hear a tale about your people's history, to that house to hear a religious tale, and to that other house to hear a purely fanciful tale. In North America, the National Storytelling Network <www .storynet.org> unites professional storytellers that also specialize: one group tells stories to connect with children and young people; another group tells stories for the purpose of healing; and another group tells stories for business management and policy development. What all of these storytellers have in common is that they work with material and in traditions that have been handed down through tens and hundreds of generations, whose authors are nameless, and whose ownership is shared by all of us.

Traditional literature is the body of stories and poems that have come to us from teller to hearer, and from hearer to teller, and whose authors are unknown. Traditional stories, rhymes, riddles, and games are so appealing and so memorable that they have been passed from generation to generation without the aid of writing.

Folk traditions are both unique and universal. We can readily identify British folktales, with their sensible talking animals and their giants; and we can distinguish them from Norwegian tales, with their trolls and hags; or Russian tales, with their witch Baba Yaga, who lives in a hut that stands on chicken feet; or Chinese tales, with their superhero Monkey King. But tales from different cultures also share similarities—sometimes strong resemblances. Thus, getting to know traditional literature is a way of getting to know other cultures, but at the same time it is a way of approaching themes that matter to people everywhere.

ILLUSTRATION 7.1   *The House That Jack Built* was the first work published by Randolph Caldecott, who is considered the father of picture books. ("This is The House That Jack Built" illustrated by Simms Taback. Used by permission of Penguin Group (USA), Inc. All rights reserved.)

The Value of Traditional Literature

Traditional stories, poems, and songs are engaging because their strong plots, contrasts of good and evil, and repeated lines invite participation. They form a rich source of multicultural and international literature, since from many areas, traditional tales are most of what is available to young American readers. Folktales have both spare details and possible symbols, and they invite the readers' own associations. They may provide safe ways to talk about emotionally frightening issues. For example, a child who feels powerless may find solace in "Jack and the Beanstalk" and "Molly Whuppie." A child who feels hemmed in by more successful siblings may bask in the success of "Cinderella." They acquaint readers with plots that will be used over and over in other works of literature. Folktales are also part of the public domain, and have appeared over and over again in versions by many retellers and illustrators. For example, the first published work of Randolph Caldecott, considered the father of picture books, was the folktale, *The House That Jack Built*.

The Evolution of Traditional Literature

In Europe and America and later in many parts of the world, traditional stories, poems, and songs were ways of passing cultural knowledge from one generation to another from prehistoric times until the mid-1700s.

In ancient times, Greek and Roman myths supplied human faces to forces of nature and human passions—from storms at sea to sexual attraction to warfare to the arts to drunkenness. Scandinavian myths did much the same (and provided English names for Tuesday through Friday). In the Middle Ages, folktales competed with biblical teachings, alleviated the suffering of poor people, made fun of powerful people, and shared the values of the common folk.

Folktales were not meant exclusively for children. Before the mid-nineteenth century, when widespread schooling separated adults' worlds from children's worlds, stories were told to mixed age groups. One account of a storytelling event from the Scottish Hebrides, some time in the late 1800s, shows how this often worked:

> The house is roomy and clean, if homely, with its bright peat fire in the middle of the floor. There are many present—men and women, boys and girls. All the women are seated, and most of the men. Girls are crouched between the knees of fathers or brothers or friends, while boys are perched wherever—boy-like—they can climb . . . The houseman is twisting twigs of heather into ropes to hold down thatch, a neighbor crofter is twining quicken roots into chords to tie cows, while another is plating bent grass into baskets to hold meal. The housewife is spinning, a daughter is carding, another daughter is teasing, while a third daughter, supposed to be working, is away in the background conversing in low whispers with the son of a neighboring crofter. Neighbor wives or neighbor daughters are knitting, sewing, or embroidering. The conversation is general . . . [The houseman is asked to tell a story, and after a while he complies.]
>
> The tale is full of incident, action, and pathos. It is told simply yet graphically, and at times dramatically—compelling the undivided attention of the listener. At the pathetic scenes and distressful events the bosoms of the women may be seen to heave and their silent tears to fall. Truth overcomes craft, skill conquers strength, and bravery is rewarded . . . When the story is ended it is discussed and commented upon, and the different characters praised or blamed according to their merits and the views of the critics.
>
> —From Alexander Carmichael, quoted in Briggs, 1970, p. 10

How could the same story appeal to so many different age groups? Partly by being sparing in the details. As D. L. Ashliman (2004) points out, by leaving description to a minimum, storytellers left their audience members free to construct their own images and interpretations of parts of the story. However, spare suggestions also carry innuendos that are understood by some in the audience but not others. For example, in the version of "Rapunzel" from the first edition of the Grimms' tales, after several visits from her lover, the girl in the tower complains to her witch stepmother that her clothes no longer fit her. In a rage, the witch cuts off Rapunzel's hair. Only the mature listeners will know why Rapunzel's clothes didn't fit and also that cutting off a young woman's hair is the traditional punishment for forbidden intimacy.

Stories can work on several levels, too, by using symbols. Many adult listeners are pleased to recognize that the dove leading Hansel and Gretel through the woods represents a benevolent spirit, and that the swan's carrying first Gretel, then Hansel, across a river on their way home symbolizes a transition from one stage of life to another. Young listeners miss those connections, but they enjoy the story anyway.

By the mid-1700s, the spread of public schooling, literacy, and scholarly knowledge were pushing folk beliefs to the periphery. And by the 1820s, folktales were being collected by professional scholars of folklore, much like old farm implements that are gathered up and placed in museums—except, as we shall see, folktale collections became enormously popular among the literate public, and with children in particular.

One reason folktales were originally collected was to save remnants of folk cultures that were succumbing to the spread of education and regimentation of factory life. Another reason was the rise of nationalism. The 1800s were a time when nationalist moods were growing stronger and stronger in people's hearts. Germany was fragmented into dozens of principalities, and there, the Brothers Grimm, who were serious linguists and patriotic lawyers, asserted German-ness by collecting folk stories from storytellers. Collectors in other European countries were soon inspired by the Grimms to make their own national folktale collections, often inspired by the same nationalistic political motives as the Grimms'.

Categories of Traditional Literature

The categories of traditional literature are not simple to map out.

A rough distinction can be made between *literary tales*, stories that were written by known authors who used traditional patterns, and *traditional tales*, those created by unknown authors that were kept alive through the oral tradition until they were written down. That's a blurry line, though, since many collectors of folktales did considerable rewriting of their source material.

Another distinction can be made between *folktales*, traditional tales without pronounced magical elements, and *fairy tales*, which do not necessarily feature fairies, but do have magical elements and were never believed to be true (Ashliman, 2004). That distinction is blurred, too, though, by the many stories with magical elements that *were* believed by some groups—such as the selchie stories about "seal people" from Scotland and the Scottish islands (see page 177).

Other categories of traditional literature include *cumulative tales, animal tales, trickster tales, humorous tales, tall tales, ghost stories, legends, epics and ballads, fables, myths, pourquoi tales,* and *religious stories*. Please see Table 7.1 for definitions of some kinds of traditional tales of stories.

for ENGLISH LANGUAGE LEARNERS

- In many parts of the world, folktales are the only form of literature we have that speak of life in those places. Choose folktales that come from the countries of origin of your English language learners. Invite those students, or members of their families or their friends, to tell other stories of their culture, too.

- Search folktales from other cultures for details about people's ways of life that are taken for granted by that culture. Use the tale to surface those traditions. For example, in many West African stories, instead of competition between a girl and her stepmother and stepsisters (such as "Cinderella" and its variants), there is more likely to be competition between the younger wife and older wives of the same husband, as in the Nigerian tale, "The Lost Heir" (in Jane Yolen's *Favorite Folktales from Around the World*). In many Western folktales, old women are portrayed as witches, but in many more societies, older women are revered for their wisdom.

- Use folktales as opportunities to research social traditions from around the world. Invite English language learners or members of their families to talk about traditions from different cultures. Give English language learners the opportunity to be experts on their cultures, or interpreters for other guests who come to speak about those cultures.

- When the class is reading folktales that seem to have a message or teach a moral, invite English language learners to tell those stories to their parents and grandparents. See if their relatives can think of stories that make the same points, or of stories that have different messages to share on the same themes. Talk about the cultural values— same and different—that the different stories bring to light.

TABLE 7.1 *Subgenres of Folktales*

SUBGENRE	DEFINITION	EXAMPLES
Folktales	Folktales often involve simple folk who get the better of people who are richer or more powerful. All but the last of the following are subtypes of folktales.	
Cumulative Tales	These tales are created by repeating phrases or events and adding to them.	"The House That Jack Built," "There Was an Old Lady Who Swallowed a Fly," "The Old Woman and Her Pig," *The Bossy Gallito, Toad Is the Uncle of Heaven*
Animal Tales	In these tales, animals talk and have human characteristics.	"Goldilocks and the Three Bears," "The Fox and the Grapes," "The Lion and the Mouse"
Trickster Tales	These tales feature characters who try to trick others, and sometimes bring calamity on themselves. The characters are often human-like animals.	"Ananse the Spider," "Why the Leopard Has Spots," "Brer Rabbit and Brer Fox," "The Tale of Rabbit and Coyote"
Numbskull Tales	These tales feature one or more prodigiously stupid or silly characters, who often win the day anyway.	"Juan Bobo," "Jack and the Three Sillies," "Hans Clodhopper"
Tall Tales	These tales are greatly exaggerated accounts of the exploits of local heroes—often members of a work group such as cowboys, sailors, or lumberjacks.	"Paul Bunyan and Babe, the Blue Ox" (about a lumberjack), "Pecos Bill" (about a cowboy), and "Stormalong" (about a sailor)
Ghost Stories	These are spooky tales, usually about the supernatural and often about the undead.	"The Tailypo," "Wiley and the Hairy Man"
Fairy Tales	Fairy tales are folk stories that involve the intervention of magic (a "faerie" element) in the plot.	"Cinderella," "The Sleeping Beauty in the Woods," "Snow White and the Seven Dwarves," "The Frog Prince," "Vasilisa the Beautiful," "The Talking Eggs"
Realistic Tales	These are folk stories with colorful events that *could have* happened.	"The Parson and the Sexton," "Old Dry Fry," "Half a Blanket"
Legends	These are stories from the oral tradition, often about national heroes and other great people; the stories are believed to have some basis in history.	"King Arthur and the Knights of the Round Table," "Robin Hood," "El Cid," "Johnny Appleseed"
Religious Stories	Religious stories overlap *legends* as a category of folktales. They are tales of saints and other holy figures, sometimes adapted from sacred texts. They may be told to promote or reinforce religious beliefs. They may be moral tales, and sometimes they are just good stories.	Children's book versions are *The Story of Jesus*, by Brian Wildsmith; *Mohammed, The Legend of the Lao Tzu and the Tao Te Ching*, all by Demi
Ballads	These are long narratives in verse, and sometimes are sung.	"Ballad of Robin Hood," "The Streets of Laredo," "The Ballad of Jesse James"
Epics	These long narrative poems are about heroes whose exploits are important to a nation, told in an elevated style.	"Beowulf," "The Odyssey"
Fables	These brief dramatic tales, often with animal characters, illustrate clear lessons.	"The Fox and the Grapes," "The Hare and the Tortoise," "The Town Mouse and the Country Mouse"
Myths	These stories from the oral tradition seek to explain how the physical and social world came to be.	"Prometheus," "Orpheus and Eurydice," "Jason and the Golden Fleece," "The World on the Turtle's Back"
Pourquoi Stories	This is a subgroup of myths with a more limited scope, explaining how day-to-day phenomena came to be.	Children's book versions are *The Orphan Boy*, by Tololwa Mollel; *Medio Pollito/Half-Chicken* by Alma Flor Ada; *Why Mosquitoes Buzz in People's Ears*, by Verna Aardema
Literary Tales	These stories by known authors are told in the form and manner of traditional tales, although they may be written with more elaborate descriptions than traditional tales.	"Belle et la Bête," ("Beauty and the Beast," by Jeanne-Marie Le Prince de Beaumont); "The Little Mermaid" (by Hans Christian Andersen), "The Happy Man's Shirt" (from Leo Tolstoy's *Fables*)
Urban Legends	These are contemporary stories, usually passed on by word of mouth, that are sometimes believed to be true.	"The Choking Doberman," "The Hook on the Door Handle," "The Microwaved Chihuahua," "The Vanishing Hitchhiker"

TECHNOLOGY in PRACTICE 7.1

RESOURCES ON THE WEB

There are several excellent Web sites devoted to folktales and folklore. Kay E. Vandergrift maintains a site useful for its access to variations of common tales on her page at at <http://www.scils.rutgers.edu>

The de Grummond Children's Literature Collection of the University of Southern Mississippi has a site at <http://www.lib.usm.edu/legacy/degrum/> that includes biographies of children's authors. There are three domains devoted to collections of scores of versions of "Jack and the Beanstalk," "Cinderella," and "Little Red Riding Hood." Many of the texts and illustrations can be viewed online.

Heidi Anne Heiner's *Sur la Lune* has annotated fairy tales—49 of them as of this writing—and there are links to the versions of the tales that are still in print and available from Amazon.com. The address of her site is <http://www.surlalunefairytales.com>.

Folk Literature from Many Cultures

Folktales can be identified with the countries in which they have been frequently told. Bear in mind, though, that naming any one country as the source of a story may be misleading, because variations of the same stories turn up in many places. "Cinderella," for instance, has more than 700 versions, found in China, Korea, many parts of Europe, and even among the Algonquin tribe in the United States. We consider the source of "Cinderella" to be France, because the French version published by Charles Perrault in 1697 is the one that is most popular with American readers.

Folktales from Italy

Early versions of "Little Red Riding Hood," "Rapunzel," "Sleeping Beauty," "Hansel and Gretel," and "Puss in Boots" were told in Italy, and were collected from the oral tradition and published in the 1500s and 1600s. Europe's first folktale collection was published in Italy by **Giovanni Francisco Straporola** (c. 1480–c. 1557). He was followed by **Giambattista Basile** (c. 1575–1632). Both writers provided the earliest written versions of "Rapunzel" and "Little Red Riding Hood." Their collections had rough and ribald elements, though. For example, in the versions of "La Finta Nonna," "The False Grandmother," the wolf—or the *bzou*, (werewolf)—kills the grandmother and tricks the little girl into eating her flesh. The version of that story that was to become popular with children was "Little Red Riding Hood," scrubbed up and retold by authors from France, Germany, and England.

In 1992, the distinguished Italian literary scholar **Italo Calvino** published a collection of 200 Italian folktales aptly named *Italian Folktales*. Calvino meant for his collection to do for Italian tales what the Grimms had done for German tales, Joseph Jacobs for English tales, and Yeats for Irish tales—except he undertook his project between a century and a century and a half after most of them.

Folktales from France

The versions of "Cinderella," "The Sleeping Beauty in the Woods," "Little Red Riding Hood," "Puss in Boots" and "Bluebeard" that are most popular with American children came from France, thanks to Charles Perrault.

Charles Perrault (1628–1703), the most famous purveyor of French traditional tales, published *Histoires ou Contes du Temps Passé, Avec des Moralités: Contes de Ma Mère l'Oye (Stories or Tales of Times Past, With Morals: Tales of My Mother Goose)*, which gave us popular versions of "Cinderella," "The Sleeping Beauty in the Woods," "Little Red Riding Hood," "Puss in Boots," and "Bluebeard." Perrault served in the court of Louis XIV, "the Sun King," so he observed firsthand the sumptuous balls that are described in his stories.

In 1989, **Jack Zipes** published the largest available collection of French fairy tales in his own translations, *Beauties, Beasts, And Enchantment: Classic French Fairy Tales*.

Folktales from Germany

From Germany come the best-known versions of "Hansel and Gretel," "Snow White," "Little Red Riding Hood," "Rumpelstiltskin," and "The Frog Prince." In German tales, children and young people are often threatened by deadly forces, but through courage and perseverance—and often the intervention of magic—they are richly rewarded. One famous German tale, "The Pied Piper of Hamelin," is based on an actual event. Historical records of Hameln, Germany, state that in the year 1284 a strangely dressed piper led all the children out of the town, and they were never seen again.

The major collectors of German folktales were two linguists and jurists, **Jacob Grimm** (1785–1863) and his brother **Wilhelm Grimm** (1786–1859). They were motivated by a desire to rekindle a spirit of German nationalism, in response to both Napoleon's invasion of Germany in 1812 and the fragmentation of the German nation into a dozen principalities in the early nineteenth century. The Grimms' efforts started a wave of folktale collecting in many other countries of Europe. They published *Kinder und Hausmärchen (Nursery and Household Tales)* in 1812, and followed it with six more editions through 1857—with each edition getting more reworked to fit middle class sentiments and children's sensibilities. The best known German folktales are "Hansel and Gretel," "Snow White and the Seven Dwarfs," "The Frog Prince," and "Iron John." All were published in the *Grimms' Fairy Tales*, as the books are known in English. The Grimms also published versions of tales that were told in other countries, such as "Rapunzel" from Italy, "Cinderella," from France and elsewhere, and "Little Red Cap," which was known in Italy and France as "Little Red Riding Hood."

Folktales from Wales, Ireland, Scotland, and England

England got its name from the Angles, who along with Saxons, Danes, and Jutes came over from the continent in the fifth century. They pushed the native Celtic peoples, who included the Britons, from whom the name Great Britain derives, to the north and west, to what are now Wales, Ireland, and Scotland. In all three places, varieties of Celtic language are still spoken, and, indeed, the local languages are today being revived and taught in schools.

TEACHING IDEA 7.1

TALES OF TRANSFORMATION

> COMMON CORE STANDARD:
> *Integration of Knowledge and Ideas, STANDARD 9*

For children in grade three and up, read them either "The Selchie" from Jane Yolen's *Favorite Folktales From Around the World*, or any of Duncan Williamson's stories from *Tales of the Seal People*. Later, have them read either Molly Bang's *Dawn* or *The Crane Wife*, retold by Odds Bodkin. Discuss each story, and enter the students' responses to the questions on a chart like the one below.

	Who changed?	What made the person change?	What made the person change back?	How do we feel about what happened?
Selchie Story				
The Crane Wife				

The Welsh, people descended from Celts living in the southwestern part of the British mainland, had a rich tradition of folklore. History and mythology were long blended together in Wales, since the history was passed on orally from one Druid to another (Druids were Celtic priests). The stories they passed on were long and complex, and learning them took a Druid fifteen years. The Welsh oral traditions gave us the first tales of Arthur, king of the Britons—although Arthur's existence cannot be firmly established. Many Welsh tales were collected in the *Mabinogion*, which has inspired the imaginations of other storytellers such as Lloyd Alexander, but has rarely been reproduced in children's books read in North America.

The Celtic Britons settled Ireland, too. St. Patrick, the Patron Saint of Ireland, was a Briton who was taken to Ireland as a slave in his youth, escaped back to England, and later returned to Ireland as its first Christian bishop. Irish tales have leprechauns—the "good people" who hide just out of sight of humans, but will have to reward you with gold if you catch one; and also "changelings"—the good people's ageless babies they sometimes secretly exchange for your human ones. (If your baby eats voraciously and has a *really* cranky temperament, chances are he's a changeling—or so goes the folk belief.) Irish storytelling is still a thriving tradition, so there are many sources for collectors. The earliest collection, in 1824, was by **Crofton Croker** who got his tales from original sources around Ireland. Shortly after came collections from **Samuel Lover** and **William Carleton**, and toward the end of the nineteenth century, **Lady Augusta Gregory**. In 1888, the great Irish poet **William Butler Yeats** (1865–1939) published *Fairy and Folk Tales of the Irish Peasantry*, a collection of 90 tales, mostly from other sources, including those just mentioned.

The Australian/English collector **Joseph Jacobs** (1854–1916) published *Celtic Fairy Tales* in 1892. Those two dozen tales contain many from Ireland, but also Scottish and Welsh tales, with some details traded among them.

Scotland has its share of magical folk beliefs. The *brownie* was one—a helpful fairy who lived out of sight of humans, but helped with the chores around a farmhouse. (Scottish farm families traditionally left an empty chair near the fire for the brownie.) The brownies gave their name to the Brownie Scouts. Scottish folk who lived near the shore had their *selchies* or *silkies,* creatures that are sometimes seals and sometimes humans.

Sir George Douglas (1856–1935) published a rich collection called *Scottish Fairy and Folk Tales* in 1901. **Ruth Manning-Sanders** (1886–1988) published eighteen *Scottish Folktales* in 1976. She published 90 folktale collections in all. **Duncan Williamson** (1928–2007), a tinker (a Scottish itinerant worker), published a collection of stories in 1998 about selchies, called *Tales of the Seal People.*

English folktales are often about simple folk who triumph through pluck (like "Jack and the Beanstalk" and "Kate Crackernuts") and luck (like "The Pedlar of Swaffham"). There are tales of foolishness ("Henny Penny," "The Three Sillies") and practicality ("The Little Red Hen," "The Three Little Pigs"). Many of the tales have animal characters. Some (like "Kate Crackernuts" and "Molly Whuppie") have strong female protagonists.

In England, folktales have found some of their best expression through the works of poets, such as Robert Browning's long poem "The Pied Piper of Hamelin" (a German tale) and Robert Southey's prose tale "The Three Bears." The latter originally had a disagreeable old woman invading the bears' cottage and sampling their bowls of porridge, chairs, and beds. The little girl Goldilocks with her bright curls replaced the old woman in the story in 1849, in a version by Joseph Cundall.

Joseph Jacobs (see above) was the first notable collector of English folktales. He wanted to put good English tales up against the tales from the Continent (primarily Charles Perrault's and the Grimms' collections) that were flooding the English market. He published several editions of *English Fairy Tales* from 1890 through 1912. **Andrew Lang** (1844–1912) published a series of twelve fairy tale collections, from *The Blue Fairy Book* in 1899 through *The Lilac Fairy Book* in 1910. These books drew on sources from all over the world, not only England. They were enormously popular in England and North America, and many are still in print.

Folktales from Russia

Russian tales feature Baba Yaga (pronounced "ya-GAH"), the amazing witch who lives in a hut on chicken feet and flies in a mortar while steering with a pestle; and also adventures that take their heroes to "the thrice-ninth kingdom beyond the thrice-ninth land." The most famous stories, at least to Western audiences, are "Vasilisa the Beautiful," "Baba Yaga," "Ivan, the Grey Wolf, and the Firebird," and "Sister Alionushka and Brother Ivanushka."

Alexandr Afanas'ev (1826–1871) published a massive collection of *Russian Fairy Tales* in eight volumes between 1855 and 1863. His motives were similar to the Grimms', but with a twist: The Russian upper classes placed more value in things European, including the French language, than they did their own culture. Afanas'ev sought to encourage interest in the folk culture of Russia as well as the Russian language. Trained as a lawyer but working as a journalist, Afanas'ev produced the most extensive collection of folktales from a single country, yet his radical political affiliations kept him in trouble with Russian authorities. After selling all his books to buy food, he died of tuberculosis at the age of 46.

ILLUSTRATION 7.2   In *The Tale of the Firebird*, Gennady Spirin uses a rich palette to bring this Russian hero tale to life. ("The Tale of the Firebird" retold and illustrated by Gennady Spirin. Used by permission of Penguin Group (USA), Inc. All rights reserved.)

Folktales from Norway

"The Three Billy Goats Gruff" and "East of the Sun, West of the Moon" come to us from Norway, along with many other colorful stories about hags, trolls, and clever married partners. Dominated by neighboring Denmark, Norway was struggling for its identity, and Norwegian was not yet recognized as a separate language. Then Peter Asbjornsen (1812–1885), a high school teacher, and Jørgen Moe (1813–1882), a priest, hiked around their country collecting tales from rural folk, which made Norwegians proud of their culture and helped establish their own language. Asbjornsen and Moe's tales were published in 1845 and 1848. These included "East of the Sun, West of the Moon," "The Man Who Kept House," and "The Three Billy Goats Gruff." They were soon translated into English by George Dasent, and quickly became popular in England and America.

Folktales from the United States

Most of the folktales that are popular in the United States came over from Europe, mainly from the sources already mentioned. Among the truly American tales are African American stories, tales from Native American peoples, tall tales, and cowboy stories.

African American tales were recorded by a white newspaperman from Georgia named **Joel Chandler Harris** (1845–1908). His collection, called *Tales of Uncle Remus*, included stories that Harris remembered hearing slaves tell when he was a child. This collection gave us the characters of Brer Rabbit, Brer Bear, and the Tar Baby.

Harris tried to capture the slaves' manner of speech with unique spellings:

> "'Mawnin'!' sez Brer Rabbit, sezee—'nice wedder dis mawnin',' sezee.
> "Tar-Baby ain't sayin' nuthin', en Brer Fox he lay low.
> "'How duz yo' sym'tums seem ter segashuate?' sez Brer Rabbit, sezee.
> "Brer Fox, he wink his eye slow, en lay low, en de Tar-Baby, she ain't sayin' nuthin'.
> (Harris, 1880/2012)

Versions of these stories that are more pleasing to the contemporary ear have been retold by **Julius Lester.**

Ask *the* Reteller . . . Joseph Bruchac

You are a scholar of comparative literature as well as an accomplished collector and reteller of traditional Native American tales. When we read your "The Boy Who Lived with the Bears," we are struck by the parallel to the European tale "Hansel and Gretel." Are you struck by the similarities of some of their tales to tales told among other cultures far removed from them?

As a storyteller and student of comparative mythology, I am struck by the parallels that are often found in stories from very different cultures and different continents. That may be because there are so many things that all humans have in common—family, the importance of caring for our children, and so on.

In this case, however, I think there are more differences than similarities. Unlike Hansel and Gretel, the boy who is abandoned in the Iroquois tale is not threatened by some exterior malevolent force, but endangered by the bad action of his own uncle. The natural world, in the form of a Mother Bear, rescues the boy and also provides a lesson for the Uncle (who is reformed at the tale's end)

in the proper way that adults and relatives should care for children. Further, it establishes and deepens the familial connection between animals and humans—not as separate, with humans dominating the natural world, but as co-equal beings. In fact, the animals serve as teachers to the humans. This exemplifies the Iroquois worldview of humans being part of the natural world, of animals being not mindless creatures, but "animal people."

Joseph Bruchac is a writer and storyteller whose work often reflects his Abenaki Indian ancestry. He and his wife Carol live in the same house he was raised in by his grandparents in the Adirondack Mountains foothills town of Greenfield Center, New York. His books and those co-authored with his older son Jim (who, like his dad, is a martial arts teacher) have won many awards.

Native American stories were collected and recorded in the nineteenth and early twentieth centuries by missionaries, and also by the early anthropologists Franz Boas, Edward Sapir, and others. Prominent among contemporary retellers of Native American stories are **Joseph Bruchac, Gayle Ross,** and **Paul Goble.**

John Lomax (1867–1948) and his son **Alan Lomax** (1915–2002) collected folk songs—first, the cowboy songs that were still being sung by veterans of the great cattle drives (1870s–1890s), and then songs from African American farmers, rail workers, prisoners, church choir leaders, and blues singers. Their *Folk Songs of North America* is still in print.

J. Frank Dobie (1888–1964) collected hundreds of true stories as well as numerous imaginative tales from old cowboys whom he got to know in Texas in the early 1900s. *The Longhorns, Up the Train from Texas, Rattlesnakes,* and *I'll Tell You a Tale* are a few of his popular titles.

During the Great Depression, the Federal Writers Project sent writers out into rural America to collect folktales. **Benjamin Botkin** (1901–1975) participated in the effort, and his *Treasury of American Folklore* contained the original versions of "Wiley and the Hairy Man," "The Tailypo," and "Little Eight John" among hundreds of others.

Folktales from Latin America

Latin American tales offer a fusion of Spanish religious stories and indigenous beliefs, sometimes mixed with street humor. For example, there is a Guatemalan tale in which Jesus, imprisoned, is accused of smoking in jail. When the guards come to investigate, Jesus has disappeared and what was thought to be a burning cigar was a firefly. There are tales of outwitting the devil, as well spooky tales and a folk song about a ghost woman, "La Llorona," who drowned her own children in life in order to become eligible to marry a well-born man who spurned her, and now roams about at night, wailing and moaning and seeking children to snatch.

From Puerto Rico come humorous tales of the noodlehead, Juan Bobo; and from the nearby Dominican Republic comes the ghost story of the Ciguapa, a hairy woman with feet mounted backwards (to confuse trackers) who kidnaps males who happen to be walking in the hills at night.

John Bierhorst (1936–) edited the largest collection of Latin American tales in English. **Alma Flor Ada** and **Isabel Campoy** rewrote several tales in both English and Spanish in *Tales Our Abuelitas Told*. **Marisa Montes** has brought out picture book versions of two stories featuring Juan Bobo: *Juan Bobo Goes to Work* and *Juan Bobo Goes Up and Down Hill*.

Folktales from Africa

Tales from Africa are often animal tales of cleverness and wisdom. Stories of the trickster, Ananse the Spider, originated in the Ashante country of Ghana, West Africa. In that region, a request for a story still yields, "One day, Spider . . ." From South Africa come philosophical tales such as the snake who was rescued from a rock—and then went to bite his rescuer. (Moral: you cannot change a creature's nature.) From Zimbabwe came the Cinderella story John Steptoe retold as *Mufaro's Beautiful Daughters*.

African stories were first recorded in the nineteenth century by European missionaries and colonial administrators. Contemporary collections have been compiled by folklore scholars **Roger Abrahams** (*African Folktales*) and **Harold Courlander** (*Yoruba Tales*). The late **Nelson Mandela** had a collection, too: *Nelson Mandela's Favorite African Folktales*.

Baba Wagué Diakité, from Mali, West Africa, has written and illustrated several West African folktales including *The Magic Gourd, The Hatseller and the Monkeys, The Hunterman and the Crocodile,* and *The Pot of Wisdom: Ananse Stories*.

Tololwa Mollel, from Tanzania, East Africa, has retold folktales from both East and West Africa, including *The Orphan Boy, The Flying Tortoise: An Igbo Tale, Ananse's Feast: An Ashanti Tale,* and *The Princess Who Lost Her Hair: An Akamba Tale*.

Verna Aardema (1911–2000), from Michigan, United States, was a schoolteacher for 30 years before she became an author of books for children. She chose traditional stories from Africa and Mexico because she wanted to acquaint American children with other cultures, and her works were and continue to be popular with children. *Why Mosquitoes Buzz in People's Ears* (illustrated by Leo and Diane Dillon) won a Caldecott Award in 1976. She also published *Bimwili & the Zimwi: A Tale from Zanzibar, Who's in Rabbit's House? A Masai Tale,* and many others.

Folktales from the Jewish Diaspora

Jews have kept alive one of the world's really old cultures. Ancient Jewish stories, recorded in the Torah and also in the Christian Old Testament, tell of Creation, of the Fall from Paradise, and of the Great Flood and Noah's Ark. Jewish culture today carries traces from the mix of the places Jews have lived: principally Germany, Russia, Central and Eastern Europe, Spain, North Africa, and the South Caucasus, as well as the United States. For example, the legend of the Golem tells of a powerful ogre formed from clay and given life by Rabbi Loew in sixteenth century Prague.

Many Yiddish tales of charmingly foolish people are set in the imaginary village of Chelm (pronounced "Helm"), somewhere in present day Poland or Ukraine.

The Hebrew language coalesced with German to yield the creole language, **Yiddish**. Yiddish stories became something of their own genre in Jewish folklore, and a great many that originated in Eastern Europe in the nineteenth and early twentieth centuries are still told. Many Jewish tales from Eastern Europe were told in Yiddish, and still contain Yiddish words. For example, they tell of life in the *shtetl*, a poor village where many *klutzes* (clumsy people) *schmooze*, *kibitz* (gossip), and *kvetch* (complain about nothing).

Nobel Prize winner **Isaac Bashevis Singer** (1902–1991) retold and also created stories from the Jewish oral tradition. There are stories of goodness and kindness and wisdom. The stories are moral: There is the expectation that one will do the right thing. Yet it is also acknowledged that the reader has a mind, and most often will use his or her ingenuity to discern the right course of action.

Eric Kimmel has rewritten several engaging stories from the Jewish and Yiddish traditions. They include *Hershel and the Hanukkah Goblins*, *Gershon's Monster*, *The Adventures of Hershel of Ostropol*, and *The Story of Esther: A Purim Tale*.

Folktales from the Middle East

Flying carpets, magic lanterns, and genies—all of these are found in **The Arabian Nights**, 1001 tales composed over hundreds of years with contributions from Persia, Egypt, and Arabia.

A famous wise man from Turkey, **Nasreddin Hoca** (1208–1284), composed tales exalting human qualities such as piety, simplicity, and charity, as well as humor. The often-witty tales have been told throughout the Muslim world for seven hundred years; many of the stories now attributed to him actually were made up by others.

A rich source of tales of wisdom are the Sufis, a group of Muslim mystics who have for centuries spun tales that are allegories of how we should live. The tales are for adults more than for children, but many appeal to readers of all ages.

Folktales from the Middle East and the Muslim world are still underrepresented in North America. One of the charming, wise, and humorous stories from the Mullah Nasrudin Hoca is found in **Demi's** *The Hungry Coat*. The late **Idries Shah**, himself a Muslim Sufi from Iran, published a longer collection in *Pleasantries of the Incredible Mullah Nasrudin*.

ILLUSTRATION 7.3 In this tale sometimes described as a "mathematical folktale," Demi tells the story of a woman who outsmarts a greedy raja. (Scholastic, Inc.)

Folktales from Asia

Many Asian folktales seem almost like parables. There is the Burmese story of the man who was so impatient that he pulled his rice plants up a little every day to make them as tall as those of his neighbors. Of course, the plants withered and died. There is the Chinese story of a woman who is threatened by a monster and who receives offers of help from a number of different strangers; together, they defeat the monster for good. "Cultivate virtues, especially those of prudence, modesty, and a collaborative spirit" seems to be the message of many of these tales.

A story from India, "One Grain of Rice," tells of a young woman who is offered a reward for a good deed done for the raja. She asks for only one grain of rice—on the first day, twice that much on the second day, twice again the third day, and so on for thirty days. Guess how much rice she has at the end of the month?

"The Stone Cutter" tells of a workingman who magically is allowed to trade his station in life for a series of more important ones, until at last he ends up where he started. It is a cumulative tale of sorts that closely parallels the English tale of "The Old Woman in a Vinegar Bottle," but with a kinder spirit, and it is a perennial favorite among story retellers and illustrators.

Asia held an exotic appeal for Western Europeans from the nineteenth century through the early twentieth, as British explorers and colonialists sent back colorful stories to cool, rainy England. **Andrew Lang,** the British folktale collector, published *A Chinese Wonder Book* with 15 tales, in 1919. The tales included "The Strange Case of Dr. Dog" and "How Footbinding Started." **Joseph Jacobs,** the Australian/English collector, published *Indian Fairy Tales* in 1910. **Rudyard Kipling**'s stories from India, including *The Jungle Book* (1894) and *Just So Stories* (1902), were literary tales, not folktales, but their folk elements had a huge appeal to British and American children.

Ed Young, the illustrator and author, spent his first 20 years in China before moving to the United States to study architecture. He has published several important tales from Asian sources. They include *Lon Po Po, a Little Red Riding Hood Story from China, Yeh-Shen: A Cinderella Story from China,* and *Monkey King,* His *Mulan* tells of a brave girl who put on armor and went to battle to save her people.

Myths from the Classical World

Myths are tales that explain people's origins, state their values, and personify the passions and drives they consider most important. Thousands of years or more before France, Germany, Italy, and the other countries discussed above were known as such, myths and creation stories were being told in Mesopotamia, Greece, Rome, and the Viking lands.

The oldest written story we have is the epic of Gilgamesh, a Mesopotamian king who lived in the city of Uruk, in present-day Iraq, around 2500 B.C. **Ludmila Zeman** retold and illustrated the epic of Gilgamesh, in a trilogy with the titles *Gilgamesh the King* (1998), *The Revenge of Ishtar* (1993), and *The Last Quest of Gilgamesh* (1998).

The ancient myths of Greece and Rome gave us gods and goddesses who were embodiments of human talents, aspirations, and flaws: Zeus, Hera, Demeter, Athena, Aphrodite, Apollo, Ares, Dionysus, Hades, and Poseidon. A perennially popular collection of Greek myths for children is still Ingri D'Aulaire and Edgar Parin D'Aulaire's' *Book of Greek Myths* (1992). Donna Jo Napoli, a professor of linguistics who is known for her novel-length adaptations of European fairy tales, recently published *Treasury of Greek Mythology* (2011).

Roman mythology borrowed from the Greeks and renamed their deities. Zeus became Jupiter, Hera became Juno, Aphrodite became Venus, Ares became Mars, Dionysus became Bacchus, and so on. Lise-Lunge Larsen published *Gifts from the Gods: Ancient Words and Wisdom from Greek and Roman Mythology* in 2011; otherwise, versions of Roman mythology for children are not as plentiful as are their Greek counterparts.

The Scandinavians had their gods and goddesses, too. In fact, they gave names to our days of the week: Tuesday (for Tiw, the god of war), Wednesday (for Woden, the Anglo Saxon name of the Scandinavian messenger god, Odin), Thursday (after Thor, the thunder god), and Friday (for Frigg, the goddess of beauty).

Authors who have written for children on Norse mythology are, again, Ingri and Edgar D'Aulaire, (*The D'Aulaires' Book of Norse Mythology*), and the Irish writer Padraic Colum (*Nordic Gods and Heroes*).

Religious Tales

Myths are tales that explain people's origins, state their values, and personify their drives, passions, and fears. Religious stories serve many of the same functions as

ISSUE to CONSIDER

Religious Stories in Public Schools?

Because of the constitutional separation of church and state, American teachers are in a quandary about books that tell religious stories. Religion is a major aspect of every culture in the world, has played a major role in the history of the United States, is important to millions of people including children, and provides some of our most frequently told stories. It serves no good purpose to keep religious stories out of schools. But allowing children to read stories from religious traditions does not mean that materials in schools should proselytize for a particular religion. Nor does it condone ostracizing any child who does not subscribe to majority religious views. It is possible to teach about religion with reasonable objectivity, but one must be careful about the sources, to avoid either proselytizing for religions or putting any children on the defensive because of their religious stances (or lack of them). Objectivity would compel teachers to make available books about many religious traditions, and not just Christianity.

ILLUSTRATION 7.4 Brian Wildsmith tells the life of Jesus of Nazareth for younger children. (Cover image of "Jesus" by Brian Wildsmith (OUP, 2002), copyright © Brian Wildsmith 2000, used by permission of Oxford University Press.)

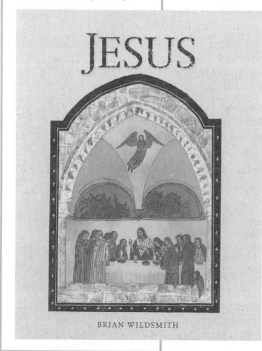

myths, except that in addition to providing explanations for the origins of people and setting out moral codes, they still guide believers and followers.

Brian Wildsmith has written and illustrated books from the Judeo-Christian tradition, including *Jesus, Mary, The Easter Story, Joseph* (of the "coat of many colors" fame), and *Exodus* (the flight of the Jews out of Egypt).

Demi has written and illustrated *Jesus, Mary, The Legend of Saint Nicholas*, and *Mother Teresa*. **Robert Sabuda** wrote and illustrated *Saint Valentine*.

There are books about other religions, too. Demi wrote and illustrated *Mohammed, Buddha*, and *The Legend of Lao Tze and Tao Te Ching*.

Derivative Folktales and Spoofs

Derivative folktales and spoofs, sometimes called *fractured fairy tales*, are stories that retell familiar folktales, usually in ways that are humorous, that surface and explode stereotypes, and that pursue the implications of features of the original tales, or do some combination of the three.

Some spoof tales hew fairly closely to the original stories, such as Jon Scieszka's *The True Story of the Three Little Pigs* and *The Frog Prince, Continued*, Philip Pullman's *I Was a Rat!*, Ellen Jackson's *Cinder Edna*, and Eugene Treviza's *Three Little Wolves and the Big, Bad Pig*, or *The Three Billy Goats Fluff*, by Rachel Mortimer.

Derivative tales use fairy story conventions in new ways, but are based on no particular story. Jay Williams' *Petronella* shockingly defied conventions when it was published in 1973 because the protagonist, the youngest of three siblings who wishes to go along on a quest, is a girl. Robert Munsch's *Paper Bag Princess* also features a female heroine who contends with a dragon to rescue Prince Ronald, who turns out not to be worth the trouble.

How Traditional Literature Works

Traditional storytellers never tell a story exactly the same way twice, but rather reconstruct it with each telling. They reconstruct a story by first sensing the story's patterns, and then using those remembered patterns to guide them as they reconstruct the story with each new telling, varying the number of details with the teller's mood and the mood of the audience as they tell it (Ong, 2002; 2005). The patterns help traditional storytellers keep hundreds of stories in their memories. Readers and listeners, too, can become sensitive to the patterns and other common features of folk literature, and those patterns help them understand, participate in, and enjoy the stories.

Below we list and describe the elements of folk stories: their openings and closings, their settings, their characters, and their motifs and tale types.

Openings and Closings

Stories meant for oral telling often have ritual openings and closings, to set the story off from day-to-day speech. In the Anglo-American tradition, we say, "Once upon a time . . ." and in Spain and Latin America, they say nearly the same thing: "Había una vez . . ." ("There was a time . . ."). In the Haitian tradition, the storyteller asks, "Kric?" and if the audience responds, "Krac," a story ensues. In the Anglo-American tradition, we once said, "Be bow bendit, My story's ended. If you don't like it, You can take it to Wales, And buy some nails And mend it." Now we say, ". . . and they lived happily ever after," while in Jamaica they may say, "Jack Mandorra, me no choose none."

Settings

In European folktales, stories are played out in a limited variety of settings, and those settings have fairly reliable associations:

> **A cottage** is where simple, unpretentious folk live. (The characters in "The Fisherman and His Wife" live in a cottage.)
> **A castle** is where people sometimes aspire to live; reaching the castle symbolizes success. (The fisherman's wife aspires to live in a castle.)
> **The forest** is where mysterious creatures live. It's a dangerous place, where unpredictable things happen. (Hansel and Gretel meet the witch in the forest. Little Red Riding Hood meets the wolf in the forest.)

TEACHING IDEA 7.2

SPOOF FAIRY TALES AND THE NARRATOR'S PERSPECTIVE

COMMON CORE STANDARD: *Craft and Structure,* STANDARD 6

Spoofs of fairy tales can be useful fare for helping young readers see narrated events from another character's point of view, as do *The True Story of the Three Little Pigs* by Jon Scieszka, *The Three Horrid Little Pigs* by Liz Pichon, or *The Three Billy Goats Fluff*, by Rachel Mortimer.

Introduce the terms *protagonist* (the main character, the one with whom the reader is led to identify) and the *antagonist*, the character who opposes or works against the protagonist and against whom the protagonist struggles.

Pair up original tales and their fractured versions: "The Three Little Pigs" and *The True Story of the Three Little Pigs*; "The Three Billy Goats Gruff" and *The Three Billy Goats Fluff*.

For each title in the pair, make a chart with four boxes (two columns and two rows). In the northwest box write, "Who is the protagonist?" In the southwest box write, "How does the protagonist look to the antagonist?" In the northeast box write, "Who is the antagonist?" And in the southeast box write, "How does the antagonist look to the protagonist?" Leave room in each box to write the class's answer. Discuss each question, and add notes to each box.

TEACHING IDEA 7.3

FINDING THE ROLES CHARACTERS PLAY

COMMON CORE STANDARD: *Key Ideas and Details,* STANDARD 2A

Review the roles of *hero, rival, helper*, and the term *goal* with the children. Then retell the story of "Jack and the Beanstalk." Ask the children to name the hero. They will probably say that Jack is the hero. Then ask what his *goal* is. Be prepared for different answers. You may ask if he wants different things at different points in the story—if so, what do the changes in his goals say about how he may be changing? Ask who the *rival* is. Then ask who the *helper* is. Be prepared for different answers. Some may name the man with the beans, and some the giant's wife.

Later, ask the children to retell the story in a new way. This time, the giant's wife is the hero. What is her goal? Who is her rival? Who is her helper? Does she achieve what she wants? Retelling the story this way can be a shocking demonstration of the way narrative directs our attention. Once we cast Jack as the hero, we are willing to forgive his misdeeds; and since the giant's wife is only a helper, we stop thinking about her once the story follows Jack and the giant down the beanstalk.

TEACHING IDEA 7.4

ROLES IN STORIES

COMMON CORE STANDARD:
Craft and Structure,
STANDARD 5

Have the students in a class brainstorm and choose a setting for a folktale. It might be a cottage in the woods, an enchanted castle, or a remote village. Next, have them name some characters that might appear in a folktale in that setting. Then, ask them to think of a goal that a character might have: It might be companionship, recognition, riches, or something to eat. Write names of possible characters on one set of cards, and words for possible goals on another set of cards. Turn the cards face down, and invite a student to draw a character card for **the hero**. Then have someone draw a card for the hero's **goal**. Next, have someone draw one of the character cards for **the rival**. Finally, have someone draw a card for **the hero's helper**. Now, either as a class or in pairs, have the students make up stories around these roles. They can compose them orally or in writing.

The **road** is a place where a character encounters new people and influences, which can change the character's life. (Jack meets the strange man with the beans along the road. The hero of Puss in Boots meets the king on the road, and his luck is transformed.)

Characters

In folktales, characters are very sparely described. "Jack and the Beanstalk," for instance, begins, "There was once upon a time a poor widow who had an only son named Jack, and a cow named Milky-white."

Main characters in folktales are contrasted in the extreme—either very good or very bad. Cinderella's stepmother was ". . . the proudest and most haughty woman that was ever seen." But Cinderella was ". . . of unparalleled goodness and sweetness of temper, which she took from her mother, who was the best creature in the world." Characters in folktales play clearly identifiable roles. We typically find a character playing *a hero*, and another playing the hero's anti-thesis, the *rival*. A minor but still important character is the *helper*, who may give the hero the magical aid she or he needs to proceed on his or her adventure (Souriau, 1955). In "Jack and the Beanstalk," we have all three: Jack as the hero, the giant as the rival, and the old man with the beans (and also the giant's wife) as the helper.

Themes

A theme is a central idea, teaching, or message that is conveyed by a work of literature. A theme may be explicit, as when it is stated plainly as a "moral" at the end of a fable by Aesop. For instance, the fable of "The Ant and the Grasshopper" concludes with, "It is better to prepare for the days of necessity," or some variation of it. Folktales usually have implicit themes that are not stated directly. In this case the reader has more work to do. If a character behaves in a certain way and is successful or unsuccessful, we can infer that the theme is that the first kind of behavior is to be imitated and the second kind to be avoided. Beauty in "Beauty and the Beast" is kind and selfless, and she is rewarded for it. Her sisters are haughty and vain, and they are not rewarded.

A theme in one folktale may be contradicted by a theme in another. For example, Jack, of the Beanstalk fame, was rewarded by following his fancy and throwing safety to the winds. But the same behavior rendered the first two little pigs meals for the wolf.

TEACHING IDEA 7.5

FINDING CONTRASTS IN STORIES

COMMON CORE STANDARD:
Key Ideas and Details,
STANDARD 3

Read the children the story of "Jack and the Beanstalk." On the board, draw a T-Chart, and label one side "Jack at Home" and label the other side "Jack in the Sky." Ask the students to help you list words that describe Jack's behavior at home and in the sky.

Ask them to think of other stories in which the hero seems different when he or she is away from home. If they need prompting, read them "Hansel and Gretel" and "The Orphan Boy and the Elk Dogs" (from Jane Yolen's *Favorite Folktales from Around the World*). How are the heroes in these stories different at home from how they are in the places they go on their adventures? Ask them to think of other stories in which the hero's demeanor and behavior is different at home than in the place where adventures happen.

Plots

Traditional tales are heavy on actions, but light on character sketches and backgrounds. While contemporary stories develop characters in great detail and provide elaborate descriptions of settings and extensive explanations of the backgrounds of the situations, folktales introduce very good characters and very bad characters and run them through a sequence of events as the problem is presented, attempts to solve it are tried, and a solution is found. In other words, folktales give prominence to plots.

Versions of the same plots occur in tale after tale, even when those tales come from different parts of the world. Why? American folklore scholar Stith Thompson (1960) says it is because "[t]he limitations of human life and the similarity of its basic situations necessarily produce tales everywhere which are much alike in all important structural aspects. They have as definite form and substance in human culture as the pot, the hoe, or the bow and arrow, and several of these narrative forms are quite as generally employed" (p. 7).

Folklore scholars for the past century have been working out ways to describe the common patterns in the plots of folktales. Antti Aarne and Stith Thompson described the shared elements and patterns of folktales in terms of motifs and tale types.

A *motif* is an element of a narrative that occurs in many different stories. As Stith Thompson explains, motifs may be *certain actors* (such as fairy godmothers, wicked stepmothers, or youngest sons or daughters), *certain objects* (such as pieces of clothing used to identify the hero, the bones of a mother that offer the heroine advice, or a carpet that flies and transports the hero), *certain actions* (such as falsely boasting about one's powers, the young hero or heroine facing impossible tasks, but succeeding with magical aid, or making a fool of oneself but making a princess laugh).

A *tale type* is a collection of elements and events that form a recognizable pattern. A tale type is a cluster of motifs, or strands of motifs woven together. For example, in "Pepelyouga," a story from Serbia, three young women sitting near a cliff are told that if one drops a spindle, her mother will be turned into a cow. The prettiest of the three does so, and when she returns home, her mother has been turned into a cow. The father remarries a cruel woman with an unattractive daughter. Immediately the step mother gives Pepelyouga impossible tasks to do. But the girl is given magical help by her cow-mother to carry out the tasks. The wicked stepmother finds out about the cow's help, and has the cow-mother killed and butchered. Everyone in the family eats the meat except for Pepelyouga, who later secretly buries her cow-mother's bones. The bones continue to give her magical aid, including special outfits to wear to the church. There, on three visits she catches the eye of the prince, but then hurries off before he can meet her (she has more impossible tasks to take care of back at home). On the third visit to the church Pepelyouga loses her golden slipper as she hurries away, and the prince finds the slipper and goes from house to house until he locates Pepelyouga, fits her with the slipper, and marries her—much to the chagrin of the stepmother and stepsisters.

Although it has some different motifs, like the dropped spindle leading to a curse and the mother turning into a cow, "Pepelyouga" shares enough motifs with "Cinderella" that they have been labeled with the same Aarne-Thompson Tale Type, number 510. In common to both is that the father remarries a wicked stepmother, the daughter is given degrading tasks along with a humiliating name, the daughter competes with an undeserving step-sister, the daughter receives magical aid from her mother after death, the daughter makes disguised visits to a ceremonial place where she enchants the prince (three times!), the daughter loses a slipper, which is later used to identify her, and the daughter and the prince marry at the end. More than 700 other stories share this pattern and are labeled with this Tale Type.

Aarne and Thompson's index allows for some 2,500 tale types and nearly 40,000 motifs. A useful online guide to stories by Tale Type is was put up by Professor D.L. Ashliman at <http://www.pitt.edu/~dash/folklinks.html#individualstories>. It is still useful, though it is no longer maintained. For those who want to see several variants of the same tale type, there are many single-volume collections available. Some are featured in Top Shelf 7.1.

TOP SHELF 7.1

BOOKS THAT SHARE MOTIFS

Motifs are devices, situations, objects, or characters that appear in several stories. Here are some motifs and some stories that share them.

The Youngest Daughter Is the Fairest

Beauty and the Beast
Vasilisa the Beautiful
East of the Sun, West of the Moon

The True Companion Is Recognized by a Tell-Tale Sign

Cinderella
The Golden Sandal: A Middle Eastern Cinderella Story
Yeh-Shen

Kind Sister and Selfish Sisters

Mufaro's Beautiful Daughters
The Talking Eggs

The Last and the Smallest One Tips the Balance

The Gigantic Turnip
"The Gecko"
(In Margaret Read Mac-Donald's *Storyteller's Start-up Book*).

Shape Shifters

The Crane Wife
Dawn
The Selkie Girl
Greyling

Wishes

The Stone Cutter
The Old Woman in the Vinegar Bottle
One Potato, Two Potato

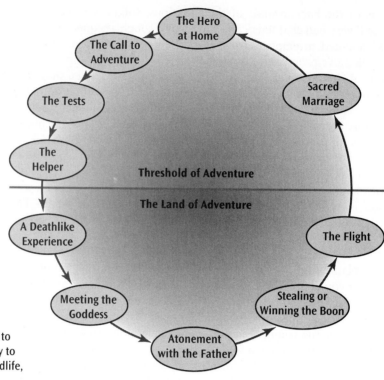

FIGURE 7.1 Campbell's hero cycle seems to tell many stories at once—a child's journey to adulthood, a rediscovery of meaning in midlife, a summary of a whole life's journey.

The Hero Cycle

Tale types and motifs give us a way of talking about similarities of folktales, and of the details they have in common. Another way to look at a great many stories told in Western cultures is the *hero cycle*. The hero cycle is a kind of plot structure that is notable for the symbolic meaning of its parts. The *hero cycle* refers to the tale of an unnoticed person who is called to a great adventure and endures many hardships before bringing some good and necessary gift back to his or her community. This kind of plot was described by the noted scholar of mythology Joseph Campbell. After studying hundreds of myths, legends, and folktales, Campbell concluded that the traditional literature of the world often tells the *same* story. Campbell called the single story told by all hero tales *the monomyth*, or single myth, and the pattern of events that comprises the monomyth *the Hero Cycle*. The Hero Cycle unfolds in several steps (see Figure 7.1).

Here we will look at each step of the cycle and illustrate it with reference to "Jack and the Beanstalk."

- **The hero at home.** In the beginning of the story, the hero is often the lowest of the low, unrecognized, but perhaps having a questioning nature or a quiet ambition to find out who he or she really is. *Jack is poor, and is often described as lazy and foolish.*

- **The call to adventure.** Soon, some problem arises that causes the hero to go on a quest. In traditional

TEACHING IDEA 7.6

DISCOVERING THE HERO CYCLE IN STORIES

COMMON CORE STANDARD: *Integration of Knowledge and Ideas, STANDARD 9*

After explaining the steps of the hero cycle, read "Hansel and Gretel" to children (in third grade or higher) and ask them to see how many matches they can find between that story and the hero cycle. Read them the stories of Hercules and of Orpheus (from the d'Aulaires' *Book of Greek Myths*), and ask them to read them again on their own. Later, see whether they can find parallels to the hero cycle in folktales such as "The Orphan Boy and the Elk Dogs" (from Jane Yolen's *Favorite Folktales from Around the World*), "East of the Sun, West of the Moon," *The Firebird* (single-volume versions have been retold and illustrated by Gennady Spirin and by Demi, and the tale also appears in Aleksandr Afanas'ev's collection of Russian folktales), and Anthony Manna's *Mr. Semolina-Simolinus* (illustrated by Giselle Potter).

literature, the hero often has to compete for the chance to go, as he or she is naturally overlooked in favor of an older or more glamorous sibling. *Jack's mother announces they are starving, and sends Jack to market to sell the cow.*

- **The tests.** Before proceeding very far on the adventure, the hero is faced with challenges or tests. If these are met with cleverness, courage, or kindness, the hero often receives some magical help that enables him or her to proceed on the quest. *On his way to the market, Jack meets an old man who asks him questions. Jack answers to the man's satisfaction.*

- **The helper.** The helper is a person or peculiar creature that provides the magical aid the hero needs to cross the threshold into the place where the object of the quest is usually found. Sometimes the helper provides other miraculous equipment that enables the hero to succeed. *The old man trades a handful of magical beans for Jack's cow.*

- **The land of adventure.** The quest leads the hero into what Campbell calls "the Land of Adventure." Like Never-Never Land, Narnia, Hogwarts School, or the land beyond the "Wrinkle in Time," this is often a magical place, impossible to reach without the aid the hero received from the helper. Once the hero is there, the adventures begin in earnest, but the hero's true powers come into play, enabling the hero to rise to the challenges. *The magical beans grow a miraculous beanstalk that enables Jack to climb up to a land in the clouds.*

- **A deathlike experience.** Once the hero arrives in the Land of Adventure, he or she may have a death and rebirth experience: The hero's childish nature must die off, and his or her more mature, heroic nature must be born. Tomb imagery is very often used at this point. *Jack finds a castle in the clouds, and persuades the Giant's wife to take him to the kitchen to eat. But when she hears the Giant coming, she forces Jack to hide in the oven.*

- **Meeting the goddess.** If the hero is male, he may encounter a beautiful but formidable female figure who may challenge or love him, but in any case, confirms him as a worthy contender. *Considering the Giant's wife as a beautiful but formidable female figure may be a stretch, but it is true that Jack somehow beguiles her into acknowledging his prowess, and that she becomes his ally.*

- **Atonement with the father.** The hero often comes up against a stern father figure who challenges him or her severely. Sometimes the hero overthrows the father figure. At the least, the hero forces the father figure to recognize his or her status as a hero. *Jack shows great courage and cool-headedness in the presence of the Giant.*

- **Stealing or winning the prize.** The object of the quest is often some magical gift or remedy that is needed back at home. The hero wins this remedy or steals it. *Jack steals the bag of gold coins, the hen that lays golden eggs, and the harp that plays music by itself.*

- **The flight.** If the hero steals the prize, the hero will escape, pursued by powerful forces. It will take more trickery and bravery to get away. *On the last trip, Jack flees down the beanstalk with the Giant close in pursuit.*

- **The return.** When the hero returns home, he or she brings what was needed to keep life going along comfortably. Sometimes the hero arrives in splendor and enters into royal marriage. Sometimes the hero slips home almost unnoticed but changed: more whole, more integrated, and proven. *Jack and his mother live well after that.*

The hero cycle fits many stories—from the story of Hercules to the Norwegian tale "East of the Sun, West of the Moon" to the Italian and French tale "Puss in

Boots," to the Iroquois tale "The Boy Who Lived with the Bears." But what gives it significance is that it seems to be a story of hope. On one level, it is an assurance to the least confident among us that she or he has a special calling, will receive help from an unexpected source provided she or he treats even the least likely helper with kindness, must move into unfamiliar territory, must leave her or his old self behind, must face up to presumed authority figures with courage and pride, and must take something good from her or his strivings and bring it back to people in the community that need it. One can go home again, but the person who is truly at home and at peace is the person who has gone forth and developed her or his talents, and has developed his or her potential.

Criteria for Evaluating Traditional Literature

- Is the story well written according to literary features discussed earlier in this chapter? Traditional literature should have spare plots, strong characters, and memorable language.
- Is the story reasonably authentic—that is, does it stay true to its source or sources? Responsible retellers usually identify the sources of their stories. And if they change them significantly, they indicate that they have done so.
- If it is an illustrated book, are the pictures consistent with the cultural setting?
- Does the book provide explanations for geographical and cultural details that may not be clear to the reader?
- Is the story retold and illustrated by a member of its culture of origin, or is it retold by a serious student of the folklore and culture of its place of origin?

EXPERIENCES FOR FURTHER LEARNING

1. Find as many variations as you can of a familiar European fairy tale. If you choose "Cinderella," you might also read *The Rough Faced Girl* by Rafe Martin, as well as these books by Shirley Climo: *The Irish Cinderlad, The Korean Cinderella, The Persian Cinderella,* and *The Egyptian Cinderella.* If you choose "Hansel and Gretel," a parallel story is Joseph Bruchac's *The Boy Who Lived With the Bears.* If you read "The Three Little Pigs," you might also read Ed Young's *Lon Po Po* and William Steig's *The Amazing Bone.* Construct a chart to illustrate what your tales have in common. Do they strike you as the "same" story? What makes each one unique to its cultural setting?

2. The folk belief in *changelings,* otherworldly babies secretly exchanged for human babies, may seem quaint and charming. But as D. L. Ashliman speculates (2006), the belief may have been used in older times to justify parents' withholding affection from an autistic child or a child with a birth defect. What might be the historical explanations for these features of folktales? Evil stepmothers. Kind, but aloof fathers. Love at first sight. Witches. A father who makes an exaggerated boast about his daughter to a potential suitor. The forest as a dangerous place.

RECOMMENDED BOOKS

* indicates a picture book; I indicates interest level
(P = preschool, YA = young adult).

Myths from Ancient Greece and Rome

*Aliki. *The Gods and Goddesses of Olympus*. HarperCollins, 1994. This book tells the story of how the gods and goddesses came to live at Olympus and provides a sketch of each of the twelve major gods and goddesses. (I: 6–10)

D'Aulaire, Ingri, and Edgar Parin D'Aulaire. *Book of Greek Myths*. Doubleday, 1962. The stories of the major Greek gods and goddesses are intelligently told and beautifully illustrated. (I: 8–12)

*Napoli, Donna Jo. *Treasury of Greek Mythology: Classic Stories of Gods, Goddesses, Heroes & Monsters*. Illustrated by Christina Balit. National Geographic, 2011. This is an accessible reference work nearly 200 pages long. (I: 8–13)

*Wells, Rosemary. *Max and Ruby in Pandora's Box*. Puffin, 1998. The characters of Max and Ruby tell the story of Pandora's box as an object lesson. You probably won't find mythology made any more accessible to younger children than it is here. (I: 5–7)

Stories of the Great Religions

*Demi. *Buddha*. Margaret K. McElderry, 1996. The story of Prince Siddhartha, who wandered out into the world and saw pain and suffering, gave up all his possessions, and founded a religion based on selflessness. (I: 9–12)

*_____. *Mary*. Margaret K. McElderry, 2006. A narrative of the life of the mother of Jesus. (I: 8–12)

*_____. *Mohammed*. Margaret K. McElderry, 2003. A narrative of the life of the prophet who founded the religion of Islam. (I: 8–12)

Wildsmith, Brian. *Jesus*. William B. Eerdmans, 2000. A book on the life of Jesus of Nazareth, for younger children (I: 6–10)

North American Tales

Chase, Richard. *The Jack Tales*. Dutton, 2003. More tales of the Appalachian tricksters Jack and Mutsmag (Jack's female counterpart) by a storyteller and folklorist who is also a consummate illustrator. (I: 8–12)

*Isaacs, Anne. *Swamp Angel*. Illustrated by Paul Zelinsky. Dutton, 1994. An original tall tale with a female character. Zelinsky painted the illustrations for the book on wood veneers for an antique look. (I: 6–9)

*Kellogg, Steven. *Johnny Appleseed*. Morrow, 1988. Active and expressive drawings illustrate this entry in Kellogg's tall tales series. See also Kellogg's *Mike Fink: A Tall Tale, Paul Bunyan,* and *Pecos Bill* (I: 6–10)

*Mora, Pat. *Doña Flor: A Tall Tale About a Giant Woman with a Great Big Heart*. Illustrated by Raúl Colon. Knopf, 2005. A tall tale about a Latina heroine from the Southwest, by the same duo who created *Tomás and the Library Lady*. (I: 6–10)

Folktales from the British Isles

*Aylesworth, Jim. *The Gingerbread Man*. Illustrated by Barbara McClintock. Scholastic, 1998. This is a lively retelling of the tale of the runaway Gingerbread Man. (I: P–8)

*Chaucer, Geoffrey. *The Canterbury Tales*. Adapted by Barbara Cohen. Illustrated by Trina Schart Hyman. Lothrop, Lee, & Shepard, 1988. Four beautifully illustrated tales from Chaucer's story of a medieval English pilgrimage to Canterbury. (I: 11–YA)

Green, Roger Lancelyn. *The Adventures of Robin Hood*. Puffin, 1995. A novel-length version of Robin Hood and his Merrie Men, drawn from many sources. (I: 8–10)

*Hodges, Margaret. *St. George and the Dragon*. Illustrated by Trina Schart Hyman. Little, Brown, 1984. A Caldecott Honor Book with stunning illustrations. (I: 8–10)

Jacobs, Joseph. *Celtic Fairy Tales*. 1st World Library, 2006. Originally published in 1890, these tales from Scotland, Ireland, and Wales are full of intricate heroism and magic. (I: 9–12)

Morris, Jackie. *The Seal Children*. Frances Lincoln Children's Books, 2003. Set in Wales, this work from the illustrator's imagination draws on the folk belief about the selchies, the seal people. (I: 9–12)

Williams, Marcia. *The Adventures of Robin Hood*. Walker Books, 2007. Eleven adventures of the man who robbed the rich and gave to the poor are retold in lively comic strip format. (I: 8–10)

Yolen, Jane. *Sword of the Rightful King*. Magic Carpet Books, 2004. A master storyteller gives us a novel-length weaving of many stories from the Arthurian legend, including "the loathly lady," and "the sword in the stone." (I: 8–12)

German Folktales

*Browne, Anthony. *Hansel and Gretel*. Walker, 2008. A version of this dark tale that will not horrify young children. (I: 7–9)

*Kimmel, Eric. *Iron John*. Illustrated by Trina Schart Hyman. Holiday House, 1994. The story of a prince who is trained in manly things by the wild man who lives in the woods. (I: 8–12)

*Zelinsky, Paul O. *Rapunzel*. Dutton, 1997. Zelinsky's elaborate retelling of this tale from the Grimms draws on elements from early French and Italian sources, and the illustrations are oil paintings from the Italian Renaissance tradition. The book won the Caldecott Medal for 1997. (I: 6–11)

*_____. *Rumpelstiltskin*. Dutton, 1986. Paul O. Zelinsky won a Caldecott Medal for this version of the world's best-known guess-my-name story. (I: 7–9)

French Folktales

*Brown, Marcia. *Cinderella*. Aladdin, 1997. This version is a reprint of Brown's Caldecott Medal winner from 1955. (I: 5–9)

*Hyman, Trina Schart. *Little Red Riding Hood*. Holiday House, 1987. Hyman won a Caldecott Honor for this fascinating retelling, with pictures within pictures on every page. (I: 5–9)

*Marshall, James. *Red Riding Hood*. Picture Puffins, 1993. Marshall's cartoony rendering brings energy and wit to this cautionary tale from Charles Perrault. (I: 5–9)

Perrault, Charles. *The Complete Fairy Tales of Charles Perrault*. Translated by Nicoletta Simboroski and Neil Philip and illustrated by Sally Holmes. Clarion, 1993. Thirteen tales, including "Cinderella," "The Sleeping Beauty," "Little Red Riding Hood," and "Bluebeard," plus a biography of Perrault, with translator's notes. (I: 6–10)

*Pinkney, Jerry. *Little Red Riding Hood*. Little, Brown, 2007. Pinkney's watercolors make Riding Hood a sympathetic character and the wolf a real threat, in this traditional retelling of Perrault's tale. (I: 5–9)

Jewish Folktales

*McGovern, Anne. *Too Much Noise*. Illustrated by Simms Taback. Sandpiper, 1992. A young children's version of the Yiddish tale, "It Could Always Be Worse." (I: 5–8)

*Taback, Simms. *Joseph Had a Little Overcoat*. Viking, 2000. Taback won a Caldecott Medal for this lively retelling in story form of a Yiddish folk song. The die-cut illustrations add to the amusement. Song lyrics and music are included. (I: All ages)

Scandinavian Folktales

Asbjørnsen, Peter Christen, and Jørgen Moe. *The Man Who Kept House*. Illustrated by Svend Otto Sorensen. Margaret McElderry, 1992. In this traditional Norse tale, a man finds that keeping house is not as easy as he had claimed. (I: 6–9)

*_____. *The Three Billy Goats Gruff*. Retold and illustrated by Paul Galdone. HMH Books, 2011. Children's book versions of this story go in and out of print. Galdone's recent version is a reliable retelling. (I: 5–9)

Russian Folktales

Afanas'ev, Aleksandr. *Russian Folk Tales*. Translated by Robert Chandler. Illustrated by Ivan Bilibin. Random House, 1984. These seven tales are perfectly illustrated by Bilibin. Children will want to hear them again and again. (I: 7–12)

*Lurie, Allison. *Baba Yaga and the Stolen Baby*. Illustrated by Jessica Souhami. Frances Lincoln, 2008. This tale by a noted children's literature scholar stays close to the original Russian tales of the witch who lives in a hut on chicken feet. (I: 5–8)

*Mayer, Marianna. *Baba Yaga and Vasilisa the Brave*. Illustrated by K. Y. Craft. Morrow, 1994. Two of children's favorite Russian characters in one story. Vasilisa succeeds with the help of the doll her dead mother gave her. (I: 6–10)

*Spirin, Gennady. *The Tale of the Firebird*. Philomel, 2002. Russian-born Spirin uses a rich palette to bring this Russian hero tale to life. (I: 5–10)

African American Tales

Galdone, Joanna C. *Tailypo!* Illustrated by Paul Galdone. Sandpiper, 1984. A man cuts off the tail of a night visitor, and it comes back to haunt him, in this traditional African American tale from rural Kentucky. (I: P–8)

Hamilton, Virginia. *Her Stories: African American Folktales, Fairy Tales, and True Tales*. Illustrated by Leo and Diane Dillon. Scholastic, 1995. Sixteen folktales and three true accounts from American black women. (I: 9–YA)

_____. *The People Could Fly: American Black Folktales*. Illustrated by Leo and Diane Dillon. Knopf, 1985. Twenty-four tales plus a bibliography; includes "Wiley, His Mother, and the Hairy Man" and "Little Eight John." Some of the stories are full of emotional power. (I: 9–YA)

Harris, Joel Chandler. *The Tales of Uncle Remus*. Adapted by Julius Lester and illustrated by Jerry Pinkney. Dial, 1987. Lester's voice makes these tales a joy to read aloud, and Pinkney's illustrations bring the characters to life. A Coretta Scott King Award Honor Book. Look for other books in this series (I: All ages)

*Lester, Julius. *John Henry*. Illustrated by Jerry Pinkney. Dial, 1994. A lively and careful retelling of this tall tale that pits human against machine. (I: 8–10)

*San Souci, Robert D. *The Talking Eggs*. Illustrated by Jerry Pinkney. Dial, 1989. An African American variant of the Cinderella story. (I: 5–10)

Native American Tales

*Bruchac, Joseph. *The First Strawberries: A Cherokee Story*. Illustrated by Anna Vojtech. Dial, 1993. A touching and lyrical story about the first man and the first woman, the overcoming of anger, and the origin of strawberries. (I: 7–10)

*_____. *The Great Ball Game: A Muskogee Story*. Illustrated by Susan L. Roth. Dial, 1994. In this *pourquoi* tale, the birds and the animals square off in a game of stickball to decide who will have dominion over the land; the bat sides with the animals and wins the game. (I: 7–10)

*Goble, Paul. *Dream Wolf*. Aladdin, 1997. In this tale, one of many from the Plains Indians, by a noted reteller and illustrator, two children lost in the hills are watched over by a kindly wolf. (I: 7–10)

*McDermott, Gerald. *Coyote: A Trickster Tale from the American Southwest*. Harcourt, 1994. A Native American trickster tale from the Zuni people, presented by a master illustrator. (I: 6–9)

*San Souci, Robert. *Sootface: An Ojibwa Cinderella Story*. Illustrated by Daniel San Souci. Bantam, 1997. In a story that closely parallels the Algonquin tale "The Rough Faced Girl," an invisible warrior chooses as his bride the young woman with the truest qualities, and this turns out to be the Sootface, she who cooks and washes for her more outwardly beautiful and vainer sisters. (I: 6–9)

Hispanic and Latin America Tales

Campoy, I., and A. F. Ada. *Tales Our Abuelitas Told: A Hispanic Folktale Collection*. Illustrated by Felipe

Dávalos Viví Escrivá, Susan Guevara, and Leyla Torres. Atheneum, 2006. Twelve tales retold by two noted Latina storytellers, with copious notes on the stories' origins and styles for telling. A Spanish-language version, *Cuentos Que Contaban Nuestras Abuelas*, is also available. (I: 6–9)

*Ehlert, Lois. *Moon Rope: A Peruvian Folktale/Un lazo a la luna: Una leyenda Peruana*. Harcourt, 1992. A *pourquoi* tale in English and Spanish that explains why Mole lives in the ground and why we see Fox's likeness in the moon. (I: 6–8)

Montes, Marisa. *Juan Bobo Goes to Work*. Illustrated by Joe Cepeda. HarperCollins, 2000. The simpleton, Juan Bobo, does everything just wrong, with humorous results. (I: 8–11)

Philip, Neil. *Horse Hooves and Chicken Feet: Mexican Folktales*. Illustrated by Jacqueline Mair. Clarion Books, 2003. These Mexican tales have some familiar forms: There is a "Cinderella" variant here, as well as a numbskull tale. There is also a mix of Catholicism, too. With an informative introduction by the anthologist. (I: 9–11)

Tales from Africa

*Aardema, Verna. *Koi and the Kola Nuts: A Tale from Liberia*. Illustrated by Joe Cepeda. Aladdin, 2003. Koi's inheritance from his father is only a kola tree, so he takes a sack of kola nuts and goes off to seek his fortune, and along the way learns that richness is not what you have, but what you give. (I: 6–10)

*Bryan, Ashley. *Beautiful Blackbird*. Atheneum, 2003. Long ago, when blackbird was voted the most beautiful bird, all the other birds asked that he decorate them with black paint. This *pourquoi* tale from Zambia explains the markings of the birds. The "songs" of birds are interwoven throughout the text. (I: 4–8)

*Kimmel, Eric. *Anansi Goes Fishing*. Illustrated by Janet Stevens. Holiday House, 1993. The tables are turned when Anansi sets out to trick his friend into doing all the work. (I: P–8). See also his *Anansi and the Talking Melon* and *Anansi and the Moss-Covered Rock*.

*Mollel, Tololwa. *The Orphan Boy*. Illustrated by Paul Morin. Clarion, 1990. A touching *pourquoi* tale from the Maasai people of East Africa, about the tragic power of overweening curiosity and the reason for the transit of Venus. (I: 6–10).

*Steptoe, John. *Mufaro's Beautiful Daughters*. Lothrop, Lee & Shepard, 1987. The humblest and kindest daughter gets the reward in this Caldecott winner. (I: 6–10)

Asian Folktales

*Casanova, Mary. *The Hunter*. Illustrated by Ed Young. Atheneum, 2000. A retelling of a Chinese tale in which a generous hunter is given a magical gift that allows him to provide for his village in a time of drought—but only if he does not reveal the source of the magic. (I: 7–11)

*Jiang, Ji-Li. *The Magical Monkey King: Mischief in Heaven*. Illustrated by Youshan Tang. Shen's Books, 2006. This is one episode from a sixteenth-century legend of the Chinese superhero, retold by the author of

The Red Scarf Girl, and illustrated in traditional brush drawings. (I: 7–11)

Ramanujan, A. K. *Folktales from India: A Selection of Oral Tales from Twenty-two Languages*. Pantheon, 1991. Over one hundred tales of wisdom and foolishness, some as short as a few paragraphs, others stringing out event after event. This collection is for adults, but there are read-alouds suitable for all ages. (I: All ages)

*Sellier, Marie. *Legend of the Chinese Dragon*. Illustrated by Catherine Louis, with calligraphy and chop marks by Wang Fei. NorthSouth Books, 2006. The book is a work of art that tells of a time when Chinese children declared war on war, and created in the Dragon a creature that combined, and trumped, all the divided people's own protective animals. (I: 7–12).

*So, Meilo. *Gobble, Gobble, Slip, Slop: A Tale of a Very Greedy Cat*. Knopf, 2004. This is a retelling of the folktale about the fat cat that eats every creature it encounters until two little crabs figure out how to save all the creatures that have been consumed. (I: 4–7)

*Young, Ed. *Lon Po Po*. Philomel, 1989. Sisters outwit the evil wolf in this Chinese variant of "Little Red Riding Hood." (I: 5–9)

Middle Eastern Folktales

*Hickox, Rebecca. *The Golden Sandal: A Middle Eastern Cinderella Story*. Illustrated by Will Hillenbrand. Holiday House, 1999. In this retelling of an Iraqi folktale "The Little Red Fish and the Clog of Gold," the Cinderella figure is named Maha, her magical helper is a fish, and the glass slipper is—can you guess? (I: 4–8)

Laird, Elizabeth. *Pea Boy and Other Stories from Iran*. Illustrated by Shirin Adl. Frances Lincoln Books, 2010. Seven lively stories, including—who knew?—a version of Miss Cockroach and Mr. Mouse, a tale that is popular in Puerto Rico. (I: 7–10)

Derivative Folktales and Spoofs

*Hartman, Bob. *The Wolf Who Cried Boy*. Illustrated by Tim Raglin. Putnam, 2002. Little Wolf longs for his favorite dish—Boy, but Boys are hard to come by. So Little Wolf entertains himself by yelling "Boy" and sending his parents on wild goose chases in search of the elusive Boy. Little Wolf has great fun—until he sees the real thing. (I: 5–8)

*Minters, Frances. *Cinder-Elly*. Illustrated by G. Brian Karas. Viking, 1994. In this story, told in a fast-moving rhyme, an urban Cinderella longs to go to the basketball game, gets there with the magical aid of a bag lady, and wins the attention of Prince Charming, the star shooter. (I: 7–11)

*Munsch, Robert. *The Paper Bag Princess*. Illustrated by Michael Martchenko. Annick Press, 1988. Canadian author Munsch created a popular tale in which a female hero, Princess Elizabeth, rescues Prince Ronald from captivity by a dragon that has burned all Elizabeth's clothes and left her draped in a paper bag. Vain Prince Ronald doesn't approve of women who dress in paper bags, even if they do save his life. Read on. (I: 7–9)

*Scieszka, Jon. *The Frog Prince, Continued*. Illustrated by Steve Johnson. Puffin, 1994. Jon Scieszka has carved out a niche for himself with his clever retellings of classic fairy tales. This one explores what might have happened if the prince really had tried to give up his froggy ways and live happily ever after with a human beauty. (I: 6–11)

*_____. *The Stinky Cheese Man and Other Fairly Stupid Tales*. Illustrated by Lane Smith. Viking, 1992. This book not only turns half a dozen classic fairy tales on their ears, but trashes the conventions of book layout, too. Scieszka is aided in this inspired assault on tradition by the artist Lane Smith and an ingenious book designer. (I: 6–11).

Vande Velde, Vivian. *The Rumpelstiltskin Problem*. Houghton Mifflin, 2000. Six different variations on the Grimms' tale explore the (many) puzzling features of the story. (I: 9–12).

Multicultural Collections

Hamilton, Martha, and Mitch Weiss. *Noodlehead Stories: World Tales Kids Can Read and Tell*. August House, 2000. Twenty-three tales from all parts of the world that can be read or told. Each story has notes on its origin, and tips for telling by the professional storytelling duo who go under the professional name of Beauty and the Beast. Beauty and the Beast promote storytelling by children. Their guide, *Children Tell Stories: Teaching and Using Storytelling in the Classroom* (2nd ed.) (Richard C. Owen, 2002), comes with a DVD showing young storytellers. Highly recommended! (I: 7–11)

_____. *Scared Witless: Thirteen Eerie Tales to Tell*. House, 2006. Ghost stories with notes and telling tips. (I: 7–11)

Hearne, Betsy, ed. *Beauties and Beasts*. Illustrated by Joanne Caroselli. Oryx Press, 1993. Hearne has researched the Beauty and the Beast tale type and has here reproduced two dozen versions of it from nearly every part of the world. (I: 7–11)

_____. *Through the Grapevine: World Tales Kids Can Read and Tell*. August House, 2001. Here are thirty-two more tales for reading or telling with notes by the authors. Many of the tales echo themes children will know from other stories. (I: 6–10)

Kaminski, Robert, and Judith Sierra, eds. *Multicultural Folktales: Stories to Tell to Young Children*. Oryx Press, 1991. Dozens of tales from most parts of the world, prefaced by instructions on telling stories and using the flannel board and accompanied by flannel board cutouts. (I: 4–7)

Collections That Challenge Stereotypes

Lurie, Alison. *Clever Gretchen and Other Forgotten Folktales*. Illustrated by Margot Tomes. Authors Guild backprint.com, 2005. Sixteen tales from the British Isles, Norway, Germany, France, and Russia, all featuring strong female protagonists. Includes well-known stories like "Molly Whuppie" and "Kate Crackernuts." Others will be welcome surprises. (I: 7–11)

Mutén, Burleigh. *Grandmother Stories: Wise Woman Tales from Many Cultures*. Barefoot Books, 2006. Illustrated by Siân Bailey. Eight stories from around the world (Senegal, Japan, Russia, Hawaii, Mexico, Ireland, Germany, and Sweden). Chosen to combat stereotypes of the old woman as a witch or a shrew, these showcase the wisdom and kindness of elderly women characters.

Ragan, Kathleen. *Fearless Girls, Wise Women, and Beloved Sisters: Heroines in Folktales from Around the World*. Norton, 1998. Over 100 stories featuring strong female protagonists, categorized by region of origin: Europe (including tales from Eastern Europe and Russia), North and South America, Asia, the Pacific, and North Africa and the Middle East. (I: 7–12)

*Yolen, Jane. *Not One Damsel in Distress: World Folktales for Strong Girls*. Illustrated by Susan Guevara. Harcourt, 2000. Thirteen stories from around the world show brave heroines in action. (I: 7–12)

*_____. *Mightier Than the Sword: World Folktales for Strong Boys*. Illustrated by Raul Colón. Harcourt, 2003. Fourteen tales from around the world portray male heroes succeeding through nonviolent means. (I: 7–12)

REFERENCES

Aarne, Antti. *The Types of the Folktale*. Translated and revised by Stith Thompson. *Folklore Fellows Communication No. 184*. Academia Scientiarum Fennica, 1961.

Ashliman, D. L. *Folk and Fairy Tales: A Handbook*. Greenwood, 2004.

Beatty, Judith S. (Ed.). *La Llorona: Encounters With the Weeping Woman*. Sunstone Press, 2004.

Bettelheim, Bruno. *The Uses of Enchantment*. Vintage, 1975.

Botkin, B. A. *A Treasury of American Folklore*. Random House, 1993.

Briggs, Katherine. *British Folktales*. Marboro Books, 1979.

Bronner, Simon, ed. *American Children's Folklore*. August House, 1988.

Campbell, Joseph. *The Hero with a Thousand Faces*. Bollingen, 1968.

Crossley-Holland, Kevin. *Folktales of the British Isles*. Pantheon, 1988.

Cypress, Sandra Messinger. *La Malinche in Mexican Literature: From History to Myth*. University of Texas Press, 1991.

Davis, Donald. *Southern Jack Tales*. August House, 1993.

Edmonds, Walter D. *The Matchlock Gun*. Dodd Mead, 1941.

Freud, Sigmund. *New Introductory Lectures on Psychoanalysis*. Norton, 1923.

Frye, Northrop. *Anatomy of Criticism*. Princeton University Press, 1971.

Hamilton, Virginia. *In the Beginning: Creation Stories from Around the World*. Illustrated by Barry Moser. Sandpiper, 1991.

Harris, J. C. (1880/2012). *The Wonderful Tar Baby Story*. From <http://www.uncleremus.com/tarbaby.html>

Jacobs, Joseph. *Celtic Fairy Tales*. Frederick Muller, 1958.

Jung, Carl, ed. *Man and His Symbols*. Dell, 1961.

——. *Memories, Dreams, and Reflections*. Vintage, 1989.

Larsen, L-L. *Gifts from the Gods: Ancient Words and Wisdom from Greek and Roman Mythology*. HMH Publishers, 2011.

Lipman, Doug. *Improving Your Storytelling*. August House, 2005.

Lomax, Alan. *The Folksongs of North America*. Dolphin, 1975.

Ong, Walter. *Orality and Literacy*. Routledge, 2002.

Rapaport, Roy. "Desecrating the Holy Woman: Derek Freeman's Attack on Margaret Mead." *American Scholar 55*(3) (Summer 1986): 313–347.

Shah, Idries. *Tales of the Dervishes: Teaching Stories of the Sufi Masters Over the Past Thousand Years*. Octagon Press, 1967.

Souriau, Etienne. *Les Deux Cent Milles Situations Dramatiques*. Flamarion, 1955.

Thompson, Stith. *The Folktale*. Holt, Rinehart, and Winston, 1960 (originally published in 1946).

Tolkien, J.R.R. "On Fairy-Stories." In *Essays Presented to Charles Williams*, Ed. C.S. Lewis. Grand Rapids: Eerdmans, 1966, pp. 38–89.

Williamson, Duncan. *Tales of the Seal People: Scottish Folk Tales*. Interlink, 1992.

Yolen, Jane. *Favorite Folktales from Around the World*. Pantheon, 1988.

Zipes, Jack. *Beauty and the Beast, and Other Classic French Fairy Tales*. Signet, 1997.

Modern Fantasy and Science Fiction

❝ She [Kate] said, *"Watch,"* and she dipped the funnel into the dish and blew through it, and out of the funnel grew the most magnificent bubble I have ever seen, iridescent, gleaming.*"*Look at it from here," said Kate, intent. "Just look at the light!" And in the sunlight, all the colors in the world were swimming over that glimmering sphere— swirling, glowing, achingly beautiful. Like a dancing rainbow the bubble hung there for a long moment; then it was gone. I thought: That's fantasy. I said: "I wish they didn't have to vanish so soon." "But you can always blow another," Kate said. ❞

—from *Dreams and Wishes: Essays on Writing for Children* by Susan Cooper

T his bubble metaphor comes from fantasy writer Susan Cooper, who was sitting in her study, contemplating a description of "fantasy," when her daughter Kate entered the room. It provides a visual image that shows how fantasy takes shape when a believer makes a new creation possible. Writers of fantasy do just that—they create magnificent bubbles so achingly beautiful that readers can only marvel and enjoy.

What Is Modern Fantasy? What Is Science Fiction?

Definition of Modern Fantasy

Fantasy literature has unexplainable magic, and it is this element that captures the minds and hearts of children. According to Lynn (2005),

> Fantasy has been variously described as imaginative, fanciful, visionary, strange, otherworldly, supernatural, mysterious, frightening, magical, inexplicable, wondrous, dreamlike, and, paradoxically, realistic. It has been termed an awareness of the inexplicable existence of "magic" in the everyday world, a yearning for a sudden glimpse of something strange and wonderful, and a different and perhaps truer version of reality. (p. xxi)

Jean Greenlaw (1995a) adds that fantasy literature goes beyond the known world and imaginatively creates a new or transformed world. "Nonrational phenomena" have a significant role in fantasy, as do events, settings, and creatures that don't exist in the real world. The imaginative creation must be so well crafted that readers accept the fantasy through a "willing suspension of disbelief," although this happens only when story details have internal consistency with the fantastic elements.

Fantasy extends reality into the unknown. It gives readers a way of understanding the world they live in by going beyond it to a wider, imaginative vision. Sometimes, people mistakenly think that fantasy is merely an escape from the complexity of reality into a simplistic world. On the contrary, the world created by fantasy can "refresh . . . delight . . . give a new vision," as it artfully presents rich characters and engaging and complex plots that are woven with fantastic elements (Alexander, 1971). Originality and the "capacity to incite wonder" are also critical elements (Gates, Steffel, & Molson, 2003). For some readers, the strength and depth of emotion they experience as they triumph and despair along with fantasy characters go beyond what they could experience in a realistic world.

Modern fantasy falls into two major classifications: low fantasy and high fantasy. All authors who write fantasy draw on the here and now, what Lloyd Alexander calls the "primary world"—people's knowledge and experience of real life—for "raw material" (Alexander, 1971, p. 164). Low fantasy is actually set in the primary world, but the magical elements of fantasy make the story impossible. In contrast, writers of high fantasy take information and experiences from the primary world and project this information to create images and situations of a "secondary world." Authors of high fantasy create a secondary world whose concrete elements are impossible according to the logic of the primary world, but consistent with its own laws. Some high fantasy stories remain totally in the created world, and some travel between that world and the primary world. Others involve a world within the primary world, marked by boundaries that keep the magic inside the created world (Tymn, Zahorski, & Boyer, 1979).

Definition of Science Fiction

Science fiction is a variety of fantasy in which an author, inspired by real developments in science, has conceived a version of reality different from the one we inhabit.

Science fiction writers weave into stories scientific concepts that are extrapolations of current scientific understandings, and make them plausible (Greenlaw, 1995b). In short, they make readers believe the unbelievable because they convince them that it is possible.

Because works of science fiction make readers entertain possibilities that go well beyond everyday occurrences, they have a useful role to play in educating the imagination, to borrow a phrase from the literary critic Northrop Frye (1957). The imagination, as Frye points out, is the source of all human invention. For example, people told stories about human flight for thousands of years before the Wright brothers' plane flew off a sand dune at Kitty Hawk. Humans would never have gotten off the ground if they hadn't long imagined the wonders of flight. Such imagining can be nourished by stories.

Distinction between Fantasy and Science Fiction

Greenlaw (1982) differentiates modern fantasy and science fiction this way: "Fantasy never could be. Science fiction has the possibility of being—maybe not in our time or on our planet, but the possibility of happening within some time and in some place" (p. 64). In other words, a story that is clearly impossible is called *fantasy;* a story with aspects of the improbable is called *science fiction*. The possibility that someday an invention or new knowledge could make feasible something that is seemingly improbable is what distinguishes science fiction from other forms of fantasy. In 1869, Jules Verne wrote **Twenty Thousand Leagues under the Sea**. The idea of a submarine obviously existed in Verne's imagination, but no real submarine had yet been built. A submarine might have seemed improbable at the time, but as it turned out, it was very possible.

At times, it is difficult to make a clear distinction between science fiction and fantasy because certain books have characteristics of both genres. These hybrid books may present details purported to have a scientific basis, yet they also include elements that make the story clearly impossible. The result is a type of science fiction called "science fantasy." Science fantasy includes elements that were previously considered traditional in high fantasy (such as dragons, wizards, and fairies) as well as elements that are traditional in science fiction (space travel or interplanetary exploration). Science fantasy begins with an extrapolation based on scientific understanding, but the story is predominantly a fantasy.

We will discuss modern fantasy in the first half of this chapter and science fiction in the second half. This parallel structure will allow a more focused look at each genre.

The Evolution of Modern Fantasy

Myths, legends, and folktales are predecessors of modern fantasy. For centuries, the oral tradition of storytelling passed along many tales of magical beings, fantastic occurrences, and otherworldly places. The beginning of modern fantasy as a genre can be traced to the nineteenth century, when stories that later became known as literary fairy tales were created in the style of stories from the oral tradition. These literary fairy tales included features of works from traditional folklore: generic settings in kingdoms far away in a distant time "long, long ago,"

ILLUSTRATION 8.1   In *Twenty Thousand Leagues Under the Sea,* Jules Verne created the captivating, visionary tale of Captain Nemo and his majestic *Nautilus,* an elaborate submarine—an undersea vehicle that had yet to be invented. Aboard the *Nautilus,* three captive castaways experience harrowing yet marvelous undersea adventures that test the limits of their imagination, courage, and mental resilience. (Cover from "Twenty Thousand Leagues Under the Seas" by Jules Verne, 1873 English edition by Geo. M Smith & Co., Boston.)

Jules Verne
Twenty Thousand Leagues
Under the Seas
A new translation by William Butcher
OXFORD WORLD'S CLASSICS

one-dimensional stock characters, magical elements, and, quite often, happy endings. Unlike stories from the oral tradition, however, literary fairy tales have known authors. A notable example is Hans Christian Andersen's mid-nineteenth century works such as "The Princess and the Pea." The elements of folklore are present: the setting in a time period described simply as "there once was . . .," the stock characters of a prince and a princess, the magical way in which the princess felt the pea through layers and layers of mattresses, and the "lived happily ever after" ending.

Several nineteenth-century British writers turned their attention to creating fantasy for children. Many of these early works are still enjoyed by today's children. *Alice's Adventures in Wonderland,* written by Charles Lutwidge Dodgson and published in 1865 under the pseudonym Lewis Carroll, was regarded as representing a turning point in literature for children because it was written with humor and imagination rather than with a didactic purpose. In the story, Alice falls into a rabbit hole and enters a fantastic world—a world that demands a sense of humor and an imaginative mind. Published in 1894, Rudyard Kipling's *The Jungle Book* is the story of Mowgli, a human child left in the jungle, raised by wolves, and nurtured by the wisdom of a bear, a python, and a panther.

J. M. Barrie's play *Peter and Wendy* had a large impact on fantasy literature for children when it was published in 1904; it was re-published in 1911 as *Peter Pan.* The story of how Peter teaches three children how to fly to Never Never Land so that they will never have to grow up is still well known and loved among children. In 1908, British writer Kenneth Grahame created another milestone book with personified animals, *The Wind in the Willows*. Day-to-day events chronicle woodland animals in complex friendships that reflect the trials and rewards that humans experience. A. A. Milne published *Winnie-the-Pooh,* with illustrations by Ernest Shepard, in 1926, and the book became a classic story of personified toy animals. Milne gave each character a distinct personality—Pooh, Eeyore, Tigger, Piglet, Owl, Kanga, and Roo—and young readers find the predictability of their words and actions in various circumstances reassuring. Hugh Lofting's *The Story of Doctor Dolittle,* published in 1920, depicts an animal doctor who sets off for Africa with his dog, duck, pig, parrot, and owl to cure monkeys of a disease. In P. L. Travers's *Mary Poppins*, published in 1934, a seemingly prim and proper nanny named Mary Poppins enters the Banks household, and her arrival "on the East Wind" foreshadows the magical adventures ahead for the two children.

Fantasy literature was also published in other European countries. Carlo Collodi's personified toy story *The Adventures of Pinocchio* was published in Italy in 1881. Children are still intrigued by this story of a lonely man who carves a marionette that comes to life and becomes his little boy. The two-volume edition of *The Wonderful Adventures of Nils* (1906–1907), by Selma Lagerlöf, was originally published as a geography primer for Swedish children. The story became a classic when it was translated into other languages; children around the world were enchanted by the story of how Nils Holgersson became elf-sized and traveled all over Sweden on the back of a goose. Tove Jansson's *Finn Family Moomintroll* was the first in a series of humorous books published during the 1940s and 1950s in Finland about the Moomins, imaginary troll-like creatures who held magical powers. In Sweden in 1945, Astrid Lindgren published *Pippi Longstocking,* a fantasy featuring an eccentric protagonist: a little girl who lives her life in such an uncharacteristic way that children who read of her adventures are fascinated by the possibility that a child like that might exist. Pippi is a nine-year-old who does as she pleases whenever she wants to because she lives alone with no adults to supervise her activities. Mary Norton's *The Borrowers,* the story of a family of "little people" who live by "borrowing" everyday objects from humans, was published in England in 1953 and was the beginning of a series.

The first modern fantasy for children published in the United States was *The Wonderful Wizard of Oz,* created by Frank Baum in 1900. Baum created thirteen more volumes about Oz. They were so immensely popular that after his death in

1919, his publisher hired Ruth Plumly Thompson to write nineteen more stories to satisfy the literary appetite of readers who loved the world of Oz.

Robert Lawson won the 1945 Newbery Medal for his personified animal story *Rabbit Hill.* The story takes place in the Connecticut countryside, where Father and Mother Rabbit and Little Georgie live. Rumor has it that new folks are coming to live in the big house, and all the animals who live in the surrounding area wonder what this will mean to them—how will they be treated?

A few years later, in 1952, E. B. White published a book that was to become a favorite of children around the world. *Charlotte's Web* tells the story of Wilbur, a runt pig who is rescued from slaughter and then catapulted into fame by Charlotte, a kind spider who spins words of praise for Wilbur in her web. Despite its lighthearted tone, the themes of friendships, death, and legacy are serious and enduring.

The mid-twentieth century marked the beginning of the publication of high fantasy series for children. J. R. R. Tolkien published *The Hobbit* in 1937. This book has been read by millions of children and adults, and translated into over twenty-five languages. Tolkien's thorough understanding of mythology was the basis of a trilogy entitled *The Lord of the Rings,* in which the protagonist, Frodo Baggins, goes on a quest.

The Chronicles of Narnia, a seven-volume series, was published between 1950 and 1956 by C. S. Lewis, who wove Christian allegories throughout his stories set in the fantasy world of Narnia. *The Chronicles of Prydain,* a high fantasy series by Lloyd Alexander, began in 1964 with the publication of *The Book of Three.* Robin McKinley's quest fantasy *The Hero and the Crown* was published in 1984 and won the Newbery Medal in 1985. It was unusual among high fantasy books because it featured a female protagonist. A high fantasy series featuring characters portrayed as animals is Brian Jacques's *Redwall* series, whose first volume was published in England in 1987. Philip Pullman's *Dark Materials* trilogy started with *The Golden Compass,* published in 1996, and ended with *The Amber Spyglass,* published in 2000.

Fantasy reading at the beginning of the twenty-first century is marked by extraordinary levels of readership and fervor. Terry Pratchett's books set in Discworld have been popular since the early 1980s. The publication of J. K. Rowling's *Harry Potter* books marks a phenomenon perhaps unequaled by any previously published books for children. With the first book, *Harry Potter and the Sorcerer's Stone,* readers—both children and adults—were hooked, and the seven books led to record-high levels of excitement, sales, and movies. All of this means that more people are reading and discussing fantasy than ever before, and more fantasies are being published in the twenty-first century than ever before.

ILLUSTRATION 8.2 The life of a shy runt pig is saved through the efforts of a clever, articulate spider named Charlotte in this extraordinarily popular animal fantasy by E. B. White. (Cover art copyright © renewed 1980 by the Estate of Garth Williams. Used by permission of HarperCollins Publishers.)

Categories of Modern Fantasy

This section examines several categories of fantasy. But literature is not genre formulaic. Some books fit into multiple genres. For example, Jane Yolen's *The Devil's Arithmetic* can be considered historical fiction because it is set mainly during the Holocaust; yet it might also be considered modern fantasy because the book's protagonist experiences a slip in time. Gail Carson Levine's *Ella Enchanted* is based on the fairy tale of Cinderella, yet it is a fully developed fantasy that goes far beyond the traditional tale. In addition, authors are increasingly including elements of science fiction with fantasy. Although it is hard to put books into neat categories, trying to do so allows for interesting comparisons.

Low fantasy features nonrational events that occur without explanation in the real world and is also known as light fantasy for the typically lighthearted and often humorous tone. The forms of low fantasy are discussed here in the order in which children are likely to be introduced to them, which corresponds roughly to young readers' increasingly higher levels of engagement in the fantasy elements.

Personified Animals

Stories with animals talking and behaving as humans do are often called personified animal fantasies. Typically, this is the first type of fantasy book that young children encounter. Animal characters who behave like humans are said to be anthropomorphic. In fact, many picture books for young children contain personified animals as characters, yet the situations they face and the way they deal with them are quite realistic to the children who read such books.

Beatrix Potter's many personified animals may be among the first fantasy characters children are introduced to. In *The Tale of Peter Rabbit,* Potter mixes behaviors typical of rabbits with behaviors of humans. Peter and his family live in a sand bank underneath the roots of a tree, play in the fields, eat garden vegetables, and hop away from danger—all rabbit-like behaviors. But Mrs. Rabbit talks to her children using words, and the rabbits wear clothing and drink chamomile tea—all human behaviors.

Kevin Henkes has written and illustrated many stories about personified mice. Sheila Rae, the brave older sister who suddenly panics and relies on the wits of her younger sister in *Sheila Rae, the Brave,* and Chester and Wilson, whose particular ways of doing things are disrupted by Lilly's move into the neighborhood in *Chester's Way,* are all mice. However, they not only behave like people but think like them, too. As children get older, they may encounter William Steig's personified animals. In *Doctor De Soto,* a fox gets a toothache and seeks the help of a dentist who is a mouse. This dilemma has both an animal and a human dimension: As a dentist, Dr. De Soto feels a moral obligation to help someone with a toothache, but as a mouse, he fears that the fox could have ulterior motives.

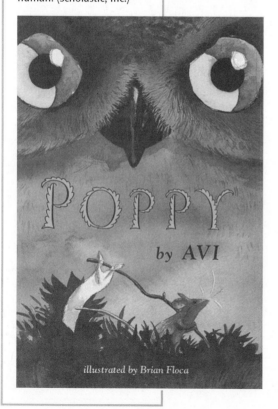

ILLUSTRATION 8.3 The situations in which the characters in *Poppy* find themselves are set in the animal world, but the solutions arise out of thoughts and behaviors that are quite human. (Scholastic, Inc.)

POPPY
by AVI
illustrated by Brian Floca

In Avi's "Tales of Dimwood Forest" stories, *Poppy,* a deer mouse, tries to convince her family to move close to a large cornfield because it could provide food for them forever. This move is thwarted when the tyrannical great horned owl, Mr. Ocax, refuses to give his consent. An unlikely group of personified animals interacts in Cynthia Rylant's *Gooseberry Park.* A Labrador retriever named Kona befriends Stumpy, a squirrel in Gooseberry Park. When Stumpy is separated from her babies during an ice storm, a bat named Murray and a hermit crab named Gwendolyn team up with Kona to reunite the newborns with their mother.

Several popular stories about personified animals center around a community of animals. *Charlotte's Web* by E. B. White is an immensely popular example. When Wilbur, the runt of the litter, is about to be slaughtered, he is rescued by a little girl named Fern. However, it is Charlotte, a spider, who calls the entire cast of barnyard animals into action to truly save Wilbur's life. As in E. B. White's books, the barnyard animals in British writer Dick King-Smith's stories such as *Babe: The Gallant Pig* become the community within which the story takes place. In *The Wind in the Willows,* by Kenneth Grahame, Ratty, Mole, Badger, and Toad form a community of animals. In *Young Fredle* by Cynthia Voigt, a kitchen mouse unexpectedly finds freedom in the greatly feared "outside world," and must learn to negotiate new ways of life with the network of animals that dwell outside of the house where his family lives.

Personified Toys

Another type of fantasy that children enjoy features personified toys (as well as other inanimate objects) that come to life. In these books, toys are able to talk and behave like humans. The toys that come to life are typically stuffed animals or dolls. The reason may be that when children play, they frequently pretend that stuffed animals and dolls have human attributes.

Perhaps the best-known personified toy story is A. A. Milne's classic work *Winnie-the-Pooh*. The story was inspired by Milne's son, Christopher Robin, and his collection of stuffed animals.

The Castle in the Attic, by Elizabeth Winthrop, is a personified toy story in which a finger-high knight in a model castle comes alive when William, the young protagonist, picks him up. But when William's desire to keep his nanny from leaving shrinks her to doll size, he, too, must enter the toy-sized life and seek to undo the magic. Lynne Reid Banks's *The Indian in the Cupboard* and other books are popular among children; however, we cannot recommend them. A toy Indian and other toys come alive when Omri puts them in a magical cupboard. Having toys come alive, seeing the unfolding adventure as the toys engage in lifelike situations, and realizing what responsibility means are all part of the drama Omri and his friend Patrick experience. Although these popular books address the question "What if toys came alive?" the toy people in them do not rise above stereotypes of Indians and cowboys, and the portrayal of the Indian is particularly problematic.

Ann Martin and Laura Godwin teamed up to create *The Doll People,* in which a hundred-year-old doll family is brought from England to America and passed down through the generations to the current owner, Kate. Eight-year-old Anabelle is a doll who reads her Aunt Sarah's journal and becomes obsessed with the need to solve the mystery of her aunt's disappearance in 1955. Humorous clashes of the ages come about with the arrival of a plastic family next door, with modern amenities such as a microwave oven. Illustrations by Brian Selznick throughout the book keep readers engagingly immersed in the doll world.

Kate DiCamillo's *The Miraculous Journey of Edward Tulane* describes a china rabbit doll who is vain, selfish, and heartless. He belongs to ten-year-old Abilene, until a disastrous series of events takes him on a long and distant journey, through

TOP SHELF 8.1

PERSONIFIED ANIMAL CHARACTERS IN PICTURE BOOKS

Lilly and friends books by Kevin Henkes

Max and Ruby books by Rosemary Wells

Peter Rabbit and friends books by Beatrix Potter

ILLUSTRATION 8.4 A clash of generations occurs in the doll world when a hundred-year-old doll family meets a modern plastic doll family. (Book cover of "The Doll People" by Ann M. Martin and Laura Godwin, pictures by Brian Selznick. Jacket Illustration © 2000 by Brian Selznick. Reprinted by permission of Disney - Hyperion Books, an imprint of Disney Book Group, LLC. All rights reserved.)

which he encounters physical damage to his toy body but a building of his emotional self through his relationships with his various owners.

Outlandish Characters and Situations

Stories that appear to be realistic fiction but have characters who behave in outrageous, highly exaggerated ways that are utterly impossible are classified as fantasy with outlandish characters. P. L. Travers created a series of stories about a character with magical abilities. The first of these was *Mary Poppins*, in which the unusual nanny arrives at the home of Jane and Michael Banks by way of an umbrella that carries her airborne on a gust of wind. Swedish writer Astrid Lindgren is known around the world as the creator of *Pippi Longstocking* and two sequels, as well as more than a hundred other books. Pippi lives alone, without any adult supervision, and displays outrageous and eccentric behavior that keeps the neighborhood children constantly amused. What makes Pippi's story a fantasy is that she is given superhuman physical abilities—for example, as a young girl, she can lift a horse.

Polly Horvath writes many books that seem to fit into both categories of magical realism and outlandish characters and situations. While all of her books are filled with exaggeration and dry humor, some, like *The Pepins and Their Problems*, have elements that are not possible, such as a cow that dispenses lemonade. Horvath uses the device of presenting the Pepins' hilariously absurd problems to readers and eliciting their suggestions for dealing with them, which prompts the sharing of the equally nonsensical responses supposedly sent in from across the United States.

Lemony Snicket's *A Series of Unfortunate Events* relies on exaggeration and humor to tell stories that are outlandish and preposterous. They parody Victorian novels, offering multiple levels of humor through the use of language play on figures of speech and vocabulary.

Magical Powers

The notion that magic might exist is an intriguing thought to children: Could there be sayings that make magical things happen, objects that hold magical powers, or other ways of bringing about magical events?

What could be more enticing than the dream that a better life than the one we live is owed to us and that we have magical powers? In J. K. Rowling's *Harry Potter and the Sorcerer's Stone*, Harry's existence is so lowly that readers are sure to recognize it as an unfair life. On the eve of his eleventh birthday, he receives an invitation to Hogwarts School of Witchcraft and Wizardry—and the news that he is the most famous wizard alive! Magical events abound throughout the Harry Potter books, and somehow all seem believable to the reader.

In Cornelia Funke's book, *Inkheart*, Meggie's father has magical power and inadvertently reads characters right out of a book and into real life, where they create havoc by engaging in the kind of criminal behavior and adventurous lifestyles they lived in the book. Meggie's burning question is: What happened to her mother, and how can they find her? What kind of magical ability will be needed to solve this mystery?

Natalie Babbitt's *Tuck Everlasting* has the ultimate magic in it: a spring that gives eternal life to those who drink from it. The source of this water is not explained, nor does the story offer an explanation of how it gives eternal life. All readers know is the magical consequences of drinking from the spring. The moral question is: Is it better to drink the water and live eternally or to live the continuous flow of the known life cycle?

Picture books also have stories with magical powers. In Chris Van Allsburg's *Jumanji*, the children play a board game, and as they land on the squares that describe their journey through the game, the jungle comes to life with lions, monsoon rains, and destructive monkeys that will not go away until the game is played out to the end. In William Steig's picture book *Sylvester and the Magic Pebble,* Sylvester is portrayed as a donkey who comes across a special pebble for his pebble collection—one that grants wishes. The problem arises when Sylvester wishes to turn into a rock temporarily to escape trouble, but cannot revert back to being a donkey. This story of personified animals includes elements of magic.

Embellished Fairy Tales

In recent years, many fairy tales have been embellished with rich character development, detailed descriptions of setting, and finely developed plot, presenting a fuller story than the original traditional tales offered. In many cases, they answer questions provoked by the original tale: Why was Rumpelstiltskin interested in the miller's daughter's child? Why was Rapunzel's mother so loving, yet so cruel in locking up her daughter? Why did Jack trade a cow for a handful of magic beans? In almost all cases, the expanded versions remain true to the essential components of the original tales as we know them, but put a new twist on or offer a different perspective to readers.

In Gail Carson Levine's *Ella Enchanted,* a gift of "obedience" is bestowed on Ella by the fairy Lucinda, and it turns out to be a curse rather than a blessing. The story explores what happens when a child must be obedient, even against her own will. The most prolific author in this category is Donna Jo Napoli. In *Zel,* she considers three perspectives on the Rapunzel story: those of the thirteen-year-old peasant daughter Zel, the nobleman who falls in love with her and wants to marry her, and the mother—who turns out to be a witch with a motive for locking up her daughter. Napoli continued her frog-turned-prince story, *Prince of the Pond,* in *Jimmy, the Pickpocket of the Palace.* Books like these offer readers opportunities to ponder what other known stories offer possibilities for embellishment.

Extraordinary Worlds

The first task of an author who creates a world that is very different from the one in which we live is to make it believable to readers. Sometimes a story begins with convincing characters in the known world who then move into an extraordinary world through various devices. For example, when Milo enters the mysterious tollbooth in Norton Juster's popular novel *The Phantom Tollbooth,* he finds an extraordinary world. In Roald Dahl's *Charlie and the Chocolate Factory,* the search for gold tickets hidden in chocolate bars takes place in the real world, but an invitation to enter a mysterious chocolate factory leads a selected few into an extraordinary world. In *Alice's Adventures in Wonderland,* Alice, a seemingly ordinary child, falls into a rabbit hole and finds an extraordinary world at the other end. In Eloise McGraw's *The Moorchild,* the human world and the "folk world" coexist side by side; the folk world is accessible only to folk, but folk can move in and out of the human world. In Eoin Colfer's *Artemis Fowl,* the twelve-year-old genius criminal mastermind must steal a fairy handbook and crack its code in an attempt to steal their gold and restock his family's fortune. The subterranean world of fairies is complex and highly

TEACHING IDEA 8.1

MAGICAL ABILITIES

Select a book that features a character with magical abilities. Would you like to possess such abilities? Why or why not? Explain what your life would be like if you had those magical abilities. Carefully consider the pros and the cons of having such abilities. How would this change your relationship with your friends, your family, and society as a whole?

TEACHING IDEA 8.2

EMBELLISH A FAIRY TALE

Select a fairy tale, and write down the essential points of the fairy tale after reading several versions in picture books and collected volumes. What are the unanswered questions? Which events make you curious? What do you wish would happen? Using the essential major points as the basis, write an expanded version of your own. Be sure to add rich details that still connect to the major points. Also check to be sure that it makes sense as to why those details were added. Illustrate to add a visual component of your story.

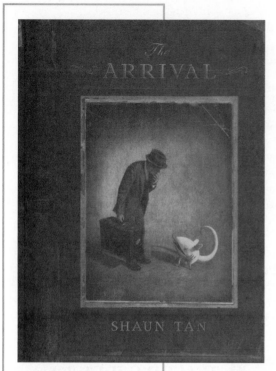

ILLUSTRATION 8.5 Shaun Tan imagines the immigrant experience by comparing it to experiencing the foreignness of the unknown fantasy world in which aliens of all kinds exist alongside humans. (Scholastic, Inc.)

guarded by the LEPrecon (Lower Elements Police reconnaissance group). Other stories are set entirely in an extraordinary world. What makes the extraordinary world believable in Mary Norton's *The Borrowers* is the author's careful attention to minute details when describing how the tiny Borrowers adapt various everyday human-size objects to their own uses. In Cornelia Funke's *Dragon Rider,* a young boy realizes his destiny of becoming a dragon rider. Set in an extraordinary world of dragons, brownies, and other creatures not in our world today, readers are treated to a fantastic world of magical happenings.

Two picture book illustrators who create some of the most extraordinary worlds are Shaun Tan and David Wiesner. Interestingly, Wiesner does so almost exclusively through illustration, with minimal text, if any. Tan uses both illustration and text to depict the extraordinary worlds he creates, although the illustrations could carry the stories, even without the text. Wiesner won the Caldecott Medal for *Tuesday,* in which flying frogs on lily pads leave the townspeople in wonder; *The Three Pigs,* in which various folk stories with pigs and wolves weave through the book in unexpected mixings; and *Flotsam,* in which an underwater world is suggested and introduced. In Shaun Tan's *The Arrival,* the utterly confusing and at times lonely experience of being an immigrant is compared to being an alien in an unknown world. In *The Lost Thing,* a boy plays with an alien creature, and, discovering it must be lost, tries to help it find its home.

Supernatural Elements

Scary stories with supernatural elements—ghosts, haunted houses, and the like—intrigue children. Margaret Mahy tells the story of a family with psychic powers in *The Haunting.* The family members struggle with what these powers do to their relationships with one another. In Mary Downing Hahn's *Wait till Helen Comes,* the ghost of Helen, who died years ago, waits by the pond to drown other children her age in hopes of getting a playmate. Molly must save her new stepsister from joining Helen.

Books with supernatural elements are not necessarily scary. Supernatural elements are taken in stride in stories such as Franny Billingsley's *The Folk Keeper.* Corinna knows that her unusual qualities would frighten some people, so she keeps them to herself and takes her "different abilities" in stride as she explains them to the reader with a matter-of-fact voice. Neil Gaiman's *The Graveyard Book* depicts the growing up of "Nobody" in a graveyard, with ghosts as parents and caretakers. But as Nobody grows up, he faces life in a world outside the protection of his cemetery home and relationships with people who are living, and not ghosts.

Among the most popular books with children today are stories that can be classified as fantasies with supernatural elements. Many children eagerly seek out these "horror stories" and "scary stories."

Time Slips

In time-slip stories, characters move from one time period to another. This element of time travel allows the author to explore themes in ways not possible in stories that take place in a single time period. Typically, the time slips allow the characters to develop an understanding that enhances their development. Barbara Elleman (1985, p. 1407) notes that "time-slip plots often center on a particular historical period, a mystery that needs to be solved, or a common problem shared across generations." Going back in time allows characters to gain firsthand experience that deepens their understanding of how historical events influence the present. Time slips in mysteries allow characters to find the clues to solve the mysteries. Sometimes, issues span generations, and in some time-slip stories, the protagonist finds ways to cope with issues by meeting others who have faced them in an earlier time.

Jon Scieszka has written a series of books about three boys who make up the Time Warp Trio: *Knights of the Kitchen Table* is the first in a series. The device that allows the boys to travel in time is a magical object, "The Book," which Joe receives as a birthday present from his uncle, a magician. When Joe and his two friends, Fred and Sam, open the book, they are whisked off to a different place and time—the medieval days of King Arthur, the days of pirates and buried treasure, the nineteenth century in the Old West, the Stone Age, the twenty-first century, or ancient Egypt.

Mary Pope Osborne's *Magic Tree House* books are a very popular series of beginning chapter books. Siblings Jack and Annie read books in their tree house and are magically transported to various times and places, where they learn historical, scientific, and cultural information. The books include time destinations as varied as the days of dinosaurs, the Revolutionary War, and Shakespeare's era.

Jane Yolen's *The Devil's Arithmetic* is a time-slip story as well as a work of historical fiction. In *The Devil's Arithmetic,* Hannah is transported to the time of the Holocaust. She returns to the present with a deeper understanding of herself as a descendant of a particular heritage and a commitment not to forget the past. In another work of historical fiction and time slip, *King of Shadows,* Susan Cooper explores the days of Shakespeare. As Nat Fields acts out his role as Puck in "A Midsummer Night's Dream," both in the present day and with Will Shakespeare himself, Nat's present-day character comes to terms with his father's death through the relationship he has with Will Shakespeare in the past time period. The device of the time slip also allows readers to see the past through a present-day character's eyes, with explanations that clarify the differences. Dan Gutman uses the device of a baseball card to allow the holder to travel back in time to the era of the person whose card he is holding. What baseball card-collecting kid wouldn't be enthralled at imagining such a thing? In *Shoeless Joe and Me,* Stosh travels back to 1919 when Shoeless Joe and others were caught "throwing" the World Series and expelled from baseball for life. Stosh hopes that if he can prevent this from happening, Shoeless Joe Jackson can be inducted into the Baseball Hall of Fame. Other ball players about whom the time travel series has been written include Jackie Robinson, Honus Wagner, Babe Ruth, and Mickey Mantle.

In Mary Hoffman's *Stravaganza* trilogy, a "Stravaganti" is someone who can traverse time periods. In the first book, *City of Masks,* Lucien lives in twenty-first century London and is undergoing chemotherapy for cancer when his father brings him a beautiful Italian notebook in which he can write and communicate when his throat hurts too much to talk. The notebook turns out to be a talisman that transports him to the time period of the stravaganti who brought it into the twenty-first century. Lucien quickly adapts to his life in the Italian Bellezza as Luciano, apprentice to a "magical" scientist Rodolfo, himself a stravaganti. Through the device of the time slip, Lucien/Luciano is able to lead a more complete life. Rebecca Stead's Newbery-winning book, *When You Reach Me,* has allusions to Madeleine L'Engle's *A Wrinkle in Time.* The book seems more like realistic fiction for much of the story, but then, things happen that remind readers that not everything is explainable in the world as we know it. Ultimately, the mystery that forms at the beginning of the story is resolved through an answer in which the device of time travel explains why certain things had to happen.

TEACHING IDEA 8.3

High Fantasy

As we mentioned earlier, high fantasy takes place in a created secondary world. Although much high fantasy is enjoyed by young adults, many middle school students and some elementary school readers are attracted to works of high fantasy. There are various categories of high fantasy: myth fantasy, gothic fantasy, epic/heroic fantasy, and sword and sorcery fantasy. Myth fantasy can be retellings of old myths, modern adaptations of old myths, or new inventions. Gothic fantasy includes elements such as fear of the unknown and the unnatural. Epic/heroic fantasy tries to recreate the world of the medieval epic and romance. Such fantasies are grand in their design and often have a strong emotional impact on readers. Heroic actions stem from the protagonist's commitment to serve "the common good." In many ways closely related to legends from the oral tradition, epic/hero fantasies often contain components of Arthurian, Welsh, Scandinavian, or other myths and legends. Sword and sorcery fantasy is similar to heroic fantasy. However, sword and sorcery fantasy is not to be confused with the "sword and sinew subgenre," which violates many of the characteristics of high fantasy. That subgenre includes a barbarian superhero, has much action, lacks thematic substance, uses a colloquial style of language, and sensationalizes violence (Egoff, 1988; Tymn, Zahorski, & Boyer, 1979).

Heroic romance is a form of high fantasy that draws from mythology and includes stories of heroes and worlds of great power. Alexander (1971) has called heroic romance a "cauldron of story" in which is found a "mythological minestrone" that combines real history with imaginary history. Included is an array of characters, events, and situations—quests, tasks, swords, dragons, and other elements of heroic romance. Because fantasy is written on many levels, Alexander suggests that readers may "ladle up whatever suits (their) taste" and "digest it, assimilate it" as thoroughly as possible.

Tymn, Zahorski, and Boyer (1979) characterize high fantasy as having "noble characters, archetypes, and elevated style." The focus on morality in high fantasy requires a hero who is compassionate, courageous, and humane and who accomplishes many good deeds. The hero is often a representative human being, "Everyman," who may be a commoner-hero or a morally ambivalent hero. The commoner-hero is at first reluctant to become involved in the events that are unfolding, but proves courageous, loyal, and generous. The morally ambivalent hero is basically good, but is more concerned with maintaining independence and individuality. The imagery for the created world is often supported by the elevated speaking style of noble characters. The themes that are explored in high fantasies usually appear unrelated to personal concerns. They are generally universal and focus on an all-out struggle between good and evil in which entire worlds are at stake. These other worlds tend to be reminiscent of medieval worlds; Tolkien's Middle-Earth, Alexander's Prydain, and Lewis's Narnia are just a few examples. Authors of high fantasy often provide readers with a detailed map of the lands in the secondary world.

Lloyd Alexander (1978, p. 442) classifies the plots in high fantasy into five categories:

- Tests of identity, endurance, and character
- Tasks, imposed or undertaken voluntarily
- Quests for marvelous objects or animals
- Escapes from death, through disguise or substitution or with help
- Journeys to other lands or worlds

Sometimes authors combine two or more of the five plot categories, either in one book or in a series of books. Although a work of high fantasy presents an impossible world, the "undercurrent of rationality" makes the story believable. The universal vitality of fantasy is timeless and eternal (Alexander, 1971). When series such as Rick Riordan's *Percy Jackson and The Olympians* incorporate many of the plot elements identified by Alexander as essential to moving fantasy stories along, and they have universal themes like loyalty, quests to save the world, and swash-buckling fight scenes depicting bravery, such elements of high appeal make it easy to understand why readers can't seem to get enough.

How Fantasy Works

Asked why anyone reads or writes fantasy, author Susan Cooper (1981) explained that fantasy goes one stage beyond realism in requiring complete intellectual surrender. Fantasy asks more of readers, and the best works of fantasy may offer readers more. She argues that the escape so often attributed to fantasy is indeed offered, but it is an inward rather than an outward escape, as readers learn to discover themselves. Cooper suggests that by going beyond the time and space of the known world, readers allow themselves to enter a dreamlike world that contains accumulated images and emotions of the human race.

Although different authors have their own thoughts on what makes a work fantasy, a number of generalizations can be made. First, fantasy includes literary elements that are characteristic of good literature, but one or more of these elements is transformed by the author into something magical or not possible in the known world. Fantasy is made believable by the consistent use of logic or laws of the created world and descriptive detail. The fantasy element cannot be brought out suddenly to magically solve problems. Whatever element makes the story a fantasy must be an integral part of the story, and all details must be consistent with that element. Fantasy is not an escape from reality, but a mirror in which reality is reflected and extended in the imagination. Finally, fantasy occurs in a secondary world created by the author, in the real world (the primary world) but with changed rules of logic, or in both worlds.

When reading fantasy, we accept the impossible by suspending disbelief. Authors engage readers in fantasy by anchoring stories in plausibility. Authors also use a combination of devices to make the fantasy elements of a story believable to readers. These devices are described within the context of the literary elements in the section that follows, applying the understanding of those elements to *Tuck Everlasting*, by Natalie Babbitt.

Setting

Many authors firmly ground a story in reality before gradually moving into fantasy. In other words, they begin the story in the primary world and move into the secondary world. Details of setting are an integral part of the story. Good authors make details so vivid that readers can see, hear, and feel the setting as they read the description. Babbitt's masterful description of the summer heat in August that opens the story is often read aloud as an exemplary passage describing the setting.

Character

Authors have one of the characters mirror the disbelief of the reader. The narrator or protagonist reassures readers that the fantastic events are normal or real. When a believable character who initially doubted the fantasy is convinced, readers are likewise convinced. Authors use consistent and distinct language for each character or group. Winnie must be kidnapped before she can have the truth revealed to her so her reaction can be monitored.

Plot

The plot must have internal consistency and logic. The idea of eternal life and never aging is a fascinating thought, but not logically consistent with our world as we know it. In order for readers to suspend disbelief in this concept and embrace the idea that in a fantasy world eternal life without aging might be a possibility, all elements of plot must be consistent with what it would be like to never age. How do people who have eternal life live among those who do not? What must be kept secret from the world, and why?

Theme

The theme must be one that matters to people in our known world. Whether we should desire eternal life or follow the life cycle as we now know it is a question that people today care about. We ponder with Winnie as to what to do with that magical potion that promises eternal life and wonder what decision we might make ourselves, if we were the ones holding that bottle of "water."

In *Tuck Everlasting,* Babbitt grounds the story in reality by first introducing a setting, a character, and a mood that are perfectly normal in the real world. Winnie Foster, the protagonist, has lost patience with the rules of all the adults in her life and considers running away from home. She is frustrated and wants more adventure. When the plot steps into the realm of the fantastic, Winnie tries to understand how people who drink special water could possibly live forever. As Winnie struggles with the decision she must make, readers are also convinced of the power of the water. They become intrigued with Winnie's dilemma and suspend disbelief in what they rationally know is not possible; they follow Winnie into the fantasy. The author has created a story with internal consistency, and the intertwining of details about characters and plot development leaves no loose threads or contradictions.

Criteria for Evaluating Modern Fantasy

- Is the story well written according to literary standards outlined in Chapter 2?
- Is the theme compelling to readers in a "real world" as well as in the fantasy world?
- Are the elements that make the story a fantasy convincing, consistent, and well developed? Does the story allow readers to suspend disbelief?
- Does the author maintain a sense of logic and order within the created world?

Major Writers of Fantasy and Their Works

AUTHOR	MAJOR WORKS INCLUDE:
Lloyd Alexander	*The Chronicles of Prydain* series
Susan Cooper	*The Dark is Rising* series; *King of Shadows*
Bruce Coville	*Jeremy Thatcher, Dragon Hatcher, My Teacher Is an Alien*
Roald Dahl	*Charlie and the Chocolate Factory, Witches*
Cornelia Funke	*The Thief Lord, Inkheart* trilogy
Brian Jacques	*Redwall* series
Diana Wynne Jones	*Chrestomanci Cycle, Howl's Moving Castle*
Philip Pullman	*The Dark Materials* trilogy
Rick Riordan	*Percy Jackson and The Olympians*
J. K. Rowling	*Harry Potter* series
Jane Yolen	*Commander Toad* series; *The Devil's Arithmetic*

Ask *the* Author . . . Bruce Coville

You have produced many audiobooks based on fantasy stories. What challenges and rewards do you find in focusing on fantasy?

When I began producing audiobooks, it seemed natural to focus on fantasy, since that was what I wrote, and also the bulk of what I read. But as it turns out, there are numerous reasons why fantasy works particularly well on audio—especially in the full cast form that I produce in, where we use a separate actor for each major character.

To begin with, fantasy grows out of the oral tradition. The roots of most fantasy novels can be found in myth, legend, and folklore—all things that were originally meant to be heard. Whether consciously or not, I think this has an effect on the writing of fantasy. Good fantasy, especially good children's fantasy, is just plain fun to listen to. It's also fun to read aloud, since the characters tend to be large (sometimes larger than life), vividly realized, and vocally interesting. So we usually have a great time in the studio!

Of course, this also represents a challenge. What, for example, does a dragon sound like? The recording is made or lost in the casting process, and over the years I have had to find actors to play everything from bunnies to dragons, with stops along the way for an effete Phoenix, a cranky toad, numerous wicked witches, a pair of talking rats, a gang of mice, and several gods from

the Greek and Norse pantheons. The actors love this—it gives them a chance to go places more realistic fiction doesn't allow for. But it does mean we spend a lot of time trying to work out how each of these creatures should sound!

One of the real joys of this form is that it allows us to bring a book to life for the child listener in a way that still leaves room for imaginative participation. Unlike film and television, where the images are set and finished, with audio the child has to engage, and create the images in his or her head. Film and television do all the work for you, and can dull the imagination. Audiobooks engage and stimulate it.

After all, no matter how good special effects become, nothing will ever beat the dragon you create in your own imagination!

Bruce Coville is the author of 90 books for children and young adults, including the international bestseller *My Teacher Is an Alien*, and the wildly popular *Unicorn Chronicles* series. He has been, at various times, a teacher, a toymaker, a magazine editor, a gravedigger, and a cookware salesman. He is also the founder of *Full Cast Audio*, an audiobook publishing company devoted to producing full cast, unabridged recordings of material for family listening. Mr. Coville lives in Syracuse, New York, with his wife, illustrator Katherine Coville.

Other Notable Writers of Modern Fantasy

There is no way to include every noteworthy author in a section on major authors and illustrators of modern fantasy. Some noted writers of fantasy are discussed in other chapters. For example, picture book creators Maurice Sendak, William Steig, and Chris Van Allsburg are featured in Chapter 3, and Laurence Yep and Virginia Hamilton are included in Chapter 4. Other writers of fantasy who are very popular include Lois Duncan, Ursula Le Guin, Anne McCaffrey, Tom McGowen, Garth Nix, Tamora Pierce, Meredith Ann Pierce, and Scott Westerfield, but much of their work is intended for and read predominantly by young adults.

Ask *the* Author . . . Jane Yolen

What do you say to those who criticize your choice to write and publish fantasy books for children?

I think that fantasy books speak to reality heart to heart. They are metaphoric shorthand. No one reading them—children or adults—is fooled into believing them word for word; that is, the reader does not believe in the actuality of dragons, unicorns, flying horses. But these stories are like points on a map, acting as a guide to life as we actually live it by showing us life as it could be lived.

For those folks who are afraid of fantasy books, seeing Satan where none exists, I tell them that they do not understand the role of metaphor in literature. But if they persist in seeing devils and the hand of hell in these stories, I cannot change their minds. And I do not try to.

What I look for in fantasy books is a strong story line, a character who changes and grows, and wonderful chewy prose. I am not interested in generic sword and sorcery, but in invention, imagination, and a prose style that sings. I have read a lot of fantasy novels in my life. So I want to be surprised, delighted, and have the little hairs on the back of my neck stand up with recognition, just as I do when I read a poem by Emily Dickinson. A fantasy book should force me to confront my real world with the imagined world.

Jane Yolen, who has been referred to as "America's Hans Christian Andersen" and the "Twentieth-Century Aesop" because of her many fairy tales and fantasy stories, is the author of over 170 books for children and adults. Her professional book *Touch Magic: Fantasy, Faerie and Folklore in the Literature of Childhood* (2000) is considered a classic reference in the field.

TECHNOLOGY in PRACTICE 8.1

The making of fantasy epics into feature-length movies has been a popular move in recent years. We have seen the Tolkien "Lord of the Rings" cycle made on a grand scale and to much fanfare. The Harry Potter books have been turned into films of enormous popularity. Even single titles like Diana Wynne Jones's *Howl's Moving Castle* is being made into a Japanese *anime* by Studio Ghibli. But what does all of this mean for the books from which these movies originate? Some argue that the movies inspire viewers to seek out the original book. They go so far as to say that movies give a context to better understand the books, many of which are several hundred pages long and quite complex. Some say movies give people the incentive to read books and they are never disappointed, unlike people who read the book first and then compare it with what was cut out or changed in the film.

Yet in an interview found on the Internet <http://www.ursulakleguin.com/Index-EarthseaMiniseries .html>, award-winning author Ursula Le Guin describes what happened to her books when they were translated into a television miniseries. The 2004 interview is entitled, "A Whitewashed Earthsea: How the Sci Fi Channel Wrecked My Books." In it, she describes how she had a contract that gave her the role of "consultant" but that, in fact, she had no say in the studio's interpretation of the books and creation of the production. In particular, she takes issue with the fact that she creates her characters as people of color in a "conscious and deliberate" decision, and that race is essential to her desire to be inclusive of people who are underrepresented in fantasy literature. Over the years, she has protested when publishers claimed that book covers featuring non-white characters "won't sell." With increasing clout, she has been able to make her statement. Yet in the film version of the book, the characters are cast as white.

This is but one difference between films and books. What are the many ways that teachers and librarians need to consider when scaffolding the discussion of students making a comparison between original books of fantasy and science fiction and their film counterparts? Written text and audio books?

TOP SHELF 8.2

POPULAR FANTASY SERIES FOR YOUNGER READERS

Artemis Fowl by Eoin Colfer

A Series of Unfortunate Events by Lemony Snicket

Spiderwick Chronicles by Tony DiTerlizzi and Holly Black

Heroes of Olympus; Percy Jackson by Rick Riordan

The Evolution of Science Fiction

The first work of science fiction may have been English author Mary Wollstonecraft Shelley's bestseller *Frankenstein*, published in 1811. This novel used medical science as the point of departure from reality and anticipated by over a century and a half the possibility of inventing new life forms and of transplanting organs.

In the mid-nineteenth century, the Frenchman Jules Verne was inspired by rapidly advancing technology to publish works of science fiction. Some of his stories anticipated later inventions. The submarine was featured in the 1869 novel *Twenty Thousand Leagues under the Sea*, and rocket travel was part of the 1865 book *From the Earth to the Moon*.

At about the same time, pulp magazines started publishing stories with science fiction themes. The term "science fiction" was coined by Hugo Gernsback, who created the magazine *Amazing Stories* in 1926; Gernsback later published Science Wonder Stories. Many notable science fiction writers got their start in those pages, including Edgar Rice Burroughs, Isaac Asimov, and Robert A. Heinlein.

Both Heinlein and Asimov owe the early nurturing of their careers to *Amazing Stories* editor John W. Campbell, who later began the magazine *Astounding Science Fiction*, helping launch the careers of many science fiction writers of the time. Robert Heinlein is credited with transforming the way science fiction stories are told. Rather than relying on pure fantasy, he researched contemporary scientific discoveries and made careful extrapolations on which he based the plots of his novels and short stories. Heinlein's 1947 book *Rocket Ship Galileo* and the twelve junior novels that were published in the succeeding years are considered to be the first children's science fiction published in the United States. Asimov's carefully researched writing allows readers—children and adults alike—to gain clear understandings of scientific and technical concepts.

Isaac Asimov coined the term "robotics" in his prolific writings about robots. He formally outlined the "Three Laws of Robotics" that have guided the way in which robots have been portrayed in science fiction ever since. With his wife, he coauthored a series about Norby, a robot.

Women often had to overcome gender bias in being accepted as writers of science fiction. Andre Norton, a pseudonym used by Alice Mary Norton, is actually a combination of two other pseudonyms that she also used: Andrew North and Allen Weston. Her use of pseudonyms arose from her conviction that masculine names would give her works credibility with male readers. At the start of her writing career in the 1930s, Norton had to convince publishers—who believed that girls would not read science fiction and that boys would not read about female protagonists in a science fiction story—to accept her work. Author of over a hundred books, often about interplanetary adventures, Norton was first published at the age of twenty and was eventually awarded the Nebula Grand Master Award for lifetime achievement in science fiction.

In 1957, the Soviet Union launched Sputnik, the first satellite, and spurred not only the U.S. space initiative but also a competition among authors to provide children with imaginative stories set in outer space. Several authors wrote "space fantasies" in the 1950s. Ellen MacGregor wrote the *Miss Pickerell* series. Jay Williams wrote a series of space fantasy stories such as *Danny Dunn and the Anti-Gravity Paint*. Louis Slobodkin's *The Space Ship under the Apple Tree*, published in 1952, was followed ten years later by *The Three-Seated Space Ship: The Latest Model of the Space Ship under the Apple Tree*. Although the limited amount of scientific information in these books is accurate, the premises of the stories are based on imagination.

In the 1960s, the movie *2001: A Space Odyssey* and the television series "Star Trek" enlarged the audience of young devotees of space fiction. In 1969 came the actual landing on the moon by manned spacecraft—a true space adventure; and in the following decade, a few well-made movies, especially *Star Wars* and *E.T.*, continued to enhance the popularity of science fiction.

In 1963, Madeleine L'Engle's *A Wrinkle in Time* was the first science fiction book to be named a winner of the Newbery Medal. Along with the prestige of the award came the recognition that science fiction had a wider readership among children than in years past.

Today, serious themes abound in science fiction for young people. Many authors of science fiction say that they choose to write in this genre because other-world settings help readers to explore serious questions about their own world from a more distant perspective and thus with clearer vision. Madeleine L'Engle, for example, explores ethical and theological questions in her books; Bernard Beckett examines questions of philosophy as well as morality. Good science fiction is entertaining, addictive, and inevitably thought provoking.

Categories of Science Fiction

Some would prefer the plural term "science fictions" for this genre of literature, for the many works labeled science fiction provide very different reading experiences. It is also interesting to note that this is one of the genres in which there is much crossover reading: adults read young adult science fiction, and older children and teens read adult science fiction.

Projecting Scientific Principles

One kind of science fiction takes one or more principles known to science, extrapolates what the principles might lead to, and plays the possibilities out in a narrative, often in an everyday setting not unlike the real world. Peter Dickinson's *Eva* is an example of a book in which a scientific principle is explored in a story about a possible future. After an accident, a young girl's body is destroyed, but her brain survives and is transplanted into a chimpanzee's body. The story probes who Eva will be: the human Eva in a chimpanzee's body or the chimpanzee Kelly with a human mind? How will she live: as a human or as a chimpanzee? *Eva* is a gripping work that questions human feelings of superiority to animals.

Utopian and Dystopian Societies

Societies different from the one we live in have been explored in adult literature for thousands of years. The biblical Eden was one of several detailed versions of an ideal society, or utopia; others were Plato's *Republic* (in the fourth century B.C.E.) and St. Augustine's *The City of God* (in the fourth century C.E.). Dante's *Inferno* (written between 1307 and 1321), a detailed account of what hell is like, provided an early example of a dystopia, a terrible place to live.

In John Christopher's *Tripod* trilogy, the Earth is conquered by alien Tripods, who cap humans' heads, thereby controlling and enslaving them by making them docile. Henry, Beanpole, and Will embark on a perilous journey to free the humans and rescue the Earth from destruction; they will later intercede in the interplanetary war between the Tripods and the Masters. **When the Tripods Came**, about aliens landing on Earth, is the prequel to the Tripod trilogy.

The Ear, the Eye and the Arm by Nancy Farmer explores a futuristic society in Zimbabwe. What might appear initially to be utopian—a highly efficient, technologically managed society—soon shows its dystopian side as readers are introduced to the vlei people, who live in what was a city dump. Likewise, what appears to be a utopia at the beginning of Lois Lowry's *The Giver* is a supposedly ideal society where people are free from all hardship, but also lack freedom of choice. The revealed dystopia highlights the negative implications of social planning. Lowry's book makes readers stop to consider whether an ideal society is possible—or desirable.

Rodman Philbrick's *The Last Book in the Universe* has what appear to be utopian and dystopian societies; it is an action-packed story where gangs rule a futuristic society after Earth has been nearly ruined by "The Big Shake." While people are ruining their minds by injecting themselves with probes that allow them to imagine a better world, there is a secret place called Eden where only humans who have been genetically perfected are allowed to live. Spaz ventures into dangerous territory to see a dying foster sister and is joined by Ryter, an old man who owns the last book in the universe, an orphan called Little Face who seeks a family, and a genetically perfected "proov" named Lanaya. This fast-paced story carefully balances chilling moments with heartwarming ones of hope.

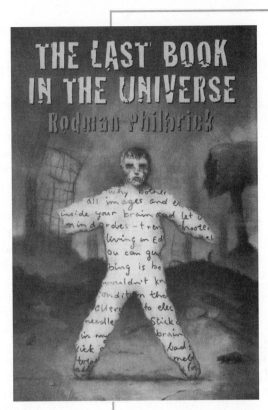

ILLUSTRATION 8.6 In a fast-paced, futuristic world after the ruin of Earth as we know it, survivors seek to build and hold on to relationships. (Scholastic, Inc.)

Surviving Environmental Catastrophes

Some science fiction deals with survival in the future, following some kind of environmental catastrophe. This catastrophe could be a nuclear holocaust, pollution, overcrowding, or destruction of other aspects of the Earth's environment.

Phoenix Rising by Karen Hesse seems to be a work of science fiction that deals with the issue of survival following an accident at a nuclear power plant. Nyle's life on a Vermont sheep farm changes as she and others in her family and community attempt to survive the effects of the fallout. She must learn to deal with contamination, illnesses, and death. However, even though something as extreme as what is described in *Phoenix Rising* has not occurred, it is possible—and, in fact, was based on the author's response to the Chernobyl incident. This book represents a fine line between realistic fiction and science fiction, but because the theme and issues are more relevant to those found in other books about surviving environmental catastrophes, *Phoenix Rising* is best discussed here.

Science Fantasies

Books that include extrapolations of scientific understandings but are based predominantly on imagination are classified as science fantasy. What some have previously called space fantasy—books about space travel, interplanetary exploration, alien visitors—are also included in this category. In *Company's Coming*, Arthur Yorinks writes about a spaceship whose alien passengers are invited for dinner. (James) Edward Marshall's extraterrestrial creature in *Space Case* is mistaken for a Halloween trick-or-treater. Paula Danziger's *This Place Has No Atmosphere* is a humorous story about a family's move from the Earth to the Moon in the twenty-first century.

William Sleator's *Interstellar Pig* is another example of science fantasy. Barney, the hero of Sleator's book, gradually discovers that his new neighbors in an isolated Cape Cod beach setting are shape-shifting aliens, involved in a deadly game of keep-away that has been going on for over a century. As the tale of the aliens' game unfolds, readers are led to imagine the many possible consequences of contact between humans and creatures who have a far greater variety of body forms, a larger territorial range, and more complex relationships to time.

How Science Fiction Works

One of the questions readers ask themselves when they encounter a new book is what genre it belongs to. Some works of science fiction identify their genre right away. For example, because Monica Hughes's *The Keeper of the Isis Light* occurs on a remote planet, readers know from the beginning that they are reading science fiction. Other works plant ambiguous clues. William Sleator's *The Boy Who Reversed Himself* raises readers' curiosity when the protagonist creates mirror writing, but they don't discover until further into the book that, through some scientific process, the boy has reversed himself and can go into the fourth dimension. Like other works from Sleator, this book gives readers an extra taste of suspense before the genre is made clear, making them wonder not only about the explanations behind events but also about the kind of reality those explanations belong to: Is it the logic of daily life or the more imaginative realm of fantasy or science fiction?

It is easy for an author of science fiction to get caught up in the adventure of the plot or the setting and give insufficient thought to developing the characters. The best works of science fiction, then, are those that draw believable characters—with complex but understandable feelings and perceptions—even when those characters are members of some invented species. Good science fiction makes its premises plausible: There is a logic to the setting, the characters, and the situation that is accessible to young readers so that they can "think their way around" in the work just as they could in any other sort of fiction. Finally, good science fiction does not merely dazzle the reader with bizarre details, but instead plants clues and invites the reader to guess and predict what is happening or what will happen.

Once a work has opened up the possibility of the fantastic—scientific or otherwise—readers interpret events in the work within that realm of possibility and even reconstruct the parts of the work they read earlier in light of fantastic explanations. But even fantasy or science fiction is based on reality. Readers must have some points of identification with a work—something they find familiar and understandable—or they are not likely to be able to comprehend what they read.

ISSUE *to* CONSIDER

Can Reading Fantasy Be Inappropriate for Children?

Fantasy literature has often been the subject of controversy. Some adults do not consider children capable of distinguishing between reality and fantasy, even though school curricula often state (and psychological studies hold) that children in the primary grades should be able to make that distinction. Others worry that fantasy is a genre that allows an escape from reality and that reading works of fantasy takes time away from more important kinds of reading that children need to be doing. Still others complain that fantasy literature is inappropriate for children because it refers to the supernatural.

In recent years, parents and others in some communities have opposed the reading of fantasy literature in schools and have called for censorship of certain types of books. In his experiences with such groups, school administrator Rick

Traw (1996) found that the presence of magic, witchcraft, and animism caused the most concern. Traw found that even the slightest hint of the supernatural caused a book to appear on the list of censored materials. For example, a reference to Halloween or a story about a city witch and a country witch might get the work into trouble.

Michael Tunnell (1994) writes about fantasy and censorship as the "double-edged sword." He believes that "fantasy is fundamentally the most important kind of story to share with [children]." He also believes that "children vicariously vent frustrations in healthy ways by subconsciously identifying with . . . heroes." In addition, Tunnell believes that fantasy gives children "a sense of hope about their ultimate abilities to succeed in the world."
What do you think?

Understanding the remote and strange in terms of the familiar is a challenge that readers face not only in science fiction, but also to some degree in all literature. Authors often begin with familiar details and lead readers gradually into the unfamiliar.

Science fiction plays on the wonderful human capacity to project from real experiences to otherworldly ones. At its best, it allows us to touch the stars from our own living rooms.

Criteria for Evaluating Science Fiction

- Is the story well written according to literary standards outlined in Chapter 2?
- Has the author made clear how the characters feel about their world and their dilemmas?
- Are there clear plot threads for the reader to follow in the invented world?
- Are there familiar guideposts that serve as jumping-off places from reality to imagination for the reader?
- Does the author allow the reader to feel a sense of delight (even if it is tinged with fear and suspense) that encourages him or her to continue reading about an imaginary place?

Major Creators of Science Fiction

AUTHOR	MAJOR WORKS INCLUDE:
Suzanne Collins	*Hunger Games* series
Peter Dickinson	*The Changes* trilogy
Jeanne DuPrau	*The Books of Ember* series
Margaret Peterson Haddix	*The Shadow Children* series
Madeleine L'Engle	*A Wrinkle in Time* trilogy, *A Ring of Endless Light*
Kenneth Oppel	*Silverwing Saga*
Susan Beth Pfeffer	*Life as We Knew It* series
William Sleator	*Interstellar Pig, Strange Attractors*

EXPERIENCES FOR FURTHER LEARNING

1. Fantasy books have often been censored as dangerous and inappropriate reading material for children. Others regard fantasy books as frivolous when there is so much for children to learn through their reading. As the popularity of books such as those in the *Harry Potter* series grows, the objections also increase. Consider these objections, and try to identify through popular media the reasoning behind them. If you encountered parents who objected to their children's reading fantasy in school, how might you respond? Research the plan that a local school district has for parents and local citizens to file complaints on books. Discuss how you would go about finding out the information you would need to respond to such complaints.

2. Select a book with personified animals. Think about the author's choice of particular animals to represent certain personality traits. Which animal traits do you find that

are carried over to a particular animal character in personified animal stories? Now find a picture book that has human characters in it. If you were to select an animal to represent each character, what would you select, and why?

3. A recurring statement made by female authors of fantasy and science fiction is that their publishers have asked them to adopt a male pseudonym to mask their gender. The belief that "boys won't want to read fantasy/science fiction by female writers" prevails even today, as the extraordinarily popular author of the *Harry Potter* series was asked to use the initials "J. K." instead of the name under which she submitted her manuscript, Joanne Rowling. How does this belief in the male gender appeal of this genre play out in classrooms filled predominantly with female teachers and school librarians?

RECOMMENDED BOOKS: FANTASY

* indicates a picture book; I indicates interest level (P = preschool, YA = young adult)

Personified Animals

Avi. *Poppy*. Illustrated by Brian Floca. Orchard, 1995. Poppy the deer mouse tries to convince her family to move closer to a large cornfield that could provide plentiful food. The frightening king of the forest, a great horned owl, denies them permission to make the move. First in a series. (I: 9–12)

Bond, Michael. *A Bear Called Paddington*. Illustrated by Peggy Fortnum. Houghton Mifflin, 1960. This is the first of a series of more than twenty books about the adventures of a bear found at Paddington train station and adopted by the Brown family. (I: 5–8)

Cleary, Beverly. *The Mouse and the Motorcycle*. Illustrated by Louis Darling. Morrow, 1965. A boy named Keith shows Ralph, a mouse, how to ride a toy motorcycle. First in a series. (I: 7–9)

DiCamillo, Kate. *The Tale of Despereaux: Being the Story of a Mouse, a Princess, Some Soup, and a Spool of Thread*. Illustrated by Timothy B. Ering. Candlewick Press, 2003. A mouse named Despereaux falls in love with the human Princess Pea and is banished to the dungeon by the other mice for his unmouse-like behavior. Good overcomes evil while hope and forgiveness persevere in this story. (I: 9–12)

Grahame, Kenneth. *The Wind in the Willows*. Illustrated by E. H. Shepard. Scribner's, 1908/1933. Rat, Mole, Badger, and Toad of Toad Hall, a group of loyal friends with very distinct personalities, enjoy various adventures in the outdoors. (I: 7–11)

*Henkes, Kevin. *Chester's Way*. Greenwillow, 1988. Chester and Wilson are very particular about how things are done. One day, Lilly moves into the neighborhood, and she is full of surprises. (I: P–8)

*_____. *Sheila Rae, the Brave*. Greenwillow, 1987. Sheila Rae is quite proud of how brave she is, but when she gets lost, she discovers she is not as fearless as she thought. (I: P–8)

Howe, James, and Deborah Howe. *Bunnicula*. Illustrated by Leslie Morrill. Atheneum, 1979. In this humorous fantasy, two family pets believe the newest arrival, a rabbit, is actually a vampire bunny. First in a series. (I: 8–10)

King-Smith, Dick. *Babe: The Gallant Pig*. Illustrated by Mary Rayner. Crown, 1985. This story is about a barnyard community and how Babe, a pig, learns to be a champion sheepherder. (I: 8–11)

Oppel, Kenneth. *Silverwing*. Simon & Schuster, 1997. Shade, the runt of the Silverwing bat colony, is separated from the others during a storm and must rejoin them on their dangerous migration South. First in a series. (I: 10 and up)

*Potter, Beatrix. *The Tale of Peter Rabbit*. Warne, 1902. This is the classic story of a rabbit who finds himself in trouble when he gets caught sneaking into Mr. McGregor's garden. First of many. (I: P–7)

Rylant, Cynthia. *Gooseberry Park*. Illustrated by Arthur Howard. Harcourt, 1995. A Labrador retriever, a hermit crab, and a bat must work together to come to the aid of their friend, a squirrel, who has become separated from her babies during an ice storm. (I: 7–10)

Voigt, Cynthia. *Young Fredle*. Illustrated by Louise Yates. Knopf, 2011. Mice communities in kitchens, cellars, and fields live and survive differently, and Young Fredle must learn to find his way in the world. (I: 7–10)

White, E. B. *Charlotte's Web*. Illustrated by Garth Williams. Harper & Row, 1952. A runt pig named Wilbur is saved by Fern, who wants to show him at the fair. Meanwhile, Charlotte the spider enlists the barnyard animals in a campaign to keep Wilbur alive. (I: 7–11)

Personified Toys

Collodi, Carlo. *The Adventures of Pinocchio*. Translated by M. L. Rosenthal. Illustrated by Troy Howell. Lothrop, Lee & Shepard, 1881/1983. This classic story is about a wooden puppet named Pinocchio whose creator is lonely and longs for company. When Pinocchio comes alive, his naïveté lands him in an adventure that forces him to learn about truthfulness. (I: 9–12)

DiCamillo, Kate. *The Miraculous Journey of Edward Tulane*. Illustrated by Bagram Ibatoulline. Candlewick, 2006. A vain and heartless china rabbit doll ends up on a journey that tears at his physical beauty but builds his emotional heart. (I: 8–12)

Godden, Rumer. *The Doll's House*. Illustrated by Tasha Tudor. Penguin, 1947/1976. The arrival of a new doll upsets the resident dolls of a Victorian dollhouse. (I: 7–10)

Martin, Ann M., and Laura Godwin. *The Doll People*. Hyperion, 2000. Anabelle, a doll, is determined to solve the mystery of her Aunt Sarah, who has been missing for nearly fifty years. The arrival of the plastic family next door provides a friend and fellow sleuth, Tiffany. The story continues in *The Meanest Doll in the World* (2003). (I: 8–12)

Milne, A. A. *Winnie-the-Pooh*. Illustrated by Ernest H. Shepard. Dutton, 1926. Christopher Robin and his friends Winnie-the-Pooh, Eeyore, Piglet, Owl, Tigger, Kanga, and Roo share many adventures in the Hundred Acre Wood. The sequel is *The House at Pooh Corner* (1928). (I: P–10)

Waugh, Sylvia. *The Mennyms*. Greenwillow, 1994. In England, a family of life-sized rag dolls have continued to live in the house of their deceased creator for forty years, but now the new homeowner intends to come for a visit. First in a series. (I: 10 and up)

*Williams, Margery. *The Velveteen Rabbit*. Illustrated by Michael Hague. Holt, 1922/1983. A well-loved toy rabbit is discarded and then transformed into a real rabbit. (I: 6–9)

Winthrop, Elizabeth. *The Castle in the Attic*. Illustrated by Donna Green. Holiday House, 1985. William receives a wooden model of a castle and discovers that the silver knight comes alive in his hands. Sir Simon leads William on an adventure in which they battle a fiery dragon and an evil wizard. The sequel is *The Battle for the Castle* (1993). (I: 9–11)

Outlandish Characters and Situations

Babbitt, Natalie. *The Search for Delicious*. Farrar, 1969. Twelve-year-old Gaylen is sent out to seek the true meaning of the word "delicious" when there is disagreement among members of the court. What he discovers is a secret plot to take over the kingdom. (I: 8–11)

Horvath, Polly. *The Pepins and Their Problems*. The Pepins are unable to solve a variety of unusual problems, so readers are asked to submit their suggestions in this humorous set of stories. (I: 8–11)

Lindgren, Astrid. *Pippi Longstocking*. Illustrated by Louis S. Glanzman. Viking, 1945/1950. Pippi Longstocking lives without adult supervision in a town in Sweden. She leads an outrageous lifestyle and keeps the neighborhood children entertained. The sequel is *Pippi in the South Seas* (1959). (I: 7–11)

Snicket, Lemony. *The Bad Beginning*. HarperCollins, 1999. This first volume in a series of books about the Baudelaire children begins with the worst news: Their parents and everything in their home have been lost in a fire. The deadpan humor of absurdly impossible events continues in a total of 13 books in this "Series of Unfortunate Events." (I: 9–12)

Travers, Pamela L. *Mary Poppins*. Illustrated by Mary Shepard. Harcourt, 1934/1962. Mary Poppins arrives with the East Wind to care for the Banks children. The nanny's unusual ways surprise and delight the children. The first in a series. (I: 7–11)

Magical Powers

Babbitt, Natalie. *Tuck Everlasting*. Farrar, 1975. Winnie discovers that the Tuck family drank from a spring that has given them eternal life. When the Tucks reveal their feelings about having eternal life, an enterprising man overhears the secret and attempts to capitalize on it by selling the water. (I: 8–12)

Coville, Bruce. *Jeremy Thatcher, Dragon Hatcher*. Harcourt, 1991. When Jeremy stumbles on Mr. Eilve's Magic Shop, a beautiful ball from the store turns out to be a dragon's egg. Many adventures follow as the dragon grows larger and larger. (I: 9–12)

Funke, Cornelia. *Inkheart*. Translated from German by Anthea Bell. Chicken House/Scholastic, 2003. When Meggie's father Mo reads aloud, some characters magically come to life. When these villains enter their real world, Meggie and Mo find themselves in the middle of the fast-paced adventure. The trilogy continues in *Inkspell* (2005) and *Inkdeath* (2008). (I: 10 and up)

_____. *The Thief Lord*. Translated from German by Oliver Latsch. Chicken House/Scholastic, 2002. A thirteen-year-old "Thief Lord" serves as a leader for a group of runaway and homeless children in Venice. (I: 10 and up)

Jones, Diana Wynne. *A Charmed Life*. Greenwillow, 1977. Witchcraft enables Gwen to trade places with a twentieth-century girl in this time-travel story. This is the first volume in a series about a young boy magician who is manipulated by his sister. (I: 11–YA)

_____. *Dark Lord of Derkholm*. Greenwillow, 1998. The story tells of a popular tourist destination, where lords and wizards role-play the parts of the dark lord and a wizard while tourists follow their fate as members of Pilgrim Parties. The sequel is *Year of the Griffin* (2000). (I: 12 and up)

Nimmo, Jennie. *Midnight for Charlie Bone*. Scholastic, 2003. When ten-year-old Charlie realizes that he can hear people talking in pictures as though he were present when the picture was taken, this is recognized as a sign that he has been bestowed with a "gift" as a half-descendant of the Red King family line. His enrollment in a school for the education of "bestowed" children leads to many adventures. First in a series. (I: 9–12)

Pierce, Tamora. *Magic Steps*. Scholastic, 2000. In this first book in the *The Circle Opens* quartet, Sandry, a young mage, discovers a boy dancing a spell and becomes his new teacher. The two team up to rid the power of invisible killers. (I: 11–YA)

———. *Sandry's Book*. Scholastic, 1997. In the *Circle of Magic* quartet, four mages-in-training practice the art of magic. (I: 11–YA)

Pratchett, Terry. *The Wee Free Men*. Harper, 2003. Nine-year-old witch-to-be Tiffany Aching defeats the Queen of Fairyland and rescues her kidnapped brother, bravely making her way through the constantly changing landscape of Fairyland, armed with a frying pan and with the aid of six-inch high Nac Mac Feegle. First in the Tiffany Aching Adventures. (I: 10–13)

*Ringgold, Faith. *Aunt Harriet's Underground Railroad in the Sky*. Crown, 1992. While flying around one day, Cassie and her brother Be Be find a train in the sky. The woman conductor is Harriet Tubman, and she leads Cassie on the Underground Railroad so that Cassie will never forget the experiences of her ancestors. (I: 6–9)

Rowling, J. K. *Harry Potter and the Sorcerer's Stone*. Scholastic, 1998. An orphaned boy discovers that he is the most famous wizard alive and begins his education at Hogwarts School of Witchcraft and Wizardry. First in the series. (I: 9–14)

Sage, Angie. *Septimus Heap: Magyk*. HarperCollins, 2005. An auspicious birth of the seventh son of a seventh son changes course as he is presumed to be born dead. This fast-paced story of magical creatures and much adventure marks the beginning of the fantasy series, *Septimus Heap*. (I: 9–12)

*Van Allsburg, Chris. *Jumanji*. Houghton Mifflin, 1981. Peter and Judy begin the jungle adventure board game of Jumanji, only to find that with each play, real parts of the jungle appear: Monkeys tear up the kitchen, rhinos stampede through the house, and a monsoon begins in the living room. (I: 6–10)

Vande Velde, Vivian. *Magic Can Be Murder*. Harcourt, 2000. Nola, a witch, tries to hide her magical abilities from authorities, but a crying spell and a murder threaten to reveal her. (I: 12–YA)

Wrede, Patricia C. *Dealing with Dragons*. Scholastic, 1990. Princess Cimorene, bored with palace life, voluntarily becomes a dragon's princess and fights wizards to keep them from interfering with the dragons as they choose their new king. First in the *Enchanted Forest Chronicles* series. (I: 12–YA)

Yep, Laurence. *Dragon of the Lost Sea*. HarperCollins, 1982. Shimmer is a dragon princess on a quest to find the lost sea that is her home. Although she dismisses the human Thorn as unable to help, she realizes that being

homeless, they have common bonds. First in a series. (I: 12–YA)

Embellished Fairy Tales

Hale, Shannon. *The Goose Girl*. Bloomsbury, 2003. When the crown princess is sent to be a bride in another kingdom, her entourage betrays her and she must rely on her gift of communicating with animals as she takes on the identity of "Goose Girl" before she can claim her rightful place. (I: 9–12)

Levine, Gail Carson. *Ella Enchanted*. HarperCollins, 1997. Ella is given the gift of obedience at the celebration of her birth, and this gift turns out to be more of a curse, as Ella cannot control her obedience. This story has an underlying Cinderella tale, but offers readers more depth and richness in this embellished book version. (I: 10 and up)

McKinley, Robin. *Rose Daughter*. Greenwillow, 1997. The author of *Beauty* (1978) once again takes up the story of Beauty and the Beast, expanding it into a full novel of her own creation. (I: 11 and up)

———. *Spindle's End*. Putnam, 2000. In this lengthy expansion of the Sleeping Beauty story, Rosie is rescued from the palace and raised by an apprentice fairy who gives her the gift of talking to animals. (I: 12 and up)

Napoli, Donna Jo. *Beast*. Atheneum, 2000. In this story set in ancient Persia, a curse changes Prince Orasmyn into a lion. He struggles to remain true to his human belief in Islamic principles as he travels from India to France, seeking redemption and love. (I: YA)

———. *Jimmy, the Pickpocket of the Palace*. Illustrated by Judith Byron Schachner. Dutton, 1995. When a princess kisses a frog, he turns into a human boy. To revert back into a frog, he must somehow obtain a ring that does not belong to him. A related title is *Prince of the Pond* (1992). (I: 9–12)

———. *Zel*. Dutton, 1996. The story of Rapunzel is explored from three perspectives: the thirteen-year-old peasant girl Zel, the nobleman who falls in love with her, and the mother who loves her daughter too much to let her go. (I: 12–YA)

Pullman, Philip. *I Was a Rat*. Knopf, 2000. Illustrated by Kevin Hawkes. A rat who had been turned into a human boy to serve as Cinderella's coachman missed his midnight curfew and must now make his way in the world of people. (I: 8–12)

Vande Velde, Vivian. *The Rumpelstiltskin Problem*. Houghton Mifflin, 2000. Six alternative versions explore the "holes" in the traditional Rumpelstiltskin tale: Why did the miller tell the king his daughter could spin straw into gold? Why did Rumpelstiltskin want a baby anyway? (I: 10–YA)

Extraordinary Worlds

Baum, L. Frank. *The Wonderful Wizard of Oz*. Oxford University. Press, 1900/1997. Dorothy is transported from her home in Kansas to the Land of Oz by way of a tornado. In her search for a way home, she meets a scarecrow who wants a brain, a tin man who wants a heart, and a lion who wants courage. To get their wishes, they must kill the Wicked Witch of the West. First in a series. (I: 9–12)

Carroll, Lewis. *Alice's Adventures in Wonderland*. Castle Books, 1865/1978. Alice follows a rabbit down a rabbit hole and finds herself in an extraordinary world. (I: 10–YA)

_____. *Through the Looking Glass and What Alice Found There*. Macmillan, 1872. When Alice steps through a mirror, she finds herself in a backwards world. (I: 11–YA)

Colfer, Eoin. *Artemis Fowl*. Hyperion, 2001. Twelve-year-old Artemis Fowl is a genius son in a family of criminals. In this high-action adventure story, he manages the impossible feat of obtaining a fairy handbook and decoding it in order to reach his goal of stealing fairy gold. First in a series. (I: 10 and up)

Collins, Suzanne. *Gregor the Overlander*. Scholastic, 2003. Eleven-year-old Gregor and his two-year-old sister fall through the laundry grate in their apartment building into "Underland," an underground world of overgrown rodents and cockroaches, and they discover that their long-missing father is being held captive. First in a series. (I: 9–12)

Dahl, Roald. *Charlie and the Chocolate Factory*. Illustrated by John Schindelman. Knopf, 1964. Charlie is one of five lucky winners who find a golden ticket that allows them to tour Willy Wonka's mysterious chocolate factory. Inside the factory are imaginative processes for creating Wonka chocolate. (I: 8–10)

_____. *James and the Giant Peach*. Knopf, 1961/1996. James's unhappy life takes a turn when the magical contents of a bag make a peach grow large enough to enter and garden insects grow large enough to be his friends. (I: 7–11)

DiTerlizzi, Tony, and Holly Black. *The Field Guide*. Simon, 2003. The five-book series of the *Spiderwick Chronicles* begins when thirteen-year-old Mallory and twin nine-year-olds Jared and Simon move into the Spiderwick Estate and enter the world of faeries and fantastic creatures. (I: 7–11)

Funke, Cornelia. *Dragon Rider*. Translated by Anthea Bell. Chicken House/Scholastic, 2004. Set in a world of dragons, brownies, and other fantastic creatures, a boy becomes the Dragon Rider of a silver dragon who derives energy from moonlight. (I: 8–12)

Gaiman, Neil. *Coraline*. HarperCollins, 2002. One day, the fourteenth door in Coraline's house leads her into an eerily "mirror" apartment—and her alternate mother and father want to keep her on *their* side of the door. (I: 11–YA)

Ibbotson, Eva. *The Secret of Platform 13*. Dutton, 1998. A doorway at a railway station in London serves as the entrance to a magical island kingdom where fantastical creatures like mermaids and ogres live. This doorway is open for only nine days every nine years, and the infant heir to the kingdom is kidnapped. (I: 10 and up)

_____. *Island of the Aunts*. Illustrated by Kevin Hawkes. Dutton, 2000. Sisters who find they need help caring for an island full of magical and unusual creatures decide they must kidnap three children who can help them out. (I: 8–11)

Juster, Norton. *The Phantom Tollbooth*. Illustrated by Jules Feiffer. Random House, 1961. Milo thinks that learning is a waste of time and there's never anything to do. Entering a tollbooth, he finds himself in the Kingdom of Wisdom, where he learns to seek Rhyme and Reason and not to jump to Conclusions; Tock teaches Milo not to waste time. (I: 9–11)

McGraw, Eloise. *The Moorchild*. Simon & Schuster, 1996. Saaski is a child of the "folk," who live in a secret world along the moor, but travel invisibly within the human world. When she is traded by the folk for a human child, she grows up realizing that she is not human like her "parents," yet not fully folk either. (I: 10–14)

Norton, Mary. *The Borrowers*. Illustrated by Beth and Joe Krush. Harcourt, 1953. Pod, Homily, and Arietty Clock are a family of little people who "borrow" everyday items from a human family and use them in ways that suit people their size. When Arietty befriends a human boy, the family fears for their safety. First in a series. (I: 8–11)

Pratchett, Terry. *Nation*. HarperCollins, 2008. Two young teens of vastly different backgrounds must figure out how to live in a world that has been completely changed by a destructive tsunami. When other survivors start arriving and looking up to them for answers, they must put aside what they knew about how the world should work and create new ways of understanding how to live. (I: 13–YA)

*Tan, Shaun. *The Arrival*. Scholastic, 2008. (Australia). This beautifully designed book wordlessly explores what it means to be an immigrant in a new land, at times, depicting the setting as if it is an alien world. (I: 9–12).

*_____. *The Lost Thing*. Scholastic, 2011 as part of *Lost and Found: Three* by Shaun Tan. A lost creature is helped in locating where it belongs, but the world is completely alien to it. (I: 7–9)

*Wiesner, David. *Flotsam*. Clarion, 2006. When a camera washes up on a beach, a young boy develops the film inside and discovers mysterious and surprising images suggesting a world unlike what we know exists. What will he make of these images, and who will be the next in imagining the stories? (I: 6–12)

Supernatural Elements

Almond, David. *Skellig*. Delacorte, 1999. Michael's life is uncertain: His parents are occupied with his baby sister's fight for life, and his family has just moved to a new home. He discovers a "Skellig" in the rundown garage and, with the help of a new friend, must decide how to help the Skellig stay alive. (I: 10–14)

Billingsley, Franny. *The Folk Keeper*. Simon & Schuster, 1989. Based on Selkie lore, this is the story of Corinna, who hides her identity to take the job of the Folk Keeper—risking her own safety and well-being to keep the Folk that live underground from doing harm to the world. Her truest identity is revealed through unexpected events, described in journal entry format. (I: 10–14)

Gaiman, Neil. *The Graveyard Book*. HarperCollins, 2008. An orphan named Nobody is raised by the ghosts who inhabit a cemetery when his own family is killed in a triple murder at the start of the story. (I: 9–12)

Hahn, Mary Downing. *Wait till Helen Comes*. Clarion, 1986. Helen is a ghost from the nineteenth century who is trying to convince another child to drown in the same lake that she did so they can be playmates. (I: 8–12)

Hunter, Mollie. *The Kelpie's Pearls*. Blackie & Son, 1964. An aging loner becomes friendly with a kelpie, whose gift of pearls sets off a series of troublesome events. (I: 9–12)

_____. *A Stranger Came Ashore: A Story of Suspense*. HarperTrophy, 1975/1994. In a suspenseful story based on Selkie lore, twelve-year-old Robbie suspects that the stranger who came ashore during a terrible storm and was befriended by his family is an evil Selkie. (I: 9–12)

Kindl, Patrice. *Owl in Love*. Houghton, 1993. Fourteen-year-old Owl is a "were-owl"—a girl by day, facing the challenges of a schoolgirl crush on a teacher and being an owl by night. (I: 10–13)

Peck, Richard. *The Ghost Belonged to Me*. Viking, 1975. Richard tries to solve the mystery of a missing girl and ends up unwillingly receiving the assistance of Blossom Culp, his nemesis. First in a series. (I: 10–YA)

Time Slips

Boston, L. M. *The Children of Green Knowe*. Illustrated by Peter Boston. Harcourt, 1989. A lonely boy moves to his grandmother's old English house, only to find that various children who played in the house over the years reappear to be his playmates. First in a series. (I: 9–11)

Cooper, Susan. *King of Shadows*. McElderry, 1999. When Nat Fielding plays the role of Puck in *A Midsummer Night's Dream*'s in the newly reconstructed Globe Theatre, he finds himself transported four hundred years back to play the same role, with Will Shakespeare as Oberon. (I: 12–YA)

Fleischman, Sid. *The 13th Floor: A Ghost Story*. Illustrated by Peter Sís. Greenwillow, 1995. Buddy Stebbins steps off an elevator on the thirteenth floor of an old building and follows his sister three hundred years back in time. They end up on a pirate ship captained by one of their own ancestors. (I: 9–12)

Gutman, Dan. *Shoeless Joe and Me*. HarperCollins, 2002. In one of the *Baseball Card Adventure* series, Stosh travels back to 1919 and attempts to stop Shoeless Joe from throwing the World Series and being expelled from baseball for life. (I: 8–11)

Hoffman, Mary. *Stravaganza: The City of Masks*. Bloomsbury, 2002. In this time-slip story in modern-day England/sixteenth-century Venice, a boy undergoing cancer treatment finds that he can travel every night to Venice and lead an exciting, cancer-free life of adventure there. The sequel is *The City of Stars*. (I: 10–YA)

McKay, Hilary. *The Amber Cat*. Simon & Schuster, 1997. In this time-slip ghost story, as Robin recovers from chickenpox, he and his friends are fascinated by his mother's stories of a mysterious girl who used to appear in her childhood. First in a series. (I: 8–11)

Osborne, Mary Pope. *Magic Tree House* series. In this beginning chapter book series, siblings Jack and Annie are magically transported from their tree house where they are reading to various times and places where they learn historical, scientific, and cultural information. (I: 7–9)

Park, Linda Sue. *Archer's Quest*. Clarion, 2006. When a king of ancient Korea suddenly appears in twelve-year-old Kevin's room, he must figure out a way to help return the king to his own time and place. (I: 10–12)

Pearce, Philippa. *Tom's Midnight Garden*. Illustrated by Susan Einzig. Harper, 1984. Tom is bored with his summer until he finds that he can visit a garden that appears only when the grandfather clock strikes thirteen every night. There, he develops a special friendship with a mysterious girl named Hatty. (I: 10–12)

Scieszka, Jon. *Knights of the Kitchen Table*. Illustrated by Lane Smith. Viking, 1991. Joe, Fred, and Sam, the Time Warp Trio, travel back to the days of King Arthur when they open "The Book" that a magician uncle sent Joe for a birthday present. First in a series. (I: 8–11)

Stead, Rebecca. *When You Reach Me*. Wendy Lamb Books/Random House, 2009. Set in 1970s New York City, a note begins a mysterious story of time slip with allusions to Madeleine L'Engle's *A Wrinkle in Time*. (I: 10–YA)

Wiseman, David. *Jeremy Visick*. Houghton Mifflin, 1981. A contemporary Cornish boy goes back in time to try to discover the location of a boy named Jeremy, who was lost in a mine accident in 1852. (I: 10–12)

Yolen, Jane. *The Devil's Arithmetic*. Viking, 1988. Hannah finds herself transported as Chaya back to the days of the Holocaust. Through the device of time travel, she grows in her understanding of her Jewish heritage. (I: 9–12)

High Fantasy

Alexander, Lloyd. *The Arkadians*. Dutton, 1995. An unlikely cast of unusual characters each tell a story filled with elements of magic and Greek mythology. Their companionship is based on bravery, loyalty, compassion, and love. (I: 11–13)

_____. *The Book of Three*. Holt, 1964/1999. *The Chronicles of Prydain* series tells of the struggle between the people of Prydain and the Lord of the Land of Death. (I: 10–13)

_____. *The Remarkable Journey of Prince Jen*. Dutton, 1991. In this coming-of-age story set in China during the Tang Dynasty, the brave Prince Jen embarks on a dangerous journey, bearing six unusual gifts. (I: 10–13)

Barron, T. A. *The Lost Years of Merlin*. Philomel, 1996. Merlin as a young boy searches for his identity. He has lost his memory and doesn't trust that the woman he is with is really his mother. His journey to discover his past introduces the reader to how Merlin gained magical sight and became a wizard. First in a series. (I: 11–YA)

Cooper, Susan. *Over Sea, Under Stone*. Illustrated by Alan E. Cover. Atheneum, 1965. A search for King Arthur's grail begins this story of fighting evil and protecting Light. First in a series. (I: 10–13)

Divakaruni, Chitra Banerjee. *The Conch Bearer*. Roaring Brook, 2003. Twelve-year-old Anan's quest begins in modern day Calcutta and takes him on a dangerous journey through the Himalayas with his companion,

Nisha, to return a magical conch to its rightful place. Book II of the *Brotherhood of the Conch: The Mirror of Fire and Dreaming* (2005). (I: 10–13)

Farmer, Nancy. *The Sea of Trolls.* Atheneum/Richard Jackson, 2004. In this epic adventure with roots based in Norse mythology, a bard's apprentice, Jack, and his little sister are kidnapped by Viking "berserkers" and he is sent on a quest across the dangerous Sea of Trolls to try and reverse a spell gone awry (I: 11–YA)

Jacques, Brian. *Redwall.* Philomel, 1987. Matthias leads the mice in protecting Redwall Abbey from Cluny the Scourge and the rats. First in a series. (I: 11–13)

Jones, Diana Wynne. *The Crown of Dalemark.* Greenwillow, 1993. This final book in a quartet about the mythical kingdom of Dalemark continues the story of Mitt, who is joined by Moril and Maewen in the quest to reunite Dalemark with Adon's gifts: the ring, the sword, and the cup. (I: 12–YA)

———. *Howl's Moving Castle.* Greenwillow, 1986. When Sophie Halter is turned into an old woman by a jealous competitor, she finds refuge in the wizard Howl's mysterious moving castle. Related title: *Castle in the Air* (1990). (I: 9–12)

Le Guin, Ursula K. *A Wizard of Earthsea.* Illustrated by Ruth Robbins. Parnassus, 1968. This first book in a series describes how Ged studies wizardry, becomes a wizard, and confronts evil. (I: 13–YA)

Lewis, C. S. *The Lion, the Witch and the Wardrobe.* Illustrated by Pauline Baynes. Macmillan, 1950. Four children discover that they can go through the back of a wardrobe to enter the magical world of Narnia. There, they meet the lion Aslan, who is trying to free Narnia from the evil spell cast by the White Witch. First in a series. (I: 9–YA)

McKinley, Robin. *The Blue Sword.* Greenwillow, 1982. Princess Aerin's mysterious powers help her to slay dragons as she fights to save her kingdom. The prequel is *The Hero and the Crown* (1984). (I: 12–YA)

Pierce, Meredith Ann. *The Darkangel.* Little, Brown, 1982. This is the first book in Pierce's *Darkangel* trilogy. Other titles are *A Gathering of Gargoyles* (1984) and *The Pearl of the Soul of the World* (1990). (I: 13–YA)

Pierce, Tamora. *Wild Magic.* Atheneum, 1992. In this first book in a series called *The Immortals,* thirteen-year-old Daine faces battle with dreadful immortal creatures. (I: 12–YA)

Pullman, Philip. *The Golden Compass.* Knopf, 1998. In this first book of *His Dark Materials,* Lyra realizes that she must find a way to prevent kidnapped children from being victimized in scientific experiments. (I: 11–YA)

Sutcliff, Rosemary. *The Sword and the Circle: King Arthur and the Knights of the Round Table.* Dutton, 1981. These stories about King Arthur, Merlin, and Sir Lancelot are mostly drawn from *Le Morte d'Arthur* by Sir Thomas Malory (1485). First in a series. (I: 11–YA)

Tolkien, J. R. R. *The Fellowship of the Ring.* Houghton Mifflin, 1955/1967. This is the first part of the *Lord of the Rings* trilogy, in which Frodo Baggins inherits a magic ring from his Uncle Bilbo (hero of *The Hobbit*) and must eventually take the ring to Mount Doom, where it will be destroyed to help the good forces win against the Dark Lord. (I: 12–YA)

———. *The Hobbit.* Houghton Mifflin, 1937. Bilbo Baggins, a peaceful Hobbit, is tricked by a wizard into going on a dangerous quest to retrieve stolen dwarf treasure from a dragon. The story of Middle Earth continues in the *Lord of the Rings* trilogy. (I: 11–YA)

Yolen, Jane. *Merlin and the Dragons.* Illustrated by Li Ming. Cobblehill/Dutton, 1995. Young King Arthur has troublesome dreams and visits Merlin, from whom he hears stories of Merlin's childhood. On hearing tales of dragons, King Vortigern, and Uther Pendragon, Arthur is reassured of his right to the crown. First in a series. (I: 8–11)

RECOMMENDED BOOKS: SCIENCE FICTION

Projecting Scientific Principles

Dickinson, Peter. *Eva*. Delacorte, 1989. Following an accident, a young girl's body is destroyed, but her brain survives and is transplanted into a chimpanzee's body. As she struggles to establish her identity, will she choose to live with her human family or with the chimps? (I: 12–YA)

Etchemendy, Nancy. *The Power of UN*. Front Street/Cricket, 2000. A mysterious old man presents Gib with an "unner"—a device that allows Gib to undo mistakes by going back in time. (I: 10–12)

Heinlein, Robert. *Farmer in the Sky*. Ballantine, 1950/1990. Bill and his father leave the overpopulated Earth and settle on Ganymede, the third moon of Jupiter, seeking better resources for living. (I: 12 and up)

Sleator, William. *The Duplicate*. Dutton, 1988. At first, sixteen-year-old David delights in having a clone, Duplicate A. Just when he realizes the complications it causes, Duplicate B arrives. (I: 11 and up)

Verne, Jules. *Twenty Thousand Leagues under the Sea*. Washington Square Press, 1976. An eccentric captain successfully makes an electric submarine. (I: YA)

Utopian and Dystopian Societies

Christopher, John. *When the Tripods Came*. Dutton, 1988. The Tripods arrive on Earth and brainwash Earthlings with hypnotic caps. Part of *The White Mountains* series. (I: 10–13)

Farmer, Nancy. *The Ear, the Eye and the Arm*. Orchard, 1994. In Zimbabwe in the year 2194, three mutants—the Ear, the Eye, and the Arm—form a detective agency and are hired to find the kidnapped children of General Matsika. (I: 11–YA)

Haddix, Margaret Peterson. *Among the Hidden*. Simon, 1998. Set in a futuristic society that enforces a "two-child only" policy, additional children are kept hidden from the community until they begin to rebel against the repression and fight for their existence. First in the *The Shadow Children* series. (I: 8–12)

Heinlein, Robert. *Citizen of the Galaxy*. Macmillan, 1957/2005. A young boy is able to leave slavery to fulfill a mission and learns that there is more to the galaxy than he realized. (I: 11–13)

Hughes, Monica. *Invitation to the Game*. Simon & Schuster, 1990. Recent high school graduates, unemployed in an overpopulated world, find themselves playing a mysterious game of survival in a different world. (I: 11–YA)

_____. *The Keeper of the Isis Light*. Macmillan, 1981. Olwen lives with a robot on a barren planet until another human lands. (I: 12–YA)

Lowry, Lois. *The Giver*. Houghton Mifflin, 1999. Knowledge is controlled in a futuristic society, and Jonah must grapple with the right to make choices when he begins to receive memories. Related books include *Gathering Blue* (2000) and *Messenger* (2003). (I: 11–YA)

Philbrick, Rodman. *The Last Book in the Universe*. Blue Sky Press/Scholastic, 2000. A mission takes four unlikely companions into dangerous territory where gangs rule a post-apocalyptic future that is nearly demolished by "The Big Shake." Meanwhile, genetically perfected humans live in the utopian world of Eden. (I: 12–YA)

Surviving Environmental Catastrophes

Beckett, Bernard. *Genesis*. Houghton Mifflin, 2006. During Anaximander's day–long oral exam in hopes of entry into "The Academy," she must reveal her thoughts on human conscience, and man vs. machine. (I: 12–YA)

DuPrau, Jeanne. *City of Ember*. Random House, 2003. First in the *Books of Ember* series, an underground city built to survive nuclear holocaust is running out of power, and two teens pursue an escape plan to leave. (I: 12 and up)

O'Brien, Robert. *Z for Zachariah*. Atheneum, 1975. Ann Burden believes that she is the only person left after a nuclear holocaust, until Mr. Loomis arrives. (I: 12–YA)

Pfeffer, Susan Beth. *Life as We Knew It*. Harcourt, 2006. This compelling series begins when an asteroid hits the moon and knocks it closer to Earth, causing worldwide disasters of nature, changing how humans lead their daily lives. (I: 12 and up)

Walsh, Jill Paton. *The Green Book*. Illustrated by Lloyd Bloom. Farrar, 1982. A group of colonists try to grow food on a hostile new planet called Shine, when the dying planet of Earth can no longer sustain life. (I: 9–12)

Science Fantasies

Coville, Bruce. *My Teacher Is an Alien*. Pocket Books, 1991. A teacher comes from outer space to study the human brain, which is believed to be defective, since humans kill one another. First in a series. (I: 8–11)

Danziger, Paula. *This Place Has No Atmosphere*. Dell, 1987. Humorous story of a move to the moon by reluctant Aurora and her family. (I: 11–YA)

Etra, Jonathan, and Stephanie Spinner. *Aliens for Lunch*. Illustrated by Steve Bjorkman. Random House, 1991. In this early chapter book, aliens appear out of the microwave, and desserts are at risk in the universe. See also *Aliens for Breakfast* (1988) and *Aliens for Dinner* (1994). (I: 7–9)

Gilmore, Kate. *The Exchange Student*. Houghton Mifflin, 1999. Fen is a seven-foot alien exchange student from a planet that is suffering from ecological disasters, including the death of animal life that would have kept the insect life under control. This loss leads to Fen's extraordinary interest in Earth's animals. (I: 12 and up)

Heinlein, Robert A. *Podkayne of Mars: Her Life and Times*. Baen, 1963/1995. Podkayne "Paddy" Fries, a Martian who aspires to be the first female starship captain, jumps at the chance to accompany her uncle on a trip to Earth by way of Venus, although she believes that Earth isn't fit for habitation. (I: 12 and up)

L'Engle, Madeleine. *A Wrinkle in Time*. Farrar, 1962. Meg and Charles Wallace go to the planet Camazotz to search for their scientist father. The sequels are *A Wind in the Door* (1973) and *A Swiftly Tilting Planet* (1978). (I: 10–YA)

*Marshall, (James) Edward. *Space Case*. Dial, 1980. An extraterrestrial creature is mistaken for a Halloween trick-or-treater. (I: P–8)

Norton, Andre. *The Time Traders*. Baen, 1958/2000. In this book in the *Time Travel* series, the protagonist, Ross Murdock, is saved from going to jail. Instead, he is sent across several periods of time and finds alien spaceships in the Bronze Age. (I: 12 and up)

O'Brien, Robert C. *Mrs. Frisby and the Rats of NIMH*. Illustrated by Zena Bernstein. Atheneum, 1971. Laboratory rats who have been made superintelligent escape and help a field mouse, Mrs. Frisby, who in turn helps them get away. O'Brien's daughter, Jane Leslie Conly, has written two sequels, illustrated by Leonard Lubin: *Racso and the Rats of NIMH* (Harper, 1986) and *R-T, Margaret, and the Rats of NIMH* (Harper, 1990). (I: 10–12)

Peck, Richard. *Lost in Cyberspace*. Dial, 1995. While working on a research paper, two sixth-grade boys discover time travel through a laptop computer. The sequel is *The Great Interactive Dream Machine* (1996). (I: 10–12)

Sleator, William. *The Boy Who Reversed Himself*. Puffin, 1998. Laura discovers that Omar has created mirror writing, and that he has reversed himself and can go into the fourth dimension. When Laura, a novice in four-space, tries to go there alone, she realizes that she doesn't know how to get back. (I: 11 and up)

Smith, Clete. *Aliens on Vacation*. Illustrated by Christian Slade. Hyperion, 2011. David discovers that his grandmother maintains a bed and breakfast in which each guest is an alien visitor and that the rooms are portals maintained by his grandmother. First in a series. (I: 8–11)

———. *Interstellar Pig*. Dutton, 1984. As Barney plays a strange board game, it becomes real. (I: 11–YA)

Yolen, Jane. *Commander Toad and the Voyage Home*. Illustrated by Bruce Degen. Putnam, 1998. Commander Toad and his homesick crew aboard the Star Warts craft are heading home, but instead land on an uncharted planet. This is another volume in the easy reader series of humorous space travel stories. (I: 7–10)

RESOURCES

Asimov, Isaac. *Asimov on Science Fiction*. Doubleday, 1981.

Barron, Neil, ed. *Anatomy of Wonder 4: A Critical Guide to Science Fiction*. R. R. Bowker, 1995.

———. *What Fantastic Fiction Do I Read Next? A Reader's Guide to Recent Fantasy, Horror, and Science Fiction*. Gale Research, 1997.

Cooper, Susan. *Dreams and Wishes: Essays on Writing for Children*. McElderry, 1996.

Le Guin, Ursula K. *The Language of the Night: Essays on Fantasy and Science Fiction*, rev. ed. HarperCollins, 1992.

Lynn, Ruth Nadelman. *Fantasy Literature for Children and Young Adults: A Comprehensive Guide* (5th ed.). Libraries Unlimited, 2005.

Sullivan, C. W. III, ed. *Science Fiction for Young Readers*. Greenwood, 1993.

Tymn, Marshall B., Kenneth J. Zahorski, and Robert H. Boyer. *Fantasy Literature: A Core Collection and Reference Guide*. R. R. Bowker, 1979.

REFERENCES

Adams, Douglas. *The Hitchhiker's Guide to The Galaxy*. Harmony, 1979.

Alexander, Lloyd. "High Fantasy and Heroic Romance." *The Horn Book 47* (December 1971): 577–594.

———. "Fantasy as Images: A Literary View." *Language Arts 55* (1978): 440–446.

———. "Future Conditional." *Children's Literature Quarterly 10.4* (Winter 1986): 164.

Andersen, Hans Christian. *The Princess and the Pea*. Houghton Mifflin, 1840/1979.

Anderson, M. T. *Feed*. Candlewick, 2002.

Asimov, Isaac, David C. Yeager, and Martin H. Greenberg, eds. *Fantastic Reading: Stories and Activities for Grades 5–8*. Scott, Foresman, 1984.

Banks, Lynne Reid. *The Indian in the Cupboard*. Doubleday, 1985.

Barrie, J. M. *Peter Pan*. Charles Scribner's Sons, 1911.

Cooper, Susan. "Escaping into Ourselves." *Celebrating Children's Books: Essays on Children's Literature in Honor of Zena Sutherland*. Ed. Betsy Hearne and Marily Kaye. Lothrop, Lee & Shepard, 1981, pp. 14–23.

Dahl, Roald. *The Witches*. Illustrated by Quentin Blake. Farrar, 1983.

de Brunhoff, Jean. *Babar*. Random House, 1937.

Egoff, Sheila A. *Worlds Within: Children's Fantasy from the Middle Ages to Today*. American Library Association, 1988.

Elleman, Barbara. "Popular Reading-Time Fantasy Update." *Booklist 81.19* (1985): 1407–1408.

Frye, Northrop. *The Educated Imagination*. Indiana University Press, 1957.

Gates, Pamela S., Susan B. Steffel, and Francis J. Molson. *Fantasy Literature for Children and Young Adults*. Scarecrow Press, 2003.

Greenlaw, M. Jean. "Fantasy." *Children's Books and Their Creators*. Ed. Anita Silvey. Houghton Mifflin, 1995a.

———. "Science Fiction." *Children's Books and Their Creators*. Ed. Anita Silvey. Houghton Mifflin, 1995b.

_____. "Science Fiction: Images of the Future, Shadows of the Past." *Top of the News* 39 (1982): 64–71.

Heinlein, Robert. *Rocket Ship Galileo*. Macmillan, 1948.

Hesse, Karen. *Phoenix Rising*. Holt, 1994.

Hunter, Mollie. *Talent Is Not Enough: Mollie Hunter on Writing for Children*. Harper, 1976.

Jansson, Tove. *Finn Family Moomintroll*. Benn, 1950.

Kipling, Rudyard. *The Jungle Book*. Macmillan, 1894.

Lagerlöf, Selma. *The Wonderful Adventures of Nils*. Dover, 1906–07/1995.

Lofting, Hugh. *The Story of Doctor Dolittle*. Stokes, 1920.

MacDonald, George. *At the Back of the North Wind*. Illustrated by Charles Mozley. Penguin, 1871/1985.

MacGregor, Ellen. *Miss Pickerell Goes to Mars*. Illustrated by Paul Galdone. McGraw Hill, 1951.

Mahy, Margaret. *The Haunting*. Macmillan, 1982.

Riordan, Rick. *Percy Jackson and The Olympians series*, Hyperion. 2005–2009.

Shelley, Mary Wollstonecraft. *Frankenstein*. Dutton, 1818/1963.

Slobodkin, Louis. *The Space Ship under the Apple Tree*. Macmillan, 1952.

_____. *The Three-Seated Space Ship: The Latest Model of the Space Ship under the Apple Tree*. Macmillan, 1962.

Steig, William. *Doctor De Soto*. FSG, 1982.

Traw, Rick. "Beware! Here There Be Beasties: Responding to Fundamentalist Censors." *The New Advocate* 9.1 (1996): 35–56.

Tunnell, Michael O. "The Double-Edged Sword: Fantasy and Censorship." *Language Arts* 71 (1994): 606–612.

Verne, Jules. *From the Earth to the Moon*. Hertzel, 1865.

Wiesner, David. *The Three Pigs*. Clarion, 2001.

_____. *Tuesday*. Clarion, 1991.

Williams, Jay. *Danny Dunn and the Anti-Gravity Paint*. McGraw, 1956.

Yolen, Jane. *Touch Magic: Fantasy, Faerie and Folklore in the Literature of Childhood* (2nd ed.). August House, 2000.

Yorinks, Arthur. *Company's Coming*. Crown, 1988.

Contemporary Realistic Fiction

> ❝ *Your room's a firetrap. It will be as neat as a pin when we're done. You'll like it. You'll see."* The tone of Henry's voice seemed to say, I know everything there is to know about anything that matters. But Fanny did not like it. Her room looked empty, less comfortable, sad even. ❞

—from *Protecting Marie* by Kevin Henkes

What Is Contemporary Realistic Fiction?

All fiction bears some relation to life as we know it. Kenneth Grahame's fanciful animal story *The Wind in the Willows* tells us much about friendship. C. S. Lewis's allegorical fantasy *The Lion, the Witch and the Wardrobe* warns that youthful selfishness can lead to corruption. Nonetheless, the trappings of such books are fanciful: We wouldn't think of learning about the driving habits of toads from reading *The Wind in the Willows*, nor would we expect to find a trapdoor in the back of our closet after reading *The Lion, the Witch and the Wardrobe* (although some of us might check, just to be sure!). Realistic fiction, however, is a different story. Although the particular characters and plots are made up, the trappings of realistic novels are drawn from the world as it is.

In the above passage from *Protecting Marie*, the father tries to help clean Fanny's room, imposing his standards of neatness on his daughter; meanwhile, she struggles with her feelings on the matter. What is amazing about this passage, and many others like it, is that Henkes masterfully depicts emotions, thoughts, and behaviors that ring true to many preteen girls. This story raises many issues: a father trying to deal with his own aging and career direction, a daughter dealing with her own adolescence, relationships among family members. But the multifaceted, complex nature of this book allows it to rise above those "problem novels" that feel didactic or have a bibliotherapeutic intent. This is a book about relationships and self-identity, in which issues are explored within the context of the family.

Contemporary realistic fiction, then, brings the same moral challenges as other types of fiction. But it presents these challenges in a here-and-now setting and in a way that says, "Hey—this is happening. You or somebody near you could be going through these very experiences."

Contemporary realistic fiction is derived from actual circumstances, with realistic settings and characters who face problems and opportunities that are within the range of what is possible in real life. It differs from historical fiction in that it is set in contemporary times; the stories could take place in the world as we know it today. In addition, the events portrayed in realistic fiction raise moral questions that a reader might face in real life. Characters in realistic fiction for children usually have certain characteristics:

- They resemble real people.
- They live in a place that is or could be real.
- They participate in a plausible, if not probable, series of events.
- They are presented with a dilemma that is of interest to children.
- They discover a realistic solution.

TEACHING IDEA 9.1

REAL LIFE VERSUS FICTION

Ask students in grades 3 through 6 to record in a diary all the events that happen to them in a single day—just the facts, without embellishment. Then have them exchange diaries with a friend and write up the friend's account as if it were a chapter in a work of realistic fiction. Encourage students to embellish the story with dialogue, details about setting, and clearly described characters. Afterward, ask the students to compare the two versions. What was added to make the fictionalized version? What was left out? How did the dramatic contour (that is, the pattern of building suspense and its resolution) of the diary version compare with that of the fictionalized version? What was made clearer about the events of the day when they were fictionalized? What was distorted?

The Value of Contemporary Realistic Fiction

Of all the genres of children's literature, realistic fiction is the one that most closely approaches the reality of children's own lives. Reading realistic fiction can benefit children in several ways:

- They may come to feel that they are not alone.
- They may learn to reflect on the choices in their own lives.

- They may develop empathy for other people.
- They may see life experiences beyond their own.
- They may take a humorous, enjoyable look at life.

When child readers recognize something in a story that is similar to their own feelings or thoughts, they realize they are not alone. Realistic fiction helps readers to empathize with other people.

Realistic fiction enables readers to see beyond the limitations of their own experience. In Frances Temple's *Tonight, by Sea*, Paulie and her family are so harassed by government-backed thugs that they take their chances and escape in a small boat in an attempt to cross the ocean. That boat eventually brings Paulie to the United States. Although most young readers are unlikely to get to know any of the many thousands of real "boat people" whom they may have heard about on the news, they get to know Paulie's story. This book extends readers' knowledge of life experiences beyond their own. Realistic fiction, then, offers readers the opportunity to see themselves reflected in the literature, as well as the opportunity to encounter people with very different lifestyles.

The Evolution of Realistic Fiction

Realistic fiction has been available for children for a long time. The first title read by children that might be called realistic fiction was Daniel Defoe's *Robinson Crusoe*, published in 1719. Although written for the general reader, it became associated with children in the mid-eighteenth century, when the philosopher Jean Jacques Rousseau recommended it for children. Rousseau's recommendation coincided with a transition publishers had already begun to make—away from merely producing books for children focused on dying and repentance and toward publishing new forms of writing, including realistic fiction.

The Nineteenth Century

The first significant works of realistic fiction written expressly for children appeared in the mid-nineteenth century in England. Meanwhile, in the United States, there was a movement away from instructional and sectarian books and toward books that could be called entertaining realistic fiction. The adventure story came into being with the works of James Fenimore Cooper. His *The Last of the Mohicans*, set on the frontier of New York state and published in 1826, is considered the first American novel. Louisa May Alcott's *Little Women* appeared in 1868. Alcott's work was the first to present the dilemma facing young women: how to balance interests inside and outside of the home.

For boys, Horatio Alger published over one hundred books, beginning in 1867 with *Ragged Dick*. These books provided strong fictional images of the American dream of lowly urban heroes getting rich through determination, cleverness, and impressing powerful people. Mark Twain's *The Adventures of Tom Sawyer* and *The Adventures of Huckleberry Finn*, published in the late nineteenth century, were considered by some to be two of the best American novels of any period (but current views point to the books as representative of the negative race portrayals of the time). Both are quintessentially American novels, complete with a strong sense of place—the Mississippi River towns, issues of race, and the conflict between overpious religion and the boisterous spirits of real people.

The first of the great realistic fiction horse stories for children, Anna Sewell's *Black Beauty*, was published in 1877 and paved the way for the continuing popularity of realistic animal stories. Although *Black Beauty* is still read today, new editions have expurgated the elements of racism found in the original.

The end of the nineteenth century saw a resurgence of sentimentalism toward the child. Frances Hodgson Burnett published *Little Lord Fauntleroy* in 1886; its somewhat saccharine plot involving a good and gentle boy who loves everyone and solves everyone's problems was a runaway success. After she moved to the United States, Burnett wrote *The Secret Garden*, a book with a more believable theme of children's redemptive effects on each other. This book is still popular with children.

The Twentieth Century

At the dawn of the twentieth century, writers continued to romanticize the innocence and beauty of children. The domestic novel flourished and was epitomized by Eleanor Potter's *Pollyanna*, who gains power over difficulties by following her father's advice to face each hardship by finding something to be glad about. "Glad" clubs formed all over the United States—their members emulating Pollyanna's unquenchably optimistic view of the world.

Perhaps the most influential development in realistic fiction for children in all of the twentieth century came when Edward Stratemeyer began a "fiction factory" in 1905. Stratemeyer generated brief plot summaries and handed them to hack writers, who completed the books under fictitious names. Hundreds of series books about the Rover Boys, the Hardy Boys, Tom Swift, the Bobbsey Twins, and others were products of Stratemeyer's fertile imagination, if not his typewriter.

Stratemeyer produced thirteen hundred of his plot summaries by the time he died in 1930, and at that point, his daughter Harriet Stratemeyer Adams began churning out the Nancy Drew series under the pen name Carolyn Keene. She is said to have written three hundred titles in the series, and two hundred million copies of them had been sold by the time she died in 1982, at age 89.

The Hardy Boys and Nancy Drew books are still updated and marketed to new generations. But today, realistic fiction book series come from the Babysitters Club, Encyclopedia Brown, Marvin Redpost, Sammy Keys, and others, which crowd the shelves of bookstores and worry some teachers, parents, and librarians because of their predictability and scant literary quality.

Between the two world wars, a host of now-classic writers and illustrators began their work. Charlotte Zolotow created picture books about relationships, such as *The Hating Book* and *The Quarreling Book*, about learning to get along with others. Robert McCloskey wrote and illustrated nature stories often set in his home state of Maine for younger children and humorous ones such as *Homer Price* for older children. A large crop of still-popular realistic fiction was published for the mid-elementary school reader, such as *The Boxcar Children* by Gertrude Warner and *The Moffats* by Eleanor Estes, both of which were followed by more books about the same characters.

From New Realism to Diverse Perspectives

Until the eve of World War II, most of the protagonists in children's realistic fiction were white and middle class. Then Florence Crannell Means, herself white, wrote some books about children of color: *Shuttered Windows*, about an African American girl in an all-white school, and *The Moved Outers*, about the World War II internment of Japanese Americans. In 1945, Jesse Jasper Jackson published *Call Me Charley*, the first children's book by an African American to openly introduce the subject of racism. The character Charley was the only person of color in an all-white school.

Sexuality appeared in books for girls before the subject was addressed for boys. *Seventeenth Summer* by Maureen Daly introduced awakening sexuality and the

TEACHING IDEA 9.2

CENSORSHIP AND PROPRIETY

This chapter referred to the struggle between some adults who defend books that contain controversial material and others who want to put such books out of the reach of children. But what do children say? Ask a group of children in grades 2 through 6 what things they think should or should not be written about in the books they read. What disagreements emerge among them? How do the children think such disagreements should be resolved? Should the books be banned? Should they be made available only to those whose parents give permission for them to read them? Or should they be made available to all students, no matter what their parents think? All libraries should have a form for reconsideration of library materials for patrons who challenge their presence in the library.

teenage romance novel. The book was enormously popular through the 1960s. In the 1970s, Judy Blume's *Are You There, God? It's Me, Margaret* and *Forever* brought loud protests from censors because of their open discussion of sexuality. John Donovan's *I'll Get There, It Better Be Worth the Trip* tells of two thirteen-year-old boys, Davy and Altschuler, who suddenly find themselves facing the question of homosexuality when they exchange a kiss.

In the 1970s, the unvarnished picture of children's life that was emerging in realistic fiction was described as "New Realism" (Root, 1977). New Realism looked at the downside of life: children suffering from poverty, racism, sexism, war, economic upheavals, and parental irresponsibility. Characters often faced unsolvable problems or moral dilemmas. New Realism focused to a large degree on adolescents as a distinct social group. Writing about problems in what became known as "problem novels" became a way of describing life.

Since then, more writers of different races, nationalities, income groups, and sexual preferences have appeared on the children's book scene, writing about life as they know it. Their themes go beyond New Realism, in that differences and hardships may be background factors in works that focus on the development of character or the pursuit of a worthwhile life. Contemporary authors of the young adult novel such as Laurie Halse Anderson, M. T. Anderson, Sonya Sones, Ellen Wittlinger, and Jacqueline Woodson sympathetically depict the culture of children and adolescents and their social and personal problems, as well as the new possibilities they face. Yet as Lambert (2008) comments, there is a continued need to expand the definition and representation of the diversity of family compositions.

The broader range of topics in contemporary realistic fiction certainly expands young readers' awareness of the varieties of possible experience. But it also gives rise to disagreements between those who would shelter children from such material and those who believe that it is healthy for young people to explore difficult real-life issues in books. In this chapter, we introduce literature that portrays perspectives that reflect diversity of all kinds—not only ethnic diversity, but also diversity based on gender, religion, socioeconomic background, political affiliation, or differing

ILLUSTRATION 9.1 The third in the Breadwinner cycle of books by Deborah Ellis, Shauzia longs to leave the Afghan refugee camp and seek a new home. (Cover of "Mud City" reproduced with permission from Groundwood Books, Toronto.)

ISSUE *to* CONSIDER

Are Contemporary Books Too Realistic?

"New" or not, realism is still a dominant element in fiction for children. Truly disturbing social problems are depicted even in books that win critical acclaim. For example, of the four 1996 Newbery Honor Books, three were works of realistic fiction. Of these, one, **What Jamie Saw** (1995) by Carolyn Coman, is about child abuse; another, **Yolonda's Genius** (1995) by Carol Fenner, portrays drug abuse, racism, and obesity. The winning books in the last few years aren't much different. In **Three Times Lucky** (2012) by Sheila Turnage, there are absent parents and a murder mystery; in **The Higher Power of Lucky** (2006) by Susan Patron, a young girl learns about the "12 step program" of addicts. You might wonder whether such books are robbing children of the joy of reading about happy childhood. And is the continuing popularity of "gentler" books, such as Laura Ingalls Wilder's **Little House** series, or **The Boxcar Children,** or the many titles by E. Nesbit, an indication that many children, parents, and teachers do not appreciate the stronger contemporary fare?

On the other hand, Katherine Paterson was probably correct when she wrote, "Children who have never felt the sting of prejudice, who laugh freely and bring their parents joy are a tiny minority of all the children in the world" (1993, p. 67). Surely, as teachers and parents, we have some obligation to expose children to the realities of life as other people live it.

What do you think? Would you advocate choosing works of contemporary realism that include tough issues for reading in school?

abilities, to name a few. If we are to work toward a world that believes in social justice, then all types of diversity must be considered and addressed.

Categories of Contemporary Realistic Fiction

Over the generations, when children have been asked what topics they enjoy in realistic fiction, their preferences have remained fairly constant. Barbara Elleman's (1986) retrospective bibliographies in *Booklist*, a publication of the American Library Association, are arranged by genres most requested by children. The most popular categories of realistic fiction are humor, mystery, and stories about survival.

It is surprising how many of these topics writers can get into one book. *Yolonda's Genius* by Carol Fenner, a 1996 Newbery Honor Book, works in the topics of school and friendship—as well as physical size and body image, music, drugs, single-parent families, and life in the city versus life in the suburbs.

The following categories are broad ones, but they are the topics of the books that children, teachers, and parents regularly seek out.

Books about Self-Discovery and Growing Up

Many works of realistic fiction enable children to explore their own thoughts, feelings, and predispositions and to compare their inner experiences with those of others. Good books about self-discovery are even available for preschoolers. *"More More More" Said the Baby*, a Caldecott Honor Book by Vera Williams, promotes self-discovery with three stories in which a baby is the center of play and is given loving attention by a father, a grandmother, and a mother. Bernard Waber created the now-classic *Ira Sleeps Over*, in which he answered unasked questions of young children, such as "Am I the only person who sleeps with a teddy?" (Ira, of course, discovers that he is not.)

Another way to discover one's self is to find one's own talents and passions. In Beverly Cleary's *Dear Mr. Henshaw*, Leigh Botts is assigned by teachers to write to an author, and soon he is writing for writing's sake. Nonetheless, given the importance of children's developing a sense of industry and competence during their early school years (an issue discussed in Chapter 1), it is lamentable that there are not more books celebrating children's development of their various talents, other than the scores of books on sports talent, which will be discussed later.

Growing up is a popular theme in children's literature. *Baseball in April and Other Stories,* by Gary Soto, depicts Mexican American young people on both sides of the mysterious threshold of adolescence, who are striving to get by in a California neighborhood where people make do with high hopes and limited means. In *Habibi,* by Naomi Shihab Nye, Liyana's family moves from St. Louis to Jerusalem to get to know the other half of her family. Growing up takes on many more complexities when you move to a country so seemingly different from where you have spent your early years.

Overcoming self-doubt is one of the aspects of growing up. Written almost seventy years ago, but still read today, *The Hundred Dresses* by Eleanor Estes is a now-classic story about overcoming the cruelty of peer prejudice. Wanda Petronski is belittled by Peggy and Maddie for wearing the same dress every day, even though she claims to have one hundred dresses at home. When Wanda's family moves away because of the prejudices they have encountered, Wanda mails Peggy and Maddie drawings of themselves, each pictured in one of the hundred dresses she has designed. Maddie's and Peggy's consciences are pricked by Wanda's responding to malevolence with kindness.

Sometimes, when life seems to be going "your way," a change in circumstances forces you to grow up. In Katherine Hannigan's first novel, *Ida B*, fourth-grader Ida B is an indulged only child; in addition, home schooling has allowed her to march to her own drummer at her own pace for her elementary years. When her mother's cancer changes their family circumstances, she must adjust to public schooling and the sale of part of their family property, resulting in sharing the land and trees she considered her own. Ida B must learn to deal with her anger and feelings of betrayal as she has lessons on growing up imposed on her.

There are many series books about self-discovery and growing up. Perhaps this is because once an author has created a strong, memorable character, readers want to know how that character handles other issues of growing up. Characters such as Beverly Cleary's Ramona Quimby, Paula Danziger's Amber Brown, Lenore Look's Alvin Ho or Ruby Lu and Sara Pennypacker's Clementine also allow readers to enjoy growing up along with their "friends" in books. These books usually offer humorous yet serious looks at daily aspects of growing up.

ILLUSTRATION 9.2 Liyana negotiates adolescent and cultural identity when she moves from St. Louis to Jerusalem after her parents decide the children should get to know the "other half" of their heritage. (Raul Colon, www.morgangaynin.com/colon)

Books about Families and Family Diversity

Family stories are important in realistic fiction because families form a child's first identity and first set of relationships, helping define who the child is in relation to the world. These stories take as many twists and turns as do families in the real world. In addition to nuclear families, extended families, alternative family structures, and new ways of considering what constitutes "family" are commonplace in today's literature. In *Shiloh*, Phyllis Reynolds Naylor has created a stable nuclear family in which each member cares about the others. Marty expresses that sense of belonging when he says, "You ask me the best place to live, I'd say right where we are, a little four-room house with hills on three sides."

Humorous accounts of growing up and dealing with family relationships are often found in books offered in series, such as *Ramona Quimby, Age 8*, one of the books in the long-running series of Ramona, Beezus, and Henry books created by Beverly Cleary. Sibling relations are at the center of *Tales of a Fourth Grade Nothing*, by Judy Blume, which features Peter Hatcher and his exasperating but endearing little brother Fudge. In a different kind of family, a single mom and her daughter lose everything in a fire in Vera Williams's picture book *A Chair for My Mother*. The family works together to save enough money to buy a soft, comfortable chair—one in which mom and daughter can snuggle together. Getting acquainted with past generations of her African American family is important to Emily in *Toning the Sweep*, by Angela Johnson. Emily videotapes the storytelling that goes on while she helps her grandmother prepare for chemotherapy and eventual death. In Hillary McKay's *Saffy's Angel*, thirteen-year-old Saffron realizes that she is adopted and tries to make sense of her personal history by putting together the pieces of her background that she and her delightfully eccentric siblings remember.

ILLUSTRATION 9.3   When a fire destroys their belongings, a little girl saves coins to help buy a chair for the mother to rest on after working all day as a waitress. (Copyright © 1982 by Vera B. Williams. Used by permission of HarperCollins Publishers.)

Parents who are incapable of taking care of their children force us to reconsider the definition of family. In Barbara O'Connor's *Moonpie and Ivy*, twelve-year-old Pearl feels rejected as her mother abandons her at the house of an aunt she hardly knew she had in the back-woods of Georgia; this is contrasted by the loving paren-tal relationship that her Aunt Ivy has with the neighbor boy, Moonpie. Although Pearl spends her summer staring down the road and waiting for her mother's car to reap-pear, she learns some family history and some reasons for her mother's erratic behavior. Difficult situations like this one have no easy resolution, but readers find hope for a future despite the circumstances.

Loss of family and seeking a place in the world are themes in Jacqueline Woodson's *Locomotion*. Lonnie is placed in a foster home while his little sister is adopted, so in *Peace, Locomotion*, he writes a series of letters to her that he plans to give to her some day so she will know what he had been thinking about during their years of separation.

Divorce, alcoholism, child abuse, and same-sex relationships—all nearly absent from books written in previous generations—are now widely treated in children's realistic fiction. The stress between family members of different generations in their extended family disturbs the youngest child in Sharon Bell Mathis's novel *The Hundred Penny Box*. In *From the Notebooks of Melanin Sun*, Jacqueline Woodson treats very sensitively a young teenage boy's discovery that his mother is a lesbian.

Books about Interpersonal Relations

Some useful works of realistic fiction revolve around the problems of getting along with others. In this area, a work of fiction can do what real life cannot: It allows us to experience the perspectives of more than one character.

In *Crazy Lady!*, a Newbery Honor Book by Jane Leslie Conly, Vernon's mother has died, and his kindly but barely literate father is unable to assist Vernon in his troubled efforts to read. Vernon meets Maxine, the neighborhood alcoholic (com-monly called the "Crazy Lady"), and her mentally challenged, mute son. As Vernon reaches out to help Maxine and her son Ronald, the relationship helps Vernon to come to terms with his learning disability as well as the loss of his mother.

In *Liar & Spy* by Rebecca Stead, seventh-grader Georges moves into a new building and ends up being part of a two-member spy club. Georges and Safer build a new friendship, based on one being the "boss" of the spy club; it tests each one's own sense of moral behavior as well as relationships with family, other tenants, and schoolmates. Full of mystery, intrigue, and ultimate surprises, this story offers op-portunities to consider many types of relationships.

Books about School

The school day is a source of constant drama for young people. School is their stage, their proving ground, their source of social contacts. There are many good works of realistic fiction that explore the pushes and tugs of schooling.

Young children just entering school worry about what the experience will be like. Amy Schwartz's *Annabelle Swift, Kindergartner* helps to answer that question for children. Annabelle's sister informs her about what she needs to know to begin kindergarten. Annabelle, however, prefers to make her own way. Schwartz creates a believable kindergarten setting in this reassuring book. A playground bully is cause for fearfulness in Alexis O'Neill's *The Recess Queen*. But when new girl Katie Sue arrives and doesn't know the "playground rules" imposed on everyone by Jean, she exuberantly invites Mean Jean to join her in jumping rope.

TOP SHELF 9.1

DEALING WITH BULLIES

Cockroach Cooties by Laurence Yep

The Hundred Dresses by Eleanor Estes

Jake Drake, Bully Buster by Andrew Clements

*The Recess Queen by Alexis O'Neill, Illustrated by Laura Huliska-Beith

No one has succeeded better at helping children see the teacher's point of view than Harry Allard in *Miss Nelson Is Missing!* and *Miss Nelson Is Back* (both illustrated by James Marshall). In the first, the children's bad behavior comes abruptly to an end when kind and gentle Miss Nelson appears to go on leave, and is replaced by a terrible disciplinarian, Miss Viola Swamp.

There are many books in series about school. Most are lighthearted and humorous looks at daily events and dilemmas faced at various grade levels. In Andrew Clements's series, eight-year-old Jake Drake must learn to deal with a bully in his fourth-grade classroom in *Jake Drake, Bully Buster*. The pitfalls of life as a middle schooler is at the core of experiences described in Jeff Kinney's *Diary of a Wimpy Kid* and its sequels. Begun as a Web cartoon, the series humorously depicts Greg Heffley's diary entries through narrative text as well as cartoon images.

Andrew Clements has written numerous school stories that are humorously told while dealing with important issues. In *The Landry News*, fifth-grader Clara Landry decides to exercise freedom of speech and writes an editorial about a formerly creative teacher who has burned out to the point of merely passing out worksheets to students. Similarly, Avi's *Nothing but the Truth* explores issues of freedom of speech in the classroom.

School experience is problematic and even traumatic for some. In Susan Shreve's *The Flunking of Joshua T. Bates*, Joshua is devastated to learn that he must repeat the third grade. He faces taunting from former classmates, but a sympathetic teacher helps him find his strengths. At other times, school or a school assignment is merely the impetus for sounding an alarm that makes people aware of problems stemming from self and family. A school assignment to keep a journal becomes a mechanism through which characters reveal some harsh truths about their home lives. In Margaret Peterson Haddix's *Don't You Dare Read This, Mrs. Dunphrey*, Tish finds her journal to be a safe place in which to spill her concerns about how to care for herself and her younger brother since her mother abandoned them.

ILLUSTRATION 9.4
Ninth-grader Philip hums along to the national anthem and ends up suspended from school for two days. The story includes news clips, diary entries, school memos, and dialogue transcriptions. (Scholastic, Inc.)

Books about Sports

Sports enthusiasts enjoy reading play-by-play accounts of athletic contests. *Shoot for the Hoop*, by Matt Christopher, satisfies this craving. Beyond merely describing basketball action, however, the author creates a hero who not only is a good basketball player but also struggles with diabetes. Matt Christopher writes voluminously—he has published over fifty sports titles—and is the focus of a fan club. Good-quality sports books such as Christopher's go beyond simply describing games and offer imaginative twists, well-developed characters, and a wide range of settings. Alfred Slote is another author who has written numerous popular sports stories for elementary school-age students. In *Hang Tough, Paul Mather*, Paul deals with his incurable blood disease by involving himself in baseball. In *Finding Buck McHenry*, a boy tries to enlist the school janitor as the Little League team coach, because he believes the janitor is a former famous baseball player from the Negro League. Tim Green has written a series called *Football Genius* and another called *Baseball Great* in which characters deal with various life issues, but with sports as the central metaphor in their lives as they grow up. Mike Lupica is a prominent sports writer for all levels of readers, and a prolific writer of sports stories for children. His *Comeback Kids* series is particularly popular.

Books about Nature and Animals

Authors who write animal and nature stories for children provide information about the natural world; they also help children build a commitment to the living things

TOP SHELF 9.2

SCHOOL STORIES WITH AN INTERNATIONAL PERSPECTIVE

The Color of Home by Mary Hoffman, Illustrated by Karin Littlewood

Elizabeti's School by Stephanie Stuve-Bodeen, Illustrated by Christy Hale

My Name is Yoon by Helen Recorvits, Illustrated by Gabi Swiatkowska

Someone Says by Carole Lexa Schaefer, Illustrated by Pierr Morgan

The Upside Down Boy by Juan Felipe Herrera, Illustrated by Elizabeth Gómez

with which they share the world. Often, animals and nature serve to teach children important lessons about their own lives.

Many realistic fiction picture books for younger children explore the multifaceted wonders of nature. In Denise Fleming's *In the Small, Small Pond*, a child watches the variety of pond life in amazement. Lois Ehlert's *Red Leaf, Yellow Leaf* has a child planting and caring for a sugar maple tree. The informational aspect of the text adds much to the story. In *Owl Moon*, John Schoenherr illustrates a night on which a father and a child go owling. Jane Yolen's text describes the setting vividly so that readers can vicariously experience the cold night and the awe of seeing the great owl.

Many children, especially girls, go through a horse story phase. Horse stories by Marguerite Henry and Walter Farley are perennial favorites. Both wrote about horses and other animals for over thirty years. Henry's *Misty of Chincoteague* and Farley's series of books about *The Black Stallion* remain justifiably popular.

A good number of Gary Paulsen's books celebrate animal life and the wilderness, especially in the cold northern lands. His *Dogsong* takes readers on a dogsled ride with Inuit boy Russell Susskit, introducing them to the interactions of dogs and humans. Another book in which Paulsen explores sled dogs is *Woodsong*, which describes the Iditarod race.

That animals provide companionship for humans is well accepted. But beyond that, animals offer life lessons for humans. That point is illuminated Kate DiCamillo's *Because of Winn-Dixie*, in which Opal adopts a stray dog from the local grocery store and names him after the store, Winn-Dixie. The friendly dog helps Opal adjust to her new community and also aids her in facing the reality of who she is and understanding that the mother who abandoned her seven years ago isn't likely to ever return.

Books about Adventure and Survival

Adventure stories are marked by fast-paced, exciting—even thrilling—action in which the main character perseveres through many struggles and overcomes the odds. Often, the adventure goes so far as to be considered a survival story. There are numerous ways of considering what constitutes survival. It could be surviving tough experiences such as peer taunting and tormenting because a child does not fit in for some reason. It could also be surviving life circumstances. But most often when we think of survival, we think of surviving life-threatening situations.

In some books for children, nature is presented as a harsh adversary; in others, nature helps characters to survive. In many books, nature is portrayed as both harsh and helpful. In Gary Paulsen's Newbery Honor Book *Hatchet*, Brian finds himself alone in the wilderness after an airplane crash, and he must come to understand nature in order to find food and shelter to stay alive. In *Julie of the Wolves*, a Newbery Medal winner by Jean Craighead George, Julie escapes from an arranged marriage in her Inuit village, surviving in the desolate Alaskan tundra by living with wolves. To be accepted by the wolves, she observes and mimics the intricacies of their behavior.

Books about Mental, Physical, Emotional, and Other Challenges

People in real life can flourish in spite of challenging mental, physical, and emotional conditions. The limiting factors they face are not just the challenging conditions, but also their own sense of the possible or the reduced expectations of those around them. The trick for authors is to create characters who can achieve success without having the disability seem to give them special powers. Books that depict this diverse perspective are also discussed in Chapter 4.

In Jack Gantos's *Joey Pigza Swallowed the Key*, the world is seen from the perspective of a third-grade boy who is "out of control"—he has attention deficit/ hyperactivity disorder. As adults, we may know what it's like to be around a child with ADHD, but how does it feel to be the child with ADHD or the classmates of the child? In one sequel, *Joey Pigza Out of Control*, Joey comes to know his previously absent father as he finds out the effects of being on and off his "meds," not just for school, but generally in day-to-day living.

In Cynthia Lord's *Rules*, twelve-year-old Catherine has many rules to live by, and she finds them necessary for living with an autistic younger brother. But a friendship with a nonverbal paraplegic helps her to realize that "normal" is not easily definable nor attainable, and perhaps living by rules is not as important as she had believed.

Multiple perspectives are effectively used in R. J. Palacio's story of Auggie, who is born with severe facial disfigurement. Following numerous surgeries and precarious health for survival, he enters school for the first time in fifth grade and faces peer reaction in *Wonder*. The theme of being kind to one another plays out as an antidote to bullying.

Books about Moral Dilemmas and Moral Responsibility

Many works of realistic fiction for young people pose moral dilemmas like those confronting people in the real world. Some are personal dilemmas that characters cannot avoid; others have to do with social issues in which characters can choose to become involved. The word "dilemma" refers to the difficulty of making choices; often, there is no clear right or wrong—just a decision with consequences.

A good example of an unavoidable personal dilemma is found in Sharon Bell Mathis's Newbery Honor Book *The Hundred Penny Box*, in which Michael, the young protagonist, is caught in the middle of a conflict between his mother and a one-hundred-year-old aunt: Does he obey his mother's rules, or does he protect Aunt Dew's memories and dignity?

A story about a character caught up in a moral dilemma of his own making is Avi's *Nothing but the Truth: A Documentary Novel*, in which high school student Phillip Malloy falsely reports that his English teacher refused to let him sing the national anthem. The book has no narrator, but rather uses diaries, newspaper clippings, memos, letters, dialogues, and radio talk-show scripts to recount the disastrous consequences of a distortion of the truth.

In *Shiloh*, Marty's desire for a dog begins the cycle of moral decision making. The dog he finds, Shiloh, belongs to someone who abuses him. Which is morally worse: Marty's "stealing" a dog that he knows has an owner (by hiding it and lying to his parents) or returning the dog to Judd Travers, who will continue to physically abuse it? Moral questions are posed throughout the book, and readers have opportunities to discuss them as they explore their own beliefs.

In Jacqueline Woodson's *Hush*, thirteen-year-old Toswiah's father is the one with the moral dilemma, and his family lives with his decision: Knowing he is receiving death threats for speaking up, is he willing to testify that a fellow police officer did not shoot and kill a boy in self-defense? This issue is complicated by race: Both Toswiah's father and the boy who was killed are African American and the officer on trial for the shooting is not. The family must immediately leave town under the Witness Protection Plan, and take on entirely new identities. The father can never be a police officer again, and each family member deals with this incredible sense of identity loss in different ways.

Carl Hiaasen takes on the tension between monetary greed at the cost of environmental conservation in both *Hoot!* and *Flush*.

ILLUSTRATION 9.5 Standing up to tell the truth means that a police officer and his family must leave their lives behind as they enter the Witness Protection Program. ("Hush" by Jacqueline Woodson, jacket art by Barry David Marcus. Used by permission of Penguin Group (USA), Inc. All rights reserved.)

In *Hoot!*, an unlikely alliance forms between a new kid in town, the tough girl who faces up to the bully attacking the new kid, and a mysterious homeless runaway boy. They work together to save the endangered baby owls when the prospective ground breaking of a franchise restaurant threatens to tear up the home of the owls. In *Flush*, a father's arrest for sinking a casino boat suspected of dumping raw sewage into the ocean leads to his two children working to find a way to prove the casino's responsibility not only to vindicate their father but also to stop the polluting of the waters of the Florida Keys. In both books, the characters walk the fine line of moral decision making in the face of the law and making moral choices about what to do.

Books about Social Diversity and Society

Getting along in different types of communities is the subject of many books written for young people. In *Amber Was Brave, Essie Was Smart*, written and illustrated by Vera B. Williams, two girls deal with their lives in poverty and their feelings of loneliness as their mother works late hours and their father is in jail for forging checks. A very different look at communities, *Smoky Night* by Eve Bunting, is based on the Los Angeles riots of 1993. The neighborhood conflicts raise questions of race and class, as the people consider basic human relations within their community. In Janet Wong's *Apple Pie, Fourth of July,* a young girl is sure that the Chinese restaurant her family owns will not get any customers on the Fourth of July because that's when they eat American foods like apple pie. To her delight, the people in her community redefine what holiday foods are when they arrive at her restaurant following the Fourth of July parade.

In *Junebug*, Alice Mead depicts the life of a boy who dreams of a big future but fears, as his tenth birthday approaches, that the local gangs and drug dealers will be pressuring him to join them. It is just this situation that worries Yolonda's mother in Carol Fenner's *Yolonda's Genius*. She moves from the inner city to the suburbs, looking for safety. However, Yolonda soon realizes that there are different types of danger to fear in different communities.

Frances Temple's *Grab Hands and Run* was fictionalized from a true account of the flight of the surviving members of a Salvadoran family from their homeland and their search for a permanent home in the North after the father has been assassinated.

Books about Aging, Death, and Dying

Realistic fiction examines many aspects of death and dying: the natural process of aging, caring for the sick, grieving for lost loved ones, and the stages that lead from grief to acceptance. The death of an animal or pet is often a child's first experience with death, although books for children also describe the deaths of peers, siblings, parents, and grandparents. The books in this section focus on relationships between the living and those who are dying or have died and are not merely about death.

Perhaps the death of a pet is a child's first introduction to such a loss. In Judith Viorst's *The Tenth Good Thing about Barney*, the protagonist's mother suggests that he think of ten good things about the cat Barney, for the family to recite at its funeral.

A Taste of Blackberries is Doris Buchanan Smith's sensitive contribution to understanding the stages of grief over the loss of a friend. When Jamie dies of an allergic reaction to a bee sting, his best friend must face the fact that Jamie will never return. The Newbery winner *Bridge to Terabithia*, by Katherine Paterson, gives the reader a rich character in Leslie, who will be remembered long after her accidental death.

The aging and death of a grandparent is a theme that allows authors to write of death as a natural phenomenon associated with age. *Blackberries in the Dark*, by Mavis Jukes, shows a child and her grandmother going through rituals as a way of remembering the grandfather. In *The Hundred Penny Box*, Michael intervenes when his mother tries to discard his great-great aunt's box of pennies she had collected, because he values the stories each penny tells.

The death of parents is most difficult for children to endure. In Cynthia Rylant's *Missing May*, the aunt who has raised Summer dies, but the loss is doubly hard because Summer has already lost her mother and father. For younger children, Eric Rohmann's *Bone Dog* offers a story of a bond that transcends the death of a beloved pet.

The treatment of death and dying varies across cultures, but there are obvious similarities. Three sixth-grade boys in Japan become curious about death in *The Friends*, by Kazumi Yumoto, and stake out an old man's house so that they may better understand what dying and death are about. However, it is their eventual friendship with the older man and their engagement in his life that enables the boys to understand death more fully.

Aging leads to death eventually. However, aging occurs years prior to death in many cases, and in other cases, age is not a factor in death. Many books include healthy portrayals of aging people. In *Wilfrid Gordon McDonald Partridge*, author Mem Fox tells about a little boy who goes in search of Miss Nancy's memory because he overhears his parents saying she's lost it. He asks the residents of the "old people's home" and gets many answers, all metaphors he interprets in his own way. His obvious affinity for Miss Nancy and his empathy for her dilemma shows another example of a good intergenerational friendship.

Mystery and Suspense Books

Mysteries enjoy wide appeal, especially among readers who enjoy the challenge of following the author's hints and diversions as they seek a solution. In an article entitled "The Scene of the Crime," Jeanette Larson (2008) cites the value of mysteries in that they "encourage readers to define problems, sequence events, look for clues, assess evidence, and reach conclusions—all valuable skills for research and learning."

Mystery books for young readers have as much variety as adult mysteries. In *The Westing Game*, a Newbery Honor Book by Ellen Raskin, the characters are involved in a battle of wits to inherit a million dollars. In her Newbery-winning adventure/mystery *From the Mixed-up Files of Mrs. Basil E. Frankweiler*, E. L. Konigsburg writes about a set of young protagonists in New York City who run away from home. Because of their familiarity with the Metropolitan Museum of Art, they figure out how to spend nights there without being detected. In a mystery set across the Atlantic Ocean, two siblings search for their missing cousin who goes up the famous ferris wheel but does not come down in Siobhan Dowd's *The London Eye Mystery*. Virginia Hamilton incorporates African American community history, which the protagonist delves into to solve a mystery in *The House of Dies Drear*, which uses the history of the Underground Railroad and a huge old house with secret passages as background for a mystery plot.

Many mysteries can be found in series. David Adler has penned many mysteries, one of which is *Cam Jansen and the Mystery of the Stolen Diamonds*. Cam uses her intellect and her photographic memory to solve the mysteries in this popular series. A "Young Cam Jansen" series introduces younger readers to mystery stories that are easy to read. The books in the Encyclopedia Brown series by Donald Sobol call for readers to get involved in solving cases along with the son of a police chief. Each book contains several short mysteries, and the solutions are in the back of the book. The "39 Clues" series, in which the Cahill family's power is secretly stored in 39 locations around the world, integrates a Web site with games and collectable cards as well.

Humorous Books

In much realistic fiction, humorous incidents serve as a release from the more serious topical themes explored by the author. Many of the books previously discussed in this chapter fit into this category.

TOP SHELF 9.3

BOOKS ABOUT AGING AND INTERGENERATIONAL RELATIONSHIPS

The Hundred Penny Box by Sharon Bell Mathis

*Singing with Momma Lou by Linda Jacobs Altman, Illustrated by Larry Johnson

Toning the Sweep by Angela Johnson

*Wilfrid Gordon McDonald Partridge by Mem Fox, Illustrated by Julie Vivas

Authors who write humorous books for children are careful not to poke fun at the natural surprises children experience—and, often, their ineptness—as they learn about life. The challenge for authors of realistic fiction is to help children empathize with others and see the humor in the plight of characters whose first stabs at life's opportunities fail. Leigh Botts's letters in **Dear Mr. Henshaw**, by Beverly Cleary, are a good example. The letters begin when Leigh is in the second grade, so his growth up to sixth grade is clear, and it is okay to laugh about what he didn't know earlier.

The first book in which author Megan McDonald introduces readers to Judy is in **Judy Moody (Was in a Mood. Not a Good Mood. A Bad Mood.)**. In this book, we see Judy in quite a range of moods in many different situations—all of which will feel familiar to readers. As a third-grader, she deals with school situations such as not wanting to cooperate with the teacher and being asked to return in a better mood the next day. At home, she deals with her little brother named Stink, who overfeeds her "favorite pet" Venus flytrap. And with her peers, she deals with a toad that pees by creating a Toad Pee Club.

Judy Blume's stories about sibling rivalry and parental approval are favorites among children—**Tales of a Fourth Grade Nothing** and **Superfudge**, in particular. In the former, Peter Hatcher is annoyed at his little brother's antics, but they are funny to the reader. Peter's unnecessary concern about his own status in the family will ring true to many young readers. When Fudge swallows Peter's pet turtle, readers can feel Peter's pain and laugh at the same time.

Beverly Cleary's characters, including Ramona and Henry Huggins, are strong, admirable children who can carry on in spite of embarrassing mistakes and goofs. Readers laugh at their misunderstandings. Throughout **Ramona the Brave**, Ramona assumes that her teacher thinks she is a nuisance. The misconception motivates her to compensate and try to win approval, and all the time the reader is enjoying her mistake. The decades that these books have been popular speak to the ongoing appeal of the endearing characters.

Annie Barrows and Sophie Blackall have created the series of stories, **Ivy and Bean**, about two seemingly opposite people who become friends: Ivy, who seems to always be reading, and Bean, who loves to play tricks and is lively. Together, they humorously turn everyday routines into fun adventures, and seal their friendship with acts of loyalty.

Sheila Greenwald's heroine, Rosy Cole, provides amusing adventures for younger readers. In **Rosy Cole: She Walks in Beauty**, Rosy tries to become a model, giving the author the opportunity to point out some of the absurdities of the modeling profession. Many series books about growing up include much humor.

Series Books

Series books are popular with children because they take the guesswork out of choosing something to read. Their very sameness, however, means that these books do less to expand a child's awareness of and appreciation for literature than one-of-a-kind books. Nonetheless, parents and teachers, eager to foster the reading habit, often forgive the shortcomings of series books in the hope that once children are "hooked on books," they may move beyond series books to more substantial reading. Teachers are also aware that reading series books may represent a sense of belonging to a group of such readers. Just as with any other books, the quality of series books varies. The worst are plagued by thin description, flat characters, and plots that pull readers from one suspenseful moment to another. The best can be funny, upbeat, and full of delightful language. One particularly popular series is *The Diary of a Wimpy Kid* by Jeff Kinney. Begun as a "webcomic," the popular series has a dedicated following, and has led to a series of movies being made as well. Middle Schooler Greg is decidedly "not cool" and keeps a journal, "handwritten" on lined notebook paper and complete with simple line illustrations.

How Contemporary Realistic Fiction Works

The term "realistic fiction" is something of a paradox. A work of fiction is contrived, yet readers are meant to believe that a work of realistic fiction is real, at least while they are engrossed in reading it. But this paradox contains some other seeming contradictions as well. Exploring two of them will clarify how realistic fiction "works."

Setting

In Kate DiCamillo's *Because of Winn-Dixie*, the story is set in the South. Details about the setting help readers to get a clear picture of how the setting influences the way the story moves along. Even the title's reference to Winn-Dixie may prove to be confusing for children who do not realize it is the name of a southern supermarket chain.

Plot

An effective work of realistic fiction makes us believe that what it describes might really have happened. Yet because it is fiction, the work is organized into a plot—and that makes it quite different from real life, in which the lion's share of our days is full of meaningless details: minutes spent waiting for traffic lights to change, minutes spent searching for lost papers or misplaced keys, minutes spent half-listening to uninteresting conversations. In contrast, just about every detail in a work of fiction is meaningful. Why aren't we aware of the difference right off?

Although realistic fiction does not resemble day-to-day reality, it does convey the ways in which we represent that reality to ourselves and others. Fiction is not like life—but it is like our stories of our lives. By taking events from life and giving them meaning, fiction shows us how we find significance and purpose in our lives.

Theme

Theme refers to the underlying meaning that is either suggested or explicitly stated within a story in a way that brings an important idea to the reader's consciousness. In realistic fiction, the theme is an issue of contemporary relevance; some are timeless and others are grounded in the current time. Many people attribute "death" as the central theme in Katherine Paterson's book, *Bridge to Terabithia*. And, indeed, the death in the story is explored in depth. However, this book is more about the themes of friendship and self-identity, and ultimately, the emotions surrounding death.

Character

Characters are created through physical descriptions, through their actions, through their thoughts and speech, and through their relationship with others. In realistic fiction, characters are developed in ways that are conceivable for people in contemporary times to live and behave. In Phyllis Reynolds Naylor's *Shiloh*, Judd Travers, a man without awareness who acts violently in the world, unthinkingly recreates the violence with which he was raised. The boy Marty makes a commitment to protect the dog Shiloh and, in so doing, goes beyond blind obedience to his father and also beyond his mother's unexamined code of ethics. Marty is aware of what he is doing. He gradually comes to understand the reasons behind his father's demands, his mother's pure but insufficient morality, and Judd Travers's brutish nature—after which he reaches his own conclusions about what he should do.

Thanks to Naylor's narrative, the reader is privileged to see these several ways of thinking through the moral issues in *Shiloh* and is allowed to make a personal judgment about them. It is not too great a step for readers to think of the issues in their lives in the complex ways Naylor reveals to them as they read *Shiloh*. It is no wonder scholars who have studied the effects of literacy have claimed that reading expands awareness (Luria, 1976; Postman, 1994; Stanovich, 1992). Over time, the habit of reading allows children to see patterns in their lives, to look into their own motives and those of others, and to see possibilities for independent action.

Point of View

A story might seem to tell "what happened," but it almost invariably makes a point that causes readers to see the events in a certain way—with a slant. Realistic fiction explores contemporary issues of significance in the characters' lives, and the point of view from which those issues are explored is particularly important in determining the ways in which reader empathy is elicited.

Adults often provide a view of the world and pass on some of the wisdom they have gained over the course of their lives. It is not surprising that even the best of writers succumb once in a while to "teaching and preaching" in realistic fiction, especially when they feel that child readers might need a little help in getting at an important idea, but it doesn't contribute to the telling of a good story. A little nudging toward an insight isn't objectionable, but if it's overdone, the writing may seem didactic. So even if the story is told from the adult point of view, we should remain wary of statements and attitudes that seem to condescend, implying that children wouldn't be capable of making their own moral judgments or of understanding the consequences of a character's actions.

Criteria for Evaluating Realistic Fiction

- Is the story well written according to literary standards outlined in Chapter 2?
- Do the characters resemble real people in our world?
- Are the events plausible? Will children believe that they could happen?
- Is the plot resolution believable—not contrived to end in a certain way?

Beyond entertainment, worthwhile realistic fiction leaves children with something to reflect on about their own lives or the lives of others.

Major Writers of Contemporary Realistic Fiction and Their Works

AUTHOR	MAJOR WORKS
Judy Blume	*Superfudge*
Andrew Clements	*Frindle*
Jack Gantos	*Joey Pigza Swallowed the Key*
E. L. Konigsburg	*From the Mixed Up Files of Mrs. Basil Frankweiler*
Phyllis Reynolds Naylor	*Shiloh*
Katherine Paterson	*Bridge to Terabithia*
Gary Paulsen	*Hatchet*
Jacqueline Woodson	*Locomotion*

Ask *the* Author. . . Sharon Creech

Most of my stories begin with the image of a person and a place, and I write to discover the story. Very early on, the main character will mention other people, and I know that these people will have their own stories to tell. It is these stories that evolve into other strands of the plot.

Weaving them together is not as difficult as it might sound, because each day I merely pick up the previous strands and go wherever it feels right to go. If I feel the need to spend some time with the main character's grandparents, for example, I will do that, and then return to the central story. That central story will be affected by what I've learned from the grandparents, and so the different strands begin to intertwine.

Often I use the image of clearing a trail to describe the writing process. Like Zinny Taylor, who clears a long trail in *Chasing Redbird*, I am only clearing a little bit of the story trail at a time. Sometimes there are side paths that look interesting, and I'll follow those and then return to the main trail.

It is wonderful when you begin to see the patterns emerge—when you can see enough of the story to sense how one part relates to another. If I tried to predict the pattern—or the course of the story trail—in advance, I don't think I'd be so willing to allow it to change and evolve, and it is this changing and evolving that becomes most interesting to me. At the end, I can see how all the parts of the trail are connected, and then I revise, clearing patches that aren't yet smooth enough.

Sometimes students worry when they're writing their own stories that they have to know the whole story before they begin. I find it more exciting to know very little at the beginning, and to run down that trail wondering what I will find along the way.

Sharon Creech is the author of *Walk Two Moons*, which received the Newbery Medal; *The Wanderer*; *Absolutely Normal Chaos*; *Bloomability*; *Pleasing the Ghost*; and *Chasing Redbird*. After spending eighteen years teaching and writing in Europe, Sharon Creech returned with her family to the United States to live.

EXPERIENCES FOR FURTHER LEARNING

1. Within the genre of contemporary realistic fiction, select a controversial issue (child abuse, abandonment by parents, parents/partners of the same gender, reference to sexuality, etc.). Gather a sampling of books related to that issue. Consider how that issue is treated in each book, and in what ways it is or is not believable. Consider what makes the issue more controversial and likely for censorship in some books and why it may be less controversial in the way it is presented in other books. Then gather some books of the same or related theme from other genres (poetry, informational books, etc.). Discuss how thinking about potentially controversial issues by reading widely across genres influences the reader.

2. Read a work of contemporary realistic fiction that is set in an area of which you have intimate knowledge. In what ways does the author establish authenticity of the locale through the theme, plot, or characters? Find details in both illustrations and text that let you know that the author also knows this setting well and confirms for you the reality of the setting. How do these details influence the believability of the setting?

RECOMMENDED BOOKS

* indicates a picture book; I indicates interest level (P = preschool, 6–10 = age 6 through 10, YA = young adult)

Books about Self-Discovery and Growing Up

Choldenko, Gennifer. *Notes from a Liar and Her Dog*. Putnam, 2001. Antonia lies constantly and writes to her "real parents" in a notebook because she is sure she must be adopted. Only her dog, Pistachio, and best friend Harrison are real to her as she seeks to understand her identity and searches for a sense of belonging. (I: 10–12)

Cleary, Beverly. *Beezus and Ramona*. Morrow, 1955. The first of a series about the indomitable and spirited Ramona and her older sister; here Ramona is a preschooler. (I: 8–10)

_____. *Dear Mr. Henshaw*. Illustrated by Paul Zelinsky. Morrow, 1983. Lee first writes to an author as part of a school assignment. In the continued correspondence, Lee increasingly confides in Mr. Henshaw about various issues that concern him—his parents' divorce, relationships with peers, and so on. (I: 9–11)

Danziger, Paula. *Amber Brown Is Not a Crayon*. Illustrated by Tony Ross. Putnam, 1994. In this popular series about a spunky girl's dilemmas as she grows up, Amber's best friend Justin is moving away. First in a series. (I: 8–11)

Estes, Eleanor. *The Hundred Dresses*. Harcourt, 1944. Wanda acts with kindness toward those who ridiculed her for wearing the same dress every day. (I: 7–10)

Gantos, Jack. *Joey Pigza Swallowed the Key*. Farrar, Straus, & Giroux, 1998. Joey knows that he is "wired," and his behavior is out of control unless he is on his medication for ADHD. First in a series. (I: 9–12)

Guest, Elissa Haden. *Iris and Walter* series. Illustrated by Christine Davenier. In this easy reader series, Iris and Walter celebrate friendship, face a range of school situations, and generally deal with the emotions of growing up. (I: 6–9)

Haddix, Margaret Peterson. *Don't You Dare Read This, Mrs. Dunphrey*. Simon & Schuster, 1996. Tish confides in her school-assigned journal her fears about her mother's whereabouts and how she will cope with caring for herself and her younger brother in their mother's absence. (I: 12–YA)

Hannigan, Katherine. *Ida B*. Greenwillow/HarperCollins, 2004. Home-schooled, only-child Ida B faces major life change when her mother's cancer means she must go to public schools and share the trees and land she considered to be her own with the family that buys their property. (I: 8–12)

Henkes, Kevin. *The Year of Billy Miller*. Greenwillow, 2013. After an accident that leaves Billy worried about himself, he faces the beginning of second grade with trepidation. Warm and supportive family relationships help him deal with issues a young child faces while growing up. (I: 6–9)

*Hoffman, Mary. *Amazing Grace*. Dial, 1991. Illustrated by Caroline Binch. Grace has an amazing ability to act, but she is told by classmates that she cannot be Peter Pan in the class play because she is a girl and she is black. The sequel is *Boundless Grace* (1995), and a related chapter book is *Starring Grace* (2000). (I: P–7)

Lowry, Lois. *Anastasia Krupnik*. Houghton Mifflin, 1979. In this first book in the series of many titles about Anastasia, the ten-year-old girl faces her first love and the news that she will soon have a baby brother. (I: 9–12)

MacLachlan, Patricia. *The Facts and Fictions of Minna Pratt*. HarperCollins, 1988. Minna plays the cello and learns about life and passions from her family, friends, and Mozart. (I: 10–YA)

_____. *Journey*. Delacorte, 1991. When two children are left by their mother, the grandparents make a home for them. (I: 9–12)

Mori, Kyoko. *Shizuko's Daughter*. Holt, 1993. Following her mother's suicide, twelve-year-old Yuki must face her adolescent years amidst difficult relationships with her father and stepmother, as her creative spirit rebels against a culture that restricts her individuality. (I: 12 and up)

Myers, Walter Dean. *Darnell Rock Reporting*. Delacorte, 1994. A thirteen-year-old's family and friends doubt that Darnell will make it as a writer for the school newspaper. (I: 11–YA)

Myracle, Lauren. *The Winnie Years Series*. Beginning with the book entitled *Ten* to reflect the age of the protagonist, the series continues with a book for each year of Winnie's life until *Thirteen + 1*. Many contemporary issues of growing up are raised and realistically dealt with. (I: 8–13)

Paulsen, Gary. *Harris and Me: A Summer Remembered*. Harcourt, 1993. A city boy goes to live with his distant cousin on a farm, where he finds love and hilarious adventures. (I: 9–12)

Soto, Gary. *Baseball in April and Other Stories*. Harcourt, 1990. Tender stories of children fitting into families and of the Latino culture of California. (I: 10–YA)

Books about Families

Birdsall, Jeanne. *The Penderwicks: A Summer Tale of Four Sisters, Two Rabbits, and a Very Interesting Boy*. Knopf, 2005. This National Book Award Winner is the first in a series of books about four sisters, a companion friend, and their adventures in a summer estate. (I: 8–12)

Blume, Judy. *Tales of a Fourth Grade Nothing*. Dutton, 1972. Readers will laugh and sympathize with Peter Hatcher's embarrassment over and envy of his pesky two-year-old brother, Fudge. Sequels include *Superfudge* (1980). (I: 7–9)

Cleary, Beverly. *Ramona Quimby, Age 8*. Morrow, 1981. As a third-grader, Ramona finds that her life changes drastically when her father goes back to school. See also *Ramona and Her Father* (1977), in which Ramona campaigns to get her father to quit smoking, and *Ramona's World* (HarperCollins, 2001). (I: 7–9)

Creech, Sharon. *Walk Two Moons*. HarperCollins, 1994. A thirteen-year-old girl and her grandparents follow the journey of her mother after she leaves them. (I: 10–YA)

*Gauch, Patricia Lee. *Christina Katerina and the Time She Quit the Family*. Illustrated by Elise Primavera. Putnam, 1987. Christina Katerina decides to "quit" her family so that she can do things her own way, but discovers that being part of a family isn't so bad after all. A sequel is *Christina Katerina and the Great Bear Train* (1990). (I: 6–9)

Henkes, Kevin. *Protecting Marie*. Greenwillow, 1995. Twelve-year-old Fanny, who is dealing with adolescence, and her temperamental artist father, who is trying to handle turning 60, have a tenuous relationship; a pet dog helps to establish trust. (I: 10–YA)

Johnson, Angela. *Toning the Sweep*. Orchard, 1993. Three generations of women come together and share memories of the past as the dying grandmother prepares to move in with her daughter and granddaughter. (I: 11–YA)

*Jukes, Mavis. *Like Jake and Me*. Illustrated by Lloyd Bloom. Knopf, 1984. A spider brings Alex and his step-father closer together. (I: 8–10)

Lisle, Janet Taylor. *Afternoon of the Elves*. Orchard, 1989. Fascinated by her friend Sara-Kate's imagination and careful caring for her creation, a playground for "elves," Kate worries about who takes care of Sara-Kate. (I: 9–12)

Mathis, Sharon Bell. *The Hundred Penny Box*. Viking Press, 1975. Michael intercedes when his mother tries to toss out his beloved great-great Aunt Dew's memorabilia. (I: 8–10)

McKay, Hillary. *Saffy's Angel*. McElderry/Simon & Schuster, 2002. Saffy realizes that she is adopted, and with the help of her loving and eccentric siblings, she tries to make sense of the mystery of her past. (I: 9–12)

Myers, Walter Dean. *Me, Mop, and the Moondance Kid*. Delacorte, 1988. Two adopted boys remain friends with an orphan girl who seeks to be adopted, too. (I: 9–12)

Naylor, Phyllis Reynolds. *Alice in April*. Atheneum, 1993. Thirteen-year-old Alice demands more appreciation from her father and older brother. First in a series. (I: 10–13)

O'Connor, Barbara. *Moonpie and Ivy*. Farrar, Straus, & Giroux, 2001. When twelve-year-old Pearl's mother abandons her at the home of an aunt she didn't even know she had, Pearl struggles to define what family means as she observes the relationship between the neighbor boy, Moonpie, and her Aunt Ivy. (I: 11–13)

*Okimoto, Jean Davies, and Elaine Aoki. *The White Swan Express: A Story About Adoption*. Illustrated by Meilo So. Clarion, 2002. Four families travel to China to meet the babies they have adopted. (I: 6–8)

Paterson, Katherine. *The Same Stuff as Stars*. Clarion, 2002. Neglected by her mother and with a father in prison, eleven-year-old Angel has long been the stable feature in her brother Bernie's life. But when their mother abandons them at the home of their great-grandmother, Angel's responsibilities seem staggering until a mysterious star man and a kind librarian reach out to help. (I: 10–14)

*Rylant, Cynthia. *The Relatives Came*. Bradbury, 1985. Family members come from various places to gather for a family reunion in this Appalachian setting. (I: P–8)

*Williams, Vera. *A Chair for My Mother*. Greenwillow, 1983. After all their furniture is lost in a fire, the family saves their spare change to buy a chair for mother. See also *Cherries and Cherry Pits* (1986), *Music, Music, for Everyone* (1984), and *Something Special for Me* (1983). (I: P–8)

Williams-Garcia, Rita. *Like Sisters on the Homefront*. Lodestar, 1995. A troubled teenager is sent South to live with relatives and experiences the healing power of family roots. (I: 12–YA)

Woodson, Jacqueline. *From the Notebooks of Melanin Sun*. Blue Sky/Scholastic, 1995. A teenage boy copes with the news that his mother is in love with another woman. (I: YA)

_____. *Locomotion*. Putnam, 2003. Lonnie C. Motion has a good family life when he is suddenly orphaned and sent to live in a foster home while his younger sister is adopted and her new family resists her seeing him. Sequel: *Peace, Locomotion* (2009).

Books about Interpersonal Relationships

DiCamillo, Kate. *Because of Winn-Dixie*. Candlewick, 2000. Ten-year-old Opal encounters a friendly stray dog at the grocery store and, through him, learns to adapt to her new community in small-town Florida and comes to peace with her mother's leaving. (I: 9–12)

*McKissack, Patricia C. *The Honest-to-Goodness Truth*. Illustrated by Giselle Potter. Anne Schwartz/Atheneum, 2000. Libby's vow to only tell the truth backfires when her honesty reveals embarrassing situations for her friends. (I: 6–9)

Mohr, Nicholasa. *Felita*. Dial, 1979. Felita is an eight-year-old Puerto Rican girl growing up in a close-knit urban community; she is confronted with racism when her family moves to a new neighborhood. (I: 7–9)

Paterson, Katherine. *Bridge to Terabithia*. Crowell, 1977. Despite their different backgrounds, Jess and Leslie forge an unexpected and special friendship when tragedy strikes. (I: 9–12)

Stead, Rebecca. *Liar & Spy*. Random House, 2012. Seventh-grader Georges moves to a new building and joins Safer in his detective adventure as they spy and try to solve mysteries. (I: 10–13)

White, Ruth. *Buttermilk Hill*. FSG, 2006. Piper's parents divorce; her father is busy with his new family and her mother is consumed with developing her new identity. She turns to writing and poetry to find solace and develop her own talents. (I: 10–13)

Woodson, Jacqueline. *I Hadn't Meant to Tell You This*. Delacorte, 1994. Racial and class barriers are overcome as two girls who have both lost their mothers bond in a friendship that allows them to confront the sexual abuse by one girl's father. (I: 12–YA)

_____. *Maizon at Blue Hill*. Delacorte, 1992/2004. Winning a scholarship at a boarding school does not ensure Maizon's acceptance by the almost all-white student body. Companion books are *Last Summer with Maizon* (1992/2004) and *Between Madison and Palmetto* (1995/2004). (I: 12–YA)

Books about School

Ada, Alma Flor. *My Name is María Isabel*. Simon & Schuster, 1993. When Maria Isabel enters a new school, the teacher decides to nickname her "Mary"—-an identity that María Isabel does not find familiar. (I: 8–10)

*Allard, Harry. *Miss Nelson Is Missing!* Illustrated by James Marshall. Houghton Mifflin, 1985. Their beloved and kind teacher, Miss Nelson, is missing, and the strange substitute teacher, Viola Swamp, has the class worried. First of three. (I: 7–10)

Clements, Andrew. *Frindle*. Simon & Schuster, 1996. Ten-year-old Nick likes to create distractions in school. As a challenge to his vocabulary-loving teacher, he attempts to introduce a new word into the English language. Among the many school stories Clements has written are *The Landry News* (1999), *The Janitor's Boy* (2000), *The School Story* (2001), and *A Week in the Woods* (2002). (I: 8–11)

———. *Jake Drake, Bully Buster*. Simon & Schuster, 2001. When SuperBully Link Baxter moves to the neighborhood, Jake Drake must learn how to stand up for himself. See also other Jake Drake books in the series. (I: 8–10)

Greene, Stephanie. *Owen Foote, Second Grade Strongman*. Illustrated by Dee De Rosa. Clarion, 1996. Owen does not like being called a "pipsqueak" by the school nurse on height-and-weight measuring day and becomes a class hero by defending his friend when the nurse calls him "too fat." First of many. (I: 6–9)

Gutman, Dan. *The Homework Machine*. Simon & Schuster, 2006. In a series of first-person entries, fifth-grade students, teacher, and even a police chief consider the ethics and the draw of a "homework machine" in contemporary days of computer use, updating the idea popularized by *Danny Dunn and the Homework Machine* back in 1958. (I: 9–12)

*Herrera, Juan Felipe. *The Upside Down Boy/El niño de cabeza*. Illustrated by Elizabeth Gómez. A Spanish-speaking boy fears starting a new school where he must learn a new language, thinking he might feel "upside down." (I: 6–9)

*Hoffman, Mary. *The Color of Home*. Illustrated by Karin Littlewood. Fogelman/Penguin Putnam, 2002. Hassan is a new child from Somalia and draws a picture of his homeland. An interpreter comes and helps him to communicate his picture verbally to his classmates. (I: P–7)

Kinney, Jeff. *Diary of a Wimpy Kid*. Abrams, 2007. Begun as a Web book on <www.funbrain.com>, this humorous story tells of a middle schooler's trials and triumphs through this "novel in cartoons." Sequels: *Roderick Rules* (2008), *Do-It-Yourself-Book* (2008), *The Last Straw* (2009), *Dog Days* (2009). (I: 9–12)

Konigsburg, E. L. *The View from Saturday*. Atheneum, 1996. Four "gifted" and eccentric sixth-graders form the school's winning Academic Bowl Team. Their lives and stories intersect in interesting ways. (I: 10–13)

*O'Neill, Alexis. *The Recess Queen*. Illustrated by Laura Huliska-Beith. Scholastic, 2002. "Mean Jean" is the recess queen—the bully of the playground—until a new girl comes and exuberantly invites Jean to play. (I: P–8)

*Schwartz, Amy. *Annabelle Swift, Kindergartner*. Orchard, 1988. Annabelle's older sister Lucy teaches her what to expect in kindergarten, but when Annabelle gets there, her knowledge sparks laughter among the children. Ultimately, Annabelle wins the classmates' approval. (I: P–7)

Smith, Greg Leitich. *Ninjas, Piranhas, and Galileo*. Little Brown, 2003. This humorously told story is about three seventh-graders who fret over their school science fair experiment gone awry, a budding romantic triangle, and a strong friendship that endures through it all. (I: 9–12)

*Stuve-Bodeen, Stephanie. *Elizabeti's School*. Illustrated by Christy Hale. Lee & Low, 2002. Set in modern-day Tanzania, Elizabeti misses being at home, but enjoys her first day of school. (I: 6–9)

Books about Sports

Avi. *S.O.R. Losers*. Bradbury, 1984. The South Orange River soccer team is composed of unlikely seventh-grade athletes, who strive for an all-losing season. (I: 12–YA)

Bloor, Edward. *Tangerine*. Harcourt Brace, 1997. Despite the fact that Paul is legally blind, he convinces his parents to hide his disability so that he can use his amazing skill as a master soccer goalie. His ability to "see" life in ways to which others seem oblivious allows him to realize what's really wrong with his football hero older brother. (I: 11–YA)

Christopher, Matt. *Penalty Shot*. Little, Brown, 1997. Jeff is a talented soccer player who gets suspended from the team for bad grades. His attempts to rejoin the team are sabotaged, and he must figure out a way to rectify the situation. There are many books in the series of sports stories by this author, including *Shoot for the Hoop* (1995). (I: 9–12)

Cohen, Barbara. *Thank You, Jackie Robinson*. Lothrop, 1974. The love of baseball helps a fatherless boy, Sam, cross boundaries of race, age, and religion to become close friends with a hotel cook named Davy. As Davy lies in a hospital bed dying, Sam brings him an autographed ball from Jackie Robinson. (I: 9–11)

Green, Tim. *Force Out*. HarperCollins, 2013. The popular author of the *Football Genius* series and the *Baseball Great* series tells the story of two sixth-grade boys who have shared goals of playing in the Little League championships but scheming and lying lead to dealing with guilt and remorse as their friendship is challenged. (I: 8–12)

Lupica, Mike. *Comeback Kids Series*. Ranging from basketball, football, soccer, baseball, and more, each book features a different sport, but all focus on the importance of teamwork. (I: 8–12)

Slote, Alfred. *Finding Buck McHenry*. HarperCollins, 1991. A boy tries to enlist the school janitor he believes is a former famous baseball player from the Negro League to be the Little League team coach. See also: *Hang Tough, Paul Mather*. HarperTrophy, 1973/1993. (I: 9–12)

Soto, Gary. *Taking Sides*. Harcourt, 1991. Lincoln Mendoza moves to a white neighborhood and has to take sides on the basketball court. The sequel is *Pacific Crossing* (1992). (I: 9–12)

Spinelli, Jerry. *Crash*. Knopf, 1996. Crash earned his name by being a star athlete from babyhood to middle school, but he earned friendship through different behaviors. (I: 10–YA)

Books about Nature and Animals

Farley, Walter. *The Black Stallion*. Random House, 1941/1991. When Alec is shipwrecked on a deserted island, he and a black stallion form a bond as he works to tame and then train him. This is the first of a series. (I: 9–12)

Henry, Marguerite. *Misty of Chincoteague*. Illustrated by Wesley Dennis. Simon & Schuster, 1990. Paul and Maureen obtain a wild horse and her colt on the island of Chincoteague, off the eastern shore of Virginia. Sequels are *Sea Star* (1949/1991) and *Stormy, Misty's Foal* (1963/1991). (I: 9–11)

Hesse, Karen. *Sable*. Illustrated by Marcia Sewall. Holt, 1994. Sable, ten-year-old Tate's dog, is constantly stealing things and must be given away to a friend. Tate is determined to show responsibility and earn the right to keep her dog. (I: 7–9)

Mikaelsen, Ben. *Stranded*. Hyperion, 1995. Twelve-year-old Koby saves the lives of two injured pilot whales in the Florida Keys. In doing so, she confronts her feelings about her own injury that resulted in an artificial foot and the resulting tensions between her parents. (I: 10–YA)

*Yolen, Jane. *Owl Moon*. Illustrated by John Schoenherr. Putnam, 1987. A father and child go owling on a winter night. (I: P–8)

Books about Adventure and Survival

Farmer, Nancy. *A Girl Named Disaster*. Orchard, 1996. Eleven-year-old Nhamo flees from her village in Mozambique to escape an arranged marriage to a cruel man. She travels alone to Zimbabwe in search of a father she does not know. (I: 10–YA)

George, Jean Craighead. *Julie of the Wolves*. Harper & Row, 1972. Running away from marriage at age thirteen means learning to live with wolves to survive. Sequels are *Julie* (1996) and *Julie's Wolf Pack* (1997). (I: 9–12)

_____. *My Side of the Mountain*. Penguin, 1959/1988. When Sam runs away to the Catskill Mountains, an old hollow tree becomes his home and a falcon and weasel his companions in the struggle for survival in the wilderness. The trilogy continues with *On the Far Side of the Mountain* (1990) and *Frightful's Mountain* (Dutton, 1999). (I: 10–12)

Hobbs, Will. *Far North*. Morrow, 1996. Fifteen-year-old Gabe, his Dene Indian roommate Raymond, and Dene elder Johnny Raven are stranded in the Canadian wilderness after a plane crash. The boys learn the skills they need to survive the harsh winter weather, the animals, and other dangers. See also *The Maze* (1998). (I: 12–YA)

Paulsen, Gary. *Hatchet*. Viking, 1987. Surviving fifty-three days in the wilderness helps Brian learn to cope with his parents' divorce. Companion books are *The River* (1991), *Brian's Winter* (1996), and *Brian's Return* (1996). (I: 9–12)

_____. *Dogsong* (2007) takes readers on a dogsled ride with Inuit boy Russell Susskit, introducing them to the interactions of dogs and humans. See also: *Woodsong* (2007).

Books about Mental, Physical, Emotional, and Other Challenges

See also other titles in the Chapter 4 bibliography.

Byars, Betsy. *The Summer of the Swans*. Viking, 1970. Sara is self-conscious about her brother, who is mentally disabled, but reconsiders her feelings when he gets lost searching for the wild swans that return each year. (I: 10–YA)

*Fleming, Violet. *Be Good to Eddie Lee*. Illustrated by Floyd Cooper. Philomel, 1993. Eddie Lee is able to see flowers and frog's eggs better than other children. (I: 7–9)

Lord, Cynthia. *Rules*. Scholastic, 2006. Twelve-year-old Catherine reconsiders the importance of rules in living with an autistic younger brother when a friendship with a nonverbal paraplegic helps her to question what it means to be "normal." (I: 9–12)

*Millman, Isaac. *Moses Goes to School*. Farrar, Straus, & Giroux, 2000. Moses and his friends attend a special school for children who are deaf, where adaptations include typing a letter into a computer that translates into standard spoken English. All of the Moses books are accompanied by American Sign Language. (I: P–8)

Palacio, R. J. *Wonder*. Knopf, 2012. Born with severe facial disfigurement that is profoundly noticeable following multiple surgeries to survive, fifth-grader Auggie enters school for the first time and is confronted with peer reactions. (I: 9–12)

Pennypacker, Sara. *Clementine*. Illustrated by Marla Frazee. Hyperion, 2006. Third-grader Clementine has good intentions, but her inability to pay attention means that things often go awry. Other books include: *The Talented Clementine* (2007), *Clementine's Letter* (2008). (I: 8–10)

Books about Moral Dilemmas and Moral Responsibility

Bauer, Marion Dane. *On My Honor*. Clarion, 1986. After promising "on his honor" to his father that he will not go swimming, Joel feels responsible for Tony's drowning when the two friends break the promise. (I: 10–YA)

Ellis, Deborah. *Mud City*. Third in the Breadwinner series, Shauzia longs to leave the Afghan refugee camp where she has gone to live for survival. (I: 9–12)

Hiaasen, Carl. *Flush*. Knopf, 2005. When Dad is arrested for sinking a casino boat he suspects is responsible for dumping raw sewage directly into the ocean, a brother and sister team up to solve the mystery and help put a stop to the polluting of the water surrounding the Florida Keys. (I: 10–YA)

_____. *Hoot!* Knopf, 2002. A cast of three unlikely friends—a boy who has just moved to the town, a homeless runaway, and a bully-confronting tough girl—work together to save an endangered species of owls from having their home destroyed by the construction of a franchise pancake restaurant. (I: 10–YA)

Naylor, Phyllis Reynolds. *Shiloh*. Atheneum, 1991. Marty's desire to keep a mistreated beagle that he found in the hills surrounding his West Virginia home causes him to make many moral decisions about what's right and what's wrong. First in a series. (I: 9–12)

Woodson, Jacqueline. *Hush*. Putnam, 2002. When a police officer testifies that a fellow officer was not acting in self-defense when he shot and killed a boy, his family must enter the Witness Protection Program and their lives are forever changed. (I: 12–YA)

_____. *Miracle's Boys*. Putnam, 2000. When their father's drowning and their mother's death from diabetes leave three brothers orphans, Ty'ree gives up his college plans and focuses on trying to keep Charlie from a life of crime and Lafayette from inward withdrawal. (I: 12–YA)

Books about Social Diversity and Society

See also other titles in the Chapter 4 bibliography.

*Boelts, Maribeth. *Those Shoes*. Illustrated by Noah Jones. Candlewick, 2009. Jeremy's desire for expensive shoes others are wearing lead him to make an unwise decision for a too-small pair at a resale shop. (I: K–7)

Fenner, Carol. *Yolonda's Genius*. McElderry, 1995. When Yolonda's mother moves her children from the dangers of city life to a rural area, Yolonda's genius lies in discovering not only her own but also her brother's talent. (I: 10–YA)

Fleischman, Paul. *Seedfolks*. Illustrated by Judy Pedersen. Harper, 1997. Suspicious neighbors become inspired by one another to transform a trash-filled city lot into a beautiful garden. (I: 12–YA)

Holt, Kimberly Willis. *Dancing in Cadillac Light*. Holt, 2002. A story of small town life depicting relationships and dealing with life issues among those who have—and those who do not. (I: 9–12)

Mead, Alice. *Junebug*. Farrar, 1995. Junebug has dreams of a better life and of becoming a boat captain someday, but worries that his tenth birthday will bring pressures to join the gang of older boys in his housing project. (I: 9–12)

Temple, Frances. *Grab Hands and Run*. Orchard, 1993. A Salvadoran family struggles to escape oppression and move to Canada. (I: 10–YA)

Williams, Vera B. *Amber Was Brave, Essie Was Smart*. Greenwillow, 2001. Two sisters share a loving relationship while trying to deal with poverty, latchkey loneliness, their mother's long hours at work, and father away at jail for forging checks. (I: 7–10)

Books about Aging, Death, and Dying

*Clifton, Lucille. *Everett Anderson's Goodbye*. Illustrated by Ann Grifalconi. Holt, 1983. A story of Everett's grief at losing his father, told in rhyme. (I: P–7)

*Fox, Mem. *Sophie*. Illustrated by Aminah Brenda Lynn Robinson. Harcourt Brace, 1989. Sophie holds on to her grandfather's hand as she grows up. He holds on to hers as he gets smaller and older. (I: P–6)

*_____. *Wilfrid Gordon McDonald Partridge*. Illustrated by Julie Vivas. Kane Miller, 1985. A little boy is concerned when he hears that his elderly friend, Miss Nancy, has lost her memory. (I: P–9)

Jukes, Mavis. *Blackberries in the Dark*. Knopf, 1985/1993. Following his grandfather's death, Austin goes to visit his grandmother, and they share their sadness as they work through their grief. (I: 8–11)

Park, Barbara. *Mick Harte Was Here*. Knopf, 1995. Thirteen-year-old Phoebe Harte narrates the story of losing her younger brother to a bike accident. (I: 9–12)

*Rohmann, Eric. *Bone Dog*. Roaring Brook, 2011. An old dog promises his boy to always be there for him, and after his death, his spirit returns to give the boy courage when he is faced with a scary situation on Halloween night. (I: 6–9)

Smith, Doris Buchanan. *A Taste of Blackberries*. Crowell, 1973. Jamie dies of an allergic reaction to a bee sting suffered while out picking blackberries, and his best friend grieves. (I: 8–10)

*Viorst, Judith. *The Tenth Good Thing about Barney*. Illustrated by Erik Blegvad. Macmillan, 1971. At a funeral in his backyard, a little boy tries to think of ten good things to remember about his cat, Barney. (I: P–8)

Yumoto, Kazumi. *The Friends*. Translated by Cathy Hirano. Farrar, Straus, & Giroux, 1996. (Originally published in Japan as *Natsu no niwa*, Fukutake Publishing, 1992.) Three boys are curious about death and spend their summer keeping surveillance on a man they are sure is old enough to die soon. Through the ensuing intergenerational friendship, the boys learn about life, living, and aging before they encounter death. (I: 10–YA)

Mystery and Suspense Books

Adler, David. *Cam Jansen and the Ghostly Mystery*. Viking, 2008. A photographic memory helps Cam solve mysteries, and in this case, a ticket booth is robbed while selling rock concert tickets. There are many other Cam Jansen mysteries in this series. (I: 8–11)

Byars, Betsy. *The Dark Stairs: A Herculeah Jones Mystery*. Viking, 1994. Thirteen-year-old Herculeah Jones, daughter of a police officer and a private investigator, and her partner Meat investigate the disappearance of the owner of Dead Oaks, an old house surrounded by stories of murder and insanity. Others in the Herculeah Jones Mystery series include *Tarot Says Beware* (1995), *Dead Letter* (1996), *Disappearing Acts* (1998), and *King of Murder* (2006). (I: 9–12)

Dowd, Siobhan. *The London Eye Mystery*. Fickling, 2008. Twelve-year-old Ted has Asperger Syndrome, and his obsessions play into his search to make sense of the world when he and his sister join together to solve the mystery of the disappearance of his visiting cousin who goes up in a capsule of the London Eye Ferris wheel, but is not in it when it comes back down. (I: 10–13)

Hamilton, Virginia. *The House of Dies Drear*. Silver Burdett Ginn, 1968. Members of an African American family find themselves dealing with a number of "ghosts" when they move into an old house where slaves used to be harbored in an Underground Railroad station. The sequel is *The Mystery of Drear House* (1987). (I: 10–YA)

Kline, Suzy. *Horrible Harry Cracks the Code*. Illustrated by Frank Remkiewicz. Viking, 2007. Horrible Harry sets out to solve a mystery of a mathematical code to prove to his classmates that he is second only to Sherlock Holmes. (I: 7–9)

Konigsburg, E. L. *From the Mixed-up Files of Mrs. Basil E. Frankweiler*. Atheneum, 1967. Siblings determine to remain hidden in the Metropolitan Museum of Art until they discover who created a mysterious sculpture. (I: 9–11)

Nixon, Joan Lowery. *The Other Side of Dark*. Delacorte, 1986. Lisa was thirteen when a gunshot put her into a four-year coma. When she wakes up, she realizes that she is the only witness to the identity of her mother's murderer. This book won the Edgar Allan Poe Mystery Writer's Award. (I: 12–YA)

Raskin, Ellen. *The Westing Game*. Dutton, 1978. When millionaire Sam Westing dies, he leaves words to the song "America the Beautiful" as clues for sixteen heirs to work out an intricate riddle and identify his murderer. (I: 9–12)

Sobol, Donald. *Encyclopedia Brown and the Case of the Slippery Salamander*. Delacorte, 1999. This is one in a series of detective stories starring ten-year-old Encyclopedia Brown and his partner Sally. Ten short cases are presented, challenging readers to figure out how they were solved, with answers at the back of the book. (I: 9–12)

Tate, Eleanora E. *The Secret of Gumbo Grove*. Watts, 1987. Raisin loves hearing stories of African Americans in the "old days," but while helping to clean up the church cemetery, she stumbles onto a mystery. (I: 9–12)

Humorous Books

Barrows, Annie. *Ivy and Bean*. Illustrated by Sophie Blackall. Chronicle, 2007. Bean loves to play tricks, and when the seemingly quiet new neighbor, Ivy, saves her from a trick gone wrong, the two seal the beginning of a wonderful friendship. Sequels: *Ivy and Bean and the Ghost that Had to Go* (2006), *Break the Fossil Record* (2007), *Take Care of the Babysitter* (2008). (I: 6–9)

Bauer, Joan. *Squashed*. Delacorte, 1992. In a humorous story, sixteen-year-old Lisa competes in a pumpkin-growing contest, trying to get her pumpkin, Max, to put on 200 pounds while she herself loses 20 pounds. (I: 12–YA)

Cameron, Ann. *The Stories Julian Tells*. Illustrated by Ann Strugnell. Knopf, 1981. Six short stories humorously describe events in Julian's life as he grows up. Other titles are *More Stories Julian Tells* (1986), *The Stories Huey Tells* (1995), and *More Stories Huey Tells* (1997). (I: 6–8)

Cleary, Beverly. *Ramona the Brave*. Morrow, 1975. This Ramona story has some of the funniest episodes in the series, including Ramona's breaking a raw egg on her head. (I: 9–12)

Greenwald, Sheila. *Rosy Cole: She Grows and Graduates*. Orchard, 1997. Rosy is now an eighth-grader, and she and her friends are in the midst of making a decision about where to attend high school. Earlier titles include *Give Us a Great Big Smile, Rosy Cole* (1981), *Write on, Rosy!* (1988), and *Rosy Cole: She Walks in Beauty* (1994). (I: 10–12)

McDonald, Megan. *Judy Moody (Was in a Mood. Not a Good Mood. A Bad Mood.)*. Illustrated by Peter Reynolds. Candlewick, 2000. Judy starts third grade in a bad mood, and her teacher asks her to return with a better mood the next day. Among the many sequels are *Judy Moody Saves the World* (2002), *Judy Moody Gets Famous* (2003), *Judy Moody, M.D.: The Doctor Is In* (2004). (I: 6–9)

Robinson, Barbara. *The Best Christmas Pageant Ever*. Tyndale House, 1972. The six rowdy Herdman siblings find themselves in the community Christmas pageant. The sequel is *The Best School Year Ever* (1994). (I: 8–12)

Rockwell, Thomas. *How to Eat Fried Worms*. Franklin Watts, 1973. Ten-year-old Billy decides on a bet to eat fifteen worms in fifteen days to earn $50 toward buying a new minibike. Luckily, his friends help by creating new concoctions each day. (I: 9–12)

RESOURCES AND REFERENCES

Alcott, Louisa May. *Little Women*. Macmillan, 1868/1962.

Alger, Horatio. *Ragged Dick, and Mark, the Match Boy*. Collier, 1897/1962.

Avi. *Nothing but the Truth: A Documentary Novel*. Orchard, 1991.

Blume, Judy. *Are You There, God? It's Me, Margaret*. Richard Jackson/Atheneum, 1970.

——. *Forever*. Bradbury, 1975.

Bunting, Eve. *Smoky Night*. Illustrated by David Diaz. Harcourt, 1994.

Burnett, Frances Hodgson. *Little Lord Fauntleroy*. Scribner, 1886.

——. *The Secret Garden*. Lippincott, 1910/1962.

Conly, Jane Leslie. *Crazy Lady!* HarperCollins, 1993.

Cooper, James Fenimore. *The Last of the Mohicans*. Scott, Foresman, 1826/1950.

Daly, Maureen. *Seventeenth Summer*. Dodd, 1942.

Defoe, Daniel. *Robinson Crusoe*. Running Press, 1719/1991.

Dodge, Mary Mapes. *Hans Brinker, or the Silver Skates*. Doubleday, 1865/1932.

Donovan, John. *I'll Get There, It Better Be Worth the Trip*. Harper, 1969.

Ehlert, Lois. *Red Leaf, Yellow Leaf*. Harcourt, 1991.

Elleman, Barbara. "Introduction." *Popular Reading for Children, II*. American Library Association, 1986, pp. v–vi.

Estes, Eleanor. *The Moffats*. Harcourt, 1941.

Grahame, Kenneth. *Wind in the Willows*. Scribner's, 1933.

Jackson, Jesse Jasper. *Call Me Charley*. Harper, 1945.

Lambert, Megan. "Reading about Families in My Family." *Hornbook*, 84(4) (May/June 2008), 261–263.

Larson, Jeanette. "The Scene of the Crime: Investigating New Mysteries." *Book Links*, 17(3) (2008): 24–28.

Lewis, C. S. *The Lion, the Witch and the Wardrobe: A Story for Children*. Macmillan, 1950.

Luria, A. R. *Cognitive Development: Its Cultural and Social Foundations*. Harvard University Press, 1976.

McCloskey, Robert. *Homer Price*. Viking, 1943.

Means, Florence. *The Moved Outers*. Houghton Mifflin, 1945.

——. *Shuttered Windows*. Houghton Mifflin, 1938.

Patron, Susan. *The Higher Power of Lucky*. Illustrated by Matt Phelan. Simon & Schuster, 2006.

Porter, Eleanor. *Pollyanna*. L. C. Page, 1913.

Postman, Neil. *The Disappearance of Childhood*. Delacorte, 1994.

Root, Shelton. "The New Realism: Some Personal Reflections." *Language Arts* 54.1 (1977): 19–24.

Rylant, Cynthia. *Missing May*. Dell, 1992.

Sewell, Anna. *Black Beauty: The Autobiography of a Horse*. Dodd, Mead, 1877/1941.

Shreve, Susan. *The Flunking of Joshua T. Bates*. Illustrated by Diane DeGroat. Knopf, 1984.

Spyri, Joanna. *Heidi*. Scribner's, 1884/1946.

Stanovich, Keith. "Are We Overselling Literacy?" *Stories and Readers: New Perspectives on Literature in the Elementary Classroom.* Ed. Charles Temple and Patrick Collins. Christopher-Gordon, 1992, p. 217.

Temple, Frances. *Tonight, by Sea.* Orchard, 1995.

Turnage, Shelia. *Three Times Lucky.* Dial, 2012.

Twain, Mark. *The Adventures of Huckleberry Finn.* Chanticleer, 1885/1950.

_____. *The Adventures of Tom Sawyer.* Scott, Foresman, 1876/1949.

Waber, Bernard. *Ira Sleeps Over.* Houghton Mifflin, 1972.

Warner, Gertrude Chandler. *The Boxcar Children.* Scott, Foresman, 1950.

Williams, Vera B. *"More, More, More" Said the Baby: 3 Love Stories.* Greenwillow, 1990.

Wong, Janet. *Apple Pie, 4th of July.* Illustrated by Margaret Chodos-Irvine. Harcourt, 2002.

Zolotow, Charlotte. *The Hating Book.* Illustrated by Ben Schechter. HarperTrophy, 1969/1989.

_____. *The Quarreling Book.* Illustrated by Arnold Lobel. HarperCollins, 1963/1982.

Historical Fiction

“ *Today I moved to a
twelve-acre rock covered
with cement, topped with
bird turd and surrounded
by water. . . . And there are
twenty-three other kids who
live on the island because
their dads work as guards or
cooks or doctors or electricians
for the prison like my dad does.
Plus there are a ton of murderers,
rapists, hit men, con men, stickup
men, embezzlers, connivers, burglars,
kidnappers and maybe even an
innocent man or two, though I
doubt it.* ”

—from *Al Capone Does My Shirts* (2004)
by Gennifer Choldenko

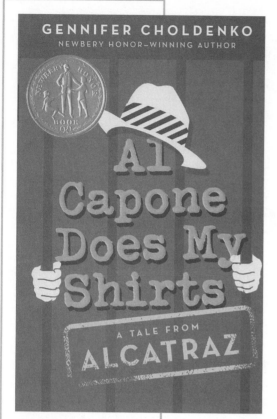

ennifer Choldenko set her story about Moose Flanagan in 1935 on the island of Alcatraz. The setting of the book is far removed from the world of today's young readers. After all, how many grow up on an isolated prison island where notorious criminals are housed? And yet readers can empathize with Moose. Most have—at one time or another—been uprooted from the place they call home and found themselves in a new school where they really did not want to be! Writers of fine historical fiction are able to help readers feel connected to people and situations from the past, which is what makes historical fiction an important tool in the classroom.

ILLUSTRATION 10.1 When Moose moves with his family to Alcatraz so his disabled sister can attend a special school nearby, he soon discovers the many complications that come with life on the famous prison island. ("Al Capone Does My Shirts" by Gennifer Choldenko. Used by permission of Penguin Group (USA) LLC. All rights reserved.)

What Is Historical Fiction?

Historical fiction is broadly defined as a work of fiction set in a time prior to when it was written. How far in the past must a story be set to qualify as historical fiction? Some say twenty-five years; others say fifty. For our purposes, the precise number of years doesn't matter. What matters most is the child's perspective. To a child, a story set forty years ago qualifies as being about "olden times." So a book such as Rita Williams-Garcia's *One Crazy Summer* falls into the realm of historical fiction, even though many adults view the Civil Rights era of the 1960s as something that happened "just yesterday."

Even the general definition given here may sometimes be too limiting. Some books feature events that were contemporary at the time they were written, but with the passing of time, the situations have gained historical significance. One such book is Beverly Naidoo's *Journey to Jo'burg*, which details the journey of two black South African children who experience the harsh realities of apartheid as they travel from their homeland to Johannesburg. At the time of its publication, the book described contemporary conditions in South Africa. However, the apartheid system has since been dismantled, so today, the events in Naidoo's book are significant from an historical perspective. Books like this one can be considered historical fiction rather than contemporary realistic fiction.

Time Periods Emphasized in Historical Fiction

Authors in the United States who write historical fiction have typically chosen to write about the United States. This means that comparatively little historical fiction set in other parts of the world is readily available to American audiences. There is also an imbalance in the subjects and time periods about which American authors have chosen to write. Some topics and periods in American history that have been written about most extensively include the American Revolutionary War, slavery and the Civil War, the westward movement, immigration, and World War II. (Lists of Recommended Books at the end of this chapter are organized by major historical periods.) One way to broaden historical perspectives for American students is to include international literature in the array of historical fiction made available in the classroom. Many works of historical fiction are included among the winners of the Mildred L. Batchelder Award given by the American Library Association for books originally published in a foreign language and subsequently translated into English and published in the United States.

Value of Historical Fiction

Why should teachers introduce children to historical fiction? First, many works of historical fiction present wonderful stories that offer children a rich aesthetic experience. After all, who can read Helen Frost's beautifully crafted verse in *The Braid* and not be touched by the plight of twins separated through immigration? Readers of Laurie Halse Anderson's *Chains*, set during the American Revolution, will be touched by the irony of a young girl's struggle to escape slavery and find personal freedom in the midst of a broader struggle by the patriots to win freedom for their homeland. Who won't chuckle over Brock Cole's *The Money We'll Save*, a picture book in which a family tries to raise a turkey in an already crowded, nineteenth-century New York tenement?

There are other reasons, as well, to incorporate historical fiction into the curriculum. Ten plus years of No Child Left Behind have resulted in a narrowing of the curriculum (Lewis, 2008; Whelan, 2006). This means that subjects—including social studies—receive far less attention in today's schools. The inclusion of historical fiction in the curriculum is one way of combating this problem. Quality historical fiction is well researched and can serve as a valuable vehicle for learning about the past, especially because historical fiction engages readers in the *drama* of historical events. This dramatic element is something too often missing from textbooks. Carl M. Tomlinson, Michael O. Tunnell, and Donald J. Richgels (1993) argue that readers need "historical empathy" to develop historical understanding. That is, readers "must be able to perceive past events and issues as they were experienced by the people at the time" (p. 54). Helping readers develop such empathy is what historical fiction does best, by lifting up ordinary people and emphasizing human motives.

Historical fiction is important for another reason as well: Many works of historical fiction are natural companions to nonfiction. For example, students who read Katherine Paterson's *Bread and Roses, Too*, the story of two children enmeshed in the struggle between the working poor and the rich mill owners of Lawrence, Massachusetts, may well make connections to and pose questions about the economic issues facing our contemporary society. In seeking answers to their questions, students can turn to the many readily available nonfiction sources (including digital ones) that explore this topic. This link between historical fiction and nonfiction is particularly significant in light of the growing recognition that students need to engage in far more extensive reading of nonfiction. Chapter 11 of this textbook features many quality nonfiction books and biographies that can serve as outstanding companion pieces to works of historical fiction.

The Evolution of Historical Fiction

It is not possible to identify a single creator for most literary genres, but this is not the case with historical fiction. Sir Walter Scott is generally believed to be the first person to write a work of what we now call historical fiction (Blos, 1993). *Waverly*, Scott's first piece of historical fiction, was

ISSUE *to* CONSIDER

Does Historical Fiction Have a Place in the Study of History?

Those who argue that historical fiction is an important tool in history instruction maintain that students "encounter the complexities of historical events, where facts from the past become living, breathing drama, significant beyond their own time" (Levstik, 1989, p. 136). Further, advocates argue that because writers of historical fiction do extensive research on the eras about which they write, literature is often a rich source of information.

On the opposing side are those who argue that literature must not be expected to bear the burden of social studies instruction. Literature is a fragile medium, they remind us, and it can readily be crushed if it is forced to bear too heavy an informational load. When students are asked to read literature for the purpose of learning about the past, they may fail to enter the story world on aesthetic terms.

What do you think? Should historical fiction serve as a springboard for learning about the past? Or should readers primarily be encouraged to read historical fiction for a rich literary experience? If you have read *The Midwife's Apprentice*, would you want students to read the book primarily as a means of learning about medieval times, or would you choose to have students explore the theme of living a fulfilling life through this book?

published in 1810 and was followed by others, including *Ivanhoe*. Although Scott didn't write specifically for children, his books were read by young and old alike.

Early works set in past eras were quite different than today's historical fiction. These early works consisted primarily of adventure stories, and they contained lengthy descriptive passages and many historical inaccuracies. The early authors of historical fiction who wrote specifically for children had their own agenda: teaching students historical information. By the 1930s, many of these works presented romantic, highly idealized views of the past that contained an overwhelming amount of information (Tomlinson, Tunnell, & Richgels, 1993).

Fortunately, historical fiction has changed considerably. The genre is no longer viewed primarily as a vehicle for conveying historical information. Rather, writers strive to tell stories—stories that show how living in a particular time and place in the past shaped the lives of people, especially ordinary people. And although ordinary people sometimes become caught up in major historical events, historical fiction, in large part, is not about those events.

Style

The style of writing used in historical fiction has also changed. Gone are the ornate descriptions, the archaic language, and the lengthy factual passages found in early works of historical fiction. Today's writers may choose to capture the flavor of an earlier era by infusing words and phrases of the period into their stories as Karen Cushman does throughout *Alchemy and Meggy Swann*, a story set in Elizabethan London. Yet they also make every effort to ensure that their stories are told in language that is accessible to children. Readers have no trouble understanding Meggy's intent when she counters the taunts of an unkind lad by retorting, "Cease your bibble-babble, you gleeking goat's bladder!"

Historical Perspective

One of the most striking changes in historical fiction for children is in the perspective from which stories are told. Today's writers are less likely to assume idealized views of the past. Joel Taxel (1983) analyzed thirty-two pieces of historical fiction about the American Revolution written between 1899 and 1976, and discussed two of these books at length. The first, Esther Forbes's *Johnny Tremain*, which was published in 1943, encapsulates an idealized view of the American Revolution: The American patriots are viewed as a united people involved in a divinely inspired struggle for freedom and equality. The perspective in James and Christopher Collier's *My Brother Sam Is Dead*, written in 1974, stands in marked contrast: The colonists are a divided people, with many remaining loyal to the king of England. Tim Meeker, the book's protagonist, questions the values of the revolutionaries, eventually choosing not to become part of the revolutionary fervor. Differing perspectives can be explained, in part, by the times in which authors live and write. *Johnny Tremain* was written in the midst of the patriotic fervor of World War II, whereas *My Brother Sam Is Dead* was published in 1974, when the United States was waging an unpopular war in Vietnam.

In recent historical fiction for children, many new perspectives have emerged. For example, in *Encounter,* Jane Yolen used a picture book format to show the arrival of Columbus through the eyes of a Taino child who tries to warn his people of the coming destruction he has seen in a dream. *Morning Girl* is a chapter book that also explores the Columbus story from the Taino point of view. This book is told in alternating voices between two siblings, one enthusiastic about the coming of the white men and the other more cautious. Perspectives on pioneer times have also changed in historical fiction for children. In earlier years, the common perspective on pioneer life was of the sort seen in the *Little House* books: Although times

TOP SHELF 10.1

INTERNATIONAL BOOKS SET IN THE WORLD WAR II ERA

Rose Blanche by Christophe Gallaz. Illustrated by Roberto Innocenti

The Island on Bird Street by Uri Orlev

The Man from the Other Side by Uri Orlev

Run, Boy, Run by Uri Orlev

The Book Thief by Marcus Zusak

were hard, a warm, united family was an ever-present, sustaining force. More recent books, such as Eve Bunting's *Dandelions*, explore the loneliness and isolation of pioneer life from a woman's perspective.

Subject Matter

The subject matter of historical fiction for children has also changed. Authors of historical fiction are writing about less well-known historical events, periods, and places. Christopher Paul Curtis sets *Elijah of Buxton* in Buxton Settlement, a haven for freed slaves established in 1849 in Canada. Candace Fleming's picture book *Boxes for Katje* tells the story of how an American town reached out to help alleviate the severe shortages suffered by a community in post–World War II Holland. In *The Porcupine Year*, set in 1852, Louise Erdrich tells the story of an Ojibwe girl and her family who have been displaced by the American government and are in search of a new home.

Writers of earlier times adhered to an unspoken code that children needed to be protected from the less savory aspects of the past (Tunnell, 1993). This is no longer true. Mildred Taylor and other writers have written about the senseless prejudice and violence that African Americans have faced. In *Journey to Topaz,* Yoshiko Uchida wrote movingly about the experiences of Japanese Americans in internment camps during World War II. In *Malka,* Mirjam Pressler tells the story of seven-year-old Malka trying to survive the horrors of Nazi-occupied Poland on her own. Julius Lester's *Day of Tears* tells the story of the largest slave auction in the United States and the way it impacted the lives of those touched by the sale. In *Breaking Stalin's Nose,* Eugene Yelchin presents a chilling portrait of oppression in the Soviet Union under Stalin's rule. The increasing availability of historical fiction of this type makes it an important tool for launching classroom discussions about issues of social justice.

Historical fiction about other parts of the world, especially developing countries, is increasingly available to American audiences. For example, in Minfong Ho's *Rice without Rain,* Jinda and her family are caught up in the turbulence of the 1945 student movement in Thailand as they struggle to survive the drought that has hit their homeland. Margarita Engle's *The Surrender Tree: Poems of Cuba's Struggle for Freedom* centers around Cuba's wars for independence. There is still too little historical fiction about other countries and cultures available to young American readers, but this situation is beginning to change.

Picture Books

The emergence in recent years of many works of historical fiction in picture book format is a noteworthy change. Some of these stories, such as Michael Tunnell's *Mailing May,* are appropriate for children as young as five, whereas stories such as Yin's *Coolies,* about the bigotry and harsh treatment faced by two Chinese boys who are helping to build the transcontinental railroad in the United States, are better suited for older elementary children. Still other picture books, such as Margaree Mitchell's *Uncle Jed's Barbershop,* a story about the segregated South during the Depression era, is even appropriate for students in middle school and beyond. Many readers especially enjoy the picture book format because illustrations can bring hard-to-imagine settings to life and can help readers to develop a feeling for bygone eras that words alone may not be able to evoke.

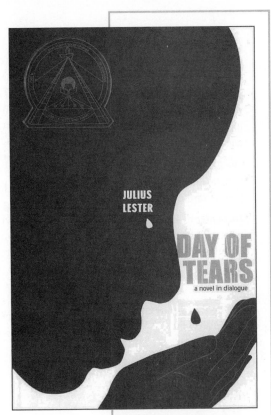

ILLUSTRATION 10.2 *Day of Tears* is the dramatic story of the biggest slave auction in American history. (Lester, Julius. From "Day of Tears." Hyperion Books, an imprint of Disney Book Group, 2005. Copyright 2005 Hyperion Books, an imprint of Disney Book Group. All rights reserved. Reproduced by permission.)

 TOP SHELF 10.2

HISTORICAL FICTION PICTURE BOOKS

Sweet Clara and the Freedom Quilt by Deborah Hopkinson. Illustrated by James Ransome

Mailing May by Michael Tunnell. Illustrated by Ted Rand

The Money We'll Save by Brock Cole

The Gardener by Sarah Stewart. Illustrated by David Small

(Continue)

The Greatest Skating Race by Louise Borden. Illustrated by Niki Daly

The Cats in Krakinski Square by Karen Hesse. Illustrated by Wendy Watson

The Bracelet by Yoshiko Uchida. Illustrated by Joanna Yardley

Encounter by Jane Yolen. Illustrated by David Shannon

Pink and Say by Patricia Polacco

The Bobbin Girl by Emily Arnold McCully

Historical Fiction Series

Historical fiction series, which emerged as a strong trend in the 1990s, continue to be very popular today. These include *Dear America, Orphan Train Children, American Diaries, My America, My Name Is America,* and the *Royal Diary* series. Although the quality of series books varies, major children's authors have contributed to the literary quality of some of these series. For example, Kathryn Lasky, Jim Murphy, Patricia McKissack, and Karen Hesse are among the authors who have written books in the *Dear America* series. Many historical fiction series books have been pitched toward a younger audience and have featured female protagonists more often than male protagonists. Many educators have welcomed the arrival of these series, claiming that they have awakened a new interest in history and cultivated a devoted following, especially among young girls.

All the changes in the genre in recent decades make for a bright future for children's historical fiction. Certainly, books in this genre have been awarded an impressive number of Newbery Medals in recent years: Karen Cushman's *The Midwife's Apprentice* (1995), Karen Hesse's *Out of the Dust* (1997), Christopher Curtis's *Bud, Not Buddy* (1999), Richard Peck's *A Year Down Yonder* (2001), Linda Sue Park's *A Single Shard* (2002), Avi's *Crispin* (2003), Laura Amy Schlitz's *Good Masters! Sweet Ladies!* (2007), Clare Vanderpool's *Moon*

Ask *the* Author. . . Richard Peck

Your works of historical fiction run the gamut from the humor of A Year Down Yonder *to the gravity that infuses* The River Between Us. *What inspires such diverse stories?*

I fell in love with the Civil War not in history class but in the pages in *Gone with the Wind* and *The Red Badge of Courage*. These were two radically different views of a mythic war, a reminder that many roads lead to the past. The great need is to bring as many young readers as possible along on the travel through time in the knowledge that no single book wins them all. I look high and low for new ways to lure the young into the past. Humor works. It certainly did for Mark Twain. His *The Adventures of Huckleberry Finn* has been called the first real American novel. But it was an historical novel too, written after the Civil War about a vanished ante-bellum world. In fact, it was nostalgia with a sting in its tail—my favorite thing. Mark Twain reminds us of the uses of humor, and how humor is anger that was sent to finishing school. And so in a good many of my novels, *The Teacher's Funeral, Fair Weather, A Long Way from Chicago,* the historical content is dramatized in a series of comic scenes.

Not all of history can be lightly told. But the past has a glamour that eludes the history textbook. In a book of mine about the Civil War, *The River Between Us,* there's limited scope for lightness and less for laughter. I turn, instead, to suspense and a secret. But the story takes place on Twain's own river, flowing like history itself, and it turns out to be about a family secret.

All of our stories are family stories, written to invite the young to look back at the traditions of their own families. And all of our stories are about how history repeats, written for readers too young to have seen that for themselves.

Richard Peck has written thirty novels, and is the only children's book author ever to have received a National Humanities Medal. In addition, he has won a number of other major awards for the body of his work, including the Margaret A. Edwards Award, the ALAN Award, and the Medallion from the University of Southern Mississippi. Virtually every publication and association in the field of children's literature has recommended his books. His *A Year Down Under* won the 2001 Newbery Medal. Its prequel, *A Long Way from Chicago,* was a National Book Award finalist and Newbery Honor Book.

Over Manifest (2011), and Jack Gantos's *Dead End in Norvelt* (2012). Given the special values of historical fiction, many teachers look forward to even more books of this caliber.

Categories of Historical Fiction

Joan Blos (1993) identifies three types of historical fiction: (1) fictionalized memoirs, (2) fictionalized family history, and (3) fiction based on research. The author's relationship to the material is different for each type.

Fictionalized Memoirs

Fictionalized memoirs are not actual memoirs. Rather, they are works of fiction set in an era in which the author actually lived. Hence, the authors of fictionalized memoirs are able to draw, at least in part, on their own experiences in crafting their narratives. The result is often a story that is full of extraordinarily rich details about daily life and that offers a special sense of immediacy to the reader. For example, it is easy to imagine how, in writing *Countdown,* Deborah Wiles drew on personal memories to describe the complex emotions associated with living through the 1962 Cuban missile crisis. Yet while writers of fictionalized memoirs may draw on personal memories, these memories are seen from an historical perspective, because the time period about which the authors write may be vastly different from the time in which they are writing. You may wonder why fictionalized memoirs are not considered biography if personal experiences serve as the inspiration for them. The reason is, quite simply, that the writers fictionalize their personal experiences.

Fictionalized Family History

Many families treasure a tradition of passing family stories from one generation to the next, and family stories have fed the historical fiction of many writers. Sometimes historical fiction develops from only the barest snippet of a family story. Such was the case for writer Ann Turner. As Turner and her aunt looked at an old trunk, her aunt remembered another old trunk (Turner, 1993):

> "You know, there used to be a very old trunk in Grandpa's house, in the basement . . . . It was an eighteenth-century trunk . . . a big, black domed thing covered with leather . . . . And there were two stories about it. One was that during the early period of settlement some of our ancestors escaped from an Indian attack in that trunk. The other story is that when the rebels came, some children were hidden in that trunk and escaped the rebels."
> "You mean we were Tories?" . . .
> "Oh, yes, some were . . . Anyway, I wonder what happened to that trunk." (p. 11)

From this fleeting exchange grew *Katie's Trunk,* a story set during the American Revolution in which a Tory child hides in the family trunk when a band of patriots comes to her house.

In other instances, relatively well-developed stories are passed down, stories that writers can use with only a little fleshing out. According to Patricia Polacco, *Pink and Say,* her story of the friendship between a black Union soldier and a white Union soldier, was passed down through her family from her great-great-grandfather, who happened to be the white soldier in the story. In writing *Our Only May Amelia,* Jennifer Holm drew on the actual diary written by her great aunt to fashion this

TOP SHELF 10.3

PAIRING RELATED PICTURE BOOKS AND LENGTHIER WORKS OF HISTORICAL FICTION

American Revolution
Katie's Trunk by Ann Turner. Illustrated by Ron Himler

My Brother Sam Is Dead by James Collier and Christopher Collier

Slavery and the Civil War
Pink and Say by Patricia Polacco

Silent Thunder by Andrea Pinkney

The Secret to Freedom by Marcia Vaughan. Illustrated by Larry Johnson

Elijah of Buxton by Christopher Paul Curtis

Westward Movement in the United States
Train to Somewhere by Eve Bunting. Illustrated by Ronald Himler

Rodzina by Karen Cushman

Coolies by Yin. Illustrated by Chris Soentpiet

Dragon's Gate by Laurence Yep

World War II
The Butterfly by Patricia Polacco

Number the Stars by Lois Lowry

Baseball Saved Us by Ken Mochizuki. Illustrated by Dom Lee

Journey to Topaz by Yohiko Uchida

TECHNOLOGY
in PRACTICE 10.1

Visit the teachingbooks.net Web site to hear Christopher Paul Curtis talk about some of the questions he asked when doing research for *Elijah of Buxton*, a work of historical fiction set in Buxton Settlement, a haven for freed slaves in Canada.

story about a young Finnish-American girl born on the Nasel River in Washington during the late nineteenth century.

Fiction Based on Research

Probably the bulk of historical fiction for children fits into the third category—fiction based on research. Writers who set their stories in eras about which they have no firsthand knowledge must engage in research to ensure authenticity. The amount of information available to writers can vary extensively. Writers who feature cultures with no writing systems frequently have only scant anthropological evidence from which to draw. Michael Dorris faced this situation when writing *Morning Girl*. Set on a Bahamian island in 1492, the book centers on a sister and brother of the Taino tribe. The story ends as Morning Girl greets the white visitors who paddle to shore—men from Columbus's ship. Dorris (1992) noted that the Tainos had no writing system, and within a generation or two of Columbus's coming, the tribe was wiped out by disease. The only written reference to these people was one entry Columbus included in his journal. By contrast, writers who focus on literate societies often have a wealth of original sources as well as extensive reference material from which to draw their information. Frances Temple (1994) described the research she did in writing *The Ramsay Scallop*, a story about a couple's religious pilgrimage, set in Europe in 1300:

> More than seventy books turn up cited in my notes for *The Ramsay Scallop*, some in English, some in French or Spanish, some in medieval French . . . . One source led to another: art books; religious meditations; playscripts; a guidebook written in 1190 by a priest, with tips on where to find clean water and what to use to discourage fleas; histories, where I found a picture of Nana Sybille in her wheelbarrow; and song books. (p. 18)

Research can take other forms as well. In writing *The Apprenticeship of Lucas Whitaker*, a book about the devastation caused by consumption 150 years ago, author Cynthia DeFelice interviewed a pathologist and an archaeologist, examined old burial grounds using radar technology, and spent a day in an anthropologist's lab learning about folk medical practices (DeFelice, 1998).

For **ENGLISH LANGUAGE LEARNERS**

- Make books available for classroom discussion that shed light on the countries and cultures of origin of your English language learners. If books on the history of a particular country are not available, books on those children's cultures still may be. (For example, you might find a book on the history of Islam, if not on Somalia). Such books give your English language learners points of connection to the classroom, and also give their classmates a better understanding of where these students come from.

- When discussing a book about an English language learner's country of origin, put the student in the role of the expert. Teachers should support the English language learner in making her explanations and should model for the other children ways of respectful inquiry.
- When reading books based in U.S. or European history, make sure that the English language learners have the background knowledge of historical periods and geographical settings that other students may take for granted.

Major Writers of Historical Fiction

WRITER	PRIMARILY WRITES . . .	MAJOR WORKS INCLUDE
Christopher Paul Curtis	Curtis's award-winning chapter books, filled with both humor and drama, focus on the African American experience in distinctly different time periods.	• *The Watsons Go to Birmingham—1963* • *Bud, Not Buddy* • *Elijah of Buxton*
Karen Cushman	Cushman creates strong female protagonists in books set in a variety of time periods including medieval England, the California Gold Rush, and Elizabethan England.	• *Catherine, Called Birdy* • *The Midwife's Apprentice* • *The Ballad of Lucy Whipple* • *Rodzina* • *The Loud Silence of Francine Green* • *Alchemy and Meggy Swann*
Karen Hesse	Hesse writes about wide-ranging historical topics including immigration, the Depression, World War II, and the Ku Klux Klan. She uses a variety of distinctive formats and crafting techniques (e.g., letters, free verse novels, picture books).	• *Letters from Rifka* • *Out of the Dust* • *Witness* • *Stowaway* • *Aleutian Sparrow* • *The Cats in Krasinski Square*
Uri Orlev	Orlev has said that the Holocaust was his childhood, and he has written about that tragic time for young people, focusing on the Jewish resistance and on struggles to survive during the Holocaust.	• *The Island on Bird Street* • *The Man from the Other Side* • *Run, Boy, Run*
Linda Sue Park	Park's historical fiction is set in Korea in a variety of eras. These works give young American readers a glimpse into worlds about which most will know little.	• *A Single Shard* • *Seesaw Girl* • *The Kite Fighters* • *When My Name Was Keoko*
Richard Peck	Much of Peck's historical fiction is marked by its humor, strong story lines, and richly drawn characters.	• *A Long Way from Chicago* • *A Year Down Yonder* • *Fair Weather* • *The Teacher's Funeral: A Comedy in Three Parts* • *The River Between Us*
Mildred Taylor	Taylor has given a special gift to children's literature: the gift of the Logan family, an African American family living in rural Mississippi during the Depression.	• *Roll of Thunder, Hear My Cry* • *Let the Circle Be Unbroken* • *The Friendship* • *The Gold Cadillac* • *Mississippi Bridge* • *The Well* • *The Land*

TOP SHELF 10.4

How Historical Fiction Works

Historical fiction differs—at least in some ways—from other genres. In particular, a work of historical fiction contains "time markers" that clearly situate it in a particular time period. Let's consider some of the critical aspects of historical fiction, which affect both how it is written and how it should be read.

Setting

Because historical fiction takes place in a time removed from the reader, setting is an especially important element in this genre. The writer's obligation is to bring place and time to life for the reader by providing details that are neither romanticized nor distorted, but are as authentic as possible, given what is known about the era in which the story is set. Research is the most likely means by which the writer obtains these details.

The importance of rich details of setting is evident in Karen Cushman's *Alchemy and Meggy Swann*. As young Meggy struggles to maneuver the streets of Elizabethan London using "walking sticks" (i.e., homemade crutches), she stumbles over the carcass of a dead dog left to rot in the street and expresses her frustration by shouting, "Fie upon this dirty city . . . home to every kind of dirt, muck, and slime God ever created" (p. 55). But the response of Roger, her companion, reveals another side of the teeming city:

> "That may be so, but you will come to love her as I do," Roger said. "London is a fair that lasts all year. Around every corner is something wondrous—here a man with a dancing monkey, yon our good Queen Bess in silks and satins on a fine white horse. This way there's a hanging at Tyburn, that way fire eaters and rope dancers and the puppeteers in Fleet Street." Gesturing grandly, he nearly knocked Meggy into the teeming gutter. (pp. 55–56)

The details that Cushman includes make it easy for the reader to envision how dramatically different London of the 1500s must have been from London today. Details about setting are crucial in historical fiction, although it is equally important not to include so many as to overwhelm the story. Setting details must also advance the story, as they do in *Alchemy and Meggy Swann*. Meggy's attention to her new

TECHNOLOGY in PRACTICE 10.2

Many teachers are finding multiple uses for software programs that allow teachers and students to easily create graphic organizers that can be applied in any number of subject areas. Ready-made templates can be used, or designs can be customized.

Using such a program, create a Venn diagram of overlapping circles to compare a period of history with today. On one circle, write the things that were unique to the historical time period (e.g., traveling by wagon). In the other circle, write descriptors for the way things are today (e.g., traveling by car). In the center section created by the overlapping circles, write down things that both times have in common (e.g., going to school). Topics such as transportation, clothing, occupations, and men's and women's roles can be addressed. Comparisons between cultures can be made. Creating their own Venn diagrams engages students in the subject matter in more complex ways.

surroundings helps the reader to understand just how challenging the streets of London are for a young girl disabled from birth.

Setting is also a crucial element in Deborah Wiles's *Countdown*. The immediate story of Franny and her family plays out in a suburb of Washington, D.C., but the broader backdrop of the story is the Cuban missile crisis and the Civil Rights Movement of the early 1960s. Wiles uses an innovative approach to effectively convey the tensions that existed at the national level during this period, tensions that directly impact Franny's life. She intersperses her narrative with dramatic black and white photographs and newspaper clippings from that time, quotes from major political players, advertisements for fallout shelters, vignettes about famous figures of the day, and other period memorabilia. *Countdown* has been described as a documentary novel and can be considered an example of genre blurring because of the blending of the narrative storyline with the diverse array of reminders of the era.

Plot

The writer of historical fiction must create a conflict that grows out of the time in which the story takes place. In *Moon Over Manifest*, author Clare Vanderpool weaves together two plot strands. Set in the midst of the Great Depression, the central story strand centers around Abilene, who arrives in Manifest, Kansas, having been sent there to live with her father's old friend, Pastor Shady Howard. Abilene has no idea when (or if) her father will return for her, nor does she understand why she can no longer follow her father around the country as he travels by rail in search of employment. The second plot strand, which emerges through stories told to Abilene by Madame Sadie, takes place in 1917/1918. Events in this strand are shaped by World War I, the influenza outbreak of 1918, Prohibition, and even a Ku Klux Klan campaign against immigrants. Only as Madame Sadie's story draws to its conclusion does Abilene come to understand the actions of her father, her own place in the world, and her relationship with her father.

In historical fiction, the writer not only must create a conflict that grows out of the time in which the story is set but also must ensure that events unfold plausibly and that the conflict is resolved in a manner consistent with the historical time period. Jacqueline Kelly's *The Evolution of Calpurnia Tate* offers an example of such a plot. Young Calpurnia Tate discovers that her growing interest in nature and science is not deemed an acceptable interest for a young girl in a rural Texas community in 1899. Her mother's pressure to make Calpurnia into a proper lady is counterbalanced only by the support of her grandfather, an amateur naturalist.

Character

More often than not, the characters in historical fiction are ordinary people rather than figures of historical importance. Sometimes, they are swept up in great historical events of their time, as happens in Laurie Halse Anderson's *Chains*, a story in which a young slave seeks freedom in the midst of the American Revolution. More

TEACHING IDEA 10.1

JACKDAWS FOR INTRODUCING HISTORICAL FICTION

COMMON CORE STANDARD: *Integration Of Knowledge and Ideas, STANDARD 7*

In order to introduce a story and the period of history in which it is set, assemble a collection of artifacts that represent important facets of the story. One by one, pull the artifacts from a bag or box and encourage the students to ask questions and make guesses about the role of the object in the story. As each object is revealed, ask students to consider how the artifacts might be related. Students will likely be motivated to make some predictions about the setting or context for the artifacts—who uses them and how they might be used.

For example, before one teacher introduced *Sarah, Plain and Tall*, she filled a brown paper bag with a map, a bonnet, a toy seal, and seashells. She pulled one item out at a time, inviting her students to make predictions about the story. All their predictions were accepted. In doing so, the teacher not only motivated the students' interest in the story but also was able to informally assess students' background knowledge about the story setting and establish a purpose for reading—to find out if their predictions were accurate or not.

TEACHING IDEA 10.2

HEAD, HEART, HANDS: NURTURING CHARACTER EMPATHY

COMMON CORE STANDARD: *Key Ideas and Details,* **STANDARD 3**

Since one of the benefits of reading historical fiction involves being able to empathize with a character experiencing a particular time in history, make a Head, Heart, and Hands chart about a character from historical fiction. Divide a piece of paper into thirds from top to bottom. In the top section, or the "head," write about what the character knows as the story unfolds. In the middle "heart" section, write about what the character feels. And in the bottom "hand" section, write about what the character does.

In Patricia Polacco's *The Butterfly*, Monique finds out (knows/head) about the secret room in her own home and has conflicting feelings (heart) about the purpose of the room until she joins (what she does/hands) her mother in helping a Jewish family escape from Nazi-occupied France.

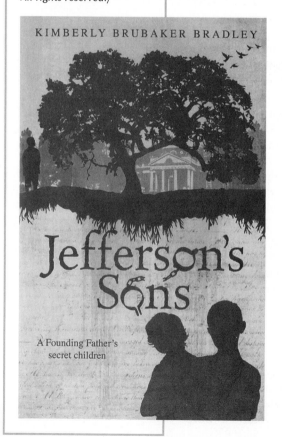

ILLUSTRATION 10.3 *Jefferson's Sons* is the story of Thomas Jefferson's secret children told from the perspective of the sons he sired with Sally Hemings. ("Jefferson's Sons: A Founding Father's Secret Children" by Kimberly Brubaker Bradley. Used by permission of Penguin Group (USA) LLC. All rights reserved.)

often than not though, the characters in historical fiction are living what can be best described as commonplace lives. For example, Laura Amy Schlitz's **Good Masters! Sweet Ladies!** features monologues by ordinary young people living in a medieval village—the plowboy, the blacksmith's daughter, the glassblower's apprentice, and the village beggar, among others. At times, though, major historical figures do enter into works of historical fiction. For example, Thomas Jefferson is a character in Kimberly Brubaker Bradley's *Jefferson's Sons,* and Frederick Douglass appears briefly in Christopher Paul Curtis's *Elijah of Buxton.*

Whether their characters are ordinary people or important historical figures, writers of historical fiction strive to create authentic characters who behave in ways that are consistent with the time period in which the story is set. Karen Cushman's *The Midwife's Apprentice* takes place in medieval England, a time when daily life was harsh and even cruel for those who were not members of the privileged classes. As this story begins, the reader is introduced to a homeless waif who has burrowed in a dung heap for warmth in order to survive a cold winter's night. Early on in the story, the daily realities of survival so completely dominate the reality of the protagonist that "she dreamed of nothing, for she hoped for nothing and expected nothing. It was as cold and dark inside her as out in the frosty night" (p. 2).

Theme

We can discern a great deal about life by learning about our past, and writers of historical fiction frequently explore themes that are significant not only for the historical period of the story but also for the present. In a listing of the themes that she explored in her Newbery Medal winner *A Gathering of Days: A New England Girl's Journal, 1830–1832,* Joan Blos (1993) includes "parent loss, death, remarriage, teacher accountability, community control, civil rights, moral responsibility versus personal loyalty" (p. 14). All are still relevant today.

The themes found in historical fiction are diverse and significant: the senselessness of prejudice and violence, the importance of family and community, the destructiveness of oppression, the need for freedom and independence, the importance of loyalty, faith and honor, the need to reach out to others. Kathy Broderick (1994) observed that "we learn about the present from studying the past. Though some of the problems of the past have been solved, there are questions that the characters in . . . [books] ask that we are still asking today" (p. 19). For this reason, historical fiction can often be used to launch rich and relevant discussions focused on issues of social justice.

Criteria for Evaluating Historical Fiction

- Is the story well written according to literary standards outlined in Chapter 2?
- Does the writer bring the setting to life through the inclusion of authentic details that do not overwhelm the story?
- Do the characters behave in ways that are believable, given the time period in which they live?
- Are the conflicts in the story plausible in light of the time period in which the story is set?
- Although the story is set in the past, are themes still relevant for today's readers?

EXPERIENCES FOR FURTHER LEARNING

1. Have you ever read a work of historical fiction and, after completing it, been convinced that you really understood the historical period featured in the story? In fact, after reading the book, you may have felt like an expert on life during the Middle Ages or on the challenges of crossing the continent in a covered wagon. Writers of historical fiction sweep us back in time into the lives of the famous, the infamous, and the common people and convince us we were there with them.

    How well does a fictional work reflect history? Read a book such as *Crispin* or *Fever 1793*. Then create a T-chart. On the left side of the chart, list information included in the story that you believe accurately reflects history. To try and verify what you have included on your chart, read informational texts about the period. Then, on the right side of the chart opposite each of your original statements, indicate if your original state-

ment was verified through your research or, if any statements were not verified, write a corrected statement opposite the original statement. To what extent does it appear that the author grounded the story in careful research?

2. More and more historical fiction is being published in picture book format, and some of these picture books explore potentially disturbing subject matter. Teachers must make judgments about whether these books are appropriate for their students. Read a sampling of historical fiction picture books, and discuss with your classmates the most appropriate audience for these books. You might want to read *The Whispering Cloth* by Pegi Shea and *Rose Blanche* by Christophe Gallaz. Then discuss how reading aloud a picture book and engaging the class in a discussion can build background knowledge and set the stage for reading a related novel.

RECOMMENDED BOOKS

* indicates a picture book; I indicates interest level
(P = preschool, YA = young adult)

Ancient Times through the Medieval Period

Avi. *Crispin: The Cross of Lead*. Hyperion, 2002. Accused of a crime he did not commit and having lost his mother—his only living relative—Crispin must flee his village. Pursued by unknown enemies, Crispin joins up with a juggler named Bear and finds himself swept up in the political intrigues of medieval England. Sequel: *Crispin: At the Edge of the World*. (I: 10 and up)

Cushman, Karen. *Catherine, Called Birdy*. Clarion, 1994. Through her journal, a young girl chronicles her daily life in medieval England. (I: 11–YA)

———. *The Midwife's Apprentice*. Clarion, 1995. A homeless waif in medieval England is given the opportunity to become a midwife's apprentice. (I: 10–14)

de Angeli, Marguerite. *The Door in the Wall*. Doubleday, 1949/1989. A young boy loses the use of his legs and is still able to save the town and serve the king. (I: 8–12)

Ellis, Deborah. *A Company of Fools*. Fitzhenry & Whiteside, 2002. Henre's quiet life behind the abbey walls changes when street urchin Micah arrives at the abbey. Together, the boys face unfathomable despair when the plague sweeps through Paris and their abbey. (I: 10 and up)

Park, Linda Sue. *A Single Shard*. Clarion, 2001. Though a homeless orphan, Tree-ear's life with his friend Craneman had always felt satisfying—until he discovers the pottery made by the master Min. This story of a boy's pursuit of his dream is set in twelfth-century Korea. (I: 10 and up)

Schlitz, Laura Amy. *Good Masters! Sweet Ladies!: Voices from a Medieval Village*. Illustrated by Robert Byrd. Candlewick, 2007. In this series of monologues set in the Middle Ages, children and young adults from various stations in life step forward to tell their tales. (I: 10 and up)

Spradlin, Michael P. *Keeper of the Grail*. Putnam, 2008. An orphan raised by monks, Tristan's world changes forever when he becomes a squire to Sir Thomas, a respected knight of the Templars, and is caught up in the political intrigue of the period. Sequels: *Trail of Fate, Orphan of Destiny*. (I: 10 and up)

Temple, Frances. *The Ramsay Scallop*. Orchard, 1994. A young couple's pilgrimage from England to Spain transforms their views of the world and each other. (I: 11–YA)

The European Renaissance

Blackwood, Gary. *The Shakespeare Stealer*. Dutton, 1998. Ordered by a cruel master to steal the script of *Hamlet* from the Globe Theatre, Widge confronts a new world when he is taken in and befriended by the Globe company members. (I: 10 and up)

Cushman, Karen. *Alchemy and Meggy Swann*. Clarion, 2010. Sent to live with a father who does not want her in a city that is hostile to those with disabilities, Meggy Swann sets out to change her life circumstances for the better. (I: 10 and up)

Gilson, Jamie. *Stink Alley*. HarperCollins, 2002. Orphaned in Holland where her family had moved with William Brewster and his English followers, strong-willed Lizzy is unable to fit in with her Pilgrim community and becomes friends with a precocious young Dutch artist who has an even greater mischievous streak than Lizzy's. (I: 8–11)

Hesse, Karen. *Stowaway*. Margaret K. McElderry, 2000. This fictionalized diary documents the actual journey of an eleven-year-old stowaway on Captain Cook's ship, the *Endeavour*. (I: 8–11)

Meyer, Carolyn. *Beware, Princess Elizabeth*. Harcourt, 2001. When Henry VIII dies, Princess Elizabeth's brother and sister—both of whom assume power before her—take steps to keep Elizabeth from ever inheriting the throne. This work of historical fiction is based on the early life of Elizabeth. (I: 11 and up)

Richardson, V. A. *The House of Windjammer*. Bloomsbury, 2003. When his father dies and debtors threaten to take over the family shipping business, Adam struggles to maintain the family honor and hold the House of Windjammer together. The story is set in 1636 in Amsterdam. (I: 12 and up)

Sturtevant, Katherine. *A True and Faithful Narrative*. Farrar, Straus, & Giroux, 2006. Meg longs to be a writer—something women do not become in 1681. Yet it is only when her friend's brother is sold into slavery in North Africa that she comes to understand the real power of words. (I: 12 and up)

The Americas before the Revolution

Dorris, Michael. *Morning Girl*. Hyperion, 1992. Life on an island is described by two Taino children prior to and on the day that Columbus lands. (I: 8–12)

*Yolen, Jane. *Encounter*. Illustrated by David Shannon. Harcourt, 1992. A Taino boy tries to warn his people of coming destruction when Columbus arrives on their island. (I: 8–12)

The American Colonies, 1600–1774

*Bruchac, Joseph. *Squanto's Journey*. Illustrated by Greg Shed. Harcourt, 2000. This is the story of the Native American who befriended the settlers of Plymouth, despite his own suffering at the hands of the Europeans. (I: 8–11)

Rinaldi, Ann. *A Break with Charity: A Story about the Salem Witch Trials*. Harcourt, 1992. A young girl struggles to find the courage to tell the truth about the Salem witch hunt. (I: YA)

Speare, Elizabeth George. *The Witch of Blackbird Pond*. Houghton Mifflin, 1958. A girl is accused of witchcraft in colonial New England. (I: 10–YA)

The American Revolution

Anderson, Laurie Halse. *Fever 1793*. Simon & Schuster, 2000. The future looks bright to Mattie, who helps her mother run a coffeehouse in the bustling capital of the newly formed United States. Then, yellow fever strikes Philadelphia, and Mattie's life turns into a living nightmare. (I: 10–14)

_____. *Chains*. Atheneum, 2010. In the midst of the American Revolution, Isabel is sold to a cruel master and struggles to find a way to escape slavery and be reunited with her younger sister. Sequel: *Forge*. (I: 12 and up)

Collier, James Lincoln, and Christopher Collier. *My Brother Sam Is Dead*. Simon & Schuster, 1974/1984. A family is torn apart as members take different sides during the American Revolution. (I: 10–YA)

Rinaldi, Ann. *Finishing Becca*. Harcourt, 1994. Becca, sent to work for a wealthy family in Philadelphia, finds herself caught up in the intrigues of the American Revolution. (I: YA)

*Turner, Ann. *Katie's Trunk*. Illustrated by Ron Himler. Macmillan, 1992. A Tory child hides in a trunk when patriots come to her home. (I: 5–9)

Life in the Early to Mid-Nineteenth Century

Blos, Joan W. *A Gathering of Days: A New England Girls' Journal, 1830–32*. Atheneum, 1990. Told in diary format, the book documents two years in the life of a girl growing up in New Hampshire. (I: 10 and up)

Bradley, Kimberly Brubaker. *Jefferson's Sons*. Dial, 2011. The story of Thomas Jefferson's secret children is told from the perspective of the sons he sired with Sally Hemings. (I: 10 and up)

DeFelice, Cynthia. *The Apprenticeship of Lucas Whitaker*. Farrar, Straus, & Giroux, 1996. Having lost his family to consumption, Lucas becomes a physician's apprentice and hopes to save his new community from consumption with a macabre folk remedy. (I: 10–13)

Giff, Patricia Reilly. *Nory Ryan's Song*. Delacorte, 2000. Faced with uncompromising English landlords and a blight that destroys the potato crop throughout Ireland, Nory must find a way to save herself and her family from starvation. Sequel: *Maggie's Door* (2003). (I: 10–13)

Slavery, the Civil War, and Reconstruction

Curtis, Christopher Paul. *Elijah of Buxton*. Scholastic, 2007. The first free child born in the Buxton Settlement, a Canadian haven established in 1849 for freed slaves, Elijah comes to understand the horrors of slavery when he journeys to America to help a friend. (I: 9–12)

Fleischman, Paul. *Bull Run*. HarperCollins, 1993. The first battle of the Civil War is described from the perspectives of sixteen different characters. (I: 10–YA)

*Hopkinson, Deborah. *Sweet Clara and the Freedom Quilt*. Illustrated by James Ransome. Knopf, 1993. Determined to escape from slavery, Clara sews a quilt that maps the way to freedom. (I: 8–12)

Lester, Julius. *Day of Tears*. Hyperion, 2005. This dramatic story of the biggest slave auction in American history can easily be adapted for readers' theater. (I: 12 and up)

Matas, Carol. *The War Within: A Novel of the Civil War*. Simon & Schuster, 2001. Because Hannah has always viewed herself first as a Southerner and then as a Jew, she can't understand how her sister could fall in love with one of the Yankees occupying their town, even if he is Jewish. Then, when General Grant orders the evacuation of all Israelites, Hannah begins to question what she has always held to be the truth. (I: 10 and up)

Paterson, Katherine. *Jip, His Story*. Puffin, 1998. Jip, an orphan who has grown up on a poor farm in Vermont, is caught up in the struggles between slave owners and abolitionists. (I: 10 and up)

Peck, Richard. *The River Between Us*. Dial, 2003. With the Civil War rapidly approaching, Tilly and her family do not know what to expect when a steamboat docks in their small Illinois town, bringing a glamorous young lady and her black servant from the South. The upheavals in their lives come from both the war and the newcomers. (I: 11 and up)

*Polacco, Patricia. *Pink and Say*. Philomel, 1994. During the Civil War, an African American Union soldier befriends a white one. (I: 8–12)

*Vaughan, Marcia. *The Secret to Freedom*. Illustrated by Larry Johnson. Lee & Low, 2001. Using quilts as part of a secret code, a young slave girl and her brother help their fellow slaves escape on the Underground Railroad. (I: 8–10)

Westward Movement in the United States

Avi. *The Barn*. Orchard, 1994. Set in the Oregon territory, this story tells of three children who build a barn in a vain attempt to keep a promise to their dying father. (I: 10–12)

Bruchac, Joseph. *Sacajawea*. Harcourt, 2000. This fictional account of the Lewis and Clark expedition is told alternately from the viewpoints of William Clark and Sacajawea, the Indian translator and guide who accompanied the explorers. (I: 10–14)

*Bunting, Eve. *Dandelions*. Illustrated by Greg Shed. Harcourt, 1995. A family experiences mixed emotions as they travel across the prairie to settle in the Nebraska territory. (I: 8–12)

*_____. *Train to Somewhere*. Illustrated by Ronald Himler. Clarion, 1996. A story of New York orphans taken by train to the West to be placed with families. (I: 8–11)

Cushman, Karen. *The Ballad of Lucy Whipple*. Clarion, 1996. When Lucy, her mother, and her siblings arrive in California in the midst of the gold rush, Lucy directs every waking thought to figuring out how she will get back home to Massachusetts. (I: 10–12)

_____. *Rodzina*. Clarion, 2003. After her parents die, Rodzina begins a lonely journey west on an orphan train, sure that she will be one of the orphans no one will want. (I: 9–12)

Erdrich, Louise. *The Birchbark House*. Hyperion, 2002. Readers follow an Ojibwe girl and her family through the cycle of four seasons, including a devastating outbreak of smallpox. Sequels: *The Game of Silence* and *The Porcupine Year*. (I: 9–12)

Holm, Jennifer. *Boston Jane: An Adventure*. HarperCollins, 2001. Schooled to become a lady, Jane Peck leaves her native Philadelphia and travels to the Washington Territory to wed her childhood idol. When she learns her fiancé has moved on, Jane has no choice but to move in with a group of scruffy men and make her own way in an alien world. Sequels: *Boston Jane: Wilderness Days, Boston Jane: The Claim, Boston Jane: An Adventure*. (I: 9–12)

Yep, Laurence. *Dragon's Gate*. HarperCollins, 1993. A Chinese boy joins his father in America, where he works under dire conditions to build the transcontinental railroad. (I: 10–YA)

Yin. *Coolies*. Illustrated by Chris Soentpiet. Philomel, 2001. Shek and Little Wong have come to America to help build the railroad across the West. Only the love and loyalty between the two brothers enables them to endure the bigotry and harsh treatment they find in this new country. (I: 9–12)

Industrialization

*McCully, E. A. *The Bobbin Girl*. Dial, 1996. Faced with poor working conditions at the cotton mill, Rebecca finds the courage to join the protest. (I: 9–12)

Paterson, Katherine. *Bread and Roses, Too*. Clarion, 2006. Two children—one whose family is caught up in a 1912 labor strike in Lawrence, Massachusetts, and the other the victim of extreme poverty—find compassion when they go to live with a family in Barre, Vermont. (I: 9–12)

_____. *Lyddie*. Dutton, 1991. After losing her parents and being separated from her brother and sister, Lyddie works in the textile mills to earn money to reunite her siblings. (I: 10–YA)

Immigration

Cole, Brock. *The Money We'll Save*. Farrar, Straus, & Giroux, 2011. A family tries to raise a turkey in an already crowded, nineteenth-century New York tenement. (I: 5–9)

Frost, Helen. *The Braid*. Farrar, Straus, & Giroux, 2006. Written in verse, this is the story of twins separated when most of the family, evicted from the Western Isles of Scotland, chooses to immigrate to America. (I: 10 and up)

Giff, Patricia Reilly. *Maggie's Door*. Wendy Lamb Books/Random House, 2003. In this sequel to *Nory Ryan's Song,* Nory and Sean leave Ireland and survive a harrowing trip across the Atlantic to finally be reunited with surviving members of their families. (I: 9–12)

Hesse, Karen. *Letters from Rifka*. Puffin, 1993. Rifka writes about fleeing Russia and having to stay behind in Belgium when her family goes on to the United States. (I: 9–12)

*Hest, Amy. *When Jessie Came Across the Sea*. Illustrated by P. J. Lynch. Candlewick, 1997. A thirteen-year-old Jewish orphan reluctantly leaves her grandmother and immigrates to New York City, where she works for three years sewing lace to earn money to bring her grandmother to the United States. (I: 8–12)

Life in the Late Nineteenth Century and Early Twentieth Century

Avi. *The Secret School*. Harcourt, 2001. When the teacher of her one-room school leaves her position before the end of the school year, Ida fears how the situation will impact her future. If she can't attend high school, Ida will be unable to prepare for the teaching profession. Determined to realize her dream, Ida commits to secretly keeping the school open and serving as the children's teacher. (I: 10–12)

Choldenko, Gennifer. *Al Capone Does My Shirts*. Putnam, 2004. Moose moves with his family to Alcatraz where his father will be a guard so his disabled sister can attend a special school. He soon discovers that all kinds of complications come with life on Alcatraz. Sequels: *Al Capone Shines My Shoes* and *Al Capone Does My Homework*. (I: 9–14)

Curtis, Christopher Paul. *Bud, Not Buddy*. Delacorte, 1999. Bud's mother has died, and the placements the orphanage finds for him never work out. So Bud sets out to find the man he is convinced must be his father. (I: 8–12)

_____. *The Mighty Miss Malone*. Wendy Lamb/Random House, 2012. When Deza's father loses his job in the midst of the Great Depression and leaves home seeking a job, the Malone family sets out in his wake, seeking to reunite the family during these turbulent times. (I: 8–12).

Henson, Heather. *That Book Woman*. Illustrated by David Small. Atheneum, 2008. Cal isn't interested in books. Still no matter the season or the weather, the book woman keeps coming by horseback, bringing the books his sister loves to read—until Cal finally decides maybe he should at least try out this reading. (I: 6–9)

Hesse, Karen. *Out of the Dust*. Scholastic, 1997. In free-verse poetry, Billie Jo chronicles the seeming hopelessness of her Depression-era life during the dust storms in the Oklahoma panhandle. (I: YA)

_____. *Witness*. Hyperion, 2001. Told in free verse, this story documents the Ku Klux Klan's attempt to recruit members in a small Vermont town in 1924. (I: 10 and up)

Holm, Jennifer. *Our Only May Amelia*. HarperCollins, 1999. May Amelia, the only girl ever born on the Nasel River in Washington, finds adventure, joy, and tragedy in her Finnish-American frontier community. Sequel: *The Trouble with May Amelia*. (I: 8–12)

_____. *Turtle in Paradise*. Random House, 2010. When Turtle is sent to Key West to live with relatives during the Great Depression, a new world opens up for her. (I: 9–12)

*Houston, Gloria. *The Year of the Perfect Christmas Tree*. Illustrated by Barbara Cooney. Dial, 1988. Because her father is away at war, Ruthie and her mom deliver the Christmas tree to the church. (I: 5–9)

*Judge, Lita. *Pennies for Elephants*. Hyperion, 2009. It is 1914, and the children of Boston are determined to raise $6,000 to ensure that three trained elephants will be housed in the Boston Zoo. (I: 4–8)

Kelly, Jacqueline. *The Evolution of Calpurnia Tate.* Henry Holt, 2009. As she strives to follow in the footsteps of her beloved grandfather, an amateur naturalist, Calpurnia Tate discovers that society holds very different expectations for young women in rural Texas in 1899. (I: 10 and up)

Larson, Kirby. *Hattie Big Sky.* Delacorte, 2007. Sixteen-year-old Hattie travels alone to Montana where she faces incredible odds as she struggles to keep the homestead she has inherited. (I: 12 and up)

Levine, Gail Carson. *Dave at Night.* HarperCollins, 1999. When Dave is placed in the Hebrew Home for Boys, an orphanage known also as the Hell Hole for Brats, he encounters cruelty, friendship, and (beyond the orphanage) the joys of the Harlem Renaissance. (I: 9–12)

MacLachlan, Patricia. *Sarah, Plain and Tall.* Harper, 1985. A brother and sister hope that Sarah will choose to stay on the prairie and become their mother. Sequels: *Skylark, Caleb's Story, More Perfect than the Moon.* (I: 9–12)

*Mitchell, Margaree. *Uncle Jed's Barbershop.* Illustrated by James Ransome. Simon & Schuster, 1993. Even in the face of racial prejudice and economic hardship caused by the Depression, Uncle Jed pursues his dream of owning his own barbershop. (I: 9 and up)

Paterson, Katherine. *Preacher's Boy.* Clarion, 1999. Robbie's high-spirited ways often land him in the doghouse with his preacher father, but when one of his schemes endangers the life of someone else, Robbie finds the courage to face up to the consequences of his actions. (I: 9–12)

Peck, Richard. *A Long Way from Chicago.* Dial, 1998. Joey and his sister spend summers with their outrageous trickster grandmother. Sequel: *A Year Down Yonder.* (I: 9–12)

———. *Fair Weather.* Dial, 2001. It is 1893, the year of the World's Columbian Exposition, and Rosie Beckett's aunt has invited Rosie and her siblings to Chicago to see all the wonders of the fair. A world of wonder and adventure await the Beckett family. (I: 9–12)

———. *The Teacher's Funeral: A Comedy in Three Parts.* Dial, 2004. Convinced the school board won't be able to replace the teacher who died in August, Russell looks forward to running away to the Dakotas—until his own sister takes over their one-room schoolhouse. (I: 9–12)

Ryan, Pam Muñoz. *Esperanza Rising.* Scholastic, 2000. When tragedy strikes her well-to-do Mexican family, Esperanza and her mother must flee to California in the midst of the Great Depression. In a Mexican farm labor camp, Esperanza learns to relinquish her past and embrace the future in her new community. (I: 11 and up)

*Rylant, Cynthia. *When I Was Young in the Mountains.* Illustrated by Diane Goode. Dutton, 1982. The memories of a young girl growing up in the Appalachian Mountains. (I: 5–9)

Schmidt, Gary D. *Lizzie Bright and the Buckminster Boy.* Clarion, 2004. Turner hates being the new boy in town—and the minister's son. But life takes a positive turn for Turner when he is befriended by Lizzie, a descendent of slaves who lives on an island off the Maine coast—until the town elders determine to force Lizzie and her people off their island home. (I: 9–12)

*Stewart, Sarah. *The Gardener.* Illustrated by David Small. Square Fish, 2007. When Lydia goes to the city to live with a grumpy uncle during the Great Depression, she finds a way to bring joy and beauty into his life. (I: 6–9)

Taylor, Mildred D. *Roll of Thunder, Hear My Cry.* Dial, 1976. An African American family faces prejudice and discrimination in the South. Other books about the Logan family: *Let the Circle Be Unbroken, The Friendship, Mississippi Bridge, The Well, The Land, Song of the Trees.* (I: 10–12)

*Tunnell, Michael O. *Mailing May.* Illustrated by Ted Rand. Greenwillow, 1997. In 1914, a young girl is mailed (by train) to see her grandmother because her family cannot afford a train ticket. (I: 5–9)

Vanderpool, Clare. *Moon Over Manifest.* Delacorte, 2010. Only as she gradually learns of events from 1917/1918 does Abilene come to understand why her father has sent her to live in the town of his youth while he travels the country seeking work during the Great Depression. (I: 10 and up)

Yep, Laurence. *Dragonwings.* Harper, 1975. The story of a Chinese boy immigrating to San Francisco to join his father. (I: YA)

World War II

*Borden, Louise. *The Greatest Skating Race.* Illustrated by Niki Daly. Margaret K. McElderry, 2004. A Dutch boy dreams of becoming a great skater racing along the frozen canals of the Netherlands. He gets an unexpected chance to become a hero when his neighbors are threatened by the Germans and he must skate with them to safety in Brussels. (I: 8–12)

Coerr, Eleanor. *Sadako and the Thousand Paper Cranes.* Putnam, 1977. The story of a survivor of the Hiroshima bombing who tries to create a thousand paper cranes to make her wish for health come true. The picture book version, *Sadako*, was illustrated by Ed Young: *Sadako* (1993). (I: 10–12)

*Fleming, Candace. *Boxes for Katje.* Farrar, Straus, & Giroux, 2003. An American town reaches out to help alleviate the suffering of a Dutch community following World War II. (I: 6–9)

*Gallaz, Christophe. *Rose Blanche.* Illustrated by Robert Innocenti. Translated by Martha Coventry and Richard Craglia. Creative Education, 1985. A young German girl stumbles upon a concentration camp outside her town and discovers its horrors. (I: 10 and up)

Giff, Patricia Reilly. *Lily's Crossing.* Delacorte, 1997. Feeling alone when her father enlists in the army, Lily befriends a refugee from the Nazis. Sequel: *Willow Run* (2005). (I: 9–12)

Hahn, Mary Downing. *Stepping on the Cracks.* Clarion, 1991. While her brother is away at war, Elizabeth befriends an army deserter. Sequel: *As Ever, Gordy* (1998). (I: 10–12)

*Hesse, Karen. *The Cats in Krasinski Square.* Illustrated by Wendy Watson. Scholastic, 2004. When a young Jewish girl and her sister learn of a Gestapo plan to arrest people smuggling food into the Warsaw Ghetto, they devise their own plan to foil the Gestapo. (I: 9–12)

*Judge, Lita. *One Thousand Tracings: Healing the Wounds of World War II*. Hyperion, 2007. In the aftermath of World War II, an American family galvanizes friends and neighbors to donate shoes and other goods to alleviate the sufferings of European war victims. (I: 6–10)

Klages, Ellen. *The Green Glass Sea*. Viking, 2006. In 1943, Dewey Kerrigan goes to live with her father in Los Alamos, New Mexico, a town that does not officially exist but where the work of the Manhattan Project is destined to change the world. (I: 10–12)

Lowry, Lois. *Number the Stars*. Houghton Mifflin, 1989. A story of how the Danes aided Jews in their flights to freedom. (I: 10–12)

*Mochizuki, Ken. *Baseball Saved Us*. Illustrated by Dom Lee. Lee & Low, 1993. A Japanese American boy's memories of life in an internment camp. (I: 8–12)

Orlev, Uri. *The Island on Bird Street*. Translated by Hillel Halkin. Houghton Mifflin, 1984. A boy struggles to survive in the Warsaw ghetto as he waits for his father to return. (I: 11–YA)

———. *The Man from the Other Side*. Translated by Hillel Halkin. Houghton Mifflin, 1991. A man and his son risk their own lives to help the Jews in the Warsaw ghetto. (I: YA)

———. *Run, Boy, Run*. Translated by Hillel Halkin. Houghton Mifflin, 2007. This is the story of a ghetto survivor who escapes into the Polish countryside and adopts a Catholic identity in order to survive. (I: 10 and up)

Park, Linda Sue. *When My Name Was Keoko*. Clarion, 2002. Two siblings struggle to maintain their dignity during the Japanese occupation of Korea prior to and during World War II. (I: 10 and up)

*Polacco, Patricia. *The Butterfly*. Philomel, 2000. When Monique discovers the Jewish family her mother has hidden in their basement, she joins her mother to defy the Nazis who occupy their French village. (I: 10 and up)

Pressler, Mirjam. *Malka*. Philomel, 2003. Seeking to escape the Nazi persecution of Jews in Poland, Malka's family is split apart, and seven-year-old Malka must survive the horrors of Nazi-occupied Poland on her own. (I: 12 and up)

Spinelli, Jerry. *Milkweed*. Knopf, 2003. Set in the Warsaw ghetto, this is the story of an orphan who doesn't even know his name, yet is determined to be part of a family and community while living in the midst of the horror and devastation of the Nazi regime. (I: YA)

Uchida, Yoshiko. *Journey to Topaz*. Creative Arts, 1988. A Japanese American family is sent away to an internment camp when World War II breaks out. Sequel: *Journey Home*. (I: 10–12)

* ———. *The Bracelet*. Illustrated by Joanna Yardley. Philomel, 1993. Sent away to an internment camp during World War II, a young Japanese American girl discovers the power of memory. (I: 7–11)

Wolff, Virginia Euwer. *Bat 6*. Scholastic, 1998. For 49 years the sixth-grade girls from Barlow and Bear Creek Ridge have met for an annual softball game—a game played to bring the two communities together. But the prejudices that linger in the aftermath of World War II have set this year's teams on a collision course. (I: 11 and up)

*Zee, Ruth Vander. *Erika's Story*. Illustrated by Roberto Innocenti. Creative Editions, 2003. This is the story of an infant thrown from a train bound for a concentration camp who was rescued by a German woman who raised the baby as her own. (I: 9 and up)

Zusak, Markus. *The Book Thief*. Knopf, 2006. Through the love and support of her beloved foster father, Liesel finds the courage to take her own stand against injustice in Nazi Germany. (I: YA)

The Mid-Twentieth Century

Almond, David. *The Fire-Eaters*. Delacorte, 2003. Bobby Burns sees many faces of suffering in his small English town—McNulty the fire-eater whose life was misshapen by World War II, the cruelty inflicted on children by school masters, and the fear sparked by the Cuban missile crisis. Yet in the midst of suffering, Bobby and his family find hope. (I: 10 and up)

English, Karen. *Francie*. Farrar, 1999. Francie longs for the time when she and her family can leave behind their life in Noble, Alabama, and all the prejudices and hardships the town holds for African Americans. (I: 10 and up)

Gantos, Jack. *Dead End in Norvelt*. Farrar, Straus, and Giroux 2011. Grounded by his parents, Jack's summer takes an unexpected turn when he is loaned out by his mother to help an elderly neighbor write obituaries for residents of Norvelt, a New Deal community once supported by Eleanor Roosevelt. (I: 10 and up)

*Harrington, Janice. *Going North*. Illustrated by Jerome Lagarrigue. Farrar, Straus, and Giroux, 2004. Jessie resents having to leave her home in Alabama, but on the family car trip through the segregated South, she comes to understand why her parents believe a better life awaits them in the North. (I: 6–10)

Ho, Minfong. *Rice without Rain*. Lothrop, 1990. As Jinda and her family struggle to survive the drought that has hit Thailand, strangers from the city seem to offer a way to survive, but soon Jinda and her family are caught up in the turbulence of the 1945 student movement. (I: YA)

Holt, Kimberly Willis. *When Zachary Beaver Came to Town*. Holt, 1999. Toby is having a hard summer, with his mother having left for Nashville and his best friend's brother in Vietnam. Then, when the "fattest boy in the world" comes to his small Texas town, Toby's summer becomes like no other he has ever known. (I: 10 and up)

*Johnson, Angela. *Just Like Josh Gibson*. Illustrated by Beth Peck. Simon & Schuster, 2004. In an era when little girls couldn't join baseball teams, an African American girl dreams of being just like Josh Gibson, the hero of the Negro Leagues. (I: 6–9)

Martin, Ann M. *Belle Teal*. Scholastic, 2001. Unexpected events shape Belle Teal's year in fifth grade with Miss Casey. Her grandmother's mind is slipping; the new girl in school won't give Belle Teal any peace, and African American students enroll in the school for the first time ever. (I: 9–12)

Naidoo, Beverley. *Journey to Jo'burg: A South African Story*. HarperCollins, 1987. A brother and sister are caught up in the cruelty of apartheid when they journey to Johannesburg to find their mother. (I: 10–12)

Schmidt, Gary. *The Wednesday Wars*. Clarion, 2007. When his classmates attend Wednesday religious school, Holling is left alone with his seventh grade teacher, whom he is convinced hates him. However, the year holds surprises for Holling. (I: 11 and up)

*Shea, Pegi Deitz. *The Whispering Cloth: A Refugee's Story*. Illustrated by Anita Riggio. Stitched by You Yang. Boyds Mill Press, 1994. A young Hmong refugee stitches her own story on her first "story cloth." (I: 7–11)

Taylor, Mildred. *The Gold Cadillac*. Illustrated by Michael Hays. Dial, 1987. An African American family from the North experiences prejudice when they visit the South. (I: 9–12)

*Wiles, Deborah. *Freedom Summer*. Illustrated by Jerome Lagarrigue. Atheneum, 2001. Joe and John Henry are best friends. They play marbles and swim together in the creek, and both boys want to be firefighters. But Joe is white and John Henry is African American, and in the 1960s in the deep South, that means there are some things Joe and John Henry cannot do together. (I: 6–9)

_____. *Countdown*. Scholastic, 2010. Franny's world is in disarray; she is feuding with her best friend; her sister is involved with a mysterious political group; her uncle is embarrassing the family in front of the whole neighborhood, and all this is happening in the midst of the Cuban missile crisis. (I: 10–12)

Williams-Garcia, Rita. *One Crazy Summer*. Amistad/HarperCollins, 2010. Delphine and her sisters are sent to spend the summer in Oakland with a mother who doesn't welcome them and sends them to a summer camp run by the Black Panthers. (I: 10–12)

*Woodson, Jacqueline. *The Other Side*. Illustrated by E. B. Lewis. Putnam, 2001. Clover wonders why a fence separates the black side of town from the white side. Then summer comes, and when a white girl begins to sit on the fence each day, Clover discovers a new friend from the other side. (I: 6–10)

Yelchin, Eugene. *Breaking Stalin's Nose*. Square Fish, 2013. A young boy devoted to Stalin and Communism discovers, over a two-day period, the chilling truth about the Soviet Union under Stalin's rule. (I: 9–12)

Other Books

Engle, Margarita. *The Surrender Tree: Poems of Cuba's Struggle for Freedom*. Henry Holt, 2008. Written in verse, this novel focuses on the sacrifices of Rosa and her husband, who care for those fighting for Cuba's independence during three nineteenth-century wars. (I: 12 and up)

RESOURCES AND REFERENCES

Albright, Lettie K., and Sylvia M. Vardell. "1950 to 2000 in Picture Books." *Book Links 13.1* (2003): 21–25.

Bachrach, Susan. *Tell Them We Remember: The Story of the Holocaust*. Little, Brown, 1994.

Beck, Cathy, Shari Nelson-Faulkner, and Kathryn Mitchell Pierce. "Talking about Books: Historical Fiction: Teaching Tool or Literary Experience?" *Language Arts 77* (2000): 546–555.

Bial, Raymond. *One-Room School*. Houghton Mifflin, 1999.

Blos, Joan W. "Perspectives on Historical Fiction." *The Story of Ourselves: Teaching History through Children's Literature*. Eds. Michael O. Tunnell and Richard Ammon. Heinemann, 1993, pp. 11–17.

Broderick, Kathy. "*The Ramsay Scallop* by Frances Temple." *Book Links 4.2* (November 1994): 19.

Conrad, Pam. "Finding Ourselves in History." *The Story of Ourselves: Teaching History through Children's Literature*. Eds. Michael O. Tunnell and Richard Ammon. Heinemann, 1993, pp. 33–38.

Cooper, Michael L. *Dust to Eat: Drought and Depression in the 1930s*. Clarion, 2004.

DeFelice, Cynthia. "The Bones Beneath the Flesh of Historical Fiction." *Book Links 8.2* (November 1998): 30–34.

Dorris, Michael. "On Writing *Morning Girl*." *Book Links 4.1* (September 1992): 32–33.

Elleman, Barbara. "The Columbus Encounter—Update." *Book Links 2.1* (1992): 31–34.

Forbes, Esther. *Johnny Tremain*. Houghton Mifflin, 1943.

Freedman, Russell. *Immigrant Kids*. Puffin, 1995.

Freedman, Russell. *Kids at Work: Lewis Hine and the Crusade Against Child Labor*. Clarion, 1998.

Fritz, Jean. "There Once Was." *The Horn Book Magazine* (July/August 1986): 432–435.

Harris, Violet. "Historical Fact and Fiction: Using Informational Books to Provide Background for Using Multicultural Literature." *Teaching for Lifelong Learning*, 85th Annual Convention of the National Council of Teachers of English, San Diego, November 1995.

Hopkins, Lee Bennett, ed. *More Books by More People*. Citation, 1974.

Levstik, Linda. "A Gift of Time: Children's Historical Fiction." *Children's Literature in the Classroom: Weaving Charlotte's Web*. Eds. Janet Hickman and Bernice E. Cullinan. Christopher-Gordon, 1989, pp. 135–145.

Lewis, A. (2008, April). Effects of NCLB's focus on reading and math. *The Education Digest*, 73(8), 71–72. Retrieved January 10, 2012, from Research Library. (Document ID: 1451909161)

Murphy, Jim. *An American Plague: The True and Terrifying Story of the Yellow Fever Epidemic of 1793*. Clarion, 2003.

Murphy, Jim. *The Boys' War: Confederate and Union Soldiers Talk about the Civil War*. Clarion, 1993.

Scott, Sir Walter. *Ivanhoe*. Edited by Graham Tulloch. Penguin, 2000.

_____. *Waverly*. Edited by Andrew Hook. Viking, 1981.

Taxel, Joel. "The American Revolution in Children's Fiction." *Research in the Teaching of English 17* (1983): 61–83.

Temple, Frances. "Researching *The Ramsay Scallop*." *Book Links* 4.2 (November 1994): 18.

Tomlinson, Carl M., Michael O. Tunnell, and Donald J. Richgels. "The Content and Writing of History in Textbooks and Trade Books." *The Story of Ourselves: Teaching History through Children's Literature*. Eds. Michael O. Tunnell and Richard Ammon. Heinemann, 1993, pp. 51–62.

Tunnell, Michael O., and Richard Ammon, eds. *The Story of Ourselves: Teaching History through Children's Literature*. Heinemann, 1993.

Tunnell, Michael O. "Unmasking the Fiction of History: Children's Historical Literature Begins to Come of Age." *The Story of Ourselves: Teaching History through Children's Literature*. Eds. Michael O. Tunnell and Richard Ammon. Heinemann, 1993, pp. 79–90.

Turner, Ann. "On Writing Katie's Trunk." *Book Links* 2.5 (May 1993): 11.

Whelan, Debra Lau. (2006, May). Schools narrowing their curriculums. *School Library Journal, 52*(5), 17. Retrieved January 10, 2012, from ABI/INFORM Global. (Document ID: 1041606191)

Nonfiction

> 66 *...Give me your tired,
> your poor, Your huddled
> masses yearning to breathe
> free, The wretched refuse
> of your teeming shore...* 99

—excerpt from a poem by Emma Lazarus

A uthor Ann Bausum opens her nonfiction book, *Denied, Detained, Deported: Stories from the Dark Side of American Immigration*, with two poems—the one that appears above by Emma Lazarus is likely to be familiar to readers. By the side of this poem sits an excerpt from a poem by Naomi Shihab Nye entitled "Statue of Liberty Dreams of Emma Lazarus, Awakens with Tears on Her Cheeks." In her poem, Nye indicates that America does indeed welcome the tired and the poor—as long as they are not too tired and too poor. The irony created by placing these two poems side by side is unmistakable and is likely to spur readers on to explore what promise to be some of the lesser known stories about immigration to the United States. This is just what good nonfiction does; it makes readers want to read and keep reading to learn more about their world. In this chapter we explore various types of nonfiction and the ways in which the genre works.

What Is Nonfiction?

Nonfiction is "a genre created mainly to inform" (Mitchell, 2003, p. 326) about a particular subject, issue, or idea. Yet high quality nonfiction does much more: It arouses curiosity; it opens the world; it engages readers in learning and thinking. Author Russell Freedman, who has written many notable works of nonfiction for children, describes his mission this way: "Certainly the basic purpose of nonfiction is to inform, to instruct, hopefully to enlighten. But that's not enough. An effective nonfiction book must animate its subject—infuse it with life. It must create a vivid and believable world that the reader will enter willingly and leave only with reluctance" (Freedman, 1992, p. 3).

Scholars sometimes disagree on the best name for this literary genre, with some arguing for the label "nonfiction" while others advocate for the label "informational" (Colman, 2007). We have chosen to use "nonfiction" as an umbrella term. Under this umbrella we include books that explore people's lives—biography, autobiography, and memoir, as well as books written by experts that are meant to inform about subjects, issues, or details. In the first part of this chapter we explore books intended to inform about various subjects or ideas, and in the latter part we focus on biography, autobiography, and memoir.

Value of Nonfiction

It is essential to put nonfiction into the hands of children—for many reasons. First, children want to know about the world around them, as evidenced by the wide array of questions they pose: How can birds fly? What is a black hole? Why did Thomas Jefferson have slaves? Nonfiction books are wonderful resources for children seeking answers to genuine questions. Further, wide reading in nonfiction helps to extend children's experiences beyond their home and immediate community. These literacy experiences contribute to building rich stores of world knowledge that are critical to success in school. There is another reason as well for putting nonfiction in the hands of children: some children simply prefer nonfiction, and teachers have documented success with reluctant readers when they share nonfiction books that are of interest to these students (Caswell & Duke, 1998; Jobe & Dayton-Sakari, 2002).

It is also important for children to read widely in nonfiction to become familiar with the structures of the genre. In the same way that coming to know story structure enables students to read stories more successfully, having familiarity with expository text patterns enables readers to comprehend nonfiction more successfully. Wise teachers say, "Children learn to read by reading." It is particularly true that children learn to read nonfiction by reading the genre. This knowledge of informational text structures is essential as children move into upper elementary grades and middle school where they are required to read many different types of nonfiction texts in a wide variety of subject areas. In fact, by sixth grade 75% of school reading involves non-narrative material (Moss, 2008).

Nonfiction also invites readers to engage in critical thinking as they are called on to distinguish fact from opinion and theory. Readers should consider the author's spirit of inquiry and what kind of research and investigation went into the book. Authors of quality nonfiction carefully research their material. This research may take many forms—authors may experience firsthand the topic they are writing about; they may consult primary source materials such as original letters, diary entries, or newspaper accounts; they may travel to libraries, museums, or historical sites in other cities to secure the information they need; they may interview experts in the field; and they may consult secondary sources such as books and contemporary articles about the topic. In a "Note from the Author," Sally M. Walker discusses her research process in order to write *Secrets of a Civil War Submarine: Solving the Mysteries of the H. L. Hunley.* She traveled to Washington, D.C. and Charleston, interviewed people by phone and in person, toured the *Hunley,* and observed a conservator at work. Authors have their own points of view and perspectives, and readers must decide whether the author has engaged in substantive research and has presented a balanced discussion or biased it in some way. After gleaning all the information in the book, readers must make inferences and reach their own conclusions.

TECHNOLOGY in PRACTICE 11.1

Increasingly, apps related to nonfiction are available for tablets such as the iPad. For example, *Skulls,* an app created by Touch Press, offers more than 300 high-resolution skulls that the viewer can rotate 360°. A double tap on a skull reveals a 3-D view. The app is a valuable companion tool for Sally M. Walker's *Written in Bone: Buried Lives of Jamestown and Colonial Maryland,* an archeological investigation of human and material remains of the early settlers.

Perhaps the most important reason to infuse classrooms with nonfiction is to prepare children for their future beyond school. As Penny Colman (2007) has observed, "Nonfiction is everywhere. It is the stuff of everyday life" (p. 257).

Given all the benefits of reading nonfiction, it is not surprising that the Common Core Standards call for the wide reading in the genre to build knowledge, extend experience, and broaden worldviews. Yet nonfiction is too often neglected in schools (Duke, 2000; Venezky, 2000). Penny Colman (2007) believes this neglect is evident in a variety of ways: (1) classroom libraries are overwhelmingly stocked with fiction; (2) summer reading lists frequently have no nonfiction titles; and (3) nonfiction writers for children are rarely invited for school visits. This neglect is really indefensible given children's interests and needs, as well as the high quality of nonfiction trade books available for children today.

Topics Addressed in Nonfiction

There is a wide array of nonfiction for children. The diversity in the genre is evident in the topics that authors address, in the scope of books, and in the formats in which authors write. Authors of nonfiction for children often write about infrequently addressed topics. For example, in *The Camping Trip that Changed America,* author Barb Rosenstock tells the story of the camping trip that Theodore Roosevelt and John Muir made into the Yosemite wilderness, a trip that inspired President Roosevelt to establish America's national park system. The many diverse topics

ILLUSTRATION 11.1 In *The Camping Trip that Changed America*, author Barb Rosenstock tells the story of the camping trip that inspired President Roosevelt to establish America's national park system. ("The Camping Trip that Changed America" by Barb Rosenstock and illustrated by Mordicai Gerstein. Used by permission of Penguin Group (USA) LLC. All rights reserved.)

addressed in nonfiction for children range from the human quest for gold to the experiences of Japanese American children in concentration camps during World War II to the race to save the legendary Ivory-billed Woodpecker. Table 11.1 lists major topics explored in nonfiction for children and includes brief descriptions of each. The recommended titles at the end of this chapter are organized by these same topics.

There is also variation in the scope of nonfiction for children. Some authors present a comprehensive view of their subject while others discuss a single facet of a topic in depth. For example, in *Let Me Play: The Story of Title IX, the Law that Changed the Future of Girls in America,* author Karen Blumenthal documents the long history of Title IX, the law that opened the world of sports for girls in the United States. Blumenthal situates her book in the broader context of the struggle for women's rights from the early twentieth century to contemporary times. By contrast, the scope of *Blizzard of Glass: The Halifax Explosion of 1917* by Sally M. Walker is far more limited. In this gripping account of the largest man-made explosion prior to the first detonation of the atomic bomb, Walker documents in chilling detail the immediate events leading up to the Halifax explosion and events in the immediate aftermath of the disaster.

Formats of Nonfiction

Nonfiction books for young readers come in diverse formats. Many are in a chapter book format that allows for an in-depth exploration of a topic. Others are in picture book format, and some of these are appropriate for very young children. For example, *First the Egg* by Laura Vaccaro Seeger was named both a Caldecott Honor Book and a Theodor Seuss Geisel honor book. In this simple picture book, containing only 41 words, die-cuts reveal a string of transformations: first the egg, then the chicken; first the tadpole then the frog.

TABLE 11.1 *Topics Explored in Nonfiction Books for Young Readers*

TOPIC	PURPOSE
History	Through these books, children can glimpse people, places, and events of the past and better understand factors that shaped the past.
Peoples and Cultures	These books introduce children to people who come from particular cultures in the United States or from other parts of the world. They help children understand the concept of culture and appreciate similarities and differences among peoples around the world.
Nature	These books, which explore the natural world, form a particularly large category of books for children. They lead children to discoveries about animals, plants, geology, geography, and the human body.
Arts	This category of books explores different facets of art, music, drama, and dance and the people engaged in these arts.
How Things Work	Children are naturally curious about how things work, and books in this category help children discover answers to some of the questions they may have about topics as diverse as the working of machines, electricity, the digital domain, and much, much more.
Sports, Recreation, and How-to Books	Children enamored with sports will find a wealth of books to satiate their interests. Books in this category also address other recreational interests of children such as cooking, photography and drawing.

Nonfiction books also come in the format of the photo essay. George Ancona has created numerous books for children in this format, including *¡Ole Flamenco!*, in which he uses photographs and text to explore the rich history, traditions, and techniques of the dance. Other writers use an alphabet format to convey information. In *O Is for Old Dominion* Pamela Duncan Edwards uses the alphabet to organize historical information about Virginia.

The Evolution of Nonfiction

Orbis Sensualium Pictus ("The Visible World in Pictures"), written by Moravian (present day Slovak) bishop Johannes Amos Comenius and published in 1657, is considered the first informational book for children. This picture dictionary illustrated with woodcuts focused on natural history and was used as a textbook throughout Europe until the late eighteenth century. The format established by Comenius (pictures accompanied by brief descriptions) proved to be highly influential and remained popular over the next century and a half (Kiefer, 2011).

While nonfiction for children has been published for centuries, until recent years the genre had the reputation of being boring, best used for report work, and unpleasantly difficult for children to read. There were, of course, notable exceptions. The first Newbery Medal was awarded in 1922 to a work of nonfiction, *The Story of Mankind* by Hendrik Willem Van Loon, and in 1942, *Paddle-to-the-Sea* by Holling C. Holling broke new ground by informing through lavish illustrations. This fictionalized but geographically accurate account of an expedition through the Great Lakes to the Atlantic Ocean was named a Caldecott Honor book.

Despite these (and other) exceptions, Horning (2010) argues that the decade of the 1980s marks the significant turning point in nonfiction for children, largely because of increased recognition of the genre by award committees. During this decade, three nonfiction books won Newbery honors: *Sugaring Time* by Kathryn Lasky, *Commodore Perry in the Land of the Shogun* by Rhoda Blumberg, and *Volcano: The Eruption and Healing of Mount St. Helens* by Patricia Lauber.

Horning describes three additional changes in the genre that occurred during the 1980s. First, there was greater attention to visual elements and the design of nonfiction books. One such book was *The Glorious Flight: Across the Channel with Louis Blériot, July 25, 1909* by Alice and Martin Provensen, which received the Caldecott Medal in 1984. This book's carefully researched paintings recreate France in the early twentieth century, the flying machines developed by Blériot, and his dramatic flight across the English Channel in 1909. In this same period, new standards for evaluating nonfiction books for the young began to emerge. In earlier decades the fictionalization within the genre was considered acceptable. These attitudes began to change in the 1980s, resulting in higher quality books for young readers. Finally, during this decade writers began to publish increasing numbers of nonfiction books for younger audiences such as the titles in the Let's Read and Find Out science series.

Since the 1980s, nonfiction books for children have continued to gain momentum, establishing their position as a popular and important genre in children's literature. Several recent trends in the genre reflect the lives of today's visually oriented children living in a digital age. While earlier works of nonfiction tended to be text-dense, both overall design and visuals are likely to assume a more prominent place in today's books (Isaacs, 2011). For example, Sally Walker's Sibert Award winning *Secrets of a Civil War Submarine: Solving the Mysteries of the H. L. Hunley* is a beautifully designed book with endpapers featuring small

ISSUE *to* CONSIDER

Is It Acceptable to Fictionalize Nonfiction?

A relatively new issue with regard to informational books is the value of a hybrid type often referred to as an *informational storybook*. Although the primary purpose of these books is to inform, they also contain fictionalized elements. The popular *Magic School Bus* books written by Joanna Cole and illustrated by Bruce Degen fit in this category. In these books, Ms. Frizzle and her class experience a fantasy adventure while they learn about the subject of the book, such as the waterworks, dinosaurs, or hurricanes. Because accuracy and authenticity are critical criteria in selecting nonfiction, this mixing of genres has become a controversial issue. Sayers (1982) stated, "The outstanding tenet of writing for children . . . is the insistence on first-hand authenticity in science, the arts, history, biography, and travel" (p. 97).

The blurring of the lines between fact and fiction is not a new issue. Margery Fisher (1982) has written that "the distinction between fiction and nonfiction is blurred and constantly shifting, but we still use it and need it" (p. 13). Mixed-genre or blended books are the focus of debate because of their popularity with children on the one hand and their potential to mislead and confuse children on the other.

On the positive side, Leal (1993) points out some benefits of informational storybooks. They enable readers to "become involved in an engaging story" (pp. 63–64), identify with a main character, activate prior knowledge about the topic, generate interest for further content study, participate in discussion, and experience a model of process writing. Leal's research has confirmed children's positive responses to informational storybooks. On the other hand, Zarnowski (1995) believes that informational storybooks "introduce irrelevant, distracting, and potentially confusing 'information'" (p. 185). According to this view, students may have difficulty distinguishing fact from fiction in the story and thus may come away confused or with inaccurate information on the subject.

What do you think? Supporters and detractors of informational storybooks present compelling arguments.

---

sketches of the focus submarine drawn from different perspectives. Printed on high quality paper, the first 38 pages of the book, which feature the design and construction of the submarine and its disastrous mission, are printed on cream-colored paper. The color of the paper changes when the focus of the book shifts to the modern day archeological quest to solve the mystery of the submarine's disastrous mission.

Digital influences are increasingly apparent in contemporary nonfiction books. Kerper (2003) has described some of the changes in the genre that reflect digital influences: nonlinear formats, varied arrangements of text on the page, unusual fonts, and the nonsequential exploration of information through sidebars, boxed information, and marginal material.

We are also seeing an increase in information conveyed through a blending of genres. The *Magic School Bus* series, with its blending of fantasy and information, is an earlier example of this trend. A more recent example is Joyce Sidman's Newbery honor book, ***The Dark Emperor and Other Poems of the Night,*** in which she writes about nocturnal creatures such as owls, porcupines, bats, and crickets. On double-page spreads, beautifully crafted relief prints are accompanied by a poem about the featured creature on one side of the spread, while on the facing page an informational paragraph about the creature is displayed.

In recent years we have also witnessed a proliferation of nonfiction series. Series books are developed by publishers to provide works about related topics. The books have a specified format, which means that every book in the series is organized in the same way. One popular series is HarperCollins' *Let's Read and Find Out* science series; the first books in this series were published in the 1970s, and the series has continued to grow. Other popular series include Houghton Mifflin's *Scientists in the Field* and National Geographic's *Face to Face with Animals* series. We are also seeing more and more series targeting beginning and emergent readers, series such as Carolrhoda's *Baby Animals* series.

TOP SHELF 11.1

QUALITY INFORMATION SERIES

Face to Face with Animals published by National Geographic

Insiders published by Simon and Schuster

National Geographic Readers published by National Geographic

Scientists in the Field published by Houghton Mifflin

Vanishing Cultures published by Lee & Low

Today nonfiction books for children abound—they cover a myriad of topics and display exciting, aesthetically appealing designs and strong, expressive writing. The establishment of prestigious awards specifically dedicated to nonfiction titles, such as the Orbis Pictus Award for Outstanding Nonfiction for Children and the Robert F. Sibert Informational Book Award, are further testament to the important place of informational books as a literary genre.

Categories of Nonfiction

In this section we discuss three major categories of nonfiction—factual, interpretive, and the nonfiction of inquiry.

Factual Nonfiction

Factual nonfiction is marked by its straightforward presentation of known facts. With new discoveries, factual information can change, of course. Nonetheless, there are many topics that have been extensively researched and about which there are commonly agreed-upon findings. For example, if you compare the contents of *Nic Bishop's Spiders*, *Spiders* by Laura Marsh, and *Time for Kids: Spiders* by Nicole Iorio, you will find many commonalities in content (e.g., information on the body parts of spiders, the ways in which spiders create webs, and where spiders are found). Factual books may vary in terms of the amount of detail, as well as design and visuals; nonetheless, readers are likely to find considerable overlap in information in factual books addressing the same topic.

Interpretive Nonfiction

Interpretive informational books present researched information with interpretation. Marc Aronson (2012) describes these books as ones that "take you on a journey." Many chapter-length works of nonfiction are of this nature. Susan Campbell Bartoletti's *They Called Themselves the K. K. K.* is such a work. In this book Bartoletti tells the story of the Ku Klux Klan—its origins, organization, and impact on the South in the years following the Civil War. She takes readers on a journey to witness the physical and psychological terror that was rained down on former slaves and others who opposed the tactics of this terrorist organization. To tell the story, Bartoletti conducted extensive research, turning to some 8,000 pages of congressional documents, 2,300 slave narratives, memoirs, diaries, period newspapers, and a host of scholarly texts about the Klan and the era of Reconstruction. As part of her investigation, she even attended a present-day Klan Congress held in the Ozark Mountains. Bartoletti then had to synthesize and interpret this voluminous research in order to craft the journey on which she takes her readers.

It is also important to recognize that authors who interpret and synthesize information may be trying intentionally to persuade readers to embrace a particular perspective. For example, both *The Down-to-Earth Guide To Global Warming* by Laurie David and Cambria Gordon (a summary for children of Al Gore's *An Inconvenient Truth: The Crisis of Global Warming*), and *The Sky's Not Falling: Why It's OK to Chill about Global Warming* by Holly Fretwell synthesize and interpret information. However, the two author teams are clearly advocating different positions about the prospect of global warming. These books serve as an example of why it is important for readers to consider author purpose and to look carefully at the credentials of authors and try to determine how thoroughly they have researched their topics. In the section below entitled Organizational

ILLUSTRATION 11.2 *If Stones Could Speak*, a book about why Stonehenge was built, emphasizes the investigative process. (Courtesy of National Geographic Books.)

and Support Tools, we discuss tools frequently found in informational books that readers can turn to in making these kinds of assessments.

Nonfiction of Inquiry

The final category of nonfiction is the nonfiction of inquiry. Zarnowski and Turkel (2011) describe this type of book as the "literature of inquiry" (p. 31). These books actually have much in common with interpretive nonfiction in that both typically require in-depth research, the findings of which must be synthesized and interpreted. What sets the nonfiction of inquiry apart is the way in which the author makes explicit the investigative process undertaken to reveal the knowledge. Zarnowski and Turkel (2011) argue that the nonfiction of inquiry can help young readers better understand the inquiry process. Marc Aronson's *If Stones Could Speak: Unlocking the Secrets of Stonehenge* is one such example. Aronson's emphasis on the investigative process is evident almost from the beginning when he states: "This is a book about questioning what others believe to be true, not accepting ideas just because famous people say they are right" (p. 8). Aronson then documents a research team's attempt to unlock the secrets of why the ancient circle of stones was constructed. Susan Campbell Bartoletti's *Black Potatoes: The Story of the Great Irish Famine, 1845–1850* is another example of the nonfiction of inquiry that not only informs readers but also allows them to think along with a gifted writer conducting an historical inquiry.

Major Writers of Nonfiction for Children

WRITER	PRIMARILY WRITES...	MAJOR WORKS INCLUDE
George Ancona	Ancona has written and/or photographed more than 75 books for children. He is particularly known for his photo essays, many of which focus on his Mexican heritage.	• *El piñatero/The Piñata Maker* • *Pablo Remembers: The Fiesta of the Day of the Dead* • *Powwow* • *¡Olé Flamenco!*
Marc Aronson	Aronson approaches history as a detective story that can yield answers through meticulous research. In many of his books, the process by which he uncovers answers is made explicit.	• *Sugar Changed the World: A Story of Magic, Spice, Slavery, Freedom, and Science* • *Trapped: How the World Rescued 33 Miners from 2,000 Feet Below the Chilean Desert* • *If Stones Could Speak: Unlocking the Secrets of Stonehenge* • *Race*
Susan Campbell Bartoletti	Author of both fiction and nonfiction, Bartoletti has won extensive recognition for her meticulously researched historical nonfiction.	• *Hitler Youth: Growing Up in Hitler's Shadow* • *They Called Themselves the K.K.K.: The Birth of an American Terrorist Group* • *Black Potatoes: The Story of the Great Irish Famine, 1845-1850*
Nic Bishop	Bishop has written numerous books about animals around the world. Each is accompanied by remarkable photographs taken by the author. In addition, his photographs can be found in outstanding works of nonfiction written by other authors.	• *Nic Bishop Spiders* • *Nic Bishop: Marsupials* • *Nic Bishop: Lizards* • *Frogs*

James Cross Giblin	As a writer of children's informational books, Giblin is known for his imaginative and engaging treatment of unusual topics. He does careful research, not only for the text of his books but also for the illustrations, which are carefully selected photographs, prints, and drawings.	• *The Riddle of the Rosetta Stone: Key to Ancient Egypt* • *Chimney Sweeps: Yesterday and Today* • *Good Brother, Bad Brother: The Story of Edwin Booth and John Wilkes Booth* • *The Life and Death of Adolf Hitler*
Steve Jenkins	In picture books illustrated with cut paper collage, Jenkins explores many facets of the natural world. His books are at once informative, engaging, and playful.	• *What Do You Do with a Tail Like This?* • *Actual Size* • *Prehistoric Actual Size* • *Bones: Skeletons and How They Work*
Jim Murphy	Murphy has penned more than 30 books, many of which focus on topics related to American history. Many of his books feature children. His books usually are illustrated with carefully researched archival photographs and they have received many prestigious awards.	• *The Great Fire* • *An American Plague* • *Truce: The Day Soldiers Stopped Fighting* • *Across America on an Emigrant Train*
Laurence Pringle	Laurence Pringle has contributed significantly to informational science books for children. Drawing on his degrees in wildlife biology, Pringle has written more than 100 books that focus primarily on nature, wildlife, and ecology and environmental issues.	• *Whales! Strange and Wonderful* • *Billions of Years, Amazing Changes: The Story of Evolution* • *Crows: Strange and Wonderful*

How Nonfiction Works

Nonfiction works in ways quite different from fictional genres. In this section we differentiate between nonfiction books that are narrative in nature and those that rely on expository structures. In addition, we explore the following elements of nonfiction books: particular expository structures, organizational tools, style, and visuals.

Structure

Authors of nonfiction must organize the information they gather in a way that is appealing and accessible to their readers. Some writers present their information in a narrative style (sometimes called narrative nonfiction). In this type of nonfiction book, the writer utilizes some of the features of fiction to convey information—features such as suspense and careful pacing. This is just what Don Brown does in *America Is Under Attack*, the story of the attack on the Twin Towers on September 11. In this gripping work, Brown narrates the stories of individuals caught up in the nightmare. Just as writers of fiction often do, Brown builds his story to a dramatic moment and then shifts the scene. For example, readers are introduced to Stanley Praimnath. As Praimnath sees the second jet hurtling toward his office window in the South Tower of the World Trade Center, he dives beneath his desk. At this point readers learn that Praimnath has survived, but they are left wondering how or whether he will escape the destruction that surrounds him. Only after focusing his storytelling on other victims of the attack does Brown finally return to chronicle the miraculous rescue of Praimnath.

While some nonfiction books are written in a narrative style, most authors of nonfiction employ an expository style of writing to explain, inform, or describe. Expository writing uses various organizational patterns to present information including description, sequence, comparison/contrast, problem-solution, and cause/effect. Each of these patterns is defined in Table 11.2. For example, Jim Murphy organizes *Across America on an Emigrant Train* sequentially; readers follow Robert Louis Stevenson's travels from Scotland to San Francisco in search of his true love. Sometimes the title of a book signals the book's global structure. For example, the title of Kathleen Zoehfeld's *How Mountains Are Made*, a book in the Let's Read and Find

TOP SHELF 11.2

NONFICTION OF INQUIRY

The Hive Detectives: Chronicle of a Bee Catastrophe by Loree Griffin Burns and illustrated by Ellen Harasimowicz

Thanksgiving: The True Story by Penny Colman

The Chimpanzees I Love: Saving Their World and Ours by Jane Goodall

Kakapo Rescue: Saving the World's Strangest Parrot by Sy Montgomery and illustrated by Nic Bishop

Ain't Nothing but a Man: My Quest to Find the Real John Henry by Scott Reynolds Nelson with Marc Aronson

Secrets of a Civil War Submarine: Solving the Mysteries of the H. L. Hunley by Sally M. Walker

Ask *the* Author . . . James Cross Giblin

How do you take complex informational material and make it both understandable and appealing to a child audience?

The first thing I do when I begin to research a new nonfiction book is to look for the story line in the material. For every subject—whether it's a biography, or a history of plagues, or the life cycle of the woolly mammoth—has an implicit story line within it, just as every novel has a plot. It's what keeps readers turning the pages, eager to find out what comes next.

A good example of a nonfiction story line can be found in my biography of Charles A. Lindbergh. It embraces the entire sweep of Lindbergh's life, from his historic nonstop flight across the Atlantic in 1927, to the kidnapping and death of his firstborn son, to his determined efforts to keep the United States out of World War II. The story line reaches its climax when Lindbergh became involved late in life with the conservation movement, saying, "I would rather have birds than airplanes."

Young people today are exposed to every facet of a public figure's personality via television and the Internet. In light of this, I believe writers for children have an obligation to present a full and rounded picture of the people and events they explore in their books. That's why I decided to discuss Lindbergh's controversial views in the years before World War II and why I subtitled the biography "A Human Hero." I hoped the phrase would suggest that even a hero like Charles Lindbergh may not always act in a heroic fashion.

When I research a book, I always keep my eye out for details that will flesh out the subject and bring it to life for young readers. Examples of such details are the lavatory facilities (or lack of them) aboard Lindbergh's plane, *The Spirit of St. Louis,* and the way that rats, and the fleas they hosted, spread the deadly Black Death in the Middle Ages. I described the latter in *When Plague Strikes: The Black Death, Smallpox, AIDS.*

Every informational book I research and write is first of all a voyage of discovery for me, the author. And if I shape the material in a lively and dramatic way, I hope it will be just as entertaining and informative a voyage for my readers.

James Cross Giblin is the author of many well-received books for children and young adults. Among his books include *Good Brother, Bad Brother: The Story of Edwin Booth and John Wilkes Booth* and *The Life and Death of Adolf Hitler.* When Jim isn't writing, he enjoys reading; going to plays, art exhibits, and movies; and exploring New York City, where he lives.

Out series, signals the book's cause and effect structure. Similarly, the title of Laura Vaccaro Seeger's *First the Egg* signals a sequential pattern of organization: "First the egg then the chicken. First the tadpole then the frog" (n. p.). These patterns of text organization reflect the line of thinking put forth by the author of a book; hence recognizing the structure of a nonfiction book is essential to comprehension. So it is critical that teachers help children be attuned to the way(s) in which an author has organized his or her work.

Authors may even choose to use a combination of narrative and expository structures. In the Orbis Pictus honor book, *Birmingham Sunday,* author Larry Dane Brimner begins with narratives of the final morning of each of the four young girls who were killed in the Sixteenth Street Baptist Church bombing in 1963. He then shifts to the use of expository text organized sequentially to document key events that led up to the fateful bombing and events that transpired after the bombing. The book concludes with brief biographies of the major participants in the events related to the Birmingham bombing.

TABLE 11.2   *Organizational Patterns Commonly Used in Nonfiction for Young Readers*

ORGANIZATIONAL PATTERN	DEFINITION
Description	This pattern provides information about an object, event, or person (e.g., facts, features, traits), often qualifying the listing in terms of criteria such as size or importance.
Sequence	This pattern puts information (e.g., events, facts, steps) into a sequence.
Comparison/Contrast	This pattern reveals likenesses and differences between two or more things.
Problem/Solution	This pattern identifies a problem and provides a possible solution or solutions to the problem.
Cause and Effect	This pattern shows how events, facts, or ideas occur as a result of other events, facts, or concepts.

Organizational and Support Tools

A variety of organizational tools are often included in nonfiction, such as a table of contents, index, glossary, timeline, and appendices. In addition, many nonfiction books contain support tools that document the research done by the author. These tools comprise the front matter and end matter of a nonfiction book. They are intended to facilitate reading and provide a basis for evaluating the thoroughness of the author's research—if the reader understands the purpose of the tool. Table 11.3 lists features that may be found in nonfiction books and the ways in which each can facilitate reading. For example, the table of contents provides an overview of the contents of the book and may even reveal the organizational structure of the book. Not all books contain these tools; they are most likely to be found in longer books aimed at older readers. Yet even shorter nonfiction books for younger readers may contain some organizational tools. For example, *Nic Bishop's Spiders* has both a glossary and an index.

In addition to including front matter and end matter, many nonfiction books are organized into chapters. Chapter titles, as well as the headings and sub-headings within chapters, can guide a reader by highlighting major ideas. Teachers can prepare children for the extensive nonfiction reading they will be required to do by providing them with rich experiences with quality informational trade books and by helping them learn to use organizational tools to support their reading.

Style

Authors of nonfiction must generate and maintain readers' interest. Writers use a variety of literary techniques to engage readers: crafting an intriguing title, "slicing" a topic in an unusual way, posing a question, crafting engaging introductions, addressing the reader directly as "you," employing humor, and using highly descriptive language and imagery. In *A Black Hole Is Not a Hole*, author Carolyn Cinami DeCristofano relies on several of these techniques. The title is one that engages, and in response to this title readers are likely to ask, "Then what is it?" For those who don't respond in this way, this question is actually posed on the cover—as a speech bubble

TEACHING IDEA 11.1

CRITICALLY REVIEWING BOOKS ON THE SAME TOPIC

COMMON CORE STANDARD: CRAFT AND STRUCTURE, STANDARD 6

Ask children to select a topic and read at least two books about it. For example, students can compare *Shipwreck at the Bottom of the World* by Jennifer Armstrong with *Ice Story: Shackleton's Lost Expedition* by Elizabeth Cody Kimmel. Have children develop categories for comparison and chart the similarities and differences in the books. This idea can also be applied to biographies. Ask children to read two or more biographies about an individual and chart their similarities and differences.

TABLE 11.3 *Organizational and Support Tools Often Found in the Front Matter and End Matter of Nonfiction Books and Biographies*

ORGANIZATIONAL TOOL	PURPOSE(S)
Table of contents	• Provides a road map to the book's content • Signals the structure of a book • Helps in locating information within a book
Index	• Helps in locating information within a book
Glossary	• Provides definitions of challenging words important to understanding information
Timeline	• Provides an overview of important events and the order in which they occurred
Bibliography and source notes	• Provides information readers can use in evaluating the thoroughness of an author's research
Note about the author	• Provides information about the author's credentials

for what appears to be a planet in space! The book then begins with a humorous introduction that is likely to pull in even the most reluctant readers:

> From the headlines, you'd think black holes were beasts with endless appetites, lying in wait for the next meal. By some reports they are "runaway," out-of-control "predators" that "feed" on galaxies, only to "belch" and "spit out" what they don't eat. They "lurk" in the shadows, "mangling" stars and "gobbling" them up. In short, they have a nasty reputation for being monsters "gone mad." (p. 1)

As DeCristofano continues to explore her admittedly complex topic, one technique she uses to help readers grasp complex concepts is the simile: "Even though [a black hole] is like a whirlpool, a black hole is not a whirlpool."

In their Caldecott Honor book, *What Do You Do with a Tail Like This?*, Steve Jenkins and Robin Page create a game-like format that immediately engages readers. Readers move through the book looking at "pairs" of double-page spreads. On the first spread appears the focus body part (e.g., tail, nose, ears, eyes) of five animals with an accompanying question: "What do you do with a _____ like this?" At this point readers are bound to engage in trying to guess the animals to which the featured body parts belong. Then, upon turning the page, readers not only discover if their guesses were right when they view complete pictures of each animal, they also learn how the featured animals use their tails (or noses or ears or eyes).

Graphic and Visual Features

In contemporary nonfiction books for children, visuals (or graphics) play a central role. According to Barbara Moss (2008), some experts argue that "graphics hold more meaning in today's texts than words" (p. 395). Visuals take many forms, including photographs, paintings, drawings, charts, diagrams, graphs, maps, and copies of documents, as well as the captions that may accompany these features. These visuals play such an important role in informational books that they must be as carefully researched as text (Tavares, 2011). They can help to clarify abstract concepts; they can convey specific facts and clarify specialized vocabulary, or they can present a realistic rendering of a concept. They can also help to provide the background knowledge necessary for readers' understanding. The diversity of visuals is one of the noteworthy features of *Secrets of a Civil War Submarine: Solving the Mysteries of the H. L. Hunley* which includes historic and contemporary photographs, maps, design sketches, copies of original documents, laser and CT scans, and x-rays. *Into the Unknown: How Great Explorers Found Their Way by Land, Sea, and Air*, written by Stewart Ross and illustrated by Stephen Biesty, relates the stories of 14 explorers (from Pytheas the Greek in 340 BC to Neil Armstrong and Buzz Aldrin in 1969) who left their homes to explore the unknown. The visuals in this book include dramatic foldout cross sections that convey information about technology, places, and concepts.

In nonfiction picture books the visuals contribute even more than those in longer books. In Steve Jenkins' *Bones*, the illustrations on some openings can almost stand alone without any text. For example, on one double-page spread, readers see six skeletal arms, each labeled with the name of the animal to which the skeleton belongs. The visual information alone shows the commonalities in structure of arms belonging to very different creatures—information confirmed by the text.

TEACHING IDEA 11.2

ARCHIVAL PHOTOGRAPHS

COMMON CORE STANDARD: *INTEGRATION OF KNOWLEDGE AND IDEAS, STANDARD 7*

Organize children into small groups, and give each group a book illustrated with archival photographs. Ask children to "read" these photographs and to compile a list of the facts and concepts that they learned from carefully viewing the photographs.

Criteria for Evaluating Nonfiction

- Is the book accurate and authentic in conveying factual, documented material?
- Is the information presented in an organized way?
- Is the format and design of the book appealing and accessible to children?
- Is the author's writing style clear, and does it generate enthusiasm for the topic?

What Is Biography?

Some of the oldest books for children are biographies—works that feature the lives of real individuals. In earlier periods, it was common to expose children to the (sometimes idealized) lives of national and cultural heroes. The practice still exists, but in a somewhat altered form. For one thing, in the United States, there is growing recognition that the society is made up of more than one culture, so the goal of many writers of biography has become promoting a more inclusive view of noteworthy Americans. For another thing, the trend toward exposure-oriented journalism—journalism that delves below the surface—has become steadily stronger since the Vietnam War era. Thus, today's children are less likely than previous generations to believe larger-than-life accounts of heroes. Finally, the study of history has become less preoccupied with famous people and great events and more focused on ordinary people and the ambience of the times in which they lived. Thus, even though a biography might have a well-known person as its subject, the author is likely to explain that person in the context of his or her time, along with the concerns, available choices, and social movements of the day.

Who are the subjects of biographies for children? Biographies have been written about people from both the past and the present day. Authors have written about the lives of scientists and inventors, political leaders, individuals who have contributed to society through the arts, and individuals who have faced and overcome persecution and hardship. Biographers have also described the lives of everyday individuals, often children, whose experiences have touched us in some way.

How does biography differ from historical fiction? Biographies that focus on famous individuals from the past offer insight into historical times just as historical

TOP SHELF 11.3

PICTURE BOOK BIOGRAPHIES OF INDIVIDUALS WHO OVERCAME ADVERSITY

Fly High! The Story of Bessie Coleman by Louise Borden and Mary Kay Kroeger, illustrated by Teresa Flavin

Rosa by Nikki Giovanni, illustrated by Bryan Collier

Playing to Win: The Story of Althea Gibson by Karen Deans, illustrated by Elbrite Brown

Harvesting Hope: The Story of Cesar Chavez by Kathleen Krull, illustrated by Yuyi Morales

When Marian Sang by Pam Muñoz Ryan, illustrated by Brian Selznick

Martin's Big Words: The Life of Dr. Martin Luther King, Jr. by Doreen Rappaport, illustrated by Bryan Collier

fiction does. However, unlike historical fiction, the information presented in a biography is based on known facts about the individual and her or his time period. Incidents, dialogue, and people are not invented or imagined, as they are in historical fiction. Autobiographies and memoirs differ from biographies in that their authors are writing about themselves.

Value of Biography

Biographies have some unique features that justify their inclusion in a literature program. First, they help children learn from the lives of others. In a biography, children can see how choices a person makes early in life can bear fruit later on or how inauspicious beginnings can lead to a good outcome. Reading biographies can also encourage children to recognize links between people's lives and the social and historical times in which they lived. For instance, in her biography *You Want Women to Vote, Lizzie Stanton?* Jean Fritz writes, "Yes, Elizabeth Cady Stanton did want women to vote. It was an outlandish idea, but that's what she wanted. Not at first. As a child, she knew that girls didn't count for much, but she didn't expect to change that. First she had to grow up" (p. 1). This biography of Stanton, who dedicated her life to women's suffrage in the United States, describes gender roles during the nineteenth century and gives reasons for people's beliefs about women's suffrage. Through biographies, children come to understand the people who have shaped history, created inventions, discovered scientific principles, composed music, crafted works of art, and contributed to their local communities. Children realize that they, too, can make a difference in the world.

Major Writers of Biography

WRITER	PRIMARILY WRITES...	MAJOR WORKS INCLUDE
Russell Freedman	In his long career as an author, Freedman has written both biographies and informational books. His books illuminate complex topics in ways that are accessible for young readers.	• *Lincoln: A Photobiography* • *The Voice that Challenged a Nation: Marian Anderson and the Struggle for Equal Rights* • *The Wright Brothers: How They Invented the Airplane* • *Kids at Work: Lewis Hine and the Crusade against Child Labor* • *Eleanor Roosevelt: A Life of Discovery*
Candace Fleming	Fleming writes in various genres of children's literature, but her love of storytelling and history are the essential ingredients for the well-researched and engaging biographies she writes. Her books are structured in notable ways.	• *Amelia Lost: The Life and Disappearance of Amelia Earhart* • *The Great and Only Barnum: The Tremendous, Stupendous Life of Showman P.T. Barnum* • *The Lincolns: A Scrapbook Look at Abraham and Mary* • *Our Eleanor: A Scrapbook Look at Eleanor Roosevelt's Remarkable Life*
Barbara Kerley	Kerley has teamed with a variety of talented illustrators to create exuberant picture book biographies about historic and literary figures.	• *The Extraordinary Mark Twain (According to Susy)* • *The Dinosaurs of Waterhouse Hawkins: An Illuminating History of Mr. Waterhouse Hawkins, Artist and Lecturer* • *What to Do about Alice? How Alice Roosevelt Broke the Rules, Charmed the World, and Drove Her Father Teddy Crazy!* • *Walt Whitman: Words for America*
Diane Stanley	Stanley has achieved prominence for her picture book biographies for children in the upper elementary grades. She transferred her talent for detailed, realistic drawing and painting to children's books.	• *Peter the Great* • *Cleopatra* • *Bard of Avon: The Story of William Shakespeare* • *Leonardo da Vinci*
Jean Fritz	Fritz wrote biographies for children for more than 35 years. Attention to detail, the use of humor, and the ability to present historical figures in an interesting, appealing way are characteristics of her work.	• *Will You Sign Here, John Hancock?* • *Stonewall* • *The Great Little Madison* • *And Then What Happened, Paul Revere?*

The Evolution of Biography

In the past, biographies for children were criticized for poor writing, invented details, and exaggeration of the positive side of their subjects. Moreover, in the first half of the twentieth century, the subjects of biographies were mostly limited to white males who were political leaders or who had made some other historical contribution to society. The prevailing thought—alive and well since ancient times—was that children should hear or read biographies of individuals who displayed admirable virtues and thus could serve as role models to emulate. These individuals were idealized—presented as being morally perfect. Because societal norms dictated that children should not be exposed to the less savory realities of life, such as discrimination, violence, or abuse, early biographies were bland and unrealistic.

Fictionalization was also an accepted practice in earlier children's biographies. For instance, authors routinely invented conversations and scenes for which there was no historic basis. True, authors had good motives for these distortions. In explaining why he fictionalized biography for children, F. M. Monjo (1982) pointed out that he used a child associated with the "great figure" as narrator because it "makes possible a casual intimacy which, I believe, young readers find congenial" (p. 99). Author Robert Lawson included fantastic elements in his fictionalized biographies. His biography of Benjamin Franklin, *Ben & Me*, was told by a mouse named Amos. Although Lawson's books were popular with children, they raised the question of whether it was necessary to fictionalize biographies to make them palatable to young readers. The answer was decades away.

As with nonfiction books in general, critical recognition of biographies for children was slow in coming. The first Newbery Medal for a work of biography was awarded in 1934 to *Invincible Louisa,* a biography of Louisa May Alcott written by Cornelia Meigs. In 1940, James Daugherty received the Newbery Medal for *Daniel Boone.* (Contemporary readers, however, may be appalled at the book's portrayal of Native Americans.) In the same year, the Caldecott Medal for the best illustrated book of the year went to a biography, *Abraham Lincoln,* by Ingri D'Aulaire and Edgar Parin D'Aulaire. Still, biographies for children had a long way to go.

The 1970s were a turning point for children's biographies. With the publication of *And Then What Happened, Paul Revere?* in 1973, author Jean Fritz set a new standard. Fritz created an authentic biography for children without any invented dialogue; she also included "Notes from the Author," containing additional facts keyed to various pages of the book. Fritz did not rely on fictionalizing to make her books congenial to young readers. Her conversational, humorous, and easily accessible writing style—as well as her focus on one or two interesting events—is what drew and still draws readers to her works.

Since the early 1970s, biographies have advanced further, to give children wider representation of noteworthy people. Biographies written in the past four decades have featured men, women, and children of many ethnic and racial backgrounds engaging in a variety of occupations and contributing in many different ways to society. For example, *Harvesting Hope: The Story of Cesar Chavez* by Kathleen Krull describes the Mexican American leader who organized the National Farm Workers Association;

TECHNOLOGY IN PRACTICE 11.2

Many books naturally connect to technology. Jean Fritz's *Leonardo's Horse* intertwines two true stories: one of long ago about Leonardo da Vinci's drawings and model for a horse that never was cast into bronze, and the other of our present day about Charles Dent's dream to recreate Leonardo's horse as a gift to the city of Milan. The book encourages curiosity, inquiry, and problem solving. There is reference to a Web site: <www .leonardoshorse.org> that includes extensive information about all aspects of Leonardo da Vinci's horse. Students may also want to check a search engine and type in "Leonardo's Horse." Many other Web sites can then be visited along with an article from *Smithsonian Magazine*, a reference to a 1977 *National Geographic* article, and other interesting material. Through these other references, students can engage in greater depth to learn about Leonardo da Vinci, Charles Dent, the famous horse, and the city of Milan.

When Marian Sang by Pam Muñoz Ryan highlights the life of Marian Anderson, the talented singer who was the first African American to perform with the Metropolitan Opera.

During the 1980s, the picture book biography became more recognized as a format to chronicle an individual's life. For instance, Alice and Martin Provensen skillfully combined illustrations and text in a unique pop-up book about the life of Leonardo da Vinci, *Leonardo da Vinci: The Artist, Inventor, Scientist in Three-Dimensional Movable Pictures.* In the 1990s, more and more authors chose to write partial biographies about the childhoods of famous individuals.

In 1988, Russell Freedman received the Newbery Medal for *Lincoln: A Photobiography,* establishing a new era for the prestige and recognition of authentic biography for children. James Cross Giblin explains that the significance of *Lincoln* in the evolution of children's biography is that it offers a "fresh approach to familiar material, demythologizing Lincoln without debunking him," telling "a dramatic true story," emphasizing the visual with its photo-essay format, and providing an "accessible yet literate text" (1992, p. 25).

In 1999, the Caldecott Medal was awarded to *Snowflake Bentley,* written by Jacqueline Briggs Martin and illustrated by Mary Azarian. This picture book biography describes the life of Wilson Bentley, whose fascination with snowflakes led to his dedicated work photographing snowflakes, documenting the unique features of each one, and becoming an authority on them. Azarian's woodcut illustrations, hand-tinted with watercolors, document Bentley's life and the beauty of snowflakes.

In the past decade alone, seven biographies have been designated as Caldecott Honor books. Included in this list are the 2002 Honor book, *Martin's Big Words: The Life of Martin Luther King, Jr.* by Doreen Rappaport, with watercolor and cut paper illustrations by Bryan Collier, and the 2009 Honor book, *A River of Words: The Story of William Carlos Williams* written by Jen Bryant and illustrated by Melissa Sweet using a creative blending of watercolors, mixed media, and collage. The impressive number of award-winning biographies reflects the established place of the genre in the field of children's literature.

A current trend in children's biographies is the publication of series biographies. These biographies follow a specified format and include the same types of information for each individual. For example, Holiday House has its *Picture Book Biographies* by David Adler. Viking's *Giants of Science* series offers critically acclaimed biographies of scientists written by Kathleen Krull, including works about greats such as Leonardo da Vinci, Marie Curie, Albert Einstein, and Charles Darwin.

Categories of Biography

Partial Biographies

Instead of presenting an entire life, a writer may create a more interesting work by selecting one segment from the person's life and exploring it in depth. Jean Fritz's biographies of famous early Americans are good examples of partial biographies. For example, in *Why Don't You Get a Horse, Sam Adams?* Fritz recounts how patriot Samuel Adams walked the streets of pre-Revolutionary Boston promoting independence from England. Another example of a partial biography is *Dave the Potter: Artist, Poet, Slave* written by Laban Carrick Hill and illustrated by Bryan Collier. This Caldecott Honor book chronicles the adult life of Dave, a slave living in South Carolina, who crafted masterful pots into which he carved his own poetry.

Complete Biographies

In a complete biography, the author recounts a person's life from birth to the present or to the person's death if he or she is no longer living. Candace Fleming chronicles the life of beloved first lady Eleanor Roosevelt in *Our Eleanor: A Scrapbook Look at Eleanor Roosevelt's Remarkable Life*. Archival photographs, diary entries, and letters combine with the text in documenting the life of Eleanor Roosevelt.

Collective Biographies

A collective biography is a book describing the lives of several people who have something in common. In *Uncommon Champions: Fifteen Athletes Who Battled Back*, Marty Kaminsky tells the story of athletes who overcame serious illnesses, physical disabilities, and other adversity to achieve in various sports. Kaminsky points out in the introduction that these athletes "are remarkable not just for their achievements on the playing fields, courts, and tracks, but for the tremendous courage they demonstrated while overcoming major obstacles in their lives" (p. 9).

Another approach to collective biography is seen in the collaborative work of author Kathleen Krull and illustrator Kathryn Hewitt. They have produced many collective biographies, including *Lives of the Musicians: Good Times, Bad Times (and What the Neighbors Thought)* and *Lives of Extraordinary Women: Rulers, Rebels (and What the Neighbors Thought)*. The format of these appealing and humorous books includes biographical sketches of the individuals accompanied by watercolor illustrations. Krull has carefully researched each individual, discovering little-known information that will fascinate readers.

ILLUSTRATION 11.3 *Dave the Potter* tells the story of a slave in South Carolina who lovingly crafted masterful pots into which he carved his own poetry. ("Dave the Potter: Artist, Poet, Slave" by Laban Carrick Hill, illustrated by Bryan Collier. Little, Brown and Company, a division of Hachette Book Group, Inc.)

Autobiographies and Memoirs

In an autobiography, a person writes about his or her own life. Many children's authors have written their autobiographies, and children who delight in these authors' books will enjoy reading about their childhoods and how they became writers.

A memoir differs from an autobiography in that it shares events from the author's life based on his or her recollection. Often, a memoir focuses on one particular event or time period in the person's life and reflects on the meaning of that event for the author. Memoirs are becoming increasingly popular in children's literature. In *Drawing from Memory*, Allen Say uses an innovative format to tell the story of how he became an artist. Say illustrates his books with paintings, drawings, and photographs, and in parts of the book utilizes a graphic novel format. Siena Cherson Siegel shares her childhood learning to dance in *To Dance: A Ballerina's Graphic Novel*, illustrated by Mark Siegel. This memoir, with its graphic novel format, seamlessly combines text and illustrations as the author describes her early life and training at the School of American Ballet.

Ordinary individuals often experience extraordinary events or inspire others with their courage and determination. Ruby Bridges gives readers a glimpse into her childhood in *Through My Eyes*. Ruby was six years old in 1960 when federal marshals escorted her to school. Ruby's historic childhood as the young girl who integrated the New Orleans public school system is shared in this award-winning book. Ibtisam Barakat recounts her early years living under Israeli occupation in *Tasting the Sky: A Palestinian Childhood*.

Picture Book Biographies

The number of picture book biographies written for children continues to increase. In the picture book biography, the illustrations and text join together in portraying a person's life. There are picture book biographies that appeal to younger readers, as well as ones for older children. In *Jazz Age Josephine,* Jonah Winter tells the story of dance great Josephine Baker from her impoverished childhood to her rise to fame in Paris. Marjorie Priceman's gouache illustrations convey the energy and movement that was Josephine Baker.

The life of 2004 Nobel Peace Prize recipient Wangari Maathai is portrayed in text and illustrations in Claire A. Nivola's *Planting the Trees of Kenya: The Story of Wangari Maathai.* Nivola's watercolor illustrations complement the text about the life of the woman who began the Green Belt Movement. A picture book biography for older children is *The Tree of Life* written and illustrated by Peter Sís. The life of Charles Darwin is recreated through intricate and detailed illustrations, along with text from Darwin's own diaries, letters, and writings.

How Biography Works

Earlier we noted that nonfiction works in ways quite different from fiction. This is not entirely true of biographies. Rather, biographies have at least some elements more closely associated with fiction.

Characterization

Biographies are stories about real people. Like the writer of any good story, the biographer must create a main character about whom children care and want to learn more. Biographers develop their subjects' personalities and recreate their lives by describing their actions and interactions with others, what they say, and the ways in which others talk about them. Although biographers strive to bring individuals to life, these individuals are real people. So the work of the biographer must be based on careful research. Yet they must also interpret facts and events. As Zarnowski (1990) points out:

> While biographers do gather all the information they can, they also filter that information through their minds. Biographers are active decision makers, deciding what to include and what to omit, what to highlight, and what to place in the background, and what to claim as truth and what to suggest as informed speculation. Biographers are interpreters of the information they collect. (p. 9)

For example, most children's biographies of Amelia Earhart highlight the dramatic achievements of the famous aviator, but in *Amelia Lost: The Life and Disappearance of Amelia Earhart,* author Candace Fleming does this and more. She also details the ways in which Earhart and her husband worked to exploit her celebrity, taking what Fleming describes as "an active role in mythologizing her . . . life" (p. viii).

Just as biographers interpret information, readers must interpret critically what they are reading. They must decide whether the portrait of the person is balanced, whether any aspects of the person's life have been fictionalized, whether dialogue is authentic, and whether the person is presented in a believable way. Close inspection of the author's bibliography and source notes can help making these determinations.

Structure

Like authors of other nonfiction books, those who write biographies must organize information in an appealing and accessible way. Because they are telling a story, the story of an individual's life, biographers often utilize a narrative style of writing. Hester Bass begins her picture book biography, *The Secret World of Walter Anderson*, in this way:

> There once was a man whose love of nature was as wide as the world.
> There once was an artist who needed to paint as much as he needed to breathe.
> There once was an islander who lived in a cottage at the edge of Mississippi, where the sea meets the earth and the sky.
> His name was Walter Anderson.

Regardless of whether writers of biography utilize a narrative or expository style of writing (or some combination of the two), biographers often rely on a sequential pattern of organization, telling the subject's life story from childhood into adulthood. Yet not all biographies proceed in a straightforward sequence. Candace Fleming begins *Amelia Lost: The Life and Disappearance of Amelia Earhart* not by focusing on Earhart's childhood but by recounting the tense moments as the crew of a Coast Guard cutter waited—in vain—for Earhart to land on Howland Island on her flight around the world.

Visuals

As is true of other works of nonfiction, visuals play an important role in most biographies. In *Good Brother Bad Brother,* James Cross Giblin tells the story of Edwin Booth and his notorious brother John Wilkes Booth. The biography is replete with old photographs, engravings, playbills, and even a poster offering a reward for John Wilkes Booth.

In picture book biographies, as in fictional picture books, text and pictures, as well as design elements, work together to tell the story of the subject. *Balloons Over Broadway*, written and illustrated by Melissa Sweet, is a biography of Anthony Sarg, the puppeteer who first envisioned and created the gigantic balloon creatures that appear in the famous Macy's Thanksgiving Day Parade. Sweet conveys the playful and imaginative nature of Sarg through word and illustrations. Every element in this delightful book—including cover, endpapers, and title page, as well as Sweet's mixed media collages embellished with handmade dolls—capture the joyful essence of the puppeteer's work.

---

for **ENGLISH LANGUAGE LEARNERS**

Biographies are available today that address individuals from many backgrounds and cultures. For this reason, the genre can be used to help English language learners feel connected to their classroom experiences. Teachers working with Mexican American students might, for example, choose to use biographies about important Mexican American labor leaders such as *Harvesting Hope: The Story of Cesar Chavez* by Kathleen Krull and *That's Not Fair!: Emma Tenayuca's Struggle for Justice* by Carmen Tafolla and Sharyll Teneyuca.

Many contemporary informational books and biographies for children have organizational features and rich visuals that can support the comprehension of English language learners. (See Table 11.3 for a list of these features.) However, teachers must be intentional in helping English language learners learn to use these devices to support reading comprehension.

Organizational and Support Tools

Biographies are likely to contain many of the same organizational and support tools found in informational books. These may include a table of contents, index, glossary, chapter headings and sub-headings, as well as support tools such as a bibliography, author's note, and source notes. See Table 11.1 for a listing of these tools and ways in which they can support reading.

Criteria for Evaluating Biography

- Is the person someone whose life will be of interest to young readers?
- Has the author presented the person in such a way that readers can identify with him or her as an authentic, believable human being?
- Is the information about the person accurate and authentic?
- Has the author written in an engaging style that maintains readers' attention?

EXPERIENCES FOR FURTHER LEARNING

1. Select a topic that interests you—say, wolves. Compare the treatment of the topic in a nonfiction book (such as *When the Wolves Returned* by Dorothy Hinshaw Patent) to its treatment in other genres such as novels (for example, *Julie of the Wolves* by Jean Craighead George), picture books (*Wolf's Favor* by Fulvio Testa), and folktales (*Peter and the Wolf* retold by Selina Hastings). How do different genres contribute to your understanding of the topic?

2. Select two nonfiction books on the same topic. For example, for the civil rights movement, you could use *Freedom Walkers: The Story of the Montgomery Bus Boycott* by Russell Freedman, and *Freedom Riders: John Lewis and Jim Zwerg on the Front Lines of the Civil Rights Movement* by Ann Bausum. Review the archival photographs in each book. How do the photographs convey information? What kind of information is presented? What design features do you notice in each book? Compare the photographs and design features on a chart, with a column for each book. Share your findings with classmates.

RECOMMENDED BOOKS

* indicates a picture book; **I** indicates interest level (P = preschool, YA = young adult)

History

Armstrong, Jennifer. *Shipwreck at the Bottom of the World: The Extraordinary True Story of Shackleton and the Endurance*. Crown, 1998. Chronicles the 1914 expedition to Antarctica led by Ernest Shackleton and the perils he and his crew experienced. (I: 10–YA)

Aronson, Marc. *If Stones Could Speak: Unlocking the Secrets of Stonehenge*. National Geographic, 2010. A documentation of the investigative quest to determine why Stonehenge was created. (I: 9–12)

———. *Trapped: How the World Rescued 33 Miners from 2,000 Feet Below the Chilean Desert*. Atheneum, 2011. A riveting account of the accident that trapped 33 Chilean miners and how the rescue was accomplished. (I: 10–YA)

Aronson, Marc and Marina Budhos. *Sugar Changed the World: A Story of Magic, Spice, Slavery, Freedom, and Science*. Clarion, 2010. A sweeping story detailing the negative impact of the sugar trade on historical events of the past 200 years. (I: 12 and up)

Bartoletti, Susan Campbell. *Black Potatoes: The Story of the Great Irish Famine, 1845–1850*. Houghton Mifflin, 2001. Primary source material was consulted to document the potato blight in Ireland. (I: 9–14)

————. *Hitler Youth: Growing Up in Hitler's Shadow.* Scholastic, 2005. This book discusses the children and teenagers who participated in the Nazi Party as Hitler Youth between 1933 and 1945. (I: 10–YA)

————. *They Called Themselves the K. K. K.: The Birth of an American Terrorist Group.* Houghton Mifflin, 2010. The story of the Ku Klux Klan—its origins, organization, and impact on the South in the years following the Civil War. (I: 11–YA)

Bausum, Ann. *Freedom Riders: John Lewis and Jim Zwerg on the Front Lines of the Civil Rights Movement.* National Geographic, 2006. The story of the Freedom Riders from the perspective of two participants. (I: 9–14)

————. *Denied, Detained, Deported: Stories from the Dark Side of American Immigration.* National Geographic, 2009. Some of the lesser known (and unhappier) stories of American immigration. (I: 10–YA)

Blumberg, Rhoda. *Commodore Perry in the Land of the Shogun.* Lothrop, Lee & Shepard, 1985. Describes Matthew Perry's important voyage to Japan to open trade and whaling ports to America. (I: 10–YA)

Brimner, Larry Dane. *Birmingham Sunday.* Boyds Mill, 2010. Brimner documents the events that occurred on the Sunday of the tragic bombing, as well as subsequent events. (I: 10–YA)

Brown, Don. *America Is Under Attack: September 11, 2001: The Day the Towers Fell.* Flash Point, 2011. Brown tells the story of the attack on the World Trade Center Twin Towers. (I: 9–12)

Colman, Penny. *Thanksgiving: The True Story.* Holt, 2008. A well-researched look at the history of this national holiday. (I: 9–14)

*Edwards, Pamela Duncan. *O Is for Old Dominion: A Virginia Alphabet.* Sleeping Bear Press, 2005. Duncan highlights places, people, and objects associated with the history of Virginia. (I: 6–10)

*Floca, Brian. *Lightship.* Atheneum, 2007. Floca tells the story of lightships, the "floating lighthouses" once used where lighthouses could not be built. (I: 6–9)

Freedman, Russell. *Children of the Great Depression.* Clarion, 2005. Archival photographs help to convey what life was like for children during the Depression. (I: 9–14)

————. *Freedom Walkers: The Story of the Montgomery Boycott.* Holiday House, 2006. Archival photographs and text convey information about the Montgomery bus boycott in the 1950s. (I: 9–14)

Giblin, James Cross. *The Riddle of the Rosetta Stone: Key to Ancient Egypt.* Crowell, 1990. The story of the discovery of the ancient Rosetta Stone and the deciphering of its hieroglyphics. (I: 8–12)

————. *Good Brother, Bad Brother: The Story of Edwin Booth and John Wilkes Booth.* Clarion, 2005. Although they were both actors, one brother would assassinate Abraham Lincoln. (I: 10–YA)

————. *Secrets of the Sphinx.* Illustrated by Bagram Ibatoulline. Scholastic, 2004. Egypt's most famous sites and the theories about their origins are detailed. (I: 9–14)

Hopkinson, Deborah. *Shutting Out the Sky: Life in the Tenements of New York 1880–1924.* Orchard, 2003. The lives of five immigrants living on the Lower East Side of New York are described. (I: 9–YA)

*Jurmain, Suzanne Tripp. *Worst of Friends.* Illustrated by Larry Day. Dutton, 2011. The story of Thomas Jefferson and John Adams—their collaborations, their quarrels, and their eventual reconciliation. (I: 7–10)

*Kerley, Barbara. *Those Rebels John and Tom.* Illustrated by Edwin Fotheringham. Scholastic, 2012. The story of how Thomas Jefferson and John Adams, two men from dramatically different backgrounds, worked together to shape American history. (I: 7–10)

Kimmel, Elizabeth Cody. *Ice Story: Shackleton's Lost Expedition.* Clarion, 1999. When Shackleton's boat, the *Endurance,* is crushed, he and his crew brave a dangerous journey to land. (I: 10–YA)

Lawrence, Jacob. *The Great Migration: An American Story.* HarperCollins, 1993. A narrative sequence of vibrant paintings helps to tell the story of African Americans' migration from the South to the North around World War I. (I: 8–12)

Murphy, Jim. *Across America on an Emigrant Train.* Clarion, 1993. The story of Robert Louis Stevenson's trip from Scotland to San Francisco in 1879 in search of his true love is combined with a history of the railroad. (I: 10–YA)

————. *An American Plague: The True and Terrifying Story of the Yellow Fever Epidemic.* Clarion, 2003. A detailed account of the Yellow Fever epidemic that hit Philadelphia in the eighteenth century. (I: 10–YA)

————. *The Great Fire.* Scholastic, 1995. Describes the Chicago fire of 1871 and its effects on individual people and the city. (I: 10–YA)

————. *Truce: The Day the Soldiers Stopped Fighting.* Scholastic, 2009. Documents the Christmas Day during World War I when German and American soldiers stopped fighting and celebrated together. (I: 9–12)

Nelson, Scott Reynolds with Marc Aronson. *Ain't Nothing But a Man: My Quest to Find the Real John Henry.* National Geographic, 2008. As he leads readers through historical research, the author describes how the railroad was built in the South and how he learned the truth about the legendary John Henry. (I: 9–14)

*Provensen, Alice, and Martin Provensen. *The Glorious Flight: Across the Channel with Louis Blériot.* Viking, 1983. In 1909, Blériot flies across the English Channel from France to England in thirty-seven minutes. (I: 7–10)

*Rosenstock, Barb. *The Camping Trip that Changed America.* Illustrated by Mordicai Gerstein. Dial, 2012. This is the story of the camping trip that Theodore Roosevelt and John Muir made into the Yosemite wilderness, a trip that inspired President Roosevelt to establish America's national park system. (I: 6–10)

Ross, Stewart. *Into the Unknown: How Great Explorers Found Their Way by Land, Sea, and Air.* Illustrated by Stephen Biesty. Candlewick, 2011. Ross relates the stories of 14 brave explorers. The first story focuses on a Greek who set sail for the Arctic Circle in 340 BC, while the final story documents the moon exploration of astronauts Armstrong and Aldrin in 1969. (I: 9–12)

*St. George, Judith. *So You Want to be President?* Illustrated by David Small. Philomel, 2000. A humorous discussion of the U.S. presidency from George Washington to Bill Clinton. (I: 6–12)

Stanley, Jerry. *Children of the Dust Bowl: The True Story of the School at Weedpatch Camp.* Crown, 1992. The inspirational story of how educator Leo Hart and Okie children built their own school during the Depression in California. (I: 10–YA)

Walker, Sally M. *Blizzard of Glass: The Halifax Explosion of 1917.* Henry Holt, 2011. A gripping account of the largest man-made explosion prior to the detonation of the first atomic bomb. (I: 10 and up)

———. *Secrets of a Civil War Submarine: Solving the Mysteries of the H. L. Hunley.* Carolrhoda, 2005. The mysteries of the buried Civil War submarine are revealed in this book. (I: 8–12)

Understanding Peoples and Cultures

*Ancona, George. *Barrio: José's Neighborhood.* Harcourt Brace, 1998. This photo-essay describes the daily life of an eight-year-old Mexican American boy living in the Mission District of San Francisco. (I: 6–10)

*———. *Pablo Remembers: The Fiesta of the Day of the Dead.* Lothrop, Lee & Shepard, 1993. Pablo remembers his grandmother in the three-day Mexican celebration. (I: 6–10)

*———. *The Piñata Maker/El piñatero.* Harcourt Brace, 1994. This bilingual text describes how Don Ricardo crafts piñatas in southern Mexico. (I: 6–10)

*———. *Powwow.* Sandpiper, 1993. This photo-essay details the experience of the Native American powwow. (I: 6–10)

Aronson, Marc. *Race: A History Beyond Black and White.* Atheneum, 2007. Aronson tackles hard questions about race and prejudice. (I: 12–YA)

*Cha, Dia. *Dia's Story Cloth: The Hmong People's Journey of Freedom.* Stitched by Chue and Nhia Thao Cha. Lee & Low, 1996. A hand-embroidered story cloth recounts the story of the Hmong people of ancient China and Laos and their emigration to the United States. (I: 8–12)

*Chocolate, Debbi. *Kente Colors.* Illustrated by John Ward. Walker, 1996. Chocolate explains the meaning of the colors and patterns of the kente cloth worn by Ashanti and Ewe peoples. (I: P–8)

Giblin, James Cross. *When Plague Strikes: The Black Death, Smallpox, AIDS.* HarperCollins, 1995. Giblin discusses epidemic diseases and their political, social, religious, and cultural consequences. (I: 10–YA)

*Hoyt-Goldsmith, Diane. *Cinco de Mayo: Celebrating the Traditions of Mexico.* Photographs by Lawrence Migdale. Holiday House, 2008. Rosie and her family celebrate Mexican history and traditions. (I: 7–12)

———. *Celebrating Ramadan.* Photographs by Lawrence Migdale. Holiday House, 2001. Ibraheem introduces readers to his Muslim heritage and the fast of Ramadan. (I: 7–12)

*Morris, Ann. *Families.* HarperCollins, 2000. Explains how families around the world are alike and different. (I: P–8)

*Morris, Ann, and Heidi Larson. *Tsunami: Helping Each Other.* Lerner, 2005. This photographic essay describes the 2004 Indian Ocean tsunami from the perspective of two brothers. (I: 8–12)

*Nivola, Claire A. *Orani: My Father's Village.* Farrar Straus Giroux, 2011. A memoir of the author's visits to her father's village in Sardinia. (I: 6–10)

Osborne, Mary Pope. *One World, Many Religions: The Ways We Worship.* Knopf, 1996. Photographs and text describe the world's major religions: Judaism, Christianity, Islam, Hinduism, Buddhism, Confucianism, and Taoism. (I: 8–YA)

Sís, Peter. *Tibet Through the Red Box.* Farrar, Straus, & Giroux, 1998. The diary of the author's father, a filmmaker who was lost in Tibet for many years, guides readers on a travel expedition to this country. (I: 9–14)

United Nations Children's Fund. *A Life Like Mine: How Children Live Around the World.* Dorling Kindersley, 2002. Organized around the four themes of survival, development, protection, and participation, this photographic essay takes readers on a journey to meet children around the globe. (I: 6–12)

Science and Nature

*Berger, Melvin, and Gilda Berger. *Where Have All the Pandas Gone?* Scholastic, 2001. Information is provided about endangered species in a question-and-answer format. (I: 5–10)

*Bishop, Nic. *Spiders.* Scholastic, 2007. Amazing color photographs combine with the text to present information about spiders. See also *Lizards, Frogs, Butterflies and Moths,* and *Marsupials.* (I: 4–9)

*Burleigh, Robert. *Chocolate: Riches from the Rainforest.* Harry N. Abrams, 2002. Published in association with Chicago's Field Museum, the book presents a history of chocolate. (I: 8–12)

Burns, Loree G. *The Hive Detectives: Chronicle of a Bee Catastrophe.* Illustrated by Ellen Harasimowicz. Houghton Mifflin, 2010. The author documents the investigation of scientists seeking to understand the cause of colony collapse disorder. (I: 10 and up)

*Cherry, Lynne. *A River Ran Wild: An Environmental History.* Harcourt Brace, 1992. This book traces the history of the Nashua River from 7,000 years ago until recent times, with double-spread pages featuring significant influences on the river. (I: 9–12)

*Cowley, Joy. *Chameleon, Chameleon.* Photography by Nic Bishop. Scholastic, 2005. A simple introduction to the chameleon, with outstanding photographs. (I: 4–7)

David, Laurie, and Cambria Gordon. *The Down-to-Earth Guide To Global Warming.* Orchard, 2007. A summary for children of Al Gore's *An Inconvenient Truth: The Crisis of Global Warming.* (I: 9 and up)

DeCristofano, Carolyn Cinami. *A Black Hole Is Not a Hole.* Charlesbridge, 2012. Through the use of visuals and clearly written text, the author explains just what a black hole is. (I: 10 and up)

*Gibbons, Gail. *Spiders.* Holiday House, 1993. A picture book examination of different kinds of spiders and their characteristics. (I: P–8)

*Halfmann, Janet. *Eggs 1, 2, 3: Who Will the Babies Be?* Illustrated by Betsy Thompson. Blue Apple, 2012. In a riddle format with answers revealed by lifting flaps, readers are introduced to a variety of creatures that all emerge from eggs. (I: 3–7)

*Hatkoff, Isabella, Craig Hatkoff, and Dr. Paula Kahumbu. *Owen & Mzee: The True Story of a Remarkable Friendship*. Photographs by Peter Greste. Scholastic, 2006. An orphaned baby hippo befriends a giant tortoise in a Kenyan nature preserve. See also *Owen & Mzee: The Language of Friendship*. (I: P–10)

Hoose, Phillip. *The Race to Save the Lord God Bird*. Farrar, 2004. The attempts to save the Ivory-billed Woodpecker from extinction are described in this compelling book. (I: 10–YA)

*Iorio, Nicole. *Time for Kids: Spiders*. HarperCollins, 2005. Factual information about spiders is accompanied by dramatic photographs. (I: 6–10)

*Jenkins, Martin. *Can We Save the Tiger?* Illustrated by Vicky White. Candlewick, 2011. Jenkins introduces the readers to a variety of animals and plants facing extinction in the modern world. (I: 6 and up)

*Jenkins, Steve. *Actual Size*. Houghton Mifflin, 2004. Animals and their body parts are illustrated in their actual size. See also *Prehistoric Actual Size*. (I: P–8)

*———. *Bones: Skeletons and How They Work*. Scholastic, 2010. Utilizing extensive pictorial information, this book features skeletons and shows how they work. (I: 6–10)

*———, and Robin Page. *What Do You Do With a Tail Like This?* Houghton Mifflin, 2003. Information about animals' sense organs is discussed in question-and-answer format. (I: P–8)

Lasky, Kathryn. *Sugaring Time*. Photographs by Christopher Knight. Macmillan, 1983. Lasky describes maple sugar time on a Vermont family farm. (I: 8–12)

Lauber, Patricia. *Volcano: The Eruption and Healing of Mount St. Helens*. Simon & Schuster, 1993. Lauber describes the biological succession and geological changes that have occurred since the eruption of Mount St. Helens. (I: 8–12)

*Marsh, Laura. *Spiders*. National Geographic Children's Books, 2011. Part of the National Geographic Kids series, this book is an introduction to spiders for beginning readers. (I: 5–8)

*McLimans, David. *Gone Wild: An Endangered Animal Alphabet*. Walker, 2006. Information about 26 endangered species is presented in alphabetical order. (I: 6–10)

Montgomery, Sy. *Kakapo Rescue: Saving the World's Strangest Parrot*. Photographs by Nic Bishop. Houghton Mifflin, 2010. Montgomery documents the efforts of a team of experts to save the kakapo, an endangered parrot once found all over New Zealand. (I: 10–14)

———. *Quest for the Tree Kangaroo: An Expedition to the Cloud Forest of New Guinea*. Photographs by Nic Bishop. Houghton Mifflin, 2006. Montgomery chronicles the amazing journey to learn more about Matschie's tree kangaroo. (I: 9–14)

Patent, Dorothy Hinshaw. *When the Wolves Returned: Restoring Nature's Balance in Yellowstone*. Photographs by Dan Hartman and Cassie Hartman. Walker, 2008. Patent discusses the reintroduction of wolves to Yellowstone National Park in 1995 to restore the balance of nature. (I: 6–12)

*Peterson, Cris. *Clarabelle: Making Milk and So Much More*. Photographs by David R. Lundquist. Boyds Mill, 2007. This is the story of Clarabelle and her newborn calf who live on a Wisconsin dairy farm. (I: P–8)

*Pfeffer, Wendy, and Steve Jenkins. *Wiggling Worms at Work*. HarperCollins, 2004. A Let's-Read-and-Find-Out Science book that tells all about earthworms. (I: P–8)

*Pringle, Laurence. *Billions of Years, Amazing Changes: The Story of Evolution*. Illustrated by Steve Jenkins. Boyds Mill, 2011. Pringle provides a straightforward account of the process of evolution along with the supporting evidence. (I: 8–11)

———. *Whales!: Strange and Wonderful*. Illustrated by Meryl Henderson. Boyds Mill, 2003. This book provides information about a variety of different kinds of whales. See also *Crows!: Strange and Wonderful*. (I: 7–10)

*Seeger, Laura Vaccaro. *First the Egg*. Roaring Brook Press, 2007. Through the use of die-cuts, Seeger presents a number of transformations in nature (first the egg, then the chicken). (I: 3–7)

*Sidman, Joyce. *Dark Emperor and Other Poems of the Night*. Illustrated by Rick Allen. Houghton Mifflin, 2010. Through poetry and informational text, Sidman explores the lives and habits of various nocturnal creatures. (I: 8–12)

*Stewart, Melissa. *Ants*. National Geographic, 2010. This simple introduction to ants for young children contains some of the organizational tools more commonly associated with books intended for an older audience. (I: 5–8)

Walker, Sally M. *Written in Bone: Buried Lives of Jamestown and Colonial Maryland*. Carolrhoda, 2009. Walker shares the results of an archeological investigation of human and material remains of the early settlers. (I: 10 and up)

Zoehfeld, Kathleen Weidner. *How Mountains Are Made*. Collins, 1995. Replete with visuals, this book, part of the Let's Read and Find Out series, explains how mountains are made. (I: 7–10)

The Arts

*Aliki. *William Shakespeare & the Globe*. HarperCollins, 1999. Discusses Shakespeare's life, the famous Globe Theatre of London, and recent efforts to reconstruct it. (I: 8–12)

*Brown, Monica. *My Name Is Celia: Me Llamo Celia*. Illustrated by Rafael López. Luna Rising, 2004. The story of the Cuban-born queen of salsa. (I: 5–10)

Desnoëttes, Caroline. *Look Closer: Art Masterpieces through the Ages*. Walker, 2006. Readers have an interactive experience lifting flaps to learn about famous paintings. (I: 8–12)

Fleming, Candace. *The Great and Only Barnum: The Tremendous, Stupendous Life of Showman P. T. Barnum*. Illustrated by Ray Fenwick. Schwartz and Wade, 2009. Fleming documents both the private and public life of the famous showman. (I: 10 and up)

Fritz, Jean. *Leonardo's Horse*. Illustrated by Hudson Talbott. Putnam, 2001. This book is two stories in one—Leonard da Vinci's unfinished work on a bronze horse for the duke of Milan, and the dream of Charles Dent to create Leonardo's horse as a gift from the American people to Italy. (I: 6–12)

*Greenberg, Jan, and Sandra Jordan. *Ballet for Martha: Making Appalachian Spring*. Illustrated by Brian Floca. Roaring Brook, 2010. The story of how a choreographer, a composer, and an artist collaborated to create the American masterpiece, *Appalachian Spring*. (I: 6–10)

*Stone, Tanya Lee. *Sandy's Circus*. Illustrated by Boris Bulikov. Viking, 2008. This is the story of the magical, moveable circus created by Alexander Calder. (I: 6–10)

How Things Work

*Gibbons, Gail. *Ice Cream: The Full Scoop*. Holiday House, 2006. Illustrations and text convey the history of ice cream and how it is made today. (I: 4–10)

*Hudson, Cheryl Willis. *Construction Zone*. Photographs by Richard Sobol. Candlewick, 2006. Documents how a building is constructed over a three-year period. (I: 4–8)

Macaulay, David. *Castle*. Houghton Mifflin, 1977. Detailed description of how a thirteenth-century Welsh castle was constructed. (I: 9–YA)

———. *The New Way Things Work*. Houghton Mifflin, 1998. A tribute to technology, this book explains how all kinds of machines work. (I: 10–YA)

Simon, Seymour. *Lungs: Your Respiratory System*. HarperCollins, 2007. Explains how the lungs and respiratory system work. (I: 8–12)

Thimmesh, Catherine. *Team Moon: How 400,000 People Landed Apollo 11 on the Moon*. Houghton Mifflin, 2006. The behind-the-scenes story of the successful mission of Apollo 11. (I: 8–14)

Sports, Recreation, and How-to Books

Blumenthal, Karen. *Let Me Play: The Story of Title IX, the Law that Changed the Future of Girls in America*. Atheneum, 2005. The history of the 1972 Title IX legislation and its impact. (I: 9–14)

Macy, Sue. *Freeze Frame: A Photographic History of the Winter Olympics*. National Geographic, 2006. This book presents a comprehensive history of the Winter Olympics. (I: 8–12)

Nelson, Kadir. *We Are the Ship: The Story of Negro League Baseball*. Hyperion, 2008. Beautiful paintings and text recount the story of the Negro Baseball league. (I: 6–12)

Ripkin, Cal, Jr. *The Longest Season*. Illustrated by Ron Mazellan. Philomel, 2007. The Hall of Fame baseball player describes the Orioles' 1988 losing season. (I: 5–10)

*Wick, Walter. *Can You See What I See? Once Upon a Time*. Scholastic, 2006. Subtitled "Picture Puzzles to Search and Solve," this interactive book invites readers to use their imagination to search for objects from fairy tales. (I: P–10)

U.S. Political Leaders and Social Activists

Bolden, Tonya. *M.L.K.: Journey of a King*. Abrams, 2007. A well-researched biography of Dr. Martin Luther King. (I: 9–14)

*Corey, Shana. *Here Come the Girl Scouts!* Illustrated by Hadley Hooper. Scholastic, 2012. The story of Juliette Gordon Low, who founded the Girl Scouts. (I: 6–10)

Fleming, Candace. *Our Eleanor: A Scrapbook Look at Eleanor Roosevelt's Remarkable Life*. Atheneum, 2005. A comprehensive biography of the beloved and longest-serving First Lady. (I: 9–YA)

———. *The Lincolns: A Scrapbook Look at Abraham and Mary*. Schwartz and Wade, 2008. Using a scrapbook format, Fleming explores the lives of Abraham and Mary and the complex intertwining of their lives. (I: 10–YA)

Freedman, Russell. *Eleanor Roosevelt: A Life of Discovery*. Clarion, 1993. The life of a famous First Lady, wife of President Franklin Delano Roosevelt, who devoted herself to public service and worked on behalf of human rights. (I: 9–YA)

———. *Kids at Work: Lewis Hine and the Crusade against Child Labor*. Clarion, 1994. The biography of photographer and social reformer Lewis Hine, whose photographs helped ensure the passage of child labor laws. (I: 9–YA)

———. *Lincoln: A Photobiography*. Clarion, 1987. A biography of Abraham Lincoln, who was president during the Civil War. (I: 9–YA)

Fritz, Jean. *And Then What Happened, Paul Revere?* Illustrated by Margot Tomes. Coward McCann, 1973. A humorous biography of patriot Paul Revere. Other biographies include *Why Don't You Get a Horse, Sam Adams?*, *Will You Sign Here, John Hancock?*, *Stonewall*, and *The Great Little Madison*. (I: 7–12)

———. *Bully for You, Teddy Roosevelt!* Illustrated by Mike Wimmer. Putnam, 1991. A biography of the twenty-sixth president, who was also a conservationist. (I: 9–12)

———. *You Want Women to Vote, Lizzy Stanton?* Puffin, 1999. Fritz documents Stanton's role in the fight for women's rights. (I: 7–11)

*Kerley, Barbara. *What to Do About Alice?* Illustrated by Edwin Fortheringham. Scholastic, 2008. A biography of President Theodore Roosevelt's daughter, subtitled "how Alice Roosevelt broke the rules, charmed the world, and drove her father Teddy crazy!" (I: 6–10)

*Krull, Kathleen. *Harvesting Hope: The Story of Cesar Chavez*. Illustrated by Yuyi Morales. Harcourt, 2003. A picture book biography of the leader of the migrant farm workers. (I: 5–10)

Marrin, Albert. *Old Hickory: Andrew Jackson and the American People*. Dutton, 2004. A detailed biography of Andrew Jackson, whose controversial presidency included the Trail of Tears. (I: 10–YA)

*Rappaport, Doreen. *Martin's Big Words: The Life of Dr. Martin Luther King, Jr*. Illustrated by Bryan Collier. Hyperion, 2001. A picture book biography of the Nobel Peace Prize recipient, with quotations from his speeches and sermons. (I: P–12)

Tafolla, Carmen, and Sharyll Teneyuca. *That's Not Fair!: Emma Tenayuca's Struggle for Justice*. Illustrated by Terry Ibañez. Wings Press, 2008. Documents the life of Mexican American social activist Emma Tenayuca, who led a strike of pecan workers in San Antonio, Texas, in the 1920s. (I: 7–11)

World Leaders

Giblin, James Cross. *The Life and Death of Adolf Hitler.* Clarion, 2002. A carefully researched biography of the life of the German leader, who was responsible for the deaths of millions of people. (I: 10–YA)

*Grimes, Nikki. *Barack Obama: Son of Promise, Child of Hope.* Illustrated by Bryan Collier. Houghton Mifflin, 2008. This picture book biography describes Obama's life journey to the presidency. (I: 6–11)

*Johnson, Jen Cullerton. *Seeds of Change.* Illustrated by Sonia Lynn Sadler. Lee & Low, 2010. The story of Wangari Maathai, the Kenyan environmentalist who worked with the women of Kenya to plant trees throughout the land. (I: 6–10)

Krull, Kathleen. *Lives of Extraordinary Women: Ruler, Rebels (and What the Neighbors Thought).* Illustrated by Kathryn Hewitt. Harcourt, 2000. Biographical vignettes of 20 historic women leaders, including Indira Gandhi and Golda Meir. (I: 8–12)

*McDonough, Yona Zeldis. *Peaceful Protest: The Life of Nelson Mandela.* Illustrated by Malcah Zeldis. Walker, 2002. The inspiring life of the South African leader and Nobel Peace Prize recipient. (I: 6–10)

*Nivola, Claire A. *Planting the Trees of Kenya: The Story of Wangari Maathai.* Farrar, 2008. The biography of the Kenyan woman who received the 2004 Nobel Peace Prize and founded the Green Belt Movement. (I: 5–8)

Stanley, Diane. *Peter the Great.* Morrow, 1986. The life of Tsar Peter Alexeevich of Russia. (I: 10–YA)

———, and Peter Vennema. *Cleopatra.* Morrow, 1994. Full-page paintings complement the story of the famous Egyptian queen. (I: 10–YA)

Explorers and Scientists

*Borden, Louise, and Mary Kay Kroeger. *Fly High! The Story of Bessie Coleman.* Illustrated by Teresa Flavin. Simon and Schuster, 2001. The biography of the first African American to earn a pilot's license. (I: 5–10)

*Ehlrich, Amy. *Rachel: The Story of Rachel Carson.* Illustrated by Wendell Minor. Harcourt, 2003. The biography of Rachel Carson, whose book *Silent Spring* is considered the beginning of the environmental movement. (I: 5–10)

Fleming, Candace. *Amelia Lost: The Life and Disappearance of Amelia Earhart.* Schwartz & Wade, 2011. Fleming documents the remarkable achievements of Amelia Earhart, as well as the way in which she crafted her public image. (I: 10 and up)

*Floca, Brian. *Moonshot: The Flight of Apollo 11.* Atheneum, 2009. Floca captures the drama of Apollo 11's historic mission. (I: 4–8)

Freedman, Russell. *The Wright Brothers: How They Invented the Airplane.* Holiday House, 1991. The lives of Wilbur and Orville Wright. (I: 9–YA)

Kerley, Barbara. *The Dinosaurs of Waterhouse Hawkins.* Illustrated by Brian Selznick. Scholastic, 2001. The biography of Victorian artist, Waterhouse Hawkins, who built the first life-size models of dinosaurs. (I: 6–12)

*Martin, Jacqueline Briggs. *Snowflake Bentley.* Illustrated by Mary Azarian. Houghton Mifflin, 1998. The life of Wilson Bentley, a self-taught scientist who studied and photographed snowflakes. (I: 6–10)

McClafferty, Carla Killough. *Something Out of Nothing: Marie Curie and Radium.* Farrar, 2006. The life of Marie Curie, the Polish chemist who was the first woman to receive a Nobel Prize. (I: 9–14)

Old, Wendie. *To Fly: The Story of the Wright Brothers.* Illustrated by Robert Andrew Parker. Clarion, 2002. The story of the famous brothers, Orville and Wilbur Wright, and how they built and flew the first airplane. (I: 6–12)

Phelan, Matt. *Around the World.* Candlewick, 2011. Using a graphic novel format, Phelan tells the story of three nineteenth-century adventurers—Thomas Stevens, Nellie Bly, and Joshua Slocum. (I: 8–12)

*Sís, Peter. *Starry Messenger.* Farrar, Straus, & Giroux, 1996. Exquisite illustrations help recount the life of astronomer Galileo Galilei. (I: 7–11)

———. *The Tree of Life.* Farrar, Straus, & Giroux, 2003. The life of Charles Darwin, "naturalist, geologist, and thinker." (I: 9–14)

Tanaka, Shelley. *Amelia Earhart: The Legend of the Lost Aviator.* Illustrated by David Craig. Abrams, 2008. A biography of the famous pilot who disappeared in the South Pacific in 1937. (I: 8–12)

Artists and Authors

*Ancona, George. *¡Ole Flamenco!* Lee & Low, 2010. Through photographs and text, the author explores the rich history, traditions, and techniques of flamenco. (I: 8–12).

*Bass, Hester. *The Secret World of Walter Anderson.* Illustrated by E. B. Lewis. Candlewick, 2009. Documents the life of the naturalist/painter from Mississippi. (I: 6–10)

*Bryant, Jen. *A River of Words: The Story of William Carlos Williams.* Illustrated by Melissa Sweet. Eerdman's, 2008. The life story of the doctor/poet William Carlos Williams is illustrated with dramatic mixed media illustrations. (I: 7–11)

*Cooper, Floyd. *Coming Home: From the Life of Langston Hughes.* Philomel, 1994. This picture book biography focuses on the childhood of the well-known African American poet. (I: 6–12)

Freedman, Russell. *The Voice that Challenged a Nation: Marian Anderson and the Struggle for Equal Rights.* Clarion, 2004. This photobiography tells the life story of singer Marian Anderson. (I: 9–14)

*Hill, Laban Carrick. *Dave the Potter: Artist, Poet, Slave.* Illustrated by Bryan Collier. Little Brown, 2010. Chronicles the adult life of Dave, a slave living in South Carolina, who crafted masterful pots into which he carved his own poetry. (I: 6–10)

*Kerley, Barbara. *Walt Whitman: Words for America.* Illustrated by Brian Selznick. Scholastic, 2004. This biography focuses on both Whitman's formative years and his work as a Civil War nurse. (I: 8–12)

*———. *The Extraordinary Mark Twain (According to Susy).* Illustrated by Edwin Fotheringham. Scholastic, 2010. Kerley's account of Twain's life is extended by excerpts from the biography written by Twain's 13-year-old daughter. (I: 7–10)

Krull, Kathleen. *Lives of the Musicians: Good Times, Bad Times (and What the Neighbors Thought)*. Illustrated by Kathryn Hewitt. Harcourt, 1993. Biographical sketches of 20 musicians and composers, including Bach and Scott Joplin. (I: 8–12)

Lowry, Lois. *Looking Back: A Book of Memories*. Houghton Mifflin, 1998. Illustrated with family photographs, this book is an autobiography of the Newbery Award-winning author. (I: 9–14)

*Ryan, Pam Muñoz. *When Marian Sang*. Illustrated by Brian Selznick. Scholastic, 2002. The life story of contralto Marian Anderson, the first African American to sing with the Metropolitan Opera. (I: 7–12)

Say, Allen. *Drawing from Memory*. Scholastic, 2011. Say uses an innovative format to tell the story of how he became an artist. (I: 10 and up)

Siegel, Siena Cherson. *To Dance: A Ballerina's Graphic Novel*. Illustrated by Mark Siegel. Atheneum, 2006. In a graphic novel format, the author shares her early years studying at the School of American Ballet. (I: 8–14)

*Sís, Peter. *The Wall: Growing Up Behind the Iron Curtain*. Farrar, 2007. The award-winning author recounts his childhood and youth in Czechoslovakia. (I: 8–YA)

*Stanley, Diane. *Leonardo da Vinci*. Morrow, 1996. A picture book biography of the famous painter and scientist. (I: 10–YA)

*———, and Peter Vennema. *The Bard of Avon: The Story of William Shakespeare*. Morrow, 1992. A picture book biography of the most famous British playwright. (I: 10–YA)

*Sweet, Melissa. *Balloons Over Broadway: The True Story of the Puppeteer of the Macy's Parade*. Houghton Mifflin, 2011. A biography of Anthony Sarg, the puppeteer who first envisioned and created the gigantic balloon creatures that appear in the famous Macy's Thanksgiving Day's Parade. (I: 6–10)

*Winter, Jonah. *Jazz Age Josephine*. Illustrated by Marjorie Priceman. Atheneum, 2012. The story of famous dancer Josephine Baker from her impoverished childhood to her rise to fame in Paris. (I: 6–10)

People Who Overcame Adversity

Barakat, Ibtisam. *Tasting the Sky: A Palestinian Childhood*. Farrar, 2007. This memoir describes the author's childhood living under Israeli occupation. (I: 9–14)

Bolden, Tonya. *Maritcha: A Nineteenth-Century American Girl*. Abrams, 2005. The biography of a girl who overcame adversity to become the first black person to graduate from Providence Rhode Island High School in 1869. (I: 9–14)

Bridges, Ruby. *Through My Eyes*. Scholastic, 1999. The life and times of Ruby Bridges, who integrated the New Orleans schools in 1960 when she was six years old. (I: 8–12)

*Deans, Karen. *Playing to Win: The Story of Althea Gibson*. Illustrated by Elbrite Brown. Holiday House, 2007. This picture book biography describes how Althea Gibson overcame discrimination to become a champion tennis player. (I: 5–9)

*Giovanni, Nikki. *Rosa*. Illustrated by Bryan Collier. Henry Holt, 2005. This picture book biography focuses on the refusal of Rosa Parks to give up her seat on the bus. (I: 6–10)

Kaminsky, Marty. *Uncommon Champions: Fifteen Athletes Who Battled Back*. Boyds Mills Press, 2000. Inspirational biographies of 15 individuals who overcame physical and emotional challenges to achieve athletically. (I: 8–12)

Pressler, Miriam. *Anne Frank: A Hidden Life*. Translated by Anthea Bell. Dutton, 2000. A description of the life of Anne Frank and the Nazi occupation of the Netherlands during World War II. (I: 10–YA)

Robinson, Sharon. *Promises to Keep: How Jackie Robinson Changed America*. Scholastic, 2004. Jackie Robinson's daughter recounts the life of the first African American to play major league baseball in this biography extensively illustrated with photographs. (I: 8–14)

Rubin, Susan Goldman with Ela Weissberger. *The Cat with the Yellow Star: Coming of Age in Terezin*. Holiday House, 2006. Ela Weissberger shares her childhood at Terezin Concentration Camp in this memoir. (I: 9–14)

Sullivan, George. *Helen Keller: Her Life in Pictures*. Scholastic, 2007. This is a photobiography of the remarkable life of Helen Keller. (I: 8–12)

RESOURCES AND REFERENCES

Aronson, Marc. "Mad Max: Digital Nonfiction in the Graveyard of Previous (Expensive) Tools." Presentation at the International Reading Association 57th Annual Convention. Chicago, IL, April 29, 2012.

Caswell, Linda J., and Nell K. Duke. "Non-narrative as a Catalyst for Literacy Development." *Language Arts 75* (1998): 108–117.

Colman, Penny. "A New Way to Look at Literature: A Visual Model for Analyzing Fiction and Nonfiction." *Language Arts, 84* (2007): 257–268.

Daugherty, James. *Daniel Boone.* Viking, 1939.

D'Aulaire, Ingri, and Edgar Parin D'Aulaire. *Abraham Lincoln.* Doubleday, 1939.

Duke, Nell K. "3.6 Minutes Per Day: The Scarcity of Informational Texts in First Grade." *Reading Research Quarterly, 35* (2000): 202–224.

Fisher, Margery. Introduction to *Matters of Fact. Beyond Fact: Nonfiction for Children and Young People.* Ed. J. Carr. American Library Association, 1982, pp. 12–16.

Freedman, Russell. "Fact or Fiction?" *Using Nonfiction Trade Books in the Elementary Classroom: From Ants to Zeppelins.* Ed. E. B. Freeman and D. G. Person. National Council of Teachers of English, 1992, pp. 2–10.

Fretwell, Holly. *The Sky's Not Falling: Why It's OK to Chill about Global Warming.* World Ahead Publishing, 2007.

George, Jean Craighead. *Julie of the Wolves.* Harper & Row, 1972.

Giblin, James Cross. *Chimney Sweeps: Yesterday and Today.* Illustrated by Margot Tomes. HarperCollins, 1982.

———. "The Rise and Fall and Rise of Juvenile Nonfiction, 1961–1988." *Using Nonfiction in the Elementary Classroom: From Ants to Zeppelins.* Eds. E. B. Freeman and D. G. Person. National Council of Teachers of English, 1992, pp. 17–25.

Gore, Al. *An Inconvenient Truth: The Crisis of Global Warming.* Viking, 2007.

Hastings, Selina. *Peter and the Wolf.* Illustrated by Reg Cartwright. Henry Holt, 1990.

Holling, Clancy. *Paddle-to-the-Sea.* Houghton Mifflin, 1941.

Horning, Kathleen T. *From Cover to Cover.* Collins, 2010.

Isaacs, Kathleen R. "The Matter: Then to Now." *The Horn Book Magazine.* (March/April 2011): 11–18.

Jobe, Ron, and Mary Dayton-Sakari. *Info-Kids: How to Use Nonfiction to Turn Reluctant Readers into Enthusiastic Learners.* Pembroke, 2002.

Kerper, Richard. "Choosing Quality Nonfiction for Children: Examining Access Features and Visual Displays." *Making Facts Come Alive: Choosing and Using Quality Nonfiction Literature K–8.* Eds. Rosemary A. Bamford and Janice V. Kristo. Christopher Gorden, 2003, pp. 41–64.

Kiefer, Barbara, and Melissa I. Wilson. "Nonfiction Literature for Children." *Handbook of Research on Children's and Young Adult Literature.* Eds. Shelby A. Wolf, Karen Coats, Patricia Enciso, and Christine A. Jenkins. Routledge, 2011, pp. 290–301.

Lawson, Robert. *Ben & Me.* Little, Brown, 1939.

Leal, Dorothy. "Storybooks, Information Books and Informational Storybooks: An Explication of an Ambiguous Grey Genre." *The New Advocate 6* (1993): 61–70.

Meigs, Cornelia. *Invincible Louisa.* Little, Brown, 1933.

Mitchell, D. *Children's Literature: An Invitation to the World.* Boston, MA: Pearson, 2003.

Monjo, F. N. "The Ten Bad Things about History." *Beyond Fact: Nonfiction for Children and Young People.* Ed. J. Carr. American Library Association, 1982, pp. 99–103.

Moss, Barbara. "Getting the Picture: Visual Dimensions of Informational Texts." *Handbook of Research on Teaching Literacy through the Communicative and Visual Arts.* Vol. 2. Eds. James Flood, Shirley Brice Heath, and Diane Lapp. Lawrence Erlbaum, 2008, pp. 393–398.

Provensen, Alice, and Martin Provensen. *Leonardo da Vinci: The Artist, Inventor, Scientist in Three-Dimensional Movable Pictures.* New York: Random House, 1984.

Sayers, F. C. "History Books for Children." *Beyond Fact: Nonfiction for Children and Young People.* Ed. J. Carr. American Library Association, 1982, pp. 95–98.

Tavares, Matt. "A Reason for the Picture: Illustrating Nonfiction Picture Books." *The Horn Book Magazine* (March/April, 2011): 49–55.

Testa, Fulvio. *Wolf's Favor.* Dial Books, 1986.

Tunis, Edwin. *Frontier Living.* World, 1961.

van Loon, Hendrik Willem. *The Story of Mankind.* Boni & Liveright, 1921.

Venezky, Richard L. "The Origins of the Present-Day Chasm Between Adult Literacy Needs and School Literacy Instruction." *Scientific Studies of Reading, 4* (2000): 19–39.

Zarnowski, M. *Learning about Biographies: A Reading-and-Writing Approach for Children.* National Council of Teachers of English, 1990.

———. "Learning History with Informational Storybooks: A Social Studies Educator's Perspective." *The New Advocate 8* (1995): 183–196.

Zarnowski, M. and Susan Turkel. "Nonfiction Literature that Highlights Inquiry: How Real People Solve Real Problems." *Journal of Children's Literature, 37* (2011): 30–37.

Children's Book Awards

There are many more awards and prizes for children's books than are described in this appendix. In some states, children vote for books that are nominated for awards. Information about awards from children can be obtained from various state libraries. Other awards are given in specific genres, such as the Nebula Award for science fiction and the Edgar Allan Poe Award for mystery. Many cultural and ethnic organizations give awards to authors of children's books that contribute to understanding and appreciation of the many cultures within the United States.

JANE ADDAMS BOOK AWARD

The Jane Addams Children's Book Award has been presented annually since 1953 by the Women's International League for Peace and Freedom and the Jane Addams Peace Association to the children's book of the preceding year that most effectively promotes the cause of peace, social justice, and world community.

1953 *People Are Important* by Eva Knox Evans (Capital)

1954 *Stick-in-the-Mud* by Jean Ketchum (Cadmus Books, E. M. Hale)

1955 *Rainbow Round the World* by Elizabeth Yates (Bobbs-Merrill)

1956 *Story of the Negro* by Arna Bontemps (Knopf)

1957 *Blue Mystery* by Margot Benary-Isbert (Harcourt Brace)

1958 *The Perilous Road* by William O. Steele (Harcourt Brace)

1959 No award given

1960 *Champions of Peace* by Edith Patterson Meyer (Little, Brown)

1961 *What Then, Raman?* by Shirley L. Arora (Follett)

1962 *The Road to Agra* by Aimee Sommerfelt (Criterion)

1963 *The Monkey and the Wild, Wild Wind* by Ryerson Johnson (Abelard-Schuman)

1964 *Profiles in Courage: Young Readers Memorial Edition* by John F. Kennedy (Harper & Row)

1965 *Meeting with a Stranger* by Duane Bradley (Lippincott)

1966 *Berries Goodman* by Emily Cheney Neville (Harper & Row)

1967 *Queenie Peavy* by Robert Burch (Viking)

1968 *The Little Fishes* by Erik Christian Haugaard (Houghton Mifflin)

1969 *The Endless Steppe: Growing Up in Siberia* by Esther Hautzig (Crowell)

1970 *The Cay* by Theodore Taylor (Doubleday)

1971 *Jane Addams: Pioneer of Social Justice* by Cornelia Meigs (Little, Brown)

1972 *The Tamarack Tree* by Betty Underwood (Houghton Mifflin)

1973 *The Riddle of Racism* by S. Carl Hirsch (Viking)

Honor Book

The Upstairs Room by Johanna Reiss (Crowell)

1974 *Nilda* by Nicholasa Mohr (Harper & Row)

Honor Books

A Hero Ain't Nothin' but a Sandwich by Alice Childress (Coward, McCann & Geoghegan)

Men Against War by Barbara Habenstreit (Doubleday)

A Pocket Full of Seeds by Marilyn Sachs (Doubleday)

1975 *The Princess and the Admiral* by Charlotte Pomerantz (Addison-Wesley)

Honor Books

The Eye of Conscience by Milton Meltzer and Bernard Cole (Follett)

My Brother Sam Is Dead by James Lincoln Collier and Christopher Collier (Four Winds)

Viva la Raza! by Elizabeth Sutherland Martinez and Enrigueta Longeaux y Vasquez (Doubleday)

1976 *Paul Robeson* by Eloise Greenfield (Crowell)

Honor Books

Dragonwings by Laurence Yep (Harper & Row)

Song of the Trees by Mildred D. Taylor (Dial)

Z for Zachariah by Robert C. O'Brian (Atheneum)

1977 *Never to Forget: The Jews of the Holocaust* by Milton Meltzer (Harper & Row)

Honor Book

Roll of Thunder, Hear My Cry by Mildred D. Taylor (Dial)

1978 *Child of the Owl* by Laurence Yep (Harper & Row)

Honor Books

Alan and Naomi by Myron Levoy (Harper & Row)

Mischling, Second Degree: My Childhood in Nazi Germany by Ilse Koehn (Greenwillow)

Special Recognition

Amifika by Lucille Clifton (Dutton)

The Wheel of King Asoka by Ashok Davar (Follett)

1979 *Many Smokes, Many Moons: A Chronology of American History through Indian Art* by Jamake Highwater (Lippincott)

Honor Books

Escape to Freedom by Ossie Davis (Viking)

The Great Gilly Hopkins by Katherine Paterson (Crowell)

1980 *The Road from Home: The Story of an Armenian Girl* by David Kherdian (Greenwillow)

West Coast Honor Book: Woman from Hiroshima by Toshio Mori (Isthmus)

Special Recognition

Natural History by M. B. Goffstein (Farrar, Straus, & Giroux)

1981 *First Woman in Congress: Jeannette Rankin* by Florence Meiman White (Julian Messner)

Honor Books

Chase Me, Catch Nobody! by Erik Haugaard (Houghton Mifflin)

Doing Time: A Look at Crime and Prisons by Phyllis Clark and Robert Lehrman (Hastings House)

We Are Mesquakie, We Are One by Hadley Irwin (Feminist Press)

1982 *A Spirit to Ride the Whirlwind* by Athena V. Lord (Macmillan)

Honor Books

Let the Circle Be Unbroken by Mildred D. Taylor (Dial)

Lupita Mañana by Patricia Beatty (Morrow)

1983 *Hiroshima no pika* by Toshi Maruki, translated from Japanese (Lothrop, Lee & Shepard)

Honor Books

The Bomb by Sidney Lenz (Lodestar/Dutton)

If I Had a Paka: Poems in Eleven Languages by Charlotte Pomerantz (Greenwillow)

West Coast Honor Book: People at the Edge of the World: The Ohlone of Central California by Betty Morrow (Bacon)

Special Recognition

All the Colors of the Race by Arnold Adoff (Lothrop, Lee & Shepard)

Children as Teachers of Peace by Our Children (Celestial Press)

1984 *Rain of Fire* by Marion Dane Bauer (Clarion/Houghton Mifflin)

1985 *The Short Life of Sophie Scholl* by Hermann Vinke, with an interview with Ilse Aichinger, translated from German by Hedvig Pachter (Harper & Row)

Honor Books

The Island on Bird Street by Uri Orlev, translated from Hebrew by Hillel Halkin (Houghton Mifflin)

Music, Music for Everyone by Vera B. Williams (Greenwillow)

1986 *Ain't Gonna Study War No More: The Story of America's Peace Seekers* by Milton Meltzer (Harper & Row)

Honor Book

Journey to the Soviet Union by Samantha Smith (Little, Brown)

1987 *Nobody Wants a Nuclear War* by Judith Vigna (Albert Whitman)

Honor Books

All in a Day by Mitsumasa Anno (Philomel)

Children of the Maya: A Guatemalan Indian Odyssey by Brent Ashabranner, photographs by Paul Conklin (Dodd, Mead)

1988 *Waiting for the Rain: A Novel of South Africa* by Sheila Gordon (Orchard/Franklin Watts)

Honor Books

Nicolas, Where Have You Been? by Leo Lionni (Knopf)

Trouble at the Mines by Doreen Rappaport (Crowell)

1989 (tie)

Anthony Burns: The Defeat and Triumph of a Fugitive Slave by Virginia Hamilton (Knopf)

Looking Out by Victoria Boutis (Four Winds Press)

Honor Books

December Stillness by Mary Downing Hahn (Clarion)

The Most Beautiful Place in the World by Ann Cameron (Knopf)

Rescue: The Story of How Gentiles Saved Jews in the Holocaust by Milton Meltzer (Harper & Row)

1990 *A Long Hard Journey: The Story of the Pullman Porter* by Patricia and Fredrick McKissack (Walker)

Honor Books

Number the Stars by Lois Lowry (Houghton Mifflin)

Shades of Gray by Carolyn Reeder (Macmillan)

The Wednesday Surprise by Eve Bunting (Clarion)

1991 *The Big Book for Peace* edited by Ann Durell and Marilyn Sachs (Dutton)

Honor Books

The Journey: Japanese Americans, Racism and Renewal by Sheila Hamanaka (Richard Jackson/Orchard)

The Middle of Somewhere: A Story of South Africa by Sheila Gordon (Orchard)

1992 *Journey of the Sparrows* by Fran Leeper Buss with the assistance of Daisy Cubias (Lodestar)

Honor Book: Now Is Your Time! The African-American Struggle for Freedom by Walter Dean Myers (HarperCollins)

1993

Longer Books: A Taste of Salt: A Story of Modern Haiti by Frances Temple (Orchard)

Letters from a Slave Girl: The Story of Harriet Jacobs by Mary E. Lyons (Scribners)

Picture Books: Aunt Harriet's Underground Railroad in the Sky by Faith Ringgold (Crown)

Mrs. Katz and Tush by Patricia Polacco (Bantam)

1994

Longer Book: Freedom's Children: Young Civil Rights Activists Tell Their Stories by Ellen Levine (Putnam)

Picture Book: This Land Is My Land by George Littlechild (Children's Book Press)

Honor Books

Longer Book: Eleanor Roosevelt: A Life of Discovery by Russell Freedman (Clarion)

Picture Book: Soul Looks Back in Wonder by Tom Feelings (Dial)

1995

Longer Book: **Kids at Work: Lewis Hine and the Crusade against Child Labor** by Russell Freedman (Clarion)

Picture Book: **Sitti's Secrets** by Naomi Shihab Nye, illustrated by Nancy Carpenter (Four Winds Press)

Honor Books

Longer Books: **Cezanne Pinto** by Mary Stolz (Knopf)

I Hadn't Meant to Tell You This by Jacqueline Woodson (Delacorte)

Picture Book: **Bein' with You This Way** by W. Nikola-Lisa, illustrated by Michael Bryant (Lee & Low)

1996

Longer Book: **The Well** by Mildred D. Taylor (Dial)

Picture Book: No award given

Honor Books

Longer Books: **From the Notebooks of Melanin Sun** by Jacqueline Woodson (Blue Sky/Scholastic)

On the Wings of Peace: Writers and Illustrators Speak Out for Peace in Memory of Hiroshima and Nagasaki (Clarion)

The Watsons Go to Birmingham—1963 by Christopher Paul Curtis (Delacorte)

Special Commendation: **The Middle Passage** by Tom Feelings (Dial)

1997

Longer Book: **Growing Up in Coal Country** by Susan Campbell Bartoletti (Houghton Mifflin)

Picture Book: **Wilma Unlimited** by Kathleen Krull, illustrated by David Diaz (Harcourt Brace)

Honor Books

Longer Books: **Behind the Bedroom Wall** by Laura E. Williams (Milkweed)

Second Daughter: The Story of a Slave Girl by Mildred Pitts Walter (Scholastic)

Picture Book: **The Day Gogo Went to Vote** by Elinor Batezat Sisulu (Little, Brown)

1998

Longer Book: **Habibi** by Naomi Shihab Nye (Simon & Schuster)

Picture Book: **Seven Brave Women** by Betsy Hearne, illustrated by Bethanne Andersen (Greenwillow)

Honor Books

Longer Books: **The Circuit: Stories from the Life of a Migrant Child** by Francisco Jiménez (University of New Mexico Press)

Seedfolks by Paul Fleischman (HarperCollins)

Picture Books: **Celebrating Families** by Rosemarie Hausherr (Scholastic)

Passage to Freedom: The Sugihara Story by Ken Mochizuki, illustrated by Dom Lee (Lee & Low)

1999

Longer Book: **Bat 6** by Virginia Euwer Wolff (Scholastic)

Picture Book: **Painted Words/Spoken Memories: Marianthe's Story** by Aliki (Greenwillow)

Honor Books

Longer Books: **The Heart of a Chief** by Joseph Bruchac (Dial)

No More Strangers Now by Tim McKee, photographs by Anne Blackshaw (A Melanie Kroupa Book/DK Ink)

Restless Spirit: The Life and Work of Dorothea Lange by Elizabeth Partridge (Viking)

Picture Books: **Hey Little Ant** by Phillip and Hannah Hoose, illustrated by Debbie Tilley (Tricycle Press)

i see the rhythm by Toyomi Igus, illustrated by Michele Wood (Children's Book Press)

This Land Is Your Land words and music by Woodie Guthrie, illustrated by Kathy Jakobsen (Little, Brown)

2000

Longer Book: **Through My Eyes** by Ruby Bridges (Scholastic)

Picture Book: **Molly Bannaky** by Alice McGill, illustrated by Chris K. Soentpiet (Houghton Mifflin)

Honor Books

Longer Books: **The Birchbark House** by Louise Erdrich (Hyperion)

Kids on Strike! by Susan Campbell Bartoletti (Houghton Mifflin)

Picture Books: **A Band of Angels: A Story Inspired by the Jubilee Singers** by Deborah Hopkinson, illustrated by Raúl Colón (Atheneum)

When Sophie Gets Angry—Really, Really Angry . . . by Molly Bang (The Blue Sky Press/Scholastic)

2001

Longer Book: **Esperanza Rising** by Pam Muñoz Ryan (Scholastic)

Honor Books

The Color of My Words by Lynn Joseph (Joanna Cotler/ HarperCollins)

Darkness over Denmark: The Danish Resistance and the Rescue of the Jews by Ellen Levine (Holiday House)

Walking to the Bus-Rider Blues by Harriette Gillem Robinet (Jean Karl/ Atheneum/ Simon & Schuster)

Picture Book: **The Composition** by Antonio Skármeta, illustrated by Alfonso Ruano (Groundwood Books)

Honor Book: **The Yellow Star: The Legend of King Christian X of Denmark** by Carmen Agra Deedy, illustrated by Henri Sorensen (Peachtree)

2002

Book for Older Children: **The Other Side of Truth** by Beverley Naidoo (HarperCollins)

Honor Books: **A Group of One** by Rachna Gilmore (Henry Holt)

True Believer by Virginia Euwer Wolff (Atheneum/Simon & Schuster)

Picture Book: **Martin's Big Words: The Life of Dr. Martin Luther King, Jr.** by Doreen Rappaport, illustrated by Bryan Collier (Jump at the Sun/Hyperion)

Honor Book: **Amber Was Brave, Essie Was Smart,** written and illustrated by Vera B. Williams (Greenwillow/HarperCollins)

2003

Book for Older Children: **Parvana's Journey** by Deborah Ellis (Groundwood Books/Douglas & McIntyre)

Honor Books: **The Same Stuff as Stars** by Katherine Paterson (Clarion)

When My Name Was Keoko by Linda Sue Park (Clarion)

Picture Book: **Patrol: An American Soldier in Vietnam** by Walter Dean Myers, illustrated by Ann Grifalconi (HarperCollins)

¡Si, Se Puede! Yes We Can! Janitor Strike in L.A. by Diana Cohn, illustrated by Francisco Delgado (Cinco Puntos Press)

The Village That Vanished by Ann Grifalconi, illustrated by Kadir Nelson (Dial)

2004

Book for Older Children: Out of Bounds: Seven Stories of Conflict and Hope by Beverly Naidoo (HarperCollins)

Honor Books

Getting Away with Murder: The True Story of the Emmett Till Case by Chris Crowe (Phyllis Fogelman Books)

Shutting Out the Sky: Life in the Tenements of New York, 1880–1924 by Deborah Hopkinson (Orchard Books)

Picture Book: Harvesting Hope: The Story of Cesar Chavez by Kathleen Krull, illustrated by Yuyi Morales (Harcourt)

Honor Books

Girl Wonder: A Baseball Story in Nine Innings by Deborah Hopkinson, illustrated by Terry Widener (Anne Schwartz Book/Atheneum)

Luba: Angel of Bergen-Belsen, told to Michell R. McCann by Luba Trysz.nska-Frederick, illustrated by Ann Marshall (Tricycle Press)

2005

Books for Older Children: With Courage and Cloth: Winning the Fight for a Woman's Right to Vote, by Ann Bausum (National Geographic Society)

Honor Book: The Heaven Shop by Deborah Ellis (Fitzhenry & Whiteside)

Book for Younger Children: Sélavi, That is Life: A Haitian Story of Hope, written and illustrated by Youme Landowne (Cinco Puntos Press)

Honor Books: Hot Day on Abbott Avenue by Karen English, with collage art of Javaka Steptoe (Clarion Books)

Henry and the Kite Dragon, by Bruce Edward Hall, with paintings of William Low (Philomel Books/Penguin Young Readers Group)

Sequoyah: The Cherokee Man Who Gave His People Writing, by James Rumford and translated into Cherokee by Anna Sixkiller Huckaby (Houghton Mifflin Books for Children)

2006

Book for Older Children: Let Me Play: The Story of Title IX, the Law that Changed the Future of Girls in America, by Karen Blumenthal (Atheneum Books for Young Readers, an imprint of Simon & Schuster)

Honor Books: The Crazy Man, by Pamela Porter (Groundwood Books/House of Anansi Press)

Sweetgrass Basket, by Marlene Carvell (Dutton Children's Books, a Division of Penguin Young Readers Group)

Book for Younger Children: Delivering Justice: W. W. Law and the Fight for Civil Rights by Jim Haskins, illustrated by Benny Andrews (Candlewick Press)

Honor Book: Poems to Dream Together/Poemas Para Soñar Juntos by Francisco X. Alarcón, illustrated by Paula Barragán (Lee & Low Books, Inc.)

2007

Book for Older Children: Weedflower by Cynthia Kadohata, (Atheneum Books for Young Readers, an imprint of Simon & Schuster Children's Publishing)

Honor Book: Freedom Walkers by Russell Freedman (Holiday House)

Counting on Grace by Elizabeth Winthrop (Wendy Lamb Books)

Book for Younger Children: A Place Where Sunflowers Grow by Amy Lee-Tai, illustrated by Felicia Hoshino (Children's Book Press)

Honor Books: Night Boat to Freedom, written by Margot Theis Raven with pictures by E. B. Lewis (Melanie Kroupa Books)

Crossing Bok Chitto, told in written form by Choctaw storyteller, Tim Tingle, illustrated by Jeanne Rorex Bridges (Cinco Puntos Press)

2008

Book for Older Children: We Are One: The Story of Bayard Rustin by Larry Dane Brimner (Calkins Creek, an imprint of Boyds Mills Press, Inc.)

Honor Books: Rickshaw Girl by Mitali Perkins, with illustrations by Jamie Hogan (Charlesbridge)

Elijah of Buxton by Christopher Paul Curtis (Scholastic Press, an imprint of Scholastic, Inc.)

Birmingham, 1963 by Carole Boston Weatherford (Wordsong, an imprint of Boyds Mills Press)

Book for Younger Children: The Escape of Oney Judge: Martha Washington's Slave Finds Freedom, written and illustrated by Emily Arnold McCully (Farrar, Straus, & Giroux)

Honor Book: One Thousand Tracings: Healing the Wounds of World War II, written and illustrated by Lita Judge (Hyperion Books for Children)

2009

Book for Older Children: The Surrender Tree: Poems of Cuba's Struggle for Freedom by Margarita Engle (Henry Holt Books for Young Readers, an imprint of Macmillan Children's Publishing Group)

Honor Books: The Shepherd's Granddaughter by Anne Laurel Carter (Groundwood Books/House of Anansi Press)

Ain't Nothing But a Man: My Quest to Find the Real John Henry by Scott Reynolds Nelson with Marc Aronson (National Geographic)

Book for Younger Children: Planting the Trees of Kenya: The Story of Wangari Maathai, written and illustrated by Claire A. Nivola (Frances Foster Books/Farrar, Straus, & Giroux, an imprint of Macmillan Children's Publishing Group)

Honor Books: The Storyteller's Candle/La velita de los cuentos, by Story/Cuento Lucía González, illustrations/illustraciones by Lulu Delacre (Children's Book Press)

Silent Music: A Story of Baghdad written and illustrated by James Rumford (Neal Porter Book/Roaring Brook Press, an imprint of Macmillan Children's Publishing Group)

2010

Book for Older Children: Marching for Freedom: Walk Together, Children, and Don't You Grow Weary by Elizabeth Partridge (Viking Children's Books, an imprint of Penguin Young Readers Group)

Honor Books: Almost Astronauts: 13 Women Who Dared to Dream by Tanya Lee Stone (Candlewick Press)

Claudette Colvin by Phillip Hoose (Melanie Kroupa Books/Farrar Straus Giroux, an imprint of Macmillan Children's Publishing Group)

Books for Younger Children: Nasreen's Secret School: A True Story from Afghanistan, written and illustrated by Jeanette Winter (Beach Lane Books, an imprint of Simon & Schuster Children's Publishing)

Honor Books: Sojourner Truth's Step-Stomp Stride by Andrea Davis Pinkney and Brian Pinkney (Disney/Jump at the Sun Books)

You and Me and Home Sweet Home by George Ella Lyon and Stephanie Anderson (a Richard Jackson Book/Atheneum Books for Young Readers, an imprint of Simon & Schuster Children's Publishing)

2011

Book for Older Children: ***A Long Walk to Water: Based on a True Story*** by Linda Sue Park (Clarion Books, Houghton Mifflin Harcourt Publishing Company)

Honors Books: ***The Ninth Ward*** by Jewell Parker Rhodes (Little, Brown Books for Young Readers, Hachette Book Group)

Birmingham Sunday by Larry Dane Brimner (Calkins Creek, an imprint of Boyds Mills Press, Inc.)

Book for Younger Children: ***Emma's Poem: The Voice of the Statue of Liberty*** written by Linda Glaser with paintings by Claire A. Nivola (Houghton Mifflin Books for Children, Houghton Mifflin Harcourt Publishing Company)

Honor Books: ***Sit-In: How Four Friends Stood Up by Sitting Down*** by Andrea Davis Pinkney, illustrated by Brian Pinkney (Little, Brown Books)

Ruth and the Green Book by Calvin Alexander Ramsey with Gwen Strauss, illustrated by Floyd Cooper (Carolrhoda Books, a division of Lerner Publishing Group, Inc.)

2012

Book for Older Children: ***Sylvia & Aki*** by Winifred Conkling (Tricycle Press, an imprint of Random House)

Honors Books: ***Heart and Soul: The Story of America and African Americans*** written and illustrated by Kadir Nelson (Baltzer & Bray, an imprint of HarperCollins)

Inside Out & Back Again by Thanhha Lai (Harper, an imprint of HarperCollins)

Book for Younger Children: ***The Mangrove Tree: Planting Trees to Feed Families*** written by Susan L. Roth and Cindy Trumbore, illustrated by Susan L. Roth (Lee & Low)

Honor Books: ***Peaceful Pieces: Poems and Quilts about Peace*** written and illustrated by Anna Grossnickle Hines (Macmillan, an imprint of Henry Holt)

Belle, the Last Mule at Gee's Bend written by Calvin Alexander Ramsey and Bettye Stroud, illustrated by John Holyfield (Candlewick Press)

2013

Book for Older Children: ***We've Got a Job: The 1963 Birmingham Children's March*** written by Cynthia Levinson (Peachtree Publishers)

Honor Books: ***Marching to the Mountaintop: How Poverty, Labor Fights and Civil Rights Set the Stage for Martin Luther King Jr's Final Hours*** written by Ann Bausum (National Geographic)

Temple Grandin: How the Girl Who Loved Cows Embraced Autism and Changed the World by Sy Montgomery (Houghton Mifflin Books for Children)

Book for Younger Children: ***Each Kindness*** written by Jacqueline Woodson, illustrated by E. B. Lewis (Nancy Paulsen Books, an imprint of Penguin)

Honor Books: ***Dolores Huerta: A Hero to Migrant Workers***, written by Sarah Warren, illustrated by Robert Casilla (Marshall Cavendish Children)

We March written and illustrated by Shane W. Evans (Roaring Brook Press, a Neal Porter imprint of Macmillan)

AMÉRICAS AWARD FOR CHILDREN'S AND YOUNG ADULT LITERATURE

The Américas Award is given in recognition of U.S. works of fiction, poetry, folklore, or nonfiction (from picture books to works for young adults) published in the previous year in English or Spanish that authentically and engagingly portray Latin America, the Caribbean, or Latinos in the United States. By combining both languages and linking the Americas, the award reaches beyond geographic borders as well as multicultural boundaries, focusing instead on cultural heritages within the hemisphere. The award is sponsored by the national Consortium of Latin American Studies Programs (CLASP). The commended list is available at http://www.uwm.edu/dept/cla/outreach_americas.

1993 *Vejigante Masquerader* by Lulu Delacre (Scholastic)

1994 *The Mermaid's Twin Sister* by Lynn Joseph (Clarion)

1995 *Tonight, by Sea* by Frances Temple (Orchard)

1996 *In My Family/En mi familia* by Carmen Lomas Garza (Children's Book Press)

Parrot in the Oven by Victor Martinez (HarperCollins)

1997 *The Circuit* by Francisco Jiménez (University of New Mexico Press)

The Face at the Window by Regina Hanson, illustrated by Linda Saport (Clarion)

1998 *Barrio: José's Neighborhood* by George Ancona (Harcourt Brace)

Mama and Papa Have a Store by Amelia Lau Carling (Dial)

1999 *Crashboomlove* by Juan Felipe Herrera (University of New Mexico Press)

2000 *The Composition* by Antonio Skármeta, illustrated by Alfonso Ruano (Groundwood)

The Color of My Words by Lynn Joseph (HarperCollins)

2001 *A Movie in My Pillow* by Jorge Argueta, illustrated by Elizabeth Gómez (Children's Book Press)

Breaking Through by Francisco Jiménez (Houghton Mifflin Company)

2002 *Before We Were Free* by Julia Alvarez (Knopf)

2003 *Just A Minute: A Trickster Tale and Counting Book* by Yuyi Morales (Chronicle Books)

The Meaning of Consuelo by Judith Ortiz Cofer (Farrar, Straus, & Giroux)

2004 *My Name Is Celia/Me llamo Celia* by Monica Brown, illustrated by Rafael López (Luna Rising)

Sammy & Juliana in Hollywood by Benjamin Alire Sáenz (Cinco Puntos)

2005 *Cinnamon Girl: letters found inside a cereal box* by Juan Felipe Herrera (HarperCollins, Joanna Cotler Books)

2006 *Josias, Hold the Book* by Jennifer Elvgren, illustrated by Nicole Tadgell (Boyds Mill)

The Poet Slave of Cuba by Margarita Engle, illustrated by Sean Qualls (Holt)

2007 *Red Glass* by Laura Resau (Delacorte)

YUM! ¡MMMM! ¡QUE RICO!: America's Sproutings by Pat Mora, pictures by Rafael López (Lee & Low)

2008 *Just in Case: A Trickster Tale and Spanish Alphabet Book* by Yuyi Morales (Roaring Brook Press)

The Surrender Tree: Poems of Cuba's Struggle for Freedom by Margarita Engle (Holt)

2010 *Return to Sender* by Julia Alvarez (Knopf, 2009)

What Can You Do With a Paleta? / ¿Qué puedes hacer con una paleta? by Carmen Tafolla, illustrated by Magaly Morales (Tricycle Press)

2011 *Clemente!* by Willie Perdomo, illustrated by Bryan Collier (Holt, 2010)

The Dreamer by Pam Muñoz Ryan, illustrated by Peter Sís (Scholastic)

2012 *Hurricane Dancers: The First Caribbean Pirate Shipwreck* by Margarita Engle (Henry Holt)

Pablo Neruda: Poet of the People by Monica Brown, illustrated by Julie Paschkis (Henry Holt)

HANS CHRISTIAN ANDERSEN AWARD

The International Board on Books for Young People has given the Hans Christian Andersen Award biennially since 1956 (since 1966 for the illustrator award). It is awarded to one author and one illustrator in recognition of his or her entire body of work.

1956 Eleanor Farjeon, Great Britain

1958 Astrid Lindgren, Sweden

1960 Erich Kästner, Federal Republic of Germany

1962 Meindert DeJong, United States

1964 René Guillot, France

1966 *Author:* Tove Jansson, Finland

Illustrator: Alois Carigiet, Switzerland

1968 *Authors:* James Krüss, Federal Republic of Germany
José Maria Sanchez-Silva, Spain

Illustrator: Juří Trnka, Czechoslovakia

1970 *Author:* Gianni Rodari, Italy

Illustrator: Maurice Sendak, United States

1972 *Author:* Scott O'Dell, United States

Illustrator: Ib Spang Olsen, Denmark

1974 *Author:* Maria Gripe, Sweden

Illustrator: Farshid Mesghali, Iran

1976 *Author:* Cecil Bødker, Denmark

Illustrator: Tatjana Mawrina, Soviet Union

1978 *Author:* Paula Fox, United States

Illustrator: Otto S. Svend, Denmark

1980 *Author:* Bohumil R'ha, Czechoslovakia

Illustrator: Suekichi Akaba, Japan

1982 *Author:* Lygia Bojunga Nunes, Brazil

Illustrator: Zbigniew Rychlicki, Poland

1984 *Author:* Christine Nöstlinger, Austria

Illustrator: Mitsumasa Anno, Japan

1986 *Author:* Patricia Wrightson, Australia

Illustrator: Robert Ingpen, Australia

1988 *Author:* Annie M. G. Schmidt, Netherlands

Illustrator: Duŭsan Kállay, Czechoslovakia

1990 *Author:* Tormod Haugen, Norway

Illustrator: Lisbeth Zwerger, Austria

1992 *Author:* Virginia Hamilton, United States

Illustrator: Kvuětá Pacovska, Czechoslovakia

1994 *Author:* Michio Mado, Japan

Illustrator: Jorg Müller, Switzerland

1996 *Author:* Uri Orlev, Israel

Illustrator: Klaus Ensikat, Germany

1998 *Author:* Katherine Paterson, United States

Illustrator: Tomi Ungerer, France

2000 *Author:* Ana Maria Machado, Brazil

Illustrator: Anthony Browne, United Kingdom

2002 *Author:* Aidan Chambers, UK

Illustrator: Quentin Blake, UK

2004 *Author:* Martin Waddell, Ireland

Illustrator: Max Velthuijs, the Netherlands

2006 *Author:* Margaret Mahy (New Zealand)

Illustrator: Wolf Erlbruch (Germany)

2008 *Author:* Jürg Schubiger (Switzerland)

Illustrator: Roberto Innocenti (Italy)

2010 *Author:* David Almond (United Kingdom)

Illustrator: Jutta Bauer (Germany)

2012 *Author:* Maria Teresa Andruetto (Argentina)

Illustrator: Peter Sís (Czech Republic)

MILDRED L. BATCHELDER AWARD

This award honors the former executive director of the Association for Library Service to Children (ALSC), a division of the American Library Association (ALA). The citation is given annually to a U.S. publisher for a children's book (defined as any trade book for children from pre-nursery school age through eighth grade) deemed the most outstanding book originally published in a foreign language in a foreign country, and then published in the United States. (From 1968 through 1977, the award was given for a book published in the previous two years; since 1979, the award has been given to a book published in the preceding year.)

1968 *The Little Man* by Erich Kästner, translated from German by James Krikup (Knopf)

1969 *Don't Take Teddy* by Babbis Friis-Baastad, translated from Norwegian by Lise Sømme McKinnon (Scribner's)

1970 *Wildcat under Glass* by Alki Zei, translated from Greek by Edward Fenton (Holt)

1971 *In the Land of Ur, the Discovery of Ancient Mesopotamia* by Hans Baumann, translated from German by Stella Humphries (Pantheon)

1972 *Friedrich* by Hans Peter Richter, translated from German by Edite Kroll (Holt)

1973 *Pulga* by S. R. Van Iterson, translated from Dutch by Alexander and Alison Gode (Morrow)

1974 *Petro's War* by Alki Zei, translated from Greek by Edward Fenton (Dutton)

1975 *An Old Tale Carved Out of Stone* by A. Linevski, translated from Russian by Maria Polushkin (Crown)

1976 *The Cat and Mouse Who Shared a House* by Ruth Hürlimann, translated from German by Anthea Bell (Walck)

1977 *The Leopard* by Cecil Bødker, translated from Danish by Gunnar Poulsen (Atheneum)

1978 No award given

1979 *Konrad* by Christine Nöstlinger (published 1977), translated from German by Anthea Bell (Watts)

Rabbit Island by Jörg Steiner (published 1978), translated from German by Ann Conrad Lammers (Harcourt)

1980 *The Sound of the Dragon's Feet* by Alki Zei, translated from Greek by Edward Fenton (Dutton)

1981 *The Winter When Time Was Frozen* by Els Pelgrom, translated from Dutch by Maryka and Raphael Rudnik (Morrow)

1982 *The Battle Horse* by Harry Kullman, translated from Swedish by George Blecher and Lone Thygesen Blecher (Bradbury)

1983 *Hiroshima no pika* by Toshi Maruki, translated from Japanese through Kurita-Bando Literary Agency (Lothrop)

1984 *Ronia, the Robber's Daughter* by Astrid Lindgren, translated from Swedish by Patricia Crampton (Viking)

1985 *The Island on Bird Street* by Uri Orlev, translated from Hebrew by Hillel Halkin (Houghton Mifflin)

1986 *Rose Blanche* by Christophe Gallaz and Robert Innocenti, translated from Italian by Martha Coventry and Richard Craglia (Creative Education)

1987 *No Hero for the Kaiser* by Rudolf Frank, translated from German by Patricia Crampton (Lothrop)

1988 *If You Didn't Have Me* by Ulf Nilsson, translated from Swedish by Lone Thygesen Blecher and George Blecher (McElderry)

1989 *Crutches* by Peter Härtling, translated from German by Elizabeth D. Crawford (Lothrop)

1990 *Buster's World* by Bjarne Reuter, translated from Danish by Anthea Bell (Dutton)

1991 *A Hand Full of Stars* by Rafik Schami, translated from German by Rika Lesser (Dutton)

1992 *The Man from the Other Side* by Uri Orlev, translated from Hebrew by Hillel Halkin (Houghton Mifflin)

1993 No award given

1994 *The Apprentice* by Pilar M. Llorente, translated from Spanish by Robin Longshaw (Farrar)

Honor Books

The Princess in the Kitchen Garden by Annemie and Margaret Heymans, translated from Dutch by Johanna H. Prins and Johanna W. Prins (Farrar)

Anne Frank Beyond the Diary: A Photographic Remembrance by Ruud van der Rol and Rian Verhoeven, translated from Dutch by Tony Langham and Plym Peters (Viking)

1995 *Boys from St. Petri* by Bjarne Reuter, translated from Danish by Anthea Bell (Dutton)

Honor Book: Sister Shako and Kolo the Goat: Memories of My Childhood in Turkey by Vedat Dalokay, translated from Turkish by Gýner Ener (Lothrop)

1996 *The Lady with the Hat* by Uri Orlev, translated from Hebrew by Hillel Halkin (Houghton Mifflin)

Honor Books

Star of Fear, Star of Hope by Jo Hoestlandt, translated from French by Mark Polizzotti (Walker)

Damned Strong Love: The True Story of Willi G. and Stephan K. by Lutz van Dijk, translated from German by Elizabeth D. Crawford (Holt)

1997 *The Friends* by Kazumi Yumoto, translated from Japanese by Cathy Hirano (Farrar)

1998 *The Robber and Me* by Josef Holub, translated from German by Elizabeth D. Crawford (Holt)

Honor Books

Hostage to War: A True Story by Tatjana Wassiljewa, translated from German by Anna Trenter (Scholastic)

Nero Corleone: A Cat's Story by Elke Heidenrich, translated from German by Doris Orgel (Viking)

1999 *Thanks to My Mother* by Schoschana Rabinovici, translated from German by James Skofield (Dial)

Honor Book: Secret Letters from 0 to 10 by Susie Morgenstern, translated from French by Gill Rosner (Viking)

2000 *The Baboon King* by Anton Quintana, translated from Dutch by John Nieuwenhuizen (Walker and Company)

Honor Books

Collector of Moments by Quint Buchholz, translated from German by Peter F. Neumeyer (Farrar)

Asphalt Angels by Ineke Holtwijk, translated from Dutch by Wanda Boeke (Front Street)

Vendela in Venice by Christina Björk, illustrated by Inga-Karin Eriksson, translated from Swedish by Patricia Crampton (R&S Books)

2001 *Samir and Yonatan* by Daniella Carmi, translated from Hebrew by Yael Lotan (Arthur A. Levine/Scholastic)

Honor Book: Ultimate Game by Christian Lehmann, translated from French by William Rodarmor (David R. Godine)

2002 *How I Became an American* by Karin Gündisch, translated by James Skofield (Cricket Books/Carus Publishing)

Honor Book: A Book of Coupons by Susie Morgenstern with illustrations by Serge Bloch, translated from the French by Gill Rosner (Viking Press)

2003 *The Thief Lord* by Cornelia Funke, translated by Oliver Latsch (The Chicken House/Scholastic Publishing)

Honor Book: Henrietta and the Golden Eggs by Hanna Johansen, illustrated by Käthi Bhend, and translated by John Barrett (David R. Godine)

2004 *Run, Boy, Run* by Uri Orlev, translated Hillel Halkin (Walter Lorraine Books/Houghton Mifflin)

Honor Book: The Man Who Went to the Far Side of the Moon: The Story of Apollo 11 Astronaut Michael Collins by Bea Uusma Schyffert, translated by Emi Guner (Chronicle Books)

2005 *Shadows of Ghadames* by Joelle Stolz, translated by Catherine Temerson (Delacorte Press/Random House)

Honor Books

The Crow-Girl: The Children of Crow Cove by Bodil Bredsdorff, translated by Faith Ingwersen (Farrar, Straus, & Giroux)

Daniel Half Human and the Good Nazi by David Chotjewitz, translated by Doris Orgel (A Richard Jackson Book, Atheneum Books for Young Readers/ Simon & Schuster)

2006 *An Innocent Soldier* by Josef Holub, translated by Michael Hofmann (German) (Arthur A. Levine Books)

Honor Books

Nicholas by Rene Goscinny, translated by Anthea Bell (French) (Phaidon Press Limited)

When I Was a Soldier by Valerie Zenatti, translated by Adriana Hunter (French) (Bloomsbury Children's Books)

2007 *The Pull of the Ocean* by Jean-Claude Mourlevat, translated by Ymaudet (French) (Delacorte Press)

Honor Books

The Killer's Tears by Anne-Laure Bondoux, translated by Y. Maudet (French) (Delacorte Press)

The Last Dragon by Silvana De Mari, translated by Shaun Whiteside (Italian) (Hyperion/Miramax)

2008 *Brave Story* by Miyuki Miyabe, translated by Alexander O. Smith (Japanese) (VIZ Media)

Honor Books

The Cat: Or, How I Lost Eternity by Jutta Richter, translated by Anna Brailovsky (German) (Milkweed Editions)

Nicholas and the Gang by Rene Goscinny, translated by Anthea Bell (French) (Phaidon Press)

2009 *Moribito: Guardian of the Spirit* by Nahoko Uehashi, translated by Cathy Hirano (Japanese) (Arthur A. Levine Books)

Honor Books

Garmann's Summer by Stian Hole, translated by Don Bartlett (Norwegian) (Eerdmans Books for Young Readers)

Tiger Moon by Antonia Michaelis, translated by Anthea Bell (German) (Amulet Books)

2010 *A Faraway Island* by Annika Thor, translated by Linda Schenck (Swedish) (Delacorte Press, an imprint of Random House Children's Books)

Honor Books

Big Wolf and Little Wolf by Nadine Brun-Cosme, illustrated by Olivier Tallec, translated by Claudia Bedrick (Enchanted Lion Books)

Eidi by Bodil Bredsdorff, translated by Kathryn Mahaffy (Farrar, Straus, & Giroux)

Moribito II: Guardian of the Darkness by Nahoko Uehashi, illustrated by Yuko Shimizu, translated by Cathy Hirano (Arthur A. Levine Books, an imprint of Scholastic)

2011 *A Time of Miracles* by Anne-Laure Bondoux, translated by Y. Maudet (Delacorte Press, an imprint of Random House Children's Books)

Honor Books

Departure Time by Truus Matti, translated by Nancy Forest-Flier (Namelos)

Nothing by Janne Teller, translated by Martin Aitken (Atheneum Books for Young Readers, an imprint of Simon & Schuster)

2012 *Soldier Bear* by Bibi Dumon Tak, illustrated by Philip Hopman, translated by Laura Watkinson (Eerdmans Books for Young Readers)

Honor Books

The Lily Pond by Annika Thor, translated by Linda Schenck (Delacorte Press, an imprint of Random House Children's Books)

2013 *My Family for the War* by Anne C. Voorhoeve, translated by Tammi Reichel (Dial Books, an imprint of Penguin Group)

Honor Books

A Game for Swallows: To Die, To Leave, To Return written and illustrated by Zeina Abirached, translated by Edward Gauvin (Graphic Universe, a division of Lerner Publishing Group)

Son of a Gun written and translated by Anne de Graaf (Eerdmans Books for Young Readers, an imprint of Wm. B. Eerdmans Publishing)

THE PURA BELPRÉ AWARD

The Pura Belpré Award, established in 1996, is presented to a Latino/Latina writer and illustrator whose work best portrays, affirms, and celebrates the Latino cultural experience in an outstanding work of literature for children and youth. It is co-sponsored by the Association for Library Service to Children (ALSC), a division of the American Library Association (ALA), and the National Association to Promote Library Services to the Spanish Speaking (REFORMA), an ALA affiliate.

1996

Narrative: An Island Like You: Stories of the Barrio by Judith Ortiz Cofer (Melanie Kroupa/Orchard)

Illustration: Chato's Kitchen by Gary Soto, illustrated by Susan Guevara (Putnam)

Honor Books

Narrative: The Bossy Gallito/El gallo de bodas: A Traditional Cuban Folktale by Lucía González, illustrated by Lulu Delacre (Scholastic)

Baseball in April, and Other Stories by Gary Soto (Harcourt)

Illustration: Pablo Remembers: The Fiesta of the Day of the Dead, illustrated by George Ancona (also published in a Spanish language edition: *Pablo recuenta: La fiesta de día d'a de los muertos*) (Lothrop)

The Bossy Gallito/El gallo de bodas: A Traditional Cuban Folktale by Lucía González, illustrated by Lulu Delacre (Scholastic)

Family Pictures/Cuadros de familia by Carmen Lomas Garza, Spanish language text by Rosalma Zubizaretta, illustrated by Carmen Lomas Garza (Children's Book Press)

1998

Narrative: Parrot in the Oven: Mi vida by Victor Martinez (Joanna Cotler/HarperCollins)

Illustration: Snapshots from the Wedding by Gary Soto, illustrated by Stephanie Garcia (Putnam)

Honor Books

Narrative: Laughing Tomatoes and Other Spring Poems/ Jitomates risueños y otros poemas de primavera by Francisco Alarcón, illustrated by Maya Christina Gonzalez (Children's Book Press)

Spirits of the High Mesa by Floyd Martinez (Arte Püblico)

Illustration: In My Family/En mi familia by Carmen Lomas Garza (Children's Book Press)

The Golden Flower: A Taino Myth from Puerto Rico by Nina Jaffe, illustrated by Enrique O. Sánchez (Simon & Schuster)

Gathering the Sun: An Alphabet in Spanish and English by Alma Flor Ada, English translation by Rosa Zubizarreta, illustrated by Simón Silva (Lothrop)

2000

Narrative: Under the Royal Palms: A Childhood in Cuba by Alma Flor Ada (Atheneum)

Illustration: Magic Windows by Carmen Lomas Garza (Children's Book Press)

Honor Books

Narrative: From the Bellybutton of the Moon and Other Summer Poems/Del ombligo de la luna y otro poemas de verano by Francisco X. Alarcón, illustrated by Maya Christina Gonzalez (Children's Book Press)

Laughing Out Loud, I Fly: Poems in English and Spanish by Juan Felipe Herrera, illustrated by Karen Barbour (HarperCollins)

Illustration: Barrio: José's Neighborhood by George Ancona (Harcourt Brace)

The Secret Stars by Joseph Slate, illustrated by Felipe Dávalos (Marshall Cavendish)

Mama and Papa Have a Store by Amelia Lau Carling (Dial)

2002

Narrative: Esperanza Rising by Pam Munoz Ryan (Scholastic Press)

Illustration: Chato and the Party Animals by Gary Soto, illustrated by Susan Guevara (G.P. Putnam's Sons)

Honor Books

Narrative: Breaking Through by Francisco Jiménez (Houghton Mifflin Company)

Iguanas in the Snow by Francisco X. Alarcón and illustrated by Maya Christina Gonzalez (Children's Book Press)

Illustration: Juan Bobo Goes to Work retold by Marisa Montes, illustrated by Joe Cepeda (HarperCollins)

2004

Narrative: Before We Were Free by Julia Alvarez (Alfred A. Knopf)

Illustration: Just a Minute: A Trickster Tale and Counting Book by Yuyi Morales (Chronicle Books)

Honor Books

Narrative: Cuba 15 by Nancy Osa (Delacorte Press)

My Diary from Here to There/Mi Diario de Aquí Hasta Allá by Amada Irma Pérez (Children's Book Press)

Illustration: First Day in Grapes by L. King Pérez, illustrated by Robert Casilla (Lee & Low Books)

The Pot That Juan Built by Nancy Andrews-Goebel, illustrated by David Diaz (Lee & Low Books)

Harvesting Hope: The Story of Cesar Chavez by Kathleen Krull, illustrated by Yuyi Morales (Harcourt)

2006

Narrative: The Tequila Worm by Viola Canales (New York: Wendy Lamb Books)

Illustration: Doña Flor: a Tall Tale About a Giant Woman with a Great Big Heart by Pat Mora, illustrated by Raul Colón (Knopf)

Honor Books

Narrative: César: ¡Sí, Se Puede! Yes, We Can! by Carmen T. Bernier-Grand (Marshall Cavendish)

Doña Flor: a Tall Tale About a Giant Woman with a Great Big Heart by Pat Mora (Knopf)

Becoming Naomi León, by Pam Muñoz Ryan *(Scholastic)*

Illustration: Arrorró, Mi Niño: Latino Lullabies and Gentle Games selected and illustrated by Lulu Delacre (Lee & Low Books)

César: ¡Sí, Se Puede! Yes, We Can! by Carmen T. Bernier-Grand, illustrated by David Diaz (Marshall Cavendish)

My Name Is Celia/ Me Llamo Celia: The Life of Celia Cruz by Monica Brown, illustrated by Rafael López (Rising Moon)

2008

Narrative: The Poet Slave of Cuba: A Biography of Juan Francisco Manzano by Margarita Engle, illustrated by Sean Qualls (Holt)

Illustration: Los Gatos Black on Halloween by Marisa Montes, illustrated by Yuyi Morales (Holt)

Honor Books

Narrative: Frida: ¡Viva la vida! Long Live Life! by Carmen T. Bernier-Grand (Marshall Cavendish)

Martina the Beautiful Cockroach: A Cuban Folktale by Carmen Agra Deedy, illustrated by Michael Austin (Peachtree)

Los Gatos Black on Halloween by Marisa Montes, illustrated by Yuyi Morales (Holt)

Illustration: My Name is Gabito: The Life of Gabriel García Márquez/Me llamo Gabito: la vida de Gabriel García Márquez by Monica Brown, illustrated by Raul Colón (Luna Rising)

My Colors, My World/Mis colores, mi mundo by Maya Christina Gonzales (Children's Book Press)

2009

Narrative: The Surrender Tree: Poems of Cuba's Struggle for Freedom by Margarita Engle (Holt)

Illustration: Just In Case by Yuyi Morales (Roaring Brook Press)

Honor Books

Narrative: Just In Case by Yuyi Morales (Roaring Brook Press)

The Storyteller's Candle/La Velita de los Cuentos by Lucía González (Children's Book Press)

Reaching Out by Francisco Jiménez (Houghton Mifflin Company)

Illustration: Papá and Me by Arthur Dorros, illustrated by Rudy Gutierrez (Rayo/HarperCollins Publishers)

The Storyteller's Candle/La Velita de los Cuentos by Lucía González, illustrated by Lulu Delacre (Children's Book Press)

What Can You Do With a Rebozo? by Carmen Tafolla, illustrated by Amy Córdova (Tricycle Press)

2010

Narrative: Return to Sender by Julia Alvarez (Alfred A. Knopf)

Illustration: Fiesta!: Celebrate Children's Day/Book Day; Celebremos El día de los niños/El día de los libros by Pat Mora, illustrated by Rafael López (Rayo, an imprint of HarperCollins Publishers)

Honor Books

Narrative: Diego: Bigger Than Life by Carmen T. Bernier-Grand, illustrated by David Diaz (Marshall Cavendish Children)

Federico García Lorca by Georgina Lázaro, illustrated by Enrique S. Moreiro (Lectorum Publications, Inc., a subsidiary of Scholastic Inc.)

Illustration: **Diego: Bigger Than Life** by Carmen T. Bernier-Grand, illustrated by David Diaz (Marshall Cavendish Children)

My Abuelita by Tony Johnston, illustrated by Yuyi Morales (Harcourt Children's Books, Houghton Mifflin Harcourt)

Gracias Thanks by Pat Mora, illustrated by John Parra (Lee & Low Books Inc.)

2011

Narrative: **The Dreamer**, written by Pam Muñoz Ryan, illustrated by Peter Sís (Scholastic Press, an imprint of Scholastic Inc.)

Illustration: **Grandma's Gift**, written and illustrated by Eric Velasquez (Walker Publishing Company, Inc., a division of Bloomsbury Publishing, Inc.)

Honor Books

Narrative: **¡Ole! Flamenco**, written and illustrated by George Ancona (Lee & Low Books Inc.)

The Firefly Letters: A Suffragette's Journey to Cuba, written by Margarita Engle (Henry Holt and Company, LLC)

90 Miles to Havana by Enrique Flores-Galbis (Roaring Brook Press, a division of Holtzbrinck Publishing)

Illustration: **Fiesta Babies**, written by Carmen Tafolla, illustrated Amy Cordova (Tricycle Press, an imprint of the Crown Publishing Group, a division of Random House, Inc.)

Me, Frida, written by Amy Novesky, illustrated by David Diaz (Abrams Books for Young Readers, an imprint of Abrams)

Dear Primo: A Letter to My Cousin, written and illustrated by Duncan Tonatiuh (Abrams Books for Young Readers, an imprint of Abrams)

2012 *Narrative:* **Under the Mesquite** by Guadalupe Garcia McCall (Lee & Low Books Inc.)

Illustration: **Diego Rivera: His World and Ours** by Duncan Tonatiuh (Abrams Books for Young Readers, an imprint of Abrams)

Honor Books

Narrative: **Hurricane Dancers: The First Caribbean Pirate Shipwreck** by Margarita Engle (Henry Holt and Company, LLC)

Maximilian and the Mystery of the Guardian Angel: A Bilingual Lucha Libre Thriller by Xavier Garza (Cinco Puntos Press)

Illustration: **The Cazuela that the Farm Maiden Stirred** written by Samantha R. Vamos, illustrated by Rafael López (Charlesbridge)

Marisol McDonald Doesn't Match /Marisol McDonald no combina, written by Monica Brown, illustrated by Sara Palacios (Children's Book Press, an imprint of Lee & Low Books Inc.)

2013 *Narrative:* **Aristotle and Dante Discover the Secrets of the Universe** by Benjamin Alire Sáenz (Simon & Schuster Books for Young Readers, an imprint of Simon & Schuster Children's Publishing Division)

Illustration: **Martín de Porres: The Rose in the Desert** written by Gary D. Schmidt, illustrated by David Diaz (Clarion Books, an imprint of Houghton Mifflin Harcourt Publishing Company)

Honor Book

Narrative: **The Revolution of Evelyn Serrano** by Sonia Manzano (Scholastic Press, an imprint of Scholastic Inc.)

No honor books for illustration were given.

BOSTON GLOBE-HORN BOOK AWARD

This award, which was established in 1967, is cosponsored by the *Boston Globe* and the *Horn Book Magazine.* Originally, the award was given for text and illustration, but in 1976, the categories were changed. Currently, the award goes to one outstanding example of fiction, nonfiction, and illustration each year. The recipients of the awards need not be U.S. citizens; however, the books must have been published in the United States.

1967 *Text:* **The Little Fishes** by Erik Christian Haugaard (Houghton Mifflin)

Illustration: **London Bridge Is Falling Down** by Peter Spier (Doubleday)

1968 *Text:* **The Spring Rider** by John Lawson (Crowell)

Illustration: **Tikki Tikki Tembo** by Arlene Mosel, illustrated by Blair Lent (Holt)

1969 *Text:* **A Wizard of Earthsea** by Ursula K. Le Guin (Houghton Mifflin)

Illustration: **The Adventures of Paddy Pork** by John S. Goodall (Harcourt)

1970 *Text:* **The Intruder** by John Rowe Townsend (Lippincott)

Illustration: **Hi, Cat!** by Ezra Jack Keats (Macmillan)

1971 *Text:* **A Room Made of Windows** by Eleanor Cameron (Atlantic/Little, Brown)

Illustration: **If I Built a Village** by Kazue Mizumura (Crowell)

1972 *Text:* **Tristan and Iseult** by Rosemary Sutcliff (Dutton)

Illustration: **Mr. Gumpy's Outing** by John Burningham (Holt)

1973 *Text:* **The Dark Is Rising** by Susan Cooper (Atheneum/McElderry)

Illustration: **King Stork** by Trina Schart Hyman (Little, Brown)

1974 *Text:* **M. C. Higgins, the Great** by Virginia Hamilton (Macmillan)

Illustration: **Jambo Means Hello** by Muriel Feelings, illustrated by Tom Feelings (Dial)

1975 *Text:* **Transport 7-41-R** by T. Degens (Viking)

Illustration: **Anno's Alphabet** by Mitsumasa Anno (Crowell)

1976 *Fiction:* **Unleaving** by Jill Paton Walsh (Farrar)

Nonfiction: **Voyaging to Cathay: Americans in the China Trade** by Alfred Tamarin and Shirley Glubok (Viking)

Illustration: **Thirteen** by Remy Charlip and Jerry Joyner (Parents)

1977 *Fiction:* **Child of the Owl** by Laurence Yep (Harper)

Nonfiction: **Chance, Luck and Density** by Peter Dickinson (Atlantic/Little, Brown)

Illustration: **Granfa' Grig Had a Pig and Other Rhymes** by Wallace Tripp (Little, Brown)

1978 *Fiction:* **The Westing Game** by Ellen Raskin (Dutton)

Nonfiction: **Mischling, Second Degree: My Childhood in Nazi Germany** by Ilse Koehn (Greenwillow)

Illustration: **Anno's Journey** by Mitsumasa Anno (Philomel)

1979 *Fiction:* **Humbug Mountain** by Sid Fleischman (Atlantic/Little, Brown)

Nonfiction: **The Road from Home: The Story of an Armenian Girl** by David Kherdian (Greenwillow)

Illustration: **The Snowman** by Raymond Briggs (Random House)

1980 *Fiction: **Conrad's War*** by Andrew Davies (Crown)

*Nonfiction: **Building: The Fight against Gravity*** by Mario Salvadori (Atheneum/McElderry)

*Illustration: **The Garden of Abdul Gasazi*** by Chris Van Allsburg (Houghton Mifflin)

1981 *Fiction: **The Leaving*** by Lynn Hall (Scribner's)

*Nonfiction: **The Weaver's Gift*** by Kathryn Lasky (Warne)

*Illustration: **Outside Over There*** by Maurice Sendak (Harper)

1982 *Fiction: **Playing Beatie Bow*** by Ruth Park (Atheneum)

*Nonfiction: **Upon the Head of the Goat: A Childhood in Hungary, 1939–1944*** by Aranka Siegal (Farrar)

*Illustration: **A Visit to William Blake's Inn: Poems for Innocent and Experienced Travelers*** by Nancy Willard, illustrated by Alice and Martin Provensen (Harcourt)

1983 *Fiction: **Sweet Whispers, Brother Rush*** by Virginia Hamilton (Philomel)

*Nonfiction: **Behind Barbed Wire: The Imprisonment of Japanese Americans During World War II*** by Daniel S. Davis (Dutton)

*Illustration: **A Chair for My Mother*** by Vera B. Williams (Greenwillow)

1984 *Fiction: **A Little Fear*** by Patricia Wrightson (McElderry/ Atheneum)

*Nonfiction: **The Double Life of Pocahontas*** by Jean Fritz (Putnam)

*Illustration: **Jonah and the Great Fish*** retold and illustrated by Warwick Hutton (McElderry/Atheneum)

1985 *Fiction: **The Moves Make the Man*** by Bruce Brooks (Harper)

*Nonfiction: **Commodore Perry in the Land of the Shogun*** by Rhoda Blumberg (Lothrop)

*Illustration: **Mama Don't Allow*** by Thatcher Hurd (Harper)

1986 *Fiction: **In Summer Light*** by Zibby O'Neal (Viking)

*Nonfiction: **Auks, Rocks, and the Odd Dinosaur: Inside Stories from the Smithsonian Museum of Natural History*** by Peggy Thomson (Crowell)

*Illustration: **Paper Crane*** by Molly Bang (Greenwillow)

1987 *Fiction: **Rabble Starkey*** by Lois Lowry (Houghton Mifflin)

*Nonfiction: **Pilgrims of Plimoth*** by Marcia Sewall (Atheneum)

*Illustration: **Mufaro's Beautiful Daughters: An African Tale*** by John Steptoe (Lothrop)

1988 *Fiction: **The Friendship*** by Mildred D. Taylor (Dial)

*Nonfiction: **Anthony Burns: The Defeat and Triumph of a Fugitive Slave*** by Virginia Hamilton (Knopf)

*Illustration: **The Boy of the Three-Year Nap*** by Dianne Snyder, illustrated by Allen Say (Houghton Mifflin)

1989 *Fiction: **Village by the Sea*** by Paula Fox (Orchard)

*Nonfiction: **The Way Things Work*** by David Macaulay (Houghton Mifflin)

*Illustration: **Shy Charles*** by Rosemary Wells (Dial)

1990 *Fiction: **Maniac Magee*** by Jerry Spinelli (Little, Brown)

*Nonfiction: **Great Little Madison*** by Jean Fritz (Putnam)

*Picture Book: **Lon Po Po: A Red Riding Hood Story from China*** by Ed Young (Philomel)

Honor Books

*Fiction: **Saturnalia*** by Paul Fleischman (Harper)

Stonewords by Pam Conrad (Harper)

*Nonfiction: **Insect Metamorphosis: From Egg to Adult*** by Ron and Nancy Goor, illustrated with photographs by Ron Goor (Atheneum)

*Picture Book: **Chicka Chicka Boom Boom*** by Bill Martin, Jr. and John Archambault, illustrated by Lois Ehlert (Simon)

1991 *Fiction: **True Confessions of Charlotte Doyle*** by Avi (Orchard)

*Nonfiction: **Appalachia: The Voices of Sleeping Birds*** by Cynthia Rylant (Harcourt)

*Picture Book: **Tale of the Mandarin Ducks*** by Katherine Paterson, illustrated by Leo and Diane Dillon (Lodestar)

Honor Books

*Fiction: **Paradise Cafe and Other Stories*** by Martha Brooks (Joy Street)

Judy Scuppernong by Brenda Seabrooke (Cobblehill)

*Nonfiction: **The Wright Brothers: How They Invented the Airplane*** by Russell Freedman (Holiday House)

Good Queen Bess: The Story of Elizabeth I of England by Diane Stanley and Peter Vennema, illustrated by Diane Stanley (Four Winds)

*Picture Books: **Aardvarks, Disembark!*** by Ann Jonas (Greenwillow)

Sophie and Lou by Petra Mathers (Harper)

1992 *Fiction: **Missing May*** by Cynthia Rylant (Orchard)

*Nonfiction: **Talking with Artists*** by Pat Cummings (Bradbury)

*Picture Book: **Seven Blind Mice*** by Ed Young (Philomel)

Honor Books

*Fiction: **Nothing but the Truth*** by Avi (Jackson/Orchard)

Somewhere in the Darkness by Walter Dean Myers (Scholastic)

*Nonfiction: **Red Leaf, Yellow Leaf*** by Lois Ehlert (Harcourt)

The Handmade Alphabet by Laura Rankin (Dial)

*Picture Book: **In the Tall, Tall Grass*** by Denise Fleming (Holt)

1993 *Fiction: **Ajeemah and His Son*** by James Berry (Harper)

*Nonfiction: **Sojourner Truth: Ain't I a Woman?*** by Patricia and Fredrick McKissack (Scholastic)

*Picture Book: **Fortune Tellers*** by Lloyd Alexander, illustrated by Trina Schart Hyman (Dutton)

Honor Books

*Fiction: **The Giver*** by Lois Lowry (Houghton)

*Nonfiction: **Lives of the Musicians: Good Times, Bad Times (and What the Neighbors Thought)*** by Kathleen Krull, illustrated by Kathryn Hewitt (Harcourt)

*Picture Books: **Komodo!*** by Peter Sís (Greenwillow)

Raven: A Trickster Tale from the Pacific Northwest by Gerald McDermott (Harcourt)

1994 *Fiction: **Scooter*** by Vera Williams (Greenwillow)

*Nonfiction: **Eleanor Roosevelt: A Life of Discovery*** by Russell Freedman (Houghton Mifflin)

*Picture Book: **Grandfather's Journey*** by Allen Say (Houghton Mifflin)

Honor Books

*Fiction: **Flour Babies*** by Anne Fine (Little)

Western Wind by Paula Fox (Orchard)

Nonfiction: Unconditional Surrender: U.S. Grant and the Civil War by Albert Marrin (Atheneum)

A Tree Place and Other Poems by Constance Levy, illustrated by Robert Sabuda (McElderry)

Picture Books: Owen by Kevin Henkes (Greenwillow)

A Small Tall Tale from the Far Far North by Peter Sís (Knopf)

1995 *Fiction: Some of the Kinder Planets* by Tim Wynne-Jones (Orchard)

Nonfiction: Abigail Adams: Witness to a Revolution by Natalie S. Bober (Atheneum)

Picture Book: John Henry by Julius Lester, illustrated by Jerry Pinkney (Dial)

Honor Books

Fiction: Jericho by Janet Hickman (Greenwillow)

Earthshine by Theresa Nelson (Jackson/Orchard)

Nonfiction: It's Perfectly Normal: Changing Bodies, Growing Up, Sex, and Sexual Health by Robie H. Harris, illustrated by Michael Emberley (Candlewick)

The Great Fire by Jim Murphy (Scholastic)

Picture Book: Swamp Angel by Anne Isaacs, illustrated by Paul O. Zelinsky (Dutton)

1996 *Fiction: Poppy* by Avi, illustrated by Brian Floca (Jackson/Orchard)

Nonfiction: Orphan Train Rider: One Boy's True Story by Andrea Warren (Houghton Mifflin)

Picture Book: In the Rain with Baby Duck by Amy Hest, illustrated by Jill Barton (Candlewick)

Honor Books

Fiction: The Moorchild by Eloise McGraw (McElderry)

Belle Prater's Boy by Ruth White (Farrar)

Nonfiction: The Boy Who Lived with the Bears: And Other Iroquois Stories by Joseph Bruchac, illustrated by Murv Jacob (Harper)

Haystack by Bonnie and Arthur Geisert, illustrated by Arthur Geisert (Houghton)

Picture Books: Fanny's Dream by Caralyn Buehner, illustrated by Mark Buehner (Dial)

Home Lovely by Lynne Rae Perkins (Greenwillow)

1997 *Fiction and Poetry: The Friends* by Kazumi Yumoto (Farrar)

Nonfiction: A Drop of Water: A Book of Science and Wonder by Walter Wick (Scholastic)

Picture Book: The Adventures of Sparrowboy by Brian Pinkney (Simon & Schuster)

Honor Books

Fiction and Poetry: Lily's Crossing by Patricia Reilly Giff (Delacorte)

Harlem by Walter Dean Myers, illustrated by Christopher Myers (Scholastic Press)

Nonfiction: Lou Gehrig: The Luckiest Man by David A. Adler, illustrated by Terry Widener (Gulliver/Harcourt)

Leonardo da Vinci written and illustrated by Diane Stanley (Morrow)

Picture Books: Home on the Bayou: A Cowboy's Story written and illustrated by G. Brian Karas (Simon)

Potato: A Tale from the Great Depression by Kate Lied, illustrated by Lisa Campbell Ernst (National Geographic)

1998 *Fiction and Poetry: The Circuit: Stories from the Life of a Migrant Child* by Francisco Jiménez (University of New Mexico Press)

Nonfiction: Leon's Story by Leon Walter Tillage, illustrated by Susan L. Roth (Farrar)

Picture Book: And If the Moon Could Talk by Kate Banks, illustrated by Georg Hallensleben (Foster/Farrar)

Honor Books

Fiction and Poetry: While No One Was Watching by Jane Leslie Conly (Holt)

My Louisiana Sky by Kimberly Willis Holt (Holt)

Nonfiction: Martha Graham: A Dancer's Life by Russell Freedman (Clarion)

Chuck Close Up Close by Jan Greenberg and Sandra Jordan (DK Ink)

Picture Books: Seven Brave Women by Betsy Hearne, illustrated by Bethanne Andersen (Greenwillow)

Popcorn: Poems written and illustrated by James Stevenson (Greenwillow)

1999 *Fiction: Holes* by Louis Sachar (Foster/Farrar)

Nonfiction: The Top of the World: Climbing Mount Everest written and illustrated by Steve Jenkins (Houghton Mifflin)

Picture Book: Red-Eyed Tree Frog by Joy Cowley, illustrated with photographs by Nic Bishop (Scholastic Press)

Honor Books

Fiction: The Trolls by Polly Horvath (Farrar, Straus, & Giroux)

Monster by Walter Dean Myers, illustrated by Christopher Myers (HarperCollins)

Nonfiction: Shipwreck at the Bottom of the World: The Extraordinary True Story of Shackleton and the Endurance by Jennifer Armstrong (Crown)

William Shakespeare & the Globe written and illustrated by Aliki (HarperCollins)

Picture Books: Dance by Bill T. Jones and Susan Kuklin, illustrated with photographs by Susan Kuklin (Hyperion)

The Owl and the Pussycat by Edward Lear, illustrated by James Marshall (di Capua/HarperCollins)

Special Citation: Tibet: Through the Red Box written and illustrated by Peter Sís (Foster/Farrar)

2000 *Fiction: The Folk Keeper* by Franny Billingsley (Atheneum)

Nonfiction: Sir Walter Ralegh and the Quest for El Dorado by Marc Aronson (Clarion)

Picture Book: Henry Hikes to Fitchburg written and illustrated by D. B. Johnson (Houghton)

Honor Books

Fiction: King of Shadows by Susan Cooper (McElderry)

145th Street: Short Stories by Walter Dean Myers (Delacorte)

Nonfiction: Osceola: Memories of a Sharecropper's Daughter collected and edited by Alan Govenar, illustrated by Shane W. Evans (Jump at the Sun/Hyperion)

Sitting Bull and His World by Albert Marrin (Farrar, Straus, & Giroux)

Picture Books: Buttons written and illustrated by Brock Cole (Farrar, Straus, & Giroux)

a day, a dog illustrated by Gabrielle Vincent (Front Street)

2001 *Fiction and Poetry: Carver: A Life in Poems* by Marilyn Nelson (Front Street)

Nonfiction: **The Longitude Prize** by Joan Dash, illustrated by Dusan Petricic (Foster/Farrar)

Picture Book: **Cold Feet** by Cynthia DeFelice, illustrated by Robert Andrew Parker (DK Ink)

Honor Books

Fiction: **Everything on a Waffle** by Polly Horvath (Farrar)

Troy by Adèle Geras (Harcourt)

Nonfiction: **Rocks in His Head** by Carol Otis Hurst, illustrated by James Stevenson (Greenwillow)

Uncommon Traveler: Mary Kingsley in Africa written and illustrated by Tomek Bogacki (Foster/Farrar)

The Stray Dog retold and illustrated by Marc Simont (HarperCollins)

2002 *Fiction:* **The Lord of the Deep** by Graham Salisbury (Delacorte)

Nonfiction: **This Land Was Made for You and Me: The Life Songs of Woody Guthrie** by Elizabeth Partridge (Viking)

Picture Book: **"Let's Get a Pup!" Said Kate** written and illustrated by Bob Graham (Candlewick)

Honor Books

Fiction: **Amber Was Brave, Essie Was Smart** written and illustrated by Vera B. Williams (Greenwillow)

Saffy's Angel by Hilary McKay (McElderry)

Nonfiction: **Handel, Who Knew What He Liked** by M. T. Anderson (Candlewick)

Woody Guthrie: Poet of the People written and illustrated by Bonnie Christensen (Knopf)

Picture Book: **I Stink!** by Kate McMullen, illustrated by Jim McMullen (Cotler/HarperCollins)

Little Rat Sets Sail by Monica Bang-Campbell, illustrated by Molly Bang (Harcourt)

2003 *Fiction:* **The Jamie and Angus Stories** by Ann Fine (Candlewick)

Nonfiction: **Fireboat: the Heroic Adventures of John J. Harvey** by Maira Kalman (Putnam)

Picture Book: **Big Momma Makes the World** by Phyllis Root, illustrated by Helen Oxenbury (Candlewick)

Honor Books

Fiction: **Feed** by M. T. Andersen (Candlewick)

Locomotion by Jacqueline Woodson (Putnam)

Nonfiction: **To Fly: The Story of the Wright Brothers** by Wendy C. Old (Clarion)

Revenge of the Whale: The True Story of the Whaleship Essex by Nathaniel Philbrick (Putnam)

Picture Book: **Dahlia** by Barbara McClintock (Foster/Farrar)

blue's journey by Walter Dean Myers, illustrated by Christopher A. Myers (Holiday)

2004 *Fiction:* **The Fire Eaters** by David Almond (Delacorte)

Nonfiction: **An American Plague: the True and Terrifying Story of the Yellow Fever Epidemic of 1793** by Jim Murphy (Clarion)

Picture Book: **The Man Who Walked Between the Towers** by Mordicai Gerstien (Roaring Brook)

Honor Books

Fiction: **God Went to Beauty School** by Cynthia Rylant (HarperTempest)

The Amulet of Samarkand: The Bartimaeus Trilogy, Book One by Jonathan Stroud (Hyperion)

Nonfiction: **Surprising Sharks** by Nicola Davies (Candlewick)

The Man Who Went to the Far Side of the Moon: The Story of Apollo 11 **Astronaut Michael Collins** by Bea Uusma Schyffert (Chronicle)

Picture Book: **The Shape Game** by Anthony Browne (Farrar)

Snow Music by Lynne Rae Perkins (Greenwillow)

2005

Fiction and Poetry: **The Schwa Was Here** by Neal Schusterman (Dutton)

Honor Books

Fiction and Poetry: **Kalpana's Dream** by Judith Clarke (Front Street)

A Wreath for Emmett Till by Marilyn Nelson (Houghton)

Nonfiction: **The Race to Save the Lord God Bird** by Phillip Hoose (Kroupa/Farrar)

Honor Books

Good Brother, Bad Brother by James Cross Giblin (Clarion)

Michael Rosen's Sad Book by Michael Rosen, illustrated by Quentin Blake (Candlewick)

Picture Book: **Traction Man Is Here!** by Mini Grey (Knopf)

Honor Books

That New Animal by Emily Jenkins, illustrated by Pierre Pratt (Foster/Farrar)

The Hello, Goodbye Window by Norton Juster, illustrated by Chris Raschka (di Capua/Hyperion)

2006

Picture Book: **Leaf Man** by Lois Ehlert (Harcourt)

Honor Books

Mama: A True Story in Which a Baby Hippo Loses His Mama during a Tsunami, but Finds a New Home, and a New Mama by Jeanette Winter (Harcourt)

Sky Boys: How They Built the Empire State Building by Deborah Hopkinson, illustrated by James E. Ransome (Schwartz & Wade/Random)

Fiction and Poetry: **The Miraculous Journey of Edward Tulane** by Kate DiCamillo, illustrated by Bagram Ibatoulline (Candlewick)

Honor Books

Yellow Elephant: A Bright Bestiary by Julie Larios, illustrated by Julie Paschkis (Harcourt)

Yellow Star by Jennifer Roy (Marshall Cavendish)

Nonfiction: **If You Decide to Go to the Moon** by Faith McNulty, illustrated by Steven Kellogg (Scholastic)

Honor Books

A Mother's Journey by Sandra Markle, illustrated by Alan Marks (Charlesbridge)

Wildfire by Taylor Morrison (Lorraine/Houghton)

2007

Picture Book: **Dog and Bear: Two Friends, Three Stories** written and illustrated by Laura Vaccaro Seeger (Porter/Roaring Brook)

Honor Books

365 Penguins by Jean-Luc Fromental, illustrated by Joelle Jolivet (Abrams)

Wolves written and illustrated by Emily Gravett (Simon)

Fiction and Poetry: The Astonishing Life of Octavian Nothing, Traitor to the Nation, Volume I: The Pox Party by M. T. Anderson (Candlewick)

Honor Books

Clementine by Sara Pennypacker, illustrated by Marla Frazee (Hyperion)

Rex Zero and the End of the World by Tim Wynne-Jones (Kroupa/Farrar)

Nonfiction: The Strongest Man in the World: Louis Cyr written and illustrated by Nicolas Debon (Groundwood)

Honor Books

Tracking Trash: Flotsam, Jetsam, and the Science of Ocean Motion by Loree Griffin Burns (Houghton)

Escape! by Sid Fleischman (Greenwillow)

2008

Picture Book: At Night by Jonathan Bean (Farrar)

Honor Books

Fred Stays with Me! by Nancy Coffelt, illustrated by Tricia Tusa (Little)

A Couple of Boys Have the Best Week Ever by Marla Frazee (Harcourt)

Fiction and Poetry: The Absolutely True Diary of a Part-Time Indian by Sherman Alexie, illustrated by Ellen Forney (Little)

Honor Books

Shooting the Moon by Frances O'Roark Dowell (Atheneum)

Savvy by Ingrid Law (Walden/Dial)

Nonfiction: The Wall by Peter Sís (Foster/Farrar)

Honor Books

Frogs by Nic Bishop (Scholastic)

What to Do About Alice? by Barbara Kerley, illustrated by Edwin Fotheringham (Scholastic)

Special Citation: The Arrival by Shaun Tan (Levine/Scholastic)

2009

Picture Book: Bubble Trouble by Margaret Mahy, illustrated by Polly Dunbar (Clarion)

Honor Books

Old Bear by Kevin Henkes (Greenwillow/HarperCollins)

Higher! Higher! by Leslie Patricelli (Candlewick)

Fiction: Nation by Terry Pratchett (HarperCollins)

Honor Books

The Astonishing Life of Octavian Nothing, Traitor to the Nation, Volume II: The Kingdom on the Waves by M. T. Anderson (Candlewick)

The Graveyard Book by Neil Gaiman (HarperCollins)

Nonfiction: The Lincolns: A Scrapbook Look at Abraham and Mary by Candace Fleming (Schwartz & Wade/Random House)

Honor Books

The Way We Work by David Macaulay with Richard Walker, illustrated by David Macaulay (Lorraine/Houghton)

Almost Astronauts: 13 Women Who Dared to Dream by Tanya Lee Stone (Candlewick)

2010

Picture Book: I Know Here by Laurel Croza, illustrated by Matt James (Groundwood)

Honor Books

The Lion and the Mouse by Jerry Pinkney (Little, Brown)

It's a Secret! by John Burningham (Candlewick)

Fiction: When You Reach Me by Rebecca Stead (Lamb/Random)

Honor Books

The Dreamer by Pam Muñoz Ryan, illustrated by Peter Sís (Scholastic)

A Conspiracy of Kings by Megan Whalen Turner (Greenwillow)

Nonfiction: Marching for Freedom: Walk Together, Children, and Don't You Grow Weary by Elizabeth Partridge (Viking)

Honor Books

Anne Frank: Her Life in Words and Pictures by Menno Metselaar and Ruud van der Rol (Flash Point/Roaring Brook)

Smile by Raina Telgemeier (Graphix/Scholastic)

2011

Picture Book: Pocketful of Posies: A Treasury of Nursery Rhymes by Salley Mavor (Houghton)

Honor Books

Dark Emperor and Other Poems of the Night by Joyce Sidman, illustrated by Rick Allen (Houghton)

Pecan Pie Baby by Jacqueline Woodson, illustrated by Sophie Blackall (Putnam)

Fiction: Blink & Caution by Tim Wynne-Jones (Candlewick)

Honor Books

Chime by Franny Billingsley (Dial)

Anna Hibiscus by Atinuke (Kane Miller)

Nonfiction: The Notorious Benedict Arnold: A True Story of Adventure, Heroism, & Treachery by Steve Sheinkin (Flash Point/Roaring Brook)

Honor Books

Into the Unknown: How Great Explorers Found Their Way by Land, Sea, and Air by Stewart Ross, illustrated by Stephen Biesty (Candlewick)

Can We Save the Tiger? by Martin Jenkins, illustrated by Vicky White (Candlewick)

2012

Picture Book: Extra Yarn by Mac Barnett, illustrated by Jon Klassen (Balzer + Bray, a HarperCollins imprint)

Honor Books

And Then It's Spring by Julie Fogliano, illustrated by Erin E. Stead (Neal Porter/Roaring Brook Press, a Macmillan imprint)

And the Soldiers Sang by J. Patrick Lewis, illustrated by Gary Kelley (Creative Editions)

Fiction: No Crystal Stair: A Documentary Novel of the Life and Work of Lewis Michaux, Harlem Bookseller by Vaunda Micheaux Nelson, illustrated by R. Gregory Christie (Carolrhoda Lab, an imprint of Lerner)

Honor Books

Life: An Exploded Diagram by Mal Peet (Candlewick Press)

Code Name Verity by Elizabeth Wein (Hyperion Books for Children, a Disney imprint)

Nonfiction: Chuck Close: Face Book written and illustrated by Chuck Close (Abrams Books for Young Readers)

Honor Books

Georgia in Hawaii: When Georgia O'Keeffe Painted What She Pleased by Amy Novesky, illustrated by Yuyi Morales (Harcourt Children's Books, Houghton Mifflin Harcourt imprint)

The Elephant Scientist by Caitlin O'Connell & Donna M. Jackson, photographs by Caitlin O'Connell and Timothy Rodwell (Houghton Mifflin Books for Children, Houghton Mifflin Harcourt imprint)

2013

Picture Book: Building Our House, written and illustrated by Jonathan Bean (Farrar Straus and Giroux, an imprint of Macmillan)

Honor Books

Open This Little Book by Jesse Klausmeier, illustrated by Suzy Lee (Chronicle Books)

Black Dog written and illustrated by Levi Pinfold (Templar Books, an imprint of Candlewick Press)

Fiction: Eleanor & Park by Rainbow Rowell (St. Martin's Griffin, an imprint of Macmillan)

Honor Books

Seraphina by Rachel Hartman (Random House Books for Young Readers)

A Corner of White by Jaclyn Moriarty (Arthur A. Levine Books, an imprint of Scholastic Inc.)

Nonfiction: Electric Ben: The Amazing Life and Times of Benjamin Franklin written and illustrated by Robert Byrd (Dial Books for Young Readers, an imprint of Penguin Group)

Honor Books

Dreaming Up: A Celebration of Building written and illustrated by Christy Hale (Lee & Low Books)

Hand in Hand: Ten Black Men Who Changed America by Andrea Davis Pinkney, illustrated by Brian Pinkney (Disney/Jump at the Sun Books, an imprint of Disney Book Group)

RANDOLPH CALDECOTT MEDAL

The Randolph Caldecott Medal, named in honor of the nineteenth-century illustrator of children's books, is awarded annually under the supervision of the Association for Library Service to Children of the American Library Association. It is awarded to the illustrator of the most distinguished children's book published in the United States in the previous year. Usually, one or more Honor Books are also chosen. The award is limited to residents or citizens of the United States.

1938 *Animals of the Bible* by Helen Dean Fish, illustrated by Dorothy P. Lathrop (Lippincott)

Honor Books

Four and Twenty Blackbirds by Helen Dean Fish, illustrated by Robert Lawson (Stokes)

Seven Simeons by Boris Artzybasheff (Viking)

1939 *Mei Li* by Thomas Handforth (Doubleday)

Honor Books

Andy and the Lion by James Daugherty (Viking)

Barkis by Clare Newberry (Harper)

The Forest Pool by Laura Adams Armer (Longman)

Snow White and the Seven Dwarfs by Wanda Gág (Coward)

Wee Gillis by Munro Leaf, illustrated by Robert Lawson (Viking)

1940 *Abraham Lincoln* by Ingri and Edgar Parin D'Aulaire (Doubleday)

Honor Books

The Ageless Story by Lauren Ford (Dodd)

Cock-a-Doodle Doo by Berta and Elmer Hader (Macmillan)

Madeline by Ludwig Bemelmans (Viking)

1941 *They Were Strong and Good* by Robert Lawson (Viking)

Honor Book: April's Kittens by Clare Newberry (Harper)

1942 *Make Way for Ducklings* by Robert McCloskey (Viking)

Honor Books

An American ABC by Maud and Miska Petersham (Macmillan)

In My Mother's House by Ann Nolan Clark, illustrated by Velino Herrera (Viking)

Nothing at All by Wanda Gág (Coward)

Paddle-to-the-Sea by Holling C. Holling (Houghton Mifflin)

1943 *The Little House* by Virginia Lee Burton (Houghton Mifflin)

Honor Books

Dash and Dart by Mary and Conrad Buff (Viking)

Marshmallow by Clare Newberry (Harper)

1944 *Many Moons* by James Thurber, illustrated by Louis Slobodkin (Harcourt)

Honor Books

A Child's Good Night Book by Margaret Wise Brown, illustrated by Jean Charlot (Scott)

Good Luck Horse by Chin-Yi Chan, illustrated by Plao Chan (Whittlesey)

The Mighty Hunter by Berta and Elmer Hader (Macmillan)

Pierre Pigeon by Lee Kingman, illustrated by Arnold E. Bare (Houghton Mifflin)

Small Rain: Verses from the Bible selected by Jessie Orton Jones, illustrated by Elizabeth Orton Jones (Viking)

1945 *Prayer for a Child* by Rachel Field, illustrated by Elizabeth Orton Jones (Macmillan)

Honor Books

The Christmas Anna Angel by Ruth Sawyer, illustrated by Kate Seredy (Viking)

In the Forest by Marie Hall Ets (Viking)

Mother Goose illustrated by Tasha Tudor (Walck)

Yonie Wondernose by Marguerite de Angeli (Doubleday)

1946 *The Rooster Crows* (traditional Mother Goose) illustrated by Maud and Miska Petersham (Macmillan)

Honor Books

Little Lost Lamb by Golden MacDonald, illustrated by Leonard Weisgard (Doubleday)

My Mother Is the Most Beautiful Woman in the World by Becky Reyher, illustrated by Ruth C. Gannett (Lothrop)

Sing Mother Goose by Opal Wheeler, illustrated by Marjorie Torrey (Dutton)

You Can Write Chinese by Kurt Wiese (Viking)

1947 *The Little Island* by Golden MacDonald, illustrated by Leonard Weisgard (Doubleday)

Honor Books

Boats on the River by Marjorie Flack, illustrated by Jay Hyde Barnum (Viking)

Pedro, the Angel of Olvera Street by Leo Politi (Scribner's)

Rain Drop Splash by Alvin Tresselt, illustrated by Leonard Weisgard (Lothrop)

Sing in Praise: A Collection of the Best Loved Hymns by Opal Wheeler, illustrated by Marjorie Torrey (Dutton)

Timothy Turtle by Al Graham, illustrated by Tony Palazzo (Welch)

1948 *White Snow, Bright Snow* by Alvin Tresselt, illustrated by Roger Duvoisin (Lothrop)

Honor Books

Bambino the Clown by George Schreiber (Viking)

McElligot's Pool by Dr. Seuss (Random House)

Roger and the Fox by Lavinia Davis, illustrated by Hildegard Woodward (Doubleday)

Song of Robin Hood edited by Anne Malcolmson, illustrated by Virginia Lee Burton (Houghton Mifflin)

Stone Soup by Marcia Brown (Scribner's)

1949 *The Big Snow* by Berta and Elmer Hader (Macmillan)

Honor Books

All Around the Town by Phyllis McGinley, illustrated by Helen Stone (Lippincott)

Blueberries for Sal by Robert McCloskey (Viking)

Fish in the Air by Kurt Wiese (Viking)

Juanita by Leo Politi (Scribner's)

1950 *Song of the Swallows* by Leo Politi (Scribner's)

Honor Books

America's Ethan Allen by Stewart Holbrook, illustrated by Lynd Ward (Houghton Mifflin)

Bartholomew and the Oobleck by Dr. Seuss (Random House)

The Happy Day by Ruth Krauss, illustrated by Marc Simont (Harper)

Henry Fisherman by Marcia Brown (Scribner's)

The Wild Birthday Cake by Lavinia Davis, illustrated by Hildegard Woodward (Doubleday)

1951 *The Egg Tree* by Katherine Milhous (Scribner's)

Honor Books

Dick Whittington and His Cat by Marcia Brown (Scribner's)

If I Ran the Zoo by Dr. Seuss (Random House)

The Most Wonderful Doll in the World by Phyllis McGinley, illustrated by Helen Stone (Lippincott)

T-Bone, the Baby Sitter by Clare Newberry (Harper)

The Two Reds by Will, illustrated by Nicolas (Harcourt)

1952 *Finders Keepers* by Will, illustrated by Nicolas (Harcourt)

Honor Books

All Falling Down by Gene Zion, illustrated by Margaret Bloy Graham (Harper)

Bear Party by William Pe'ne du Bois (Viking)

Feather Mountain by Elizabeth Olds (Houghton Mifflin)

Mr. T. W. Anthony Woo by Marie Hall Ets (Viking)

Skipper John's Cook by Marcia Brown (Scribner's)

1953 *The Biggest Bear* by Lynd Ward (Houghton Mifflin)

Honor Books

Ape in a Cape by Fritz Eichenberg (Harcourt)

Five Little Monkeys by Juliet Kepes (Houghton Mifflin)

One Morning in Maine by Robert McCloskey (Viking)

Puss in Boots by Charles Perrault, illustrated by Marcia Brown (Scribner's)

The Storm Book by Charlotte Zolotow, illustrated by Margaret Bloy Graham (Harper)

1954 *Madeline's Rescue* by Ludwig Bemelmans (Viking)

Honor Books

A Very Special House by Ruth Krauss, illustrated by Maurice Sendak (Harper)

Green Eyes by A. Birnbaum (Capitol)

Journey Cake, Ho! by Ruth Sawyer, illustrated by Robert McCloskey (Viking)

The Steadfast Tin Soldier by Hans Christian Andersen, illustrated by Marcia Brown (Scribner's)

When Will the World Be Mine? by Miriam Schlein, illustrated by Jean Charlot (Scott)

1955 *Cinderella, or the Little Glass Slipper* by Charles Perrault, illustrated by Marcia Brown (Scribner's)

Honor Books

Book of Nursery and Mother Goose Rhymes illustrated by Marguerite de Angeli (Doubleday)

The Thanksgiving Story by Alice Dalgliesh, illustrated by Helen Sewell (Scribner's)

Wheel on the Chimney by Margaret Wise Brown, illustrated by Tibor Gergely (Lippincott)

1956 *Frog Went A-Courtin'* retold by John Langstaff, illustrated by Feodor Rojankovsky (Harcourt)

Honor Books

Crow Boy by Taro Yashima (Viking)

Play with Me by Marie Hall Ets (Viking)

1957 *A Tree Is Nice* by Janice May Udry, illustrated by Marc Simont (Harper)

Honor Books

Anatole by Eve Titus, illustrated by Paul Galdone (McGraw-Hill)

Gillespie and the Guards by Benjamin Elkin, illustrated by James Daugherty (Viking)

Lion by William Pe'ne du Bois (Viking)

Mr. Penny's Race Horse by Marie Hall Ets (Viking)

1 Is One by Tasha Tudor (Walck)

1958 *Time of Wonder* by Robert McCloskey (Viking)

Honor Books

Anatole and the Cat by Eve Titus, illustrated by Paul Galdone (McGraw-Hill)

Fly High, Fly Low by Don Freeman (Viking)

1959 *Chanticleer and the Fox* adapted from Chaucer, illustrated by Barbara Cooney (Crowell)

Honor Books

The House That Jack Built by Antonio Frasconi (Harcourt)

Umbrella by Taro Yashima (Viking)

What Do You Say, Dear? by Sesyle Joslin, illustrated by Maurice Sendak (Scott)

1960 *Nine Days to Christmas* by Marie Hall Ets and Aurora Labastida, illustrated by Marie Hall Ets (Viking)

Honor Books

Houses from the Sea by Alice E. Goudey, illustrated by Adrienne Adams (Scribner's)

The Moon Jumpers by Janice May Udry, illustrated by Maurice Sendak (Harper)

1961 *Baboushka and the Three Kings* by Ruth Robbins, illustrated by Nicholas Sidjakov (Parnassus)

Honor Book: Inch by Inch by Leo Lionni (Astor-Honor)

1962 *Once a Mouse* by Marcia Brown (Scribner's)

Honor Books

The Day We Saw the Sun Come Up by Alice E. Goudey, illustrated by Adrienne Adams (Scribner's)

The Fox Went Out on a Chilly Night illustrated by Peter Spier (Doubleday)

Little Bear's Visit by Else Holmelund Minarik, illustrated by Maurice Sendak (Harper)

1963 *The Snowy Day* by Ezra Jack Keats (Viking)

Honor Books

Mr. Rabbit and the Lovely Present by Charlotte Zolotow, illustrated by Maurice Sendak (Harper)

The Sun Is a Golden Earring by Natalia M. Belting, illustrated by Bernarda Bryson (Holt)

1964 *Where the Wild Things Are* by Maurice Sendak (Harper)

Honor Books

All in the Morning Early by Sorche Nic Leodhas, illustrated by Evaline Ness (Holt)

Mother Goose and Nursery Rhymes illustrated by Philip Reed (Atheneum)

Swimmy by Leo Lionni (Pantheon)

1965 *May I Bring a Friend?* by Beatrice Schenk de Regniers, illustrated by Beni Montresor (Atheneum)

Honor Books

A Pocketful of Cricket by Rebecca Caudill, illustrated by Evaline Ness (Holt)

Rain Makes Applesauce by Julian Scheer, illustrated by Marvin Bileck (Holiday House)

The Wave by Margaret Hodges, illustrated by Blair Lent (Houghton Mifflin)

1966 *Always Room for One More* by Sorche Nic Leodhas, illustrated by Nonny Hogrogian (Holt)

Honor Books

Hide and Seek Fog by Alvin Tresselt, illustrated by Roger Duvoisin (Lothrop)

Just Me by Marie Hall Ets (Viking)

Tom Tit Tot by Evaline Ness (Scribner's)

1967 *Sam, Bangs & Moonshine* by Evaline Ness (Holt)

Honor Book: One Wide River to Cross by Barbara Emberley, illustrated by Ed Emberley (Prentice-Hall)

1968 *Drummer Hoff* by Barbara Emberley, illustrated by Ed Emberley (Prentice-Hall)

Honor Books

The Emperor and the Kite by Jane Yolen, illustrated by Ed Young (World)

Frederick by Leo Lionni (Pantheon)

Seashore Story by Taro Yashima (Viking)

1969 *The Fool of the World and the Flying Ship* retold by Arthur Ransome, illustrated by Uri Shulevitz (Farrar)

Honor Book: Why the Sun and the Moon Live in the Sky by Elphinstone Dayrell, illustrated by Blair Lent (Houghton Mifflin)

1970 *Sylvester and the Magic Pebble* by William Steig (Windmill/Simon & Schuster)

Honor Books

Alexander and the Wind-Up Mouse by Leo Lionni (Pantheon)

Goggles! by Ezra Jack Keats (Macmillan)

The Judge by Harve Zemach, illustrated by Margot Zemach (Farrar)

Pop Corn & Ma Goodness by Edna Mitchell Preston, illustrated by Robert Andrew Parker (Viking)

Thy Friend, Obadiah by Brinton Turkle (Viking)

1971 *A Story, a Story* by Gail E. Haley (Atheneum)

Honor Books

The Angry Moon by William Sleator, illustrated by Blair Lent (Atlantic/Little, Brown)

Frog and Toad Are Friends by Arnold Lobel (Harper)

In the Night Kitchen by Maurice Sendak (Harper)

1972 *One Fine Day* by Nonny Hogrogian (Macmillan)

Honor Books

Hildilid's Night by Cheli Durán Ryan, illustrated by Arnold Lobel (Macmillan)

If All the Seas Were One Sea by Janina Domanska (Macmillan)

Moja Means One by Muriel Feelings, illustrated by Tom Feelings (Dial)

1973 *The Funny Little Woman* retold by Arlene Mosel, illustrated by Blair Lent (Dutton)

Honor Books

Anansi the Spider adapted and illustrated by Gerald McDermott (Holt)

Hosie's Alphabet by Hosea, Tobias, and Lisa Baskin, illustrated by Leonard Baskin (Viking)

Snow White and the Seven Dwarfs illustrated by Nancy Eckholm Burkert (Farrar)

When Clay Sings by Byrd Baylor, illustrated by Tom Bahti (Scribner's)

1974 *Duffy and the Devil* retold by Harve Zemach, illustrated by Margot Zemach (Farrar)

Honor Books

Cathedral by David Macaulay (Houghton Mifflin)

Three Jovial Huntsmen by Susan Jeffers (Bradbury)

1975 *Arrow to the Sun* by Gerald McDermott (Viking)

Honor Book: Jambo Means Hello by Muriel Feelings, illustrated by Tom Feelings (Dial)

1976 *Why Mosquitoes Buzz in People's Ears* by Verna Aardema, illustrated by Leo and Diane Dillon (Dial)

Honor Books

The Desert Is Theirs by Byrd Baylor, illustrated by Peter Parnall (Scribner's)

Strega Nona retold and illustrated by Tomie de Paola (Prentice)

1977 *Ashanti to Zulu: African Traditions* by Margaret Musgrove, illustrated by Leo and Diane Dillon (Dial)

Honor Books

The Amazing Bone by William Steig (Farrar)

The Contest retold and illustrated by Nonny Hogrogian (Greenwillow)

Fish for Supper by M. B. Goffstein (Dial)

The Golem by Beverly Brodsky McDermott (Lippincott)

Hawk, I'm Your Brother by Byrd Baylor, illustrated by Peter Parnall (Scribner's)

1978 *Noah's Ark* illustrated by Peter Spier (Doubleday)

Honor Books

Castle by David Macaulay (Houghton Mifflin)

It Could Always Be Worse by Margot Zemach (Farrar)

1979 *The Girl Who Loved Wild Horses* by Paul Goble (Bradbury)

Honor Books

Freight Train by Donald Crews (Greenwillow)

The Way to Start a Day by Byrd Baylor, illustrated by Peter Parnall (Scribner's)

1980 *Ox-Cart Man* by Donald Hall, illustrated by Barbara Cooney (Viking)

Honor Books

Ben's Trumpet by Rachel Isadora (Greenwillow)

The Garden of Abdul Gasazi by Chris Van Allsburg (Houghton Mifflin)

The Treasure by Uri Shulevitz (Farrar)

1981 *Fables* by Arnold Lobel (Harper)

Honor Books

The Bremen Town Musicians retold and illustrated by Ilse Plume (Doubleday)

The Grey Lady and the Strawberry Snatcher by Molly Bang (Four Winds)

Mice Twice by Joseph Low (McElderry)

Truck by Donald Crews (Greenwillow)

1982 *Jumanji* by Chris Van Allsburg (Houghton Mifflin)

Honor Books

On Market Street by Arnold Lobel, illustrated by Anita Lobel (Greenwillow)

Outside Over There by Maurice Sendak (Harper)

A Visit to William Blake's Inn: Poems for Innocent and Experienced Travelers by Nancy Willard, illustrated by Alice and Martin Provensen (Harcourt)

Where the Buffaloes Begin by Olaf Baker, illustrated by Stephen Gammell (Viking)

1983 *Shadow* by Blaise Cendrars, illustrated by Marcia Brown (Scribner's)

Honor Books

A Chair for My Mother by Vera B. Williams (Greenwillow)

When I Was Young in the Mountains by Cynthia Rylant, illustrated by Diane Goode (Dutton)

1984 *The Glorious Flight: Across the Channel with Louis Blériot* by Alice and Martin Provensen (Viking)

Honor Books

Little Red Riding Hood retold and illustrated by Trina Schart Hyman (Holiday House)

Ten, Nine, Eight by Molly Bang (Greenwillow)

1985 *Saint George and the Dragon* by Margaret Hodges, illustrated by Trina Schart Hyman (Little, Brown)

Honor Books

Hansel and Gretel retold by Rika Lesser, illustrated by Paul O. Zelinsky (Dodd)

Have You Seen My Duckling? by Nancy Tafuri (Greenwillow)

The Story of Jumping Mouse retold and illustrated by John Steptoe (Lothrop)

1986 *The Polar Express* by Chris Van Allsburg (Houghton Mifflin)

Honor Books

King Bidgood's in the Bathtub by Audrey Wood, illustrated by Don Wood (Harcourt)

The Relatives Came by Cynthia Rylant, illustrated by Stephen Gammell (Bradbury)

1987 *Hey, Al!* by Arthur Yorinks, illustrated by Richard Egielski (Farrar)

Honor Books

Alphabatics by Suse MacDonald (Bradbury)

Rumpelstiltskin by Paul O. Zelinsky (Dutton)

The Village of Round and Square Houses by Ann Grifalconi (Little, Brown)

1988 *Owl Moon* by Jane Yolen, illustrated by John Schoenherr (Philomel)

Honor Book: Mufaro's Beautiful Daughters: An African Tale by John Steptoe (Lothrop)

1989 *Song and Dance Man* by Karen Ackerman, illustrated by Stephen Gammell (Knopf)

Honor Books

The Boy of the Three-Year Nap by Dianne Snyder, illustrated by Allen Say (Houghton Mifflin)

Free-Fall by David Wiesner (Lothrop)

Goldilocks and the Three Bears by James Marshall (Dial)

Mirandy and Brother Wind by Patricia C. McKissack, illustrated by Jerry Pinkney (Knopf)

1990 *Lon Po Po: A Red-Riding Hood Story from China* by Ed Young (Philomel)

Honor Books

Bill Peet: An Autobiography by Bill Peet (Houghton Mifflin)

Color Zoo by Lois Ehlert (Lippincott)

Hershel and the Hanukkah Goblins by Eric Kimmel, illustrated by Trina Schart Hyman (Holiday House)

The Talking Eggs by Robert D. San Souci, illustrated by Jerry Pinkney (Dial)

1991 *Black and White* by David Macaulay (Houghton Mifflin)

Honor Books

"More More More," Said the Baby: 3 Love Stories by Vera B. Williams (Greenwillow)

Puss in Boots by Charles Perrault, translated by Malcolm Arthur, illustrated by Fred Marcellino (Farrar)

1992 *Tuesday* by David Wiesner (Clarion)

Honor Book: Tar Beach by Faith Ringgold (Crown)

1993 *Mirette on the High Wire* by Emily Arnold McCully (Putnam)

Honor Books

Seven Blind Mice by Ed Young (Philomel)

The Stinky Cheese Man and Other Fairly Stupid Tales by Jon Scieszka, illustrated by Lane Smith (Viking)

Working Cotton by Sherley Anne Williams, illustrated by Carole Byard (Harcourt)

1994 *Grandfather's Journey* by Allen Say (Houghton Mifflin)

Honor Books

Owen by Kevin Henkes (Greenwillow)

Peppe, the Lamplighter by Elisa Bartone, illustrated by Ted Lewin (Lothrop)

Raven by Gerald McDermott (Harcourt)

In the Small, Small Pond by Denise Fleming (Holt)

Yo! Yes? by Chris Raschka (Orchard)

1995 *Smoky Night* by Eve Bunting, illustrated by David Diaz (Harcourt)

Honor Books

Swamp Angel by Anne Isaacs, illustrated by Paul O. Zelinksy (Dutton)

John Henry by Julius Lester, illustrated by Jerry Pinkney (Dial)

Time Flies by Eric Rohmann (Crown)

1996 *Officer Buckle and Gloria* by Peggy Rathmann (Putnam)

Honor Books

Alphabet City by Stephen T. Johnson (Viking)

Zin! Zin! Zin! A Violin by Lloyd Moss, illustrated by Marjorie Priceman (Simon & Schuster)

The Faithful Friend by Robert D. San Souci, illustrated by Brian Pinkney (Simon & Schuster)

Tops & Bottoms by Janet Stevens (Harcourt)

1997 *Golem* by David Wisniewski (Clarion)

Honor Books

Hush! A Thai Lullaby by Minfong Ho, illustrated by Holly Meade (Kroupa/Orchard)

The Graphic Alphabet by David Pelletier (Orchard)

The Paperboy by Dav Pilkey (Jackson/Orchard)

Starry Messenger by Peter Sís (Foster/Farrar)

1998 *Rapunzel* by Paul O. Zelinsky (Dutton)

Honor Books

The Gardener by Sarah Stewart, illustrated by David Small (Farrar)

Harlem by Walter Dean Myers, illustrated by Christopher Myers (Scholastic)

There Was an Old Lady Who Swallowed a Fly by Simms Taback (Viking)

1999 *Snowflake Bentley* by Jacqueline Briggs Martin, illustrated by Mary Azarian (Houghton Mifflin)

Honor Books

Duke Ellington: The Piano Prince and the Orchestra by Andrea Davis Pinkney, illustrated by Brian Pinkney (Hyperion)

No, David! by David Shannon (Scholastic)

Snow by Uri Shulevitz (Farrar)

Tibet: Through the Red Box by Peter Sís (Foster/Farrar)

2000 *Joseph Had a Little Overcoat* by Simms Taback (Viking)

Honor Books

A Child's Calendar by John Updike, illustrated by Trina Schart Hyman (Holiday House)

Sector 7 by David Wiesner (Clarion)

When Sophie Gets Angry—Really, Really Angry . . . by Molly Bang (Scholastic)

The Ugly Duckling by Hans Christian Andersen, adapted by Jerry Pinkney, illustrated by Jerry Pinkney (Morrow)

2001 *So You Want to Be President?* by Judith St. George, illustrated by David Small (Philomel)

Honor Books

Casey at the Bat by Ernest Lawrence Thayer, illustrated by Christopher Bing (Handprint)

Click, Clack, Moo: Cows That Type by Doreen Cronin, illustrated by Betsy Lewin (Simon & Schuster)

Olivia by Ian Falconer (Atheneum)

2002 *The Three Pigs* by David Wiesner (Clarion/Houghton Mifflin)

Honor Books

The Dinosaurs of Waterhouse Hawkins illustrated by Brian Selznick, text, Barbara Kerley (Scholastic)

Martin's Big Words: The Life of Dr. Martin Luther King, Jr. illustrated by Bryan Collier, text, Doreen Rappaport (Jump at the Sun/Hyperion)

The Stray Dog by Marc Simont (HarperCollins)

2003 *My Friend Rabbit* illustrated and written by Eric Rohmann (Roaring Brook Press/ Millbrook Press)

Honor Books

The Spider and the Fly illustrated and written by Tony DiTerlizzi (Simon & Schuster)

Hondo & Fabian illustrated and written by Peter McCarty (Henry Holt)

Noah's Ark illustrated and written by Jerry Pinkney (Sea Star/ North-South Books)

2004 *The Man Who Walked Between the Towers* illustrated and written by Mordicai Gerstein (Roaring Brook Press/ Millbrook Press)

Honor Books

Ella Sarah Gets Dressed illustrated and written by Margaret Chodos-Irvine (Harcourt, Inc.)

What Do You Do with a Tail Like This? illustrated by Steve Jenkins; written by Robin Page and Steve Jenkins (Houghton Mifflin Company)

Don't Let the Pigeon Drive the Bus illustrated and written by Mo Willems (Hyperion)

2005 *Kitten's First Full Moon* illustrated and written by Kevin Henkes (Greenwillow/HarperCollins)

Honor Books

The Red Book illustrated by Barbara Lehman (Houghton Mifflin)

Coming on Home illustrated by E. B. Lewis, written by Jacqueline Woodson (Putnam)

Knuffle Bunny: A Cautionary Tale illustrated and written by Mo Willems (Hyperion)

2006 *The Hello, Goodbye Window* illustrated by Chris Raschka, written by Norton Juster (Michael di Capua/Hyperion)

Honor Books

Rosa illustrated by Bryan Collier and written by Nikki Giovanni (Holt)

Zen Shorts illustrated and written by Jon J. Muth (Scholastic Press)

Hot Air: The (Mostly) True Story of the First Hot-Air Balloon Ride illustrated and written by Marjorie Priceman (an Anne Schwartz Book/Atheneum Books for Young Readers/Simon & Schuster)

Song of the Water Boatman and Other Pond Poems illustrated by Beckie Prange, written by Joyce Sidman (Houghton Mifflin Company)

2007 *Flotsam* by David Wiesner (Clarion)

Honor Books

Gone Wild: An Endangered Animal Alphabet by David McLimans (Walker)

Moses: When Harriet Tubman Led Her People to Freedom illustrated by Kadir Nelson, written by Carole Boston Weatherford (Hyperion/Jump at the Sun)

2008 *The Invention of Hugo Cabret* by Brian Selznick (Scholastic Press, an imprint of Scholastic)

Honor Books

Henry's Freedom Box: A True Story from the Underground Railroad illustrated by Kadir Nelson, written by Ellen Levine (Scholastic Press)

First the Egg by Laura Vaccaro Seeger (Roaring Brook/Neal Porter)

The Wall: Growing Up Behind the Iron Curtain by Peter Sís (Farrar/Frances Foster)

Knuffle Bunny Too: A Case of Mistaken Identity by Mo Willems (Hyperion)

2009 *The House in the Night* illustrated by Beth Krommes, written by Susan Marie Swanson (Houghton Mifflin Company)

Honor Books

A Couple of Boys Have the Best Week Ever by Marie Frazee (Harcourt)

How I Learned Geography by Uri Shulevitz (Farrar, Straus, & Giroux)

A River of Words: The Story of William Carlos Williams, illustrated by Melissa Sweet, written by Jen Bryant (Eerdmans Books for Young Readers, an imprint of Wm. B. Eerdmans Publishing Co.)

2010 *The Lion & the Mouse* illustrated and written by Jerry Pinkney (Little, Brown and Company Books for Young Readers)

Honor Books

All the World by Liz Garton, illustrated by Marla Frazee (Beach Lane Books)

Red Sings from Treetops: A Year in Colors by Joyce Sidman, illustrated by Pamela Zagarenski (Houghton Mifflin Books for Children, Houghton Mifflin Harcourt)

2011 *A Sick Day for Amos McGee*, illustrated by Erin E. Stead, written by Philip C. Stead (A Neal Porter Book, published by Roaring Brook Press, a division of Holtzbrinck Publishing)

Honor Books

Dave the Potter: Artist, Poet, Slave, illustrated by Bryan Collier, written by Laban Carrick Hill (Little, Brown and Company, a division of Hachette Book Group, Inc.)

Interrupting Chicken by David Ezra Stein (Candlewick Press)

2012 *A Ball for Daisy* by Chris Raschka (Schwartz & Wade Books, an imprint of Random House Children's Books, a division of Random House, Inc.)

Honor Books

Blackout by John Rocco (Disney · Hyperion Books, an imprint of Disney Book Group)

Grandpa Green by Lane Smith (Roaring Brook Press, a division of Holtzbrinck Publishing Holdings Limited Partnership)

Me . . . Jane by Patrick McDonnell (Little, Brown and Company, a division of Hachette Book Group, Inc.)

2013 *This Is Not My Hat,* written and illustrated by Jon Klassen (Candlewick Press)

Honor Books

Creepy Carrots! illustrated by Peter Brown, written by Aaron Reynolds (Simon & Schuster Books for Young Readers, an imprint of Simon & Schuster Children's Publishing Division)

Extra Yarn illustrated by Jon Klassen, written by Mac Barnett (Balzer + Bray, an imprint of HarperCollins Publishers)

Green illustrated and written by Laura Vaccaro Seeger (Neal Porter Books, an imprint of Roaring Brook Press)

One Cool Friend illustrated by David Small, written by Toni Buzzeo (Dial Books for Young Readers, a division of Penguin Young Readers Group)

Sleep Like a Tiger illustrated by Pamela Zagarenski, written by Mary Logue (Houghton Mifflin Books for Children, an imprint of Houghton Mifflin Harcourt Publishing Company)

INTERNATIONAL READING ASSOCIATION CHILDREN'S BOOK AWARD

This award is given annually to honor new talent in children's literature. Publishers worldwide are invited to suggest candidates. Since 1987, an award has been given to one author who writes for older readers and one author who writes for younger readers. In 1995, a third award was added for an author of an informational book.

1975 *Transport 7-41-R* by T. Degens (Viking, United States)

1976 *Dragonwings* by Laurence Yep (Harper, United States)

1977 *A String in the Harp* by Nancy Bond (McElderry, United States)

1978 *A Summer to Die* by Lois Lowry (Houghton Mifflin, United States)

1979 *Reserved for Mark Anthony Crowder* by Alison Smith (Dutton, United States)

1980 *Words by Heart* by Ouida Sebestyen (Atlantic/Little, Brown, United States)

1981 *My Own Private Sky* by Delores Beckman (Dutton, United States)

1982 *Goodnight, Mister Tom* by Michelle Magorian (Kestrel, Great Britain)

1983 *The Darkangel* by Meredith Ann Pierce (Atlantic/Little, Brown, United States)

1984 *Ratha's Creature* by Clare Bell (McElderry, United States)

1985 *Badger on the Barge* by Janni Howker (Julia MacRae, Great Britain)

1986 *Prairie Songs* by Pam Conrad (Harper, United States)

1987 *Older Readers: After the Dancing Days* by Margaret I. Rostkowski (Harper, United States)

Younger Readers: The Line-Up Book by Marisabina Russo (Greenwillow, United States)

1988 *Older Readers: The Ruby in the Smoke and Shadow in the North* by Philip Pullman (Oxford, Great Britain)

Younger Readers: The Third-Story Cat by Leslie Baker (Little, Brown, United States)

1989 *Older Readers: Probably Still Nick Swansen* by Virginia Euwer Wolff (Holt, United States)

Younger Readers: Rechenka's Eggs by Patricia Polacco (Philomel, United States)

1990 *Older Readers: Children of the River* by Linda Crew (Delacorte, United States)

Younger Readers: No Star Nights by Anna Egan Smucker, illustrated by Steve Johnson (Knopf, United States)

1991 *Older Readers: Under the Hawthorn Tree* by Marita Conlon-McKenna (O'Brien Press, Ireland)

Younger Readers: Is This a House for Hermit Crab? by Megan McDonald, illustrated by S. D. Schindler (Orchard, United States)

1992 *Older Readers: Rescue Josh McGuire* by Ben Mikaelsen (Hyperion, United States)

Younger Readers: Ten Little Rabbits by Virginia Grossman, illustrated by Sylvia Long (Chronicle, United States)

1993 *Older Readers: Letters from Rifka* by Karen Hesse (Holt, United States)

Younger Readers: Old Turtle by Douglas Wood, illustrated by Cheng-Khee Chee (Pfeifer-Hamilton, United States)

1994 *Older Readers: Behind the Secret Window: A Memoir of a Hidden Childhood* by Nelly S. Toll (Dutton, United States)

Younger Readers: Sweet Clara and the Freedom Quilt by Deborah Hopkinson, illustrated by James E. Ransome (Knopf, United States)

1995 *Older Readers: Spite Fences* by Trudy Krisher (Bantam, United States)

Younger Readers: The Ledgerbook of Thomas Blue Eagle by Gay Matthaei and Jewel Grutman, illustrated by Adam Cvijanovic (Thomasson-Grant, United States)

Informational Book: Stranded at Plimouth Plantation 1626 by Gary Bowen (HarperCollins, United States)

1996 *Older Readers: The King's Shadow* by Elizabeth Alder (Farrar, United States)

Younger Readers: More Than Anything Else by Marie Bradby, illustrated by Chris K. Soentpiet (Orchard, United States)

Informational Book: The Case of the Mummified Pigs and Other Mysteries in Nature by Susan E. Quinlan (Boyds Mills, United States)

1997 *Older Readers: Don't You Dare Read This Mrs. Dunphrey* by Margaret Peterson Haddix (Simon & Schuster, United States)

Younger Readers: The Fabulous Flying Fandinis by Ingrid Slyder (Cobblehill, United States)

Informational Book: Brooklyn Bridge by Elizabeth Mann (Mikaya Press, United States)

1998 *Older Readers: Moving Mama to Town* by Ronder Thomas Young (Orchard, United States)

Younger Readers: Nim and the War Effort by Millie Lee and Yangsook Choi (Farrar, United States)

Informational Book: Just What the Doctor Ordered: The History of American Medicine by Brandon Marie Miller (Lerner, United States)

1999 *Older Readers: Choosing Up Sides* by John Ritter (Penguin Putnam, United States)

Younger Readers: My Freedom Trip: A Child's Escape from North Korea by Frances and Ginger Park (Boyds Mills, United States)

Informational Book: First in the Field, Baseball Hero Jackie Robinson by Derek T. Dingle (Hyperion, United States)

2000 *Older Fiction: Bud, Not Buddy* by Christopher Paul Curtis (Delacorte, United States)

Older Nonfiction: Eleanor's Story: An American Girl in Hitler's Germany by Eleanor Ramrath Garner (Peachtree Publishers, United States)

Younger Fiction: Molly Bannaky by Alice McGill (Houghton Mifflin, United States)

Younger Nonfiction: The Snake Scientist by Sy Montgomery (Houghton Mifflin, United States)

2001 *Younger Fiction: Stranger in the Woods* by Carl R. Sams II and Jean Stoick (Carl R. Sams II Photography)

Younger Nonfiction: My Season with Penguins by Sophie Webb (Houghton Mifflin

Older Fiction: Jake's Orphan by Peggy Brooke (Dorling Kindersley)

Older Nonfiction: Girls Think of Everything by Catherine Thimmesh and Melissa Sweet (Houghton Mifflin)

2002 *Primary Fiction: Silver Seeds* by Paolilli and Dan Brewer (Viking, Penguin Putnam Books)

Primary Nonfiction: Aero and Officer Mike by Joan Plummer Russell (Boyds Mills Press)

Intermediate Fiction: Coolies by Yin (Philomel, Penguin Putnam Books)

Intermediate Nonfiction: Pearl Harbor Warriors by Dorinda Makanaonalani Nicholson and Larry Nicholson (Woodson House)

Young Adult Fiction: A Step from Heaven by Ann Na (Front Street)

Young Adult Nonfiction: Meltdown: A Race Against Nuclear Disaster at Three Mile Island by Wilborn Hampton (Candlewick Press)

2003 *Primary Fiction: One Leaf Rides the Wind* by Celeste Davidson Mannis (Viking)

Primary Nonfiction: The Pot That Juan Built by Nancy Andrews-Goebel (Lee & Low Books)

Intermediate Fiction: **Who Will Tell My Brother?** by Marlene Carvell (Hyperion)

Intermediate Nonfiction: **If the World Were a Village: A Book About the World's People** by David J. Smith (Kids Can Press)

Young Adult Fiction: **Mississippi Trial, 1955** by Chris Crowe (Phyllis Fogelman Books)

Young Adult Nonfiction: **Headin' for Better Times: The Arts of the Great Depression** by Duane Damon (Lerner)

2004 *Primary Fiction:* **Mary Smith** by Andrea U'ren (Farrar, Straus, & Giroux)

Primary Nonfiction: **Uncle Andy's: A Faabbbulous Visit with Andy Warhol** by James Warhola (Penguin)

Intermediate Fiction: **Sahara Special** by Esmé Raji Codell (Hyperion Books)

Intermediate Nonfiction: **Carl Sandburg: Adventures of a Poet** by Penelope Niven (Harcourt)

Young Adult Fiction: **Buddha Boy** by Kathe Koja (Farrar, Straus, & Giroux)

Young Adult Nonfiction: **At the End of Words: A Daughter's Memoir** by Miriam Stone (Candlewick Press)

2005 *Primary Fiction:* **Miss Bridie Chose a Shovel** by Leslie Conner and illustrated by Mary Azarian (Houghton Mifflin)

Primary Nonfiction: **Eliza and the Dragonfly** by Susie Caldwell Rinehart and illustrated by Anisa Claire Hovemann (Dawn Publications)

Intermediate Fiction: **The Golden Hour** by Maiya Williams (Amulet Books)

Intermediate Nonfiction: **Buildings in Disguise** by Joan Mariea Arbogast (Amulet Books)

Young Adult Fiction: **Emako Blue** by Brenda Woods (Boyds Mill Press)

Young Adult Nonfiction: **The Burn Journals** by Brent Runyon (G.P. Putnam's Sons)

2006 *Primary Fiction:* **Russell the Sheep** by Rob Scotton (Harper Collins)

Primary Nonfiction: **Night Wonders** by Jane Ann Peddicord (Charlesbridge)

Intermediate Fiction: **The Bicycle Man** By David L. Dudley (Clarion Books)

Intermediate Nonfiction: **Americans Who Tell the Truth** by Robert Shetterly (Dutton)

Young Adult Fiction: **Black and White** by Paul Volponi (Viking Press)

Young Adult Nonfiction: **JAZZ ABZ: An A to Z Collection of Jazz Portraits** by Wynton Marsalis and Paul Rogers (Candlewick Press)

2007 *Primary Fiction:* **Tickets to Ride: An Alphabetical Amusement** by Mark Rogalski (Running Press Kids)

Primary Nonfiction: **Theodore** by Frank Keating (Paula Wiseman Book, Simon & Schuster)

Intermediate Fiction: **Blue** by Joyce Moyer Hostetter (Calkins Creek Books, Boyds Mills Press)

Intermediate Nonfiction: **Something Out of Nothing: Marie Curie and Radium** by Carla Killough McClafferty (Farrar, Straus, & Giroux)

Young Adult Fiction: **Leonardo's Shadow: Or, My Astonishing Life as Leonardo da Vinci's Servant** by Christopher Grey (Atheneum Books, Simon & Schuster)

Young Adult Nonfiction: **The Poet Slave of Cuba: A Biography of Juan Francisco Manzano** by Margarita Engle (Henry Holt)

2008 *Primary Fiction:* **One Thousand Tracings: Healing the Wounds of World War II** by Lita Judge (Hyperion)

Intermediate Fiction: **The Silver Cup** by Constance Leeds (Viking Penguin Group)

Young Adult Fiction: **Red Glass** by Laura Resau (Delacorte Random House)

Primary Nonfiction: **Louis Sockalexis: Native American Baseball Pioneer** by Bill Wise, illustrated by Bill Farnsworth (Lee & Low)

Intermediate Nonfiction: **Tracking Trash: Flotsam, Jetsam, and the Science of Ocean Motion** by Loree Griffin Burns (Houghton Mifflin)

Young Adult Nonfiction: **Tasting the Sky: A Palestinian Childhood** by Ibtisam Barakat (Melanie Kroupa Books, Farrar, Straus, & Giroux)

2009 *Primary Fiction:* **The Wheat Doll** by Alison L. Randall (Peachtree)

Intermediate Fiction: **The Leanin' Dog** by K. A. Nuzum (HarperCollins)

Young Adult Fiction: **Freeze Frame** by Heidi Ayarbe (HarperCollins)

Primary Nonfiction: **Manfish: The Story of Jacques Cousteau** by Jennifer Berne (Chronicle)

Intermediate Nonfiction: **The Raucous Royals** by Carlyn Beccia (Houghton Mifflin)

Young Adult Nonfiction: **Snow Falling in Spring** by Moying Li (Farrar, Straus, & Giroux)

2010 *Primary Fiction:* **All the World** by Liz Garton Scanlon (Beach Lane)

Primary Nonfiction: **Building on Nature: The Life of Antoni Gaudi** by Rachel Rodriguez, Photo credit: Diane Rigda (Henry Holt)

Intermediate Fiction: **The Beef Princess of Practical County** by Michelle Houts (Delacorte)

Intermediate Fiction: **The Evolution of Calpurnia Tate** by Jacqueline Kelly (Henry Holt)

Young Adult Fiction: **When You Reach Me** by Rebecca Stead (Wendy Lamb)

2011 *Primary Fiction:* **Wanted: The Perfect Pet** by Fiona Roberton (Penguin Young Readers Group)

Primary Nonfiction: **My Heart Is Like a Zoo** by Michael Hall (HarperCollins)

Intermediate Fiction: **Mockingbird** by Kathryn Erskine (Penguin Young Readers Group)

Intermediate Fiction: **Split** by Swati Avasthi (Alfred A. Knopf)

2012 *Primary Fiction:* **Where's Walrus?** by Stephen Savage (Scholastic)

Intermediate Fiction: **Sparrow Road** by Sheila O'Connor (Putnam)

Intermediate Fiction: **Flyaway** by Lucy Christopher (Chicken House/Scholastic)

Young Adult Fiction: **Between Shades of Gray** by Ruta Sepetys (Philomel)

Primary Nonfiction: **My Hands Sing the Blues: Romare Bearden's Childhood Journey** by Jeanne Walker Harvey (Marshall Cavendish)

Young Adult Nonfiction: **How They Croaked: The Awful Ends of the Awfully Famous** by Georgia Bragg (Walker)

EZRA JACK KEATS NEW WRITERS AWARD

Ezra Jack Keats (1919–1983) was a prolific illustrator of children's picture books who won the Caldecott Medal in 1963 for *The Snowy Day*. The Ezra Jack Keats award is funded by the Ezra Jack Keats Foundation and is given to a promising writer who has had six or fewer children's books published. The writer need not be the illustrator. The books must "reflect the tradition of Ezra Jack Keats," whose books portrayed strong family relationships and universal qualities of childhood; the books must also appeal to children nine years old or younger. The award is administered by the Early Childhood Resources and Information Center of the New York Public Library.

1987 *The Patchwork Quilt* by Valerie Flournoy, illustrated by Jerry Pinkney (Dial)

1989 *Jamaica's Find* by Juanita Havill, illustrated by Anne Sibley O'Brien (Houghton Mifflin)

1991 *Tell Me A Story, Mama* by Angela Johnson (Orchard)

1993 *Tar Beach* by Faith Ringgold (Crown)

1995 *Taxi, Taxi* by Cari Best, illustrated by Dale Gottlieb (Little, Brown)

1997 *Calling the Doves/El canto de las palomas* by Juan Felipé Herrera (Children's Book Press)

1999 *Elizabeti's Doll* by Stephanie Stuve-Bodeen, illustrated by Christy Hale (Lee & Low)

2000 *Dear Juno* by Soyung Pak, illustrated by Susan Kathleen Hartung (Viking)

2001 *Henry Hikes to Fitchberg* by D. B. Johnson (Houghton)

2002 *Freedom Summer* by Deborah Wiles, illustrated by James Lagarrigue (Simon & Schuster)

2003 *Ruby's Wish* by Shirim Yim Bridges, illustrated by Sophie Blackall (Chronicle)

2004 *My Name Is Yoon* illustrated by Gabi Swiatowska (Farrar, Straus, & Giroux)

2005 *Going North* by Janice N. Harrington (Farrar, Straus, & Giroux)

2006 *New Illustrator Award: Silly Chicken* illustrated by Yunmee Kyong, written by Rukhsana Khan (Viking)

New Writer Award: My Best Friend by Mary Ann Rodman, illustrated by E. B. Lewis (Viking)

2007 *New Illustrator Award: Mystery Bottle* illustrated by Kristen Balouch (Hyperion)

New Writer Award: For You Are A Kenyan Child by Kelly Cunnane, illustrated by Ana Juan (Atheneum)

2008 *New Illustrator Award: The Apple Pie that Papa Baked* illustrated by Jonathan Bean, written by Lauren Thompson (Simon & Schuster)

New Writer Award: Leaves by David Ezra Stein (G.P. Putnam's Sons)

2009 *New Illustrator Award: Bird* illustrated by Shadra Strickland, written by Zetta Elliot (Lee & Low)

New Writer Award: Garmann's Summer by Stian Hole, illustrated by Stian Hole. Translated by Don Bartlett (Eerdmans)

2010 *New Illustrator Award: Only a Witch Can Fly* illustrated by Taeeun Yoo, written by Alison McGhee (Feiwel & Friends)

New Writer Award: Most Loved in All the World written by Tonya Cherie Hegamin, illustrated by Cozbi Cabrera (Houghton Mifflin Harcourt)

2011 *New Illustrator Award: Most Loved in All the World* illustrated and written by Tao Nyeu (Dial Books for Young Readers)

New Writer Award: I Know Here written by Laurel Croza, illustrated by Matt James (Groundwood Books)

2012 *New Illustrator Award: Same, Same but Different* illustrated and written by Jenny Sue Kostecki-Shaw (Christy Ottaviano Books/ Henry Holt)

New Writer Award: Tía Isa Wants a Car illustrated and written and illustrated by Meg Medina (Candlewick Press)

2013 *New Illustrator Award: Mom, It's My First Day of Kindergarten!* illustrated and written by Hyewon Yum (Frances Foster Books/Farrar Straus Giroux)

New Writer Award: And Then It's Spring written by Julie Fogliano, illustrated by Erin E. Stead (Neal Porter Books/ Roaring Brook Press)

CORETTA SCOTT KING AWARD

The Coretta Scott King Award is presented annually by the Coretta Scott King Task Force of the American Library Association's Social Responsibilities Round Table. It has been awarded to African American authors since 1970 and also to African American illustrators since 1974 for books that encourage understanding and appreciation of people of all cultures and their pursuit of the "American dream." The award celebrates the life of Martin Luther King, Jr., and honors his widow, Coretta Scott King, for her strength and dedication in continuing the fight for racial equity and universal peace. One or more Honor Books may also be chosen each year.

1970 *Author Award: Dr. Martin Luther King, Jr., Man of Peace* by Lillie Patterson (Garrard)

1971 *Author Award: Black Troubadour: Langston Hughes* by Charlemae Rollins (Rand McNally)

Honor Books

I Know Why the Caged Bird Sings by Maya Angelou (Random House)

Unbought and Unbossed by Shirley Chisholm (Houghton Mifflin)

I Am a Black Woman by Mari Evans (Morrow)

Every Man Heart Lay Down by Lorenz Graham (Crowell)

The Voice of the Children by June Jordan and Terri Bush (Holt)

Black Means by Gladys Groom and Bonnie Grossman (Hill & Wang)

Ebony Book of Black Achievement by Margaret W. Peters (Johnson)

Mary Jo's Grandmother by Janice May Udry (Whitman)

1972 *Author Award: 17 Black Artists* by Elton C. Fax (Dodd)

1973 *Author Award: I Never Had It Made: The Autobiography of Jackie Robinson* by Alfred Duckett (Putnam)

1974 *Author Award: Ray Charles* by Sharon Bell Mathis (Crowell)

Honor Books

A Hero Ain't Nothin' but a Sandwich by Alice Childress (Coward-McCann)

Don't You Remember? by Lucille Clifton (Dutton)

Ms. Africa: Profiles of Modern African Women by Louise Crane (Lippincott)

Guest in the Promised Land by Kristin Hunter (Scribner's)

Mukasa by John Nagenda (Macmillan)

Illustrator Award: Ray Charles by Sharon Bell Mathis, illustrated by George Ford (Crowell)

1975 *Author Award: The Legend of Africana* by Dorothy Robinson (Johnson)

1976 *Author Award: Duey's Tale* by Pearl Bailey (Harcourt)

Honor Books

Julius K. Nyerere: Teacher of Africa by Shirley Graham (Messner)

Paul Robeson by Eloise Greenfield (Crowell)

Fast Sam, Cool Clyde and Stuff by Walter Dean Myers (Viking)

Song of the Trees by Mildred Taylor (Dial)

1977 *Author Award: The Story of Stevie Wonder* by James Haskins (Lothrop)

Honor Books

Everett Anderson's Friend by Lucille Clifton (Holt)

Roll of Thunder, Hear My Cry by Mildred D. Taylor (Dial)

Quiz Book on Black America by Clarence N. Blake and Donald F. Martin (Houghton Mifflin)

1978 *Author Award: Africa Dreams* by Eloise Greenfield (Crowell)

Honor Books

The Days When the Animals Talked: Black Folk Tales and How They Came to Be by William J. Faulkner (Follett)

Marvin and Tige by Frankcina Glass (St. Martin's)

Mary McCleod Bethune by Eloise Greenfield (Crowell)

Barbara Jordan by James Haskins (Dial)

Coretta Scott King by Lillie Patterson (Garrard)

Portia: The Life of Portia Washington Pittman, the Daughter of Booker T. Washington by Ruth Ann Stewart (Doubleday)

1979 *Author Award: Escape to Freedom: A Play about Young Frederick Douglass* by Ossie Davis (Viking)

Honor Books

Skates of Uncle Richard by Carol Fenner (Random House)

Justice and Her Brothers by Virginia Hamilton (Greenwillow)

Benjamin Banneker by Lillie Patterson (Abingdon)

I Have a Sister, My Sister Is Deaf by Jeanne W. Peterson (Harper)

Illustrator Award: Something on My Mind by Nikkie Grimes, illustrated by Tom Feelings (Dial)

1980 *Author Award: The Young Landlords* by Walter Dean Myers (Viking)

Honor Books

Movin' Up by Berry Gordy (Harper)

Childtimes: A Three-Generation Memoir by Eloise Greenfield and Lessie Jones Little (Harper)

Andrew Young: Young Man with a Mission by James Haskins (Lothrop)

James Van Der Zee: The Picture Takin' Man by James Haskins (Dodd)

Let the Lion Eat Straw by Ellease Southerland (Scribner's)

Illustrator Award: Cornrows by Camille Yarbrough, illustrated by Carole Byard (Coward-McCann)

1981 *Author Award: This Life* by Sidney Poitier (Knopf)

Honor Books

Don't Explain: A Song of Billie Holiday by Alexis De Veaux (Harper)

Illustrator Award: Beat the Story Drum, Pum-Pum by Ashley Bryan (Atheneum)

Honor Books

Grandmama's Joy by Eloise Greenfield, illustrated by Carole Byard (Philomel)

Count on Your Fingers African Style by Claudia Zaslavsky, illustrated by Jerry Pinkney (Crowell)

1982 *Author Award: Let the Circle Be Unbroken* by Mildred D. Taylor (Dial)

Honor Books

Rainbow Jordan by Alice Childress (Coward-McCann)

Lou in the Limelight by Kristin Hunter (Scribner's)

Mary: An Autobiography by Mary E. Mebane (Viking)

Illustrator Award: Mother Crocodile: An Uncle Amadou Tale from Senegal translated by Rosa Guy, illustrated by John Steptoe (Delacorte)

Honor Book: Daydreamers by Eloise Greenfield, illustrated by Tom Feelings (Dial)

1983 *Author Award: Sweet Whispers, Brother Rush* by Virginia Hamilton (Philomel)

Honor Book: This Strange New Feeling by Julius Lester (Dial)

Illustrator Award: Black Child by Peter Magubane (Knopf)

Honor Books

All the Colors of the Race by Arnold Adoff, illustrated by John Steptoe (Lothrop)

Just Us Women by Jeannette Caines, illustrated by Pat Cummings (Harper)

1984 *Author Award: Everett Anderson's Goodbye* by Lucille Clifton (Holt)

Special Citation: The Words of Martin Luther King, Jr. compiled by Coretta Scott King (Newmarket)

Honor Books

The Magical Adventures of Pretty Pearl by Virginia Hamilton (Harper)

Lena Horne by James Haskins (Coward-McCann)

Bright Shadow by Joyce Carol Thomas (Avon)

Because We Are by Mildred Pitts Walter (Lothrop)

Illustrator Award: My Mama Needs Me by Mildred Pitts Walter, illustrated by Pat Cummings (Lothrop)

1985 *Author Award: Motown and Didi* by Walter Dean Myers (Viking)

Honor Books

Circle of Gold by Candy Dawson Boyd (Apple/Scholastic)

A Little Love by Virginia Hamilton (Philomel)

1986 *Author Award: The People Could Fly: American Black Folktales* by Virginia Hamilton (Knopf)

Honor Books

Junius Over Far by Virginia Hamilton (Harper)

Trouble's Child by Mildred Pitts Walter (Lothrop)

Illustrator Award: The Patchword Quilt by Valerie Flournoy, illustrated by Jerry Pinkney (Dial)

Honor Book: The People Could Fly: American Black Folktales retold by Virginia Hamilton, illustrated by Leo and Diane Dillon (Knopf)

1987 *Author Award: Justin and the Best Biscuits in the World* by Mildred Pitts Walter (Lothrop)

Honor Books

Lion and the Ostrich Chicks and Other African Folk Tales by Ashley Bryan (Atheneum)

Which Way Freedom? by Joyce Hansen (Walker)

Illustrator Award: Half a Moon and One Whole Star by Crescent Dragonwagon, illustrated by Jerry Pinkney (Macmillan)

Honor Books

Lion and the Ostrich Chicks and Other African Folk Tales by Ashley Bryan (Atheneum)

C.L.O.U.D.S. by Pat Cummings (Lothrop)

1988 *Author Award: The Friendship* by Mildred D. Taylor (Dial)

Honor Books

An Enchanted Hair Tale by Alexis De Veaux (Harper)

The Tales of Uncle Remus: The Adventures of Brer Rabbit by Julius Lester (Dial)

Illustrator Award: Mufaro's Beautiful Daughters by John Steptoe (Lothrop)

Honor Books

What a Morning! The Christmas Story in Black Spirituals selected by John Langstaff, illustrated by Ashley Bryan (Macmillan)

The Invisible Hunters: A Legend from the Miskito Indians of Nicaragua compiled by Harriet Rohmer et al., illustrated by Joe Sam (Children's Book Press)

1989 *Author Award: Fallen Angels* by Walter Dean Myers (Scholastic)

Honor Books

A Thief in the Village and Other Stories by James Berry (Orchard)

Anthony Burns: The Defeat and Triumph of a Fugitive Slave by Virginia Hamilton (Knopf)

Illustrator Award: Mirandy and Brother Wind by Patricia C. McKissack, illustrated by Jerry Pinkney (Knopf)

Honor Books

Under the Sunday Tree by Eloise Greenfield, illustrated by Amos Ferguson (Harper)

Storm in the Night by Mary Stolz, illustrated by Pat Cummings (Harper)

1990 *Author Award: A Long Hard Journey: The Story of the Pullman Porter* by Patricia C. McKissack and Fredrick McKissack (Walker)

Honor Books

Nathaniel Talking by Eloise Greenfield (Black Butterfly)

The Bells of Christmas by Virginia Hamilton (Harcourt)

Martin Luther King, Jr. & the Freedom Movement by Lillie Patterson (Facts on File)

Illustrator Award: Nathaniel Talking by Eloise Greenfield, illustrated by Jan Spivey Gilchrist (Black Butterfly)

Honor Book

The Talking Eggs by Robert D. San Souci, illustrated by Jerry Pinkney (Dial)

1991 *Author Award: The Road to Memphis* by Mildred D. Taylor (Dial)

Honor Books

Black Dance in America by James Haskins (Crowell)

When I Am Old with You by Angela Johnson (Orchard)

Illustrator Award: Aida by Leontyne Price, illustrated by Leo Dillon and Diane Dillon (Harcourt)

1992 *Author Award: Now Is Your Time: The African American Struggle for Freedom* by Walter Dean Myers (HarperCollins)

Honor Book: Night on Neighborhood Street by Eloise Greenfield (Dial)

Illustrator Award: Tar Beach by Faith Ringgold (Crown)

Honor Books

All Night, All Day! A Child's First Book of African American Spirituals selected by Ashley Bryan (Atheneum)

Night on Neighborhood Street by Eloise Greenfield, illustrated by Jan Spivey Gilchrist (Dial)

1993 *Author Award: The Dark-Thirty: Southern Tales of the Supernatural* by Patricia C. McKissack (Knopf)

Honor Books

Mississippi Challenge by Mildred Pitts Walter (Bradbury)

Sojourner Truth: Ain't I a Woman? by Patricia C. McKissack and Fredrick McKissack (Scholastic)

Somewhere in the Darkness by Walter Dean Myers (Scholastic)

Illustrator Award: The Origin of Life on Earth: An African Creation Myth retold by David A. Anderson, illustrated by Kathleen Atkins Wilson (Sights)

Honor Books

Little Eight John by Jan Wahl, illustrated by Wil Clay (Lodestar)

Sukey and the Mermaid by Robert D. San Souci, illustrated by Brian Pinkney (Four Winds)

Working Cotton by Sherley Anne Williams, illustrated by Carol Byard (Harcourt)

1994 *Author Award: Toning the Sweep* by Angela Johnson (Orchard)

Honor Books

Brown Honey in Broomwheat Tea by Joyce Carol Thomas (HarperCollins)

Malcolm X: By Any Means Necessary by Walter Dean Myers (Scholastic)

Illustrator Award: Soul Looks Back in Wonder: Collection of African American Poets edited by Phyllis Fogelman, illustrated by Tom Feelings (Dial)

Honor Books

Brown Honey in Broomwheat Tea by Joyce Carol Thomas, illustrated by Floyd Cooper (HarperCollins)

Uncle Jed's Barbershop by Margaree King Mitchell, illustrated by James Ransome (Simon & Schuster)

1995 *Author Award: Christmas in the Big House, Christmas in the Quarters* by Patricia C. and Fredrick L. McKissack (Scholastic)

Honor Books

Black Diamond: The Story of the Negro Baseball Leagues by Patricia C. and Fredrick L. McKissack (Scholastic)

I Hadn't Meant to Tell You This by Jacqueline Woodson (Delacorte)

The Captive by Joyce Hansen (Scholastic)

Illustrator Award: The Creation by James Weldon Johnson, illustrated by James Ransome (Holiday House)

Honor Books

Meet Danitra Brown by Nikki Grimes, illustrated by Floyd Cooper (Lothrop)

The Singing Man by Angela Shelf, illustrated by Terea Shaffer (Holiday House)

1996 *Author Award: Her Stories* by Virginia Hamilton (Blue Sky Press)

Honor Books

The Watsons Go to Birmingham—1963 by Christopher Paul Curtis (Delacorte)

Like Sisters on the Homefront by Rita Williams-Garcia (Lodestar)

From the Notebooks of Melanin Sun by Jacqueline Woodson (Blue Sky)

Illustrator Award: The Middle Passage: White Ships, Black Cargo by Tom Feelings (Dial)

Honor Books

Her Stories by Virginia Hamilton, illustrated by Leo and Diane Dillon (Blue Sky)

The Faithful Friend by Robert D. San Souci, illustrated by Brian Pinkney (Simon & Schuster)

1997 *Author Award: Slam!* by Walter Dean Myers (Scholastic)

Honor Book: Rebels against Slavery: American Slave Revolts by Patricia C. McKissack and Fredrick McKissack (Scholastic)

Illustrator Award: Minty: A Story of Young Harriet Tubman by Alan Schroeder, illustrated by Jerry Pinkney (Dial)

Honor Books

The Palm of My Heart: Poetry by African American Children by Davida Adedjouma, illustrated by Gregory Christie (Lee & Low)

Running the Road to ABC by Denize Lauture, illustrated by Reynold Ruffins (Simon & Schuster)

Neeny Coming, Neeny Going by Karen English, illustrated by Synthia Saint James (Bridgewater)

1998 *Author Award: Forged by Fire* by Sharon M. Draper (Atheneum)

I Thought My Soul Would Rise and Fly: The Diary of Patsy, a Freed Girl by Joyce Hansen (Scholastic)

Honor Book: Bayard Rustin: Behind the Scenes of the Civil Rights Movement by James Haskins (Hyperion)

Illustrator Award: In Daddy's Arms I Am Tall: African Americans Celebrating Fathers, illustrated by Javaka Steptoe (Lee & Low)

Honor Books

Ashley Bryan's ABC of African American Poetry by Ashley Bryan (Jean Karl/Atheneum)

Harlem by Walter Dean Myers, illustrated by Christopher Myers (Scholastic)

The Hunterman and the Crocodile by Baba Wagué Diakité (Scholastic)

1999 *Author Award: Heaven* by Angela Johnson (Simon & Schuster)

Honor Books

Jazmin's Notebook by Nikki Grimes (Dial)

Breaking Ground, Breaking Silence: The Story of New York's African Burial Ground by Joyce Hansen and Gary McGowan (Holt)

The Other Side: Shorter Poems by Angela Johnson (Orchard)

Illustrator Award: i see the rhythm by Toyomi Igus, illustrated by Michele Wood (Children's Book Press)

Honor Books

I Have Heard of a Land by Joyce Carol Thomas, illustrated by Floyd Cooper (Joanna Cotler/HarperCollins)

The Bat Boy and His Violin by Gavin Curtis, illustrated by E. B. Lewis (Simon & Schuster)

Duke Ellington: The Piano Prince and His Orchestra by Andrea Davis, illustrated by Brian Pinkney (Hyperion)

2000 *Author Award: Bud, Not Buddy* by Christopher Paul Curtis (Delacorte)

Honor Books

Francie by Karen English (Farrar, Straus, & Giroux)

Black Hands, White Sails: The Story of African-American Whalers by Patricia C. and Fredrick McKissack (Scholastic)

Monster by Walter Dean Myers (HarperCollins)

Illustrator Award: In the Time of the Drums by Kim L. Siegelson, illustrated by Brian Pinkney (Jump at the Sun/Hyperion)

Honor Books

My Rows and Piles of Coins by Tololwa M. Mollel, illustrated by E. B. Lewis (Clarion)

Black Cat by Christopher Myers (Scholastic)

2001 *Author Award: Miracle's Boys* by Jacqueline Woodson (Putnam)

Honor Book: Let It Shine! Stories of Black Women Freedom Fighters by Andrea Davis, illustrated by Stephen Alcorn (Gulliver/Harcourt)

Illustrator Award: Uptown by Bryan Collier (Holt)

Honor Books

Freedom River by Bryan Collier (Jump at the Sun/Hyperion)

Only Passing Through: The Story of Sojourner Truth by Anne Rockwell, illustrated by R. Gregory Christie (Random House)

Virgie Goes to School with Us Boys by Elizabeth Fitzgerald Howard, illustrated by E. B. Lewis (Simon & Schuster)

2002 *Author Award Winner: The Land* by Mildred Taylor (Phyllis Fogelman Books/Penguin Putnam)

Honor Books

Money-Hungry by Sharon G. Flake (Jump at the Sun/Hyperion)

Carver: A Life in Poems by Marilyn Nelson (Front Street)

Illustrator Award Winner: Goin' Someplace Special illustrated by Jerry Pinkney, text by Patricia McKissack (Anne Schwartz Book/Atheneum)

Honor Book: Martin's Big Words illustrated by Bryan Collier, text by Doreen Rappoport (Jump at the Sun/Hyperion)

2003 *Author Award Winner: Bronx Masquerade* by Nikki Grimes (Dial Books for Young Readers)

Honor Books

The Red Rose Box by Brenda Woods (G.P. Putnam's Sons)

Talkin' About Bessie: the Story of Aviator Elizabeth Coleman by Nikki Grimes (Orchard Books/Scholastic)

Illustrator Award: Talkin' About Bessie: the Story of Aviator Elizabeth Coleman by Nikki Grimes (Orchard Books/Scholastic)

Honor Books

Rap a Tap Tap: Here's Bojangles—Think of That illustrated by Leo and Diane Dillion (Blue Sky Press/Scholastic, Inc.)

Visiting Langston illustrated by Bryan Collier (Henry Holt & Co.)

2004 *Author Award Winner: The First Part Last* by Angela Johnson (Simon & Schuster Books for Young Readers)

Honor Books

Days of Jubilee: The End of Slavery in the United States by Patricia C. and Fredrick L. McKissack (Scholastic)

Locomotion by Jacqueline Woodson (G.P. Putnam's Sons/Penguin Young Readers Group)

The Battle of Jericho by Sharon M. Draper (Atheneum Books for Young Readers)

Illustrator Award Winner: Beautiful Blackbird by Ashley Bryan (Atheneum Books for Young Readers)

Honor Books

Almost to Freedom by Colin Bootman (Carolrhoda Books/Lerner Publishing Group)

Thunder Rose by Kadir Nelson (Silver Whistle/Harcourt)

2005 *Author Award Winner: Remember: The Journey to School Integration* by Toni Morrison (Houghton Mifflin)

Honor Books

The Legend of Buddy Bush by Shelia P. Moses (Margaret K. McElderry Books/Simon & Schuster)

Who Am I Without Him?: Short Stories About Girls and the Boys in Their Lives by Sharon G. Flake (Jump at the Sun/Hyperion Books for Children)

Fortune's Bones: The Manumission Requiem by Marilyn Nelson (Front Street)

Illustrator Award Winner: Ellington Was Not a Street by Kadir Nelson (Simon & Schuster)

Honor Books

God Bless the Child illustrated by Jerry Pinkney, written by Billie Holiday and Arthur Herzog, Jr. (Amistad/HarperCollins)

The People Could Fly: The Picture Book illustrated by Leo and Diane Dillon, written by Virginia Hamilton (Alfred A. Knopf/Random House)

2006 *Author Award Winner: Day of Tears: A Novel in Dialogue* by Julius Lester (Jump at the Sun; Reprint edition)

Honor Books

Maritcha: A Nineteenth-Century American Girl by Tonya Bolden (Harry N. Abrams)

Dark Sons by Nikki Grimes (Jump at the Sun)

A Wreath for Emmett Till by Marilyn Nelson, illustrated by Philippe Lardy (Houghton Mifflin)

Illustrator Awards

Rosa by Nikki Giovanni, illustrated by Bryan Collier (Henry Holt and Co. (BYR))

Brothers in Hope: The Story of the Lost Boys of Sudan written and illustrated by R. Gregory Christie (Lee & Low Books)

New Talent: Jimi & Me by Jaime Adoff (Jump at the Sun)

2007 *Author Winner: Copper Sun* by Sharon M. Draper (Atheneum)

Honor Book: The Road to Paris by Nikki Grimes (Putnam Juvenile)

Illustrator Award Winner: Moses: When Harriet Tubman Led Her People to Freedom illustrated by Kadir Nelson, written by Carole Boston Weatherford (Jump at the Sun)

Jazz illustrated by Christopher Myers, written by Walter Dean (Holiday House)

Poetry for Young People: Langston Hughes edited by David Roessel and Arnold Rampersad, illustrated by Benny Andrews (Sterling)

New Talent: Standing Against the Wind by Traci L. Jones (Farrar, Straus, & Giroux (BYR))

2008 *Author Award: Elijah of Buxton* by Christopher Paul Curtis (Scholastic Press)

Honor Books

November Blues by Sharon M. Draper (Atheneum)

Twelve Rounds to Glory: The Story of Muhammad Ali by Charles R. Smith Jr., illustrated by Bryan Collier (Candlewick)

Illustrator Award: Let It Shine by Ashley Bryan (Atheneum)

The Secret Olivia Told Me by N. Joy, illustrated by Nancy Devard (Just Us Books, Inc.)

Jazz On A Saturday Night by Leo and Diane Dillon (The Blue Sky Press)

New Talent: Brendan Buckley's Universe and Everything in It by Sundee T. Frazier (Delacorte Books for Young Readers)

2009 *Author Award: We Are the Ship: The Story of Negro League Baseball* written and illustrated by Kadir Nelson (Hyperion Book CH)

Honor Books

The Blacker the Berry by Joyce Carol Thomas, illustrated by Floyd Cooper (Amistad)

Keeping the Night Watch by Hope Anita Smith, illustrated by E. B. Lewis (Henry Holt and Co.)

Becoming Billie Holiday by Carole Weatherford, illustrated by Floyd Cooper (Wordsong; Library Binding edition)

Illustrator Award: The Blacker the Berry by Joyce Carol Thomas, illustrated by Floyd Cooper (Amistad)

We Are the Ship: The Story of Negro League Baseball written and illustrated by Kadir Nelson (Hyperion Book CH)

Before John Was a Jazz Giant: A Song of John Coltrane by Carole Boston Weatherford, illustrated by Sean Qualls (Henry Holt and Co.)

The Moon Over Star by Dianna Hutts Aston, illustrated by Jerry Pinkney (Dial)

New Talent: Shadra Strickland, illustrator of *Bird* by Zetta Elliott (Lee & Low Books)

2010 *Author Award: Bad News for Outlaws: The Remarkable Life of Bass Reeves, Deputy U.S. Marshal* by Vaunda Micheaux Nelson, illustrated by R. Gregory Christie (Carolrhoda Books, a division of Lerner Publishing Group, Inc.)

Honor Book

Mare's War by tanita s. davis (Alfred A. Knopf, an imprint of Random House Children's Books, a division of Random House, Inc.)

Illustrator Award: My People by Langston Hughes, illustrated by Charles R. Smith Jr. (Ginee Seo Books, Atheneum Books for Young Readers)

Honor Book

The Negro Speaks of Rivers by Langston Hughes, illustrated by E. B. Lewis (Disney/Jump at the Sun Books, an imprint of Disney Book Group)

New Talent: The Rock and the River by Kekla Magoon (Aladdin, an imprint of Simon & Schuster Children's Publishing Division)

Coretta Scott King–Virginia Hamilton Award for Lifetime Achievement: Walter Dean Myers, whose books include: *Amiri & Odette: A Love Story*, published by Scholastic Press, an imprint of Scholastic; *Fallen Angels*, published by Scholastic Press; *Monster*, published by Amistad and HarperTeen, imprints of HarperCollins Publishers; and *Sunrise Over Fallujah*, published by Scholastic Press

2011 *Author Award: One Crazy Summer* by Rita Williams-Garcia (Amistad, an imprint of HarperCollins Publishers)

Honor Books

Lockdown by Walter Dean Myers (Amistad, an imprint of HarperCollins Publishers)

Ninth Ward by Jewell Parker Rhodes (Little, Brown and Company, a division of Hachette Book Group, Inc.)

Yummy: The Last Days of a Southside Shorty written by G. Neri, illustrated by Randy DuBurke (Lee & Low Books, Inc.)

Illustrator Award: Dave the Potter: Artist, Poet, Slave illustrated by Bryan Collier, written by Laban Carrick Hill (Little, Brown and Company, a division of Hachette Book Group, Inc.)

Honor Books

Jimi: Sounds Like a Rainbow: A Story of the Young Jimi Hendrix illustrated by Javaka Steptoe, written by Gary Golio (Clarion Books, an imprint of Houghton Mifflin Harcourt Publishing Company)

Zora and Me illustrated by Victoria Bond, written by T. R. Simon (Candlewick Press)

Seeds of Change illustrated by Sonia Lynn Sadler, written by Jen Cullerton Johnson (Lee & Low Books, Inc.)

Coretta Scott King–Virginia Hamilton Award for Lifetime Achievement: Dr. Henrietta Mays Smith, professor emerita at the University of South Florida, Tampa, School of Library and Information Science

2012 *Author Award: Heart and Soul: The Story of America and African Americans*, written and illustrated by Kadir Nelson (Balzer + Bray, an imprint of HarperCollins Publishers)

Honor Books

The Great Migration: Journey to the North, written by Eloise Greenfield, illustrated by Jan Spivey Gilchrist (Amistad, an imprint of HarperCollins Publishers)

Never Forgotten, written by Patricia C. McKissack, illustrated by Leo and Diane Dillon (Schwartz & Wade Books, an imprint of Random House Children's Books)

Illustrator Award: Underground: Finding the Light to Freedom, illustrated and written by Shane W. Evans (A Neal Porter Book, published by Roaring Brook Press)

Honor Books

Heart and Soul: The Story of America and African Americans, written and illustrated by Kadir Nelson (Balzer + Bray, an imprint of HarperCollins Publishers)

Coretta Scott King–Virginia Hamilton Award for Lifetime Achievement: Ashley Bryan, storyteller, artist, author, poet, and musician whose numerous awards include the Coretta Scott King Book Award for *Let It Shine* and *Beautiful Blackbird*

NATIONAL COUNCIL OF TEACHERS OF ENGLISH (NCTE) AWARD FOR EXCELLENCE IN POETRY FOR CHILDREN

This award was given annually from 1977 to 1982 and every three years after that to a living American poet in recognition of his or her entire body of work for children ages three through thirteen.

1977 David McCord

1978 Aileen Fisher

1979 Karla Kushin

1980 Myra Cohn Livingston

1981 Eve Merriam

1982 John Ciardi

1985 Lilian Moore

1988 Arnold Adoff

1991 Valerie Worth

1994 Barbara Juster Esbensen

1997 Eloise Greenfield

2000 X. J. Kennedy

2003 Mary Ann Hoberman

2006 Nikki Grimes

2009 Lee Bennett Hopkins

2011 J. Patrick Lewis

2013 Joyce Sidman

JOHN NEWBERY MEDAL

The John Newbery Medal has been awarded annually since 1922 under the supervision of the ALA's Association for Library Service to Children. It is presented to the author of the work judged to be the most distinguished contribution to literature for children published in the United States during the previous year. One or more Honor Books are also chosen. Winners must be residents or citizens of the United States.

1922 *The Story of Mankind* by Hendrik Willem van Loon (Liveright)

Honor Books

Cedric the Forester by Bernard Marshall (Appleton)

The Golden Fleece and the Heroes Who Lived before Achilles by Padraic Colum (Macmillan)

The Great Quest by Charles Hawes (Little, Brown)

The Old Tobacco Shop by William Bowen (Macmillan)

Windy Hill by Cornelia Meigs (Macmillan)

1923 *The Voyages of Doctor Dolittle* by Hugh Lofting (Lippincott)

Honor Book No record

1924 *The Dark Frigate* by Charles Hawes (Atlantic/Little, Brown)

Honor Book No record

1925 *Tales from Silver Lands* by Charles Finger (Doubleday)

Honor Books

Dream Coach by Anne Parrish (Macmillan)

Nicholas by Anne Carroll Moore (Putnam)

1926 *Shen of the Sea* by Arthur Bowie Chrisman (Dutton)

Honor Book: Voyagers by Padraic Colum (Macmillan)

1927 *Smoky, the Cowhorse* by Will James (Scribner's)

Honor Book No record

1928 *Gayneck, the Story of a Pigeon* by Dhan Gopal Mukerji (Dutton)

Honor Books

Downright Dencey by Caroline Snedeker (Doubleday)

The Wonder Smith and His Son by Ella Young (Longmans)

1929 *The Trumpeter of Krakow* by Eric P. Kelly (Macmillan)

Honor Books

The Boy Who Was by Grace Hallock (Dutton)

Clearing Weather by Cornelia Meigs (Little, Brown)

Millions of Cats by Wanda Gág (Coward)

Pigtail of Ah Lee Ben Loo by John Bennett (Longmans)

Runaway Papoose by Grace Moon (Doubleday)

Tod of the Fens by Elinor Whitney (Macmillan)

1930 *Hitty, Her First Hundred Years* by Rachel Field (Macmillan)

Honor Books

Daughter of the Seine by Jeanette Eaton (Harper)

Jumping-Off Place by Marian Hurd McNeely (Longmans)

Little Blacknose by Hildegarde Swift (Harcourt)

Pran of Albania by Elizabeth Miller (Doubleday)

Tangle-Coated Horse and Other Tales by Ella Young (Longmans)

Vaino by Julia Davis Adams (Dutton)

1931 *The Cat Who Went to Heaven* by Elizabeth Coatsworth (Macmillan)

Honor Books

The Dark Star of Itza by Alida Malkus (Harcourt)

Floating Island by Anne Parrish (Harper)

Garram the Hunter by Herbert Best (Doubleday)

Meggy Macintosh by Elizabeth Janet Gray (Doubleday)

Mountains Are Free by Julia Davis Adams (Dutton)

Ood-Le-Uk the Wanderer by Alice Lide and Margaret Johansen (Little, Brown)

Queer Person by Ralph Hubbard (Doubleday)

Spice and the Devil's Cake by Agnes Hewes (Knopf)

1932 *Waterless Mountain* by Laura Adams Armer (Longmans)

Honor Books

Boy of the South Seas by Eunice Tietjens (Coward)

Calico Bush by Rachel Field (Macmillan)

The Fairy Circus by Dorothy P. Lathrop (Macmillan)

Jane's Island by Marjorie Allee (Houghton Mifflin)

Out of the Flames by Eloise Lownsbery (Longmans)

Truce of the Wolf and Other Tales of Old Italy by Mary Gould Davis (Harcourt)

1933 *Young Fu of the Upper Yangtze* by Elizabeth Lewis (Winston)

Honor Books

Children of the Soil by Nora Burglon (Doubleday)

The Railroad to Freedom by Hildegarde Swift (Harcourt)

Swift Rivers by Cornelia Meigs (Little, Brown)

1934 *Invincible Louisa* by Cornelia Meigs (Little, Brown)

Honor Books

ABC Bunny by Wanda Gág (Coward)

Apprentice of Florence by Anne Kyle (Houghton Mifflin)

Big Tree of Bunlahy by Padraic Colum (Macmillan)

The Forgotten Daughter by Caroline Snedeker (Doubleday)

Glory of the Seas by Agnes Hewes (Knopf)

New Land by Sarah Schmidt (McBride)

Swords of Steel by Elsie Singmaster (Houghton Mifflin)

Winged Girl of Knossos by Erik Berry (Appleton)

1935 *Dobry* by Monica Shannon (Viking)

Honor Books

Davy Crockett by Constance Rourke (Harcourt)

Day on Skates by Hilda Van Stockum (Harper)

Pageant of Chinese History by Elizabeth Seeger (Longmans)

1936 *Caddie Woodlawn* by Carol Ryrie Brink (Macmillan)

Honor Books

All Sail Set by Armstrong Sperry (Winston)

The Good Master by Kate Seredy (Viking)

Honk, The Moose by Phil Strong (Dodd)

Young Walter Scott by Elizabeth Janet Gray (Viking)

1937 *Roller Skates* by Ruth Sawyer (Viking)

Honor Books

Audubon by Constance Rourke (Harcourt)

The Codfish Musket by Agnes Hewes (Doubleday)

Golden Basket by Ludwig Bemelmans (Viking)

Phebe Fairchild: Her Book by Lois Lenski (Stokes)

Whistler's Van by Idwal Jones (Viking)

Winterbound by Margery Bianco (Viking)

1938 *The White Stag* by Kate Seredy (Viking)

Honor Books

Bright Island by Mabel Robinson (Random House)

On the Banks of Plum Creek by Laura Ingalls Wilder (Harper)

Pecos Bill by James Cloyd Bowman (Little, Brown)

1939 *Thimble Summer* by Elizabeth Enright (Rinehart)

Honor Books

Hello the Boat! by Phyllis Crawford (Holt)

Leader by Destiny: George Washington, Man and Patriot by Jeanette Eaton (Harcourt)

Mr. Popper's Penguins by Richard and Florence Atwater (Little, Brown)

Nino by Valenti Angelo (Viking)

Penn by Elizabeth Janet Gray (Viking)

1940 *Daniel Boone* by James Daugherty (Viking)

Honor Books

Boy with a Pack by Stephen W. Meader (Harcourt)

By the Shores of Silver Lake by Laura Ingalls Wilder (Harper)

Runner of the Mountain Tops by Mabel Robinson (Random House)

The Singing Tree by Kate Seredy (Viking)

1941 *Call It Courage* by Armstrong Sperry (Macmillan)

Honor Books

Blue Willow by Doris Gates (Viking)

The Long Winter by Laura Ingalls Wilder (Harper)

Nansen by Anna Gertrude Hall (Viking)

Young Mac of Fort Vancouver by Mary Jane Carr (Crowell)

1942 *The Matchlock Gun* by Walter D. Edmonds (Dodd)

Honor Books

Down Ryton Water by Eva Roe Gaggin (Viking)

George Washington's World by Genevieve Foster (Scribner's)

Indian Captive: The Story of Mary Jemison by Lois Lenski (Lippincott)

Little Town on the Prairie by Laura Ingalls Wilder (Harper)

1943 *Adam of the Road* by Elizabeth Janet Gray (Viking)

Honor Books

Have You Seen Tom Thumb? by Mabel Leigh Hunt (Lippincott)

The Middle Moffat by Eleanor Estes (Harcourt)

1944 *Johnny Tremain* by Esther Forbes (Houghton Mifflin)

Honor Books

Fog Magic by Julia Sauer (Viking)

Mountain Born by Elizabeth Yates (Coward)

Rufus M. by Eleanor Estes (Harcourt)

These Happy Golden Years by Laura Ingalls Wilder (Harper)

1945 *Rabbit Hill* by Robert Lawson (Viking)

Honor Books

Abraham Lincoln's World by Genevieve Foster (Scribner's)

The Hundred Dresses by Eleanor Estes (Harcourt)

Lone Journey: The Life of Roger Williams by Jeanette Eaton (Harcourt)

The Silver Pencil by Alice Dalgliesh (Scribner's)

1946 *Strawberry Girl* by Lois Lenski (Lippincott)

Honor Books

Bhimsa, the Dancing Bear by Christine Weston (Scribner's)

Justin Morgan Had a Horse by Marguerite Henry (Rand McNally)

The Moved-Outers by Florence Crannell Means (Houghton Mifflin)

New Found World by Katherine Shippen (Viking)

1947 *Miss Hickory* by Carolyn Sherwin Bailey (Viking)

Honor Books

The Avion My Uncle Flew by Cyrus Fisher (Appleton)

Big Tree by Mary and Conrad Buff (Viking)

The Heavenly Tenants by William Maxwell (Harper)

The Hidden Treasure of Glaston by Eleanore Jewett (Viking)

Wonderful Year by Nancy Barnes (Messner)

1948 *The Twenty-One Balloons* by William Pène du Bois (Viking)

Honor Books

The Cow-Tail Switch and Other West African Stories by Harold Courlander (Holt)

Li Lun, Lad of Courage by Carolyn Treffinger (Abingdon)

Misty of Chincoteague by Marguerite Henry (Rand McNally)

Pancakes-Paris by Claire Huchet Bishop (Viking)

The Quaint and Curious Quest of Johnny Longfoot by Catherine Besterman (Bobbs)

1949 *King of the Wind* by Marguerite Henry (Rand McNally)

Honor Books

Daughter of the Mountains by Louise Rankin (Viking)

My Father's Dragon by Ruth S. Gannett (Random House)

Seabird by Holling C. Holling (Houghton Mifflin)

Story of the Negro by Arna Bontemps (Knopf)

1950 *A Door in the Wall* by Marguerite de Angeli (Doubleday)

Honor Books

The Blue Cat of Castle Town by Catherine Coblentz (Longmans)

George Washington by Genevieve Foster (Scribner's)

Kildee House by Rutherford Montgomery (Doubleday)

Song of the Pines by Walter and Marion Havighurst (Winston)

Tree of Freedom by Rebecca Caudill (Viking)

1951 *Amos Fortune, Free Man* by Elizabeth Yates (Dutton)

Honor Books

Abraham Lincoln, Friend of the People by Clara Ingram Judson (Follett)

Better Known as Johnny Appleseed by Mabel Leigh Hunt (Lippincott)

Gandhi, Fighter without a Sword by Jeanette Eaton (Morrow)

The Story of Appleby Capple by Anne Parrish (Harper)

1952 *Ginger Pye* by Eleanor Estes (Harcourt)

Honor Books

Americans before Columbus by Elizabeth Baity (Viking)

The Apple and the Arrow by Mary and Conrad Buff (Houghton Mifflin)

The Defender by Nicholas Kalashnikoff (Scribner's)

The Light at Tern Rocks by Julia Sauer (Viking)

Minn of the Mississippi by Holling C. Holling (Houghton Mifflin)

1953 *Secret of the Andes* by Ann Nolan Clark (Viking)

Honor Books

The Bears of Hemlock Mountain by Alice Dalgliesh (Scribner's)

Birthdays of Freedom, Vol. 1 by Genevieve Foster (Scribner's)

Charlotte's Web by E. B. White (Harper)

Moccasin Trail by Eloise McGraw (Coward)

Red Sails to Capri by Ann Weil (Viking)

1954 *. . . And Now Miguel* by Joseph Krumgold (Crowell)

Honor Books

All Alone by Claire Huchet Bishop (Viking)

Hurry Home Candy by Meindert DeJong (Harper)

Magic Maize by Mary and Conrad Buff (Houghton Mifflin)

Shadrach by Meindert DeJong (Harper)

Theodore Roosevelt, Fighting Patriot by Clara Ingram Judson (Follett)

1955 *The Wheel on the School* by Meindert DeJong (Harper)

Honor Books

Banner in the Sky by James Ullman (Lippincott)

Courage of Sarah Noble by Alice Dalgliesh (Scribner's)

1956 *Carry On, Mr. Bowditch* by Jean Lee Latham (Houghton Mifflin)

Honor Books

The Golden Name Day by Jennie Lindquist (Harper)

Men, Microscopes, and Living Things by Katherine Shippen (Viking)

The Secret River by Marjorie Kinnan Rawlings (Scribner's)

1957 *Miracles on Maple Hill* by Virginia Sorensen (Harcourt)

Honor Books

Black Fox of Lorne by Marguerite de Angeli (Doubleday)

The Corn Grows Ripe by Dorothy Rhoads (Viking)

The House of Sixty Fathers by Meindert DeJong (Harper)

Mr. Justice Holmes by Clara Ingram Judson (Follett)

Old Yeller by Fred Gipson (Harper)

1958 *Rifles for Watie* by Harold Keith (Crowell)

Honor Books

Gone-Away Lake by Elizabeth Enright (Harcourt)

The Great Wheel by Robert Lawson (Viking)

The Horse Catcher by Mari Sandoz (Westminster)

Tom Paine, Freedom's Apostle by Leo Gurko (Crowell)

1959 *The Witch of Blackbird Pond* by Elizabeth George Speare (Houghton Mifflin)

Honor Books

Along Came a Dog by Meindert DeJong (Harper)

Chucaro: Wild Pony of the Pampa by Francis Kalnay (Harcourt)

The Family under the Bridge by Natalie Savage Carlson (Harper)

The Perilous Road by William O. Steele (Harcourt)

1960 *Onion John* by Joseph Krumgold (Crowell)

Honor Books

America Is Born by Gerald W. Johnson (Morrow)

The Gammage Cup by Carol Kendall (Harcourt)

My Side of the Mountain by Jean Craighead George (Dutton)

1961 *Island of the Blue Dolphins* by Scott O'Dell (Houghton Mifflin)

Honor Books

America Moves Forward by Gerald W. Johnson (Morrow)

The Cricket in Times Square by George Selden (Farrar)

Old Ramon by Jack Schaefer (Houghton Mifflin)

1962 *The Bronze Bow* by Elizabeth George Speare (Houghton Mifflin)

Honor Books

Belling the Tiger by Mary Stolz (Harper)

Frontier Living by Edwin Tunis (World)

The Golden Goblet by Eloise McGraw (Coward)

1963 *A Wrinkle in Time* by Madeleine L'Engle (Farrar)

Honor Books

Men of Athens by Olivia Coolidge (Houghton Mifflin)

Thistle and Thyme by Sorche Nic Leodhas (Holt)

1964 *It's Like This, Cat* by Emily Cheney Neville (Harper)

Honor Books

The Loner by Ester Wier (McKay)

Rascal by Sterling North (Dutton)

1965 *Shadow of a Bull* by Maia Wojciechowska (Atheneum)

Honor Book: Across Five Aprils by Irene Hunt (Follett)

1966 *I, Juan de Pareja* by Elizabeth Borten de Trevino (Farrar)

Honor Books

The Animal Family by Randall Jarrell (Pantheon)

The Black Cauldron by Lloyd Alexander (Holt)

The Noonday Friends by Mary Stolz (Harper)

1967 *Up a Road Slowly* by Irene Hunt (Follett)

Honor Books

The Jazz Man by Mary H. Weik (Atheneum)

The King's Fifth by Scott O'Dell (Houghton)

Zlateh the Goat and Other Stories by Isaac Bashevis Singer (Harper)

1968 *From the Mixed-Up Files of Mrs. Basil E. Frankweiler* by E. L. Konigsburg (Atheneum)

Honor Books

The Black Pearl by Scott O'Dell (Houghton Mifflin)

The Egypt Game by Zilpha Keatley Snyder (Atheneum)

The Fearsome Inn by Isaac Bashevis Singer (Scribner's)

Jennifer, Hecate, Macbeth, William McKinley, and Me, Elizabeth by E. L. Konigsburg (Atheneum)

1969 *The High King* by Lloyd Alexander (Holt)

Honor Books

To Be a Slave by Julius Lester (Dial)

When Sheemiel Went to Warsaw and Other Stories by Isaac Bashevis Singer (Farrar)

1970 *Sounder* by William H. Armstrong (Harper)

Honor Books

Journey Outside by Mary Q. Steele (Viking)

The Many Ways of Seeing: An Introduction to the Pleasures of Art by Janet Gaylord Moore (World)

Our Eddie by Sulamith Ish-Kishor (Pantheon)

1971 *Summer of the Swans* by Betsy Byars (Viking)

Honor Books

Enchantress from the Stars by Sylvia Louise Engdahl (Atheneum)

Knee-Knock Rise by Natalie Babbitt (Farrar)

Sing Down the Moon by Scott O'Dell (Houghton Mifflin)

1972 *Mrs. Frisby and the Rats of NIMH* by Robert C. O'Brien (Atheneum)

Honor Books

Annie and the Old One by Miska Miles (Atlantic/Little, Brown)

The Headless Cupid by Zilpha Keatley Snyder (Atheneum)

Incident at Hawk's Hill by Allan W. Eckert (Little, Brown)

The Planet of Junior Brown by Virginia Hamilton (Macmillan)

The Tombs of Atuan by Ursula K. Le Guin (Atheneum)

1973 *Julie of the Wolves* by Jean Craighead George (Harper)

Honor Books

Frog and Toad Together by Arnold Lobel (Harper)

The Upstairs Room by Johanna Reiss (Crowell)

The Witches of Worm by Zilpha Keatley Snyder (Atheneum)

1974 *The Slave Dancer* by Paula Fox (Bradbury)

Honor Book: *The Dark Is Rising* by Susan Cooper (McElderry)

1975 *M. C. Higgins, the Great* by Virginia Hamilton (Macmillan)

Honor Books

Figgs and Phantoms by Ellen Raskin (Dutton)

My Brother Sam Is Dead by James Lincoln Collier and Christopher Collier (Four Winds)

The Perilous Gard by Elizabeth Marie Pope (Houghton Mifflin)

Philip Hall Likes Me, I Reckon Maybe by Bette Greene (Dial)

1976 *The Grey King* by Susan Cooper (McElderry)

Honor Books

Dragonwings by Laurence Yep (Harper)

The Hundred Penny Box by Sharon Bell Mathis (Viking)

1977 *Roll of Thunder, Hear My Cry* by Mildred D. Taylor (Dial)

Honor Books

Abel's Island by William Steig (Farrar)

A String in the Harp by Nancy Bond (McElderry)

1978 *Bridge to Terabithia* by Katherine Paterson (Crowell)

Honor Books

Anpao: An American Indian Odyssey by Jamake Highwater (Lippincott)

Ramona and Her Father by Beverly Cleary (Morrow)

1979 *The Westing Game* by Ellen Raskin (Dutton)

Honor Book: *The Great Gilly Hopkins* by Katherine Paterson (Crowell)

1980 *A Gathering of Days: A New England Girl's Journal, 1830–1832* by Joan W. Blos (Scribner's)

Honor Book: *The Road from Home: The Story of an Armenian Girl* by David Kherdian (Greenwillow)

1981 *Jacob Have I Loved* by Katherine Paterson (Crowell)

Honor Books

The Fledgling by Jane Langton (Harper)

A Ring of Endless Light by Madeleine L'Engle (Farrar)

1982 *A Visit to William Blake's Inn: Poems for Innocent and Experienced Travelers* by Nancy Willard, illustrated by Alice and Martin Provensen (Harcourt)

Honor Books

Ramona Quimby, Age 8 by Beverly Cleary (Morrow)

Upon the Head of the Goat: A Childhood in Hungary, 1939–1944 by Aranka Siegal (Farrar)

1983 *Dicey's Song* by Cynthia Voigt (Atheneum)

Honor Books

The Blue Sword by Robin McKinley (Greenwillow)

Doctor De Soto by William Steig (Farrar)

Graven Images by Paul Fleischman (Harper)

Homesick: My Own Story by Jean Fritz (Putnam)

Sweet Whispers, Brother Rush by Virginia Hamilton (Philomel)

1984 *Dear Mr. Henshaw* by Beverly Cleary (Morrow)

Honor Books

The Sign of the Beaver by Elizabeth George Speare (Houghton Mifflin)

A Solitary Blue by Cynthia Voigt (Atheneum)

Sugaring Time by Kathryn Lasky (Macmillan)

The Wish Giver by Bill Brittain (Harper)

1985 *The Hero and the Crown* by Robin McKinley (Greenwillow)

Honor Books

Like Jake and Me by Mavis Jukes (Knopf)

The Moves Make the Man by Bruce Brooks (Harper)

One-Eyed Cat by Paula Fox (Bradbury)

1986 *Sarah, Plain and Tall* by Patricia MacLachlan (Harper)

Honor Books

Commodore Perry in the Land of the Shogun by Rhoda Blumberg (Lothrop)

Dogsong by Gary Paulsen (Bradbury)

1987 *The Whipping Boy* by Sid Fleischman (Greenwillow)

Honor Books

A Fine White Dust by Cynthia Rylant (Bradbury)

On My Honor by Marion Dane Bauer (Clarion)

Volcano: The Eruption and Healing of Mount St. Helens by Patricia Lauber (Bradbury)

1988 *Lincoln: A Photobiography* by Russell Freedman (Clarion)

Honor Books

After the Rain by Norma Fox Mazer (Morrow)

Hatchet by Gary Paulsen (Bradbury)

1989 *Joyful Noise: Poems for Two Voices* by Paul Fleischman (Harper)

Honor Books

In the Beginning: Creation Stories from Around the World by Virginia Hamilton (Harcourt)

Scorpions by Walter Dean Myers (Harper)

1990 *Number the Stars* by Lois Lowry (Houghton Mifflin)

Honor Books

Afternoon of the Elves by Janet Taylor Lisle (Orchard)

Shabanu: Daughter of the Wind by Suzanne Fisher Staples (Knopf)

The Winter Room by Gary Paulsen (Orchard)

1991 *Maniac Magee* by Jerry Spinelli (Little, Brown)

Honor Book: *The True Confessions of Charlotte Doyle* by Avi (Orchard)

1992 *Shiloh* by Phyllis Reynolds Naylor (Atheneum)

Honor Books

Nothing but the Truth: A Documentary Novel by Avi (Orchard)

The Wright Brothers: How They Invented the Airplane by Russell Freedman (Holiday House)

1993 *Missing May* by Cynthia Rylant (Orchard)

Honor Books

The Dark-Thirty: Southern Tales of the Supernatural by Patricia McKissack (Knopf)

Somewhere in the Darkness by Walter Dean Myers (Scholastic)

What Hearts by Bruce Brooks (HarperCollins)

1994 *The Giver* by Lois Lowry (Houghton Mifflin)

Honor Books

Crazy Lady! by Jane Leslie Conly (HarperCollins)

Dragon's Gate by Laurence Yep (HarperCollins)

Eleanor Roosevelt: A Life of Discovery by Russell Freedman (Clarion)

1995 *Walk Two Moons* by Sharon Creech (HarperCollins)

Honor Books

Catherine, Called Birdy by Karen Cushman (Clarion)

The Ear, the Eye and the Arm by Nancy Farmer (Richard Jackson/Orchard)

1996 *The Midwife's Apprentice* by Karen Cushman (Clarion)

Honor Books

What Jamie Saw by Carolyn Coman (Front Street)

The Watsons Go to Birmingham—1963 by Christopher Paul Curtis (Delacorte)

Yolonda's Genius by Carol Fenner (McElderry/Simon & Schuster)

The Great Fire by Jim Murphy (Scholastic)

1997 *The View from Saturday* by E. L. Konigsburg (Jean Karl/Atheneum)

Honor Books

A Girl Named Disaster by Nancy Farmer (Richard Jackson/Orchard)

Moorchild by Elois McGraw (McElderry)

The Thief by Megan Whalen Turner (Greenwillow)

Belle Prater's Boy by Ruth White (Farrar)

1998 *Out of the Dust* by Karen Hesse (Scholastic)

Honor Books

Ella Enchanted by Gail Carson Levine (HarperCollins)

Lily's Crossing by Patricia Reilly Giff (Delacorte)

Wringer by Jerry Spinelli (HarperCollins)

1999 *Holes* by Louis Sachar (Foster/Farrar)

Honor Book: A Long Way from Chicago by Richard Peck (Dial)

2000 *Bud, Not Buddy* by Christopher Paul Curtis (Delacorte)

Honor Books

Getting Near to Baby by Audrey Couloumbis (Putnam)

Our Only May Amelia by Jennifer L. Holm (HarperCollins)

26 Fairmount Avenue by Tomie dePaola (Putnam)

2001 *A Year Down Yonder* by Richard Peck (Dial)

Honor Books

Because of Winn-Dixie by Kate DiCamillo (Candlewick Press)

Hope Was Here by Joan Bauer (Putnam)

Joey Pigza Loses Control by Jack Gantos (Farrar, Straus, & Giroux)

The Wanderer by Sharon Creech (Joanne Cotler/HarperCollins)

2002 *A Single Shard* by Linda Sue Park (Clarion Books/Houghton Mifflin)

Honor Books

Everything on a Waffle by Polly Horvath (Farrar, Straus, & Giroux)

Carver: A Life In Poems by Marilyn Nelson (Front Street)

2003 *Crispin: The Cross of Lead* by Avi (Hyperion Books for Children)

Honor Books

The House of the Scorpion by Nancy Farmer (Atheneum)

Pictures of Hollis Woods by Patricia Reilly Giff (Random House/Wendy Lamb Books)

Hoot by Carl Hiaasen (Knopf)

A Corner of the Universe by Ann M. Martin (Scholastic)

Surviving the Applewhites by Stephanie S. Tolan (HarperCollins)

2004 *The Tale of Despereaux: Being the Story of a Mouse, a Princess, Some Soup, and a Spool of Thread* by Kate DiCamillo, illustrated by Timothy Basil Ering (Candlewick Press)

Honor Books

Olive's Ocean by Kevin Henkes (Greenwillow Books)

An American Plague: The True and Terrifying Story of the Yellow Fever Epidemic of 1793 by Jim Murphy (Clarion Books)

2005 *Kira-Kira* by Cynthia Kadohota (Atheneum/Simon & Schuster)

Honor Books

Lizzie Bright and the Buckminster Boy by Gary D. Schmidt (Clarion/Houghton Mifflin)

Al Capone Does My Shirts by Gennifer Choldenko (Putnam)

The Voice that Challenged a Nation: Marian Anderson and the Struggle for Equal Rights by Russell Freedman (Clarion/Houghton Mifflin)

2006 *Criss Cross* by Lynne Rae Perkins (Greenwillow Books/HarperCollins)

Honor Books

Whittington by Alan Armstrong, illustrated by S. D. Schindler (Random House)

Hitler Youth: Growing Up in Hitler's Shadow by Susan Campbell Bartoletti (Scholastic)

Princess Academy by Shannon Hale (Bloomsbury Children's Books)

Show Way by Jacqueline Woodson, illustrated by Hudson Talbott (G.P. Putnam's Sons)

2007 *The Higher Power of Lucky* by Susan Patron, illustrated by Matt Phelan (Simon & Schuster/Richard Jackson)

Honor Books

Penny from Heaven by Jennifer L. Holm (Random House)

Hattie Big Sky by Kirby Larson (Delacorte Press)

Rules by Cynthia Lord (Scholastic)

2008 *Good Masters! Sweet Ladies! Voices from a Medieval Village* by Laura Amy Schlitz (Candlewick)

Honor Books

Elijah of Buxton by Christopher Paul Curtis (Scholastic)

The Wednesday Wars by Gary D. Schmidt (Clarion)

Feathers by Jacqueline Woodson (Putnam)

2009 *The Graveyard Book* by Neil Gaiman (HarperCollins)

Honor Books

The Underneath by Kathi Appelt (Atheneum Books for Young Readers, an imprint of Simon & Schuster)

The Surrender Tree: Poems of Cuba's Struggle for Freedom by Margarita Engle (Henry Holt)

Savvy by Ingrid Law (Dial Books for Young Readers, a division of Penguin Young Readers Group in partnership with Walden Media)

After Tupac & D Foster by Jacqueline Woodson (G.P. Putnam's Sons, a division of Penguin Books for Young Readers)

2010 *You Reach Me* by Rebecca Stead (Wendy Lamb Books, an imprint of Random House Children's Books)

Honor Books

Claudette Colvin: Twice Toward Justice by Phillip Hoose (Melanie Kroupa Books/Farrar, Straus, & Giroux, an imprint of Macmillan Children's Publishing Group)

The Evolution of Calpurnia Tate by Jacqueline Kelly (Henry Holt and Company)

Where the Mountain Meets the Moon by Grace Lin (Little, Brown and Company Books for Young Readers)

The Mostly True Adventures of Homer P. Figg by Rodman Philbrick (The Blue Sky Press, an imprint of Scholastic Inc.)

2011 *Moon over Manifest* by Clare Vanderpool (Delacorte Press, an imprint of Random House Children's Books)

Honor Books

Turtle in Paradise by Jennifer L. Holm (Random House Children's Books)

Heart of a Samurai by Margi Preus (Amulet Books, an imprint of Abrams)

Dark Emperor and Other Poems of the Night by Joyce Sidman, illustrated by Rick Allen (Houghton Mifflin Books for Children, Houghton Mifflin Harcourt)

One Crazy Summer by Rita Williams-Garcia (Amistad, an imprint of HarperCollins)

2012 *Dead End in Norvelt* by Jack Gantos (Farrar Straus Giroux)

Honor Books

Inside Out & Back Again by Thanhha Lai (HarperCollins Children's Books, a division of HarperCollins Publishers)

Breaking Stalin's Nose by Eugene Yelchin (Henry Holt and Company)

2013 *The One and Only Ivan* by Katherine Applegate (HarperCollins Children's Books)

Honor Books

Splendors and Glooms by Laura Amy Schlitz (Candlewick Press)

Bomb: The Race to Build—and Steal—the World's Most Dangerous Weapon by Steve Sheinkin (Flash Point/Roaring Brook Press)

Three Times Lucky by Sheila Turnage (Dial/Penguin Young Readers Group)

ORBIS PICTUS AWARD FOR OUTSTANDING NONFICTION FOR CHILDREN

The National Council of Teachers of English (NCTE) established the Orbis Pictus Award in 1990 to recognize outstanding nonfiction for children. The annual award is named for *Orbis Pictus* (*The World in Pictures*), a 1657 work by John Amos Comenius, believed to be the first book written expressly for children.

1990 *The Great Little Madison* by Jean Fritz (Putnam)

Honor Books

The Great American Gold Rush by Rhoda Blumberg (Bradbury)

The News about Dinosaurs by Patricia Lauber (Bradbury)

1991 *Franklin Delano Roosevelt* by Russell Freedman (Clarion)

Honor Books

Arctic Memories by Normee Ekoomiak (Holt)

Seeing Earth from Space by Patricia Lauber (Orchard)

1992 *Flight: The Journey of Charles Lindbergh* by Robert Burleigh and Mike Wimmer (Philomel)

Honor Books

Now Is Your Time! The African American Struggle for Freedom by Walter Dean Myers (HarperCollins)

Prairie Visions: The Life and Times of Solomon Butcher by Pam Conrad (HarperCollins)

1993 *Children of the Dust Bowl: The True Story of the School of Weedpatch Camp* by Jerry Stanley (Crown)

Honor Books

Talking with Artists by Pat Cummings (Bradbury)

Come Back, Salmon by Molly Cone (Sierra Club)

1994 *Across America on an Emigrant Train* by Jim Murphy (Clarion)

Honor Books

To the Top of the World: Adventures with Arctic Wolves by Jim Brandenburg (Walker)

Making Sense: Animal Perception and Communication by Bruce Brooks (Farrar)

1995 *Safari Beneath the Sea: The Wonder World of the North Pacific Coast* by Diane Swanson (Sierra Club)

Honor Books

Wildlife Rescue: The Work of Dr. Kathleen Ramsay by Jennifer Owings Dewey (Boyds Mills)

Kids at Work: Lewis Hine and the Crusade against Child Labor by Russell Freedman (Clarion)

Christmas in the Big House, Christmas in the Quarters by Patricia and Fredrick McKissack (Scholastic)

1996 *The Great Fire* by Jim Murphy (Scholastic)

Honor Books

Dolphin Man: Exploring the World of Dolphins by Laurence Pringle, photos by Randall S. Wells (Atheneum)

Rosie the Riveter: Women Working on the Home Front in World War II by Penny Colman (Crown)

1997 *Leonardo da Vinci* by Diane Stanley (Morrow)

Honor Books

Full Steam Ahead: The Race to Build a Transcontinental Railroad by Rhoda Blumberg (National Geographic)

The Life and Death of Crazy Horse by Russell Freedman (Holiday House)

One World, Many Religions: The Ways We Worship by Mary Pope Osborne (Knopf)

1998 *An Extraordinary Life: The Story of a Monarch Butterfly* by Laurence Pringle (Orchard Books)

Honor Books

A Drop of Water: A Book of Science and Wonder by Walter Wick (Scholastic)

A Tree Is Growing by Arthur Dorros, illustrated by S. D. Schindler (Scholastic)

Charles Lindbergh: A Human Hero by James Cross Giblin (Clarion)

Kennedy Assassinated! The World Mourns: A Reporter's Story by Wilborn Hampton (Candlewick)

Digger: The Tragic Fate of the California Indians from the Missions to the Gold Rush by Jerry Stanley (Crown)

1999 *Shipwreck at the Bottom of the World: The Extraordinary True Story of Shackleton and the Endurance* by Jennifer Armstrong (Crown)

Honor Books

Black Whiteness: Admiral Byrd Alone in the Antarctic by Robert Burleigh, illustrated by Walter Lyon Krudop (Atheneum)

Fossil Feud: The Rivalry of the First American Dinosaur Hunters by Thom Holmes (Messner)

Hottest, Coldest, Highest, Deepest by Steve Jenkins (Houghton)

No Pretty Pictures: A Child of War by Anita Lobel (Greenwillow)

2000 *Through My Eyes* by Ruby Bridges (Scholastic)

Honor Books

At Her Majesty's Request: An African Princess in Victorian England by Walter Dean Myers (Scholastic)

Clara Schumann: Piano Virtuoso by Susanna Reich (Clarion Books)

Mapping the World by Sylvia A. Johnson (Atheneum)

The Top of the World: Climbing Mount Everest by Steve Jenkins (Houghton)

2001 *Hurry Freedom: African Americans in Gold Rush California* by Jerry Stanley (Crown)

Honor Books

The Amazing Life of Benjamin Franklin by James Cross Giblin, illustrated by Michael Dooling (Scholastic)

America's Champion Swimmer: Gertrude Ederle by David A. Adler, illustrated by Terry Widener (Gulliver Books)

Michelangelo by Diane Stanley (HarperCollins)

Osceola: Memories of a Sharecropper's Daughter by Alan B. Govenar, illustrated by Shane W. Evans (Jump at the Sun)

Wild & Swampy by Jim Amosky (HarperCollins)

2002 *Black Potatoes: The Story of the Great Irish Famine, 1845–1850* by Susan Campbell Bartoletti (Houghton)

Honor Books

The Cod's Tale by Mark Kurlansky, illustrated by S. D. Schindler (Penguin Putnam Books)

The Dinosaurs of Waterhouse Hawkins: An Illuminating History of Mr. Waterhouse Hawkins, Artist and Lecturer by Barbara Kerley, illustrated by Brian Selznick (Scholastic)

Martin's Big Words: The Life of Dr. Martin Luther King, Jr. by Doreen Rappaport, illustrated by Bryan Collier (Hyperion)

2003 *When Marian Sang: The True Recital of Marian Anderson: The Voice of a Century* by Pam Muñoz Ryan, illustrated by Brian Selznick (Scholastic)

Honor Books

Confucius: The Golden Rule by Russell Freedman, illustrated by Frederic Clement (Arthur A. Levine Books)

Emperor's Silent Army: Terracotta Warriors of Ancient China by Jane O'Connor (Viking)

Phineas Gage: A Gruesome but True Story About Brain Science by John Fleischman (Houghton)

Tenement: Immigrant Life on the Lower East Side by Raymond Bial (Houghton)

To Fly: The Story of the Wright Brothers by Wendie C. Old, illustrated by Robert Andrew Parker (Clarion)

2004 *An American Plague: The True and Terrifying Story of the Yellow Fever Epidemic of 1793* by Jim Murphy (Clarion)

Honor Books

Empire State Building: When New York Reached for the Skies by Elizabeth Mann, illustrated by Alan Witschonke (Mikaya Press)

In Defense of Liberty: The Story of America's Bill of Rights by Russell Freedman (Holiday House)

Leonardo: Beautiful Dreamer by Robert Byrd (Dutton)

The Man Who Made Time Travel by Kathryn Lasky, illustrated by Kevin Hawkes (Farrar, Straus, & Giroux)

Shutting Out the Sky: Life in the Tenements of New York, 1880–1924 by Deborah Hopkinson (Orchard Books)

2005 *York's Adventure with Lewis and Clark: An African-American's Part in the Great Expedition* by Rhoda Blumberg (HarperCollins)

Honor Books

Actual Size by Steve Jenkins (Houghton)

The Race to Save the Lord God Bird by Phillip Hoose (Farrar, Straus, & Giroux)

Secrets of the Sphinx by James Cross Giblin, illustrated by Bagram Ibatoulline (Scholastic)

Seurat and La Grande Jatte: Connecting the Dots by Robert Burleigh (Abrams Books for Young Readers)

The Voice That Challenged a Nation: Marian Anderson and the Struggle for Equal Rights by Russell Freedman (Clarion)

2006 *Children of the Great Depression* by Russell Freedman (Clarion Books)

Honor Books

ER Vets: Life in an Animal Emergency Room by Donna Jackson (Houghton Mifflin)

Forbidden Schoolhouse: The True and Dramatic Story of Prudence Crandall and Her Students by Suzanne Jurmain (Houghton Mifflin)

Genius: A Photobiography of Albert Einstein by Marfe Ferguson Delano (National Geographic)

Hitler Youth: Growing Up in Hitler's Shadow by Susan Campbell Bartoletti (Scholastic)

Mosquito Bite by Alexandra Siy and Dennis Kunkel (Charlesbridge Publishing)

2007 *Quest for the Tree Kangaroo: An Expedition to the Cloud Forest of New Guinea* by Sy Montgomery, photos by Nic Bishop (Houghton Mifflin)

Honor Books

Gregor Mendel: The Friar Who Grew Peas by Cheryl Bardoe, illustrated by Jos. A. Smith (Abrams Books for Young Readers)

Freedom Walkers: The Story of the Montgomery Bus Boycott by Russell Freedman (Holiday House)

John Muir: America's First Environmentalist by Kathryn Lasky, illustrated by Stan Fellows (Candlewick Press)

Something Out of Nothing: Marie Curie and Radium by Carla Killough McClafferty (Farrar, Straus, & Giroux)

Team Moon: How 400,000 People Landed Apollo 11 on the Moon by Catherine Thimmesh (Houghton Mifflin)

2008 *M.L.K. Journey of a King* by Tonya Bolden (Abrams Books for Children)

Honor Books

Black and White Airmen: Their True History by John Fleischman (Houghton Mifflin)

Spiders by Nic Bishop (Scholastic)

Helen Keller: Her Life in Pictures by George Sullivan (Scholastic)

Muckrakers by Ann Bausum (National Geographic)

Venom by Marilyn Singer (Darby Creek Publishing)

2009 *Amelia Earhart: The Legend of the Lost Aviator* by Shelley Tanaka, Illustrated by David Craig (Abrams Books for Young Readers)

Honor Books

George Washington Carver by Tonya Bolden (Abrams Books for Young Readers)

The Lincolns: A Scrapbook Look at Abraham and Mary by Candace Fleming (Schwartz & Wade Books)

Washington at Valley Forge by Russell Freedman (Holiday House)

We Are the Ship: The Story of Negro League Baseball by Kadir Nelson (Hyperion Books for Children)

When the Wolves Returned: Restoring Nature's Balance in Yellowstone by Dorothy Hinshaw Patent, illustrated by Dan and Cassie Hartman (Walker Books for Young Readers)

2010 *The Secret World of Walter Anderson* by Hester Bass, illustrated by E. B. Lewis (Candlewick Press)

Honor Books

Almost Astronauts: 13 Women Who Dared to Dream by Tanya Lee Stone (Candlewick Press)

Darwin: With Glimpses into His Private Journal and Letters by Alice B. McGinty (Houghton Mifflin Books for Children)

The Frog Scientist by Pamela S. Turner (Houghton Mifflin Books for Children)

How Many Baby Pandas? by Sandra Markle (Walker Books for Young Readers)

Noah Webster: Weaver of Words by Pegi Deitz Shea (Calkins Creek Books)

2011 *Ballet for Martha: Making Appalachian Spring* by Jan Greenberg and Sandra Jordan, illustrated by Brian Floca (Roaring Brook Press)

Honor Books

Birmingham Sunday by Larry Dane Brimner (Calkins Creek)

Candy Bomber: The Story of the Berlin Airlift's "Chocolate Pilot" by Michael O. Tunnell (Charlesbridge)

If Stones Could Speak: Unlocking the Secrets of Stonehenge by Mark Aronson (National Geographic)

Journey into the Deep: Discovering New Ocean Creatures by Rebecca L. Johnson (Millbrook Press)

Mammoths and Mastodons: Titans of the Ice Age by Cheryl Bardoe (Abrams Books for Young Readers)

2012 *Balloons over Broadway: The True Story of the Puppeteer of Macy's Parade* by Melissa Sweet (Houghton Mifflin Books for Children)

Honor Books

Amelia Lost: The Life and Disappearance of Amelia Earhart by Candace Fleming (Schwartz & Wade Books)

Father Abraham: Lincoln and His Sons by Harold Holzer (Calkins Creek)

Pablo Neruda: Poet of the People by Monica Brown, illustrated by Julie Paschkis (Henry Holt and Company)

Terezin: Voices from the Holocaust by Ruth Thomson (Candlewick Press)

The Mangrove Tree: Planting Trees to Feed Families by Susan L. Roth & Cindy Trumbore (Lee & Low Books Inc.)

2013 *Monsieur Marceau: Actor without Words* by Leda Schubert, illustrated by Gérard DuBois (Roaring Brook Press)

Honor Books

Citizen Scientist: Be a Part of Scientific Discovery from Your Own Backyard by Loree Griffin Burns, photos by Ellen Harasimonwicz (Henry Holt & Company)

Electric Ben: The Amazing Life and Times of Benjamin Franklin by Robert Byrd (Dial Books for Young Readers)

The Mighty Mars Rovers: The Incredible Adventures of Spirit and Opportunity by Elizabeth Rusch (Houghton Mifflin Books for Children)

Those Rebels, John & Tom by Barbara Kerley, illustrated by Edward Fotheringham (Scholastic)

We've Got a Job: The 1963 Birmingham Children's March by Cynthia Levinson (Peachtree Publishers)

SCOTT O'DELL HISTORICAL FICTION AWARD

The Scott O'Dell Historical Fiction Award was established in 1981 and is administered by the Advisory Committee of the Bulletin of the Center for Children's Books. Books must be historical fiction, have unusual literary merit, be written by a citizen of the United States, and be set in the New World. They must have been published in the previous year by a United States publisher and must be written for children or young adults.

1984 *The Sign of the Beaver* by Elizabeth George Speare (Houghton)

1985 *The Fighting Ground* by Avi (Harper)

1986 *Sarah, Plain and Tall* by Patricia MacLachlan (Harper)

1987 *Streams to the River, River to the Sea: A Novel of Sacagawea* by Scott O'Dell (Houghton)

1988 *Charley Skedaddle* by Patricia Beatty (Morrow)

1989 *The Honorable Prison* by Lyll Becerra de Jenkins (Lodestar)

1990 *Shades of Gray* by Carolyn Reeder (Macmillan)

1991 *A Time of Troubles* by Pieter VanRaven (Atheneum)

1992 *Stepping on the Cracks* by Mary Downing Hahn (Clarion)

1993 *Morning Girl* by Michael A. Dorris (Hyperion)

1994 *Bull Run* by Paul Fleischman (HarperCollins)

1995 *Under the Blood-Red Sun* by Graham Salisbury (Harcourt)

1996 *The Bomb* by Theodore Taylor (Harcourt)

1997 *Jip: His Story* by Katherine Paterson (Clarion)

1998 *Out of the Dust* by Karen Hesse (Scholastic)

1999 *Forty Acres and Maybe a Mule* by Harriette Gillem Robinet (Atheneum)

2000 *The Art of Keeping Cool* by Janet Taylor Lisle (Simon & Schuster)

2002 *The Land* by Mildred D. Taylor (Phyllis Fogelman Books)

2003 *Trouble Don't Last* by Shelley Pearsall (Alfred A. Knopf)

2004 *A River Between Us* by Richard Peck (Dial Press)

2005 *Worth* by A. LaFaye (Simon & Schuster)

2006 *The Game of Silence* by Louise Erdrich (HarperCollins Children's Books)

2007 *The Green Glass Sea* by Ellen Klages (Viking Children's Books)

2008 *Elijah of Buxton* by Christopher Paul Curtis (Scholastic)

2009 *Chains* by Laurie Halse Anderson (Simon & Schuster)

2010 *The Storm in the Barn* by Matt Phelan (Candlewick)

2011 *One Crazy Summer* by Rita Williams Garcia (Amistad)

2012 *Dead End in Norvelt* by Jack Gantos (Farrar, Straus and Giroux)

2013 *Chickadee* by Louise Erdrich (HarperCollins)

THE TOMÁS RIVERA MEXICAN AMERICAN CHILDREN'S BOOK AWARD

The Tomás Rivera Mexican American Children's Book Award, established in 1995, was founded by the College of Education at Texas State University-San Marcos. It is awarded annually to honor the most distinguished book depicting the Mexican American experience. Both fiction and nonfiction selections are eligible, as are books appropriate for children ages 0 to 16 years old. Literary quality and authenticity in representation are criteria for consideration.

1996 *Chato's Kitchen* by Gary Soto, illustrated by Susan Guevara (Putnam)

1997 *The Farolitos of Christmas* by Rudolfo Anaya, illustrated by Edward Gonzalez (Hyperion)

1998 *In My Family/En Mi Familia* written and illustrated by Carmen Lomas Garza (Children's Book Press)

1999 *Tomás and the Library Lady* by Pat Mora, illustrated by Raúl Colón (Knopf)

2000 *The Three Pigs/Los Tres Cerdos: Nacho, Tito, and Miguel* written and illustrated by Bobbi Salinas (Piñata Books)

2001 *My Land Sings: Stories of the Río Grande* by Rudolfo Anaya, illustrated by Amy Cordova (Rayo)

2002 *My Very Own Room* by Amada Irma Pérez, illustrated by Maya Christina Gonzalez (Children's Book Press)

2003 *A Library for Juana* by Pat Mora, illustrated by Beatriz Vidal (Knopf)

2004 *Just a Minute: A Trickster Tale and Counting Book* written and illustrated by Yuyi Morales (Chronicle Books)

2005 *Becoming Naomi León* by Pam Muñoz Ryan

2006 *José! Born to Dance* by Susanna Reich, illustrated by Raúl Colón

2007 *Downtown Boy* by Juan Felipe Herrera

2008 *Los Gatos Black on Halloween* by Marisa Montes, illustrated by Yuyi Morales

2009 *He Forgot to Say Goodbye* by Benjamin Alire Sáenz

The Holy Tortilla and a Pot of Beans by Carmen Tafolla

2011 *Bait* by Alex Sanchez (Simon & Schuster Books for Young Readers)

2012 *Sylvia and Aki* by Winifred Conkling (Tricycle Press)

Diego Rivera: His World and Ours by Duncan Tonatiuh (Harry N. Abrams)

2013 *Under the Mesquite* by Guadalupe García McCall (Lee & Low Books)

ROBERT F. SIBERT INFORMATIONAL BOOK AWARD

Established in 2001, the Robert F. Sibert Informational Book Award is given annually to the author of the most distinguished informational book published during the preceding year. The award is named in honor of Robert F. Sibert, the long-time president of Bound to Stay Bound Books of Jacksonville, Illinois, and is sponsored by the company. The Association for Library Service to Children, a division of the American Library Association, administers the award.

2001 *Sir Walter Ralegh and the Quest for El Dorado* by Marc Aronson (Clarion)

Honor Books

The Longitude Prize by Joan Dash, illustrated by Dusan Petricic (Frances Foster Books/Farrar, Straus, & Giroux)

Blizzard! The Storm That Changed America by Jim Murphy (Scholastic)

My Season with Penguins by Sophie Webb (Houghton Mifflin)

Pedro and Me: Friendship, Loss, and What I Learned by Judd Winick (Holt)

2002 *Black Potatoes: The Story of the Great Irish Famine, 1845–1850* by Susan Campbell Bartoletti (Houghton Mifflin)

Honor Books

Surviving Hitler: A Boy in the Nazi Death Camps by Andrea Warren (HarperCollins)

Vincent van Gogh: Portrait of an Artist by Jan Greenberg and Sandra Jordan (Delacorte)

Brooklyn Bridge by Lynn Curlee (Atheneum)

2003 *The Life and Death of Adolf Hitler* by James Cross Giblin (Clarion)

Honor Books

Six Days in October: The Stock Market Crash of 1929 by Karen Blumenthal (Atheneum Books for Young Readers)

Hole in My Life by Jack Gantos (Farrar, Straus, & Giroux)

Action Jackson by Jan Greenberg and Sandra Jordan (Roaring Brook Press)

When Marian Sang by Pam Munoz Ryan (Scholastic)

2004 *An American Plague: The True and Terrifying Story of the Yellow Fever Epidemic of 1793* by Jim Murphy (Clarion)

Honor Book: I Face the Wind by Vicki Cobb with illustrations by Julia Gorton (HarperCollins)

2005 *The Voice that Challenged a Nation: Marian Anderson and the Struggle for Equal Rights* by Russell Freedman (Clarion/Houghton Mifflin)

Honor Books

Sequoyah: The Cherokee Man Who Gave His People Writing by James Rumford, translated into Cherokee by Anna Sixkiller Huckaby (Houghton Mifflin)

The Tarantula Scientist by Sy Montgomery, photographs by Nic Bishop (Houghton Mifflin)

Walt Whitman: Words for America by Barbara Kerley, illustrated by Brian Selznick (Scholastic)

2006 *Secrets of a Civil War Submarine: Solving the Mysteries of the H. L. Hunley* by Sally M. Walker (Carolrhoda Books, Inc., a division of Lerner Publishing Group)

Honor Book: Hitler Youth: Growing Up in Hitler's Shadow by Susan Campbell Bartoletti (Scholastic Nonfiction, an imprint of Scholastic)

2007 *Team Moon: How 400,000 People Landed Apollo 11 on the Moon* by Catherine Thimmesh (Houghton Mifflin)

Honor Books

Freedom Riders: John Lewis and Jim Zwerg on the Front Lines of the Civil Rights Movement by Ann Bausum (National Geographic)

Quest for the Tree Kangaroo: An Expedition to the Cloud Forest of New Guinea by Sy Montgomery, photographs by Nic Bishop (Houghton Mifflin)

To Dance: A Ballerina's Graphic Novel by Siena Cherson Siegel, illustrated by Mark Siegel (Simon & Schuster/Richard Jackson and Simon & Schuster/Aladdin)

2008 *The Wall: Growing Up Behind the Iron Curtain* by Peter Sís (Farrar/Frances Foster)

Honor Books

Lightship, written and illustrated by Brian Floca (Simon & Schuster/Richard Jackson)

Nic Bishop Spiders, written and photographed by Nic Bishop (Scholastic Nonfiction, an imprint of Scholastic)

2009 *We Are the Ship: The Story of Negro League Baseball* by Kadir Nelson (Disney/Jump at the Sun, an imprint of the Disney Book Group)

Honor Books

Bodies from the Ice: Melting Glaciers and the Recovery of the Past by James M. Deem (Houghton Mifflin)

What to Do About Alice?: How Alice Roosevelt Broke the Rules, Charmed the World, and Drove Her Father Teddy Crazy! by Barbara Kerley, illustrated by Edwin Fotheringham (Scholastic Press)

2010 *Almost Astronauts: 13 Women Who Dared to Dream* by Tanya Lee Stone (Candlewick Press)

Honor Books

The Day-Glo Brothers: The True Story of Bob and Joe Switzer's Bright Ideas and Brand-New Colors by Chris Barton, illustrated by Tony Persiani (Charlesbridge)

Moonshot: The Flight of Apollo 11 written and illustrated by Brian Floca (Richard Jackson/Atheneum Books for Young Readers)

Claudette Colvin: Twice Toward Justice by Phillip Hoose (Melanie Kroupa/Farrar, Straus, & Giroux, an imprint of Macmillan Children's Publishing Group)

2011 *Kakapo Rescue: Saving the World's Strangest Parrot* written by Sy Montgomery, photographs by Nic Bishop (Houghton Mifflin Books for Children, an imprint of Houghton Mifflin Harcourt Publishing Company)

Honor Books

Ballet for Martha: Making Appalachian Spring written by Jan Greenberg and Sandra Jordan, illustrated by Brian Floca (A Neal Porter Book, published by Flash Point, an imprint of Roaring Brook Press)

Lafayette and the American Revolution written by Russell Freedman (Holiday House)

2012 *Balloons over Broadway: The True Story of the Puppeteer of Macy's Parade* by Melissa Sweet (Houghton Mifflin Books for Children, an imprint of Houghton Mifflin Harcourt Publishing Company)

Honor Books

Black & White: The Confrontation between Reverend Fred L. Shuttlesworth and Eugene "Bull" Connor by Larry Dane Brimner (Calkins Creek, an imprint of Boyds Mills Press)

Drawing from Memory written and illustrated by Allen Say (Scholastic Press, an imprint of Scholastic)

The Elephant Scientist written by Caitlin O'Connell and Donna M. Jackson, photographs by Caitlin O'Connell and Timothy Rodwelland (Houghton Mifflin Books for Children, an imprint of Houghton Mifflin Harcourt Publishing Company)

Witches!: The Absolutely True Tale of Disaster in Salem written and illustrated by Rosalyn Schanzer (National Geographic Society)

2013 *Bomb: The Race to Build—and Steal—the World's Most Dangerous Weapon* by Steve Sheinkin (Point, an imprint of Roaring Brook Press)

Honor Books

Electric Ben: The Amazing Life and Times of Benjamin Franklin written and illustrated by Robert Byrd (Dial Books for Young Readers, a division of Penguin Young Readers Group)

Moonbird: A Year on the Wind with the Great Survivor B95 by Phillip M. Hoose (Farrar Straus Giroux Books for Young Readers)

Titanic: Voices from the Disaster by Deborah Hopkinson (Scholastic Press, an imprint of Scholastic)

LAURA INGALLS WILDER AWARD

The Laura Ingalls Wilder Award is presented to an author or an illustrator whose books are published in the United States and have made a substantial and lasting contribution to literature for children over a period of years. The award was first presented in 1954 and was given every five years from 1960 to 1980; since then, it has been given every three years.

1954 Laura Ingalls Wilder

1960 Clara Ingram Judson

1965 Ruth Sawyer

1970 E. B. White

1975 Beverly Cleary

1980 Dr. Seuss (Theodor Seuss Geisel)

1983 Maurice B. Sendak

1986 Jean Fritz

1989 Elizabeth George Speare

1992 Marcia Brown

1995 Virginia Hamilton

1998 Russell Freedman

2001 Milton Meltzer

2003 Eric Carle

2005 Laurence Yep

2007 James Marshall

2009 Ashley Bryan

2011 Tomie dePaola

2013 Katherine Paterson

NAME/TITLE INDEX

SUBJECT INDEX

Abstract art, 65, 66
Action, characterization and, 30
Ada, Alma Flor, 87
Adults
    diverse perspectives in literature
        for, 105–106
    picture books with appeal for, 58
Adventures, realistic fiction about,
    236
Adversity, 283
Africa, folktales from, 181
African Americans, 92, 93–94, 96,
    98, 104, 146
Aging, realistic fiction about, 238–239
AIDS, 126
ALA. See American Library
    Association
Alliteration, 158
Alphabet books, early childhood,
    54
Amazon.com, 20
American Indian Youth Literature
    Award, 105
American Library Association
    (ALA), 6, 13, 14, 19
Américas Book Award for
    Children's and Young Adult
    Literature, 104
Amish, 89
Animals
    personified, 202, 203
    realistic fiction about, 235–236
Anno, Mitsumasa, 128–129
Antagonist, 185
Anthologies, poetry, 152
Appalachian Americans, 89, 98–99
Apps, 67, 273
Archival photographs, 283
Art
    abstract, 65, 66
    computer-generated, 63
    folk, 65
    of illustrators with cultural
        depictions and artistic license,
        95
    informational books about, 274
    naïve, 65, 66
    three-dimensional, 62
Artistic media, picture books and
    drawing, 61
    painting, 60–61
    paper crafts, 61–62
    scratchboard, 62
    three-dimensional art, 62
Artistic style, of picture books, 63
    cartoon, 64–65
    examples, 65
    folk art, 65
    naïve art, surrealism and abstract
        art, 65, 66
    realism, impressionism and
        expressionism, 64, 65
    romanticism and postmodernism,
        65, 66
Asia, folktales from, 182–183
Asian Americans, 92–93, 98, 103,
    104–105
Asian Pacific American Literary
    Award, 104–105
Astrid Lindgren Memorial Award,
    132

Audiobooks, fantasy, 211
Authenticity
    authors, multicultural literature
        and perspectives of, 100
    culture and, 93, 94–95
    in language, 102
Authors
    with authentic perspectives in
        multicultural literature, 100
    of biography, 284
    characterization and, 31
    of contemporary realistic fiction
        with major works, 242
    on culture, 87
    on culture and race, 96, 131
    on fantasy, 211–212
    of fantasy with major works, 210
    of historical fiction, 259
    on historical fiction, 256
    of informational books, 278–279
    on informational books, 280
    of international literature,
        128–130
    on international literature, 131
    of picture books, 50–52, 73, 74
    of science fiction, 217
Autobiographies, 287
Awards, 14, 28, 57, 96, 124, 256.
    See also specific awards
    distinguished contribution to
        children's literature, 13
    international literature, 132–134
    multicultural literature, 103–105
    new voices, 93
    for nonfiction titles, 103, 277, 286
    outstanding international books
        for children, 133–134

Biography
    autobiographies and memoirs,
        287
    categories of, 286–288
    characterization in, 288
    collective, 287
    complete, 287
    criteria for evaluating, 290
    defined, 283
    for English Language Learners,
        289
    evolution of, 285–286
    major writers of, 284
    organizational and support tools,
        290
    partial, 286
    with picture book biographies,
        283, 288
    structure and, 289
    value of, 283–284
    visuals and, 289
Bodily functions, censorship and,
    17–18
Book design
    borders, 68–69
    covers and jackets, 67–68
    endpapers, 68
    last page, 70
    page turns, 69–70
    picture books and printmaking,
        62–63
    single pages and double-page
        spreads, 69

size and shape, 67
    text layout and typeface, 69
Book fairs, 123–124
Book reviews, in journals, 19
Books. See also Book design;
    Informational books; Picture
    books; Selecting books; Series
    books; specific types of books
    about aging, 238–239
    audiobooks, 211
    comic, 6
    contemporary realistic fiction,
        232–240, 242
    early childhood, 18–19, 52–55
    easy readers and predictable,
        56–58
    ebooks and apps, 67
    fantasy, 210
    about friendship, 128
    how-to, 274
    humorous, 239–240
    immigrant stories, 101
    international books set in World
        War II, 125, 254
    international literature and origin
        of, 124
    with memorable settings, 29
    with memorable themes, 37
    multicultural, 91–92
    about multiracial characters, 88
    mystery and suspense, 239
    nonfiction of inquiry, 277, 278
    online, 20
    pairing of historical fiction and
        information, 260
    with peritextual features
        impacting story, 68
    about poetry, 153–154
    about political and social unrest,
        100, 131
    about school, 234–236
    technology and connecting to,
        285
    touchstone books for different
        ages, 18–19
    traditional literature and shared
        motifs in, 187
    translated into English, 130
    in verse, 148–149
    war depicted in picture, 128
Borders, book design and, 68–69
Bruchac, Joseph, 180
Bullies, realistic fiction about, 234

Caldecott Medal, 14, 55, 62, 103,
    286
Cartoon, as artistic style, 64–65
Catastrophes, environmental, 215
Censorship
    ALA on, 19
    in children's literature, 17–19
    comic books and, 6
    in contemporary realistic fiction,
        231
Chalk drawing, 61
Challenges, realistic fiction about,
    236–237
Characterization
    action and, 30
    author description and, 31
    in biography, 288

through plot and roles played, 31
    relations with others and, 30
    thoughts, feelings and, 30–31
    visual representation of, 71
    through words and delivery, 31
Characters
    books with multiracial, 88
    character map, 32
    conflict between, 33
    conflict between nature and,
        33–34
    conflict between society and, 34
    conflict within, 33
    in contemporary realistic fiction,
        241–242
    empathy and, 262
    fantasy, 209
    flat, 32
    in historical fiction, 261–262
    outlandish situations and, 204
    personified animals, 203
    roles, 185
    round, 32–33
    in traditional literature, 186
Children's literature
    censorship and, 17–19
    characteristics of good, 6–7
    children's reaction to, 4–6
    contemporary, 14–15
    defined, 7–10
    English Language Learners and,
        16–17
    Enlightenment and, 12–13
    genres of, 15–16
    "Golden Age" of, 13–14
    history of, 10–15
    in Middle Ages, 10
    in Puritan times, 12
    qualities of, 8–10
    race in, 92–93
    resources for, 19–20
    touchstone books for different
        ages, 18–19
Classical world, myths from, 173,
    183
Classrooms, folk music in, 146
Closings, in traditional literature,
    185
Collage
    as artistic medium, 61–62
    poem, 160
Collective biographies, 287
Color
    picture books and printing,
        49–50
    as visual literacy design element,
        59
    water color painting, 60–61
Comic books, 6
Comparisons, in poetry, 159–160
Complete biographies, 287
Composition, as visual literacy
    design element, 60
Computer-generated art, 63
Concept books, early childhood,
    53–54
Concrete poems, 150
Conflict, character, 33–34
Contemporary realistic fiction
    authors and major works of, 242
    authors on writing, 243

353

CREDITS

p. 4: Asbjornsen, Peter, and J. E. Moe. *The Three Billy Goats Gruff*. Illustrated by Glen Rounds. Holiday House, 1993. **p. 5:** Astrid Lindgren, acceptance speech for the Hans Christian Andersen Award in 1958. **p. 6:** The Comics Code Authority. **p. 7:** Hunt, Peter. *Children's Literature: An Illustrated History*. New York: Oxford University Press, 1995. **p. 10:** Watson, Victor. *The Cambridge Guide to Children's Books in English*. Cambridge University Press, 2001. **p. 11:** Betsy Hearne. **p. 12:** Thomas Parkhurst. **p. 17:** First Amendment. **p. 18:** American Library Association. **p. 28:** Richard W. Jackson. **p. 29:** Ada, Alma Flor. *My Name Is Maria Isabel*. Atheneum, 1995. **p. 29:** Cushman, Karen. *The Midwife's Apprentice*. Clarion, 1995. **p. 31:** Schmidt, Gary (2011). *OK for Now*. **p. 31:** Erskine, Kathryn. *The Mockingbird*. Puffin. **p. 31:** Rowling, J.K. *Harry Potter and the Sorcerer's Stone*. Scholastic, 1998. **p. 37:** Rebecca Lukens. **p. 37:** Temple, Frances. Personal communication. 1994. **p. 41:** Allen, Judy, and Tudor Humphreys. *Are You a Spider?* Kingfisher, 2003. **p. 41:** William Carlos Williams. **p. 41.** Mark Twain. **p. 42:** Grahame, Kenneth. *The Wind in the Willows*. Scribner's, 1908/1953. **p. 42:** Briggs, Katherine. *British Folktales*. Pantheon, 1977. **p. 42:** Temple, Frances. *Grab Hands and Run!* HarperCollins, 1995. **pp. 42 and 43:** Babbitt, Natalie. *Tuck Everlasting*. Farrar, Straus, and Giroux, 1975. **p. 43:** Schmidt, Gary. *The Wednesday Wars*. Clarion, 2007. **p. 47:** Cianciolo, Patricia J. *Picture Books for Children*. 4th ed. American Library Association, 1997. **p. 49:** Sendak, Maurice. *Caldecott and Co.* Farrar, Straus, & Giroux, 1990. **p. 51:** Gág, Wanda. *Millions of Cats*. Coward, McCann, 1929. **p. 51:** Burton, Virginia Lee. *Mike Mulligan and His Steam Shovel*. Houghton Mifflin, 1939. **p. 54:** Ehlert, Lois. *Planting a Rainbow*. Harcourt, 1988. **p. 54:** Base, Graeme. *Animalia*. Abrams, 1987. **p. 54:** Jane Bayer's *A, My Name Is Alice*. **p. 55:** Shannon, David. *No, David!* Blue Sky/Scholastic, 1998. **p. 56:** Wood, Audrey. *The Napping House*. Illustrated by Don Wood. Harcourt, 1984. **p. 61:** Fleming, Denise. *In the Small, Small Pond* (1993). **p. 63:** Chodos-Irvine, Margaret. *Ella Sarah Gets Dressed*. Harcourt. 2003. **p. 64:** Allen Say. *Grandfather's Journey*. **p. 66:** McCallum, Robyn. "Metafiction and Experimental Work." 397–409. In *International Companion Encyclopedia of Children's Literature*. Edited by Peter Hunt. London and New York: Routledge, 1996, pp. 397–409. **p. 74:** Jon Scieszka and Lane Smith. **p. 85:** *Maizon at Blue Hill* by Jacqueline Woodson. **p. 87:** Alma Flor Ada. **p. 87:** Nieto, Sonia. *Affirming Diversity*. 2nd ed. Longman, 1996. **p. 89:** Lester, Julius. *On Writing for Children & Other People*. Dial, 2004. **p. 89:** Meltzer, Milton. "The Social Responsibility of the Writer." *The New Advocate* 2.3 (1989): 155–157. **p. 89:** Haldane, Suzanne. *Helping Hands: How Monkeys Assist People Who Are Disabled*. Dutton, 1991. **p. 93:** Horning, K. T. (2008). An interview with Rudine Sims Bishop. *Hornbook*, 84(3), 247–259. **p. 94:** Harris, Violet J. "African American Children's Literature: The First One Hundred Years." *Journal of Negro Education* 59 (1990): 540–555. **p. 94:** Garza, Carmen Lomas. *Family Pictures/Cuadros de familia*. Spanish language text by Rosalma Zubizaretta. Children's Book Press, 1990. **p. 95:** Cai, Mingshui. "Can We Fly across Cultural Gaps on the Wings of Imagination? Ethnicity, Experience, and Cultural Authenticity." *The New Advocate* 8.1 (1995): 1–16. **p. 95:** Sims Bishop, Rudine. "African American Literature for Children: Anchor, Compass, and Sail." *Perspectives* 7 (1991): ix–xii. **p. 96:** Julius Lester. **p. 98:** Khorana, Meena G. Editorial. *Bookbird* 34.4 (1996): 2–3. **p. 104:** Smith, Henrietta M., ed. *The Coretta Scott King Awards: 1970–2004*. (3rd ed.). American Library Association, 2004. **p. 126:** French, Jackie. *Joesephine Wants to Dance*. Illustrated by Bruce Whatley. HarperCollins, 2006. **p. 127:** Orlev, Uri. *The Lady with the Hat*. Translated by Hillel Halkin. Houghton Mifflin, 1995. **p. 131:** Beverley Naidoo. **p. 142:** Charles Temple. **p. 142:** Mason, Walt. "Football." *The Random House Book of Poetry for Children*. Ed. Jack Prelutsky. Illustrated by Arnold Lobel. Random House, 1983. **p. 142:** White, E. B. *Charlotte's Web*. Harper Trophy, 1952. **p. 142:** Emily Dickinson. **p. 145:** Charles Temple. **p. 145:** Charles Temple. **p. 146:** Stevenson, Robert Louis. *A Child's Garden of Verses*. Illustrated by Tasha Tudor. Simon & Schuster, 1999. **p. 147:** Service, Robert W. *The Cremation of Sam McGee*. Illustrated by Ted Harrison. Kids Can Press, 2006. Originally published in 1907. **p. 147:** Thayer, Ernest L. *Casey at the Bat: A Ballad of the Republic Sung in 1888*. Illustrated C. F. Payne. Simon and Schuster, 2003. **p. 148:** Naomi Shihab Nye. **p. 148:** Edward Lear. *They Went to Sea in a Sieve*. **p. 148:** Bucksnort Trout. **p. 149:** Edward Lear. **p. 149:** Charles Temple. **p. 150:** Poetry Slam. **p. 150:** Charles Temple. **p. 151:** Charles Temple. **p. 151:** Worth, Valerie. *Small Poems Again*. Illustrated by Natalie Babbitt. Farrar, Straus, & Giroux, 1985. **p. 153:** Anonymous. **p. 153:** William Blake. *Songs of Innocence and Songs of Experience*. Dover, 1789/1992. **p. 154:** Browning, Robert. *The Pied Piper of Hamelin*. Routledge, 1888. **p. 154:** Carroll, Lewis. *Alice's Adventures in Wonderland*. Illustrated by Sir John Tenniel. Dover, 1865/1993. **p. 154:** David Bates. **p. 154:** Christina Rossetti. **p. 155:** Stevenson, Robert Louis. *A Child's Garden of Verses*. Illustrated by Tasha Tudor. Simon & Schuster, 1999. **p. 155:** Kipling, Rudyard. *Puck of Pook's Hill*. Doubleday, 1906. **p. 155:** "True Love Blues." Copyright © 1999 by Nikki Grimes. First appeared in *Hopscotch Love: A Family Treasury of Love Poems* published by HarperCollins. Reprinted by permission of Curtis Brown, Ltd. **p. 156:** McCord, David. *All Small: Poems by David McCord*. Illustrated by Madelaine Gill Linden. Little, Brown, 1986. "The Pickety Fence" from *One At A Time* by David TW McCord Trust. Copyright © 1965, 1966 by David McCord. By permission of Little, Brown and Company, Inc. **p. 157:** de la Mare, Walter. *Peacock Pie*. Holt, 1923. **p. 157:** Bucksnort Trout. **p. 158:** Christina Rossetti. **p. 158:** Copyright © by Pearson Education, Upper Saddle River, NJ. **p. 158:** Heaney, Seamus, and Ted Hughes. *The Rattle Bag*. Faber and Faber,2005. **p. 158:** Tennyson, Alfred. "The Eagle." *1851. Poems of Tennyson: 1830–1870*. Ed. T. Herbert Warren. Oxford Univ. Press, 1912. **p. 158:** Blake, William. *Songs of Innocence and Songs of Experience*. Dover, 1789/1992. **p. 160:** Anonymous. **p. 161:** Paul Janeczko's *This Delicious Day*. **p. 161:** "Famous" by Naomi Shihab Nye, *Words Under the Words: Selected Poems* (Eighth Mountain Press/Perseus, 1994), by permission of Eighth Mountain Press. **p. 162:** Prelutsky, Jack, ed. *The Random House Book of Poetry for Children*. Illustrated by Arnold Lobel. Random House, 1983. **p. 162:** Myra Cohn Livingston. **p. 164:** Nikki Grimes. **p. 173:** Alexander Carmichael quoted in Briggs, Katherine. *British Folktales*. Marboro Books, 1979. **p. 179:** Harris, Joel Chandler. *The Tales of Uncle Remus*. **p. 180:** Joseph Bruchac. **p. 187:** Thompson, Stith. *The Folktale*. Holt, Rinehart, and Winston, 1960. **p. 197:** Cooper, Susan. *Dreams and Wishes: Essays on Writing for Children*. McElderry, 1996. **p. 198:** Lynn, Ruth Nadelman. *Fantasy Literature for Children and Young Adults: A Comprehensive Guide*, (5th ed.). Libraries Unlimited, 2005. **p. 198:** Alexander, Lloyd. "High Fantasy and Heroic Romance." *The Horn Book* 47 (December 1971). **p. 199:** Greenlaw, M. Jean. "Science Fiction: Images of the Future, Shadows of the Past." *Top of the News* 39 (1982): 64–71. **p. 206:** Elleman, Barbara. "Popular Reading-Time Fantasy Update." *Booklist* 81.19 (1985): 1407–1408. **p. 208:** Alexander, Lloyd. "High Fantasy and Heroic Romance." *The Horn Book* 47 (December 1971). **p. 208:** Alexander, Lloyd. "Fantasy as Images: A Literary View." *Language Arts* 55 (1978): 440–446. **p. 211:** Bruce Coville. **p. 212:** Jane Yolen. **p. 216:** Tunnell, Michael O. "The Double-Edged Sword: Fantasy and Censorship." *Language Arts* 71 (1994): 606–612. **p. 227:** Henkes, Kevin. *Protecting Marie*.

Greenwillow, 1995. **p. 232:** Katherine Paterson. **p. 239:** Jeanette Larson. *The Scene of the Crime: Investigating New Mysteries.* **p. 243:** Sharon Creech. **p. 251:** Choldenko, Gennifer. *Al Capone Does My Shirts.* Putnam, 2004. **p. 253:** Levstik, Linda. "A Gift of Time: Children's Historical Fiction." *Children's Literature in the Classroom: Weaving Charlotte's Web.* Eds. Janet Hickman and Bernice E. Cullinan. Christopher-Gordon, 1989, pp. 135–145. **p. 253:** Tomlinson, Carl M., Michael O. Tunnell, and Donald J. Richgels. "The Content and Writing of History in Textbooks and Trade Books." *The Story of Ourselves: Teaching History through Children's Literature.* Eds. Michael O. Tunnell and Richard Ammon. Heinemann, 1993, pp. 51–62. **p. 256:** Richard Peck. **p. 257:** Turner, Ann. "On Writing Katie's Trunk." *Book Links 2.5* (May 1993): 11. **p. 258:** Temple, Frances. *The Ramsay Scallop.* Orchard, 1994. **p. 260:** Cushman, Karen. *Alchemy and Meggy Swann.* Clarion, 2010. **p. 262:** Cushman, Karen. *The Midwife's Apprentice.* Clarion, 1995. **p. 262:** Simon and Schuster. **p. 263:** Broderick, Kathy. "The Ramsay Scallop by Frances Temple." *Book Links 4.2* (November 1994): 19. **p. 271:** *The New Colossus* by Emma Lazarus. **p. 272:** Mitchell, D. *Children's Literature: An Invitation to the World.* Boston, MA: Pearson, 2003. **p. 272:** Freedman, Russell. "Fact or Fiction?" *Using Nonfiction Trade Books in the Elementary Classroom: From Ants to Zeppelins.* Ed. E. B. Freeman and D. G. Person. National Council of Teachers of English, 1992, pp. 2–10. **p. 273:** Colman, Penny. "A New Way to Look at Literature: A Visual Model for Analyzing Fiction and Nonfiction." *Language Arts, 84* (2007): 257–268. **p. 276:** Zarnowski, M. Learning History with Informational Storybooks: A Social Studies Educator's Perspective. *The New Advocate 8* (1995):

183–196. **p. 276:** Leal, Dorothy. "Storybooks, Information Books and Informational Storybooks: An Explication of an Ambiguous Grey Genre." *The New Advocate 6* (1993): 61–70. **p. 276:** Sayers, F. C. "History Books for Children." *Beyond Fact: Nonfiction for Children and Young People.* Ed. J. Carr. American Library Association, 1982, pp. 95–98. **p. 276:** Fisher, Margery. *Introduction to Matters of Fact. Beyond Fact: Nonfiction for Children and Young People.* Ed. J. Carr. American Library Association, 1982, pp. 12–16. **p. 278:** Aronson, Marc. If Stones Could Speak: Unlocking the Secrets of Stonehenge. *National Geographic,* 2010. **p. 280:** James Cross Giblin. **p. 280:** Seeger, Laura Vaccaro. *First the Egg.* Roaring Brook Press, 2007. **p. 282:** DeCristofano, Carolyn Cinami. *A Black Hole Is Not a Hole.* Charlesbridge, 2012. **p. 282:** Moss, Barbara. "Getting the Picture: Visual Dimensions of Informational Texts." *Handbook of Research on Teaching Literacy through the Communicative and Visual Arts.* Vol. 2. Eds. James Flood, Shirley Brice Heath, and Diane Lapp. Lawrence Erlbaum, 2008, pp. 393–398. **p. 284:** Fritz, Jean. *You Want Women to Vote, Lizzy Stanton?* Puffin, 1999. **p. 285:** Monjo, F. N. "The Ten Bad Things about History." *Beyond Fact: Nonfiction for Children and Young People.* Ed. J. Carr. American Library Association, 1982, pp. 99–103. **p. 287:** Kaminsky, Marty. *Uncommon Champions: Fifteen Athletes Who Battled Back.* Boyds Mills Press, 2000. **p. 288:** Zarnowski, M. *Learning about Biographies: A Reading-and-Writing Approach for Children.* National Council of Teachers of English, 1990. **p. 288:** Fleming, Candace. *Amelia Lost: The Life and Disappearance of Amelia Earhart.* Schwartz & Wade, 2011. **p. 289:** Bass, Hester. *The Secret World of Walter Anderson.* Illustrated by E. B. Lewis. Candlewick, 2009.